I0887799

# E-Retailing Challenges and Opportunities in the Global Marketplace

Shailja Dixit
*Amity University, India*

Amit Kumar Sinha
*Amity University, India*

A volume in the Advances in E-Business Research (AEBR) Book Series

BUSINESS SCIENCE Reference
An Imprint of IGI Global

Published in the United States of America by
Business Science Reference (an imprint of IGI Global)
701 E. Chocolate Avenue
Hershey PA, USA 17033
Tel: 717-533-8845
Fax: 717-533-8661
E-mail: cust@igi-global.com
Web site: http://www.igi-global.com

Copyright © 2016 by IGI Global. All rights reserved. No part of this publication may be reproduced, stored or distributed in any form or by any means, electronic or mechanical, including photocopying, without written permission from the publisher. Product or company names used in this set are for identification purposes only. Inclusion of the names of the products or companies does not indicate a claim of ownership by IGI Global of the trademark or registered trademark.

Library of Congress Cataloging-in-Publication Data

Names: Dixit, Shailja, 1975- editor. | Sinha, Amit Kumar, editor.
Title: E-retailing challenges and opportunities in the global marketplace / Shailja Dixit and Amit Kumar Sinha, editors.
Description: Hershey, PA : Business Science Reference, [2016] | Includes bibliographical references and index.
Identifiers: LCCN 2016002537| ISBN 9781466699212 (hardcover : alk. paper) | ISBN 9781466699229 (ebook : alk. paper)
Subjects: LCSH: Electronic commerce. | Retail trade--Technological innovations. | International trade.
Classification: LCC HF5548.32 .E18727 2016 | DDC 658.8/72--dc23 LC record available at http://lccn.loc.gov/2016002537

This book is published in the IGI Global book series Advances in E-Business Research (AEBR) (ISSN: 1935-2700; eISSN: 1935-2719)

British Cataloguing in Publication Data
A Cataloguing in Publication record for this book is available from the British Library.

All work contributed to this book is new, previously-unpublished material. The views expressed in this book are those of the authors, but not necessarily of the publisher.

For electronic access to this publication, please contact: eresources@igi-global.com.

# Advances in E-Business Research (AEBR) Book Series

In Lee
*Western Illinois University, USA*

ISSN: 1935-2700
EISSN: 1935-2719

## Mission

Technology has played a vital role in the emergence of e-business and its applications incorporate strategies. These processes have aided in the use of electronic transactions via telecommunications networks for collaborating with business partners, buying and selling of goods and services, and customer service. Research in this field continues to develop into a wide range of topics, including marketing, psychology, information systems, accounting, economics, and computer science.

The **Advances in E-Business Research (AEBR) Book Series** provides multidisciplinary references for researchers and practitioners in this area. Instructors, researchers, and professionals interested in the most up-to-date research on the concepts, issues, applications, and trends in the e-business field will find this collection, or individual books, extremely useful. This collection contains the highest quality academic books that advance understanding of e-business and addresses the challenges faced by researchers and practitioners.

## Coverage

- E-business strategies
- Semantic Web
- E-CRM
- E-Services
- Virtual organization
- Web advertising
- E-business standardizations
- E-Marketing
- Online consumer behavior
- B2B e-marketplaces

IGI Global is currently accepting manuscripts for publication within this series. To submit a proposal for a volume in this series, please contact our Acquisition Editors at Acquisitions@igi-global.com or visit: http://www.igi-global.com/publish/.

The Advances in E-Business Research (AEBR) Book Series (ISSN 1935-2700) is published by IGI Global, 701 E. Chocolate Avenue, Hershey, PA 17033-1240, USA, www.igi-global.com. This series is composed of titles available for purchase individually; each title is edited to be contextually exclusive from any other title within the series. For pricing and ordering information please visit http://www.igi-global.com/book-series/advances-business-research/37144. Postmaster: Send all address changes to above address. Copyright © 2016 IGI Global. All rights, including translation in other languages reserved by the publisher. No part of this series may be reproduced or used in any form or by any means – graphics, electronic, or mechanical, including photocopying, recording, taping, or information and retrieval systems – without written permission from the publisher, except for non commercial, educational use, including classroom teaching purposes. The views expressed in this series are those of the authors, but not necessarily of IGI Global.

## Titles in this Series

*For a list of additional titles in this series, please visit: www.igi-global.com*

*Successful Technological Integration for Competitive Advantage in Retail Settings*
Eleonora Pantano (Middlesex University London, UK)
Business Science Reference • copyright 2015 • 405pp • H/C (ISBN: 9781466682979) • US $200.00 (our price)

*Strategic E-Commerce Systems and Tools for Competing in the Digital Marketplace*
Mehdi Khosrow-Pour (Information Resources Management Association, USA)
Business Science Reference • copyright 2015 • 315pp • H/C (ISBN: 9781466681330) • US $185.00 (our price)

*The Evolution of the Internet in the Business Sector Web 1.0 to Web 3.0*
Pedro Isaías (Universidade Aberta (Portuguese Open University), Portugal) Piet Kommers (University of Twente, The Netherlands) and Tomayess Issa (Curtin University, Australia)
Business Science Reference • copyright 2015 • 407pp • H/C (ISBN: 9781466672628) • US $235.00 (our price)

*RFID Technology Integration for Business Performance Improvement*
In Lee (Western Illinois University, USA)
Business Science Reference • copyright 2015 • 317pp • H/C (ISBN: 9781466663084) • US $225.00 (our price)

*Integrating Social Media into Business Practice, Applications, Management, and Models*
In Lee (Western Illinois University, USA)
Business Science Reference • copyright 2014 • 325pp • H/C (ISBN: 9781466661820) • US $225.00 (our price)

*Electronic Payment Systems for Competitive Advantage in E-Commerce*
Francisco Liébana-Cabanillas (University of Granada, Spain) Francisco Muñoz-Leiva (University of Granada, Spain) Juan Sánchez-Fernández (University of Granada, Spain) and Myriam Martínez-Fiestas (ESAN University, Perú)
Business Science Reference • copyright 2014 • 393pp • H/C (ISBN: 9781466651906) • US $215.00 (our price)

*Trends in E-Business, E-Services, and E-Commerce Impact of Technology on Goods, Services, and Business Transactions*
In Lee (Western Illinois University, USA)
Business Science Reference • copyright 2014 • 347pp • H/C (ISBN: 9781466645103) • US $185.00 (our price)

*Interdisciplinary Perspectives on Business Convergence, Computing, and Legality*
Reema Khurana (Institute of Management Technology-Ghaziabad, India) and Rashmi Aggarwal (Institute of Management Technology-Ghaziabad, India)
Business Science Reference • copyright 2013 • 354pp • H/C (ISBN: 9781466642096) • US $165.00 (our price)

IGI GLOBAL
DISSEMINATOR OF KNOWLEDGE
www.igi-global.com

701 E. Chocolate Ave., Hershey, PA 17033
Order online at www.igi-global.com or call 717-533-8845 x100
To place a standing order for titles released in this series, contact: cust@igi-global.com
Mon-Fri 8:00 am - 5:00 pm (est) or fax 24 hours a day 717-533-8661

*This book is dedicated to my husband Anurag, my daughter Shreshthi and my son Yashvardhan, for their love, understanding and emotional support.*

*Shailja*

*This book is dedicated to my loving parents the late Mr. Shail Kumar Sinha & the late Mrs. Vidhya Sinha, they have been my continuous source of inspiration and motivation.*

*Amit*

# Table of Contents

# Detailed Table of Contents

in place. Hence chapter illustrates how the stakeholder theory can be considered to be consistent with value maximization. Whilst incomplete contracts provide benefits of flexibility, they have also been criticized for facilitating lack of clarity in respect of objectives, focus and accountability in the decision making process. Furthermore, through the engagement of stakeholders, as well as appropriate forms of regulation, the chapter will also, simultaneously, illustrate how a "properly constructed Balanced Scorecard" can comprehensively communicate enterprises' business strategies.



The increase in penetration of internet and information and communication technology (ICT) along with change in consumer lifestyle and growing population of internet savvy consumers presents an encouraging platform for e-retailers in emerging markets. Education, technology and growing demand from middle class consumers are further driving the growth vehicle of e-tailing in these nations. There is adequate literature available for electronic business in the context of developed nations but applying that knowledge without any consideration of the unique business environment prevalent in emerging markets may spell danger for online traders. Therefore, the proposed chapter focuses on the growth of e-tailing in emerging economies. It talks about the driving forces for success of e-tailing in various developing economies. The opportunities, challenges and unique issues associated with e-tailing in emerging markets are also discussed. The chapter ends with a discussion on the future of e-tailing in emerging nations.



E-tailing has a dynamic ecosystem different from traditional retailing. To the best of our knowledge, there are few case studies scientifically grounded yet practical. Nonetheless, this is the authors' goal with this book chapter. A case study of China's e-tailing is needed because China is the largest emerging market as well as the largest e-retailing market in the world. Moreover, e-tailing provides one of the most effective ways for foreign retailers to enter China's impressive retail market. This case study will explore the underlying reasons for the success of China's e-tailing market by investigating the elements of China's e-tailing ecosystem. This study will further investigate the major players in China's e-tailing market, with a focus on the Alibaba Group, China's largest e-tailing company. This study will address Alibaba's e-tailing strategies and practices by comparing Alibaba and its major domestic and global competitors (e.g., Amazon).

This chapter uniquely reports origin of e-commerce and holistic present scenario of online retail in India. Desk research and extant review of literature from reliable market research reports, books, journals and web has been done to decipher internet penetration, evolution of e-commerce and present scenario. Study observed that India is third largest country in terms of internet users. India will drive e-commerce in Asia pacific region after China and Indonesia. Reasons hampering India from finding place in global retail e-commerce index are also put in foreground. Sequential events leading to growth of different types of e-commerce in India are delineated into two waves to understand the evolutionary process. Out of total non-travel B2C e-commerce, online retail holds significant fifty percent share and its prospects for future growth are extremely positive. Businesses and researchers will find this chapter useful to devise future strategies to win and sustain e-commerce market in India.



The Internet has changed the way many consumers shop, not just in the digital domain, but also in the physical world. E-tailing is a subset of e-commerce, which encapsulates all "commerce" conducted via the Internet. It refers to that part of e-commerce which entails the sale of product merchandise and does not include sale of services viz. Railway tickets, airlines tickets, job portals, etc. In 2012, the size of India's e-commerce market was USD 10 billion, while that of the e-tailing market was USD 0.6 billion. The current small size of e-tailing has led to it rarely being assessed on standalone basis. It is either clubbed with e-commerce or with brick & mortar retail, which, while not incorrect, does not allow for e-tailing's evaluation on its own merit. Consumer's perception regarding shopping has been changed with the introduction of internet media. Retail industry has witnessed major revolution in the changing technology oriented business scenario of the twenty-first century in India. Internet has shrunk the entire World. The rules of the game in retailing are fast changing with the introduction of Information Technology. The e-Retailing website is the front door of the online store that interacts between the e-retailer and consumers. The electronic retailing (e-Tailing, e-Retailing, internet retailing etc.) is the model of selling of retail goods using electronic media, in particular, the internet. In this research paper the authors propose to explore the factors contributing to the growth of e–Retailing in India and to investigate conceptually the issues and challenges involved in e- Retailing An attempt in this paper will also be made to study the present scenarios of e-tailing opportunities, its market, the viabilities and trends.

chapter provides a 360 degree view about E-Tailing from a global context as also touches upon how this is influencing this sector in India. Starting from the basic premise of E-Tailing the chapter would also cover shopper behavior and the related key drivers for this business segment. It explores the various business models and their viability as also how technology impacts the shoppers and E-Tail to the extent that physical stores might no longer exist. E-Tail was based on the basic premise that this business would be more profitable than physical stores because of the savings on real estate cost as they need not open physical stores. In spite of the increasing penetration of the internet and smart phone usage, E-Tail is still in its evolution and the optimal business model is yet to be well established. The cost of fulfillment which refers to the cost required to deliver the products is turning out to be a challenge to manage and is negating the savings on real estate because of the absence of physical stores. This led to the market place model where in the E-Tailer does not hold any inventory and that is a saving for them as compared to the inventory led model where they would have to invest in the inventory. However, this has not been a major breakthrough as the investment on technology continues to be a major cost for any E-Tailer. In spite of these challenges E-Tail is considered to be the way forward largely because it is well placed to cater to some of the key shopper expectations such as - simplifying their life, value delivery, customization and speed. Although this business opportunity is aligned to some of the key customer expectations, the business model needs to be powerful as also viable and sustainable. It is in that context that any E-Tailer needs to adhere to the "Basic Retail Model" as also have a well defined revenue model. The changing dynamics of retail has led to the omni channel model where physical stores and online merge seamlessly to offer a comprehensive shopping experience. The need for this from a shopper's perspective is validated from the fact that many E-Tailers are now opening physical touch points for their customers. Clearly this is the way forward and stand alone online or offline retail might find the going tough if they do not embrace omni channel especially in the context of the changes that affect this sector such as Big Data and Analytics, Internet of things and Wearable devices, Virtual wallets and last but not the least 3D printing.



Internet has created an opportunities for businesses especially retailers to stay connected with customers in the era of globalization. The customers can make purchases in a faster and convenient manner with the use of internet. E- Retailing is becoming very prominent and is being accepted by every age group across the world over the last few decades. Customers are embracing the shift from physical store to virtual store for purchase of products. E- Commerce has been grown very fast because of many advantages associated with buying on internet because of lower transaction and search cost as compared to other types of shopping. Through online shopping consumers can buy faster, more alternatives and can order product and services with comparative lowest price. (Cuneyt and Gautam 2004). This research paper will focus on youth of different social, national cultural backgrounds and their perception and attitude towards e-retailing .This also attempts to find out the important factors that make them loyal towards a particular marketer, without personal interaction.

## Section 5
## Communicating and Delivering Value Online



The global reach of social media provides opportunities for e-Retailers. Implementing a global social media strategy maximizes the efficiency of the exchange of information between the target audience and the brand. Information acquisition provides e-Retailers with knowledge about their target audience, while information dissemination spreads awareness about the brand to the target audience. As a result, e-Retailers leveraging user content on social media enable the development of strategic global engagement to reduce cultural complexities. The REALLY framework develops a foundation to leverage user-generated content using standardization for multilayered social media campaigns for e-Retailers. Roxy's global social media campaign is used as a case example to analyze global social media strategy and internationalization.



This chapter proposes to bring forth insights as how media contributes in e-tailing. The success of online retailers owe to the role which media plays in changing the consumer mind. India's retail market value was estimated at $520 billion in 2013, and is expected to grow to $950 billion by 2018. With a CAGR currently pegged at 13%, the Indian e-commerce market is expected to grow the fastest within the Asia-Pacific Region – with its market size doubling every 2-2.5 years. This certainly gives us reason for deep introspection. While the global growth rate of online shoppers is estimated at 8-10%, India currently has more than 10 million online shoppers. With the evolution of the online marketplace, sites like Flipkart, Snapdeal, Jabong and Myntra are thriving which has risen the practice of buying goods online. The media has definitely played vital role in shaping the online retail business.



Tremendous growth of information technology led to the rise of a new form of retailing, the digital retailing, (includes e-commerce and m-commerce), which offers value, convenience and tons of information. Mostly, customers experience digital and conventional retailing distinctly. For a customer to appreciate 'The brand', it is necessary for him to experience it, no matter through which channel he interacts with 'The brand'. Here, Omnichannel strategy, which uses digital media as its backbone, is an integrated sales experience that melds the advantages of physical stores with the information rich-experience of online shopping. An Omnichannel strategy enables the customer to get what he wants anyhow, anytime and anywhere through options like Click and Collect Store, order from a public space, browse in store-order online, browse online-get at store and in-store GPS, information centre etc. From a retailer's perspective, it offers him a single customer view (SCV) that helps in understanding what the customers want. An effective integration of field intelligence and digital media data facilitates excellent control over the stocking of products. Integration of channels enables a retail store to fulfil an online order, thus the volume of products going into decline stage is reduced. Also it becomes easy to either risk pool the inventory and deliver from one point or reduce warehousing and deliver from the store. As a result, capital investment is optimised. To adopt omnichannel, it is necessary to understand the psychology of digital shoppers, customer touch points and actionable channels preferred by the customers. The SCV offered by omnichannel ensures that the brand makes its customers appreciate, enjoy and remain connected to the brand.



In the past 10 years, e-commerce and e-retailing have developed rapidly in China, the largest emerging country. Due to the increasingly more competition in this industry, a fast and reliably delivery is important to win customer satisfaction. Despite of the fact that many e-retailing companies are running virtual network by outsourcing logistics to third parties, there is also a trend for companies to establish their own logistics channels. In fact, self-owned logistics can be an effective approach of marketing and customer relationship development, and thus provide competitive advantage. This chapter focuses on how Chinese e-retailing companies compete through logistics management. It starts with an introduction of e-retailing and logistics management from practice and literature perspectives. Then, there are cases studies into successful Chinese re-retailing companies with a highlight on their logistics management models and customer satisfaction based on initial survey. Further discussion will address the critical issues of logistics management in e-retailing.



The internet has already revolutionized many aspects of modern business and living and promises to bring even more radical future changes. In contrast, tax laws are normally slow to changing realities. It is anticipated that trade in tangible (physical) goods with e- commerce will not introduce problems. However, trade in intangible (electronic or digital) goods can be problematic because they will be difficult if not impossible to track. The chapter discusses the important concepts woven around the idea of taxing e tailing transactions and aims at coming up with a conclusion which will help further to determine the appropriate tax policies for e retailers keeping in mind the global framework. The chapter aims at discussing the concept of Internet Taxation, E- Retailing laws and regulations in Global Context. The chapter also discusses broad outlines relating to taxability of E Retailing transactions from VAT and CST angle under different scenarios and arguments in favor and against of taxing the e tailing transactions. The chapter also discusses important acts passed in different economies for taxing online retailers including Marketplace Fairness Act 2013 and Internet Tax Freedom Act. It is concluded by discussing the possible effects of the online retail tax. It could be argued that e- commerce for most part will not require new tax principles. Existing principles still apply only the old ways of doing things need to be digitized. The internet and e- commerce certainly does introduce some new business models and products that would not have been possible with old technology. And in some case, new laws may be required or old laws amended. Trade in intangibles or goods that are in digital format promises to be the main problem area.

# Foreword

Just over two decades ago, the rapid growth of electronic retailing (e-retailing or e-tailing), used in world wide web as early as 1995, has progressively produced an important effect in many related fields linked to business-to-business commerce, management, marketing and other associated areas. From that time on, many corporations and businesses in all parts of the world have been trying to put into practice the sale of goods and services through the Internet.

In the second decade of the 21st century, the need for e-tailing strategies at all levels is even more pronounced. In today's turbulent globally and economically racked competitive markets, corporations are under intense pressures when it comes to use the best strategy to reach their goals.

Today, of course, it is almost two decades later. The world of e-tailing has moved to full and centre stage, ably supported by a galaxy of individual companies. Thus, I am delighted to see this edited book by Shailja Dixit and Amit Kumar Sinha with its focus upon how to manage e-tailing in the global marketplace. The subjects command the interest, imagination and needed application of the selected concept. For example (and this is just a sample), questions and issues such as:

- To identify, examine, and address global challenges encountered by e-commerce firms, especially those from emerging economies;
- To explore potential and scope for organisations willing to change their offering and communication strategy;
- To describe how education, technology, and growing demand from both middle class and youth consumers are the driving forces of e-tailing;
- To analyse how virtual communities and social media influence user motivation, adoption and usage pattern.

Many other issues are addressed in plain and understandable ways. Nor is the text entirely theoretical. Chapters are often enriched by excellent case studies and examples from known companies as well as by rigorous empirical analysis providing a vibrant backcloth for this significant book.

I am looking forward to seeing the book in print and recommend it to policy makers, practitioners and graduate students.

*Paolo Piciocchi*
*University of Salerno, Italy*

**Paolo Piciocchi**, *PhD in "Business Administration", is Associate Professor of Business and Communication Management, at the Department of Political, Social and Communication Science, University of Salerno, where he also teaches Network Dynamics. He is a member of the Research Group GSA-AIDEA (Italian Academy of Business Administration and Management) "Innovation and Creativity – Strategies to Change and Manage Complexity". He was Visiting Professor at the Westminster University of London and at IBM Almaden Research Center. He is a Board Member of the Scientific Committee at the International Conference on the Human Side of Service Engineering. He is Author of several works, including articles, papers, monographies, and international conference proceedings.*

# Foreword

The concept of e-tailing has brought together many retailers online. Features like easy search for required product, cash on delivery, home delivery services and tracking transaction status have played a crucial role in enhancing customer shopping experience. Small enterprises that specialize in niche products are entering the e-tail market to make their products available worldwide. E-tailing is being widely used in the retail sector and is growing rapidly due to increasing penetration of mobile phones and broadband, cash on delivery, 3G/4G rollout and internet banking. Furthermore, e-tailing eliminates the need to build and maintain expensive showrooms, thus reducing cost and increasing profit for retailers. However, lack of internet usage, complex website design, lack of graphical presentations, high cost of acquisition of customers, e-retailers' ability to charge premium for services are some of the challenges the industry is facing.

The e-commerce industry is an exciting place with the interplay of social, mobility, analytics, cloud (SMAC), digital, 3D and, virtualization. The current high valuations, in spite of losses, perhaps, are indicative of the future potential.

The big retailers are increasingly focusing on their digital strategies in order to gain the obvious benefits of online platforms. The e-commerce companies are concentrating their efforts on increasing the penetration of their mobile apps for higher growth.

This book provides theoretical perspective and the latest empirical research findings on the topic related to the change that is occurring. In the book "E-Retailing Challenges and Opportunities in the Global Marketplace", Shailja and Amit have edited the quintessential collection of research articles that address many of the major issues related to the study and research in relation to e tailing and e commerce.

I hope that the book shall prove to be beneficial for scholars, researchers, academicians, practitioners and entrepreneurs.

*Sharad Kumar Venkta*
*Toonz Retail India Pvt. Ltd., India*

**Sharad Kumar Venkta** *is Managing Director for Toonz Retail India Pvt. Ltd.*

# Preface

With rapid growth of the Internet and globalization of market, the retail sector has become an increasingly competitive and dynamic in nature. Business and marketing activities are affected by the infusion of Internet technologies and are revolutionizing constantly all aspects of marketing. E-marketing and E-commerce are the two important terms in the new Internet-based business domain. E-tailing a sub domain is defined as retailing conducted online. The e-tailing industry is expanding rapidly with strong early life cycle growth. Globally over the past five years, online retail has grown at a 17% Compounded Annual Growth Rate (CAGR), with growth particularly strong in Latin America (27%) and Asia Pacific (25%).

Despite the recent economic slowdown, the e-tailing sector enjoys continued growth due to increasing worldwide internet penetration, in fact posing a threat to Brick and Mortar stores. The retail industry is in the midst of a revolution. In this ever increasing digital world, the retail store as we know is changing. Globalisation, evolving technology, big data, e-commerce and sustainability are just some of the forces driving the change. Retailers are increasingly leveraging their presence across channels of catalogue, web, stores and kiosks, to increase their share of the customer's wallet and expand across consumer segments. The bricks-and-mortar format has begun to look different from the store of five years ago and distribution channels are no longer singular or even multi – they are fusing. Terms such as cross-channel and omni-channel are now synonymous with this change and integral to driving the retail landscape of the future.

Globally, an "achievement-oriented society" has consolidated and the customer has become smart and hybrid in nature. Manufacturers are able to predict customers' wishes with remarkable accuracy as a result of the automated evaluation of purchasing and search patterns. The increased Internet connectivity of domestic appliances and building technology also provides a clearer insight into consumer behavior. This leads to highly personalized consumer profiles, which companies can utilize in order to make precise product recommendations and transmit individualized promotional messages.

Globally, the merger of stationary retailing and e-commerce has made major advances. So-called Everywhere Commerce is now widespread. The retail sector targets customers through a variety of channels. Showrooms with a range of delivery options are a common sight in cities.

Shopping is possible at any time and the goods are delivered to the designated address immediately. Recent studies on consumer shopping behaviour indicate that multichannel shoppers show a significantly higher value and frequency of purchase than single channel shoppers.

## ABOUT THE BOOK

This book has been woven with global economy as its loom and e-tailing as its thread. This is the result of collective work among a numbers of researchers in the United State of America, Italy, China, Muscat, South Africa, Bangkok, Malaysia and India. This is a unique effort that gives an in-depth and global insight in to the way e-commerce, e-tailing and online marketing has evolved over a period of time. The book provides not only strong managerial insight but also plenty of empirical research evidence, as well as fresh conceptualizations to comprehend the intricacies of the fast changing world of e-tailing. The diversity of global perspective presented in this book with major emphasis on emerging markets like India and China will help to illuminate the sphere of e-tailing in a way that cannot be found in a text book. We hope the content of the chapter will be useful for Managers, Researchers, Students and Policy Makers.

A key feature of the book is that it taps into the latest research studies from across the globe and in some cases it comes up with the new research findings. This aspect helps to ensure that book is most up to-date possible and has the sharpest edge in discussing best practices in e-retailing.

The book intelligently has been engraved to be equally valuable for individuals, organizations, and society as a whole. It provides new prologues and new perceptions to use e tailing to those familiar with the concept and to beginner with same ease. It aims to aid the marketing strategist emphasizing the use of e-tailing in producing, communicating, and delivering online offerings to the consumer. The book through online marketing intelligence helps in identifying useful models for customer motivations and aspirations for using e-retailing.

## BOOK ORGANIZATION

The book has been efficiently organized to give a clear understanding on the subject. It has 6 Sections that are concluding with Case Study at the end. The book covers both developed and developing economies in relation to the growth and trend of e-tailing.

Section 1 has two chapters which enhances the understating of the subject. Chapter 1, the introductory chapter provides background and tools for a strong comprehensive understanding of the concepts pertaining to electronic commerce and electronic business. The author argues that the adoption of e-business has helped companies to gain a competitive edge over their peers in terms of reduced costs, increased revenue streams, and greater customer satisfaction. Chapter 2 basically contributes to identify, analyze, and address global challenges encountered by E-commerce firms in selected Jurisdictions across the globe. It is argued by the author that both principal and agent should be actively engaged in the mediation process - which includes contract formation stages and other phases highlighted within the chapter.

Section 2 has 4 chapters which focus on the E-Tailing Opportunities & Challenges in Emerging Economies. This context is extremely timely for emerging economies where E-Tailing Opportunities are rapidly spreading, has huge potential and scope for organizations willing to change their offering and communication strategy. The section covers two biggest Emerging economies: India and China for discussing the subject.

Chapter 3 provides insights on how E-tailing is catching up quickly with the offline stores and expanding its reach in emerging economies. The Author describes how Education, technology, and growing demand from middle class consumers are the driving forces of e-tailing in emerging nations. Chapter 4 is in a form of case study and discusses how China's e-tailing market been growing at an astonishing rate and discusses the importance of cultural and social factors that differentiate China's e-tailing success from other global players. The author believes that e-tailing might become one of the most effective ways for foreign retailers to enter the Chinese retail market. Chapter 5 & Chapter 6 focus on the Indian market and provide stepwise penetration of e-commerce and e-retailing in the Indian market. The various modes of commerce and net penetration impact have been demonstrated in the chapters. The authors have suggested that by understanding the utility of e-commerce technology, learning lessons from evolutionary past and knowing absolved present position, this additive knowledge can be extrapolated by electronic retailers to capture golden opportunity in near future.

Section 3 has 2 Chapters which focus on the Virtual communities: The people power in E-Retailing. Virtual communities collect individuals to come together for making relationships, sharing common goals and interests, as well as getting social supports.

Chapter 7 explains how virtual communities influences user motivation, adoption and usage pattern. Members in virtual communities mutually discuss products or brands from multiple dimensions, such as prices, effectiveness, reputation, usage experiences, or potential problems thus impacting buying and disposing of products and services.

Chapter 8 empirically explains how online opinion leaders influence the purchase intentions in e-retailing. The author believes that Opinion leaders still play an important role in buying decisions, although this role needs to be interpreted in relation to the changes in market dynamics and consumer behavior introduced by Web 2.0. The author argues that aspects of trust, remains the central elements in the marketing methods used by e-retailers.

Section 4 has 2 chapters discussing the issues of Hybrid Consumer Behavior in Digital World. Consumers benefit from access to a wider variety of goods and sellers, greater convenience, improved possibilities to compare products and prices, and in some instances, lower prices. In addition, all users potentially benefit from better access to content and information, lower transaction costs, reduced environmental costs and wider benefits such as improved learning, innovation, and creativity. These variables frequently disrupt and change the behavior of consumer decision making.

Chapter 9 critically views how changing dynamics of retail has led to the omni channel model where physical stores and online merge seamlessly to offer a comprehensive shopping experience to attract consumers. Thus, the business model needs to be powerful as also viable and sustainable. The author argues that E-Tailer needs to adhere to the "Basic Retail Model" as also have a well-defined revenue model so that a balance can be strike between revenue generation and super offerings to attract and retain the hybrid consumer. Chapter 10 discusses significantly the young consumer towards e tailing. The Author suggests that different researches should be conducted to understand the e-behavior and pattern of e-purchasing behavior of youth as they promise to be the most potential segment.

Section 5 contains 5 chapters which elaborates how to communicate and deliver the additional value in the online offering to the customers above what they already receive from their present suppliers via various channel i.e. Communicating and Delivering Value Online. Chapter 11 comprehends on global strategic approaches to social media campaigns to leverage UGC (User Generated Content) across all social media channels across various countries. The Author mentions that to capitalize on the efficiency of social media and its global reach, e-Retailers should use a global strategy instead of looking at social media contrasts in an individual country approach. Chapter 12 identifies the significant role of Media cannot be denied in the overall marketing of online retailing. Most of the social Medias are maximizing the utility of online retailers in current Market.

Chapter 13 discusses the relevance of Omni channel retailing in order to satisfy and retain the customers of online retail. The author suggests that to adopt Omni channel, it is necessary to understand the psychology of digital shoppers, customer touch points, and actionable channels preferred by the customers. Chapter 14 analyses and compares the various logistic e-retailing logistics management companies in China. It discusses how the success of e-retailing depends on the successful logistics of the company. The author suggests that E-commerce companies or logistics companies should focus on 3 networks: physical logistics network, virtual network and customer marketing network.

Chapter 15 aims at discussing the concept of Internet Taxation, E-Retailing laws and regulations in Global Context. The Author also discusses broad outlines relating to taxability of E-Retailing transactions from VAT and CST angle under different scenarios and arguments in favor and against of taxing the e tailing transactions.

Section 6 is a case study of an online enterprise which failed in its operation. The case study mentions how a business model is absolutely important to the success of any e-tailing business. The author suggests that building the trust with online customers, since the company is living in the virtual web and making a personal ‘connection’ can do wonders. Investing significantly in customer service and winning their ‘trust’ is the key to the success of any e-tailing firm.

*Shailja Dixit*
*Amity University, India*

*Amit Kumar Sinha*
*Amity University, India*

# Acknowledgment

This book bears the imprint of so many people.

From Shailja Dixit: The Almighty God should be Thanked the first for this life. I could never have done this without the faith I have in You. My overriding debt continues to be for my husband Anurag Dixit for providing me with the time, support and inspiration for writing this book. My children, daughter Shreshthi and son Yashvardan, were very supportive and loving throughout the assignment. I shall never have enough words to express my gratitude towards my in-laws, my parents, and my other family members who have always supported and motivated me throughout my life personally and professionally .I want to thank my dearest friend Divya who has been my mentor since childhood.

My colleagues and associates at Amity University continue to have an important impact on my academic and research orientation. My friend and critique Archana Sharma and Sana Moid needs special mention for their consistent support in my journey. I continually benefit from the wisdom my colleague and Co-Editor Amit K. Sinha.

From Amit Kumar Sinha: First and foremost, I would like to express my gratitude towards my Spiritual Guru (Preacher) Shri Narayan Mahaprabhu Ji for her divine blessings. I would like to thank my wife Sonal for standing beside me throughout my career and writing this book. She has been my inspiration and motivation for continuing to improve my knowledge and move my career forward. I also thank my wonderful daughters Adwita & Anvita who are just about the best daughter a father could hope. I am appreciative to my Co-Editor Dr. Shailja Dixit for continuous support and trusting me throughout the project.

From Both Editors: We owe a considerable amount of gratitude to our University Pro Vice Chancellor Major Gen K K Ohri for his encouragement and our Head of the Institute Prof Vijay Pratap Sahi for believing in our capabilities and their unconditional support without which this book could not have been completed. We most indebtly and gratefully acknowledge our Research Mentor Prof Manoj Joshi for helping us in enhancing our research acumen and thought process. We are indeed obliged to Prof R P Gupta, Prof Anil Dubey and Prof Ashok Kumar for guiding and motivating us. Apoorva Srivastava needs special mention for his research insight and support he provided for our book.

We are grateful to all our wonderful authors and reviewers who that took part in the review process. Without their support, this book would not have become a reality. We thank them for their unrelenting support and promptness that has helped in the timely completion of the book. Our sincere gratitude goes to the chapter's authors who contributed their time and expertise to this book. We also appreciate the valuable contributions of the reviewers regarding the improvement of quality, coherence, and content presentation of chapters. Most of the authors also served as referees; we highly appreciate their double task.

The talented staff at IGI deserves praise for their consistent support. We would like to thank our Project Manager Janine Haughton, Courtney Tychinski and Erin O'Dea for ensuring that everything is in proper way. We benefitted greatly from their superb help.

We also thank the team at IGI Global for their excellent support and help in the publication of the book.

*Shailja Dixit*
*Amity University, India*

*Amit Kumar Sinha*
*Amity University, India*

# Section 1

# Introduction:
## E-Tailing Global Challenges and Opportunities

# Chapter 1
# Advocating Electronic Business and Electronic Commerce in the Global Marketplace

**Kijpokin Kasemsap**
*Suan Sunandha Rajabhat University, Thailand*

## ABSTRACT

*This chapter describes the overview of electronic business (e-business), the multifaceted applications of e-business, the importance of e-business in the global marketplace, the overview of electronic commerce (e-commerce), the emerging trends of e-commerce, and the importance of e-commerce in the global marketplace. The utilization of e-business and e-commerce is required for modern organizations that seek to serve suppliers and customers, improve business performance, reinforce competitiveness, and gain continuous effectiveness in the global marketplace. Therefore, it is necessary for modern organizations to advocate their e-business and e-commerce and establish a strategic plan to regularly check their practical advancements toward satisfying customer requirements. The chapter argues that advocating e-business and e-commerce has the potential to enhance organizational performance and gain sustainable competitive advantage in the global marketplace.*

## INTRODUCTION

E-business is the transformation of vital business processes through the utilization of web-based technologies (Katsanakis & Kossyva, 2012). E-business offers a business solution that allows companies to share databases, forecasts, inventory plans, product information, and financial data (Nguyen, 2013). The presence of e-business has brought a significant impact on business practice (Janita & Chong, 2013). E-business capabilities have a significant impact on internationalization performance (Raymond, Bergeron, Croteau, & St-Pierre, 2015). E-business revolutionizes the procedure of effective communication between internal and external customers within an organization (Kasemsap, 2015a). Technological, organizational, and environmental contextual factors alter the ability of e-businesses to derive value from competitive strategies-dynamic capabilities alignment (Rashidirad, Soltani, & Salimian, 2014).

DOI: 10.4018/978-1-4666-9921-2.ch001

Copyright © 2016, IGI Global. Copying or distributing in print or electronic forms without written permission of IGI Global is prohibited.

E-commerce has become the most important commercial activity (Yan, Lee, & Lee, 2015). Both virtual businesses and e-commerce operations enable organizations to have fluid structures, modify the changing conditions, lower expenses, access to new markets, and attain new consumers in the global marketplace (Gökmen, 2012). Many companies have recognized the importance of developing an online platform with the objective of having a higher interaction with the client, and influence them in the e-commerce, through the buying process (Ibarra, Partida, & Aguilar, 2015). E-commerce can be recognized as a dynamic capability (Hua, Morosan, & DeFranco, 2015). E-commerce increases the commercial ability toward customer satisfaction, thus maintaining competitive costs and pricing in modern business (Kasemsap, 2015b).

## BACKGROUND

In a dynamic business environment, firms must be able to continually evolve their capabilities to facilitate e-business innovation (Lin & Hsia, 2011). The three main types of e-business are business-to-business (B2B), business-to-consumer (B2C), and business-to-government (B2G) (Volusion, 2006). B2B is the largest form of e-business in terms of money spent. B2B allows trading to take place between businesses, using a low-cost sales channel for the sale of goods and services and is responsible for constantly changing corporate buying habits (Volusion, 2006).

The most widely recognized form of e-business, B2C is the exchange of information, products, and services taking place between a business and a consumer over the Internet. As the Internet develops, B2C is continually changing the way consumers acquire information, the way products are compared against one another, and the way in which they are purchased. B2G is the online exchange of information and transactions between businesses and government agencies, also known as e-governance. B2G allows government agencies and businesses to utilize the electronic method to conduct business and interact with each other over the Internet (Volusion, 2006).

E-commerce is considered as an innovation for organizations because it is embedded in the organization's core business processes or is extending basic business products and services, and integrating suppliers and customers in the value chain (Hong & Zhu, 2006). Traditional commerce has been converted to e-commerce by new technologies (Safa & Ismail, 2013). The consolidation of the World Wide Web as an everyday technology has allowed the emergence of a new competitive environment where firms can develop their business processes (Laudon & Laudon, 2005) to deal with customers (Turban, Lee, King, & Chung, 2000). The applications and opportunities for e-commerce are increasing (Huang, Lee, & Lee, 2009). Firms across the globe have adopted e-commerce in their operations and have gained various benefits (Vaithianathan, 2010).

## ADVOCATING ELECTRONIC BUSINESS AND ELECTRONIC COMMERCE IN THE GLOBAL MARKETPLACE

This section describes the overview of e-business, the multifaceted applications of e-business, the importance of e-business in the global marketplace, the overview of e-commerce, the emerging trends of e-commerce, and the importance of e-commerce in the global marketplace.

## Overview of Electronic Business

E-business technologies have distributed in the last decade, and many practitioners claim that they are the ultimate solution to the information exchange problem among firms' enterprise systems (Hsu, 2013). E-business technologies are defined as the Internet-based technologies (e.g., Extranets, electronic data interchange (EDI), and websites) toward linking many firms for performing e-business functions, such as online selling, online purchasing, online coordination, and online information sharing (Banker, Bardhan, Chang, & Lin, 2006). E-business organizations must frequently face changes in their systems to stay competitive (Leyton, Pino, & Ochoa, 2015).

E-business refers to the application of information and communications technology (ICT) to improve business activities toward enhancing services and managing business operations (Beynon-Davies, 2004). Regional policy frameworks need to focus on strengthening the ICT infrastructure, clarifying market rules to build user confidence, developing networks, facilitating ICT-enabled clustering and infrastructure sharing (Thomas, Miller, & Simmons, 2015). Firms are increasingly using e-business tools to transform channel relationships in order to achieve competitive advantage (Theodosiou & Katsikea, 2012). E-business has enabled businesses to evolve from physical, or linked computer-based, organizations to organizations where different business parties (e.g., customers, suppliers, and other counterparties) at different locations interact only, or mainly, using the Internet and the Web 2.0 (Kotb, Roberts, & Stoner, 2013).

The uses of e-business tools effectively offer new benefits and drive value to the business parties in the relationship (Osmonbekov & Gruen, 2013). In a highly competitive business characterized by time constraints and information management, the use of ICT has become vital for services differentiation and diversification (Evangelista & Sweeney, 2006). ICT affects the global economy and the business world (Seo, Lee, Hur, & Kim, 2012). The information system (IS) has been considered the main catalyst for stimulating business transformations that trigger considerable changes in business processes and performance outcomes (Markus, 2004). The relationship between information technology (IT) applications and organizational change is an important concern in the field of IS (Fichman, 2004).

Organizations aiming to achieve business goals should focus on developing IT, technical alignment, and IS effectiveness (Kasemsap, 2015c). Business intelligence, an emerging business technology, enlarges business performance, thus leading to the higher level of efficiency, effective quality outputs, and improved marketing decisions (Kasemsap, 2015d). Business analytics can be utilized to validate the causal relationships within business input, process, and output toward gaining business success (Kasemsap, 2015e). Applying data mining for business intelligence in the knowledge management environments has the potential to achieve business goals in the digital age (Kasemsap, 2015f). New uses of IS have the potential for significant transformations in applications development, organizational business processes, and organizational performance (Markus, 2004). To realize the successful development of e-business schemes, implementation management is an important issue (Iizuka, Iizuka, & Suematsu, 2013).

## Multifaceted Applications of Electronic Business

New technology-based firms, particularly those that develop their business around a new technological platform, are likely to be impacted by globalization, in terms of both pace of innovation and pressure of competition (Onetti, Zucchella, Jones, & McDougall-Covin, 2012). With the rapid growth of the Internet, there has been a greater need to discover the dynamics of e-business networks in the virtual world (Mishra, 2011). In the e-business context, applications and software systems should be interoperable (Papazoglou & Ribbers, 2006). Ubiquitous e-business is one of the major topics in intelligent manufacturing systems (Oh, 2010). In the Internet-based e-business environment, most business data are distributed, heterogeneous, and private (Liu, Cao, & He, 2011).

E-business enables organizations to reduce costs, increase demand, and create new business models (Singh & Byrne, 2006). E-business models usually involve a wide range of business processes across different business functions with complex activities, events, and documents (Wang & Wu, 2011). Emerging IT tools (e.g., cloud computing, service-oriented architecture (SOA), and the Web 2.0) increasingly affect the roots of existing IS applications, and represent a paradigm shift in developing e-business (Hirschheim, Welke, & Schwarz, 2010). An innovative e-business application can be characterized by a technical innovation in IT, an innovation of new business models, and the new ways of cooperating with stakeholders to expand business perspectives and create business value (Turban et al., 2000).

The evolution of e-business from one stage of maturity to the next requires e-business firms to continually acquire and evolve new capabilities to match the requirements of different evolutionary stages (Lin & Hsia, 2011). Most firms are increasingly engaged in business transformations that are triggered by the adoption of new IS (Lin & Hsia, 2011). The implementation of B2B e-business systems demands integration of incompatible IS infrastructures and business processes (Lee & Lim, 2005). Reinforced by the growth of e-commerce, even during the current global economic downturn, intermediated online targeted advertising (IOTA) has emerged as the promising e-business model empowered by the Web 2.0 principle (Li, Idemudia, Lin, & Yu, 2012).

B2B e-business technology can provide an efficient support for sharing information and integrating business processes between supply chain partners (Saraf, Langdon, & Gosain, 2007). As an important dimension of application capability of e-business, e-business systems development plays a significant role in establishing a high-quality B2B e-business system, thus influencing e-business service capability (Wu, Zhong, & Mei, 2011). From the project initiation to the plan deployment and to the implementing process, by developing the various levels of interorganizational project implementation teams, B2B participants can create effective communication and close cooperation, and share development knowledge and experience accumulated from previous IS implementation (Lu, Huang, & Heng, 2006).

Regarding the lower cost and greater ease of implementation, e-business technologies hold the promise of enabling information made available from enterprise resource planning (ERP) systems to be shared among firms in the extended supply chain (Swaminathan & Tayur, 2003). E-business technologies serve to extend the original value proposition of ERP (Gonzalez, 1998), offer an ERP-based organization the opportunity to build interactive relationships with its business partners (Ash & Burn, 2003), and bring together their previously separate information at a very low cost (Norris, Hurley, Hartley, Dunleavy, & Balls, 2000). The decision to adopt e-business should take into account not only the benefits, but also the costs of adoption, maintenance, and financial constraints (Nguyen, 2013).

## Importance of Electronic Business in the Global Marketplace

The rapid deployment of e-business is an economically significant issue for modern business (Raisinghani, Meade, & Schkade, 2007). E-business promotes rapid industrial growth (Lai, Kan, & Ulhas, 2013). E-business adoption resulted in tangible financial benefits for small and medium-sized enterprises (SMEs) in customer development and electronic marketing (Grant, Edgar, Sukumar, & Meyer, 2014).

Evans and Wurster (1997) stated that businesses can obtain several benefits by participating in e-business (e.g., identify new market, improve interorganizational communication, engage better relationship with suppliers, and have more opportunities to have larger field with other larger companies).

The business model has become a popular concept in business and management fields (Klang, Wallnöfer, & Hacklin, 2014). Wang (2001) defined e-business model as a competition strategy for marketplace and the structure of business processes for the entire electronic trade course including marketing and advertising, negotiation, purchasing, logistics of products and service delivery, payment with the method of security, post-sales service, and post-sales intelligence. The key factors that establish an e-business innovation are grouped into three perspectives (i.e., IT applications, business models, and collaboration with stakeholders) (Wu & Hsia, 2008). Using B2B e-business to create IT business value needs the high-quality IT support service (DeLoan & McLean, 2004).

Several studies have examined the relationship between e-business technologies and organizational performance (Hsu, 2013). There is a positive relationship between e-business utilization and organizational performance (Zhu & Kraemer, 2005). Poon and Swatman (1998) stated that there are five main benefits linked to the adoption of e-business (e.g., ability to have wider exposure in the global marketplace, direct and indirect marketing, lower communication cost, capture more market, and enhance company image). Competitive advantage in the transport and logistics sector effectively creates value chains enhanced by e-business (Marchet, Perego, & Perotti, 2009).

The literature has identified various factors inhibiting e-business adoption (Nguyen, 2013). These factors include large initial cost (Evangelista & Sweeney, 2006), running cost and customers' adaptability to the new service (Samar & Robert, 2004), company size (Nurmilaakso, 2008), the compatibility and standard of the new system, management's support and security (Gunasekaran & Ngai, 2008), uncertain return on investment (ROI) due to the higher competition level resulting from the higher product return rate due to online customers unable to inspect the physical conditions of the product (Samar & Robert, 2004). E-business leverages organizational network capability and technologies to interact with customers, suppliers, and employees in order to sustain competitive advantage (Holsapple & Singh, 2000). Collaboration is recognized as a necessary strategy for the survival of small firms, and a strategy that enhances the competitive positioning of larger firms (Beckett, 2005).

In order to remain competitive and sustainable in the ever-changing business environments, organizations need to frequently make changes to their business activities and the corresponding business process models (Dam & Ghose, 2015). The business model is defined as a locus of e-business innovation (Amit & Zott, 2001). The business model is the business logic by which a specific company uses its resources to create customer value with a mediating link between IT-enabled e-business innovation and business value implementation (Osterwalder, Pigneur, & Tucci, 2005). The business model involves four interlocking elements (i.e., value proposition, profit formula, key resources, and key processes), thus creating business value (Johnson, Christensen, & Kagermann, 2008).

Regarding e-business, the business value network is a business configuration that describes the collaborative architecture of sourcing agreements and alliances that firms implement to gain complementary resources from other firms for the execution of business value-generating activities (Rai, Sambamurthy, & Agarwal, 2008). Because the separation between firms and their surrounding environments is increasingly more blurred in e-business environments, the collaborative network is a source of innovation and business growth (Pisano & Verganti, 2008). It is essential for modern organizations to develop a sustainable network of cooperative agreements with partners to arrange resources and create business value (Lin & Hsia, 2011).

E-business has a number of applications that vary in complexity and can be defined as the use of the Internet or any other electronic medium for the arrangement of transactions, the support of business processes, and the development of collaboration opportunities with other businesses or clients (Matopoulos, Vlachopoulou, & Manthou, 2007). The interorganizational transaction efficiency and accuracy, interorganizational collaboration, and interorganizational independency among business partners in supply chain are important collaborative advantage derived from B2B e-business investment (Rai, Patnayakuni, & Seth, 2006).

As most established organizations realize that they need to form alliances with their customers and suppliers over electronic networks, integrating e-business technologies with ERP systems become a critical management issue (Ash & Burn, 2003). Many IS researchers have identified ERP and e-business integration, as one of the most important IS topics for future research (Bendoly, Soni, & Venkataramanan, 2004). ERP system is particularly useful in providing management with the types of information necessary for making business decisions (Kasemsap, 2015g). Reconfiguring and integrating ERP systems with front-end web-based systems to support e-business initiatives should be at the top of the list for IS executives (Straub & Watson, 2001).

The goal of B2B e-business is to provide IT support for supply chain collaboration, thus diffusing products and services worldwide, improving resource use efficiency, and reducing supply chain uncertainty (Kumar & van Dissel, 1996). B2B e-business, by facilitating sharing knowledge between supply chain partners, can enable manufacturing firms to effectively respond to customer demand, achieve higher customer satisfaction and loyalty, thus leading to the long-term financial performance (Rai et al., 2006). E-business service capability adds value through the availability of more current information regarding orders shared with suppliers enabling the coordination of inbound logistics processes, thus reducing inventory levels and increasing profitability (Dehning, Richardson, & Zmud, 2007).

## Overview of Electronic Commerce

In the competitive e-commerce landscape, the ability of an e-commerce firm to form a single function is an important determinant of organizational performance and business value (Tan, Pan, & Zuo, 2014). Castro-Schez et al. (2011) stated that e-commerce technologies have introduced new ways to do business. E-commerce is an evolution through the adoption of Web 2.0 capabilities to enhance customer participation and achieve greater economic value (Huang & Benyoucef, 2013). Web 2.0 refers to a platform for controlling collective intelligence (Kaplan & Haenlein, 2010). The rapid development of Web 2.0 has provided a huge potential to transform e-commerce from a product-oriented environment to a customer-centered environment (Wigand, Benjamin, & Birkland, 2008).

E-commerce involves different aspects (e.g., technological, economic, and legal perspectives) regarding the characteristics of the e-commerce transactions (Palopoli, Rosaci, & Ursino, 2006). E-commerce systems provide users with a browser-based interface to acquire the details of products and services (Fang, Zhang, Sensoy, & Magnenat-Thalmann, 2014). E-commerce transactions between a merchant and a customer are recognized as B2C processes that can be compared to the retail trade of traditional commerce (Rosaci & Sarne, 2014). B2B e-commerce enhances time-based delivery performance (Karthik, Richard, & Gary, 2004). Organizational ability in conducting e-commerce transaction and collaboration with business partners over B2B e-commerce can have a strategic impact on organizational performance (Subramani, 2004).

In the recent decade, the consumer-to-consumer (C2C) e-commerce has developed very fast and played a key role in the Internet transaction (Tian, Ye, Yan, & Sun, 2015). Through the Internet, e-commerce has a worldwide reach, with a potential customer base around the globe, providing attractive and promotional information, including C2C interactions (Morosan, 2014), thus allowing organizations to create more effective business models. Papaioannou et al. (2013) stated that C2C electronic market has become the most active segment of electronic markets. Hartono et al. (2014) stated that the Internet technology and the variety of the resulting applications have revolutionized the way customers do business and interact with sellers of commercial products and services.

Organizations recognizing the importance of e-commerce have started to create task forces to boost the implementation of their online strategies (Hua et al., 2015). The three core business processes that must be well-coordinated in e-commerce firms are the forecasting and planning, order processing, and product development and management (Kalakota & Robinson, 2001). E-commerce adoption process is a sequence of stages through which a potential e-commerce adopter evaluates the new idea (Shih, 2012).

## Emerging Trends of Electronic Commerce

E-commerce is a new evolution by adopting a variety of Web 2.0 features, functions and capabilities in order to enhance customer participation (Kim & Srivastava, 2007), promote customer relationships (Liang, Ho, Li, & Turban, 2011), and achieve greater economic value (Parise & Guinan, 2008). Swamynathan et al. (2008) indicated that Web 2.0 significantly influences business transactions and the reliability of business reputation systems. Web 2.0 can strengthen business relationships with customers, increase traffic to company websites, identify new business opportunities, and support brand development (Michaelidou, Siamagka, & Christodoulides, 2011).

In the development of e-commerce, security has been the important issue (Zhang, Deng, Wei, & Deng, 2012). Many researchers conducted a variety of security technologies, such as e-commerce protocols (Ogata & Futatsugi, 2010), user authentication (Lin & Chang, 2009), electronic signatures (Srivastava, 2009), and electronic payment (Guan, Tan, & Hua, 2004). A number of e-commerce security issues should be take into consideration to increase the whole security of e-commerce, such as physical security (Furnell, 2004) and managerial security (Tomlinson, 2000). Yousafzai et al. (2003) offered the insights into the role of perceived security, perceived privacy, and perceived trustworthiness related to trust in electronic banking. Chellappa and Pavlou (2002) indicated that the security has a positive relationship with the trust. Perceived security has a positive effect on trust, along with loyalty which is influenced by user satisfaction (Flavian & Cuinaliu, 2006).

The growth of the Internet has been accompanied by the increasing interest in the concept of trust (Sillence, Briggs, Harris, & Fishwick, 2006). Lack of trust between commercial entities and purchasers can restrict the potential of e-commerce (Antoniou & Batten, 2011). McKnight et al. (2002) stated that trust is a strategic imperative for online service providers because it strongly influences the consumers' purchasing intentions when consumers interact with unfamiliar vendors through the Internet. Trust has been identified as a key factor in promoting B2B ecommerce (Lee & Lim, 2005). Regarding tourism industry, many consumers still tend to be reluctant to purchase tourism products and services online, especially the high-priced or luxury invisible tourism products and services since they are likely to be less trustful of e-commerce (Kim, Chung, & Lee, 2011). Transaction cost has positive relationship with trust and consumers' willingness to buy online (Teo & Yu, 2005). Rabinovich et al. (2007) explored transaction cost in the e-commerce firms with logistics service and found that the role of transaction costs is very important.

Trust plays a crucial role in the formation of dependent relationships represented by online transactions (Li, Pieńkowski, van Moorsel, & Smith, 2012). Trust in the context of relationships between consumers and online service providers is influenced by user privacy and perceived security (Fam, Foscht, & Collins, 2004). Customers are unlikely to complete a transaction if they do not trust the website that they are shopping at (Chang & Chen, 2008). Hwang and Kim (2007) stated that the practitioners and researchers for e-commerce should understand and promote the trust paradigm in the context of e-commerce. Bai et al. (2008) empirically tested that website quality has a positive impact on user satisfaction, and that user satisfaction has a positive impact on repurchase intention. Mutual trust between trading partners increases IT customization for supply chain coordination and improves strategic information sharing about capacity planning, production scheduling, and marketing strategies (Klein, Rai, & Straub, 2007).

## Importance of Electronic Commerce in the Global Marketplace

Innovations associated with ICT have opened up new opportunities for the global economy and delivered in the age of e-commerce (Ho, Kauffman, & Liang, 2011). Given the tremendous success of the Internet and e-commerce in developed countries, emerging economies are quickly embracing IT (Agarwal & Wu, 2015). Globalization is the tendency of investment funds and businesses to move beyond domestic and national markets to other markets around the globe, allowing them to become interconnected with different markets (Savrul, Incekara, & Sener, 2014). Customers are of great importance to e-commerce in intense competition (Cao, Yu, & Zhang, 2015). B2B e-commerce adoption enables SMEs to sustain competitive advantage in a dynamic competitive environment (Hamad, Elbeltagi, Jones, & El-Gohary, 2015).

An ever-increasing use of Internet has greatly been affecting the importance of e-commerce websites (Sohrabi, Mahmoudian, & Raeesi, 2012). Having a good understanding of users' interests has become increasingly important for online retailers hoping to create a personalized service for a target market (Su & Chen, 2015). The use of the Internet as the additional sales channel offers traditional retailers opportunities to reach expanded markets while improving the efficiency of their operations (Xia & Zhang, 2010). SMEs can benefit the new environment via e-commerce (Savrul et al., 2014). Organizations with proper e-commerce support should continue to refine their internal and external resource allocation to explore business opportunities and showcase the features of dynamic capabilities (Wheeler, 2002).

With the popularity of the Internet, more and more enterprises and individuals are involved in e-commerce (Tian, Zhang, & Guan, 2013). The Internet has provided great convenience for online shoppers and has presented unprecedented opportunities for online retailers to understand their customers (Wu, Li, & Xu, 2014). The rapid development of e-commerce platforms has allowed retailers to introduce online product recommendations toward attracting consumers in their purchase decisions (Lin, 2014). The decision support systems literature has a strong tradition in studying the relationship between channels and consumer decision making (Chiu, Kao, & Lo, 2010). Most websites utilize text and images to provide consumers with the required information (Stableford & Mettger, 2007).

For successful e-commerce practices, online shoppers need to reach a state of mind where they engage with the website with total involvement, concentration, and enjoyment (Bilgihan, Okumus, Nusair, & Bujisic, 2014). The most prominent form of recommendations is the digitalized user recommendations or word-of-mouth communication (WOM) recommendations (Dellarocas, 2003). The economic impact of system recommendations has attracted the academic interest (Lin, 2014). System recommendations influence consumer decision-making process (Zhang, Agarwal, & Lucas, 2011), product sales (Pathak, Garfinkel, Gopal, Venkatesan, & Yin, 2010), and product sales diversity (Fleder & Hosanagar, 2009). Having a larger volume of user recommendations can make such recommendations seem more trustworthy (Zhu & Zhang, 2010), which is more likely to drive product sales.

E-commerce is essential for enterprises because it improves their understanding of customer needs and of the products and services available in the global marketplace (Zhu, 2004). Enterprise systems have become a necessary component of IT infrastructure in modern organizations (Ahmad, Haleem, & Syed, 2012). By conducting e-commerce, manufacturers can eliminate distributors and wholesalers; optimize internal processes; reduce the production period, inventory, and circulation (Chun, Rhee, Park, & Kim, 2011); and obtain higher margins (Laudon & Traver, 2009). Online businesses are able to capture customers' behaviors, which gives them insights into their shopping experiences and expectations, and helps them develop successful business strategies (Constantinides & Fountain, 2008).

In the e-commerce environment, Web 2.0 can enable businesses to provide the high-quality products, place them in a better position to predict market trends, and maximize the effectiveness of their marketing campaigns (Constantinides, Romero, & Boria, 2008). Web 2.0 can affect the marketing aspects, such as customer control and value creation (Huang & Benyoucef, 2013). Regarding Web 2.0, customers' perceptions, preferences, and decisions are not only based on information presented on e-commerce websites, but are also influenced by content generated by people on social networks (Constantinides & Fountain, 2008). The value created by customers is significantly enhanced through Web 2.0 since the collaborative efforts of networked customers usually lead to better outputs (Kaplan & Haenlein, 2010).

## FUTURE RESEARCH DIRECTIONS

The strength of this chapter is on the thorough literature consolidation of e-business and e-commerce. The extant literature of e-business and e-commerce provides a contribution to practitioners and researchers by describing the multifaceted applications of e-business and e-commerce to appeal to the different segments of e-business and e-commerce in order to maximize the business impact of e-business and e-commerce in the global marketplace. The classification of the extant literature in the domains of e-business and e-commerce will provide the potential opportunities for future research. Future research direction should broaden the perspectives in the implementation of e-business and e-commerce to be utilized in the knowledge-based organizations.

Practitioners and researchers should recognize the suitability of a more multidisciplinary approach toward research activities in implementing e-business and e-commerce in terms of knowledge management-related variables (e.g., knowledge sharing behavior, knowledge creation, organizational learning, learning orientation, and motivation to learn). It will be useful to bring the additional disciplines together (e.g., strategic management, marketing, finance, and human resources) to support a more holistic examination of e-business and e-commerce in order to transfer the existing theories and approaches to inquiry in this area.

## CONCLUSION

This chapter described the overview of e-business, the multifaceted applications of e-business, the importance of e-business in the global marketplace, the overview of e-commerce, the emerging trends of e-commerce, and the importance of e-commerce in the global marketplace. E-business makes it easier, faster, and cheaper for businesses to communicate with their suppliers and their customers. Using e-mail and online ordering systems, communication and transactions can instantly occur between companies situated anywhere in the world. Improved customer service has nurtured better relations between retail outlets and customers, ensuring that customers remain loyal to the outlets. The adoption of e-business has helped companies gain a competitive edge over their peers in terms of reduced costs, increased revenue streams, and greater customer satisfaction.

The adoption of e-business has improved communication in the competitive retailing industry. Companies using websites in the competitive retailing industry are able to offer the after-sales services to their clients without the need for a physical presence or storefront. Companies that have adopted e-business have a faster product development cycle, enabling them to quickly respond to market needs. Companies using e-business take advantage of being market leaders to increase revenues before their competitors can enter the market. Operational costs (e.g., the maintenance of inventory and transaction costs) have reduced concerning e-business adoption. Companies using e-business have a wider online presence in the global marketplace.

E-commerce is beneficial to both business and consumer wise as payment and documentations can be completed with greater efficiency. E-commerce proves its importance based on the fact where time is the essence. To both consumers and business, connectivity plays an important part as it is the important factor determining the whole business. From the business point of view, e-commerce provides better connectivity for its potential customer as their respective website can be virtually accessed from anywhere through Internet. In the commercial markets, time plays an important role to both business and consumers.

In the global marketplace perspective, the appearance of e-commerce as a pioneer has promoted various business opportunities for companies and investors. Due to the growth of e-commerce, more organizational resources are being directed into electronic securities, Internet facilities, business plans, and new technologies. Concerning e-commerce phenomenon, new markets have emerged from e-commerce toward giving a boost to the global marketplace. The utilization of e-business and e-commerce is required for modern organizations that seek to serve suppliers and customers, improve business performance, reinforce competitiveness, and gain continuous effectiveness in the global marketplace. Advocating e-business and e-commerce has the potential to enhance organizational performance and gain sustainable competitive advantage in the global marketplace.

## REFERENCES

Agarwal, J., & Wu, T. (2015). Factors influencing growth potential of e-commerce in emerging economies: An institution-based N-OLI framework and research propositions. *Thunderbird International Business Review*, *57*(3), 197–215. doi:10.1002/tie.21694

Ahmad, N., Haleem, A., & Syed, A. A. (2012). Compilation of critical success factors in implementation of enterprise systems: A study on Indian organisations. *Global Journal of Flexible Systems Management, 13*(4), 217–232. doi:10.1007/s40171-013-0019-8

Amit, R., & Zott, C. (2001). Value creation in e-business. *Strategic Management Journal, 22*(6/7), 493–520. doi:10.1002/smj.187

Antoniou, G., & Batten, L. (2011). E-commerce: Protecting purchaser privacy to enforce trust. *Electronic Commerce Research, 11*(4), 421–456. doi:10.1007/s10660-011-9083-3

Ash, C., & Burn, J. (2003). Assessing the benefits from e-business transformation through effective enterprise management. *European Journal of Information Systems, 12*(4), 297–308. doi:10.1057/palgrave.ejis.3000476

Bai, B., Law, R., & Wen, I. (2008). The impact of website quality on customer satisfaction and purchase intentions: Evidence from Chinese online visitors. *International Journal of Hospitality Management, 27*(3), 391–402. doi:10.1016/j.ijhm.2007.10.008

Banker, R., Bardhan, I. R., Chang, H., & Lin, S. (2006). Plant information systems, manufacturing capabilities, and plant performance. *Management Information Systems Quarterly, 30*(2), 315–337. doi: 10.2307/25148733

Beckett, R. C. (2005). Collaboration now a strategic necessity. Handbook of Business Strategy, 6(1), 327–332. doi: 10.1108/08944310510558124

Bendoly, E., Soni, A., & Venkataramanan, M. A. (2004). Value chain resource planning: Adding value with systems beyond the enterprise. *Business Horizons, 47*(2), 79–86. doi:10.1016/j.bushor.2003.08.004

Beynon-Davies, P. (2004). *E-business*. New York, NY: Palgrave Macmillan.

Bilgihan, A., Okumus, F., Nusair, K., & Bujisic, M. (2014). Online experiences: Flow theory, measuring online customer experience in e-commerce and managerial implications for the lodging industry. *Information Technology & Tourism, 14*(1), 49–71. doi:10.1007/s40558-013-0003-3

Cao, J., Yu, X., & Zhang, Z. (2015). Integrating OWA and data mining for analyzing customers churn in e-commerce. *Journal of Systems Science and Complexity, 28*(2), 381–392. doi:10.1007/s11424-015-3268-0

Castro-Schez, J. J., Miguel, R., Vallejo, D., & Lopez-Lopez, L. M. (2011). A highly adaptive recommender system based on fuzzy logic for B2C e-commerce portals. *Expert Systems with Applications, 38*(3), 2441–2454. doi:10.1016/j.eswa.2010.08.033

Chang, H. H., & Chen, S. W. (2008). The impact of online store environment cues on purchase intention: Trust and perceived risk as a mediator. *Online Information Review, 32*(6), 818–841. doi:10.1108/14684520810923953

Chellappa, R. K., & Pavlou, P. A. (2002). Perceived information security, financial liability and consumer trust in electronic commerce transactions. *Logistics Information Management, 15*(5/6), 358–368. doi:10.1108/09576050210447046

Chiu, P. H., Kao, G. Y. M., & Lo, C. C. (2010). Personalized blog content recommender system for mobile phone users. *International Journal of Human-Computer Studies*, *68*(8), 496–507. doi:10.1016/j.ijhcs.2010.03.005

Chun, S. H., Rhee, B. D., Park, S. Y., & Kim, J. C. (2011). Emerging dual channel system and manufacturer's direct retail channel strategy. *International Review of Economics & Finance*, *20*(4), 812–825. doi:10.1016/j.iref.2011.02.006

Constantinides, E., & Fountain, S. J. (2008). Web 2.0: Conceptual foundations and marketing issues. *Journal of Direct, Data and Digital Marketing Practice*, *9*(3), 231–244. doi:10.1057/palgrave.dddmp.4350098

Constantinides, E., Romero, L. R., & Boria, M. A. G. (2008). Social media: A new frontier for retailers? *European Retail Research*, *22*(1), 1–28. doi:10.1007/978-3-8349-8099-1_1

Cui, M., & Pan, S. L. (2015). Developing focal capabilities for e-commerce adoption: A resource orchestration perspective. *Information & Management*, *52*(2), 200–209. doi:10.1016/j.im.2014.08.006

Dam, H. K., & Ghose, A. (2015). Mining version histories for change impact analysis in business process model repositories. *Computers in Industry*, *67*, 72–85. doi:10.1016/j.compind.2014.10.005

Dehning, B., Richardson, V. J., & Zmud, R. W. (2007). The financial performance effects of IT-based supply chain management systems in manufacturing firms. *Journal of Operations Management*, *25*(4), 806–824. doi:10.1016/j.jom.2006.09.001

Dellarocas, C. (2003). The digitization of word of mouth: Promise and challenges of online feedback mechanisms. *Management Science*, *49*(10), 1407–1424. doi:10.1287/mnsc.49.10.1407.17308

DeLone, W. H., & McLean, E. R. (2004). Measuring e-commerce success: Applying the DeLone & McLean information systems success model. *International Journal of Electronic Commerce*, *9*(1), 31–47. doi: 10.1080/10864415.2004.11044317

Evangelista, P., & Sweeney, E. (2006). Technology usage in the supply chain: The case of small 3PLs. *International Journal of Logistics Management*, *17*(1), 55–74. doi:10.1108/09574090610663437

Evans, P. B., & Wurster, B. S. (1997). Strategy and the new economics of information. *Harvard Business Review*, *75*(5), 70–83. PMID:10170332

Fam, K. S., Foscht, T., & Collins, R. D. (2004). Trust and the online relationship: An exploratory study from New Zealand. *Tourism Management*, *25*(2), 195–207. doi:10.1016/S0261-5177(03)00084-0

Fang, H., Zhang, J., Sensoy, M., & Magnenat-Thalmann, N. (2014). Reputation mechanism for e-commerce in virtual reality environments. *Electronic Commerce Research and Applications*, *13*(6), 409–422. doi:10.1016/j.elerap.2014.08.002

Fichman, R. (2004). Going beyond the dominant paradigm for information technology innovation research: Emerging concepts and methods. *Journal of the Association for Information Systems*, *5*(8), 314–355.

Flavián, C., & Guinalíu, M. (2006). Consumer trust, perceived security and privacy policy: Three basic elements of loyalty to a web site. *Industrial Management & Data Systems*, *106*(5), 601–620. doi:10.1108/02635570610666403

Fleder, D., & Hosanagar, K. (2009). Blockbuster culture's next rise or fall: The impact of recommender systems on sales diversity. *Management Science*, *55*(5), 697–712. doi:10.1287/mnsc.1080.0974

Furnell, S. (2004). E-commerce security: A question of trust. *Computer Fraud & Security*, *2004*(10), 10–14.

Gökmen, A. (2012). Virtual business operations, e-commerce & its significance and the case of Turkey: Current situation and its potential. *Electronic Commerce Research*, *12*(1), 31–51. doi:10.1007/s10660-011-9084-2

Gonzalez, J. S. (1998). *The 21st century Intranet*. Upper Saddle River, NJ: Prentice Hall.

Grant, K., Edgar, D., Sukumar, A., & Meyer, M. (2014). "Risky business": Perceptions of e-business risk by UK small and medium sized enterprises (SMEs). *International Journal of Information Management*, *34*(2), 99–122. doi:10.1016/j.ijinfomgt.2013.11.001

Guan, S. U., Tan, S. L., & Hua, F. (2004). A modularized electronic payment system for agent-based e-commerce. *Journal of Research and Practice in Information Technology*, *36*(2), 67–87.

Gunasekaran, A., & Ngai, E. W. T. (2008). Adoption of e-procurement in Hong Kong: An empirical research. *International Journal of Production Economics*, *113*(1), 159–175. doi:10.1016/j.ijpe.2007.04.012

Hamad, H., Elbeltagi, I., Jones, P., & El-Gohary, H. (2015). Antecedents of B2B e-commerce adoption and its effect on competitive advantage in manufacturing SMEs. *Strategic Change*, *24*(5), 405–428. doi:10.1002/jsc.2019

Hartono, E., Holsapple, C. W., Kim, K. Y., Na, K. S., & Simpson, J. T. (2014). Measuring perceived security in B2C electronic commerce website usage: A respecification and validation. *Decision Support Systems*, *62*, 11–21. doi:10.1016/j.dss.2014.02.006

Hirschheim, R., Welke, R., & Schwarz, A. (2010). Service-oriented architecture: Myths, realities, and a maturity model. *MIS Quarterly Executive*, *9*(1), 37–48.

Ho, S. C., Kauffman, R. J., & Liang, T. P. (2011). Internet-based selling technology and e-commerce growth: A hybrid growth theory approach with cross-model inference. *Information Technology & Management*, *12*(4), 409–429. doi:10.1007/s10799-010-0078-x

Holsapple, C. W., & Singh, M. (2000). Toward a unified view of electronic commerce, electronic business, and collaborative commerce: A knowledge management approach. *Knowledge and Process Management*, *7*(3), 151–164. doi:10.1002/1099-1441(200007/09)7:3<151::AID-KPM83>3.0.CO;2-U

Hong, W., & Zhu, K. (2006). Migrating to Internet-based e-commerce: Factors affecting e-commerce adoption and migration at the firm level. *Information & Management*, *43*(2), 204–221. doi:10.1016/j.im.2005.06.003

Hsu, P. F. (2013). Integrating ERP and e-business: Resource complementarity in business value creation. *Decision Support Systems*, *56*, 334–347. doi:10.1016/j.dss.2013.06.013

Hua, N., Morosan, C., & DeFranco, A. (2015). The other side of technology adoption: Examining the relationships between e-commerce expenses and hotel performance. *International Journal of Hospitality Management*, *45*, 109–120. doi:10.1016/j.ijhm.2014.12.001

Huang, C. Y., Tzeng, G. H., & Ho, W. R. J. (2011). System on chip design service e-business value maximization through a novel MCDM framework. *Expert Systems with Applications*, *38*(7), 7947–7962. doi:10.1016/j.eswa.2010.12.022

Huang, T. C., Lee, T. J., & Lee, K. H. (2009). Innovative e-commerce model for food tourism products. *International Journal of Tourism Research*, *11*(6), 595–600. doi:10.1002/jtr.731

Huang, Z., & Benyoucef, M. (2013). From e-commerce to social commerce: A close look at design features. *Electronic Commerce Research and Applications*, *12*(4), 246–259. doi:10.1016/j.elerap.2012.12.003

Hwang, Y., & Kim, D. J. (2007). Customer self-service systems: The effects of perceived web quality with service contents on enjoyment, anxiety, and e-trust. *Decision Support Systems*, *43*(3), 746–760. doi:10.1016/j.dss.2006.12.008

Ibarra, L., Partida, A., & Aguilar, D. (2015). Electronic commerce as a business strategy: Impact in consumption habits in Hermosillo, Sonora's inhabitants. *Procedia: Social and Behavioral Sciences*, *175*, 275–282. doi:10.1016/j.sbspro.2015.01.1201

Iizuka, K., Iizuka, Y., & Suematsu, C. (2013). E-business process modeling issues: From the viewpoint of inter-organizational process efficiency and information sharing. *Procedia Computer Science*, *22*, 820–827. doi:10.1016/j.procs.2013.09.164

Iyer, K. N. S., Germain, R., & Frankwick, G. L. (2004). Supply chain B2B e-commerce and time-based delivery performance. *International Journal of Physical Distribution & Logistics Management*, *34*(8), 645–661. doi:10.1108/09600030410557776

Janita, I., & Chong, W. K. (2013). Barriers of B2B e-business adoption in Indonesian SMEs: A literature analysis. *Procedia Computer Science*, *17*, 571–578. doi:10.1016/j.procs.2013.05.073

Johnson, M. W., Christensen, C. M., & Kagermann, H. (2008). Reinventing your business model. *Harvard Business Review*, *86*(12), 51–59. PMID:18543808

Kalakota, R., & Robinson, M. (2001). *E-business 2.0: Roadmap for success*. Boston, MA: Addison–Wesley.

Kaplan, A. M., & Haenlein, M. (2010). Users of the world, unite! The challenges and opportunities of Social Media. *Business Horizons*, *53*(1), 59–68. doi:10.1016/j.bushor.2009.09.003

Kasemsap, K. (2015a). The role of e-business adoption in the business world. In N. Ray, D. Das, S. Chaudhuri, & A. Ghosh (Eds.), *Strategic infrastructure development for economic growth and social change* (pp. 51–63). Hershey, PA, USA: IGI Global. doi:10.4018/978-1-4666-7470-7.ch005

Kasemsap, K. (2015b). The role of electronic commerce in the global business environments. In F. Cipolla-Ficarra (Ed.), *Handbook of research on interactive information quality in expanding social network communications* (pp. 304–324). Hershey, PA, USA: IGI Global. doi:10.4018/978-1-4666-7377-9.ch019

Kasemsap, K. (2015c). The role of information system within enterprise architecture and their impact on business performance. In M. Wadhwa & A. Harper (Eds.), *Technology, innovation, and enterprise transformation* (pp. 262–284). Hershey, PA, USA: IGI Global. doi:10.4018/978-1-4666-6473-9.ch012

Kasemsap, K. (2015d). Implementing business intelligence in contemporary organizations. In A. Haider (Ed.), Business technologies in contemporary organizations: Adoption, assimilation, and institutionalization (pp. 177–192). Hershey, PA, USA: IGI Global. doi:10.4018/978-1-4666-6623-8.ch008

Kasemsap, K. (2015e). The role of business analytics in performance management. In M. Tavana & K. Puranam (Eds.), *Handbook of research on organizational transformations through big data analytics* (pp. 126–145). Hershey, PA, USA: IGI Global. doi:10.4018/978-1-4666-7272-7.ch010

Kasemsap, K. (2015f). The role of data mining for business intelligence in knowledge management. In A. Azevedo & M. Santos (Eds.), *Integration of data mining in business intelligence systems* (pp. 12–33). Hershey, PA, USA: IGI Global. doi:10.4018/978-1-4666-6477-7.ch002

Kasemsap, K. (2015g). Implementing enterprise resource planning. In M. Khosrow-Pour (Ed.), *Encyclopedia of information science and technology* (3rd ed., pp. 798–807). Hershey, PA, USA: IGI Global. doi:10.4018/978-1-4666-5888-2.ch076

Katsanakis, I., & Kossyva, D. (2012). C-business: A theoretical framework for the implementation of co-opetition strategy in e-business. *Procedia: Social and Behavioral Sciences*, *58*, 259–268. doi:10.1016/j.sbspro.2012.09.1000

Kim, M. J., Chung, N., & Lee, C. K. (2011). The effect of perceived trust on electronic commerce: Shopping online for tourism products and services in South Korea. *Tourism Management*, *32*(2), 256–265. doi:10.1016/j.tourman.2010.01.011

Klang, D., Wallnöfer, M., & Hacklin, F. (2014). The business model paradox: A systematic review and exploration of antecedents. *International Journal of Management Reviews*, *16*(4), 454–478. doi:10.1111/ijmr.12030

Klein, R., Rai, A., & Straub, D. W. (2007). Competitive and cooperative positioning in supply chain logistics relationships. *Decision Sciences*, *38*(4), 611–646. doi:10.1111/j.1540-5915.2007.00172.x

Kotb, A., Roberts, C., & Stoner, G. (2013). E-business in accounting education in the UK and Ireland: Influences on inclusion in the curriculum. *The International Journal of Management Education*, *11*(3), 150–162. doi:10.1016/j.ijme.2013.05.002

Kumar, K., & van Dissel, H. G. (1996). Sustainable collaboration: Managing conflict and cooperation in interorganizational systems. *Management Information Systems Quarterly*, *20*(3), 279–300. doi:10.2307/249657

Lai, J. Y., Kan, C. W., & Ulhas, K. R. (2013). Impacts of employee participation and trust on e-business readiness, benefits, and satisfaction. *Information Systems and e-Business Management, 11*(2), 265–285.

Laudon, K. C., & Laudon, J. P. (2005). *Management information systems: Managing the digital firm.* Upper Saddle River, NJ: Prentice Hall.

Laudon, K. C., & Traver, C. G. (2009). *E-commerce: Business, technology and society*. Upper Saddle River, NJ: Prentice Hall.

Lee, S., & Lim, G. G. (2005). The impact of partnership attributes on EDI implementation success. *Information & Management*, *42*(4), 503–516. doi:10.1016/S0378-7206(03)00153-8

Leyton, D., Pino, J. A., & Ochoa, S. F. (2015). EBTAM: Technology acceptance in e-business environments. *Information Systems and e-Business Management*, *13*(2), 211–234. doi: 10.1007/s10257-014-0255-2

Li, F., Pieńkowski, D., van Moorsel, A., & Smith, C. (2012). A holistic framework for trust in online transactions. *International Journal of Management Reviews*, *14*(1), 85–103. doi:10.1111/j.1468-2370.2011.00311.x

Li, K., Idemudia, E. C., Lin, Z., & Yu, Y. (2012). A framework for intermediated online targeted advertising with banner ranking mechanism. *Information Systems and e-Business Management*, *10*(2), 183–200. doi:10.1007/s10257-010-0134-4

Liang, T., Ho, Y., Li, Y., & Turban, E. (2011). What drives social commerce: The role of social support and relationship quality. *International Journal of Electronic Commerce*, *16*(2), 69–90. doi:10.2753/JEC1086-4415160204

Lin, I. C., & Chang, C. C. (2009). A countable and time-bound password-based user authentication scheme for the applications of electronic commerce. *Information Science*, *179*(9), 1269–1277. doi:10.1016/j.ins.2008.12.026

Lin, L. M., & Hsia, T. L. (2011). Core capabilities for practitioners in achieving e-business innovation. *Computers in Human Behavior*, *27*(5), 1884–1891. doi:10.1016/j.chb.2011.04.012

Lin, Z. (2014). An empirical investigation of user and system recommendations in e-commerce. *Decision Support Systems*, *68*, 111–124. doi:10.1016/j.dss.2014.10.003

Liu, B., Cao, S. G., & He, W. (2011). Distributed data mining for e-business. *Information Technology Management*, *12*(2), 67–79. doi:10.1007/s10799-011-0091-8

Lu, X. H., Huang, L. H., & Heng, M. S. H. (2006). Critical success factors of inter-organizational information systems: A case study of Cisco and Xiao Tong in China. *Information & Management*, *43*(3), 395–408. doi:10.1016/j.im.2005.06.007

Maity, M., & Dass, M. (2014). Consumer decision-making across modern and traditional channels: E-commerce, m-commerce, in-store. *Decision Support Systems*, *61*, 34–46. doi:10.1016/j.dss.2014.01.008

Marchet, G., Perego, A., & Perotti, S. (2009). An exploratory study of ICT adoption in the Italian freight transportation industry. *International Journal of Physical Distribution & Logistics Management*, *39*(9), 785–812. doi:10.1108/09600030911008201

Markus, M. L. (2004). Technology management: Using IT to drive organizational change. *Journal of Information Technology*, *19*(1), 4–20. doi:10.1057/palgrave.jit.2000002

Matopoulos, A., Vlachopoulou, M., & Manthou, V. (2007). Exploring the impact of e-business adoption on logistics processes: Empirical evidence from the food industry. *International Journal of Logistics Research and Applications*, *10*(2), 109–122. doi:10.1080/13675560701427270

McKnight, D. H., Choudhury, V., & Kacmar, C. (2002). The impact of initial consumer trust on intentions to transaction with a website: A trust building model. *The Journal of Strategic Information Systems*, *11*(3/4), 297–323. doi:10.1016/S0963-8687(02)00020-3

Michaelidou, N., Siamagka, N. T., & Christodoulides, G. (2011). Usage, barriers and measurement of social media marketing: An exploratory investigation of small and medium B2B brands. *Industrial Marketing Management*, *40*(7), 1153–1159. doi:10.1016/j.indmarman.2011.09.009

Mishra, V. (2011). The influence of e-business alliance network on e-business firm's performance: An exploratory study. *Journal of Service Science Research*, *3*(2), 153–184. doi: 10.1007/s12927-011-0007-5

Morosan, C. (2014). Toward an integrated model of adoption of mobile phones for purchasing ancillary services in air travel. *International Journal of Contemporary Hospitality Management*, *26*(2), 246–271. doi:10.1108/IJCHM-11-2012-0221

Mukhopadhyay, S. K., & Setoputro, R. (2004). Reverse logistics in e-business: Optimal price and return policy. *International Journal of Physical Distribution & Logistics Management*, *34*(1), 70–89. doi:10.1108/09600030410515691

Nguyen, H. O. (2013). Critical factors in e-business adoption: Evidence from Australian transport and logistics companies. *International Journal of Production Economics*, *146*(1), 300–312. doi:10.1016/j.ijpe.2013.07.014

Norris, G., Hurley, J., Hartley, K., Dunleavy, J., & Balls, J. (2000). *E-business and ERP: Transforming the enterprise*. New York, NY: John Wiley & Sons.

Nurmilaakso, J. M. (2008). Adoption of e-business functions and migration from EDI-based to XML-based e-business frameworks in supply chain integration. *International Journal of Production Economics*, *113*(2), 721–733. doi:10.1016/j.ijpe.2007.11.001

Ogata, K., & Futatsugi, K. (2010). Proof score approach to analysis of electronic commerce protocols. *International Journal of Software Engineering and Knowledge Engineering*, *20*(2), 253–287. doi:10.1142/S0218194010004712

Oh, S. (2010). New role-based access control in ubiquitous e-business environment. *Journal of Intelligent Manufacturing*, *21*(5), 607–612. doi:10.1007/s10845-008-0208-z

Onetti, A., Zucchella, A., Jones, M. V., & McDougall-Covin, P. P. (2012). Internationalization, innovation and entrepreneurship: Business models for new technology-based firms. *Journal of Management and Governance*, *16*(3), 337–368. doi:10.1007/s10997-010-9154-1

Osmonbekov, T., & Gruen, T. (2013). Manufacturer–reseller e-business arrangements: The impact of inequity on relationship performance and the moderating role of dependence. *Industrial Marketing Management*, *42*(6), 872–879. doi:10.1016/j.indmarman.2013.05.013

Osterwalder, A., Pigneur, Y., & Tucci, C. L. (2005). Clarifying business models: Origins, present, and future of the concept. *Communications of the Association for Information Systems, 16*(1), 1–25.

Palopoli, L., Rosaci, D., & Ursino, D. (2006). Agents' roles in B2C e-commerce. *AI Communications, 19*(2), 95–126.

Papaioannou, E., Assimakopoulos, C., Sarmaniotis, C., & Georgiadis, C. K. (2013). Investigating customer satisfaction dimensions with service quality of online auctions: An empirical investigation of e-Bay. *Information Systems and e-Business Management, 11*(2), 313–330. doi:10.1007/s10257-012-0202-z

Papazoglou, M. P., & Ribbers, P. M. A. (2006). *E-business: Organizational and technical foundations*. Chichester, UK: John Wiley & Sons.

Parise, S., & Guinan, P. J. (2008). Marketing using Web 2.0. In *Proceedings of the 41st Hawaii International Conference on System Sciences*. Washington, DC: IEEE Computer Society Press.

Pathak, B., Garfinkel, R., Gopal, R. D., Venkatesan, R., & Yin, F. (2010). Empirical analysis of the impact of recommender systems on sales. *Journal of Management Information Systems, 27*(2), 159–188. doi:10.2753/MIS0742-1222270205

Pisano, G. P., & Verganti, R. (2008). Which kind of collaboration is right for you? *Harvard Business Review, 86*(12), 78–86.

Poon, S., & Swatman, P. M. C. (1998). A combined-method study of small business Internet commerce. *International Journal of Electronic Commerce, 2*(3), 31–46. doi:10.1080/10864415.1998.11518314

Qu, W. G., Pinsonneault, A., Tomiuk, D., Wang, S., & Liu, Y. (2015). The impacts of social trust on open and closed B2B e-commerce: A Europe-based study. *Information & Management, 52*(2), 151–159. doi:10.1016/j.im.2014.07.002

Rabinovich, E., Knemeyer, A. M., & Mayer, C. M. (2007). Why do Internet commerce firms incorporate logistics service providers in their distribution channels? The role of transaction costs and network strength. *Journal of Operations Management, 25*(3), 661–681. doi:10.1016/j.jom.2006.05.012

Rai, A., Patnayakuni, R., & Seth, N. (2006). Firm performance impacts of digitally enabled supply chain integration capabilities. *Management Information Systems Quarterly, 30*(2), 225–246.

Rai, A., Sambamurthy, V., & Agarwal, R. (2008). How CIOs can enable governance of value nets. *MIS Quarterly Executive, 7*(4), 193–204.

Raisinghani, M. S., Meade, L., & Schkade, L. L. (2007). Strategic e-business decision analysis using the Analytic Network Process. *IEEE Transactions on Engineering Management, 54*(4), 673–686. doi:10.1109/TEM.2007.906857

Rashidirad, M., Soltani, E., & Salimian, H. (2014). Do contextual factors matter? A missing link between competitive strategies–dynamic capabilities alignment and e-business value. *Strategic Change, 23*(1/2), 81–92. doi:10.1002/jsc.1961

Raymond, L., Bergeron, F., Croteau, A. M., & St-Pierre, J. (2015). Developing absorptive capacity through e-business: The case of international SMEs. *Journal of Small Business Management*, *53*, 75–94. doi:10.1111/jsbm.12192

Rezaei, R., Chiew, T. K., & Lee, S. P. (2014). A review on e-business interoperability frameworks. *Journal of Systems and Software*, *93*, 199–216. doi:10.1016/j.jss.2014.02.004

Rosaci, D., & Sarne, G. M. L. (2014). Multi-agent technology and ontologies to support personalization in B2C e-commerce. *Electronic Commerce Research and Applications*, *13*(1), 13–23. doi:10.1016/j.elerap.2013.07.003

Safa, N. S., & Ismail, M. A. (2013). A customer loyalty formation model in electronic commerce. *Economic Modelling*, *35*, 559–564. doi:10.1016/j.econmod.2013.08.011

Saraf, N., Langdon, C. S., & Gosain, S. (2007). IS application capabilities and relational value in interfirm partnerships. *Information Systems Research*, *18*(3), 320–339. doi:10.1287/isre.1070.0133

Savrul, M., Incekara, A., & Sener, S. (2014). The potential of e-commerce for SMEs in a globalizing business environment. *Procedia: Social and Behavioral Sciences*, *150*, 35–45. doi:10.1016/j.sbspro.2014.09.005

Seo, H. J., Lee, Y. S., Hur, J. J., & Kim, J. K. (2012). The impact of information and communication technology on skilled labor and organization types. *Information Systems Frontiers*, *14*(2), 445–455. doi:10.1007/s10796-010-9276-7

Shih, H. Y. (2012). The dynamics of local and interactive effects on innovation adoption: The case of electronic commerce. *Journal of Engineering and Technology Management*, *29*(3), 434–452. doi:10.1016/j.jengtecman.2012.06.001

Sillence, E., Briggs, P., Harris, P., & Fishwick, L. (2006). A framework for understanding trust factors in web-based health advice. *International Journal of Human-Computer Studies*, *64*(8), 697–713. doi:10.1016/j.ijhcs.2006.02.007

Singh, M., & Byrne, J. (2006). Performance evaluation of e-business in Australia. *The Electronic Journal of Information Systems Evaluation*, *8*(1), 71–80.

Sohrabi, B., Mahmoudian, P., & Raeesi, I. (2012). A framework for improving e-commerce websites usability using a hybrid genetic algorithm and neural network system. *Neural Computing & Applications*, *21*(5), 1017–1029. doi:10.1007/s00521-011-0674-7

Srivastava, A. (2009). Electronic signatures and security issues: An empirical study. *Computer Law & Security Report*, *25*(5), 432–446. doi:10.1016/j.clsr.2009.05.007

Stableford, S., & Mettger, W. (2007). Plain language: A strategic response to the health literacy challenge. *Journal of Public Health Policy*, *28*(1), 71–93. doi:10.1057/palgrave.jphp.3200102 PMID:17363939

Straub, D., & Watson, R. (2001). Research commentary: Transformational issues in researching IS and net-enabled organizations. *Information Systems Research*, *12*(4), 337–345. doi:10.1287/isre.12.4.337.9706

Su, Q., & Chen, L. (2015). A method for discovering clusters of e-commerce interest patterns using click-stream data. *Electronic Commerce Research and Applications*, *14*(1), 1–13. doi:10.1016/j.elerap.2014.10.002

Subramani, M. R. (2004). How do suppliers benefit from IT use in supply chain relationships? *Management Information Systems Quarterly*, *28*(1), 45–74.

Swamynathan, G., Wilson, C., Boe, B., Almeroth, K., & Zhao, B. (2008). Do social networks improve e-commerce? A study on social marketplaces. In *Proceedings of the First Workshop on Online Social Networks*. New York, NY: ACM Press. doi:10.1145/1397735.1397737

Tan, F. T. C., Pan, S. L., & Zuo, M. (2014). The role of organisational interdependencies and asset orchestration in business integration: A case study of M.com. *International Journal of Information Management*, *34*(6), 780–784. doi:10.1016/j.ijinfomgt.2014.07.004

Teo, T. S. H., & Yu, Y. (2005). Online buying behavior: A transaction cost economics perspective. *Omega: The International Journal of Management Science*, *33*(5), 451–465. doi:10.1016/j.omega.2004.06.002

Theodosiou, M., & Katsikea, E. (2012). Antecedents and performance of electronic business adoption in the hotel industry. *European Journal of Marketing*, *46*(1/2), 258–283. doi:10.1108/03090561211189329

Thomas, B., Miller, C., & Simmons, G. (2015). An examination of regional policy implications pertaining to SME e-business adoption in South-East Wales. *Strategic Change*, *24*(5), 429–446. doi:10.1002/jsc.2020

Tian, Y., Ye, Z., Yan, Y., & Sun, M. (2015). A practical model to predict the repeat purchasing pattern of consumers in the C2C e-commerce. *Electronic Commerce Research*, *15*(4), 571–583. doi:10.1007/s10660-015-9201-8

Tian, Z., Zhang, Z., & Guan, X. (2013). A new evolution model for B2C e-commerce market. *Information Technology Management*, *14*(3), 205–215. doi:10.1007/s10799-013-0159-8

Tomlinson, M. (2000). Tackling e-commerce security issues head on. *Computer Fraud & Security*, *2000*(11), 10–13. doi:10.1016/S1361-3723(00)11017-6

Turban, E., Lee, J., King, D., & Chung, H. M. (2000). *Electronic commerce: A managerial perspective*. Upper Saddle River, NJ: Prentice Hall.

Vaithianathan, S. (2010). A review of e-commerce literature on India and research agenda for the future. *Electronic Commerce Research*, *10*(1), 83–97. doi:10.1007/s10660-010-9046-0

Volusion. (2006). *Ebusiness and its significance in today's marketplace*. Retrieved from http://www.volusion.com/ecommerce-blog/articles/e-business-solution-e-commerce

Wang, H. J., & Wu, H. (2011). Supporting process design for e-business via an integrated process repository. *Information Technology & Management*, *12*(2), 97–109. doi:10.1007/s10799-010-0076-z

Wang, S. (2001). Designing information systems for electronic commerce. *Industrial Management & Data Systems*, *101*(6), 304–314. doi:10.1108/EUM0000000005580

Wheeler, B. C. (2002). NEBIC: A dynamic capabilities theory for assessing net-enablement. *Information Systems Research*, *13*(2), 125–146. doi:10.1287/isre.13.2.125.89

Wigand, R. T., Benjamin, R. I., & Birkland, J. (2008). Web 2.0 and beyond: Implications for electronic commerce. In *Proceedings of the 10th International Conference on Electronic Commerce*. New York, NY: ACM Press. doi:10.1145/1409540.1409550

Wu, J., Li, L., & Xu, L. D. (2014). A randomized pricing decision support system in electronic commerce. *Decision Support Systems*, *58*, 43–52. doi:10.1016/j.dss.2013.01.015

Wu, J. H., & Hisa, T. L. (2008). Developing e-business dynamic capabilities: An analysis of e-commerce innovation from I-, M-, to U-commerce. *Journal of Organizational Computing and Electronic Commerce*, *18*(2), 1–17. doi:10.1080/10919390701807525

Wu, J. N., Zhong, W. J., & Mei, S. E. (2011). Application capability of e-business, e-business success, and organizational performance: Empirical evidence from China. *Technological Forecasting and Social Change*, *78*(8), 1412–1425. doi:10.1016/j.techfore.2011.03.023

Xia, Y., & Zhang, G. P. (2010). The impact of the online channel on retailers' performances: An empirical evaluation. *Decision Sciences*, *41*(3), 517–546. doi:10.1111/j.1540-5915.2010.00279.x

Yan, B. N., Lee, T. S., & Lee, T. P. (2015). Analysis of research papers on e-commerce (2000–2013): Based on a text mining approach. *Scientometrics*, *105*(1), 403–417. doi:10.1007/s11192-015-1675-6

Yousafzai, S. Y., Pallister, J. G., & Foxall, G. R. (2003). A proposed model of e-trust for electronic banking. *Technovation*, *23*(11), 847–860. doi:10.1016/S0166-4972(03)00130-5

Zhang, T., Agarwal, R., & Lucas, H. C. (2011). The value of IT-enabled retailer learning: Personalized product recommendations and customer store loyalty in electronic markets. *Management Information Systems Quarterly*, *35*(4), 859–881.

Zhang, Y., Deng, X., Wei, D., & Deng, Y. (2012). Assessment of e-commerce security using AHP and evidential reasoning. *Expert Systems with Applications*, *39*(3), 3611–3623. doi:10.1016/j.eswa.2011.09.051

Zhu, F., & Zhang, X. (2010). Impact of online consumer reviews on sales: The moderating role of product and consumer characteristics. *Journal of Marketing*, *74*(2), 133–148. doi:10.1509/jmkg.74.2.133

Zhu, K. (2004). The complementarity of information technology infrastructure and ecommerce capability: A resource-based assessment of their business value. *Journal of Management Information Systems*, *21*(1), 167–202.

Zhu, K., & Kraemer, K. L. (2005). Post-adoption variations in usage and value of e-business by organizations: Cross-country evidence from the retail industry. *Information Systems Research*, *16*(1), 61–84. doi:10.1287/isre.1050.0045

Zuo, W., Huang, Q., Fan, C., & Zhang, Z. (2013). Quality management of B2C e-commerce service based on human factors engineering. *Electronic Commerce Research and Applications*, *12*(5), 309–320. doi:10.1016/j.elerap.2013.03.005

## ADDITIONAL READING


Agudo-Peregrina, A. F., Pascual-Miguel, F. J., & Chaparro-Peláez, J. (2014). It's never the same: The role of homogeneity in online services. *Service Business*, *8*(3), 453–464. doi:10.1007/s11628-014-0249-7

Andoh-Baidoo, F. K., Osei-Bryson, K. M., & Amoako-Gyampah, K. (2012). Effects of firm and IT characteristics on the value of e-commerce initiatives: An inductive theoretical framework. *Information Systems Frontiers*, *14*(2), 237–259. doi:10.1007/s10796-010-9234-4

Banerjee, P. K., & Ma, L. C. (2012). Routinisation of B2B e-commerce by small firms: A process perspective. *Information Systems Frontiers*, *14*(5), 1033–1046. doi:10.1007/s10796-011-9329-6

Blasco-Arcas, L., Hernandez-Ortega, B., & Jimenez-Martinez, J. (2013). Adopting television as a new channel for e-commerce. The influence of interactive technologies on consumer behavior. *Electronic Commerce Research*, *13*(4), 457–475. doi:10.1007/s10660-013-9132-1

Capece, G., Calabrese, A., Di Pillo, F., Costa, R., & Crisciotti, V. (2013). The impact of national culture on e-commerce acceptance: The Italian case. *Knowledge and Process Management*, *20*(2), 102–112. doi:10.1002/kpm.1413

Chen, M. Y., & Teng, C. I. (2013). A comprehensive model of the effects of online store image on purchase intention in an e-commerce environment. *Electronic Commerce Research*, *13*(1), 1–23. doi:10.1007/s10660-013-9104-5

Costa, A. A., & Tavares, L. V. (2014). Social e-business as support for construction e-procurement: E-procurement network dynamics. *Automation in Construction*, *43*, 180–186. doi:10.1016/j.autcon.2014.03.019

Dakhlia, S., & Strauss, R. P. (2013). Should sales taxes be imposed on e-commerce? *Journal of Public Economic Theory*, *15*(6), 803–828.

Fauska, P., Kryvinska, N., & Strauss, C. (2014). Agile management of complex goods & services bundles for B2B e-commerce by global narrow-specialized companies. *Global Journal of Flexible Systems Management*, *15*(1), 5–23. doi:10.1007/s40171-013-0054-5

Georgiadis, C. K., Stiakakis, E., & Ravindran, A. R. (2013). Editorial for the special issue: Digital economy and e-commerce technology. *Operations Research*, *13*(1), 1–4. doi:10.1007/s12351-011-0122-6

Gómez-López, M. T., Gasca, R. M., & Pérez-Álvarez, J. M. (2015). Compliance validation and diagnosis of business data constraints in business processes at runtime. *Information Systems*, *48*, 26–43. doi:10.1016/j.is.2014.07.007

Hu, L., Lin, K., Hassan, M. M., Alamri, A., & Alelaiwi, A. (2015). CFSF: On cloud-based recommendation for large-scale e-commerce. *Mobile Networks and Applications*, *20*(3), 380–390. doi:10.1007/s11036-014-0560-5

Lai, J. Y., Ulhas, K. R., & Lin, J. D. (2014). Assessing and managing e-commerce service convenience. *Information Systems Frontiers*, *16*(2), 273–289. doi:10.1007/s10796-012-9344-2

Luo, X. R., Xu, H., & Yao, L. J. (2012). E-commerce intelligence development and research in the Greater China Region. *Electronic Markets*, *22*(2), 71–72. doi:10.1007/s12525-012-0100-8

Otim, S., & Grover, V. (2012). Resolving uncertainty and creating value from the exercise of e-commerce investment options. *Information Systems Journal*, *22*(4), 261–287. doi:10.1111/j.1365-2575.2011.00385.x

Papastavrou, S., Chrysanthis, P. K., & Samaras, G. (2014). Performance vs. freshness in web database applications. *World Wide Web (Bussum)*, *17*(5), 969–995. doi:10.1007/s11280-013-0262-0

Peng, L., & Lai, L. (2014). A service innovation evaluation framework for tourism e-commerce in China based on BP neural network. *Electronic Markets*, *24*(1), 37–46. doi:10.1007/s12525-013-0148-0

Piva, F., & Dahab, R. (2013). E-commerce of digital items and the problem of item validation: Introducing the concept of reversible degradation. *Applicable Algebra in Engineering Communication and Computing*, *24*(3/4), 277–308. doi:10.1007/s00200-013-0197-9

Qiu, J., Lin, Z., & Li, Y. (2015). Predicting customer purchase behavior in the e-commerce context. *Electronic Commerce Research*, *15*(4), 427–452. doi:10.1007/s10660-015-9191-6

Rawat, S., & Divekar, R. (2014). Developing a social media presence strategy for an e-commerce business. *Procedia Economics and Finance*, *11*, 626–634. doi:10.1016/S2212-5671(14)00228-7

Shiau, W. L., & Dwivedi, Y. K. (2013). Citation and co-citation analysis to identify core and emerging knowledge in electronic commerce research. *Scientometrics*, *94*(3), 1317–1337. doi:10.1007/s11192-012-0807-5

Shojaiemehr, B., & Rafsanjani, M. K. (2014). A fuzzy system approach to multilateral automated negotiation in B2C e-commerce. *Neural Computing & Applications*, *25*(2), 367–377. doi:10.1007/s00521-013-1491-y

Sigman, B. P., & Boston, B. J. (2013). Digital discernment: An e-commerce web site evaluation tool. *Decision Sciences Journal of Innovative Education*, *11*(1), 29–46. doi:10.1111/j.1540-4609.2012.00367.x

Sila, I. (2013). Factors affecting the adoption of B2B e-commerce technologies. *Electronic Commerce Research*, *13*(2), 199–236. doi:10.1007/s10660-013-9110-7

Weitzenboeck, E. M. (2015). Looking back to see ahead: The changing face of users in European e-commerce law. *Artificial Intelligence and Law*, *23*(3), 201–215. doi:10.1007/s10506-015-9170-1

Zhang, D., Yan, Z., Jiang, H., & Kim, T. (2014). A domain-feature enhanced classification model for the detection of Chinese phishing e-business websites. *Information & Management*, *51*(7), 845–853. doi:10.1016/j.im.2014.08.003

## KEY TERMS AND DEFINITIONS

**Business-to-Business:** The trading between firms characterized by relatively large volumes, competitive prices, and fast delivery times.

**Electronic Business:** The application of information and communications technology in support of all the activities of business.

**Electronic Commerce:** The business that is transacted by transferring data electronically, especially over the Internet.

**Information and Communications Technology:** The creation of computer systems and applications, especially those that move data around a computer network, between clients and servers, or over the Internet.

**Information System:** A combination of hardware, software, infrastructure, and trained personnel organized to facilitate planning, control, coordination, and decision making in an organization.

**Information Technology:** The development, implementation, and maintenance of computer hardware and software systems to organize and communicate information electronically.

**Internet:** A process of connecting a computer to any other computer anywhere in the world via dedicated routers and servers.

**Marketing:** The management process through which products and services move from concept to the customer.

# Chapter 2
# E Commerce as a Tool for Resource Expansion:
## Postal Partnerships, Data Protection Legislation and the Mitigation of Implementation Gaps

**Marianne Ojo**
*North-West University, South Africa*

## ABSTRACT

*This chapter is aimed at illustrating how the potential of E commerce as a tool for resource expansion, can be maximized where information gaps, asymmetries, and more specifically, implementation gaps are addressed and mitigated. Engaging stakeholders, as well as bright line rules - distinguished from principles, at relevant phases and stages of mediation process between agents and stakeholders, would not only serve to foster greater accountability, but also ensure that better enforcement mechanisms are in place. Hence chapter illustrates how the stakeholder theory can be considered to be consistent with value maximization. Whilst incomplete contracts provide benefits of flexibility, they have also been criticized for facilitating lack of clarity in respect of objectives, focus and accountability in the decision making process. Furthermore, through the engagement of stakeholders, as well as appropriate forms of regulation, the chapter will also, simultaneously, illustrate how a "properly constructed Balanced Scorecard" can comprehensively communicate enterprises' business strategies.*

## INTRODUCTION

E commerce is generally considered to relate to "the purchase and sale of goods and services over the internet, whether business to consumer (B2C) or business to business (B2B)." As well as constituting part of the "multi-channel business model" its expansion to incorporate "m-commerce", namely, shopping via mobile devices, as well as "s-commerce", namely, shopping via social media networks, is highlighted (Department for Business Innovation & Skills, 2013, p. 8).

DOI: 10.4018/978-1-4666-9921-2.ch002

Copyright © 2016, IGI Global. Copying or distributing in print or electronic forms without written permission of IGI Global is prohibited.

The importance of facilitating successful delivery from the source to consumer, across the various distribution channels is crucial to a firm's progress or success in implementing an enterprise's E commerce goals and objectives. As well as identifying challenges which could hinder, or are presently hindering the fulfillment of desired objectives - by way of continuous acquisition and refinement of information, effective knowledge sharing and management - fostered through partnership with distributive agents, it is also essential to have adequate resources to facilitate the execution and transformation of such knowledge resource and asset into desired outcomes. "The best marketing in the world won't help you if the carrier leaves the package out in the rain or the bottles are broken" (E-commerce Europe, 2013).

In selecting the aims and objectives of this chapter, vital areas and issues which relate to the above-mentioned statements have been taken into consideration: namely, (i) the importance of successful delivery following the ordering of products on the internet (be it from originating business to a business firm or to a consumer), (ii) addressing global challenges faced by selected jurisdictions across the globe as a means of ensuring successful realization of E commerce goals, as well as iii) means whereby successful partnership arrangements can be forged and fostered between the originating firm, distributing channels and the all-important postal carrier.

## Objectives of Chapter

The objectives of the chapter are hereby highlighted as follows:

1. To identify, analyze and address global challenges encountered by E commerce firms in selected jurisdictions across the globe.
2. To investigate and propose means of harnessing Ecommerce as a tool for resource expansion.
3. To investigate the extent to which informational gap in executing Ecommerce goals has been mitigated over the years and also investigate if there is a corresponding decrease or increase in level of implementation gaps, as well as reasons for such increased or decreased gaps.

The first three objectives will primarily be facilitated through a discussion of a vital issue confronting the theories which constitute the focal point of discussion in this chapter. The issue referred to being information asymmetries and the theories being the principal-agent theory and the broader stakeholder theory. An incorporation of the role of corporate social responsibility will assist in facilitating the objective of illustrating how E commerce can be used as a tool for resource expansion.

4. Investigating gaps in data privacy and protection legislation and directives as means of proposing ways whereby greater trust can be fostered between the originating business, distributing channels and consumer.
5. To investigate buyer spending habits, consumer preferences and behaviors across the globe as a means of proposing how e commerce businesses can better understand and address consumer needs, hence also mitigating costs which could be incurred through returns.

In investigating and addressing the above-mentioned objectives, the chapter will also attempt to contribute to the existing and previous literature on why certain jurisdictions have been more successful with their E tailing business models, as well as make recommendations aimed at addressing present concerns which may relate to implementation, strategy and design, and environmental concerns.

## Background

In line with the first objective, the scope of the chapter will embrace jurisdictional considerations from all continents around the globe (that is Africa, Asia, North America, Europe, Latin America and Australia), as well as harness the success results achieved in certain jurisdictions as a means of promoting development in other jurisdictions where such information may prove to be priceless. For example, security issues, which constitutes a principal challenge in several jurisdictions in Africa, Asia, and Latin America, has been considered to be a success story in Australia.

As regards the second objective, E commerce whilst constituting a threat and challenge to certain businesses, namely SMEs and postal firms, has also provided revenue generating opportunities which these firms and enterprises can exploit. From this perspective, its significance in serving as a potential means of cost reduction and innovation will be highlighted through investigative analyses aimed at exploring how partnerships between E commerce firms, SMEs and postal agencies could maximize economic efficiencies, achieve profit maximization objectives - in developed as well as, developing countries.

Furthermore, the significance of the second objective also lies in its potential to providing the answer to how knowledge spillovers can be gained from information sharing and successful partnership arrangements. This is also crucially linked to the third objective: the goal of mitigating the "implementation gap".

In relation to the third objective, namely how the "implementation gap" in successfully executing and incorporating informational resources could be mitigated, through better knowledge management techniques, the main question to be addressed here not being what to do, but how to go about achieving goals of successfully implementing and deriving benefits that can be generated from E commerce.

In relation to the fourth objective, which focuses on data privacy, protection legislation and directives, this will involve a global and international comparison of applicable legislation. It will do so as a means of investigating concerns relating to privacy laws, and consider ways whereby trust can be fostered or regained by consumers in these jurisdictions, as well as other jurisdictions. It will also attempt to investigate the extent to which data privacy and protection legislation has impacted consumer decisions to engage in social networks and other vital Ecommerce channels. In relation to the fifth objective, late deliveries, damaged goods or poor quality (poorer than expected quality of delivered good), may constitute reasons for returns and correspondingly lower revenues.

Furthermore, accessibility to E commerce, through m commerce or s commerce devices, determines the extent to which certain jurisdictions are engaged in E commerce. Even though certain target audiences in particular jurisdictions spend several hours and considerable time on social networks, lack of trust and confidentiality in data protection, high fraud levels, as well as in availability of certain E commerce products, such as Kindle Direct products (Amazon) in certain areas, may discourage such audiences from engaging in respective E commerce transactions.

In South East Asia, for example, it is contended that "a major market gap stems from the extent of Amazon.com's presence in the B2C market segment" (Greene, 2014). Furthermore, in many countries where feature phones are still very popular, in comparison to more sophisticated smart phones used by some other jurisdictions, E commerce businesses may be wise in seeking other advertising avenues - such as attractive and captivating billboards and shopping malls to captivate their target audiences. In addressing the stated aims and objectives, this chapter, it is hoped, will make a substantial contribution to the existing and previous literature on the topic as well as recommend innovative solutions to the most up-to-date trends in the E commerce field and global market.

## Concepts and Definitions

As well as the definitions provided under the introductory section, namely that:

- E commerce is the purchase and sale of goods and services over the internet, whether business to consumer (B2C) or business to business (B2B)" two further definitions, provided by UNCTAD (2015, p. 4) are as follows:
- C2C is the modern version of using the classified advertising section in a local newspaper or going to an auction, as well as embracing online auction platforms such as EBay - offering possibilities for informal enterprises to engage in Ecommerce.
- B2G is similar to B2B except that, in this case, buyer is a government entity - such as public E procurement.

## Distinguishing between Information and Implementation Gaps

Information gap can be defined as the gap between knowledge which is actually required to successfully launch an Ecommerce product (goods or services) and knowledge which business or enterprise actually commands or is in possession of, in engaging in a successful or profitable launch. On the other hand, implementation gap may be defined as the gap between knowledge actually required by the business or enterprise to successfully launch an Ecommerce product - as well as the manufacturing and technological facilities and expertise which the enterprise requires in successfully launching the E commerce product whilst sustaining a long term based successful launch, and actual knowledge, expertise and technological facilities with which business or enterprise is equipped with in sustaining a long term based profitable or successful launch.

Within the context of the above mentioned definitions, informational resources is distinguished from those resources and facilities required to convert knowledge base and information into desired outcome. Hence implementation involves the know-how as well as facilities to convert information into desired outcome.

Some contributory factors to informational gaps

1. Degree of information or knowledge about target group
   That is, preferences or tastes of those businesses or consumers who constitute the focus of the enterprise's profit maximization goals
2. Technological factors
   Degree of information about the technology or facilities required to launch the E commerce product
3. Economic factors
   Information actually acquired by the enterprise in respect of its competitors
4. Environmental, political and religious factors
   Information about environment and jurisdictional related matters which may affect a successful launch - particularly over a longer term
5. Legal factors
   Legal, institutional arrangements which may impact the successful launch of the product
6. Social and cultural factors

## Launching a Product

Stages of a product launch

1) Production -------------------> 2) Marketing-------------------->3) Distribution

In certain cases the business or enterprise may or may not be involved in all the stages. For example with Amazon, books may commence from stage one, whilst in certain other cases it may choose to serve simply as a distribution channel.

Advertising may be involved within the marketing as well as distribution phases and in these phases, the business may well inquire into whether better advertisement would be carried out by a distribution outlet or decide that it is better endowed with information from the production stage and marketing stages, namely the generation of reviews in advertising the product.

It would also investigate the consequences that outsourcing any of the stages would have as regards marginally or significantly contributing to the revenues generated by the enterprise.

According to UNCTAD (2015, p. 4), E commerce can be divided into four stages namely:

- Information gathering
- Agreement
- Transaction
- Delivery

This chapter will aim to illustrate how stakeholders can be effectively engaged in each of the above-mentioned stages in achieving the goals of profit maximization, as well as corporate social goals. And whilst it might appear that multiple goals and objectives could divert the focus of the firm's agents, as regards planning, decision making and control, it will also be highlighted that effective negotiation at all levels of the above mentioned four stages, can help eliminate inefficiencies, which in turn would transform to value adding attributes, as well as a realization of the principal objective of profit maximization.

With respect to the goal of profit maximization - particularly for small enterprises who find it burdensome to afford costs associated with the compliance and monitoring of rules, taxes and regulations, it may be worth exploring how each of the above-mentioned stages may be exploited through the utilization of E commerce as resource and expansion generating tool. This would embrace such innovations as how stakeholders can be incorporated into the information gathering phase with the ultimate goal of reducing information asymmetries, as well generating value adding knowledge base and expertise which would facilitate a successful longer term horizon whilst mitigating implementation gaps in the process.

With respect to agreements, the relevance of federal, state regulations and tailor made regulations which are particularized to individual firms requires consideration. Even though it is argued that "compliance costs place small businesses at a competitive disadvantage - with the cost disadvantage confronting small businesses being driven by environmental regulations, tax compliance, occupational safety and health and homeland security regulations" (Crain & Crain, 2010, p. 57), large firms are also acknowledged to frequently bear the cost of economic regulations - this being considered to be applicable to nearly every sector - with the exception of health care (Crain & Crain, 2010, p. 58). Tax breaks could also be introduced - particularly with regards to smaller enterprises who find it cumbersome to sustain associated compliance and regulatory costs.

As regards matters of direct taxation, the main challenges raised by the digital economy, according to the OECD (2014, p. 125), are classified under three headings:

- **Nexus:** Elaborated on as "the continual increase in the potential of digital technologies and the reduced need in many cases for extensive physical presence in order to carry on business, combined with the increasing role of network effects generated by customer interactions", which are also considered by the OECD to raise questions as to whether the current rules to determine nexus with a jurisdiction for tax purposes are appropriate.
- **Data:** "The growth in sophistication of information technologies" which is considered by the OECD to have permitted companies in the digital economy to gather and use information across borders to an unprecedented degree which is also considered to raise the issues of how to attribute value created from the generation of data through digital products and services, and of how to characterize for tax purposes a person or entity's supply of data in a transaction, for example, as a free supply of a good, as a barter transaction, or some other way.
- **Characterization:** "The development of new digital products or means of delivering services", which in the OECD's view, creates uncertainties in relation to the proper characterization of payments made in the context of new business models, particularly in relation to cloud computing.

As regards delivery, the role of postal agencies and the effectiveness which such agencies can contribute in facilitating value adding benefits and contributions to the chain has been acknowledged. As well as the potential to improve access and avenues for deliveries - particularly in those jurisdictions where postal coverage is poor and the use of postal codes is not even in operation, postal agencies can serve as an expansion generating tool by contributing such expertise and resource to E commerce. Collaborations between local postal agencies, furthermore can serve as an expansion-generating avenue for such local agencies with partnerships being facilitated - not only with respect to the E commerce products being distributed, but also as advertising platforms for E commerce products, products being sold by local postal agencies and E commerce designated postal carriers. Websites with links incorporating the partnership whilst facilitating the advertising of all products constituting the focus of a possible tripartite arrangement between E commerce business, E commerce designated postal carrier, and local postal agencies.

## MAIN FOCUS OF THE CHAPTER

### Role of Corporate Social Responsibility as a Corporate Governance Mechanism: Reconciling Theories

In applying the role of corporate social responsibility, as well as the impact which stakeholder engagement in the E commerce process could generate, in mitigating informational asymmetries and fostering value maximization, reference will be specifically made to Sacconi's model of corporate social responsibility as an extension of corporate governance (2004), and also the role of self-regulation in the mediation process. This particularly being the case where small and medium enterprises are concerned.

According to Sacconi (2004, p. 6), corporate social responsibility can be defined as:

*A model of extended corporate governance whereby those in control of the firm have responsibilities that range from the fulfillment of their fiduciary duties owed towards the owners (principal) to the fulfillment of analogous fiduciary duties owed towards all the firm's stakeholders."*

Jensen (2002, p. 13), argues that:

*To the extent that the stakeholder theory says that firms should pay attention to all their constituencies, that the theory is unassailable, and that to this extent, the theory is completely consistent with value maximization or value-seeking behavior."*

In seeking to reconcile both views, it will be illustrated that firms can effectively involve the engagement of stakeholders as a means of attaining value maximization objectives - even under the stakeholder theory, where corporate social responsibility is involved and where certain other considerations which involve the effective implementation of self-regulation, bright line rules and principles are appropriately incorporated in facilitating better communication between the principal and stakeholders of the firm.

In illustrating the role of corporate social responsibility as "a model of extended corporate governance" reference is made by Sacconi (2004, p. 24) to the self-regulation approach to corporate social responsibility which he distinguishes into:

- Self-regulation based on a discretionary approach
- Self-regulation based on voluntary compliance with explicit norms

Whilst the discretionary approach is more synonymous with principles based regulation, the second approach lies in between a principles based approach and a bright line rules approach since the term "voluntary" denotes a persuasive - as distinguished from a mandatory approach to regulatory enforcement.

In consolidating on the reasons attributable to pessimistic views about the degree of accountability accorded by the corporate social responsibility model, Jensen (2002, p. 9) adds that:

*Whereas value maximization provides corporate managers with a single objective, stakeholder theory directs corporate managers to serve many masters - with resulting consequences of managerial confusion, conflict inefficiency, and probably competitive failure - given the absence as well as the operation of a clear objective.*

In drawing a conclusion about the stakeholder theory he adds that (see 2002, p. 21):

*If widely adopted, the stakeholder theory will reduce social welfare - even though it is claimed by its advocates to increase it."*

Even though the above arguments are well founded on the bases of Jensen's arguments (see 2002, p. 14), namely the assertions that stakeholder theory leaves board of directors and executives in firms with "no principled criterion for decision making," as well as the reasoning that the theory is popular with managers and directors of firms since it encourages them to pursue short term interests, with less accountability for stewardship of firm's resources,

If adopted with the engagement of stakeholders at appropriate stages, as well as the incorporation of applicable and most suitable forms of rules during such phases of the mediation process between agents and stakeholders, such that flexibility is facilitated in the process to allow for contingencies whilst also compelling effective enforcement and compliance mechanisms, corporate social responsibility should be fostered through the outcomes emanating from better, focused planning, control, decision making, as well as more effective accountability, compliance and enforcement mechanisms. Crucial to achieving these outcomes, is the ability to allocate between persuasive rules which should be incorporated to facilitate flexibility, or more penal based rules which should foster better compliance and enforcement.

According to Sacconi (2004, p. 32), stakeholders should be engaged in all phases of the CSR management function, with effective dialogue taking place within these stages:

1. Creating and establishment of the social contract (which clearly stipulates the firm's fiduciary duties towards its stakeholders).
2. Internal management and implementation - with the presence of external members on internal board or committees - both corporate board of directors or those set up "ad-hoc" to address corporate social responsibility.
3. Social accountability - this stage aiming to identify areas of effective interest of stakeholders.
4. Verification by an independent third party - as distinguished from auditors - with an independent third party controlling the verification of this phase .

Parker (2007, p. 31) defines meta regulation as:

- The proliferation of different forms of regulation, be it tools of state law or non-law mechanisms, each regulating one another.

Meta regulation, it is further added, can:

- Also entail any form of regulation (whether by tools of state law or other mechanisms) that regulates any other form of regulation. This might include legal regulation of self-regulation (establishing an oversight board above a self-regulatory professional association), non-legal methods of regulating internal corporate self-regulation or management, or the regulation of national law making by transitional bodies, and so on (see Sacconi, 2004, p. 7).

## Advantages of Self-Regulation

Some potential advantages of self-regulation as identified by Coglianese and others (2004, p. 6) are as follows:

- **Proximity:** Self-regulatory organizations are considered to be closer to the industry being regulated.
- **Flexibility.**
- **Compliance:** Self-regulation is considered to have the potential to contribute to a higher level of compliance with rules since the involvement of industry in establishing those rules facilitates greater acceptance of such rules by individual firms.

- **Resources:** Self-regulatory bodies are considered to have greater potential to secure required facilities and funding

Identified disadvantages include (see Coglianese et al, 2004, p. 7, 8):

- **Conflicts of Interest:** Which is attributed to "the very proximity which can help self-regulators acquire useful information" – since knowledge of a particular industry does not necessarily imply that the incentives of the self-regulator are projected in the right direction to enable such a regulator regulate more effectively
- **Inadequate Sanctions:** The advantage attributed to flexibility is also considered to have the potential to result in effective level of sanctions being imposed on serious perpetrators.
- Level of enforceability and insufficient monitoring of compliance with rules.

In addition to the level of accountability which has already been highlighted as a disadvantage previously, tendencies for regulatory capture - which are attributed to the proximity between the regulator and the regulated, constitutes another principal disadvantage which is associated with self regulation. In terms of flexibility, compliance, enforcement and accountability, the Enforced Self Regulation model is considered to confer greater benefits than self regulation. Under Enforced Self Regulation, greater compliance would be fostered, not only because "rules would be tailored to match the company – hence, i) rules could be simpler and have greater specificity of meaning, ii) the dangers of complexity and blandness may be avoided when rules relate to a finite and known set of circumstances rather than to an infinite and unknown range of business activities, but also because companies would be more committed to rules they wrote (Ayres and Braithwaite, 2001, p. 110,113)."

In comparing and contrasting advantages and disadvantages associated with regulatory competition to those associated with Enforced Self Regulation and how these could complement each other to address disadvantages attributed to self regulation, reference will now be made to a model based on Cooperative and Competitive Enforced Self Regulation (see Ojo, 2010 and 2011), which should not only offer greater flexibility, but also more accountability mechanisms which would facilitate compliance.

Such a model is represented diagrammatically below:

Basel Committee-----> Meta Regulation ----->State ------ >Enforced Self Regulation ---- >Firm

Meta regulation is carried out by the Basel Committee on Banking Supervision, whilst the State is involved in imposing Enforced Self Regulation on individual firms.

Enforced Self Regulation (in the form of binding regulations) is required – not only because the Basel Committee is in need of stronger enforcement mechanisms, but because the "race to bottom effects" attributed to unfettered regulatory competition needs to be addressed. Regulatory competition also offers flexibility in facilitating the modification of regulations - which not only helps in "optimally matching the interests of those that bear the cost and incur the benefit of regulation," but also helps regulators in facilitating more superior regulation (Pan, 2003, p. 3).

In highlighting why entrepreneurs choose to stay with an existing firm or rather compete with it, Spulber (2014, p. 16) makes reference to the "innovation game" which can be related to the Co-operative and Competitive Enforced Self Regulation Model and is illustrated thus:[1]

1. **Through Co-Operation:** In which case, he exemplifies as "technology transfer contract" whereby an existing firm which operates in a market with initial technology acquires discovery from the inventor and implements innovation and
2. **Through Competition:** In which case he refers to this scenario as "creative destruction" (2014, p. 172) since in his view, the inventor creates invention and formulates a new strategy which competes with the existing firm.

The above- mentioned, "strategic innovation game", according to Spulber, also implies a Coasian theorem - which will be discussed later on in the chapter in context with the discussion on transaction, monitoring costs and property rights in information. Further discussion on a consideration of transaction and monitoring costs, and the firm's decision to collaborate with an entrepreneur or stakeholder, taking into consideration, self regulatory costs, should highlight the role of self regulation, and particularly government enforced self regulation in determining why entrepreneurs choose to set up new firms or rather save costs by collaborating with existing firm - given those costs also associated with regulation.

Clearly defined property rights help to mitigate incidences of information asymmetries - which constitute an issue under incomplete contracts where the residual rights to control as regards information need to be allocated based on decisions which are contingent upon unforeseen circumstances. Whilst incomplete contracts are inevitable, monitoring costs as well as other costs associated with lack of clear definition of property rights, will be illustrated later on in the chapter.

Value Maximization: Reduction of Monitoring Costs Through Information Sharing and Stakeholder Engagement Monitoring costs could be reduced whilst making it easier or accessible for the principal to get engaged in the monitoring process. Whilst the information gathering process could involve the engagement of charitable organizations, board and shareholder meetings in the form of audit committees, could involve the representation of board and shareholder interests with a 50:50 representation. In such a case, whilst board representatives would require adequate compensation, shareholder representatives may be compensated for their services through the acquisition of enterprise or company shares or as voted by shareholders or recommended by the external auditor (with large firms).

According to Maher and Andersson (1999),

*...if owner-controlled firms are more profitable than manager-controlled firms, it would seem that insider systems have an advantage in that they provide better monitoring which leads to better performance. The vast majority of empirical studies, it turns out, do seem to favor the beneficial effects of enhanced monitoring as a result of higher ownership concentration.*

This also accords with several arguments put forward in support of value maximization and principal agent theory goal of firm maximization as providing more clarity as regards firm's objective - in contrast to the stakeholder theory, which is argued by Jensen (2002, p. 9), to result in managerial confusion, conflict, inefficiency and probably competitive failure - given the absence and operation of a clear objective which value maximization provides.

In this sense value maximization would appear better aligned, not just with the principal agent theory - whereby fiduciary duties are owed by the agents to a narrower range of stakeholders, but more specifically to concentrated ownership structures. Several studies also support the contention that information asymmetries are better managed under concentrated ownership structures and whilst that may well be case, the use and applicability of the Balanced Scorecard under the stakeholder theory, should serve to facilitate firm performance measures and monitoring. However, this is also argued not to be the case.

*The Balanced Scorecard is best described not as a scorecard, but as a dashboard or instrument panel. It can tell managers many interesting things about their business, but it does not give a score for the organization's performance, or even for the performance of its business units. It does not allow us to distinguish winners from losers. (Jensen, 2002, p. 19).*

The feasibility of the goal of value maximization, however does not necessarily imply that a firm has to operate within the narrower ambit of the principal agent theory. Nor does it imply that firms with more independent boards achieve better performance results - as the following results from several investigations demonstrate.

Based on their findings, Bhagat and Bolton (2009, p. 25) arrive at the following conclusions:

- That there has been a shift in the relationship between board independence and firm performance since 2002 (this being the year when the SOX legislation was introduced).
- A negative relationship between board independence and operating performance was documented by them prior to 2002. After 2002, a positive relationship between independence and operating performance was concluded.

As well as making reference to several studies whereby it is concluded that firms with independent boards do not necessarily perform better, they also make references to models (Renee & Ferreira, 2007) which support the view that greater board independence might be detrimental to firm value given the reluctance of CEOs to share information with more independent boards or given the fact that such boards may be too pre-occupied with trying to replace CEOs or addressing compensation issues.

In consolidating upon the discussion relating to the reliability of performance measures, such as the Balance Scorecard, as well as questions relating to dispersed and concentrated ownership structures and systems, and which of these systems better address information asymmetries - given the level of importance attached to corporate governance mechanisms such as audits and audit committees, will now be considered.

Concentrated ownership systems and structures are considered to better address information asymmetries than dispersed ownership structures and systems. However, it is also widely acknowledged in the academic literature, that capital markets - which constitute a dominant feature of dispersed ownership systems and structures, have in operation, audits and audit committees in contrast to family owned and concentrated ownership systems and structures.

Since audits and audit committees serve, or rather should serve, as effective corporate governance mechanisms and monitoring devices, with the audit serving as a vital signaling mechanism (Ojo, 2013) in communicating information to stakeholders about the performance or prospects of a firm, then it would appear that dispersed ownership systems and structures are also well equipped to address information asymmetries. Thus depending on the level of credibility of audits, they should serve to mitigate information asymmetries between the principal and the agent. However, the reliability of performance measures and monitoring initiatives, as highlighted with the Balance Scorecard and argued by Jensen, cannot always be confirmed.

Those deficiencies highlighted under the stakeholder theory, namely managerial confusion and lack of clarity as regards firm objectives, as well as questions regarding the applicability of the Balanced Scorecard, as an effective performance measure, could be addressed where stakeholders are effectively engaged, as previously highlighted (Sacconi, 2004, p. 32), in mitigating the informational gaps and asymmetries which appear to be wider under the stakeholder theory, and particularly given the operation of incomplete contracts under both principal agent and stakeholder theories.

It would appear that the degree of incompleteness of contracts is wider under the stakeholder theory than under the traditional principal agent theory. Whilst this could be regarded as principally contributing to the extent of informational asymmetries under the stakeholder model, the degree of flexibility offered by such incomplete contracts could also provide avenues whereby more profitable bargaining, as well as better alignment of agents' objectives (with those of the principal), occur - where stakeholders are effectively engaged in dialogues and communication at crucial and relevant stages of the contract and implementation processes. In this respect, timing, completeness and accuracy of information communicated between both parties is paramount.

Hence whilst avenues for opportunistic behaviors on the part of the agents, may appear evident during the early stages of the contract formation process, such gaps or deficiencies may be mitigated with the involvement of stakeholders in the contract process, as well as their involvement in vital organization decisions - through their involvement in committees such as that described previously whereby audit committees comprising both board and shareholder interests on a 50:50 based composition are introduced.

If contracts governing golden handshakes and pension funds are designed in such a way that clauses or provisos which impact these figures are incorporated - in the event of reckless and excessively undue risk taking events, managers and particularly those within the strategic levels, would be more cautious with decision making, control and planning procedures. Such clauses and provisions could be negotiated between designated stakeholders and management in the early stages of the contract formation process. As regards the free-rider argument, particularly that advanced by Maher and Andersson (1999, p. 8), namely that there are less incentives with shareholders to undertake monitoring in dispersed ownership structures, given the fact that benefits are (equally) shared with all shareholders, whereas, the full costs of monitoring are incurred by those who monitor, it could also be said that consequences of a firm's demise could even be more detrimental for those stakeholders considered to have insignificant stakes or are unable to afford monitoring - hence such stakeholders should have greater incentives to monitor - even if they do not have the means.

As concluded by Maher and Andersson (1999, p. 8):

*The competitiveness and ultimate success of a corporation is the result of teamwork that embodies contributions from a range of different resource providers including investors, employees, creditors, suppliers, distributors, and customers. Corporate governance and economic performance will be affected by the relationships among these various stakeholders in the firm. According to this line of argument, any assessment of the strengths, weaknesses, and economic implications of different corporate governance frameworks needs a broader analytical framework which includes the incentives and disincentives faced by all stakeholders.*

In highlighting the role of the large shareholder, Shleifer and Vishny's investigations include a large shareholder who does not participate in management, and they do not consider "strategic interactions between large shareholders (1986, p. 463)." Under their model, the large shareholder is considered to have such a large stake that it is worthwhile undertaking some monitoring responsibilities and all shareholders enjoy benefits from gains on their shares. As well as highlighting that even though the returns (see 1986, p. 463) made by the large shareholder are sufficient enough to cover his monitoring costs, that too little monitoring or take-over occurs since the gains are internalized only to his shares, they also argue that if the large shareholder is valued, small shareholders may favor the payment of dividends to ensure that he stays with the firm (see 1986, p. 461-488).

## Issues, Controversies, Problems

### Bridging the Gap between Information and Implementation Gaps: Distinguishing between Information Gaps and Information Asymmetries

In considering the distinction between information gaps and information asymmetries, a consideration of the principal agent theory is required. Whilst information gaps focus solely on the principal's ability to gather and acquire adequate information required to successfully launch a product for goal maximizing purposes, information asymmetries arise as a result of information which is known by the principal but not disclosed to the agent or wider stakeholders of an enterprise, and as a result involves both the principal and the agent/stakeholders.

Hence bridging the gap between information and implementation gaps would require an involvement of not just the principal, but also stakeholders, since by definition, the implementation gap is aimed at profit maximization on the long term as a result of converting informational resources into desired outcomes, namely profit maximization and other goals, which embrace corporate social responsibility. Whilst the traditional principal agent theory incorporates basically the principal and the agent with profit maximization as its central focus, the stakeholder theory embraces not just the principal, but a wider range of stakeholders - and extending beyond the profit maximization goal, by incorporating goals which include corporate social responsibility concerns.

As a result, stakeholders would also be involved in the information gathering and acquisition process – in collaboration with the agent's technological and informational expertise, in a collaboration aimed at maximizing not only firms' profit goals, but also aimed at benefiting society, whilst reducing implementation gaps in the process.

Whereas under the information gap scenario, only the principal might be involved, given the earlier stages of the conception of un translated ideas (into goals), information asymmetries - as well as implementation gaps, principally relate to the principal as well as the agent and/or the society at large, since goal maximization, investors and desired outcomes are *actively* involved.

Hence the involvement of stakeholders or the principal in the process should mitigate the information- implementation gap. Information asymmetries whilst arising as a result of information known to the agent, but not the principal or stakeholders, could also be mitigated through effective corporate governance mechanisms which involve the representation of shareholders or stakeholders as part of the audit committee.

In so doing information asymmetries are not only mitigated, the issue relating to monitoring costs, could also be addressed. The mitigation of implementation gaps through the involvement of stakeholders of an enterprise - and its application to corporate social responsibility function as means of extended corporate governance will now be considered (See Sacconi 2004, p. 32).

## Monitoring and Transaction Costs: The Mitigation of Implementation Gaps

### How Should the Principal be Encouraged to Get Involved in the Information Gathering and Monitoring Process?

Stakeholder engagement should be regarded as a tool, not only in mitigating information asymmetries, but also in compelling greater accountability on the part of the agents, facilitating avenues and platforms whereby incentives are created, as well as establishing negotiations and agreements which constitute the bases on which longer term based planning, goals, decision making and control are realized. Through such a tool and platform, the agent's incentives and objectives should be better aligned with those of the principal - hence discouraging the pursuit of short term interests on the part of the agents.

Furthermore, the stages during which hard law and principles should be incorporated in the mediation process between stakeholders and their agents, should involve a careful consideration of the role of certainty and predictability at those stages. Since incomplete contracts are inevitable and are necessary to facilitate flexibility - given unforeseen contingencies that need to be provided for, principles should constitute the basis for regulation where events which have a greater degree of unpredictability and uncertainty are concerned.

As regards those matters which involve greater certainty, bright line rules which should facilitate greater enforcement mechanisms (Ojo, 2010 and 2011), should be incorporated. It could very well be the case that the earlier stages of the mediation process, for example, the contract formation process, would involve more bright line rules being incorporated at this stage, since this process or stages involves, should involve or should require greater certainty than is the case with those decisions or stages which are best left to "residual property right owners" to decide.

As regards who retains property rights to valuable information, it is argued by Carlton and Fischel that

*...whether insider trading is beneficial, depends on whether the property right in information is more valuable to the form's managers or to the firm's investors and that; in either case, parties can engage in value maximizing exchange through the allocation of property right in information to the highest valuing user.*

*Why should a determination be made in respect of who values at most, the property rights in information - particularly if the agent's goals and incentives should be closely aligned with those of the principal?*

The importance of the engagement of both parties in the value maximizing exchange, as highlighted above, is noteworthy. The determination and allocation of property right in information appears more contentious.

Such a determination becomes necessary because the ideal assumption that goals of the agents will be closely aligned with those of the principal, does not always hold. Neither does the ideal objective of aiming to align the agent's goals and objectives with those of the principal - however, a means of facilitating the realization of goal alignment should be sought and encouraged - and this would be better fostered where both the principal and agent are equally considered to have the firm's interests of value maximization at heart - even though varying degrees of interests and values are actually attached to the firm.

In attempting to bridge the gap between actual diverging interests, shareholder representatives who are easily discernible as having huge stakes and shareholdings in the firm could be engaged in value maximization negotiations, as part of an internally established committee, with designated board representatives whose stakes in the firm could be consolidated or increased through the grant of shares, as well as other incentives. Such grants or incentives, being not only aimed at ensuring that short term focus or interests are merely promoted, but that tendencies towards high risk taking activities or ventures are discouraged.

Such "value maximizing exchange" as that described by Carlton and Fischel (1983, p. 863), which in their opinion should involve the allocation to the highest valuing user, could hence, also take place between shareholder and board representatives at a higher level - since ultimately, both parties should, given their interests and stakes in the firm, equally have the interest of value maximization at heart.

An allocation of property right in information to the highest valuing user, as well as the discussion of residual property rights being also connected with the issue of incomplete contracts - a major contributing factor to information asymmetries between the principal and agents of the firm.

"The residual right of control" is also considered by Sacconi (2004, p. 8) to confer upon the holder of such a right, the privilege to decide what should be done about decisions "left over" from the original contract and that become decided upon when unforeseen situations occur - in the case where contracts are lacking of provisos which are contingent upon unforeseen events.

How easy or accurate then is it to discern "the highest valuing user" or entitlement to the "residual right of control"? This in itself could also involve information asymmetries in the sense that not all information may be readily disclosed (or disclosed at all), that is, information about stakeholders may also be incomplete, inaccurate or unreliable – thus aggravating the information asymmetry problem which should be addressed.

The need for discernment of the highest valuing user, as well as the entitlement to the residual right of control can be justified on the grounds of measures necessary to mitigate tendencies to abuse or misuse information for self-dealing interests or personal gains - both being intricately linked through the information asymmetry problem. However the highest valuing user or the "entitled" to the residual right of control could also have other undisclosed conflicting interests - for which reason it is vital to incorporate additional safeguards, in the form of principal and agent involvement as a committee which represents both interests.

Addressing information asymmetries between the principal and the agent through a mitigation of such asymmetries should hence principally focus on the engagement of both parties rather than a determination of entitlement - which could hinge on subjective or undisclosed factors. For example, an explicit outright ownership of shares or high stakes in a firm may not necessarily imply that such a stakeholder is more interested in the firm's value maximization goals than another stakeholder with less shares. This being particularly the case where such a significant holding stakeholder has other undisclosed interests in another jurisdiction or enterprise - whose material value could be considerably higher than those held in the firm in which he is considered to be the highest valuing user. At the same time, such a stakeholder could well indeed be the highest valuing user in the sense that such information provides opportunistic means to exploit information in consolidating on stake holdings held in the other firm where interests are held - particularly where such a firm is competing with the firm in question. Furthermore, a stakeholder objectively considered to have insignificant interests or stakes may have invested his entire life's aspirations and goals in the firm. Hence value attached to a firm by a stakeholder is not only relative, but also subject to external factors and influences.

The rationale for a collaboration between stakeholders (whether such include inventors of new design or technology) and agents of a firm, lies in the efficiency gains that could be derived from such a collaboration.

The "strategic innovation game", according to Spulber (2014, p. 172) also implies a Coasian theorem which he states thus,

*...when property rights are well defined, and when there are no transaction costs, the creators of a nuisance externality and the parties harmed by the nuisance will negotiate an efficient allocation. If the creators of a nuisance have property rights, the parties harmed by the nuisance will pay the creators of the nuisance to abate. If the parties harmed by the nuisance have property rights, the creators of the nuisance will need to pay them compensation and choose to abate.*

He then consolidates on Coase's findings that "firms combine activities when internal governance costs are less than market transaction costs," and adds that for Coarse, the firm expands its activities up to a point where further expansion would raise governance costs above market transaction costs - and that firm outsources activities when market transactions are more efficient. Spulber (2014, p. 173)

In applying the above findings with how it applies to an E commerce enterprise or inventor considering expansion - both in respect of collaborating with an existing firm or with a more specialized entrepreneur, the components of transaction costs, as highlighted, will now be considered.

Transaction costs are considered by Spulber (2014, p. 173) to include the following:

- **Costs of Communication and Information Processing:** The magnitude of such costs being considered to vary according to whether discoveries involve complex scientific and technological innovations.
- Costs of searching and matching
- **Costs of Bargaining between Investors and Potential Adopters of Product or Technology:** With costs of designing and monitoring contingent contracts being included under this heading.
- **Moral Hazard Related Costs:** It is further added that moral hazard problems exist where inventor's efforts are highly specialized and prove difficult to monitor.

In applying the above to knowledge or technological transfer, in the form of "residual property rights of information", we can relate such a situation to moral hazard because the stakeholder acquiring such a position may not be as equipped, as regards expertise to effectively assume such a role - as is case with those agents of the firm who most likely had been employed to undertake such a role and would have exercised such specialized capacity. Furthermore those stakeholder/s allocated "residual property rights of information" may find it difficult to monitor because of the inability to undertake duties or fulfil obligations owing to a lack of expertise or experience or inadequate informational and/or technological resources to undertake such a role.

According to Maher and Andersson (1999, p. 7), modes of aligning the interests and objectives of managers with those of shareholders and overcoming problems of monitoring are as follows:

- Attempting to induce managers to carry out efficient management by directly aligning managers interests with those of shareholders e.g. executive compensation plans, stock options, direct monitoring by boards, etc.

- Consolidating shareholder's rights so shareholders have both a greater incentive and ability to monitor management. In their view, this approach enhances the rights of investors through legal protection from expropriation by managers e.g. protection and enforcement of shareholder rights, prohibitions against insider-dealing, etc.
- Implementing indirect means of corporate control such as that provided by capital markets, managerial labor markets, and markets for corporate control e.g. take-overs.

This is not to disprove the principle and rationale behind "residual property rights of information" or ascertaining the highest valuing user, but rather to highlight the importance of engaging such stakeholders in collaborative efforts with management, who are most likely to be better specialized, through internal committees, to generate more productive results.

Hence monitoring costs for inexperienced stakeholders with "residual property rights of information" may be high owing to the inability to effectively monitor agents - hence resulting in productive inefficiencies. In certain cases, it may well be the case that the stakeholder is an "innovative and highly specialized" inventor or entrepreneur - in which case it could be questioned as regards why such an innovative inventor does not choose to start a new firm. In such a case, determinants of the entrepreneur's decision to start a new firm or rather stay with an existing firm which can effectively implement new discoveries or strategies hinges on other factors which have already been discussed under the model of Cooperative and Competitive Enforced Self Regulation.

From the above examples, the engagement of managers, as well as shareholders, is evident and is also increasingly appearing to be the norm in several jurisdictions where shareholder rights and involvement in the firm has gradually increased over the years. Such involvement have assumed the grant and assignment of greater voting powers to shareholders as regards executive compensation. Further initiatives involve the representation of shareholder interests as part of internal committees. Given lessons drawn from corporate collapse over the years, it appears that there is increasing recognition that a balance needs to be drawn between awarding or remunerating executives in such a way whereby reckless risk taking incentives are unduly encouraged, and involving those whose interests are more likely to be affected owing to longer lasting and damaging repercussions. Whereas many agents escape the damaging and life changing repercussions of an enterprise' demise, with some even receiving golden handshakes and life secured pensions, stakeholders are left to pick the pieces.

## Postal Partnerships: Value Maximization and the Engagement of Stakeholders

Whilst reports by Reuters, highlight the impact of the rise of the Internet on postal services, "a heavy toll on first-class mail, the USPS's most profitable product" (Reuters, 2014), other reports highlight challenges also faces in several parts of the world - for example in Europe, where partial privatization is occurring with government post offices in a bid aimed at facilitating their competitiveness and enhancing their efficiency (Spelich, 2014).

Reports also highlight innovative initiatives being undertaken as regards postal agencies in Belgium, where E commerce products are specifically being designed to meet the demands and requirements of E Commerce (Spelich, 2014). In certain countries such as the UK, collaborations are being forged between post offices and bookstores - highlighting the impact of the crisis encountered by these entities as a result of the rise in internet and Ecommerce. Discounts are linked to purchases associated with these collaborations - where a consumer purchases a product from either the bookstore (WH Smith) or the post office.

From the illustrations above, the need for efforts on the part of postal agencies, in a bid to make them more competitive, cannot be over emphasized. These particularly relating to speed of delivery, as well as accessibility which E consumers have in easily, more affordably downloading products such as E books with instant delivery.

Postal agencies would be well advised to forge partnerships with their E commerce competitors in areas where both could symbiotically benefit from collaborative relationships and successful partnerships. The key to this being innovation as well as responsive to recognize the potential to benefit from the strengths or weaknesses of the other. In the sense that the strength of the other becomes a vehicle to develop one's weakness and in the sense where the other's weakness provides a forum for assisting and contributing to the partnership. To elaborate, where innovative and design expertise could be provided by a party, and the other is equipped with technological facilities such as the know-how to deliver promptly and efficiently, and another endowed with local knowledge and/or resources to facilitate and develop trust between consumer and E commerce enterprise, this could generate better results in terms of less returns, damaged products - owing to on-time deliveries - as well as higher levels of consumer satisfaction and results which are attributed to having tailor made the Ecommerce products to specifically meet consumer needs and preferences.

The above illustrates how collaborative and cooperative partnerships can actively engage stakeholders in the E commerce process as well as eliminate informational asymmetries which could result in a high level of product returns or poor consumer satisfaction results. We can also apply the illustration to the ambit of corporate social responsibility in the sense that those local postal agencies with whom collaborations are being forged should have the interests of the local stakeholders at heart in according a level of expected accountability for revenues generated and how such revenues have been expended to develop postal agencies or services in that area.

Furthermore, the role of Ecommerce as a tool for resources expansion is demonstrated with such local and external collaborations resulting in the development and facilitation of better resources, as well as a value maximizing and profit maximizing avenue:

- From the E commerce enterprise perspective (origin of transaction)
- From the postal carrier perspective; as well as
- Local postal agencies (destination); and
- Consumers

The above stages involve a wider range of stakeholders than the traditional principal agency model and the positive environmental benefits which could be generated for consumers through such collaborations -particularly in those rural areas with under developed postal code systems should not be underestimated.

## Data Protection Legislation

According to UNCTAD (2015:71), the main international reference frameworks used for privacy and data protection are:

- The OECD Guidelines
- The European Union Data Protection Directive
- Asia-Pacific Economic Cooperation Privacy Framework

The need for harmonization in respect of the above mentioned regulations, as well as basic principles, is an area which is highlighted as being in dire need of attention - this also being the case with the African Union Convention on Cyber Security and Personal Data Protection, which was adopted just in June 2014 (UNCTAD, 2015, p. 58).

In Central America, the need for laws and regulations related to data protection and cybercrime is highlighted in the Information Economy Report - even though 7 out of 8 countries are confirmed as having consumer protection legislation in place (UNCTAD, 2015, p. 58). Furthermore, Middle Africa was confirmed as being the region with the weakest coverage of E commerce legislation - with 2 of 9 countries having laws relating to e transactions, consumer protection (online) and data protection whilst only one country has cybercrime legislation in place (UNCTAD, 2015, p. 58).

These are contrasted with the previously mentioned case of Australia where security issues, which constitutes a principal challenge in jurisdictions namely, Africa, Asia, and Latin America, has been considered to be a success story.

It needs to be added that even though security issues constitute a major challenge in the above mentioned jurisdictions, data from the OECD (2012) and UNCTAD also reveal major challenges in jurisdictions such as Australia, the United States and the EU as reflected by Table 1.

According to the OECD Report on Consumer Protection in Online and Mobile Payments (2012, p. 25):

- Problems related to non-delivery, late delivery, non-conforming and faulty products have been linked to payments through government regulation and/or by payment providers, particularly in the area of dispute resolution
- The levels of protection available vary significantly from country to country - with only a few OECD countries (including Finland, Greece, Japan, Korea, Norway, the United Kingdom, and the United States), for example, having developed specific legal or regulatory provisions protecting cardholders in cases of non-delivery of goods or non-performance of services.
- As regards non-conforming products, specific legislation is in place in only a few countries as well (including Finland, Greece, Japan, Korea, Norway, the United Kingdom, and the United States) to provide consumers with redress mechanisms.

*Table 1. Top ten locations of consumers and companies involved in online complaints*

| Top Consumer Locations | Number of Complaints | Top Company Locations | Number of Complaints |
|---|---|---|---|
| United States | 13 445 | United States | 4 731 |
| Australia | 1 914 | China | 3 996 |
| France | 1 100 | United Kingdom | 1213 |
| United Kingdom | 767 | India | 469 |
| Canada | 694 | Canada | 285 |
| Brazil | 555 | Australia | 264 |
| Argentina | 341 | Germany | 220 |
| India | 311 | Mexico | 158 |
| Spain | 295 | Spain | 144 |

Source: econsumer.gov/Federal Trade Commission ; UNCTAD "Unlocking the Potential of E commerce for Developing Countries" Information Economy Report 2015 at page 71 Figure V.3)

Table 2 highlights those areas where consumers have experienced the most problematic issues as regards E commerce transactions - namely security and privacy issues which embrace secure online – as well as offline protection mechanisms and controls

## SOLUTIONS AND RECOMMENDATIONS

Notable observations made by the OECD, particularly with regards to future work that could be reviewed by the Committee on Consumer Policy, as highlighted in key points in its Conference on Empowering E-Consumers: Strengthening Consumer Protection in the Internet Economy, include the following (OECD, 2010, p. 11):

- The need to strengthen payment protection in the mobile commerce industry
- The need to explore modes of enhancing transparency in the collection, storage, sharing, and use of consumers' personal information
- The need to explore means of enhancing the transparency and clarity of contracts
- The need to identify trends and consumer challenges - particularly with respect to C-2-C transactions
- As regards digital content products, the identification of the type of information needed by consumers to make informed choices in the purchase of digital content products, as well as the development of adequate redress mechanisms for consumers and the exploration of consumer protection implications resulting from inter-operability were highlighted.
- The need for improved enforcement mechanisms

*Table 2. Incidents by type of data exposed*

| | (%) |
|---|---|
| Credit card number | 10.4 |
| Date of birth | 12.2 |
| Medical | 13.3 |
| Telephone number | 13.3 |
| Miscellaneous | 15.6 |
| Social security number | 18.5 |
| Address | 18.7 |
| User name | 37.4 |
| Email | 39 |
| Name | 41.4 |
| Password | 47.8 |

Source Risk Based Security, "Data Breach Quickview: An Executive's Guide to 2013 Data Breach Trends https://www.riskbasedsecurity.com/reports/2013-DataBreachQuickView.pdf;

UNCTAD "Unlocking the Potential of E commerce for Developing Countries" Information Economy Report 2015 and particularly Figure V.5 "Incidents By Type of Data Exposed" at page 72

The need for improved enforcement mechanisms which will not only foster compliance, but also better accountability through self-regulation, constitutes a focal theme for this chapter. Self-regulation, has been highlighted, as well as elaborated on under the background to the study - given compliance costs for small businesses and enterprises who may find it cumbersome to meet the cost and compliance requirements and demands imposed by government regulations. Whilst self-regulation has its weaknesses, which primarily relates to the level of accountability which could be encouraged under this means of regulation, notable advantages relate to the flexibility it confers on the firm in respect of tailor made rules which are generated and which accord better with the enterprise's needs and requirements.

## FUTURE RESEARCH DIRECTIONS

Having briefly considered the role of audits and audit committees are vital corporate governance mechanisms in dispersed ownership systems and structures, it would be worth exploring how liquidity can be implemented to address informational asymmetries under family owned and concentrated ownership systems and structures.

Addressing information asymmetries between the principal and the agent through a mitigation of such asymmetries should ideally principally focus on the engagement of both parties rather than a determination of entitlement - which could hinge on subjective or undisclosed factors.

Even though it is argued by the author that both principal and agent should be actively engaged in the mediation process - which includes contract formation stages and other phases highlighted within the chapter, and that the discernment of the highest valuing user or who is entitled to residual rights of control should take secondary priority to the engagement of principal and agent in the information sharing process, the impact of strategic interactions between large shareholders, and whether such can indeed be considered to have entitlement to residual rights of control, constitutes an area which could be investigated for future research.

## CONCLUSION

Given the non-binding effects of governing principles established under such international frameworks as the OECD, European Union Data Directive and Asia Pacific Economic Cooperation Privacy Framework, there is need to incorporate and introduce more binding standards which would not only foster greater compliance (with rules and standards), as well as enforcement, but also ensure that these rules and standards are applied consistently, objectively, and harmoniously across jurisdictions.

Hence at supranational level, a collaborative framework for rule drafting, implementation and enforcement, could be developed between international bodies such as the OECD, UNCTAD and WTO, and regional supranational authorities with the aim of establishing and implementing legal frameworks which have more binding and authoritative applications as merely opposed to persuasive effects.

Such a framework can be illustrated by way of reference to the Co operative and Competitive Enforced Self Regulation Model, which was illustrated in this chapter:

Supranational collaboration-----> Meta Regulation -----> State ------ > Enforced Self Regulation ---- > Firm

Further, as highlighted previously, meta regulation will involve the use of more binding rules, standards or regulations. Such standards, whilst aiming to facilitate a better means of addressing specific consumer needs and concerns, in matters relating particularly to data protection and privacy, should also aim to enhance clarity, transparency, as well as consistency in their interpretation and application.

E commerce is likely to be encouraged even in those areas or parts of the world where less facilities or access exist to particular E commerce products where initiatives are undertaken by Ecommerce businesses and enterprises to innovate and develop products which not only provide competitive attributes - by virtue of the ease with which such products can be easily obtained, the availability of options and channels whereby the product can be obtained, the range of payment modes offered - whether these are debit, credit card type transactions, bank transfer or mediating systems such as PayPal, as well as discounts attached to such products and offered specifically to jurisdictions which have limited or reduced access to such products. However, whilst means of facilitating and encouraging E commerce transactions - as well as E commerce expansion, are to be commended, of greater concerns are major obstacles to the successful implementation of E commerce goals - which primarily relate to security, data protection and privacy matters.

If adopted with the engagement of stakeholders at appropriate stages, as well as the incorporation of applicable and most suitable forms of rules during such phases of the mediation process between agents and stakeholders, such that flexibility is facilitated in the process to allow for contingencies whilst also compelling effective enforcement and compliance mechanisms, corporate social responsibility should be fostered through the outcomes emanating from better, focused planning, control, decision making, as well as more effective accountability, compliance and enforcement mechanisms.

## REFERENCES

Adams, R. B., & Ferreira, D. (2007). A theory of friendly boards. *The Journal of Finance*, *62*(1), 217–250. doi:10.1111/j.1540-6261.2007.01206.x

Addressing the Tax Challenges of the Digital Economy. (2014). OECD Library. Retrieved from http://www.oecd-ilibrary.org/taxation/addressing-the-tax-challenges-of-the-digital-economy_9789264218789-en

Ayres, I., & Braithwaite, J. (2001). *Responsive Regulation: Transcending the Deregulation Debate*. Oxford University Press.

Bhagat, S., & Bolton, B. (2009). *Corporate Governance and Firm Performance: Recent Evidence*. Retrieved from http://www.econ.upf.edu/docs/seminars/bhagat.pdf

Carlton, D. W., & Fischel, D. R. (1983, May). The Regulation of Insider Trading. *Stanford Law Review*, *35*(5), 857–895. doi:10.2307/1228706

Coglianese, C., Healey, T. J., Keating, E. K., & Michael, M. L. (2004). *The Role of Government in Corporate Governance*. Regulatory Policy Program Center for Business and Government.

Crain, N., & Crain, W. M. (2010, September). *The Impact of Regulatory Costs on Small Firms*. Retrieved from https://www.sba.gov/sites/default/files/The%20Impact%20of%20Regulatory%20Costs%20on%20Small%20Firms%20%28Full%29.pdf

Department for Business Innovation & Skills. (2013, October). *A Strategy For Future Retail: Industry and Government Delivering in Partnership.* Retrieved from https://www.gov.uk/government/uploads/system/uploads/attachment_data/file/252383/bis-13-1204-a-strategy-for-fut ure-retail-industry-and-government-delivering-in-partnership.pdf

E-commerce Europe. (2013, October 24). *Round Table Amsterdam: E-commerce in Europe - Challenges and Opportunities.* Retrieved from http://www.ecommerce-europe.eu/news/2013/10/round-table-amsterdam-e-commerce-in-europe-challenges-and-opportunities

Fama, E. F. (1980). Agency problems and the theory of the firm. *Journal of Political Economy*, *88*(2), 288–307. doi:10.1086/260866

Greene, W. (2014, January 16). E Commerce in South east Asia: Opportunities for Continued Growth in 2014. *Tigermine.com.* Retrieved from http://www.tigermine.com/2014/01/16/e-commerce-southeast-asia-opportunities-challenges-growth-2014/

Jensen, M.C. (2002). Value Maximization, Stakeholder Theory, and the Corporate Objective Function. *Business Ethics Quarterly*, 12(1).

Jensen, M. C., & Meckling, W. H. (1976). Theory of the firm: Managerial Behavior, Agency costs and ownership structure. *ScienceDirect.* Retrieved from http://www.sciencedirect.com/science/article/pii/0304405X7690026X

Laux, V. (2008). Board independence and CEO turnover. *Journal of Accounting Research*, *46*(1), 137–171. doi:10.1111/j.1475-679X.2008.00269.x

Maher, M., & Andersson, T. (1999). Corporate Governance: Effect on Firm Performance and Economic Growth. *ECGI.* Retrieved from http://www.ecgi.org/research/accession/cgeu.pdf

Ojo, M. (2010). Building on the Trust of Management: Overcoming the Paradoxes of Principles Based Regulation. Law and Prosociality, 30(7).

Ojo, M., (2011). Co-operative and Competitive Enforced Self Regulation: The Role of Governments, Private Actors and Banks in Corporate Responsibility. *Journal of Financial Regulation and Compliance, 19*(2).

Ojo, M. (2013, December 28). *Audits, Audit Quality and Signaling Mechanisms: Concentrated Ownership Structures.* Paper presented at the 2014 IBFR Conference, May 27 - 30 2014 San Jose Costa Rica. Retrieved from http://www.theibfr.com/ARCHIVE/ISSN-1941-9589-V9-N2-2014.pdf

Organisation for Economic Co-operation and Development. (2010). Summary of Key Points and Conclusions. *Proceedings of the conference on Empowering E-Consumers: Strengthening Consumer Protection in the Internet Economy.*

Organization for Economic Co-operation and Development. (2010). Summary of Key Points and Conclusions. Proceedings of the conference on Empowering E-Consumers: Strengthening Consumer Protection in the Internet Economy.

Pan, E.J. (2003). Harmonization of U.S – E.U Securities Regulation: The Case for a Single European Securities Regulator Law and Policy in International Business

Parker, C. (2007). M eta Regulation: Legal Accountability for Corporate Social Responsibility. In D McBarnet, A Voiculescu, & T Campbell (Eds.), The New Corporate Accountability: Corporate Social Responsibility and the Law. Cambridge University Press.

Remarque, R. (2013). *Africa E commerce: Beyond the Hype*. Retrieved from http://www.siliconafrica.com/african-e-commerce/

Risk Based Security. (2013). *Data Breach Quick-view: An Executive's Guide to 2013 Data Breach Trends*. Retrieved from https://www.riskbasedsecurity.com/reports/2013-DataBreachQuickView.pdf

Sacconi, L. (2004). *Corporate Social Responsibility (CSR) as a Model of 'Extended' Corporate Governance: An Explanation Based on the Economic Theories of Social Contract*. Reputation and Reciprocal Conformism.

Shleifer, A., & Vishny, R. W. (1986). Large shareholders and corporate control. *Journal of Political Economy*, *94*(3), 461–488. http://scholar.harvard.edu/files/shleifer/files/lg_shareholders.pdf doi:10.1086/261385

Spelich, J. W. (2014). Alibaba's head has a plan to save post offices around the world. Retrieved from http://qz.com/203912/ali-babas-e-commerce-head-has-a-plan-to-save-post-offices-around-the-world/

Spulber, D. (2014). *The Innovative Entrepreneur*. New York, Cambridge: Cambridge University Press. doi:10.1017/CBO9781107239012

Tirole, J. (2006). *The Theory of Corporate Finance*. Princeton, Oxford: Princeton University Press.

UNCTAD, (2015). *Unlocking the Potential of E commerce for Developing Countries* Information Economy Report.

Section 2

# E-Tailing Opportunities and Challenges in Emerging Economies

# Chapter 3
# Challenges and Opportunities of E-Tailing in Emerging Economies

**Ritu Narang**
*University of Lucknow, India*

**Prashant Trivedi**
*University of Lucknow, India*

## ABSTRACT

*The increase in penetration of internet and information and communication technology (ICT) along with change in consumer lifestyle and growing population of internet savvy consumers presents an encouraging platform for e-retailers in emerging markets. Education, technology and growing demand from middle class consumers are further driving the growth vehicle of e-tailing in these nations. There is adequate literature available for electronic business in the context of developed nations but applying that knowledge without any consideration of the unique business environment prevalent in emerging markets may spell danger for online traders. Therefore, the proposed chapter focuses on the growth of e-tailing in emerging economies. It talks about the driving forces for success of e-tailing in various developing economies. The opportunities, challenges and unique issues associated with e-tailing in emerging markets are also discussed. The chapter ends with a discussion on the future of e-tailing in emerging nations.*

## INTRODUCTION

E-tailing is catching up quickly with the offline stores and expanding its reach in emerging economies. The last few years have seen a radical increase in traffic from traditional to online retail formats (Tong, 2010). The increase in penetration of internet and information and communication technology (ICT) has resulted in development of new distribution channels, making online presence a major requirement (Liang & Huang, 1998) for retailers to expand their geographic reach. Consequently, the national boundaries are blurring and consumers across the globe are being served by good quality products at a competitive price, at their convenience, at their door step and at their chosen paying terms.

DOI: 10.4018/978-1-4666-9921-2.ch003

Copyright © 2016, IGI Global. Copying or distributing in print or electronic forms without written permission of IGI Global is prohibited.

Market saturation and slow growth rate in developed economies has shifted the focus of the marketers in the globalised world towards the growth potential prevailing in emerging economies (Narang & Singh, 2014). They are looking forward to invest in these new markets where online retail platforms are emerging to woo the customers away from the traditional retail formats (Kearney, 2013). Among emerging nations, Brazil, Russia, India and China are turning out to be the hubs for business and economic activities because of their attractive growth forecasts, huge population and encouraging business environment. China is at the top of the global retail e-commerce index among the nations where e-tailing has shown tremendous potential. The enormous success of Alibaba, Taubau and Tmall bears testimony to this. China houses 1.36 billion people. Its 517 million internet users constitute a market worth 64 billion USD. It is poised to achieve 271 billion over the next five years (A.T. Kearney, 2013). In 2012, 54% of its consumers had made more than 20 purchases through internet. India also offers a fertile untapped potential for e-tailers. A big response received by companies like Flipkart, Amazon, Snapdeal, etc. reveals the growing interest towards e-tailers. It is the young population ranging between the age group of 15 to 35 years that constitutes the majority of online shoppers in India where internet penetration is reported to be around 19%. However, it is expected to experience a yearly growth rate of 41% (ASSOCHAM, 2012) which will provide further impetus to online purchases. Another example can be taken of Brazil which has a strong and growing middle class with 80 million online customers who spend $ 10.6 billion annually in making purchases on internet and are poised to spend 18.7 billion by 2017. Russia is not lagging far behind. It boasts of Europe's largest online population of 70 million users with 33 million consumers shopping online. Cities like St Petersburg and Moscow are the main centres of online retailing, accounting for three fourth of online retail transactions (A.T. Kearney, 2013).

Education, technology and growing demand from middle class consumers are the driving forces of e-tailing in emerging nations (Narang, 2010). Increase in disposable income and purchasing power of growing middle class consumers coupled with their changing lifestyle is set to provide huge impetus to growth of e-tailing in India (Technopak, 2012). Accompanying these facilitators are some barriers as well. They are present in the form of poor connectivity and access to internet, disparity in economic status, lack of skilled human resource, low literacy rate, restrictive business climate and government policies (Tigre, 2003; Palacios, 2003). A.T. Kearney (2012) echoes these findings by citing that underdeveloped infrastructure may also act as a hindrance for the online retail industry in emerging markets like India. Further, feelings of apprehension and distrust towards e-tailing are pervasive among e-buyers. Consumers perceive several risks associated with the e-purchase of goods in the form of financial loss, in-transit loss, loss due to incomplete transaction through web, legal risk associated with assigning responsibility and contract enforcement on improper delivery (Schoder & Yin, 2000). Nevertheless, no one can deny that emerging economies offer tremendous potential for returns on investment to the modern retailers. Yet, it would be a folly to assume that transfer of business models from the developed nations to emerging nations would translate into success. It is essential to understand the unique forces propelling e-retail expansion and the challenges that require prudent handling for success in e-business. This chapter seeks to draw attention towards such factors. The first section of the chapter throws light on the drivers for growth of e-tailing business in emerging markets. The next section outlines the challenges that loom forth before the companies in their quest for exploitation of business opportunities. The last section provides some suggestions on how to move forward in these evolving markets.

## DRIVERS FOR GROWTH OF E-TAILING BUSINESS

Youth has always favoured innovation (Schiffman & Kanuk, 2003) prompting young population in emerging markets to provide impetus to e-tailing. Younger generation is also reported to be less bothered about the security and reliability issues with internet shopping (Dholakia & Uusitalo, 2002). The users with higher education and income are more inclined towards e-tailing than groups with lower education and income (Cunningham & Cunningham, 1973) and computer proficiency is reported to be more in highly educated people (Gibbs, Kraemer & Dedrick, 2003) who tend to be less skeptical about adoption of newer technologies and methods (Zhao & Gutierrez, 2002). Earlier studies have demonstrated that online shoppers are mostly males with high income who possess university degrees (Dholakia & Uusitalo, 2002). Let us examine the factors responsible for expansion of e-business.

### Changing Demographic and Lifestyle Factors

Basu, Barik & Arokiasamy (2013) state that the growth potential of the BRIC nations depends largely upon the ability of their populace to develop skills for employment. The emerging nations like China, India, Russia and Brazil are working hard upon the growth of their citizens in terms of education and skill development. Sheng-jun (2011) also supports the role of education in driving the growth of BRIC nations, especially China and India. We find that the customers in almost all emerging nations are in a transition stage where they are seeking more education than before with chances of acquiring higher education.

Age is an important factor responsible for influencing and changing needs and attitudes. As stated earlier, it is usually the younger generation that favors the adoption of newer and innovative methods (Modahl, 2000; Schiffman & Kanuk, 2003) Emerging nations house the young populace that facilitates the adoption of newer technologies like internet, smart phones, tablets and computers. So, it is particularly the youth in India and other emerging economies that are playing a pivotal role in the rise of e-tailing. They are trend conscious and want to change their lifestyles (Narang, 2010).

Earnings of the citizens of emerging nations have experienced an upward trend. Rise in the number of working women has led to more disposable income in the hands of people with a quest for better lifestyles. Studies indicate that higher income, occupation and education positively impact the perception towards non-store shopping (Cunningham & Cunningham, 1973; Mulhern, 1997). Further, the literature on online shopping reveals that mostly it is the customers with higher incomes and education degrees from universities that patronize electronic purchases (Dholakia & Uusitalo, 2002; Joines, Scherer & Scheufele, 2003). The emergence of middle class with increased purchasing power constitutes the most important segment for e-tailers (AIMC, 2005). Demand generated by this segment has attracted many companies to look towards emerging nations as a lucrative market for their products. Internet acts as a potent medium to reach the customers dispersed all over the geographical space.

### Technology

Willingness to adopt newer methods of purchasing including online platforms depends on higher exposure to technology (Dholakia & Uusitalo, 2002; Lohse, Bellman & Johnson, 2000). Progress made in the field of communication technology has encouraged adoption and growth of online shopping (Sharma & Sheth, 2004). For instance, Chinese mobile phone giant, Xiomi claims that it was able to sell 75,000 of its smart-phone model Mi3 through exclusive online flash sales on Flipkart in eight seconds. Latest technology in the form of high speed internet (3G and 4G) is knocking at the screens of consumers in emerging nations. The customers are able to visit the store virtually, compare prices of various offerings at their own convenience.

Introduction of mobile applications has further pushed up the business of e-tailing in emerging markets (Bigne, 2005). Wireless internet through mobiles is another factor responsible for leading the change in the daily activities of the contemporary world (Sivanad, 2004). The deep penetration of internet enabled mobile phones with affordable data plans has empowered the customers, especially youth. According to a report from BCG and Internet and Mobile Association of India (IAMAI) (2015), internet growth in India has been tremendous. It has reached a figure of 100 million users within 20 years from its introduction and is poised to reach another100 million within a year. The key reason cited behind this growth is the increased affordability caused by low cost data enabled handsets. Increasing awareness and educational level has evoked the need for internet. As many as 190 million internet users were reported in India in the month of June 2014. This figure is the third largest one after US (275 million) and China (620 million). India is also reported to be one of the largest markets for social networking sites like Facebook and Linkedin.

## Political Environment

The environment prevailing in emerging markets has become attractive for business houses with promises of higher returns on investments. Online retail business is a relatively new phenomenon in emerging economies but has received a tremendous response from customers. Political scenario in emerging nations is becoming lenient towards upcoming businesses including e-retail. The governments of emerging nations are modifying their laws to promote and accelerate economic activities. For instance, governments in China, Russia and Brazil are investing in new infrastructural developments, reducing the trade barriers and raising the limits of foreign direct investments (FDI) in retail sector in their respective countries. Other drivers that act as engine for growth in e-tailing are detailed below.

## Convenience

Studies demonstrate that convenience of buying over internet is the major factor which impacts online purchase (Wang, Ye, Zhang, & Nguyen, 2005). Round the clock opportunity for online shopping provides it an edge over traditional channel of retailing (Hofacker, 2001; Wang et al., 2005). According to a study, 58% of respondents opt for online shopping as they can make purchases after store operating hours while 61% prefer it to avoid crowd and waiting lines (The Tech Faq, 2008). Rising expectations of consumers in emerging markets provides 24x7 selling opportunity for e-tailers. Promptness and ease of operations are other factors which can lead to increase in purchase frequency. The various aspects of convenience which can lead to increased frequency of online purchases have been summarised in Figure 1.They include availability of item, anytime and anywhere shopping, ease of payment and anytime service and return.

- **Availability of Item:** Online shopping offers e-tailers the convenience of making available huge variety and assortment of items of latest trends and fashion without making investment in physical infrastructure.

*Figure 1. Convenience and online purchases*

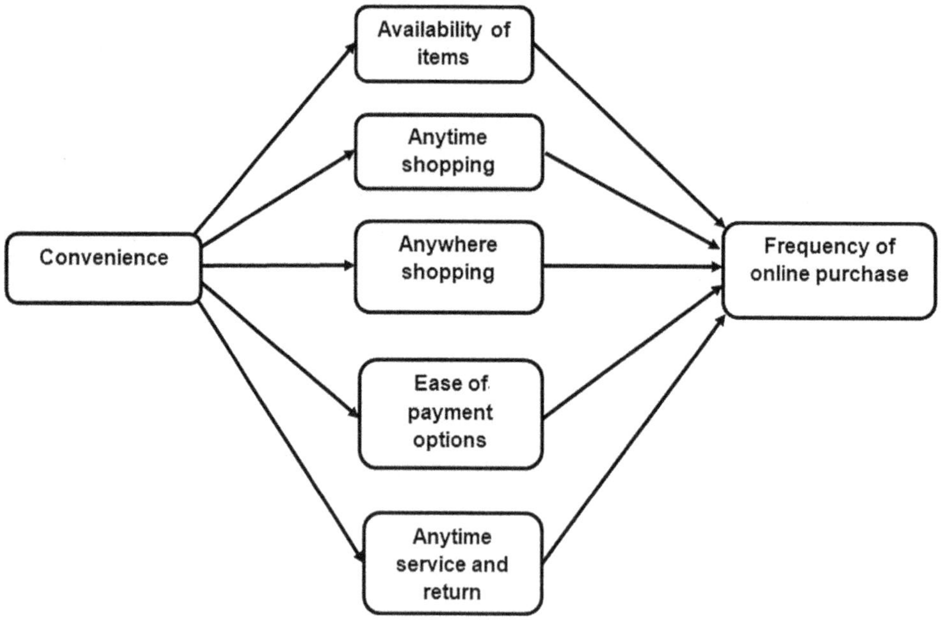


- **Anytime Shopping:** Convenience of anytime shopping provides edge to e-tailers over traditional shops (Hofacker, 2001; Wang et al., 2005) which still remain untapped.
- **Anywhere Shopping:** Convenience of anywhere shopping is almost unavailable in the context of traditional shops. Consumers can order online from anywhere even from a moving vehicle. This helps the consumers save time and boost online sales (Childers, Carr, Peck, & Carson, 2001).
- **Ease of Payment Option:** Convenience of hassle free payment option boosts affinity towards online purchase (Rox, 2007) particularly, when buyers get an opportunity to avoid long queues.
- **Anytime Service and Return:** Convenience in terms of service and smooth return policy are considered essential for online purchases. (Hermes, 2000).

Initiatives by e-tailers in above aspects of convenience provide thrust to their business growth. By taking care of consumer's expectations companies engaged in e-tailing business are able to attract and retain customers.

## Cost and Time Efficiency

It has been experienced that customers are able to buy products at a lesser price through online marketplace than the offline traditional store (Rox, 2007). Further, they get an opportunity to compare prices from different portals and choose the product with the lowest price rather than buy the highly priced product from nearby offline retail stores (Lim & Dubinsky, 2004). Bulk purchases directly from the producers result in lowering of product cost to the e-sellers. Further, lesser levels in distribution network reduce distribution cost. Operating cost tend to be comparatively lower for e-tailers because of less investment in resources such as land, labor, etc. Huge investments in showrooms, its maintenance, etc are not required by online stores. These cost advantages can be transferred to customers in the form of lower prices.

Online shopping can be done anytime from anywhere. This makes e-purchase an effortless exercise as customers do not have to travel through heavy traffics, find parking spots, wait at the checkout queues or get stuck in crowded stores (Childers et al., 2001). Further, e-tailers enjoy unlimited shelf space as the products are shown virtually to the consumers. Visual options on the website help to compare various products without having to physically move from one place to other and spend money on transport. The virtual platform offers display of different varieties and assortment of products. It has been reported that consumers usually enjoy and prefer services which reduce their psychological costs (Prasad & Aryasri, 2009). E-tailers or online sellers facilitate the customers by reducing the search cost for product features and price related information (Strader & Shaw, 1999; Bhatt & Emdad, 2001).

## Expansive Reach

Companies that adopt e-tailing as a complementary channel have an edge over their store counter parts in terms of reach and convenience. Geographical areas which were neglected earlier because of resource limitation can now be served through electronic channel. Through proper logistics e-sellers can take the advantage of untapped market spread over a large geographical area. For instance, a brick and mortar store of Levis can serve nearby customers only but an online store can cater to orders from different nooks and corners of the world. E-tailing is ideal for niche products as it can reach its target market directly. Dell computers, for instance started its operation in India by serving online only. Internet provides huge opportunity to e-tailers to communicate about their products at a minimal cost. Satisfied customer experiences with online delivery and services can help e-tailers to expand their customer base by converting more and more prospects into customers. The advantage of reaching out to more buyers can in turn, help them to reap economies of scale.

## Social Media

Social media platforms are expanding their reach, especially to young consumers who take decisions based upon the buzz created virally through these channels. Facebook, Twitter, Youtube, etc. are some of the platforms available for companies operating in emerging economies. They can use social media as channels to communicate their offerings to their customers. For instance, around 80% consumers in China have admitted that they use social media as a learning platform to enquire about the offerings and deals while 66% of them engage in writing reviews about the products (Kearney, 2013).

Consumers in Brazil also read product reviews online and request for opinions from reference groups. A.T. Kearney (2012) reports that general merchandise retailer, Magazine Luiza motivates its consumers to open their own digital Luiza stores on Facebook and sell within their social networks. It is also estimated that sales conversion rates from many social networking sites are sometimes found to be as much as 40 percent higher than from their respective websites (Kearney, 2013). Flipkart, Snapdeal, Red Bus, etc. in India have also started to utilize Facebook and other social media platforms to promote their businesses and communicate about various schemes and offers from time to time.

## CHALLENGES BEFORE E-TAILERS IN EMERGING MARKETS

There are some areas which impose huge challenges to e-tailers in emerging markets. It is important for e-tailers to understand these issues in order to serve their markets better.

### Evolving Markets

The most alarming challenge faced by e-tailers in emerging nations is that they have to operate in evolving business markets (Technopak, 2012) where there is enormous scope for change and development. The customers' shopping behaviour is also undergoing continuous modification. It means that e-tailers have to be extremely vigilant to upgrade their operations to meet the expectations of customers in order to sustain their operations in a dynamic environment. The entire supply chain has to be made efficient by further adoption of newer technology and utilization of skilled and well-organized human resource. This involves efficient delivery within the infrastructural constraints of emerging nations and yield desired results.

### Trust

Studies point out that the consumers are always concerned about security of their transactions as well as private information while making online purchases (Constantinides, 2004). Whysall (2000) suggests that customer's trust in sharing personal information is the function of his willingness to purchase and patronize the electronic seller. "Customers who do not trust an e-business will not be loyal to it even though they may be generally satisfied by the e-business" (Anderson & Srinivasan, 2003, p.128).

Most customers in emerging nations are not very familiar with internet. Their apprehension about ordering online is due to lack of trust in claims made by e-tailers. Additionally, they fear ordering items which might not perform well. Trust building in terms of reliability, quality of products, security of financial transaction, etc. is a big challenge. Closely associated with the concept of trust are the following issues that merit attention:

- **Intangibility:** Customers are unable to see and experience products physically before purchase. Therefore, quality assessment poses a great challenge to them. Additionally, customers in emerging nations seek higher value for their money which leads them to distrust the online seller. The intangible aspect of selling may be addressed through selling brands or by developing e-tailer's own brand equity (Korgaonkar & Karson, 2007). It has been generally accepted that customer's buying decisions are often effected by brand names (Lim & Dubinsky, 2004) which play an important role in building trust.
- **Privacy and Security:** On one hand, security of private information is a big challenge to online players as any leakage in data results in negative impact. On the other hand, consumers abhor intrusion of any kind into their privacy. This gets compounded particularly in emerging nations where customers are still struggling to adapt to new technology. Hence, it becomes imperative for e-tailers to assure customers that their data is secured and will never be used for any other purpose. Clarifying customer privacy policy and ensuring strict and proper adherence to it may reduce cus-

tomer fear. Use of advanced and safe technology and methods to safeguard personal information of customers and prevent any misuse of electronic mode of payments may facilitate in building trust (Prasad & Aryasri, 2009).

- **Fraud Prevention:** Fraud prevention deserves special attention in building trust. Fraud may range from receipt of poor quality product where the product actually delivered is of inferior quality to the one which was promised by the portal at the time of order placement to a situation where the customer denies payment for purchase or even refuses to accept the delivery of order. Providing wrong mailing address, identity, etc. are other examples of deception. These issues assume greater challenge in emerging nations where customers are likely to indulge in unethical practices and behaviour.
- **Secure Web Interface:** Is another stumbling block for online sellers. Recently, there was a violation of security at Microsoft India's online store which aggravated the angst of customers associated with online transactions. Security intrusion can have severe repercussion on the positioning of the portal and its brand equity. This scenario necessities continuous monitoring and improvement of portal security systems to ensure secure shopping experience.

## Customer Service and Support

The customers in emerging nations may require more guidance and instructions on purchase and usage, thereby necessitating 24x7 customer support and service. Customer service has been conceded to be as important as quality of website (Liu & Guo, 2008). A study by Hermes (2000) has also supported this by stating that 72 percent of consumers buying online consider service as a vital factor in determining satisfaction. Customers are likely to assume that online sellers are either concealing something or are unwilling to address their problems. Therefore, the reach of services to consumers (Wang et al., 2005) and provision for constant customer feedback through dynamic pages on the websites (Yu & Wu, 2007) assume great importance. Presence of interactive customer service helps the buyers approach the seller anytime at their convenience from anywhere (Lim & Dubinsky, 2004). Customer service requires inclusion of tracking system for customer retention. Building an efficient tracking mechanism is very important so that customers can get information about their orders at a click. Further, consumers across the emerging nations look for competitive offering and keep on switching among the portals to find the best offer. Understanding the unique needs of customers and building appropriate service support can help in retaining customers and building loyal towards the web portal.

Special efforts are required to reduce dissonance, attract, build and retain the large base of customers. For example, some consumers in emerging nations have complained that the quality of products, especially in apparels is not up to the mark. Colors tend to be different from images shown on web portal and standard sizes of apparels are not delivered. These causes of dissonance necessitate immediate rectification as it can lead to loss of customers and spread of negative word of mouth publicity which can dent the image of the company. For instance, Flipkart in India faced an embarrassing situation when it failed to efficiently handle orders after launching its promotional campaign, "The Big Billion Day" in the month of October, 2014 in India. Its website was not able to respond to the large number of hits with customers receiving numerous errors (TOI, Oct 2014). Negative comments started all over the Twitter, a micro blogging site. Instead of getting any advantage it caused negative publicity for the company. E-tailers need to be extremely vigilant and well prepared before launching such promotional campaigns.

## Profitability

Profitability poses another challenge in emerging nations. For instance, despite popularity and being in business for several years many e-tailers like Snapdeal, Myntra, Flipkart in India have yet to show profits in their balance sheets. This could be because acquiring market share is considered more important than profitability in the initial stages of business. The fight for a big pie in market share is driving e-tailers to acquire customers through heavy discount offers which prevent covering of all costs. Heavy advertising through mass media entails substantial expenditure leading to increased customer acquisition cost. This makes the task of developing consumer loyalty towards the portal more difficult, particularly when everyone is adopting the same weapon of price cuts. The biggest challenge is to handle the pressure of desired rate of return returns from the investors along with deeper penetration of markets and higher frequency of orders. The challenge in this aspect is twin fold. Firstly, big investment in logistics and competitive pricing environment makes the task of earning big profits difficult for the companies. Secondly, e-tailing business is in the infant stage in a number of emerging nations. Imitating the business model and marketing strategies adapted in developed nations may not assure their survival and growth as the situation prevailing there may be entirely different from their developed counterparts.

## Competition

E-tailers have to face stiff competition to stay ahead in terms of quality, service, presentation and post purchase services. To achieve and maintain superiority in these aspects, the companies have to make substantial investments. Finding the right digital strategy specific to the need of the country is another issue as any lacuna is likely to result in loss of customers to competitors. Other related challenges include trade regulations, legal issues and competition from street vendors. Being new in comparison to traditional retailing, there is always a scope for changes in regulations governing e-tailing which may have an adverse impact on current business model and plan. People in emerging nations still enjoy purchasing from the local vendors situated in their vicinity. Hence, these small retailers continue to provide competition due to their ability to offer credit facility, free home delivery, hassle free quick return of goods and good rapport with customers. Lack of human involvement raises additional concern for e-tailers, particularly when the traditional retail format thrives on personal relationships. Therefore, people providing support from call centres assume great importance for e-tailers. It is through them that the companies can try to compensate the lack of human touch in transactions.

## Order Fulfillment and Delivery

Currently, delivering goods to suburbs is an issue and companies have to establish an extensive distribution network to reach out to their customers on time. E-tailers can be accessed from anywhere and are supposed to perform accurately till the last mile of delivery. Through promotion they may increase traffic to their portal but fulfilling its demand satisfactorily is another issue. This calls for proper inventory management, investment in adequate and standard storage facilities and building fast delivery system. Delays in delivery or out of stock scenario may lead to switching over of customers to competition and spread of poor word of mouth.

## Handling Returns

Return of purchased goods is a serious concern in emerging markets especially where cash on delivery is a popular payment option. Handling this matter properly is a challenge as customers may feel cheated if there is any delay in handling return process, refund or replacement. Further, reverse logistics decision poses the following questions with respect to treatment of returned articles:

- **Destroy:** Should the returned product be destroyed?
- **Recycle:** Should it be recycled and its components utilised?
- **Refurbish:** Should it be refurbished and sent for shipping?
- **Remanufacture:** Should it be remanufactured?
- **Repackage:** Should it be repackaged?

## Channel Cannibalization

Possibility of conflict and cannibalization of some channels are some other complications that may arise for manufacturing companies. This may result in wastage of resources in case of brick and click stores. To avoid channel cannibalization, brick and mortar retailers may retaliate, which may pose another threat to e-tailers.

## Environmental Issues

Sustainability has started attracting tremendous attention across the globe. Emerging nations are no exceptions. It has become imperative to look into environmental issues like wastage handling, emission of harmful material/gases from products, over use of plastic and other non bio-degradable materials in packaging of products. Firms engaged in green operations are received well by the consumers across the globe. Increasing awareness among consumers of emerging nations is compelling firms to engage in and promote sustainability.

Programs to control and refine sustainable practices are being adopted by companies all over the world across the entire supply chain (Rao, 2002; GEMI 2004) through communication about the issue and encouragement to adopt the best practices. Sustainability entails adoption of pro-environmental practices in packaging and reverse logistics (Vachon, Klassen, & Johnson, 2001), training of suppliers, controlling supply chain practices (Rao 2002), and ensuring proper utilisation of products by customers (Snir, 2001). Similarly, e-tailers will also be expected to adhere to pro- environmental practices by ensuring proper compliance across the entire supply chain. They will be required to educate customers about contribution to this cause through recycling, refurbishing and proper disposal etc. Selling of star rated electrical and electronic products to the customers through promotional schemes etc. could be another option. To sum up, e-tailers will need to gear up to collaborate with their suppliers or customer or both (Geffen & Rothenberg 2000, Rao 2002) to address the concern for environment.

## SUGGESTIONS FOR EFFECTIVE E-TAILING IN EMERGING ECONOMIES: A WAY FORWARD

The business of e-tailing is expanding its reach by leaps and bounds. The business environment prevailing in emerging economies is different from that in developed nations. Hence, it is important to understand all those issues which are relevant or unique to these developing economies. Understanding of CCLIP, an acronym for culture, customers, logistics, internet and digital infrastructure and payment can facilitate exploitation of opportunities and handling of challenges. Keeping these factors in mind will help the marketer to decide suitable marketing strategies in developing nations. These may be encapsulated as following:

### Culture

Culture is one of the important force which controls human behaviour (Schiffman & Kanuk, 1997). It is a set of unwritten norms prevailing in a society which drive the behaviour of its people. Success of marketing endeavours depends on proper understanding of culture and values prevailing in a society (Herbig, 1998). E-tailing, is not an exception to this. Understanding of values, beliefs and norms prevailing in emerging markets is vital for e-tailers. Emerging nations like India, China, Brazil, and Russia have different cultures with distinct variations. Asians are supposed to consider family, group and clan relationships (Yau, 1988) while taking decisions. Yau (1988) also stated that the Chinese consumers show high regard for authority and anticipate people holding authority to guide them. Similarly, most Indians are affected by the opinions of their family members and traditions while the customers in developed nation are usually independent in their buying decisions. Trust towards the company in terms of product, information content, privacy, transaction, technology, and security depends upon culture (Constantinides, Romero, & Gomez, 2010). E-tailing companies need to take care of the cultural aspect and build a platform specific to the need of the region they are operating in. Understanding the differences in terms of language, colour and aesthetics could become a deciding factor in achieving success of global ventures (Jobber, 2007).

Avoiding uncertainty can be understood as the level to which the members of a culture feel apprehensive towards any unknown or uncertain situations (Hofstede, 1991). Perceived risk means consumers' perception about unlikely circumstances which may encompass the adverse result of purchasing a product (Dowling & Staelin, 1994). Consumer's information search behaviour is also influenced by their ability to tolerate uncertainty and risk (Garner & Thompson, 1986). Both perceived risk and uncertainty avoidance vary among customers across emerging nations. For instance, Indians are high on uncertainty avoidance so building and sustaining their trust assumes great importance.

The groups which an individual seeks to evaluate self and form attitudes are referred to as reference groups. Their importance may vary from culture to culture (Witt, 1970). Indian consumers, for example, prefer to obtain detailed advice about products friends and family members besides searching for the product online. Reference groups influence behaviour through three ways – informational, value expressive and utilitarian (Park & Lessig, 1977).

Ethnocentrism involves discrimination between in-group with which the consumers identify themselves and out-groups which are considered as very different (Shimp & Sharma, 1987). This is also a culture specific issue which may influence online purchases. Highly ethnocentric customers may prefer local sellers with whom they are familiar and feel connected to rather than going online for making purchases from foreign sellers. This implies that any decision pertaining to the business of e-tailing in emerging nations should be taken only after consideration of the culture prevalent in that nation as customers across emerging markets differ in their preferences, customs, rituals, aesthetics, level of ethnocentric tendencies etc. and prefer products and offerings that are compatible with their value systems.

## Customers

It has been suggested that the common user of internet is a professional, equipped with disposable income, young and adequately educated (Palumbo & Herbig, 1998). Increase in purchasing power and income are expected to lead the customers from traditional to online sellers (Comor, 2000) as time assumes greater value than money (Burke, 1997). This phenomenon is being observed in some emerging nations as well. However, the customers in these nations tend to differ because of different socio-economic environments prevailing in their respective countries. For instance, capabilities associated with using technology vary across emerging markets which affects the online business. Chinese customers are comparatively better versed in using computers than their Indian counterparts. They differ in their lifestyle as well. An understanding about the demographic characteristics, psychographics, liking, etc. of the buyers in respective nations will help in designing more interactive websites and forming better marketing strategies etc.

Price sensitivity is another aspect which requires proper treatment as customers in emerging markets are more attracted towards discounts and seek more value for money deals. In this pursuit they may switch from one website to other. Despite rise in average incomes in Asia and the growing incomes of middle class, the per capita income of consumers in emerging economies is still very less when compared to their counterparts in the developed world. This makes consumers in emerging nations very price-sensitive (Narang, 2011). The facility to compare prices online has further boosted this mindset. The e-tailers not only face competition from other online sellers but also from the traditional offline stores which run highly cost effective operations. To handle the price conscious customers various e-tailers like Flipkart, Yebhi.com and many others in India are already offering free shipping, flexible policy for returns and various promotional schemes in anticipation of serving and attracting the price conscious buyers.

Similarly, customers in Russia use search engine, Yandex heavily to locate latest offers and compare prices across various online retailers. Growing middle class in Brazil also goes for "bang for the buck" (Kearney, 2013) to get advantage of "big bargains". These price sensitive consumers are using websites such as Groupon, Piexe and Urbano which offer group buying facility. Websites like Buscape allows them to compare prices and features with respect to more than 7 million products. Even in China, a highly competitive online market compels e-tailers to reduce prices to improve their sales and increase market share (Kearney, 2013). On the occasion of Chinese New Year, online traders like Dangdang and JD.com compete heavily on prices.

## Online Experience

Atmospherics or environmental cues have been reported to play a very important role in store selection, reputation, image, customer satisfaction and loyalty (Pan and Zinkhan, 2006; Narang, Polsa, Alabi & Wei, 2015). They will be equally important in case of online purchases. Therefore, instead of being obsessed with cognitive cues such as price and quality, the e-sellers need to pay attention to the emotional aspect of shopping behaviour as well. Buyers are likely to experience emotions like pleasure, arousal, excitement, dominance, unfamiliarity, novelty (Mehrabian & Russell, 1974) and disappointment while browsing through a website. Since e-tailing lacks human element the role of atmospherics or customer experience assumes greater importance. It may be provided through dynamic web pages, user friendly interface, easier processing and proper demonstration of products through 3D images. Flash files, videos etc, may be required to familiarize the customers in emerging markets with the products as they are comparatively less versed with online buying than their counterparts in developed nations. Websites need to be designed according to the needs of customers in different nations to provide online service support both before and after sale. Choice of words for designing content would also have to be done carefully. Any ambiguity and misunderstanding needs to be avoided as quality of information and visual design have a significant impact on repeat purchase (Koo, Kim, & Lee, 2008).

It has been stated that the website image may also influence the customer's decision of choosing a website for purchase (Lim & Dubinsky, 2004). The websites created by companies need to be secure as well as more interactive and useful. E-tailers can convert a visitor into a buyer if the website provides ample information about the product, adequate customer service and ease of use and access (Laudon & Traver, 2009). Customers using online platform require more information about the products as they cannot touch or feel the product (Lim & Dubinsky, 2004). Further, they prefer information that satisfies their need (Keency, 1999) which may include feedback and reviews from current and past users. Further, it has to be ensured that only requisite information is delivered as extra and unstructured information adversely effects the purchase decision (Bigné-Alcañiz, Ruiz-Mafé, Aldás-Manzano, & Sanz-Blas, 2008).

Offering logical, comfortable and smooth web experience converts visitors into buyers (Broekhuizen & Huizingh, 2009). A customer satisfied with the service quality of the portal in terms of process and encounter tends to revisit the site and may spread positive word of mouth by share his experience through various channels including social media. Online atmospherics, can thus, make the buyers feel happy, fearless (Narang et al., 2015), warm and welcomed. Web portals like Ebay, for instance, provides opportunity for auctioning products to its customers, which transcends shopping into an interesting game of luck and convert shopping into an enjoyable activity (Prasad & Aryasri, 2009). In brief, factors impacting online experience have to be borne in mind while designing e-shops in emerging markets.

## Logistics

Inventory carrying, shipping and transaction costs get added at each level of supply chain (Delfmann, Albers, & Gehring, 2002). Proper management of logistics i.e. both upstream and downstream the supply chain can reduce cost, bring profitability and yield competitive advantage (Nicholls & Watson, 2005). Logistics is one area which may offer edge to online retailers over offline stores as they have comparatively lesser levels in their distribution network. It may help them to save big costs. Traditional retailers, on the other hand have limited access to customers and face constraints in terms of store size and inventory holding capacity (Van Vliet & Pota, 2001). However, Rowlands (2001) points out that neither multichannel retailer nor pure e-tailers are able to provide nationwide home delivery as the size of orders from small towns are not sufficient enough to justify pan country distribution. Thus, logistics of retailers limit the reach to major towns in emerging nations. For example, in Russia most of e-tailing business is concentrated in Moscow and St Petersburg. The situation is more or less similar in China, India and Brazil.

In the evolution stage, e-tailers may decide to outsource delivery network and warehousing (Rowlands, 2001). Outsourcing logistics function and focussing on promotion and other marketing activities helps them to save significant initial fixed costs (Anderson, Chatterjee, & Lakshmanan, 2003). However, outsourcing involves synchronisation issues and newer costs in the form of controlling the service level (Rabinovich & Bailey, 2004). Decisions related to the size of shipment, type of shipment, frequency of load (density), presence of delivery stores, lacuna in delivery, frequency of delivery, delivery time sensitivity, type of vehicles required and their numbers, size of vehicle, delivery cost, packaging, warehousing etc. are crucial and need proper attention as logistics can become the source of competitive edge over others and provide impetus to the success of e-tailers in emerging nations.

From the viewpoint of consumers, the services provided by e-tailers have to focus and achieve efficiencies on the following aspects of logistics:

- **Timeliness:** Pertains to delivery date choice, delivery within specified time slot, time window, etc. Delivery to the designated person on time is a very critical element of success in emerging economies. This becomes more so when companies like Flipkart are even trying to expand their reach to rural parts of India by tying up with the postal department. To deliver the products faster to the customers B2W and Walmart are establishing dedicated online warehouses and planning to invest $450 million in building efficient distribution network in Brazil. JD.com from China is known for the same day delivery in as many as 23 cities and to achieve this it has built its own logistics infrastructure with an additional investment of $580 million. In Russia, e-tailer Ozone has also invested in its own logistics network with 2,100 pickup point covering 130 cities and is set to expand further.
- **Availability:** Ensuring availability of all products at all locations of the country of operations is not possible always but presence of substitutes and display option of similar products can help the situation where customer can choose from the options available in his area.
- **Order Tracking:** Proper order tracking system is a very useful facility which helps the customers to remain assured about the delivery of the product ordered online. It provides clarity with respect to waiting time required. In case the desired product is out of stock then timely information about its availability will help to retain the customer, provided he is willing to wait.
- **Condition of Product:** Online sellers have to ensure accuracy of orders in terms of size, quantity, delivery point etc. and take necessary actions for damage prevention during transport through proper and adequate packing so that the customer receives the product in good condition. Failing this may lead to not only loss of customer but also development of negative image about the company.
- **Returns:** Decisions pertaining to channel option for return, response time, quick and timely payment collection, replacements and alternative offers will have major implications for success of e-business. Since, customer's future buying behaviour may strongly be influenced by the return policy of the company (Griffis et. al, 2012), it merits special attention in case of emerging nation. Matters pertaining to treatment of returned product and other issues such as repair, resale, etc. have also to be considered by e-tailers in emerging economies.

## Internet and Digital Infrastructure

No doubt that the role of logistics is vital in building and sustaining e-tailing in emerging markets but the challenges offered by lack of digital infrastructure are no less by any parameter. Though the penetration of internet is increasing rapidly, however, except for Malaysia and Singapore, most of the Asian population is still quite away from the internet and other digital devices. Earlier, India was not present in the global retail index of A.T. Kearney due to its poor internet penetration. However, with growing reach of broadband, smart phones and other peripheral devices like printers etc, the Indian e-retail market is set to grow rapidly. Yet the differences in terms of availability of technology penetration exist in developing nations which have their own implications for e-tailers. They need to assess and comprehend the technological environment of each of the emerging nation separately and adopt suitable strategies to reach their target markets. For instance, many online service providers missed the presence of central booking system in India. Cleartrip, for instance, upon starting its business in India found that many small airlines did not have membership of Global Distribution System GDS (a digital system which is used as a single point access to reserve air tickets). It had to build software, "ticket masters clone" to cope with the situation. Bookmyshow also faced a similar problem. To cope with the problem of little internet penetration, Redbus, a bus ticketing website in India provides an option of alternate platform from where numerous travel agents across the country are facilitated to reserve tickets for their travellers. In a country like Vietnam owning a printer is not very common among consumers so Groupon-style discount site, NhomMua has formed a team of couriers with motorbikes to deliver vouchers in Hanoi and Ho Chi Minh City to the customers.

## Payment

The process of online payment is a serious issue as it affects the willingness to pay for goods (Wang et al., 2005). Companies across the emerging nations offer various options such as cash on delivery (COD), debit cards, credit cards EMI, Mobile transfer, e-wallet etc. for making online purchases. Equated monthly instalments make COD more attractive. E-wallets help online consumers to create a digital wallet and keep money for online transactions. Debit and credit cards are other options of online payment. Consumers across the globe prefer different options depending on the ease of use, culture and availability of technology. For instance, cash on delivery is the most prominent and popular option in India.

Emerging nations in Asia are basically cash oriented societies because of limited reach of banking and credit cards facilities. This coupled with lack of consumer trust in online transactions has compelled many leaders in e-tailing like 360buy, Taobao Mall (Tmall) in China, Flipkart in India and Rakuten in Indonesia to provide COD facility. To a great extent the COD facility helps in meeting the customer expectations but it entails significant financial cost in terms of labour, handling of cash and frequent returns of already purchased items. E-tailers have to find ways to curtail these costs.

Recently, payment gateways through prepaid cards have emerged in the form of an alternative payment option. For example, Cherry Credits from Singapore, Gudang Voucher in Indonesia and Gash Plus in Taiwan allow buyers to buy pre-paid cards at retail outlets which are used for online purchases of games. There is tremendous scope for expansion of this kind of prepaid cards for purchase of various other items as well. To cope with the problem of lack of trust, Alipay in China provides escrow service that releases payments to sellers only after getting a confirmation from the customers that they are satisfied with the purchase. This payment option can be experimented in other nations as well. In Russia, Qiwi has joined hands with Visa Virtual, a service provider serving 11 million users to deposit their money in registered accounts and use them like credit cards. The upper limit for online purchase is worth $500 per transaction.

Another upcoming and effective platform for payment is mobile gateways. High mobile phone penetration and weak banking presence in many parts of Asian continent makes them highly desirable. For example, Kenya-based M-Pesa, allows complete payment through mobiles. In a nutshell, e-tailers have to design a smooth and safe payment process by adopting the new and appropriate technologies that will be readily accepted by their customers and won't burden the sellers with additional costs.

## CONCLUSION

The growth rate shown by emerging nations promises a bright future ahead for both national and international marketers. The ever increasing digital infrastructure, rising aspirations of middle class customers and their changing lifestyle will provide further impetus to retail business. The transformation of retail from brick and mortar to e-tailing has already started and is set to grow rapidly in emerging nations like India, China, Russia, Brazil etc., which are the most sought after markets.

Unique ID numbers provided to registered users are likely to ease the purchase process through integration of required information on customers with hassle free buying experience. With an increase in digital literacy customers are expected to get versed in using mobile applications and tablets to place orders by using virtual money. Better connectivity and enhanced smart mobile penetration will further help to bring about exponential growth in electronic business in the emerging economies. We may, therefore say that smart phones are likely to assume greater importance than computers and tablets with respect to purchase orders. However, it would be wrong to assume that electronic business will replace the brick and mortar retail format. In places like India where there is still a wide presence of unorganized retailers, most of the major retailers will need to employ a hybrid channel system to meet the consumers' preference for brick and click model.

Growing technology and data mining are expected to create a situation where consumers' preferences will be automatically updated to display the requisite products. With better connectivity and collaboration among the huge network of warehouses and service providers, the delivery time can be expected to reduce drastically. It is also quite possible that companies begin to develop their own distribution channels to reach economies of scale. Well secured automated system will be expected to take care of the required privacy and payment security issues. Further, it may be predicted that future competition among e-tailers is expected to shift towards issues like quality and atmospherics than prices. Therefore, it would be very meaningful to conduct empirical studies on the role of atmospherics in electronic retailing in emerging nations. It would be also interesting and useful to study the psychographic profiles of online buyers and examine the relationship between their lifestyle and e-portal selection.

## REFERENCES

AIMC - Association for the research In Communication Media. (n. d.). 15 encuesta AIMC a usuarios de Internet. Retrieved from http://www.aimc.es/-Navegantes-en-la-Red-.html

Anderson, R. E., & Srinivasan, S. S. (2003). E-satisfaction and e-loyalty: A contingency framework. *Psychology and Marketing*, *20*(2), 123–138. doi:10.1002/mar.10063

Anderson, W. P., Chatterjee, L., & Lakshmanan, T. R. (2003). E-commerce, transportation, and economic geography. *Growth and Change*, *34*(4), 415–432. doi:10.1046/j.0017-4815.2003.00228.x

ASSOCHAM. (2012). *State of e-commerce in India.* Retrieved from http://www.assocham.org/arb/general/Comscore%20ASSOCHAM-report-state-of-e-commerce-in-india.pdf

Basu, T., Barik, D., & Arokiasamy, P. (2013, August 26-31). Demographic Determinants of Economic Growth in BRICS and selected Developed Countries, *Paper presented at the XXVII IUSSP International Population Conference (IUSSP 2013)*, BEXCO, Busan, Republic of Korea.

India @ Digital Bharat. (2015). *BCG and IAMAI.* Retrieved from http://www.bcgindia.com/documents/file180687.pdf

Bhatt, G., & Emdad, A. (2001). An analysis of the virtual value chain in electronic commerce. *Logistics Information Systems, 14*(1/2), 78–84. doi:10.1108/09576050110362465

Bigne, E., Carla, R., & Sanz, S. (2005). The Impact of Internet User Shopping Patterns and Demographics. *Journal of Electronic Commerce Research, 6*(3), 193–209.

Bigné-Alcañiz, E., Ruiz-Mafé, C., Aldás-Manzano, J., & Sanz-Blas, S. (2008). Influence of online shopping information dependency and innovativeness on internet shopping adoption. *Online Information Review, 32*(5), 648–667. doi:10.1108/14684520810914025

Broekhuizen, T., & Huizingh, E. (2009). Online purchase determinants: Is their effect moderated by direct experience? *Management Research News, 32*(5), 440–457. doi:10.1108/01409170910952949

Burke, R. R.Burke & Raymond R. (1997). Do You See What I See? The Future of Virtual Shopping. *Journal of the Academy of Marketing Science, 25*(4), 352–360. doi:10.1177/0092070397254007

Childers, T. L., Carr, C. L., Peck, J., & Carson, S. (2001). Hedonic and utilitarian motivations for online retail shopping behaviour. *Journal of Retailing, 77*(4), 511–535. doi:10.1016/S0022-4359(01)00056-2

Comor, E. (2000). Household Consumption on the Internet: Income, Time, and Institutional Contradictions. *Journal of Economics, 34*(1), 105.

Constantinides, E. (2004). Influencing the online consumer's behaviour: The web experiences. *Internet Research, 2*(2), 111–126. doi:10.1108/10662240410530835

Constantinides, E., Romero, C. L., & Gomez, M. A. (2010). Effects of web experience on consumer choice: A multicultural approach. *Internet Research, 20*(2), 188–209. doi:10.1108/10662241011032245

Cunningham, I., & Cunningham, W. (1973). The urban in-home shopper: Socio-economic and attitudinal characteristics. *Journal of Retailing, 49*(1), 42–57.

Delfmann, W., Albers, S., & Gehring, M. (2002). The impact of electronic commerce on logistics service providers. *International Journal of Physical Distribution & Logistics Management, 32*(3), 203–222. doi:10.1108/09600030210426539

Dholakia, R., & Uusitalo, O. (2002). Switching to Electronic Stores: Consumer characteristics and the perception of shopping benefits. *International Journal of Retail & Distribution Management, 30*(10), 459–469. doi:10.1108/09590550210445335

Dowling, G. R., & Staelin, R. (1994). A model of perceived risk and intended risk-handling activity. *The Journal of Consumer Research, 21*(1), 119–134. doi:10.1086/209386

Economic Action Plan (2015). Retrieved from http://www.budget.gc.ca/2015/docs/plan/budget2015-eng.pdf

Garner, S.J. & Thompson H.A. (1986). Patient perceived risk in the purchase of physician services. *Journal of Professional Services Marketing*, 1, 149-159.

Geffen, C. A., & Rothenberg, S. (2000). Suppliers and environmental innovation: The automotive paint process. *International Journal of Operations & Production Management*, *20*(2), 166–186. doi:10.1108/01443570010304242

GEMI (Global Environmental Management Initiative). (2004). *Forging new links: enhancing supply chain value through environmental excellence*. Retrieved from http://www.gemi.org/supplychain/resources/ForgingNewLinks.pdf

Gibbs, J., Kraemer, K. L., & Dedrick, J. (2003). Environment and Policy Factors Shaping Global Ecommerce Diffusion: A Cross-Country Comparison. *The Information Society*, *19*(1), 5–18. doi:10.1080/01972240309472

Griffis, S. E., Rao, S., Goldsby, T. J., & Niranjan, T. T. (2012). The customer consequences of returns in online retailing: An empirical analysis. *Journal of Operations Management*, *30*(4), 282–294. doi:10.1016/j.jom.2012.02.002

Herbig, P. (1998). *Handbook of Cross-cultural Marketing*. New York, NY and London: International Business Press.

Hermes, N. (2000). Fiscal decentralisation in developing countries. *De Economist*, *148*(5), 690–692.

Hofacker, C. R. (2001). *Internet Marketing* (3rd ed.). New York: Wiley.

Hofstede, G. (1991). *Cultures and Organizations: Software of the Mind*. London: McGraw-Hill.

Jobber, D. (2007). *Principles and practice of marketing* (5th ed.). London: McGraw Hill.

Joines, J., Scherer, C., & Scheufele, D. (2003). Exploring Motivations for Consumer Web use and their implications for Ecommerce. *Journal of Consumer Marketing*, *20*(2), 90–108. doi:10.1108/07363760310464578

Kearney, A. T. (2012). *E-commerce is the next frontier in global expansion*. Retrieved from http://www.atkearney.com/documents/10192/348450/2012-E-Commerce-Index.pdf/83c81d46-fa4f-4421-850a-ef501d92afbd

Kearney, A. T. (2013). *Online retail is front and central in the quest for growth*. Retrieved from http://www.atkearney.com/documents/10192/3609951/Online+Retail+Is+Front+and+Center+in+the+Quest+for+Growth.pdf/f6693929-b2d6-459e-afaa-3a892adbf33e

Keeney, R. L. (1999). The value of internet commerce to the customer. *Management Science*, *45*(4), 533–542. doi:10.1287/mnsc.45.4.533

Koo, D. M., Kim, J. J., & Lee, S. H. (2008). Personal values as underlying motives of shopping online. *Asia Pacific Journal of Marketing and Logistics*, *20*(2), 156–173. doi:10.1108/13555850810864533

Korgaonkar, P. A., & Karson, E. J. (2007). The influence of perceived product risk on consumers' e-tailer shopping preference. *Journal of Business and Psychology*, *22*(1), 55–64. doi:10.1007/s10869-007-9044-y

Laudon, K. C., & Traver, C. G. (2009). *E-Commerce Business. Technology. Society* (5th ed.). New Jersey: Prentice Hall.

Li, N., & Zhang, P. (2002), Consumer online shopping attitudes and behavior: an assessment of research. *Proceedings of 8th Americas Conference on Information System* (pp. 508-517).

Liang, T., & Huang, J. (1998). An empirical study on consumer acceptance of products in electronic markets: A transaction cost model. *Decision Support Systems*, *24*(1), 29–43. doi:10.1016/S0167-9236(98)00061-X

Lim, H., & Dubinsky, A. J. (2004). Consumers' perceptions of e-shopping characteristics: An expectancy-value approach. *Journal of Services Marketing*, *18*(6), 500–513. doi:10.1108/08876040410561839

Liu, C., & Guo, Y. (2008). Validating the end-user computing satisfaction instrument for online shopping systems. *Journal of Organizational and End User Computing*, *20*(4), 74–96. doi:10.4018/joeuc.2008100104

Lohse, G., Bellman, S., & Johnson, E. (2000). Consumer buying behaviour on the Internet: Findings from panel data. *Journal of Interactive Marketing*, *14*(1), 15–29. doi:10.1002/(SICI)1520-6653(200024)14:1<15::AID-DIR2>3.0.CO;2-C

Mega trends 2015. (2015) *Making sense of a world in motion* Retrieved from http://www.ey.com/Publication/vwLUAssets/ey-megatrends-report-2015/$FILE/ey-megatrends-report-2015.pdf

Mehrabian, A., & Russell, J. (1974). *An Approach to Environmental Psychology.* Cambridge, MA: MIT Press.

Miller, R. R. (1998). *Selling to Newly Emerging Markets.* New York: Quorum Books.

Modahl, M. (2000). *Now or never.* New York: Harper Collins.

Mulhern, F. (1997). Retail Marketing: From distribution to integration. *International Journal of Research in Marketing*, *14*(2), 103–124. doi:10.1016/S0167-8116(96)00031-6

Narang, R. (2010). Psychographic segmentation of youth in the evolving Indian retail market. *International Review of Retail, Distribution and Consumer Research*, *20*(5), 535–557. doi:10.1080/09593969.2010.520508

Narang, R. (2011). Examining the role of various psychographic characteristics in apparel store selection: A study of Indian youth. *Young Consumers: Insights and Ideas for Responsible Marketers*, *12*(2), 133–144. doi:10.1108/17473611111141597

Narang, R., Polsa, P., Soneye, A., & Fuxiang, W. (2015). Impact of hospital atmosphere on perceived health care outcome. *International Journal of Health Care Quality Assurance*, *28*(2), 129–140. doi:10.1108/IJHCQA-12-2013-0142 PMID:26335166

Narang, R., & Singh, S. (2014). Quality of Work Life and Service Quality. In A. Goyal (Ed.), Innovation in Services Marketing and Management: Strategies for Emerging Economies (pp. 265-290). Hershey, PA, USA: IGI Global. doi:10.4018/978-1-4666-4671-1.ch015

Nicholls, A., & Watson, A. (2005). Implementing e-value strategies in UK retailing. *International Journal of Retail & Distribution Management*, *33*(6), 426–443. doi:10.1108/09590550510600852

Palacios, J. J. (2003). Globalization and e-commerce: Diffusion and impacts in Mexico. I-Ways. *Digest of Electronic Commerce Policy and Regulation*, *26*, 195–205.

Palumbo, F., & Herbig, P. (1998). International Marketing Tool: The Internet. *Industrial Management & Data Systems*, *98*(6), 253–261. doi:10.1108/02635579810228381

Pan, Y., & Zinkhan, G. M. (2006). Determinants of retail patronage: A meta-analytical perspective. *Journal of Retailing*, *82*(3), 229–244. doi:10.1016/j.jretai.2005.11.008

Park, C. W., & Lessig, V. P. (1977). Students and housewives: Differences in susceptibility to reference group influence. *The Journal of Consumer Research*, *4*(2), 102–110. doi:10.1086/208685

Prasad, C., & Aryasri, A. (2009). Determinants of shopper behaviour in e-tailing: An empirical analysis. *Paradigm*, *13*(1), 73–83. doi:10.1177/0971890720090110

Rabinovich, E., & Bailey, J. P. (2004). Physical distribution service quality in internet retailing: Service pricing, transaction attributes, and firm attributes. *Journal of Operations Management*, *21*(6), 651–672. doi:10.1016/j.jom.2003.11.004

Rao, P. (2002). Greening the supply chain: A new initiative in South East Asia. *International Journal of Operations & Production Management*, *22*(6), 632–655. doi:10.1108/01443570210427668

Rox, H. (2007). Top reasons people shop online may surprise you. *Associatecontent.com*. Retrieved from http://www.associatedcontent.com/article/459412/top_reasons_people_shop_online_may.html?cat=3

Schiffman, L., & Kanuk, L. (2003). *Consumer Behaviour* (8th ed.). New Jersey: Prentice Hall.

Schiffman, L. G., & Kanuk, L. L. (1997). Consumer Behaviour (6th ed). Englewood Cliffs, NJ: Prentice-Hall International.

Schoder, D., & Yin, P. L. (2000). Building firm trust online. *Communications of the ACM*, *43*(12), 73–79. doi:10.1145/355112.355127

Sharma, A., & Sheth, J. (2004). Web-based marketing. The coming revolution in marketing thought and strategy. *Journal of Business Research*, *57*(7), 696–702. doi:10.1016/S0148-2963(02)00350-8

Sheng-jun, Y. (2011). Educational Policies and Economic Growth in BRICs: Comparative Perspectives. *Journal of US-China Public Administration*, *8*(2), 188–197.

Shimp, T. A., & Sharma, S. (1987). Consumer ethnocentrism: Construction and validation of the CETSCALE. *JMR, Journal of Marketing Research*, *24*(August), 280–289. doi:10.2307/3151638

Sivanad, C., Geeta, M., & Sulep, M. (2004). Barriers to mobile Internet banking services adoption: An empirical study in Klang Valley of Malaysia. *Internet Business Review*, *1*, 1–17.

Snir, E. M. (2001). Liability as a catalyst for product stewardship. *Production and Operations Management*, *10*(2), 190–206. doi:10.1111/j.1937-5956.2001.tb00078.x

Strader, T. J., & Shaw, M. J. (1999). Consumer cost differences for traditional and Internet markets. *Internet Research*, *9*(2), 82–92. doi:10.1108/10662249910264819

Technopak. (2012). *E-tailing In India–pushing the retail frontier*, Retrieved from http://www.rasci.in/downloads/2012/e-tailing_%20india_pushing_retail_frontier.pdf

The Tech Faq. (2008). *Top reasons why people shop online*. Retrieved from http://www.thetechfaq.com/2008/09/29/top-reasons-why-people-shop-online/,Thetechfaq.com

Tigre, P. B. (2003). E-commerce readiness and diffusion: The case of Brazil. I-Ways. *Digest of Electronic Commerce Policy and Regulation*, *26*, 173–183.

Tong, X. (2010). A cross-national investigation of an extended technology acceptance model in the online shopping context. *International Journal of Retail & Distribution Management*, *38*(10), 742–759. doi:10.1108/09590551011076524

Vachon, S., Klassen, R. D., & Johnson, P. F. (2001). Customers as green suppliers: managing the complexity of the reverse supply chain. In J. Sarkis (Ed.), *Greening Manufacturing: From Design to Delivery and Back* (pp. 136–149). Sheffield, UK: Greenleaf Publisher. doi:10.9774/GLEAF.978-1-909493-22-3_11

Van Vliet, P., & Pota, D. (2001). Understanding online retail: A classification of online retailers. *Journal of Computer Information Systems*, *41*(2), 23–29.

Wang, C. L., Ye, L. R., Zhang, Y., & Nguyen, D. D. (2005). Subscription to fee-based online services: What makes consumer pay for online content? *Journal of Electronic Commerce Research*, *6*(4), 301–311.

Whysall, P. (2000). Retailing and the internet: A review of ethical issues. *International Journal of Retail & Distribution Management*, *28*(11), 481–489. doi:10.1108/09590550010356840

Witt, R. E. (1970). *Group Influence on Consumer Brand Choice*. The University of Texas: Bureau of Business Research.

Yau, O. H. M. (1988). Chinese cultural values: Their dimensions and marketing implications. *European Journal of Marketing*, *22*(5), 44–57. doi:10.1108/EUM0000000005285

Yu, T., & Wu, G. (2007). Determinants of internet shopping behaviour: An application of reasoned behaviour theory. *International Journal of Management*, *24*(4), 744–762.

Zhao, Z. J., & Gutierrez, J. A. (2002). Customer Service Factors Influencing the Internet Shopping in New Zealand. Retrieved from http://proceedings.informingscience.org/InSITE2004/017zhao.pdf

## KEY TERMS AND DEFINITIONS

**CCLIP:** CCLIP is an acronym for Culture, Customer, Logistics, Internet and Digital Infrastructure and Payment.

**Convenience:** Convenience is the ease of online purchase.

**Culture:** Culture here is defined as the resultant force of customer's value, belief, norms, trust and attitude.

**Customer:** Customer can be defined as the user who pays for the offering.

**Customer Dissonance:** Customer dissonance is the conflict in the mind of customers due to differing thoughts regarding purchased products.

**Digital Infrastructure:** Digital Infrastructure can be defined as the presence of adequate equipment like computers, internet facility, printers etc. to avail the internet based transactions.

**Emerging Markets:** Emerging Markets are the nations which are on the verge of development and are poised to become developed in near future based on their potential and trends recorded in their economies.

**E-Tailing:** E-tailing can be defined as the combination of retail and internet where end users are directly served through various offerings over electronic media.

**Payment:** Payment includes the various options available to customer to pay the price of the product purchased from online sellers.

**Returns:** Returns can be defined as the reverse movement of goods from buyer to e-tailers.

# Chapter 4
# China's E-Tailing Blossom:
## A Case Study

**Bo Liang**
*Saint Vincent College, USA*

**Thomas Cline**
*Saint Vincent College, USA*

**Yanbin Tu**
*Robert Morris University, USA & Jianghan University, China*

**Zhongyu Ma**
*State Information Center Beijing, China*

## ABSTRACT

*E-tailing has a dynamic ecosystem different from traditional retailing. To the best of our knowledge, there are few case studies scientifically grounded yet practical. Nonetheless, this is the authors' goal with this book chapter. A case study of China's e-tailing is needed because China is the largest emerging market as well as the largest e-retailing market in the world. Moreover, e-tailing provides one of the most effective ways for foreign retailers to enter China's impressive retail market. This case study will explore the underlying reasons for the success of China's e-tailing market by investigating the elements of China's e-tailing ecosystem. This study will further investigate the major players in China's e-tailing market, with a focus on the Alibaba Group, China's largest e-tailing company. This study will address Alibaba's e-tailing strategies and practices by comparing Alibaba and its major domestic and global competitors (e.g., Amazon).*

## INTRODUCTION

E-tailing, or online retailing, has experienced rapid growth globally during the past ten years. Global e-tailing sales are expected to reach $1.92 trillion by 2016 (as cited in Statista, 2014). E-tailing is also playing a growing role in global GDP growth. It is estimated that e-tailing will account for 1.61 percent of global GDP by 2018 (as cited in Statista, 2014).

Chinese e-tailing growth is the driving force for global e-tailing growth. China's e-tailing market has been growing at a significant rate since 2009. In 2013, china surpassed the United States as the largest e-tailing market. The major force of China's e-tailing boom is e-tailing on Singles Day (11/11) in which products on retail sites such as Tmall.com are sold at deep discounts. Singles Day was launched by

DOI: 10.4018/978-1-4666-9921-2.ch004

Copyright © 2016, IGI Global. Copying or distributing in print or electronic forms without written permission of IGI Global is prohibited.

Alibaba in 2009. Since 2012 this day has become the largest shopping day in the world, exceeding the sales volumes on Cyber Monday in the U.S. In 2012, Alibaba's sales volume on Singles Day achieved $3.1 billion, more than doubling Cyber Monday's sales for 2012. In 2013, Alibaba reached sales of $ 5.7 billion on this day, nearly tripling Cyber Monday's sales for 2013. In 2014, Alibaba recorded sales of $9.3 billion on Singles Day, an increase of 60% from 2013 sales and five times larger than Cyber Monday's sales.

In this case study, we will explore the stories behind the boom of China's e-tailing market by answering the following three, major questions:

1. Why has China's e-tailing market been growing at an astonishing rate during the past five years and is it sustainable over the next five or ten years?
2. What are the cultural and social factors that differentiate China's e-tailing success from other global players?
3. What are the effective China market entry strategies for international retailers?

# CHINA'S E-TAILING BOOM

## Introduction to China's E-Tailing Market

### An Overview of China's E-Tailing Market

This section will provide an overview of China's e-tailing market, including the elements such as market size, growth rate, and competition. We also briefly introduce the existing literature on China's e-tailing market.

In 2013, China surpassed the U.S. as the largest e-tailing market by reaching annual sales of $315.75 billion (eMarketer, 2014). It is projected that China's e-tailing sales will grow to $871.79 billion by 2017(eMarketer, 2014). Figure 1 shows China's e-tailing sales from 2012 to 2018. China's e-tailing sales contributed to nine percent of China's total GDP in 2013, an increase of seven percent from 2012 (eMarketer, 2014; The World Bank, 2015).

In contrast, the U.S.'s e-tailing sales contributed to only two percent of its total GDP in 2013 (The World Bank, 2015; U.S. Department of Commerce, 2015). Figure 2 illustrates the percentage contribution of e-tailing sales to China and the U.S.'s national from 2012 to 2014.

According to iResearch (2014), by the second quarter of 2014, China's e-tailing market has long been dominated by the consumer- to -consumer (C2C) market. However, the business -to -consumer (B2C) market has been growing much faster than has the C2C market over the past few years. Figure 3 shows the market share and projected market share of C2C and B2C e-tailing market in China from 2010 to 2017. The GMV (gross merchandise volume) of the B2C e-tailing market reached a year-over-year (YoY) growth rate of 73.1%, more than twice that of the C2C market in the second quarter of 2014 (iResearch, 2014). This suggests that Chinese consumers are becoming more mature, and thus showing more preference to branded products.

The growth rate of China's B2C e-tailing market is also much higher than that of China's overall retail market. It's estimated that China's e-tailing will account for 18% of the total retail sales in 2018, an increase of 8 percent from 2013 (Morgan Stanley, 2014).

*Figure 1. E-tailing sales in China (2012-2018)*
*Source: eMarketer, 2014.*

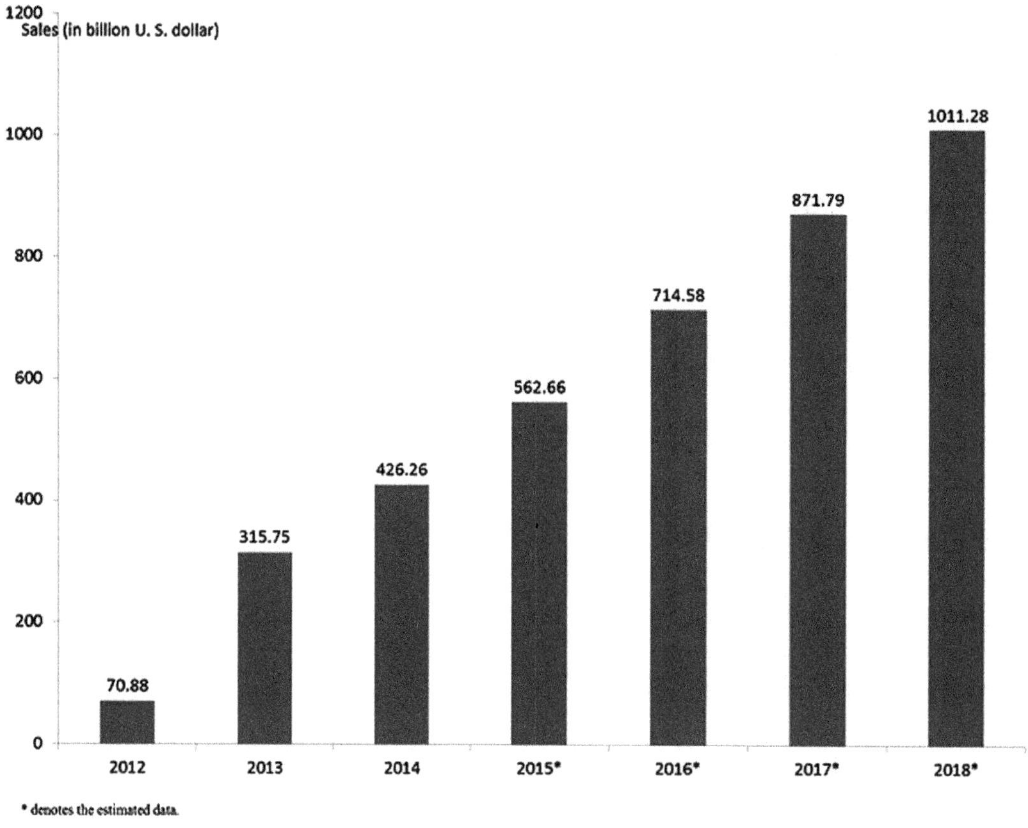


*Figure 2. Percentage contribution of e-tailing sales to national GDP: China vs. U.S. (2012-2014)*
*Source: eMarketer, 2014; The World Bank, 2015; U.S. Department of Commerce, 2015.*

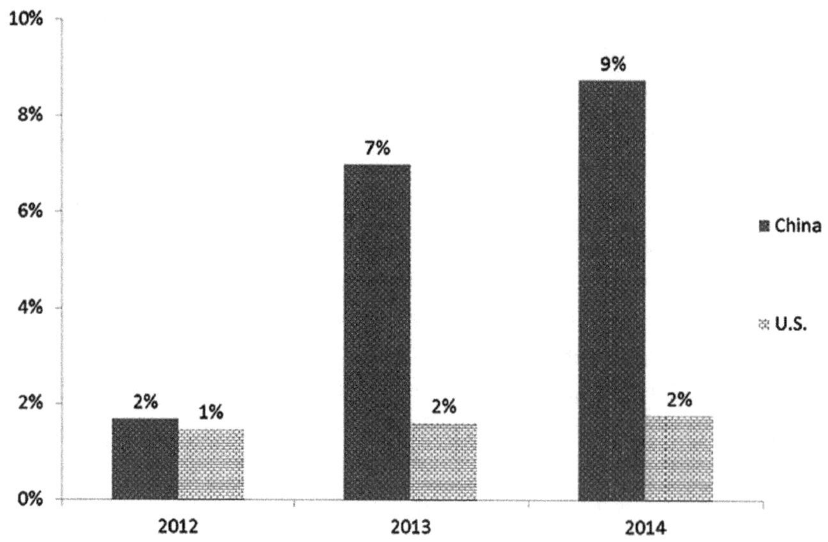

*Figure 3. Market share of C2C and B2C e-tailing market in China (2010-2017)*
*Source: iResearch, 2014.*

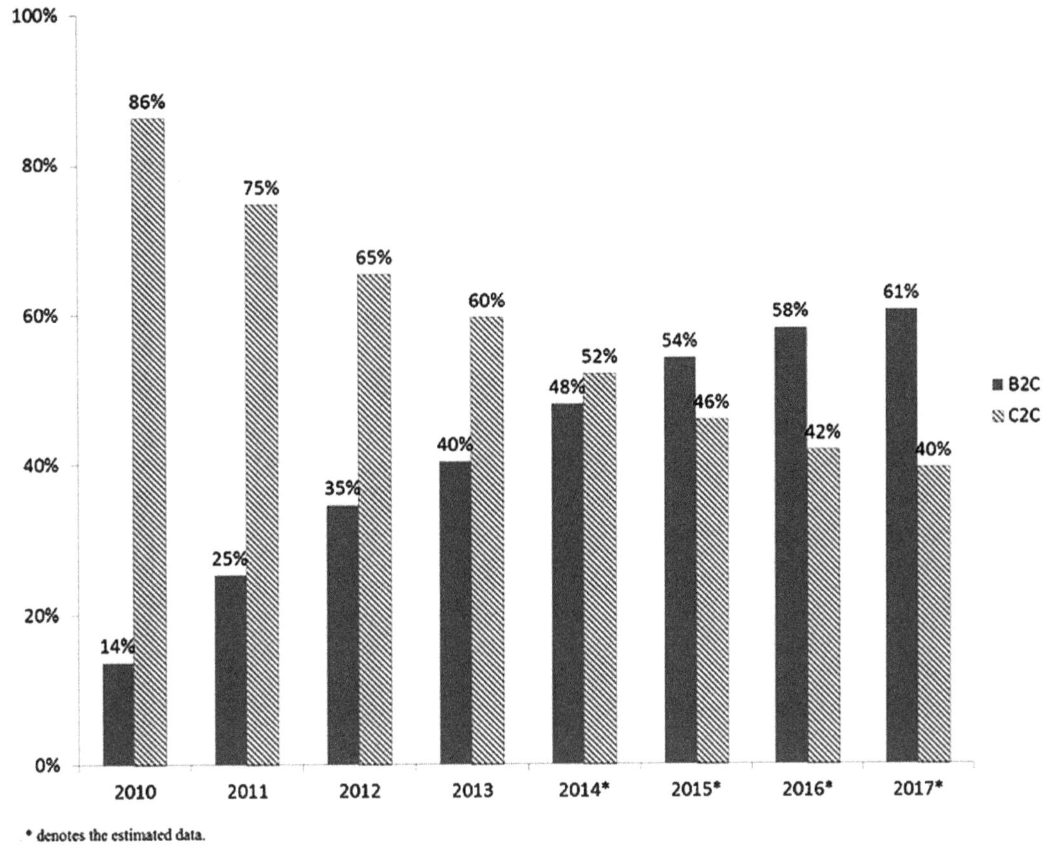


What do Chinese consumers shop for online? The most popular product category among Chinese online shoppers is the category of apparel and accessories (Nielsen, 2014; Mckinsey, 2013). The total online apparel sales in China reached ¥ (China Yuan Renminbi) 434.9 billion ($36.2 billion) in 2013, an increase of 42.6% from 2012.

## China's Mobile E-Tailing Market

One major trend in global e-tailing is that more and more consumers are shopping using mobile devices. Mobile sales in the U.S. in 2014 accounted for 23% of all online Cyber Monday sales, an increase of 27% from 2013 (IBM, 2015). Mobile sales in China have been growing at a more astonishing rate. In 2014, the penetration rate of mobile internet use in China reached 83.4%, 2.5 percent more than that of PC internet use (CNNIC, 2014). The popularity of mobile internet connection has provided consumers with opportunities for mobile shopping. China's mobile e-tailing sales reached ¥929.71 billion ($148.16 billion) in 2014, up 239% from ¥274.00 billion ($43.66 billion) in 2013 (iResearch, 2014). Mobile sales accounted for 33% of online sales in China in 2014, compared with 14.5% in 2013 (iResearch, 2014). Mobile sales are projected to exceed PC sales in 2016 and reach 61.7% of online sales in 2018 (iResearch, 2014).

## Cross-Border Shopping

With the maturity of China's e-tailing market, millions of Chinese consumers are crossing virtual borders to shop foreign goods online. China's cross-border e-tailing sales have been growing exponentially, with an average annual growth rate of 81% from 2008 to 2014. Chinese consumers spent more than $1.5 billion in cross-border shopping online in 2014(Xinhua, 2015).

## Major E-Tailing Players: Market Competition

China's e-tailing market is dominated by one company, Alibaba. During the second quarter of 2012, in the C2C market alone, Alibaba's Taobao reached a market share of 94.96%, whereas Eachnet (former Ebay in China) only had a market share of 0.1 percent (iResearch, 2012). On the B2C market, Alibaba is mainly competing with JD. In 2013, Tmall, a B2C platform by Alibaba, achieved a market share of 57.3% in the B2C market, followed by JD with a market share of 21.2% (iResearch, 2014). Figure 4 shows market share of B2C e-tailing sites in China by GMV in the second Quarter of 2014 (iResearch, 2014).

## Previous Work on China E-Retailing Market

China's e-tailing market has attracted the attention of researchers from both academia and industry. Our study will integrate relevant data and research findings from both perspectives. Academic work

*Figure 4. Market share of B2C e-tailing websites in China by GMV in Q2, 2014*
*Source: iResearch, 2014.*

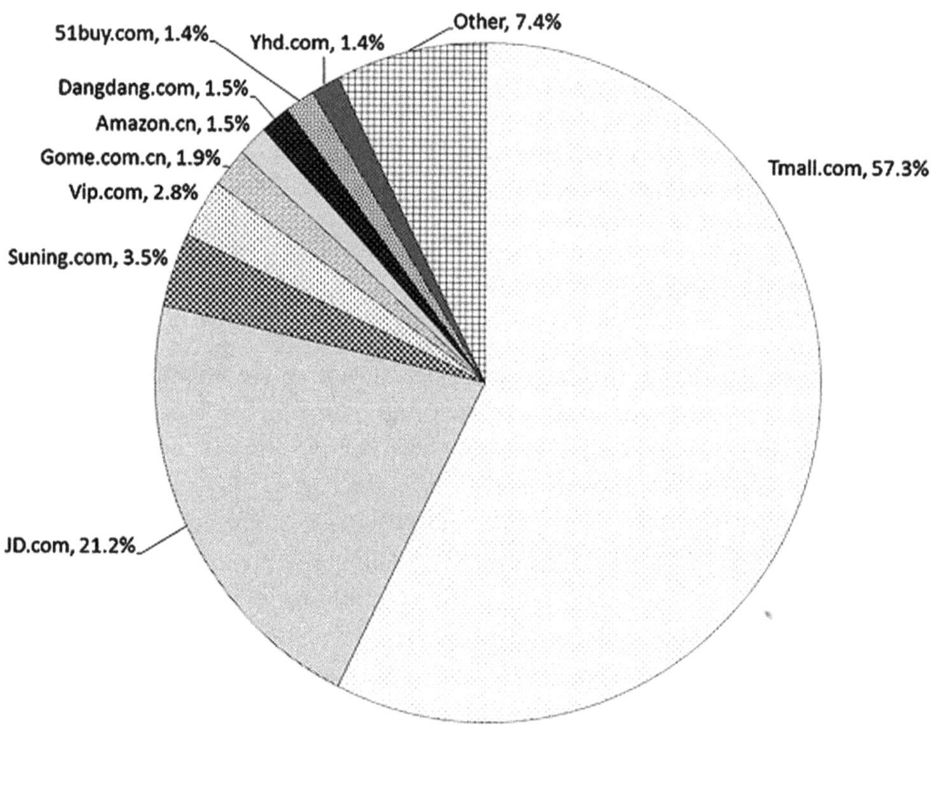

in this field has concentrated on two areas: e-tailers and e-consumers. Research on China's e-tailers has focused on the following aspects: operation (payment systems; Chen, 2012; Zhao, Savage &Chen, 2008), competitive strategies (Chen, Pan & Ouyang, 2014; Ke & Sun, 2014; Wang, 2012; Wang & Ren, 2012), performance assessment (Huang, Jiang & Tang, 2009), and social activities (Qu, Wang, Wang & Zhang, 2013). Research on China's e-consumers has investigated the following topics: (1) shoppers' interest patterns (Mummalaneni & Meng, 2009; Su & Chen, 2015; Xiao, 2010), (2) customer satisfaction (Liu, He, Gao & Xie, 2008; Omar, Bathgate & Nwankwo, 2011), and (3) the factors that may influence consumers' adoption of online shopping (Bian & Zhu, 2013; Clemes, Gan & Zhang, 2014; Fan,Lee & Kim, 2013; Pang, Yen & Tarn, 2007; Yoon, 2009). Because of limited space, this case study reviews only some of the academic literature to explore China's e-tailing market.

Marketing research and consulting companies have also conducted comprehensive research on China's e-tailing market. During our collection of data for this case study, we found valuable data from: iResearch, eMarketer, Statista, China Internet Watch, Bain, Nielsen, and McKinsey. In this case study, we organize and synthesize comprehensive data from these sources to illustrate China's e-tailing market

## China's E-Tailing Ecosystem

According to Turban et al. (2006), e-tailing is defined as retailing conducted over the internet. From a shopper's point of view, an e-tailing transaction is achieved through the following steps. First, a shopper will visit an on-line shopping site where information of products (e.g., descriptions, prices, images, reviews) is displayed. This shopper will then view the information of products, and put interesting products in a shopping cart. Next, this shopper will check out the products by filling in and submitting order information (e.g., address, payment methods). Finally, this shopper will then receive orders by logistics companies (e.g., UPS).

A successful transaction needs effort from shoppers and a variety of businesses, such as retailers, platform providers, and logistic companies. To understand the reason why china e-tailing has been growing at an outstanding rate, we need to investigate all the major elements involved in the integrated e-tailing process. From a macro point of view, these elements constitute an ecosystem of china's e-tailing market, including cultural and social influence, economic structure, logistics, policy and regulations, and online shoppers.

### Cultural and Social Influence

E-tailing is an innovative form of retailing. According to the theory of technology adoption lifecycle, consumers across countries adopt new technologies at different rates. Researchers have conducted cross-cultural studies on the adoption of online shopping by comparing consumers in China with consumers from other countries such as the U.S. (e.g., Pavlou & Chai, 2002; Yoon, 2009). Most of these studies developed their theories based on Hofstede's cultural difference theory, which proposes six dimensions of cultural difference: (1) masculinity-femininity, (2) individualism-collectivism, (3) power distance, (4) uncertainty avoidance, (5) long-term orientation, and (6) indulgence vs. restraint

Empirical research indicates that the national cultural and social influence on online shopper behaviors is based primarily on three dimensions of Hofstede's cultural difference theory: collectivism / individualism, power distance, and long-term orientation. Culture is closely associated with social relations. China is a highly collectivist culture in which people feel a strong sense of belonging to their groups. An online shopping platform is an online community in which shoppers and sellers build and maintain relationships. In China's collectivist culture, shoppers are more likely to maintain harmonious and long-term relationships with sellers than do Westerners (Pavlou & Chai, 2002; Yoon, 2009). This may be a possible reason why there are less negative online reviews on China's retailing sites (Fang, Zhang, Bao, & Zhu, 2013). Online shopping is a virtual activity that requires high levels of trust between shoppers (C2 C) and between shoppers and sellers (B2C; Grabner-Kraeuter, 2002; Guo, Wang & Leskovec, 2011; Ling & Chai, 2010; Wang, 2012). Strong relationships are the facilitators of trust between Chinese shoppers and sellers (Pavlou & Chai, 2002; Yoon, 2009). Moreover, because of the close relationships between shoppers, Chinese online shoppers are more likely to trust online reviews or Word-of-Mouth by other shoppers than are Westerners (Yu, Guo &Yao, 2011). China's collectivist online behavior contrasts sharply with more individualistic online behavior in the West, where, in general, e-tailing tends to be more transactional and less relational.

Power distance is also closely associated with social influence. Chinese perceive high levels of power distance. That is, Chinese accept that power is distributed unequally in the society. Based on the theory of technology adoption lifecycle, early majority is heavily influenced by early adopters, who may create a social demand for new technologies. For online shopping, consumers with lower power are more likely to follow the behaviors of their in-group opinion leaders, i.e., early adopters recruit more early adopters and innovations such as e-tailing diffuses more quickly (Pavlou & Chai, 2002; Yoon, 2009). In contrast, the early majority in Western Societies wait for feedback from the early adopters, hence slowing down the diffusion of e-tailing, including mobile shopping.

## Economic Forces: Information Technology Infrastructure

The growth of the e-tailing market is enabled by an economy with an emphasis on developing information technology infrastructure, including internet access and internet connection devices.

According to China Internet Network Information Center (CINIC, 2014), China had more internet users than any other countries, nearly 648.75 million internet users by 2014. In addition, China had more internet users on mobile devices than on PCs. The proportion of mobile internet users to total internet users reached 83.4% in 2014.

Online shopping, especially mobile shopping, has become a popular application by Chinese internet users. According to a survey by CINIC, the percentage of mobile shoppers among online shoppers increased from 28.9% to 38.9% from 2013 to 2014. In contrast, the penetration rate of China's internet access was only 46.03% in 2014. These data suggest an additional growth opportunity of China's e-tailing market, especially mobile e-tailing market in the near future.

## Policy and Regulation

E-tailing is a virtual marketplace in which consumers take risks from the beginning (e.g., misleading product information), to the middle (e.g., security and privacy of personal information), and to the end (e.g., condition of the delivered orders) of a complete transaction. Therefore, government regulations play a more important role to protect the interests of consumers in e-tailing than in traditional retailing. On the other hand, to ensure competition in this market, regulations are also needed on e-tailing tax and foreign investment.

Although China e-tailing market has been growing dramatically during the past few years, extant policy and regulations are not sufficient to protect the healthy growth of this market. Chinese government agencies are enforcing new and tighter regulations on e-tailing along the following dimensions: protection of consumer interests, taxation, and foreign investment.

### Protection of Consumer Interests

*The Law of the People's Republic of China on Protection of Consumer Rights and Interests* has been in effect for a decade. In March 2014, a revised version of the law was launched. The new law has added regulations on e-tailing to protect online shoppers' rights and interests. For example, the revised law regulates the liability of providers of e-tailing platforms (e.g., Alibaba and JD.com), and requires no time limitation for sending back returned products. The revised law also requires all retailers (including offline and online retailers) to maintain the confidentiality of consumers' personal information.

In December 2014, the ministry of business launched a regulation of *Online Retailing Conducted on Third-Party Platforms Transaction Rules Administrative Procedures*. The purpose of this regulation is to regulate transaction rules stipulated by third-party e-tailing platforms (e.g., Alibaba). This regulation enforces that ten sets of rules must be included in the transaction rules by third-party platform providers, including the set of rules on consumer rights protection. For any adoption or modification to its transaction rules, a third-party platform provider must display the transaction rules on its website for at least 15 days for the solicitation of public opinion. This regulation is the first administrative regulation on the transaction rules of third-party platform providers. This shows that Chinese government is making efforts to tighten the regulations on the behaviors of third-party platform providers.

### Taxation

Tax evasion by online retailers, especially in the C2C market, has long been a problem in China, causing unfair competition between offline and online retailers. In April 2013, The State Administration for Taxation started to require online retailers to issue official invoices with each transaction. In China, invoice are issued by taxation authorities and used as a proof that the proper tax has been paid on each transaction. This new policy would have a significant impact on the C2C market, especially on Alibaba Taobao, the largest C2C platform. In the B2C market, e-tailing platforms such as JD, Dangdang, and Alibaba Tmall have already issued invoices. Therefore, the new tax policy would have less impact on the B2C market.

### Foreign Investment

After China joined the World Trade Organization (WTO) in 2001, Chinese governments have lifted restrictions on foreign investment in the retail sector including both of the offline and online sectors. The Measures for Administration of Foreign Investment in the Commercial Sector (MAFICS) took effect in 2004. MAFICS allowed foreign-invested enterprises (FIEs) to undertake retailing activities in fixed places or via television, telephone, mail order, internet, and automats. In 2010, China's Ministry of Commerce (MOFCOM) issued the Circular on Several Issues Concerning the Approval and Administration of Foreign Investment in Online Sales and Automatic Vending Machines, which simplifies approval procedures of FIEs that sell products via the Internet and vending machines. All these new measures have increased competition between domestic (e.g., Alibaba) and foreign e-tailers (e.g., Amazon).

## Logistics

The key to success in e-commerce is the efficiency of logistics – order fulfillment and distribution. With the development of China's e-tailing market, online shoppers are demanding higher levels of customer service. Accordingly, many online retailers are viewing logistics as a critical competitive advantage.

The Chinese government grouped cities in China into four tiers based on their economic development and political importance. The top tier lists includes cities such as Shanghai, Beijing, Shenzhen, and Guangzhou. The geographic distribution of internet use is much faster than that of physical retail chains. With limited selection at local retail stores, consumers in lower tier cities exhibit greater demand for online products than consumers in higher tier cities. Therefore, the lower tier cities have become a fast growing e-tailing market, promising more opportunities for Chinese e-tailers.

China's express delivery industry has been growing fast as a result of explosive growth of china's e-tailing market since 2010. But this industry has not been growing at the same speed as the e-tailing industry overall. Specifically, the extension of logistics distribution network in lower tier cities and rural regions has been lagging behind. As a result, consumers in these geographic areas have suffered delayed, damaged or even lost orders, especially during promotion events such as Singles Day.

China's express delivery market is highly fragmented. By 2013, there were more than 8,000 legitimately registered express delivery service companies in China. This is in stark contrast to the U.S., where the U.S. postal service (USPS) and United Postal Service (UPS) dominate express delivery. In China, there are three groups of express companies on the market: the Express Mail Service (EMS) owned by state-owned China Post, foreign logistics companies (e.g., UPS), and private express companies. The top ten players are EMS, SF, STO, YT, ZTO, Yunda, Tiantian, HTKY, ZJS and CCES, with a combined market share of 87% of the express delivery market in China (Deloitt, 2014). Private express companies, which focus on small-scale local logistics service have been growing faster than EMS and foreign companies. These companies are able to offer services at lower rates than their state and foreign competitors. To improve logistic service, especially last mile delivery service, some large online retailers have built their own logistic operation or partnered with established express companies.

## E-Tailing Shoppers

Research in China's online shoppers has been rich and productive over the past years. The primary focus in the field is to investigate factors influencing decision-makings on online shopping adoption.

For retail shopping, consumers first need to decide where to shop, online or offline. Previous work has identified factors that may influence consumers' adoption of online shopping, including website factors (Liu & Arnett, 2000; Shergill & Chen, 2005), perceived risk (e.g., Chang, Cheung & Lai. 2005; Miyazaki & Fernandez, 2001), service quality (e.g., Lee & Lin, 2005; Yang & Jun, 2002), convenience (e.g., Childers et al., 2001; Prasad & Aryasri, 2009), price (e.g., Reibstein, 2002; Vijayasarathy & Jones, 2000), product variety (Cho, 2004; Sin & Tse; 2002), consumer resources (Shim, Eastlick, Lotz & Warrington 2001;Young & Kim, 2004), subjective norms (Foucault & Scheufele, 2002; Tan, Yan & Urquhart, 2007), product guarantee (Koyuncu & Bhattacharya 2004; Xu & Paulins, 2005), and demographic characteristics (e.g., Brashear et al.,2009; Chang & Samuel, 2004; Swinyard & Smith, 2003).

Important research shows that the following factors had more influence on China's online shoppers than other factors: (1) perceive risk or trust (Clemes, Gan & Zhang, 2014; Corbitt, Thanasankit & Yi,

2003; Kim, Ferrin & Rao, 2008), (2) consumer resources (Clemes et al., 2014; Corbitt et al., 2003), (3) service quality, (4) subjective norms, (5) product variety, (6) convenience, and (7) website factors. Clemes et al. (2014) investigated the environmental factors associated with online shopping adoption by Chinese consumers. They found Chinese are more likely to shop online if they (1) perceive lower levels of risk of online shopping (e.g., risk of online transaction, risks of information privacy), (2) have more online resources (e.g., internet connection, digital devices), and (3) are more influenced by their friends or families. They also found that Chinese online shoppers perceived the following benefits of online shopping: (1) higher quality of service, (2) a variety of products, (3) convenience, and (4) well-designed websites.

Further, Clemes et al. (2014) found that these environmental factors influence online shoppers differently based on shopper's demographic characteristics. For example, female shoppers are more likely to be influenced by their friends or families than are male shoppers. In China, consumers with high-income do not tend to shop online. The opposite is true in most Western countries.

Marketing research companies have investigated the characteristics of Chinese online shoppers. Chinese online shoppers have a low level of brand loyalty. Their shopping decisions are mostly influenced by price. They compare prices offered from different online sellers. That is the main reason why the Singles Day, biggest shopping day in China, features deeply discounted products. But a new trend suggests that more and more middle-class shoppers include online shopping in their daily lives and have become more brand focused. VANCL, a Chinese online clothing and apparel company, reported that 80% of its consumers made repeat purchases in 2012. Regarding gender difference, the majority of Chinese shoppers are female. This may explain the reason why the top products purchased online have been apparel and accessories and beauty products in China.

Social media has become a major platform in which consumers share information about their purchases. According to China Internet Watch (2014), 82% of Sina Weibo (the most popular micro-blogging platform in China) users shopped online during the third quarter of 2014. According to the surveys by BCG (2011), 40% of China's online shoppers read and post reviews about products – more than double that in the US.

Combining results from academic research and industrial research, the typical Chinese shopper is a female consumer who shops for appearance-focused products such as clothes and accessories, handbags, and shares her experience on social media.

## Domestic E-Tailing Players in China

China is currently the second largest retail market in the world, and is expected to surpass the U.S. to become the largest retail market by 2018 (PwC, 2014). One of the major differences between American retail market and Chinese retail market is the level of competition between offline and online retailers. In the U. S., e-tailers (e.g., Amazon) have been competing heavily with traditional retail chains (e.g., Walmart). Many traditional retailers have extensive geographic retail networks throughout the country and have been building online capabilities to attract more online shoppers. But in China, e-tailers, led by Alibaba, have been dominating the e-tailing market because of the underdevelopment of nationwide offline retail chains. Therefore, in this section, we examine domestic competition in China's e-tailing market by comparing Alibaba and its major competitors, including Eachnet, JD, and Yihaodian.

## The Brief History of Alibaba

For China's e-tailing market, the first and top company that has captured world-wide attention is the Alibaba Group. The company introduces itself on its homepage as follows: "Alibaba Group was established in 1999 by 18 people led by Jack Ma, a former English teacher from Hangzhou, China. From the outset, the company's founders shared a belief that the Internet would level the playing field by enabling small enterprises to leverage innovation and technology to grow and compete more effectively in the domestic and global economies. Since launching its first website helping small Chinese exporters, manufacturers and entrepreneurs to sell internationally, the Alibaba Group has grown into a global leader in online and mobile commerce. Today the company and its related companies operate leading wholesale and retail online marketplaces as well as Internet-based businesses offering advertising and marketing services, electronic payment, cloud-based computing and network services and mobile solutions, among others."

The Alibaba Group grew very quickly from a small online marketplace to an e-commerce giant in just over ten years. The important timeline for the company is listed in Table 1.

The key companies and their businesses under the umbrella of the Alibaba Group are listed as in Table 2. Among these companies, Taobao and Tmall are two major e-tailing platforms. Launched in 2003, Taobao has grown to become China's largest C2C online platform with millions of product listings from small businesses and individual entrepreneurs. Tmall, a B2C platform, was first introduced by Taobao as Taobao Mall in 2003. In 2010, Taobao Mall separated from Taobao by launching an independent web domain, Tmall.com. Tmall is currently China's largest B2C online platform. Through Tmall, brands and retailers sell products directly to the final consumers. In the past, Alibaba was well known for its Alibaba.com trading website, which connects Chinese suppliers with international businesses. But now

*Table 1. The important timeline of Alibaba*

| Year | Milestone |
|---|---|
| Dec, 1998 | Jack Ma and 17 other founders created an online marketplace, named "Alibaba Online". |
| 1999-2000 | Alibaba Group raised a total of US$25 million from SoftBank, Goldman Sachs, Fidelity and others. |
| Dec, 2001 | Alibaba.com became profitable. |
| May, 2003 | Taobao was established as a C2C marketplace. |
| Dec, 2004 | Alipay became a separate payment business from Taobao. |
| Oct, 2005 | Alibaba Group built the strategic partnership with Yahoo! and took over the operation of China Yahoo!. |
| Nov, 2007 | Alibaba.com was listed on the Hong Kong Stock Exchange. |
| April, 2008 | Taobao Mall (Tmall.com) was introduced as a retail B2C marketplace. |
| Sept, 2009 | Alibaba Cloud Computing was introduced. |
| Oct, 2010 | eTao was launched as a shopping search engine |
| Jun, 2011 | Taobao was re-organized into three separate companies: Taobao Marketplace, Taobao Mall (Tmall.com) and eTao |
| Jul, 2011 | Alibaba released its own mobile operating system, Aliyun OS. |
| May, 2014 | Alibaba Group filed registration documents to go public in the US. |
| Sep, 2014 | Alibaba became the biggest initial public offerings in American history, and its shares (BABA) began trading on the NYSE. |

*Table 2. Key companies in Alibaba Group*

| # | Company Name | Brief Description | Est. Year |
|---|---|---|---|
| 1 | Alibaba.com | Leading international supply chain platform for buyers and suppliers. | 1999 |
| 2 | 1688.com | Leading wholesale marketplace for small businesses located in China. | 1999 |
| 3 | Taobao.com | The biggest online C2C marketplace in China. | 2003 |
| 4 | Alipay.com | Dominant online payment solution in China. | 2004 |
| 5 | Tmall.com | The biggest online B2C marketplace in China. | 2008 |
| 6 | Aliyun.com | Clouding computing and data analytical services. | 2009 |
| 7 | Juhuasuan.com | Famous online group buying site with big discounts. | 2010 |
| 8 | AliExpress | Logistics services to customers in globe. | 2010 |

Alibaba.com accounts for only a small part of its revenues. Taobao and Tmall contribute to the majority of Alibaba's group revenue. For the year ending March 31, 2013, the combined GMV of Taobao and Tmall exceeded ¥ 1 trillion (iResearch, 2014).

## Domestic Competition in the C2C Market: Alibaba Taobao vs. EachNet

In the C2C e-tailing market, Alibaba Taobao has reached a market share of nearly 95% by the second quarter of 2012 (iResearch, 2012). The success of Taobao has played a key role in the fast growth of Alibaba and China's e-tailing market. A challenging question is: how did Taobao achieve success by defeating EachNet, China's eBay?

China's C2C e-tailing market started to take off at the end of 1990s. Inspired by the success of eBay, EachNet was co-founded by two Chinese born Harvard MBA graduates Bo Shao and Haiyin Tan in 1999. By the middle of 2001, EachNet held 90% of China's C2C e-tailing market. EBay entered China in 2002 by acquiring 33% stake in EachNet and fully acquired EachNet in 2003. During that time, China was the second largest e-tailing market worldwide. Lured by the size of China's e-tailing market, Alibaba launched Taobao to compete with EachNet in China's C2C e-tailing market.

Taobao's key competitive advantage over EachNet is its customer-focused value proposition. First, Taobao uses a more customer-focused revenue generation strategy. Taobao, which has more than seven million sellers and 800 million product listings, doesn't collect any fees on listings and transactions from sellers or buyers (Osawa, 2013). This strategy may have lowered sellers and buyers' perceived risks of the adoption of online shopping technologies. In contrast, EachNet charges listing and transaction fees from sellers.

But, how does Taobao make money while providing free transaction service? Taobao makes money from merchants' payments for on-site advertising; merchants want to be listed atop among several million merchants and attract consumers. Alibaba developed Taobao's own search engine, eTao, and prohibits Google indexing Taobao product listings. Just like Google, Taobao's site shows not only organic results but also sponsor ads for products associated to the keywords.

Second, Taobao offers a secure and trusted online payment system, which may also have lowered the perceived risk of adopting online shopping technologies. In 2004, Alibaba launched Alipay, an escrow-based online payment platform. Escrow allows buyers to pay securely online without exposing their credit card details. Buyers can also track delivery of their orders, and payment is only released to the supplier after buyers confirm that they have received their orders. Alipay is the preferred payment solution for transactions on Taobao. In 2013, Alipay reported 300 million registered users and 12.5 billion transactions. Alipay eventually overtook PayPal as the largest mobile payment platform in the world with 100 million mobile registered users and over 2.78 billion transactions. Before 2007, EachNet used eBay's payment system-PayPal through which buyers pay directly to sellers without any middle transaction. It was not until 2007 that EachNet started to provide an escrow-based payment system—"An Fu Tong".

Finally, Taobao provides users convenient tools for communication. With a special cultural and social background as discussed earlier, Chinese shoppers are willing to build positive and long-term relationships with sellers and other shoppers. Thus, for e-tailers, providing timely and convenient communication tools is an important approach to success. Alibaba provides an online messaging service called "Ali-Wangwang for instant online communication between buyers and sellers. Further, since Chinese consumers are sophisticated mobile users, Taobao provides mobile communication tools (e.g., instant messaging and voice mail) to buyers and sellers. However, EachNet lacked tools for convenient communication between buyers and sellers.

With all of its marketing efforts, Taobao gained significant market share, from 8% to 59%, whereas EachNet lost market share, from 79% to 36%, from 2003 to 2005 (The Economist, 2006). By 2006, ebay finally pulled out of China and sold EachNet to Tom online, a mobile Internet company in China. Since 2009, Taobao launched marketing campaigns, including the campaigns for Singles Day, and introduced new features and services to create better customer experience (e.g., Taobao app and Taobao agents). As of April, 2015, Taobao is the ninth most visited website in the world and the second most visited website in China (Alexa, 2015). According to iResearch (2014), Taobao Marketplace was China's largest online shopping destination in terms of GMV in 2013.

However, Taobao is also facing big challenges on the domestic e-tailing market. A substantial number of sellers are selling counterfeit products for huge profit margins and using predatory pricing on Taobao. From the White Paper published by Chinese government agents on Jan 23, 2015, the ratio of genuine products to sampling products on Taobao is 37.25%, or approximately 2.68 counterfeit products for every one genuine product. The negative news led to the loss of US$30 billion on Alibaba's market cap during one day. Counterfeited products hurt buyers' interest and confidence at the marketplace, and eventually hurt Alibaba's reputation. The two new regulations on protection of consumer interest discussed earlier will push Alibaba to establish more policies to protect consumers and impose more restrictions on sellers. Tax evasion by small-sized sellers on Taobao is also hurting Alibaba's reputation. The new tax policy on the use of invoices for online transactions will have a big impact ton Taobao's small-sized sellers. These sellers may raise product prices to offset rising costs. As a result, more consumers may switch from the C2C market to the B2C market for more authentic products with reasonable prices.

## Domestic Competition in the B2C Market

### *Alibaba Tmall vs. JD*

After Taobao's huge success in the C2C market, Alibaba launched Tmall to compete in the B2C market in 2008. Tmall provides a number of services to retailers from design, to operation, to marketing, to payment, and to order fulfillment and logistics. Tmall achieved a market share of 57.3% in the B2C market in 2013 (iResearch, 2014). In 2014, Alibaba announced its intent to reposition Tmall as a venue for premium brands. Over 4,000 global brands such as Apple, Burberry, Estee Lauder, Costco have set up stores on Tmall.

JD.com or Jingdong Mall is a major competitor of Tmall. JD is the largest online direct sales company and the second largest online B2C company in China. The company was founded as a magneto-optical store by Liu Qiangdong in 1998 in Beijing. Its B2C platform went online as jdlaser.com in 2004. Soon, the company diversified its product categories to offer electronics, computers, and other products. The company changed its domain name to 360buy.com in 2007, and to JD.com in 2013. In 2013, JD reached a market share of 46.5% in the online direct sales market and a market share of around 20% in the online B2C market (iResearch, 2014).

Tmall has two major advantages over JD. One advantage lies in the business model used to generate revenue. Tmall uses a "platform" business model, by which revenue is generated from transaction fees from third-party merchants. Tmall's transaction fee is comprised of four parts: security deposit, annual technology and service fee, customer loyalty program fee, and a commission on each transaction. However, JD uses a mix of "platform" and "direct sale" business model with a focus on "direct sale". With a "direct sale" business model, revenue is earned from the mark-up for products sold to consumers. The "platform" business model generates much higher gross profit margin than does the "direct sale" business model. In 2014, JD's "direct" business gross profit margin was only seven percent, and the "platform" business gross profit margin reached 70%. JD's overall profit margin was around 11.6%, whereas Alibaba's overall profit margin was around 70% in 2014.

The other advantage of Tmall over JD is the diversity of products and brands sold on its platform. Tmall offers a wide range of products and brands from domestic and global retailers through two channels: "Tmall" (Tmall.com) and "Tmall Global" (Tmall.HK). "Tmall" sells products from retailers that have business entities located in Mainland China, whereas "Tmall Global" sells products from overseas retailers directly to Chinese consumers. JD offers products primarily in 3Cs (Cameras, Computers and Cell Phones) and appliances with over 63% of market share (Yipitdata, 2014). JD has expanded its market share in other product categories beyond the market of appliances and electronics. The number of products (stock keeping units) JD offers has grown 26 times from 2011 to 2014. To compete with "Tmall Global", JD launched a new cross-border e-commerce platform: "JD Worldwide", providing Chinese consumers with a convenient and safe way to purchase authentic and imported products. Through this platform, overseas sellers are able to sell directly to Chinese consumers without any physical presence in China. JD also launched a pilot platform with eBay: "Best of eBay Deals," in which Chinese consumers are allowed to buy products from eBay's global inventory.

JD's logistics strength is a key advantage over Tmall. JD started to build and operate a nationwide fulfillment infrastructure in 2007. By 2014, JD has been operating seven large logistics centers, 123 large warehouses, 3,210 self- distribution stations, 1,620 delivery stations, and 214 pickup stations in 495 cities across China. The entire logistics network covers 1,860 districts and counties. With a strong fulfillment infrastructure, JD started to provide same-day delivery in 43 cities and next-day delivery in another 256 cities across China in 2014. The company also provides high-speed delivery services such as Night Delivery and Three-Hour Delivery in six major cities. Through Night Delivery service, customers can receive an order in the same evening between 7PM and 10PM, if they place the order before 3PM. By Three-Hour Delivery service, customers can receive an order within three hours of placing the order. The company's last-mile delivery network offers customized delivery options (e.g., same-day, next-day) and flexible payment options (e.g., cash on delivery) to customers in more than 150 cities across China.

Unlike its rival, Alibaba does not directly own physical logistics infrastructure and primarily relies on third-party logistics companies to serve geographically dispersed Chinese consumers. However, Alibaba has been taking significant steps to build its logistics capability. In 2013, Alibaba initiated two major moves to build its logistic strength. One move is the "China Smart Logistic Network" in which Alibaba works with industry partners to establish a logistics network with a 24-hour domestic delivery capability. The major industry partners include large express delivery companies (e.g., SF Express and Yunda Express) and retailer Yintai Holdings (owns a department store chain in China). This logistic network is planned to be finished in five to eight years. The goal of this network is to deliver parcels among 2,000 of China's major cities within 24 hours. The other move is a joint venture logistics business between Alibaba and Hairer, one of China's biggest manufacturers and distributors of household appliances. Alibaba invested US $360 million into this joint venture with 9.9% stake. This deal would combine Alibaba's online retail platform and Haier's Goodaymart logistics unit, which covered 2,800 districts and counties nationwide with 83 warehouses and over 6,000 star service centers.

To compete with Tmall, JD has built strategic alliance with Tencent. Tencent is one of the largest Internet companies in the world and serves the largest online community in China. In 2014, Tencent acquired a 15% stake in JD. Meanwhile JD acquired 100% interests in QQ Wanggou and PaiPai, and a minority stake in Yixun. QQ Wanggou and Yixun are Tencent's two B2C businesses, and PaiPai is Tencent's C2C business. Chinese e-shoppers are active users of social media platforms such as Weixin and Weibo. Tencent announced to promote JD's services prominently on its mobile social media platform--WeChat -- with more than 270 million monthly active users. The strategic partnership enables JD to tap Tencent's significant mobile and Internet user base, and cutting-edge technologies in mobile and web development.

With all the efforts taken by JD, the gap between JD and Alibaba is decreasing. In 2014, the total number of active users on JD.com reached 96.6 million, an increase of 104% from 2013. This accounted for 29% of the number of the total active users on Alibaba (Taobao and Tmall). As of December 31, 2014, there were over 60,000 third-party sellers over JD online marketplace. The GMV from online marketplace increased from ¥31.8 billion in 2013 to ¥100.9 billion (US$16.3 billion) in 2014, a growth rate of more than 217%. GMV from the online direct sales totaled ¥159.3 billion an increase of 70% from 2013. JD's total GMV increased from ¥125.5 billion in 2013 to ¥260.2 billion (US$41.9 billion) in 2014, an increase of 107% from 2013 and 11.45% of Alibaba's GMV.

### *Alibaba Tmall vs. Yihaodian*

Yihaodian is the first B2C online grocery business in china. The company was founded by Gang Yu and Junling Liu in 2008 with an aim to establish an online supermarket. Yihaodian currently offers more than 8,000,000 products, covering 14 product lines. Walmart first invested in Yihaodian in 2011. In 2012, Walmart increased its investment in Yihaodian, bringing Walmart's total ownership stake to approximately 51%, a controlling interest

Yihaodian uses the same business model as JD.com: a mix of "platform" and "direct sale" business model with a focus on "direct sale". Although it maintains a small market share in China's B2C e-tailing market (1.4 percent in 2014), Yihaodian is a major competitor of Tmall in China's booming online grocery market. Chinese consumers perceive that imported food is higher quality than domestic food. . In 2013, Yihaodian sold 250 million units of imported foods, motivated primarily because of safety concerns on baby milk powder. Imported milk accounted for 37.2% of total imported goods sold on Yihaodian in 2013.

Since its launch, Yihaodian has been growing at a rapid rate. Yihaodian's registered users grew from 29 million in 2013 to 57 million in 2013. According to iResearch, Yihaodian reached a much higher year to year (YoY) growth rate than the B2C sector in China from 2013 to 2014Yihaodian is also expanding its product lines beyond grocery products to attract more customers in the e-tailing market. Yihaodian's current product lines include products in cosmetics and personal care, apparel, appliances and others.

Unlike in the U.S., grocery shopping is a frequent and repetitive activity in China. Therefore, one of the key factors for online grocery retailers is an efficient logistics system. Targeting young professionals in big cities, Yihaodian has distribution centers in seven large cities, including: Shanghai, Beijing, Guangzhou, Wuhan, Chengdu, Xi'an and Shenyang. Yihaodian announced that it will open 110 new facilities in China from 2013 to 2016and expand into Tier-2, -3, and -4 cities. Yihaodian offers same-day delivery to customers in the seven distribution centers, and next-day delivery to customers in over 100 cities in China. To integrate online and offline experience, Yihaodian launched virtual supermarkets in subway stations in Shanghai, Beijing and Guangzhou in 2011. These virtual supermarkets allow shoppers to use cameras on their mobile phones to scan the QR codes of the products and get the goods delivered to doorsteps within 48 hours. In the following year (2012), Yihaodian built 1,000 more "virtual stores" with an augmented-reality mobile app across China. These "stores" are open public spaces where shoppers can use their smartphones to view a virtual supermarket with 1,200 meters of floor space and 1,000 items in stock.

Tmall has a 22% market share in the online grocery business. For fresh food products (including fresh fruits, seafood and meat), Tmall introduced a "pre-sales" channel of the website: yushou.tmall.com. Through this channel, customers place advance orders during specific promotion periods and get later delivery within specified time periods. To supply fresh food, Tmall has initiated a series of joint promotions with trade offices of foreign governments. For example, during the 2013 Chinese New Year, Tmall launched a promotion event in which more than 120,000 consumers spent more than ¥ 20 million on imported foods from 25 countries (e.g., blueberries from Chile, lamb from New Zealand). In 2013, Tmall also launched two online promotion events with the U.S. Department of Agriculture during which a wide variety of U.S. products were sold including pork, seafood, fresh fruit, snack foods and others. As a result of such initiatives, according to Tmall officials (Alizila, 2014), sales of imported food on Tmall increased 500% in the first half of 2013.

We present a comparison of Tmall, JD, and Yihaodian in key areas such as business models and logistics in Table 3.

*Table 3. Comparison of Tmall, JD.com and Yihaodian*

| | Tmall | JD.com | Yihaodian |
|---|---|---|---|
| B2C market share [1] | 57.3% | 21.2% | 1.4% |
| Business model[2] | platform | a mix of platform and direct sale (focus: direct sale) | a mix of platform and direct sale (focus: direct sale) |
| Product categories | wide | wide (focus: 3Cs and appliances) | wide(focus: grocery products) |
| Brands | domestic and global | domestic and global | domestic and global |
| Profit margin | 70% | 11.60% | unavailable |
| Logistics | Partnership with third-party logistic companies | nationwide fulfillment centers | fulfillment centers in seven cities |

Notes:

1. Market share of B2C e-tailing sites in China in the second Quarter of 2014 (iResearch, 2014)
2. Gross profit margin in 2014

In summary, given massive customer base and huge profits, Alibaba will continue to dominate China's e-tailing market over the next five to ten years. However, Alibaba will face more fierce competition from domestic e-tailers such as JD and Yihaodian. To survive and thrive the competition, e-tailers need to interact effectively with the factors in China's e-tailing ecosystem as discussed earlier. For example, like Alibaba, e-tailers need to understand Chines e-shoppers and establish customer-focused propositions. With the growing popularity of mobile devices (e.g., smartphone, tablet) and mobile software applications (e.g., Wechat), e-tailers need to build mobile capabilities or form strategic alliances with major mobile service providers such as Tencent.

## Alibaba, Amazon, and eBay: An International Comparison

In this section, we briefly compare Alibaba, Amazon and eBay. We choose Alibaba as a representative of China's e-commerce firms because it is the biggest one and it's a public listing company at New York Stock Exchange. We choose Amazon and eBay as the representatives of American e-commerce firms because they are best known to American consumers and they are also public listing firms in America.

### The Brief History of Amazon and eBay

#### *Amazon.com*

The company was founded in 1994. In 1994, Jeff Bezos left his employment as vice-president of D. E. Shaw & Co., a Wall Street firm, and he moved to Seattle. He began to work on a business plan for what would eventually become Amazon.com. Bezos incorporated the company as "Cadabra" on July 5, 1994, and the site went online as Amazon.com in 1995. It sounded too much like cadaver. Additionally, a name begins with "A". "Amazon" was a place that was "exotic and different" just as he planned for his store to be, a river he noted was by far the "biggest" river in the world (according to volume, not length), and he planned to make his store the biggest in the world. The company began as an online bookstore. In the first two months of business, Amazon sold to all 50 states and over 45 countries. Within two months, Amazon's sales were up to $20,000/week. By early 2001, Amazon had three distinct operating segments: 1) U.S. Mature Businesses; 2) Early-Stage Businesses and Others; 3) International. Since 2000, Amazon's logotype has featured a curved arrow leading from A to Z, representing that they carry every product from A to Z, with the arrow shaped like a smile. After eight, long years in business, Amazon final earned profits in 2003.

Amazon is a global e-commerce giant now. It has business operations in more than 20 countries including Amazon.cn in China. Amazon expanded its business scales and scopes through a series of merges and acquisitions. Amazon had acquired more than 50 companies by 2009. After 2009, Amazon kept acquiring and investing 20 companies including Woot, Quidsi, BuyVIP, Amie Street, Yap, Kiva Systems, Teachstreet Evi, IVONA Software, Goodreads, Liquavista, and Twitch.

#### *eBay.com*

eBay was originally called AuctionWeb which was founded by Pierre Omidyar in 1995. It then became www.ebay.com, short for Echo Bay Technology Group, the name of Omidyar's consulting firm. The ebay logo is the combination of "Echo" and "Bay" where each letter is in different colors suggesting various choices and shopping fun. In 1996 eBay became profitable, and it hired Jeffrey Skoll, a Stanford

MBA. In 1997, the company raised $5 million in venture capital funding. With the help of Meg Whitman from Harvard Business School in 1998, eBay could sustain its success. Meg helped build the vision for eBay-- the business of connecting people, not selling them things. With vast growth and strong branding, eBay became a dominant player in online auction marketplaces. To facilitate payments and protect eBay users from fraudulent, eBay purchased Billpoint and renamed it eBay Payments. eBay bought PayPal late in 2002. PayPal is now widely used by millions of eBay users and thousands of firms for online transactions. However, on September 30, 2014, eBay announced it would split into two independent public companies: eBay and PayPal by the end of 2015.

## The Similarities and Differences among Alibaba, Amazon, and eBay

At first glance, the e-commerce giants Alibaba, Amazon, and eBay seem to have a lot in common. These companies are IT firms with rapid growth rates in the past, and focus on helping people buy a vast variety of products at low prices without stepping into a physical store. Like Amazon and eBay, Alibaba has built up a massive customer base and data infrastructure and has emerged as the dominant player in its home market (Sawhney & Khosla, 2014). They are all public listing companies in the United States. In fact, after studying each company carefully, we can find that these e-commerce giants are different in many aspects. As a starting point, let's look at their basic data in Table 4.

Table 4 lists firm data, and Amazon.com is No.1 in terms of total assets, total revenues and total employee number. Alibaba Group is No.1 in the areas of total profits and total market cap. eBay.com is ranked No.2 in the areas of total profits and employee number.

Many people call Alibaba as China's Amazon.com, but this is misleading (Riley, 2014). First, Amazon.com has its company Amazon.cn presenting in China (we have discussed Amazon.cn in previous sections). Second, Alibaba's business model is different from Amazon, eBay or any other U.S. e-commerce competitors (Osawa, 2013). Alibaba itself doesn't sell products, nor does Alibaba operate its own online store. The main business operation of Alibaba is to build marketplaces where millions of merchants and individuals can sell products to consumers and business customers (both B2C and C2C). Note that eBay is primarily C2C, and Amazon is primarily B2C.

Alibaba understands the demands of Chinese consumers in terms of tone, approach, and product variety. It handles well the intricacies of Chinese regulations and policies, and it knows the best way to work with governments in various levels. In contrast, Amazon is a guru in logistics and supply chain management. It also establishes its own brands such as Kindle Fire devices and AmazonBasics (Sawhney

*Table 4. The basic firm data in 2014/15*

| Company | Assets Size | Revenues | Profits | Employees | Market Cap |
|---|---|---|---|---|---|
| Alibaba GP | CN¥255.434 | CN¥76.204 | CN¥24.32 | 26,845 | US$213.91 |
| Amazon.com | US$ 54.505 | US$ 88.988 | US$ -0.241 | 154,100 | US$ 201.69 |
| eBay.com | US$ 45.13 | US$ 17.90 | US$ 0.046 | 34,600 | US$ 71.48 |
| Who is No. 1? | Amazon.com | Amazon.com | Alibaba GP | Amazon.com | Alibaba GP |

Note: US$ and CN¥ in Billion; Alibaba Data in Q1, 2015, Amazon and eBay Data in Q4, 2014; US$1.00= CN¥6.21

& Khosla, 2014). Amazon's sales for the second quarter in 2014 reached to \$15.7 billion from \$12.8 billion a year earlier. Amazon also inked a net loss of \$7 million in the same quarter. With an operating profit of \$79 million, Amazon's operating profit margin was a meager 0.5%, in stark contrast to Alibaba's 49% operating profit margin. Alibaba's revenue is much smaller than Amazon's. eBay, meanwhile, had its revenue increased by 14% to \$3.88 billion in the second quarter in 2014. But its net profit decreased by 7.5% to \$640 million from a year earlier (Osawa, 2013).

In terms of marketplace maker, Alibaba is more like eBay as both online shopping sites (Taobao and Tmall) are marketplaces where buyers and sellers can meet to conduct transactions. Similar to eBay's PayPal, Alibaba's Alipay, has also emerged as a huge player in China's e-commerce payment systems. Alipay is widely used by millions of merchants and online users. It has a money-market fund, and it even does micro lending to small business. The payment system has allowed the company to collect a big data on small businesses, consumers and their online transactions, which offers tremendous values for business intelligence discoveries (Juro, 2014).

So, the best equation used for Alibaba's business model is *Alibaba (Tmall + Taobao + Alipay + eTao) = A Mix of (Amazon + eBay + PayPal + Google).*

Compared with Amazon and eBay, Alibaba is behind in terms of globalization. Currently, about 10% of Alibaba's revenue comes from its international unit which is low compared to Amazon which runs business in more than 20 countries. But Alibaba's overseas sales are increasing rapidly, up 32% in the second quarter of 2014 (Pressman, 2014). Alibaba is a public listing company in the NYSE, which provides opportunities to promote Alibaba globally. With huge cash in hand, Alibaba needs to look at modest opportunities in the United States, while expanding cross-country trade flows. There are discussions about the potential threats of Alibaba to Amazon and eBay (Berman, 2014; Loed, 2014). In fact, it already helps cherry farmers in Washington and fisherman in Alaska sell to Chinese consumers. Alibaba has acquired 11main.com in America. Alibaba is also working with Apple, Costco and Amazon, helping them explore China's markets. Another opportunity for Alibaba's international expansion is in fast-growing markets with less developed physical retail ecosystems, such as Brazil. One of the BRIC countries, Brazil is one of the fastest growing e-commerce markets in the world. It has demand potential for Chinese-made products, because Brazil has a strong middle class with up-scale consumption habits. Alibaba is well-positioned to conduct e-commerce in Brazil, following its Portuguese e-commerce site 201

Regarding international competition, Alibaba also faces various challenges in its business operations. In January 2015, Chinese officials accused Alibaba of selling fake products and misleading consumers on Taobao. Several months later, western brands sued Alibaba over counterfeit products. Alibaba notes this challenge, and in its IPO filing Alibaba writes "The first risk Alibaba displays, which typically means its most important for investors, is the 'trusted status of our ecosystem' ... If we fail to balance the interests of all participants in our ecosystem, buyers, sellers and other participants may stop visiting our marketplaces, conduct fewer transactions or use alternative platforms…" (Popper, 2014). Making and trading counterfeited products are very common in China. At times, the local Chinese governments have protected, not crack down this crime due to the local tax revenue advantage counterfeit products offer. Many Chinese consumers might be tolerant of counterfeit products because of low prices. However, Western consumers are less tolerant. Reversing this trend will be a major challenge under the unique ecosystems in China. It will require a comprehensive effort by e-commerce companies, consumers, sellers, local governments, and law enforcements.

## CHINA'S E-TAILING: ITS OPPORTUNITIES AND CHALLENGES

China's economy presents both opportunities and challenges for Alibaba. China has the largest population in the world, with a rising number of middle class. The overall stage of e-tailing is still in the growth phase, and there are a lot of opportunities to expand China's e-tailing in both depth and breadth. The speed of the Internet and penetration of mobile users will also help boost the e-tailing growth. The urbanization in rural country brings extra business opportunities. In fact, China's e-tailing revenue grew 45% over Q2 2013, as e-tailers such as Alibaba push into more rural areas where there is less competition from physical stores (Pressman, 2014). But, the slowdown of China's economic growth from double digits to 7% and lower, sluggish personal income growth, low ratio of personal consumption over investment and crossing-board purchases present some challenges to China's e-tailing.

From the perspective of industrial lifecycle, China's e-tailing is still in the growth stage while American e-tailing might be relatively mature. Alibaba sells four times as much product in dollar terms as eBay does, and it's growing much faster than eBay. Alibaba grew 50% annually in GMV (the value of all merchandise) from 2012 to 2013. At the same period, eBay's growth was about 15% (Smith 2014). Figure 5 shows the trading size of Alibaba and eBay.

The growth stage of China's e-tailing vs. the mature stage of American e-tailing is also reflected in the online user growth. In Q2 2012, Alibaba had 150 million active users and eBay had 140 active ones. But in Q2 2014, Alibaba had 280 million active users, and eBay had 150 million active users. The rapid growth stage of China's e-tailing will help foreign companies sustain their business growth if they enter into China's market appropriately.

To enter China's e-tailing market successfully, foreign e-tailing firms must first understand the ecosystem of China's e-tailing. This ecosystem includes cultural and social influence, economic structure, logistics, policy and regulations, and buyers. Each of these factors has been discussed in this chapter. eBay's has yet to match China's e-tailing success story. Jack Ma famously said that "eBay is a shark in the ocean. We are a crocodile in the Yangtze River. If we fight in the ocean we will lose, but if we fight in the river we will win."(Popper, 2014). To survive in China, foreign firms need to know that the

*Figure 5. GMV in $B*

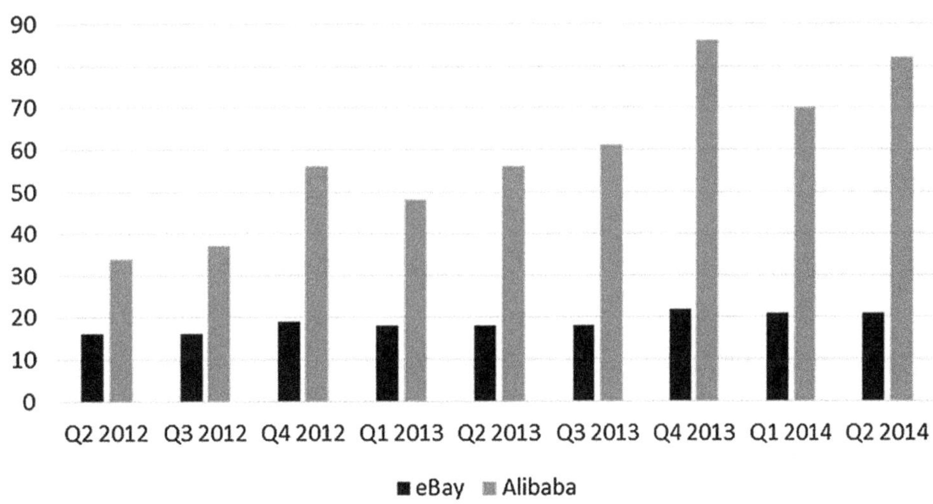

Yangtze River is different from the ocean. You can well fight in the ocean, but this does not mean you can swim in the Yangtze River. Second, foreign firms need to understand the market competitions in China. We have previously analyzed the major e-tailing players in China. They need to correctly select their marketing strategy, differentiate them from others, and try to fully utilize the advantages which they have in their domestic markets. They either use the current marketplace available in China, or they can expand their business by developing new Chinese segments. Recently, Amazon.com chose the former by opening a store at Tmall.com in China. The latter will require more time and risk. Alternatively, foreign companies could partner with Chinese local e-tailers to penetrate China's market. One example is Costco partnering with Alibaba to sell health food and supplement products into China. As the Chinese middle-class increases, their demand for quality products from the Western countries will increase. The overall longtime trend is that the e-tailing will help link the demands and supplies across borders, and price differences will decrease due to the integration of global e-tailing markets.

## CONCLUSION

In this chapter, we introduce the general picture of China's e-tailing market. China has experienced rapid growth of economy and e-tailing during the past ten years. Chinese e-tailing annual sales reached $ 301 billion in 2013, a more than 650% increase from 2008 (China E-commerce Center). Behind the rapid growth, we investigated the unique dynamic ecosystem of China's e-tailing. This ecosystem includes cultural and social influence, economic structure, logistics, policy and regulations, and buyers. We introduce major e-tailing firms in China, and analyze the competitions among these market players. At present, Alibaba Group dominates China's e-tailing market, and JD is the second large e-tailer with more than 60,000 employees. Because Alibaba is the largest e-tailer in China, and its stocks are listed and traded at NYSE, we compare Alibaba with American e-tailing giants such as Amazon.com and eBay.com. Alibaba is not China's Amazon, or eBay, or others. More accurately we can state that is Alibaba is a mix of (Amazon + eBay + PayPal + Google). We also addressed challenges for China's e-tailing, including international partnerships and counterfeit products sold by Taobao and Tmall. Lastly, we discussed the future of China's e-tailing and suggest a few marketing entering strategies for foreign companies. We believe that a case study of Chinese e-tailing like ours is needed because China is the largest emerging market as well as the largest e-tailing market. Moreover, e-tailing might become one of the most effective ways for foreign retailers to enter the Chinese retail market. We hope that this chapter provides readers with a comprehensive introduction to e-tailing in China.

## REFERENCES

2014 China mobile shopping report (brief edition). (2014). *iResearch.* Retrieved from http://www.iresearchchina.com/samplereports/6112.html

B2C e-commerce as percentage of global GDP from 2009 to 2018. (2014). *Statista*. Retrieved from http://www.statista.com/statistics/324612/b2c-e-commerce-as-percentage-of-gdp-worldwide/

B2C e-commerce sales worldwide from 2012 to 2018. (2014). *Statista*. Retrieved from http://www.statista.com/statistics/261245/b2c-e-commerce-sales-worldwide/

The world's next e-commerce superpower. (2011). BCG (The Boston Consulting Group). Retrieved from https://www.bcg.com/documents/file91905.pdf

Berman, J. (2014). Alibaba's Opportunities May Spell Trouble for eBay and Amazon. *TheStreet.com.* Retrieved from http://www.thestreet.com/story/12968357/1/alibabas-challenges-and-opportunities-may-spell-trouble-for-ebay-and-amazon.html

Brashear, T. G., Kashyap, V., Musante, M. D., & Donthu, N. (2009). A profile of the Internet shopper: Evidence from six countries. *Journal of Marketing Theory and Practice*, *17*(3), 267–282. doi:10.2753/MTP1069-6679170305

Chang, J., & Samuel, N. (2004). Internet shopper demographics and buying behavior in Australia. *Journal of American Academy of Business*, *5*(1/2), 171–176.

Chang, M. K., Cheung, W., & Lai, V. S. (2005). Literature derived reference models for the adoption of online shopping. *Information & Management*, *42*(4), 543–559. doi:10.1016/S0378-7206(04)00051-5

Chen, G. (2012). The use of electronic brokerage systems in China: A modified e-Commerce model. *Canadian Journal of Administrative Sciences*, *29*(1), 99–109. doi:10.1002/cjas.213

Chen, J. E., Pan, S. L., & Ouyang, T. H. (2014). Routine reconfiguration in traditional companies' e-commerce strategy implementation: A trajectory perspective. *Information & Management*, *51*(2), 270–282. doi:10.1016/j.im.2013.11.008

Childers, T. L., Carr, C. L., Peck, J., & Carson, S. (2001). Hedonic and utilitarian motivations for online retail shopping behavior. *Journal of Retailing*, *77*(4), 511–535. doi:10.1016/S0022-4359(01)00056-2

Statistical report on Internet development in China internet report. (2014). *China Internet Network Information Center (CNNIC)*. Retrieved from http://www1.cnnic.cn/IDR/ReportDownloads/201404/U020140417607531610855.pdf

82% Sina Weibo users shop online. (2014). *China Internet Watch*. Retrieved from http://www.chinainternetwatch.com/11199/sina-weibo-users-shop-online/

China mobile shopping market GMV hit RMB167.64 Bn in 2013 with fast growing penetration. (2014). *iResearch.* Retrieved from http://www.iresearchchina.com/views/5405.html

China online shopping GMV soars 47.1%. (2014). *iResearch.* Retrieved from http://www.iresearchchina.com/views/5826.html

China online shopping market slows down while mobile buying outbursts. (2014). *iResearch*. Retrieved from http://www.iresearchchina.com/views/5548.html

China sees more sophisticated online shoppers. (2014). *Nielsen*. Retrieved from http://www.nielsen.com/content/dam/nielsenglobal/cn/docs/Nielsen%202014%20China%20online%20shopper%20trends_EN_Client%20Version.PDF

China's pied piper. (2006). *The Economist.* Retrieved from http://www.economist.com/node/7942225

Chinese spend big on cross-border Internet shopping. (2015). *Xinhua*. Retrieved from http://www.china.org.cn/business/2015-03/31/content_35211611.htm

Cho, J. (2004). Likelihood to abort an online transaction: Influences from cognitive evaluations, attitudes, and behavioral variables. *Information & Management*, *41*(7), 827–838. doi:10.1016/j.im.2003.08.013

Clemes, M. D., Gan, C., & Zhang, J. (2014). An empirical analysis of online shopping adoption in Beijing, China. *Journal of Retailing and Consumer Services*, *21*(3), 364–375. doi:10.1016/j.jretconser.2013.08.003

Corbitt, B. J., Thanasankit, T., & Yi, H. (2003). Trust and e-commerce: A study of consumer perceptions. *Electronic Commerce Research and Applications*, *2*(3), 203–215. doi:10.1016/S1567-4223(03)00024-3

Fan, Q., Yul Lee, J., & In Kim, J. (2013). The impact of web site quality on flow-related online shopping behaviors in C2C e-marketplaces: A cross-national study. *Managing Service Quality: An International Journal*, *23*(5), 364–387. doi:10.1108/MSQ-11-2012-0150

Fang, H., Zhang, J., Bao, Y., & Zhu, Q. (2013). Towards effective online review systems in the Chinese context: A cross-cultural empirical study. *Electronic Commerce Research and Applications*, *12*(3), 208–220. doi:10.1016/j.elerap.2013.03.001

Foucault, B. E., & Scheufele, D. A. (2002). Web vs campus store? Why students buy textbooks online. *Journal of Consumer Marketing*, *19*(5), 409–423. doi:10.1108/07363760210437632

GMV of China online shopping hit unexpected 268.37 billion Yuan in Q2 2012. (2012). *iResearch*. Retrieved from http://www.iresearchchina.com/views/4394.html

Grabner-Kraeuter, S. (2002). The role of consumers' trust in online-shopping. *Journal of Business Ethics*, *39*(1-2), 43–50. doi:10.1023/A:1016323815802

Guo, S., Wang, M., & Leskovec, J. (2011, June). The role of social networks in online shopping: information passing, price of trust, and consumer choice. *Proceedings of the 12th ACM conference on Electronic commerce,* San Jose, CA (pp. 157-166). ACM. doi:10.1145/1993574.1993598

How Tmall.com fills China's dinner tables with global. (2014). *Alizila*. Retrieved from http://www.alizila.com/how-tmallcom-fills-chinas-dinner-tables-global-food

Huang, J., Jiang, X., & Tang, Q. (2009). An e-commerce performance assessment model: Its development and an initial test on e-commerce applications in the retail sector of China. *Information & Management*, *46*(2), 100–108. doi:10.1016/j.im.2008.12.003

Holiday benchmark data alert. (2015, January 5). IBM. Retrieved from http://www-01.ibm.com/software/marketing-solutions/benchmark-hub/alert.html

Ke, X., & Sun, Q. (2014). Study of CSF in China's B2C E-commerce based on expert evaluation. *Journal of Electronic Commerce in Organizations*, *12*(2), 31–45. doi:10.4018/jeco.2014040103

Kim, D. J., Ferrin, D. L., & Rao, H. R. (2008). A trust-based consumer decision-making model in electronic commerce: The role of trust, perceived risk, and their antecedents. *Decision Support Systems*, *44*(2), 544–564. doi:10.1016/j.dss.2007.07.001

Koyuncu, C., & Bhattacharya, G. (2004). The impacts of quickness, price, payment risk, and delivery issues on on-line shopping. *Journal of Socio-Economics*, *33*(2), 241–251. doi:10.1016/j.socec.2003.12.011

Lee, G. G., & Lin, H. F. (2005). Customer perceptions of e-service quality in online shopping. *International Journal of Retail & Distribution Management*, *33*(2), 161–176. doi:10.1108/09590550510581485

Ling, K. C., Chai, L. T., & Piew, T. H. (2010). The effects of shopping orientations, online trust and prior online purchase experience toward customers' online purchase intention. *International Business Research*, *3*(3), 63–75. doi:10.5539/ibr.v3n3p63

Liu, C., & Arnett, K. P. (2000). Exploring the factors associated with website success in the context of electronic commerce. *Information & Management*, *38*(1), 23–33. doi:10.1016/S0378-7206(00)00049-5

Liu, X., He, M., Gao, F., & Xie, P. (2008). An empirical study of online shopping customer satisfaction in China: A holistic perspective. *International Journal of Retail & Distribution Management*, *36*(11), 919–940. doi:10.1108/09590550810911683

Loed, W. (2014). 10 reasons why Alibaba blows away Amazon and EBay. *Forbes.com.* Retrieved from http://www.forbes.com/sites/walterloeb/2014/04/11/10-reasons-why-alibaba-is-a-worldwide-leader-in-e-commerce/

China's e-tail revolution: Online shopping as a catalyst for growth. (2013). Mckinsey & Co. Retrieved from https://www.mckinsey.com/~/media/McKinsey/dotcom/Insights%20and%20pubs/MGI/Research/Productivity%20Competitiveness%20and%20Growth/China%20e-tailing/MGI_China_e-tailing_Full_report_March_2013.ashx

Miyazaki, A. D., & Fernandez, A. (2001). Consumer perceptions of privacy and security risks for online shopping. *The Journal of Consumer Affairs*, *35*(1), 27–44. doi:10.1111/j.1745-6606.2001.tb00101.x

eCommerce: China's consumption growth engine. (2014). *Morgan Stanley*. Retrieved from http://online.barrons.com/articles/ecommerce-chinas-consumption-growth-engine-1415323378

Mummalaneni, V., & Meng, J. (2009). An exploratory study of young Chinese customers' online shopping behaviors and service quality perceptions. *Young Consumers*, *10*(2), 157–169. doi:10.1108/17473610910964732

Omar, M., Bathgate, I., & Nwankwo, S. (2011). Internet marketing and customer satisfaction in emerging markets: The case of Chinese online shoppers. *Competitiveness Review: An International Business Journal*, *21*(2), 224–237. doi:10.1108/10595421111117489

Osawa, J. (2013). Alibaba isn't the Amazon of China. *Wall Street Journal.* Retrieved from http://blogs.wsj.com/digits/2013/10/16/alibaba-isnt-the-amazon-of-china/

Osawa, J. (2014). Alibaba: A mix of Amazon, eBay and PayPal with a dash of Google- how the Chinese company came to dominate Chinese e-commerce. *Wall Street Journal.* Retrieved from http://www.wsj.com/articles/SB10001424052702303546204579440472954450720

Osawa, J. (2014). How to understand Alibaba's business model. *Marketwatch.com.* Retrieved from http://www.marketwatch.com/story/how-to-understand-alibabas-business-model-2014-03-15-94855847

Pang, C., Yen, D. C., & Tarn, J. M. (2007). Exploring online shoppers'e-trust in China. *Human Systems Management*, *26*(3), 193–198.

Popper, B. (2014). Alibaba has more sales than Amazon and eBay combined, but will Americans trust it? China's biggest internet company has filed for its US IPO. *The Verge.com*. Retrieved from http://www.theverge.com/2014/5/7/5690596/meet-alibaba-the-ecommerce-giant-with-more-sales-than-amazon-and-ebay

Posts tagged 'Tmall'. (2014). *Yipitdata*. Retrieved from http://yipitdata.com/tag/tmall/

Prasad, C. J., & Aryasri, A. R. (2009). Determinants of shopper behavior in e-tailing: An empirical analysis. *Paradigm*, *13*(1), 73–83. doi:10.1177/0971890720090110

Pressman, A. (2014). Alibaba a threat to eBay, Amazon outside the U.S., not within. *Yahoo Finance*. Retrieved from http://finance.yahoo.com/news/alibaba-aims-at-ebay-and-amazon-outside-of-the-united-states-173757037.html

A new era in buying Retail in China's digital age. (2013). *PwC (PricewaterhouseCoopers)*. Retrieved from http://www.pwccn.com/webmedia/doc/635334251818697593_consulting-retail-china.pdf

Qu, Z., Wang, Y., Wang, S., & Zhang, Y. (2013). Implications of online social activities for e-tailers' business performance. *European Journal of Marketing*, *47*(8), 1190–1212. doi:10.1108/03090561311324282

Reibstein, D. J. (2002). What attracts customers to online stores, and what keeps them coming back? *Journal of the Academy of Marketing Science*, *30*(4), 465–473. doi:10.1177/009207002236918

Retail sales worldwide will top $22 trillion this year. (2014). *eMarketer*. Retrieved from http://www.emarketer.com/Article/Retail-Sales-Worldwide-Will-Top-22-Trillion-This-Year/1011765

Riley, C. (2014). Alibaba is not the Amazon of China. *CNN Money*. Retrieved from http://money.cnn.com/2014/09/15/investing/alibaba-amazon-china/

Sawhney, M., & Khosla, S. (2014). Alibaba vs. Amazon: Who will win the global e-commerce war? *Forbes.com*. Retrieved from http://www.forbes.com/sites/forbesleadershipforum/2014/09/22/alibaba-vs-amazon-who-will-win-the-global-e-commerce-war/

Shergill, G. S., & Chen, Z. (2005). Web-based shopping: Consumers' attitudes towards online shopping in New Zealand. *Journal of Electronic Commerce Research*, *6*(2), 79–94.

Shim, S., Eastlick, M. A., Lotz, S. L., & Warrington, P. (2001). An online prepurchase intentions model: The role of intention to search. *Journal of Retailing*, *77*(3), 397–416. doi:10.1016/S0022-4359(01)00051-3

Sin, L., & Tse, A. (2002). Profiling internet shoppers in Hong Kong: Demographic, psychographic, attitudinal and experiential factors. *Journal of International Consumer Marketing*, *15*(1), 7–29. doi:10.1300/J046v15n01_02

Smith, C. (2014). Here's why Alibaba is becoming a huge threat to Amazon and eBay. *BusinessInsider.com*. Retrieved from http://www.businessinsider.com/why-alibaba-is-becoming-a-huge-threat-to-amazon-and-ebay-2014-8

Su, Q., & Chen, L. (2014). A method for discovering clusters of e-commerce interest patterns using click-stream data. *Electronic Commerce Research and Applications*, *14*(1), 1–13. doi:10.1016/j.elerap.2014.10.002

Swinyard, W. R., & Smith, S. M. (2003). Why people (don't) shop online: A lifestyle study of the Internet consumer. *Psychology and Marketing*, *20*(7), 567–597. doi:10.1002/mar.10087

Tan, F. B., Yan, L., & Urquhart, C. (2007). The effect of cultural differences on attitude, peer influence, external influence and self-efficacy in actual online shopping behavior. *Journal of Information Science and Technology*, *4*(1).

GDP Data. (2015). *The World Bank*. Retrieved from http://data.worldbank.org/indicator/NY.GDP.MKTP.CD

Tong, X. (2010). A cross-national investigation of an extended technology acceptance model in the online shopping context. *International Journal of Retail & Distribution Management*, *38*(10), 742–759. doi:10.1108/09590551011076524

Turban, E., King, D., Lee, J. K., & Viehland, D. (2006). *Electronic commerce: A managerial perspective*. Upper Saddle River, New Jersey: Prentice Hall.

Quarterly Retail E-commerce Sales. (2015). *U.S. Department of Commerce*. Retrieved from https://www.census.gov/retail/mrts/www/data/pdf/ec_current.pdf

Vijayasarathy, L. R., & Jones, J. M. (2000). Print and Internet catalog shopping: Assessing attitudes and intentions. *Internet Research*, *10*(3), 191–202. doi:10.1108/10662240010331948

Wang, S. (2012). A dynamic model of trust in online shopping. *Proceedings of the 2012 AICI International Conference on Artificial Intelligence and Computational Intelligence* (pp. 296-303). Berlin Heidelberg: Springer. doi:10.1007/978-3-642-34240-0_39

Wang, X. (2012). Foreign direct investment and innovation in China's e-commerce sector. *Journal of Asian Economics*, *23*(3), 288–301. doi:10.1016/j.asieco.2010.11.007

Wang, X., & Ren, Z. J. (2012). How to compete in China's E-commerce market. *Sloan Review*. Retrieved from http://sloanreview.mit.edu/article/how-to-compete-in-chinas-e-commerce-market/

Xu, Y., & Paulins, V. A. (2005). College students' attitudes toward shopping online for apparel products: Exploring a rural versus urban campus. *Journal of Fashion Marketing and Management*, *9*(4), 420–433. doi:10.1108/13612020510620795

Yang, Z., & Jun, M. (2002). Consumer perception of e-service quality: From internet purchaser and non-purchaser perspectives. *The Journal of Business Strategy*, *19*(1), 19–41.

Yoon, C. (2009). The effects of national culture values on consumer acceptance of e-commerce: Online shoppers in China. *Information & Management*, *46*(5), 294–301. doi:10.1016/j.im.2009.06.001

Youderian, A. (2014). Alibaba vs. Amazon: An in-depth comparison of two eCommerce giants. *Ecommercefuel.com*. Retrieved from http://www.ecommercefuel.com/alibaba-vs-amazon/

Young Kim, E., & Kim, Y. K. (2004). Predicting online purchase intentions for clothing products. *European Journal of Marketing*, *38*(7), 883–897. doi:10.1108/03090560410539302

Yu, X. H., Guo, X. T., & Yao, Q. Y. (2011). The effect of online word-of-mouth in electronic markets: An investigation of the culture differences in the Chinese and US contexts. *Proceedings of the 2011 International Conference on Management Science and Engineering (ICMSE),* Piscataway, New Jersey (pp. 34-40). IEEE.

Zhang, Y., Bian, J., & Zhu, W. (2013). Trust fraud: A crucial challenge for China's e-commerce market. *Electronic Commerce Research and Applications*, *12*(5), 299–308. doi:10.1016/j.elerap.2012.11.005

Zhao, D., Savage, S. J., & Chen, Y. (2008). Ownership, location and prices in Chinese electronic commerce markets. *Information Economics and Policy*, *20*(2), 192–207. doi:10.1016/j.infoecopol.2008.02.001

# Chapter 5
# E-Commerce in India: Evolution and Revolution of Online Retail

**Prateek Kalia**
*I.K Gujral Punjab Technical University, India*

**Navdeep Kaur**
*Guru Nanak Dev Engineering College, India*

**Tejinderpal Singh**
*Panjab University, India*

## ABSTRACT

*This chapter uniquely reports origin of e-commerce and holistic present scenario of online retail in India. Desk research and extant review of literature from reliable market research reports, books, journals and web has been done to decipher internet penetration, evolution of e-commerce and present scenario. Study observed that India is third largest country in terms of internet users. India will drive e-commerce in Asia pacific region after China and Indonesia. Reasons hampering India from finding place in global retail e-commerce index are also put in foreground. Sequential events leading to growth of different types of e-commerce in India are delineated into two waves to understand the evolutionary process. Out of total non-travel B2C e-commerce, online retail holds significant fifty percent share and its prospects for future growth are extremely positive. Businesses and researchers will find this chapter useful to devise future strategies to win and sustain e-commerce market in India.*

## INTRODUCTION

In India, online consumer base is increasing dramatically, as gadgets like smartphones and tablets are available at reasonable prices and access to 3G and broadband is easy. This technology adoption by masses has fueled the success of domestic e-commerce players like Flipkart and Snapdeal, and lured international players like Amazon and Alibaba into Indian market (PWC, 2015). While domestic companies are experimenting with their business models to attract and expand their customer base (Awad, 2012; Chaffey, 2013; Kalia, n.d.; Laudon & Traver, 2007; Schneider, 2012), international companies

DOI: 10.4018/978-1-4666-9921-2.ch005

Copyright © 2016, IGI Global. Copying or distributing in print or electronic forms without written permission of IGI Global is prohibited.

are banking on their deep pockets, strong domain knowledge and international exposure. One of the fastest growing segments of e-commerce is online retail. Significant funding is required in India due to underdeveloped e-commerce ecosystem (Kalia, Kaur, & Singh, 2015) and e-retailers are deploying large chunks of their investments to build infrastructure like fulfillment and logistics on their own (PWC & ASSOCHAM, 2014).

Young population, growing internet penetration and upwardly rising middle class will propel e-commerce and overall retail business in India in coming years (PWC, 2015). But this opportunity can only be encashed by e-commerce business if they have significant understanding of evolution and current scenario of the Indian e-commerce market which has seen a dotcom burst earlier in 2000 (Kumar & Mahadevan, 2003). Extant review of literature from reliable market research reports, books, journals and web has been done covered in this chapter to present evolution and current status quo of e-retail market in India.

## INTERNET PENETRATION: WORLD VS. INDIA

From 1% in 1999, internet penetration has reached 40% of the world population in 2014. Landmark of first billion internet users was reached in 2005, second in 2010 and third is expected by end of 2014. Global internet users by per year since 1993 are mentioned in table 1.

As seen in the figure 1, Asia has almost half of internet users i.e. holds 48% (1322491069) of total internet user population. Americas (North and South) comprises 22% (596331291), Europe has 19% (520381481), Africa 10% (268209162) and Oceania holds 1% (25109590) of total internet user population.

In 2014, top 20 countries comprise almost 75% (2.1 billion) of all internet users in the world (2.8 billion). Rest of 25% (0.7 billion) is held among the other 178 countries, each representing less than 1% of total users. China, is on the top of the list with 22% (642 million users in 2014), this user base is more than combined user base of next three countries (United States, India, and Japan). United States, Germany, France, U.K., and Canada have the highest penetration: over 80% of population in these countries has an internet connection. India has lowest penetration (19%) in top 20 countries but highest yearly growth rate (14%). Despite such low penetration rate India ranks third with 243,198,922 users (Table 2). Because of tremendous growth of internet in India there is enormous potential for e-commerce (Joseph, 2012).

## B2C ELECTRONIC COMMERCE: WORLD VS. INDIA

Worldwide business-to-consumer (B2C) e-commerce sales will grow by 17.7% this year to reach $1.771 trillion (Figure 2). This growth is attributed to increase in number of online and mobile users in emerging markets, boom in mobile commerce, better shipping and payment options, and entry of major brands in international markets (Emarketer.com, 2014).

Asia-Pacific will become largest regional e-commerce market in the world in 2014, as B2C e-commerce sales in the region will grow to $525.2 billion as compared to $482.6 billion in North America (Table 3) (Emarketer.com, 2014).

In 2014 Asia-Pacific will hold 46% of worldwide digital buyers; these users are just 16.9% of the region's population. This explains that emerging markets are getting strength out of their huge population

*Table 1. Internet users in the world*

| Year | Internet Users | Users Growth | World Population | Population Growth | Penetration (% of Pop. with Internet) |
|---|---|---|---|---|---|
| 2014 | 2925249355 | 7.9% | 7243784121 | 1.14% | 40.40% |
| 2013 | 2712239573 | 8.0% | 7162119430 | 1.16% | 37.90% |
| 2012 | 2511615523 | 10.5% | 7080072420 | 1.17% | 35.50% |
| 2011 | 2272463038 | 11.7% | 6997998760 | 1.18% | 32.50% |
| 2010 | 2034259368 | 16.1% | 6916183480 | 1.19% | 29.40% |
| 2009 | 1752333178 | 12.2% | 6834721930 | 1.20% | 25.60% |
| 2008 | 1562067594 | 13.8% | 6753649230 | 1.21% | 23.10% |
| 2007 | 1373040542 | 18.6% | 6673105940 | 1.21% | 20.60% |
| 2006 | 1157500065 | 12.4% | 6593227980 | 1.21% | 17.60% |
| 2005 | 1029717906 | 13.1% | 6514094610 | 1.22% | 15.80% |
| 2004 | 910060180 | 16.9% | 6435705600 | 1.22% | 14.10% |
| 2003 | 778555680 | 17.5% | 6357991750 | 1.23% | 12.20% |
| 2002 | 662663600 | 32.4% | 6280853820 | 1.24% | 10.60% |
| 2001 | 500609240 | 21.1% | 6204147030 | 1.25% | 8.10% |
| 2000 | 413425190 | 47.2% | 6127700430 | 1.26% | 6.70% |
| 1999 | 280866670 | 49.4% | 6051478010 | 1.27% | 4.60% |
| 1998 | 188023930 | 55.7% | 5975303660 | 1.30% | 3.10% |
| 1997 | 120758310 | 56.0% | 5898688340 | 1.33% | 2.00% |
| 1996 | 77433860 | 72.7% | 5821016750 | 1.38% | 1.30% |
| 1995 | 44838900 | 76.2% | 5741822410 | 1.43% | 0.80% |
| 1994 | 25454590 | 79.7% | 5661086350 | 1.47% | 0.40% |
| 1993 | 14161570 | | 5578865110 | | 0.30% |

*Source:* Internetlivestats.com, 2014

*Figure 1. Internet users by region*
*Source: Internetlivestats.com, 2014*

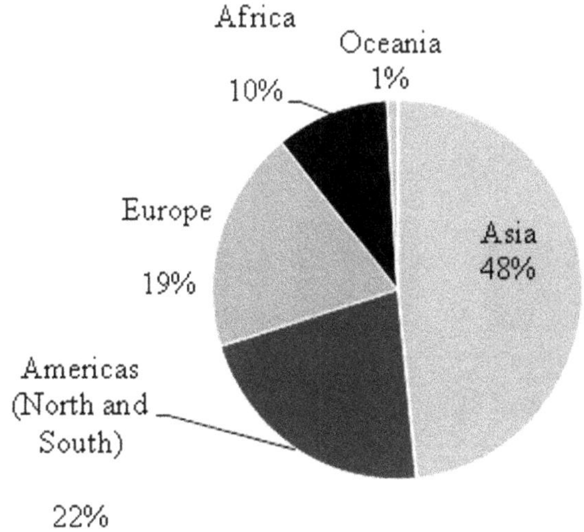

*Table 2. List of countries by internet usage (2014)*

| Rank | Country | Internet Users | 1 Year Growth % | 1 Year User Growth | Total Country Population | 1 Yr Population Change (%) | Penetration (% of Pop. with Internet) | Country's share of World Population | Country's share of World Internet Users |
|---|---|---|---|---|---|---|---|---|---|
| 1 | China | 641601070 | 4.00% | 24021070 | 1393783836 | 0.59% | 46.03% | 19.24% | 21.97% |
| 2 | United States | 279834232 | 7.00% | 17754869 | 322583006 | 0.79% | 86.75% | 4.45% | 9.58% |
| **3** | **India** | **243198922** | **14.00%** | **29859598** | **1267401849** | **1.22%** | **19.19%** | **17.50%** | **8.33%** |
| 4 | Japan | 109252912 | 8.00% | 7668535 | 126999808 | -0.11% | 86.03% | 1.75% | 3.74% |
| 5 | Brazil | 107822831 | 7.00% | 6884333 | 202033670 | 0.83% | 53.37% | 2.79% | 3.69% |
| 6 | Russia | 84437793 | 10.00% | 7494536 | 142467651 | -0.26% | 59.27% | 1.97% | 2.89% |
| 7 | Germany | 71727551 | 2.00% | 1525829 | 82652256 | -0.09% | 86.78% | 1.14% | 2.46% |
| 8 | Nigeria | 67101452 | 16.00% | 9365590 | 178516904 | 2.82% | 37.59% | 2.46% | 2.30% |
| 9 | UK | 57075826 | 3.00% | 1574653 | 63489234 | 0.56% | 89.90% | 0.88% | 1.95% |
| 10 | France | 55429382 | 3.00% | 1521369 | 64641279 | 0.54% | 85.75% | 0.89% | 1.90% |
| 11 | Mexico | 50923060 | 7.00% | 3423153 | 123799215 | 1.20% | 41.13% | 1.71% | 1.74% |
| 12 | South Korea | 45314248 | 8.00% | 3440213 | 49512026 | 0.51% | 91.52% | 0.68% | 1.55% |
| 13 | Indonesia | 42258824 | 9.00% | 3468057 | 252812245 | 1.18% | 16.72% | 3.49% | 1.45% |
| 14 | Egypt | 40311562 | 10.00% | 3748271 | 83386739 | 1.62% | 48.34% | 1.15% | 1.38% |
| 15 | Vietnam | 39772424 | 9.00% | 3180007 | 92547959 | 0.95% | 42.97% | 1.28% | 1.36% |
| 16 | Philippines | 39470845 | 10.00% | 3435654 | 100096496 | 1.73% | 39.43% | 1.38% | 1.35% |
| 17 | Italy | 36593969 | 2.00% | 857489 | 61070224 | 0.13% | 59.92% | 0.84% | 1.25% |
| 18 | Turkey | 35358888 | 3.00% | 1195610 | 75837020 | 1.21% | 46.62% | 1.05% | 1.21% |
| 19 | Spain | 35010273 | 3.00% | 876986 | 47066402 | 0.30% | 74.38% | 0.65% | 1.20% |
| 20 | Canada | 33000381 | 7.00% | 2150061 | 35524732 | 0.98% | 92.89% | 0.49% | 1.13% |

*Source:* Internetlivestats.com, 2014

*Figure 2. B2C e-commerce sales worldwide, 2012-2017*
*Note: CAGR(2012-2017)=17.4%; includes products and services ordered and leisure and unmanaged business travel sales booked using the internet via any device, regardless of the method of payment or fulfillment.*
*Source: Emarketer.com, 2014*

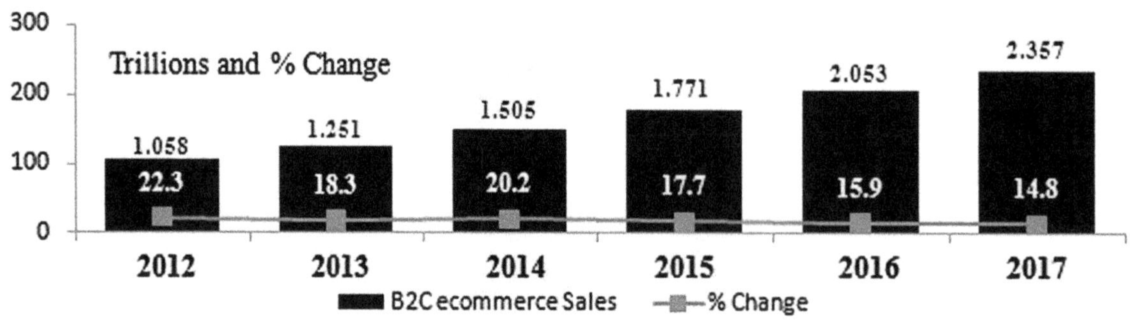

*Table 3. B2C e-commerce sales worldwide, by region (billions), 2012-2017*

| Region/Year | 2012 | 2013 | 2014 | 2015 | 2016 | 2017 |
|---|---|---|---|---|---|---|
| Asia Pacific | $301.2 | $383.9 | $525.2 | $681.2 | $855.7 | $1,052 |
| North America | $379.8 | $431.0 | $482.6 | $538.3 | $597.9 | $660.4 |
| Western Europe | $277.5 | $312.0 | $347.4 | $382.7 | $414.2 | $445.0 |
| Central and Eastern Europe | $41.5 | $49.5 | $58.0 | $64.4 | $68.9 | $73.1 |
| Latin America | $37.6 | $48.1 | $57.7 | $64.9 | $70.6 | $74.6 |
| Middle East and Africa | $20.6 | $27.0 | $33.8 | $39.6 | $45.5 | $51.4 |
| **Worldwide** | **$1,058.2** | **$1,251.4** | **$1,504.6** | **$1,771.0** | **$2,052.7** | **$2,357.4** |

*Source:* Emarketer.com, 2014

base that come and shop online for the first time. There will be low penetration in Central and Eastern Europe, Latin America, and the Middle East and Africa. Most of the occupants of North America and Western Europe will continue to shop through digital channels.

China is emerging as undisputed leader of digital global market. China has 60% of e-commerce in Asia Pacific and second only to the US. Asia pacific growth will be driven by China, along with India and Indonesia (Table 4). China will sweep over the US in spending in 2016 (Emarketer.com, 2014).

## GLOBAL RETAIL E-COMMERCE INDEX

A.T. Kearney, a global management consulting firm has formulated "*Global retail e-commerce index*" which ranks online retail market attractiveness of countries on a 0-to-100-point scale. Higher scores reflect higher growth potential in that country. This index is based on following metrics (ATKearney, 2012, 2013) -

- **Online Market Size (40 percent):** Current online retail sales. The higher the rating shows greater current online retail market size.
- **Technology Adoption and Consumer Behavior (20 percent):** Indicates online consumer behavior, like Internet penetration, purchasing trends, and technology adoption. Higher ratings, depicts that country's consumer base is favorable for transacting online.
- **Infrastructure (20 Percent):** Indicates development of financial and logistical infrastructure, it includes credit cards per household and availability and quality of logistics providers. High ratings signals conducive infrastructure for online purchasing.
- **Growth Potential (20 Percent):** Projected online retail sales growth. The higher is the rating, greater is the projected growth rate.

### The Index Findings

Both developed and developing countries find their place in the index rankings. Top position is held by China followed by the G8 countries (Japan, United States, United Kingdom, Germany, France, Canada,

*Table 4. B2C e-commerce sales growth worldwide (% change),by region and country, 2011-2017*

| Region/Country | 2011 | 2012 | 2013 | 2014 | 2015 | 2016 | 2017 |
|---|---|---|---|---|---|---|---|
| **Middle East and Africa** | **70.00%** | **43.00%** | **31.00%** | **25.00%** | **17.20%** | **15.00%** | **13.00%** |
| **Asia-Pacific** | **37.20%** | **32.80%** | **23.10%** | **29.00%** | **20.90%** | **16.70%** | **14.20%** |
| Indonesia | 104.50% | 85.00% | 71.30% | 45.10% | 37.20% | 26.00% | 22.00% |
| China* | 103.70% | 94.10% | 65.10% | 51.20% | 30.60% | 22.60% | 18.30% |
| India** | 47.20% | 39.70% | 34.60% | 27.10% | 23.70% | 18.20% | 16.60% |
| South Korea | 17.60% | 6.00% | 6.90% | 9.30% | 8.30% | 8.20% | 7.30% |
| Australia | 11.00% | 10.50% | 6.00% | 5.70% | 5.10% | 5.00% | 4.20% |
| Japan | 27.10% | 13.20% | 7.20% | 7.10% | 6.70% | 5.60% | 5.00% |
| Other | 23.90% | 12.40% | 12.70% | 12.00% | 11.90% | 11.00% | 10.20% |
| **Latin America** | **38.50%** | **33.00%** | **22.10%** | **21.70%** | **12.70%** | **10.40%** | **8.40%** |
| Mexico | 46.70% | 47.30% | 29.60% | 23.80% | 15.40% | 13.30% | 10.30% |
| Brazil | 32.90% | 21.80% | 16.50% | 19.10% | 8.50% | 6.90% | 6.00% |
| Argentina | 40.60% | 31.00% | 14.90% | 24.00% | 18.00% | 12.00% | 10.00% |
| Other | 44.50% | 46.20% | 28.60% | 23.40% | 15.20% | 12.70% | 9.80% |
| **Central and Eastern Europe** | **41.60%** | **30.10%** | **20.90%** | **19.40%** | **11.00%** | **7.00%** | **6.10%** |
| Russia | 43.00% | 30.10% | 21.10% | 19.30% | 10.80% | 6.90% | 5.20% |
| Other | 40.80% | 30.10% | 20.70% | 19.40% | 11.20% | 7.10% | 6.60% |
| **Western Europe** | **17.10%** | **17.10%** | **14.00%** | **11.90%** | **9.90%** | **8.30%** | **7.50%** |
| Italy | 32.10% | 25.50% | 22.60% | 20.30% | 16.80% | 12.40% | 12.00% |
| Spain | 22.40% | 18.80% | 16.20% | 13.80% | 11.90% | 10.00% | 8.00% |
| Sweden | 22.00% | 18.40% | 16.20% | 13.30% | 10.30% | 9.00% | 8.40% |
| Norway | 21.80% | 17.10% | 15.30% | 13.30% | 10.50% | 7.40% | 6.40% |
| Finland | 20.10% | 16.10% | 14.70% | 11.20% | 9.00% | 7.20% | 6.30% |
| UK | 14.20% | 13.70% | 13.70% | 12.20% | 10.20% | 8.20% | 7.30% |
| Germany | 17.40% | 23.40% | 12.80% | 9.40% | 6.90% | 6.50% | 6.10% |
| Denmark | 16.50% | 14.30% | 12.40% | 10.60% | 8.90% | 6.50% | 5.90% |
| Netherlands | 20.20% | 14.00% | 12.40% | 10.10% | 9.00% | 6.70% | 5.70% |
| France | 12.20% | 12.30% | 11.00% | 9.10% | 8.00% | 7.60% | 7.10% |
| Other | 19.60% | 20.30% | 14.70% | 12.10% | 10.10% | 8.90% | 8.00% |
| **North America** | **15.00%** | **14.00%** | **12.50%** | **11.90%** | **11.40%** | **10.90%** | **10.30%** |
| Canada | 12.00% | 14.30% | 14.20% | 13.60% | 12.60% | 11.00% | 10.00% |
| US*** | 15.20% | 14.00% | 12.40% | 11.80% | 11.30% | 10.90% | 10.40% |
| **Worldwide** | **23.30%** | **21.70%** | **17.10%** | **18.30%** | **14.50%** | **12.40%** | **11.00%** |

*Source:* Emarketer.com, 2013

Russia, and Italy) which are within top 15 positions. 10 out of 30 spots have been occupied by developing countries, with China holding starry first position. Consumers are rapidly adopting new age consumer behavior in developing countries thereby accelerating transformation of traditional markets into more organized or online markets.

## India's Unharnessed Online Retail Potential

Online retailing has become buzz word in India; still India doesn't feature in top 30 countries in 2013 Global Retail E-commerce Index (Table 5). India is second most populous country in the world (1.2 billion people) and ranks third in world in term of number of internet users (243,198,922), still it fails to reach among top 30 countries of the index because of following constraints (Kearney, 2013) -

*Table 5. The 2013 global retail e-commerce index*

| Rank | Country | Market Type | Online Market Size (40%) | Consumer Behavior (20%) | Growth Potential (20%) | Infrastructure (20%) | Online Market attractiveness Score |
|---|---|---|---|---|---|---|---|
| 1 | **China** | Next Generation | 100 | 68.8 | 100 | 51.1 | **84** |
| 2 | **Japan** | Digital DNA | 100 | 100 | 17.2 | 99.1 | **83.3** |
| 3 | **United States** | Established and Growing | 100 | 77.6 | 39.8 | 96.5 | **82.8** |
| 4 | **United Kingdom** | Established and Growing | 100 | 77.5 | 14.7 | 86.3 | **75.7** |
| 5 | **South Korea** | Digital DNA | 79.6 | 97.4 | 9.3 | 95.1 | **72.2** |
| 6 | **Germany** | Established and Growing | 90.3 | 78.3 | 28.1 | 65.1 | **70.4** |
| 7 | **France** | Established and Growing | 85.5 | 75.7 | 7.4 | 71.6 | **65.2** |
| 8 | **Brazil** | Next Generation | 37.2 | 51.2 | 64.7 | 64.1 | **50.9** |
| 9 | **Australia** | Established and Growing | 15.7 | 89.4 | 46.2 | 86.9 | **50.8** |
| 10 | **Canada** | Established and Growing | 17.7 | 73.5 | 48.3 | 91.5 | **49.7** |
| 11 | **Singapore** | Digital DNA | 2.3 | 93.1 | 28.9 | 100 | **45.3** |
| 12 | **Argentina** | Next Generation | 9.2 | 59.1 | 75.7 | 68 | **44.2** |
| 13 | **Russia** | Next Generation | 34.9 | 51.8 | 56.4 | 42.3 | **44.1** |
| 14 | **Hong Kong** | Digital DNA | 3.2 | 93.7 | 17.2 | 100 | **43.4** |
| 15 | **Italy** | Next Generation | 16.1 | 52.2 | 64.3 | 60.7 | **41.9** |
| 16 | **Sweden** | Established and Growing | 12.1 | 77.5 | 21.7 | 85.7 | **41.8** |
| 17 | **Slovakia** | Next Generation | 2 | 71.5 | 86.4 | 44.3 | **41.2** |
| 18 | **New Zealand** | Digital DNA | 2.5 | 92.3 | 28.1 | 78.5 | **40.8** |
| 19 | **Netherlands** | Established and Growing | 16.2 | 77.5 | 17.4 | 73.9 | **40.2** |
| 20 | **Chile** | Next Generation | 3.9 | 61 | 56.5 | 74.8 | **40** |
| 21 | **Finland** | Established and Growing | 13.3 | 77.2 | 13.6 | 82.1 | **39.9** |
| 22 | **Turkey** | Next Generation | 10.7 | 26.6 | 72.9 | 78.4 | **39.9** |
| 23 | **Venezuela** | Next Generation | 2.5 | 49.5 | 100 | 42.1 | **39.3** |
| 24 | **Belgium** | Established and Growing | 9.8 | 70.6 | 26.5 | 73.1 | **38** |
| 25 | **UAE** | Next Generation | 0.9 | 50.3 | 49.2 | 87.8 | **37.8** |
| 26 | **Norway** | Established and Growing | 12.3 | 77.5 | 9.7 | 75.7 | **37.5** |
| 27 | **Ireland** | Next Generation | 7.2 | 62.3 | 42.2 | 67.9 | **37.4** |
| 28 | **Denmark** | Established and Growing | 10.2 | 78.3 | 14.1 | 73 | **37.2** |
| 29 | **Switzerland** | Established and Growing | 13.2 | 68.2 | 10.9 | 79.4 | **37** |
| 30 | **Malaysia** | Next Generation | 1 | 63 | 44.2 | 75 | **36.8** |

*Source:* ATKearney, 2013

- **Poor Internet Penetration:** India has just 19.9% internet penetration, which is even low than Nigeria which has 37.59% penetration to its total population (Internetlivestats.com, 2014). Only 20% of 930.20 million mobile phone users have smartphones (Bgr.in, 2014; Deloitte, 2014; Statista.com, 2014). Increase in smartphone usage, mobile broadband and National Optical Fibre Network plan by government can increase internet penetration considerably.
- **Infrastructure Constraints:** Improvement in roads and highways in tier 2 cities can improve the base of online consumers. Poor transportation and logistics makes timely delivery difficult (Kalia, 2013; McKinsey & Company, 2010).
- **Low Credit Card Penetration:** Only 2% of Indians hold credit card (Sutherland Insights, 2014), which hinders online retail transactions. For the reason Cash on delivery (COD) is getting popular in India (Agarwal, 2014; Das, 2014).
- **Complex Tax Laws:** Online retailers find it difficult to put accurate taxes to online order because of complex state and local tax laws. Introduction of Goods and Services Tax (GST) is expected to improve online retail efficiency in the future by taking off tax complexity across states (Nishith Desai Associates, 2015; Patnia, 2014; Schneider, 2012).
- **Paucity of Funds:** Because of capital intensive nature of the business, about 70-80% of electronic commerce companies require funds. Many e-commerce companies and startups are on the verge of closing or being acquired by larger companies as venture capitalists and investors have their interest in successful and larger companies (The Economist, 2014). A relaxed FDI (Foreign Direct Investment) policy will certainly help Indian retailers.

## INDIAN SCENARIO

### Types of Electronic Commerce

There are several ways to characterize different types of electronic commerce. Here five major type of electronic commerce are discussed based on nature of market relationship-who is selling to whom and technology based P2P and m-commerce (Laudon & Traver, 2007) (Figure 3).

- **B2B:** Business-to-business or B2B electronic commerce is normally used to describe complete range of product or service e-commerce transactions occurring between two organizations (Industrial manufacturers, partners and retailers). B2B includes activities like procurement, sup-

*Figure 3. Types of electronic commerce*

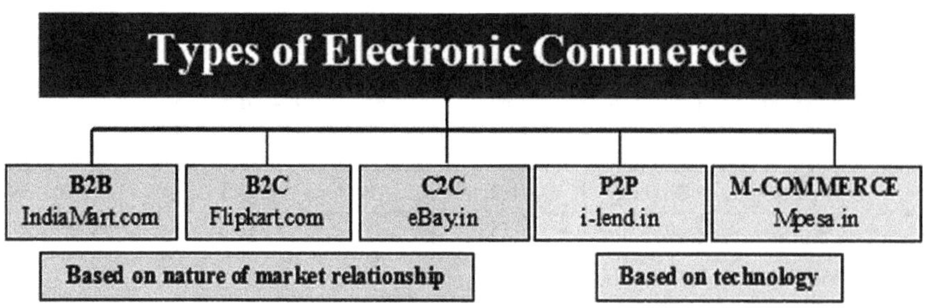

plier management, inventory management, channel management, sales activities, payment management, and service and support (Awad, 2012; Kalakota & Whinston, 2009). Scope of B2B has enhanced over the years form sales to promotion of investment, stock trade and financial alliances. B2B is largest form of e-commerce in the world. B2B transactions in India has shown growth of over 30-40% and soon to reach mark of $100 billion (MSLGroup, 2012). Some of the leading B2B exchanges in India are Tradeindia.com (India's largest B2B portal), AuctionIndia.com, Indiamart.com, Fastparts and FreeMarkets.

- **B2C:** Direct commercial transactions between businesses and consumers are termed under Business-to-Consumer e-commerce (Awad, 2012; Schneider, 2012). This new genre of e-commerce bagged popularity in late 1990s after internet became more accessible. B2C e-commerce includes online travel, online retail/e-tailing, online classifieds, digital downloads and financial services. In India online travel holds 71% of B2C market but online retail is also significantly catching up with 16% of total B2C market (IAMAI, 2013). Flipkart.com, myntra.com, Jabong.com, Shoppoing.indiatimes.com and Homeshop18.com are few of the leading online retailers. Since past few years online services like hotel booking, matrimonial classifieds, banking, and bill payment are also gaining grounds.
- **C2C:** Consumer-to-consumer commerce is prevalent since ages, even before internet, it has just transformed into a global phenomenon due to world wide connectivity. In Consumer-to-consumer e-commerce consumer can sell to each other on an auction site/common platform provided by an online market maker (Schneider, 2012). Customer make a listing of the product on the website and relies on the market maker, who catalogs, optimize search engines, set transaction procedures so that product gets displayed, sold and paid for with ease. eBay.in is one of the leading C2C e-commerce market maker in India.
- **P2P:** Internet users can share computer resources and files without any central web server through peer-to-peer technology (Laudon & Traver, 2007). Hence no intermediary is required. User can search content on P2P network using P2P software. End users computer system act as nodes (peers) in such network.napstar.com, became extremely popular for finding and sharing MP3 files of popular songs. BitTorrent also works on same technology.
- **M-commerce:** Mobile or m-commerce uses wireless technology to deliver electronic commerce capabilities directly into the consumer's hand. Now users equipped with mobile phones and other hand held devices like tablets can conduct diverse kind of e-commerce transactions like banking, travel booking, stocks or online shopping etc while on move (Laudon & Traver, 2007; Schneider, 2012). Almost all the leading businesses are developing mobile websites to market and sell their products and services. Mpesa.in is mobile service by Vodafone, where user can send, receive or withdraw money or pay bills using mobile phone. Mobile commerce is going to be next big thing in India with number of mobile internet users expected to reach 185 million by June 2014 (Bgr.in, 2014)

## Key Stakeholders Engaged in the E-Commerce Sector

To amplify the e-commerce effect and get ahead of competition stakeholders are innovating and differentiating themselves to give consumers a worthy online experience. Every business is striving to join e-commerce bandwagon, and the list of e-commerce players is increasing. Call centres, logistic players, financial intermediaries, social networking websites, network service providers and internet service providers act as enablers, working and adjusting themselves in the background as per strategies of online businesses. With customer centric focus, all stakeholders coordinate with each other to facilitate three flows of e-commerce transactions i.e. *product flow*, movement of goods and services from business to final consumer through logistic providers; *information flow*, flow of information of order from customers and later transmission of order status/tracking from business to consumer; *monetary flow*, flow of payments through financial intermediaries; from consumers to online business players and suppliers and vice-versa (Figure 4) (Ernst & Young, 2013; Kalakota & Whinston, 2009; Rajaraman, 2011).

## Origin of E-Commerce in India

Indian e-commerce industry has seen a rollercoaster ride (Figure 5). Initially market was restricted to just print media (classified advertisements), and now with more than 243,198,922 internet users (Internetlivestats.com, 2014), Indian e-commerce is soaring high. New business models like group buying and social commerce are emerging. Evolution of Indian e-commerce took place in two major phases; these phases with significant events are discussed below (Ernst & Young, 2013).

- **First Wave:** Seeds of internet evolution in India were sown long back in 1982 when DataQuest-India's first IT publication (Dqindia.com, 2014) was launched and establishment of one of first networks of India – ERNET. This network was collaborative effort of five IITs, IISc, NCST and DIT in 1986 (Ernet.in, 2014). This initiative led to formation of ERNET India and it connected 800 institutions and 100,000 users by 1996. Formally in 1995, first wave of e-commerce revolution swayed. VSNL introduced dial-up internet in 6 cities in India (Economictimes.indiatimes.com, 2014b). Launch of economic liberalization, end of license regime, and high taxes and import restrictions and relaxed policies led to growth of SMEs and information technology industry, who adopted internet at early stage.

*Figure 4. Multiple stakeholders engaged in e-commerce sector*
*Source: Ernst & Young, 2013*

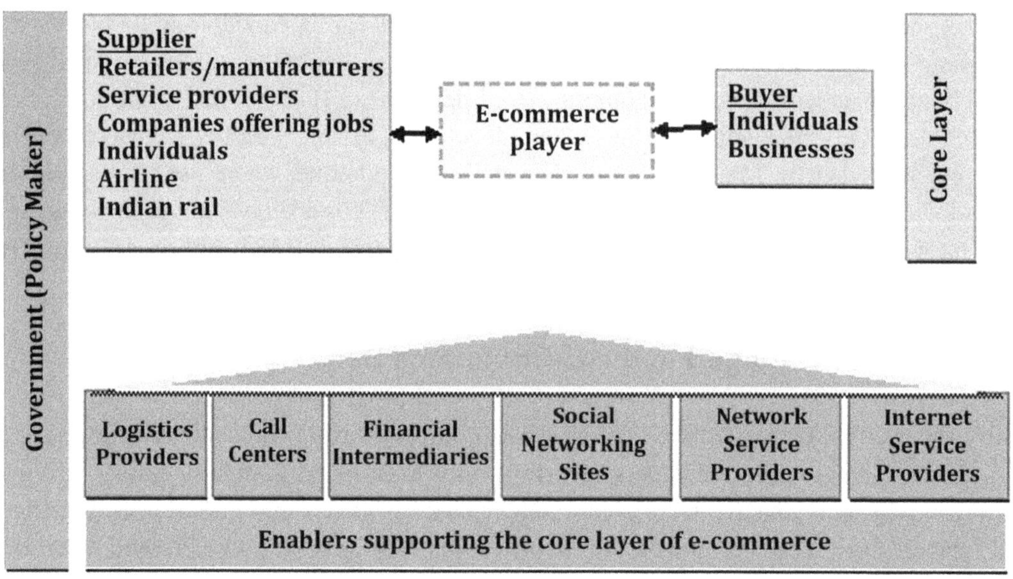

*Figure 5. Two waves of e-commerce evolution in India*
*Source: Ernst & Young, 2013*

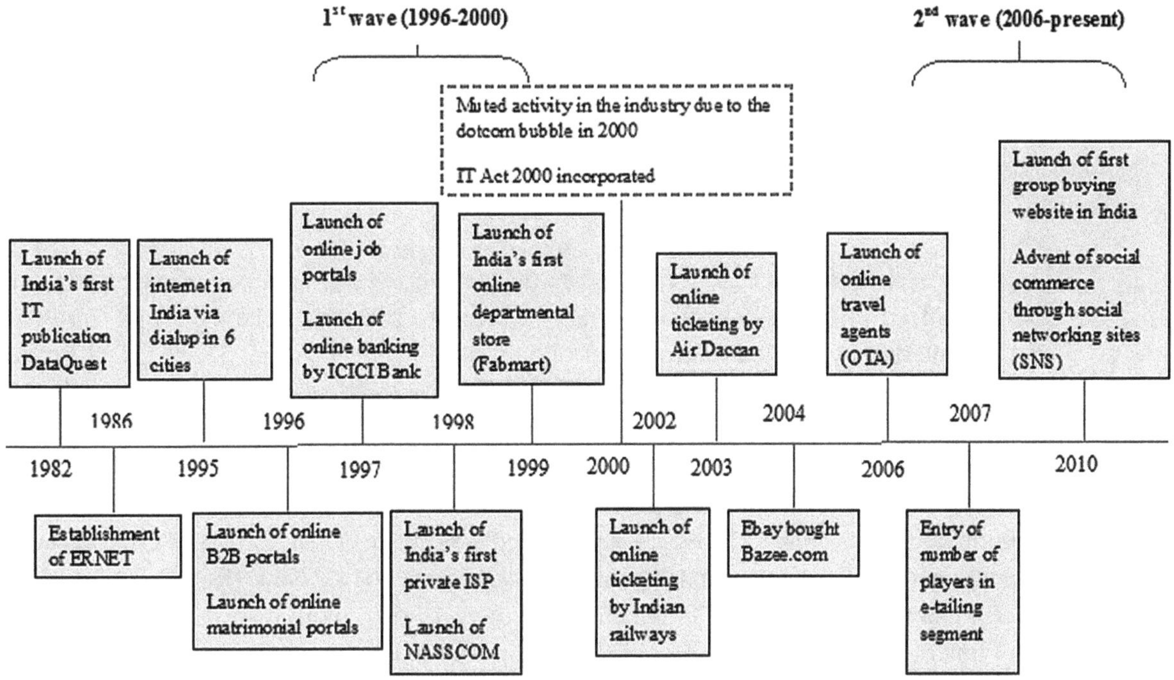


- **B2B Directory:** Liberalized trade policies stimulated the growth of B2B online portal. IndiaMART.com by Dinesh Agarwal and TradeIndia.com by Bikki Khosla emerged as India's first B2B in 1996 (Indiamart.com, 2014; Tradeindia.com, 2014).
- **Online Matrimonial:** Sagaai.com, popularly known as Shaadi.com was founded by Anupam Mittal in 1996. This revolutionized concept of finding matrimonial matches online. Now shaadi.com has become World's largest matrimonial portal (Shaadi.com, 2014).
- **Online Recruitment:** Economic reforms of 1991 created huge number of jobs. Till 1997, employment news, megazines and notifications in the newspapers were the only source for employers and job aspirants. Sanjeev Bikhchandani sensing this huge opportunity created Naukari.com in 1997 to connect employers and job seekers (Infoedge.in, 2014).
- **Online Classified:** One of the primary reasons for instant popularity of online classified was simplicity of use, as there were no headaches regarding delivery, logistics or taxation.

Apart from these developments few significant events happened like launch of India's first online banking site by ICICI bank in 1997 (Economictimes.indiatimes.com, 2014a), Sify became India's first private ISP in 1998 (Kannan, 2011), NASSCOM was launched to promote IT industry in 1998 (NASSCOM, 2014) and India's first online departmental store, Fabmart.com (earlier known as Fabmall or indramall, which was later rebranded to Indiaplaza.com) came into existence in 1999 (Kumar & Mahadevan, 2003; Kurian, 2000). First wave of Indian e-commerce crumpled to low internet penetration, menial online shopper base, slower internet, inadequate infrastructure support and little acceptance of internet shopping concept. This dot-com burst was marked by crumple of more than 1000 e-commerce business in

India. 2000-2005 was silent era of Indian e-commerce with few developments like incorporation of IT Act 2000 ("IT Act," 2000), Launch of online ticketing by Indian Railways (J. Singh, 2011), Bazee.com was acquired by eBay.in (eBay.in, 2005).

- **Second Wave:** Second wave of e-commerce in India was marked by advent of low cost carriers (LCCs) in the Indian aviation sector in 2005 (Ahmed & Mahfooz, n.d.). People found online ticket booking more reliable, cheaper and simple. This success overcame the initial inertia felt by online shoppers and lead to growth of online retail.
    - **Online Travel:** Before 2005-06, masses had this perception that air travel is luxury and only rich can afford it. LCCs (low cost carriers) decided to sell their tickets through third parties and internet, which led to growth of online travel agents (OTAs). These OTAs further developed their websites to increase their sales. Within three years of its incorporation; in 2002 IRCTC implemented e-ticketing and in 2005 it churned 63% of e-commerce (22feet-tribalworldwide.com, 2014). At the time when the e-commerce market was trying to spring up in 2009, IRCTC became largest contributor and accounted for over a third of the total e-commerce (Chowdhury, 2009). A new record was made when 5.80 lakh e-tickets were booked on IRCTC website on 19 March 2014 (Mehta, 2014). Now IRCTC is one of the biggest e-commerce portal of India, churning revenue even more than famous e-retail site like Flipkart (Factsninfo.com, 2014). Not just on national level, IRCTC has also emerged as fastest growing e-commerce website in entire Asia-Pacific region in terms of online money transactions (J. Singh, 2011).
    - **Online Retail:** In 2007, convenience and changing lifestyles of consumers paved way for online retailers who are innovative and strive to achieve delightful customer experience. These retailers adapted and duplicated global business models for profit and growth.
    - **Group Buying:** Since 2010, Indian e-commerce is following global trend and daily deals and group buying websites are substantially getting more number of visitors and members every day. Venture capitalists see it as huge investment opportunity.
    - **Social Networking Actively Used by Organizations to Reach Out to Customers:** Because of huge mass appeal of social networking sites e-commerce players are strategically using these websites to target potential customers. Companies upload latest product information, try to create product loyalty, advertise, create hype and receive feedbacks, and keep connected to their customers. Social commerce is emerging as phenomenon (Figure 6).

## Present: B2C Electronic Commerce Market Size from 2009-2013

Digital commerce market in India has been dominated by online travel throughout its evolution, but online retail is catching up and more and more online users are showing interest in making purchase online. Another category which has shown upward trend is financial services. Based on total transactions done through personal computer and mobile (Table 6) (IAMAI, 2013) -

- Online travel transactions have been leading digital commerce industry with 73% share (INR 345.44 billion), and it was predicted to grow further at the rate of 30% to cross INR 449.07 billion by the end of year 2013.

*Figure 6. Social networking captures large share of pc screen time in India*
*Source: ComScore, 2013*

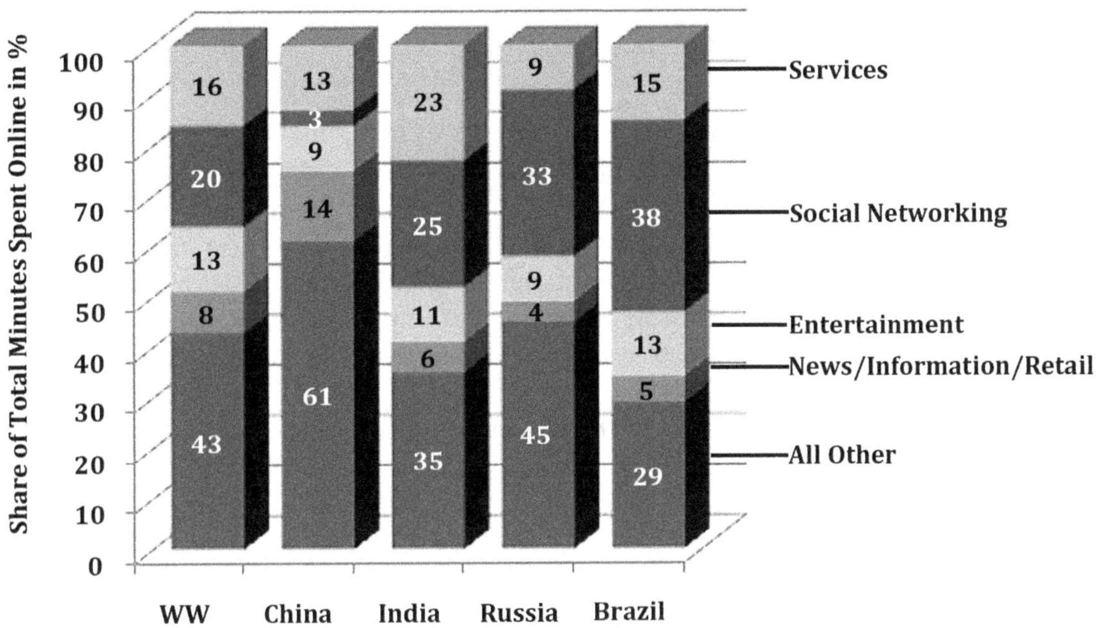


*Table 6. Digital commerce market size from 2009-2013 (Figures in billions, percentages indicate share of overall market size)*

| Year | Dec-09 | Dec-10 | Dec-11 | Dec-12 | Dec-13 |
|---|---|---|---|---|---|
| **Total Market Size** | 192.49 | 262.63 | 351.42 | 473.49 | 629.67 |
| **Online Travel Industry** | 149.53 (78%) | 204.40 (78%) | 265.72 (76%) | 345.44 (73%) | 449.07 (71%) |
| **Online Non- Travel Industry** | 42.96 (22%) | 58.23 (22%) | 85.70 (24%) | 128.05 (27%) | 180.60 (29%) |
| *E-tailing* | 15.50 | 23.72 | 38.42 | 64.54 | 100.04 |
| *Financial Services* | 15.40 | 18.48 | 22.55 | 28.86 | 36.07 |
| *Classifieds* | 7.75 | 10.85 | 16.82 | 23.54 | 30.61 |
| *Other Online Services* | 4.31 | 5.18 | 7.92 | 11.10 | 13.88 |

*Source*: IAMAI, 2013

- Non-travel transactions chip in remaining 27% (INR 128.05 billion), out of which -
    - E-tailing claims first position with nearly 50% share (INR 64.54 billion)
    - Financial services take second spot with 23% share (INR 28.86 billion)
    - Classifieds segment get hold of 18% of the whole non-travel industry pie (INR 23.54 billion)
    - Other online services sum up to the remaining 9% (INR 11.10 billion)

It was anticipated that the non-travel industry segment will mature by 41% and reach up to INR 180.60 billion by December 2013.

## Categorizing B2C Electronic Commerce in India

Digital market in India is divided into two major segments: Online travel and non-online travel, which are discussed below (Figure 7) (IAMAI, 2013) -

- **Online Travel:** This industry segment consists of domestic and international air tickets, railway tickets, bus tickets, hotel bookings and tour packages/travel insurance.
- **Non-Online Travel**
  - **E-Tailing:** This includes electronic retailing of consumer items like books, apparels and footwear, jewellery and personal/healthcare accessories, camera and camera accessories, consumer durables and kitchen appliances, home furnishings, mobile phones and mobile accessories, laptops/net books/tablets and other products such as vouchers/coupons, toys, gifts, flowers, handicrafts, stationary etc.
  - **Financial Services:** The elements here include insurance related services, utility bill payments including mobile bill payments and online transactions for shares and securities trading.
  - **Classifieds:** This category includes B2C Classifieds like online jobs and matrimony, other B2C categories like car, real estate and B2B classifieds.
  - **Other Online Services:** This comprises emerging online services like online entertainment ticketing, online food and grocery delivery.

*Figure 7. Components of digital commerce market, 2012 (INR 473.49 billion)*
*Source: IAMAI, 2013*

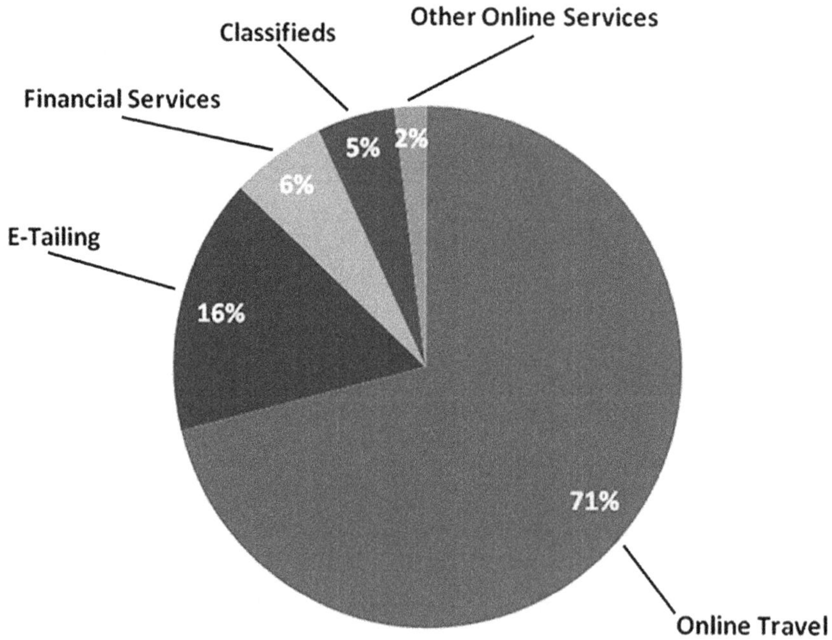

## Indian Online Retail Market Size and Growth

Indian population has enormous enthusiasm towards internet therefore it has become fundamental element of our speedy lifestyle. Internet has evolving from just a medium for communication to consumer-centric e-marketplace, where consumer can buy latest products and services at best price and convenience. With changing lifestyles and growing internet penetration in last 5 years, India's online retail industry has grown nine folds from around Rs 15 billion revenues in 2007-08 to Rs 139 billion in 2012-13. This compounded annual growth rate (CAGR) of over 56 per cent is propelled by sales of books electronics and apparel. New businesses are focusing on niche segments like grocery, jewellery, furniture and apparel will further drive the market at healthy 50-55 per cent CAGR to Rs 504 billion by 2015-16 (Figure 8) (CRISIL, 2014). Fueled by substantial price discounts from online retailers and backed with manufacturers' guarantees, online shopping is bound to increase (Gopalan & Ranganathan, 2014).

## Total Retail vs. Online Retail

Potential of India's online retail industry can be estimated from the fact that it's very small in comparison to organised and overall (organised plus unorganised) retail in the country. It is expected that industry's revenue will grow to more than double to around 18 per cent of organised retail by 2016 from around 8 per cent in 2013. Still its share will be just 1% of the overall retail (organised plus unorganised) pie (Figure 9 & 10), which is very low as compared to 9-10% in the US and UK, and around 4-5% in China (CRISIL, 2014).

## E-Tailing

E-tailing comprises of buying consumer items such as books, apparels and footwear, jewellery, mobiles, cameras, computers (desktops/laptops/net books/tablets), home and kitchen appliances, home furnishings, vouchers/coupons, flowers and toys, gifts online. The e-tailing category has grown from INR 15.50 billion in the year 2009 (Jan-Dec 2009) to INR 64.54 billion in year 2012 (Jan-Dec 2012). This category was estimated to cross the 100.00 billion mark in the year 2013 (Figure 11) (IAMAI, 2013).

*Figure 8. Indian online retail market size and growth*
*Source: CRISIL, 2014*

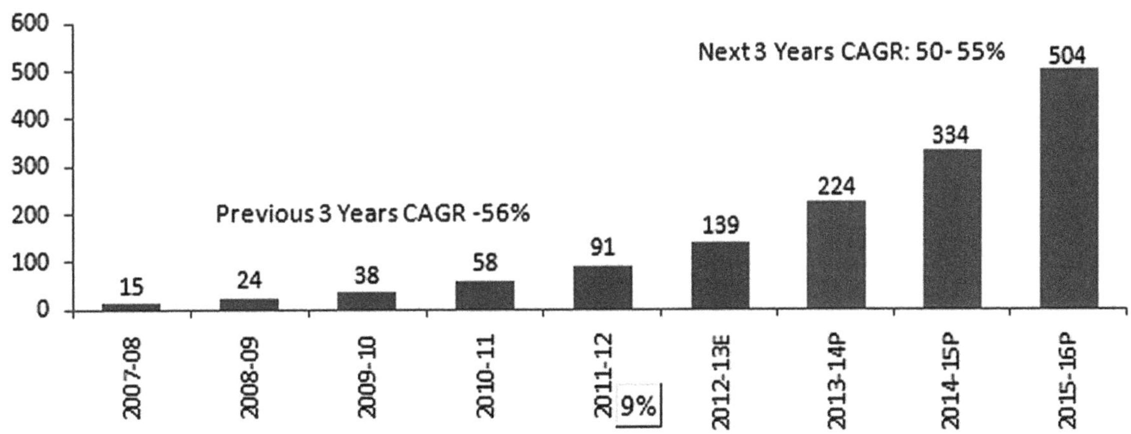

*Figure 9. Comparative picture overall Vs online retail 2012-13*
*Source: CRISIL, 2014*

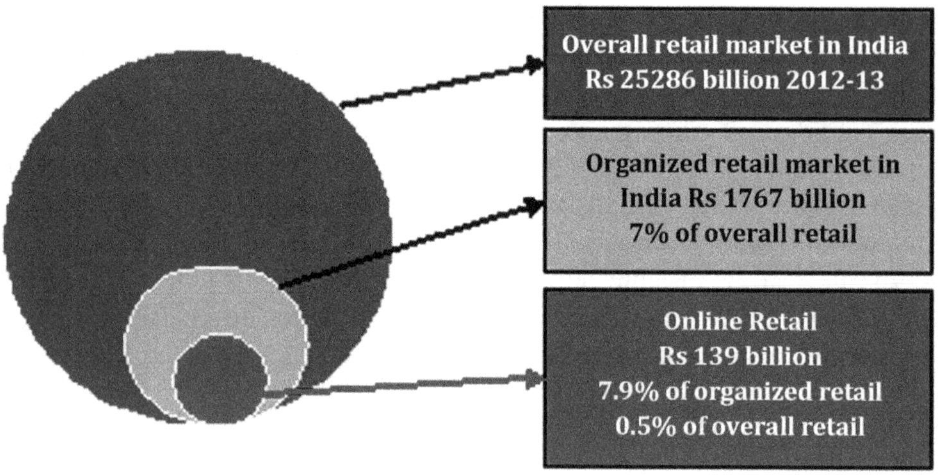


*Figure 10. Online retail Vs total retail in India*
*Source: The Boston Consulting Group, 2012*

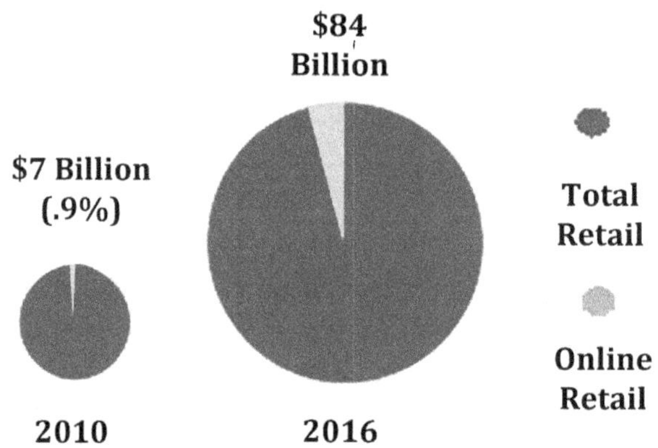


## Components Share of E-Tailing, Jan-Dec 2012

Top components that take nearly 78% of total e-tail market are Laptops/Net-books/Tablets 24.5% (INR 15.79 billion), followed by apparels and footwear which contribute 20.6% (INR 13.31 billion) and mobile phones, cameras, mobile and camera accessories contributing another 33% (INR 21.31 billion). Remaining 20% (INR 14.13 billion) of the total e-tailing pie is constituted by consumer durables and kitchen appliances, books and home furnishings, i.e. INR 5.00 billion, INR 2.88 billion and INR 2.00 billion respectively. Only about 3% is contributed by nascent category comprising products like deals/ coupons, toys, gifts, handicrafts, flowers etc. (Table 7 (IAMAI, 2013).

*Figure 11. Growth of e-tail in India, 2009-2013 (figures in INR billions)*
*Source: IAMAI, 2013*

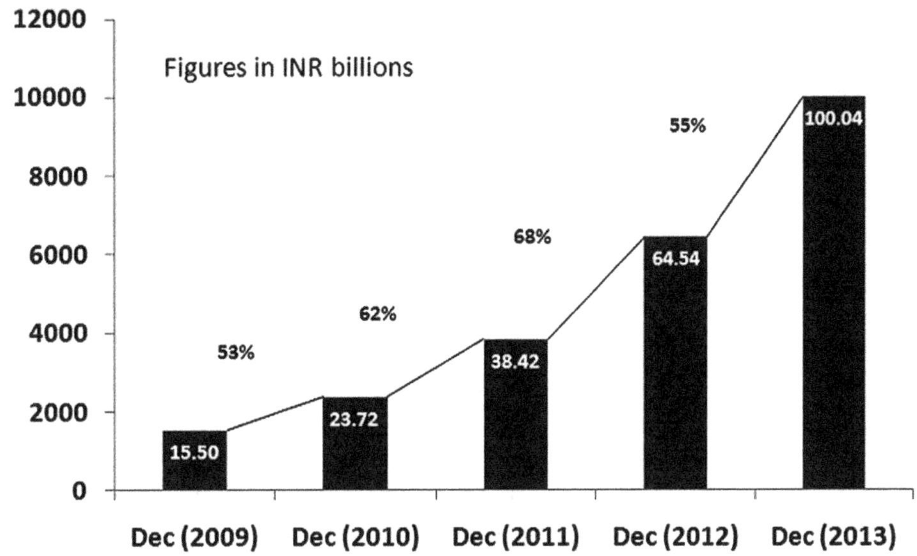


*Table 7. Components share of e-tailing, Jan-Dec 2012*

| Component | Percentage (%) | Market size (INR in billions) |
|---|---|---|
| Books | 4.50% | 2.88 |
| Apparels + Footwear | 20.60% | 13.31 |
| Jewellery + Personal/Health Care Accessories | 3.70% | 2.40 |
| Cameras + Camera Accessories | 14.10% | 9.14 |
| Consumer Durables + Kitchen Appliances | 7.80% | 5.00 |
| Home Furnishings | 3.10% | 2.00 |
| Mobile Phone + Mobile Accessories | 18.90% | 12.17 |
| Laptops/Netbooks/Tablets | 24.50% | 15.79 |
| Other Products (Voucher, Coupon, Toys, Gifts, Handicrafts, Stationary, Etc | 2.80% | 1.85 |

*Source*: IAMAI, 2013

## CONCLUSION

Electronic commerce is becoming popular because it offers unique and variety of features to its user. Consumer can buy latest products and services at best price with convenience. Precursor of e-commerce, i.e. internet is fast becoming an essential part of our lives; it has evolved from just a medium for communication to consumer-centric e-marketplace. Almost forty percent of world population is using internet, and half of it is from Asia. After China and US, India has highest number of Internet users. This tremendous growth of internet in India incites enormous potential for e-commerce.

It is estimated that worldwide business-to-consumer (B2C) e-commerce sales will grow by 20.1% to reach $1.500 trillion in 2014 and Asia-Pacific will become largest regional e-commerce market in the world. This explains that emerging markets are getting strength out of their huge population base that come and shop online for the first time. Asia pacific growth will be driven by China, along with India and Indonesia.

Despite of its huge population and entrancing forecasts discussed in the paper, India fails to reach among top 30 countries of Global Retail E-Commerce Index because of poor internet penetration, infrastructure constraints, low credit card penetration, complex tax laws and paucity of funds. Even during evolution of e-commerce in India, which occurred in two waves; first wave in (1996-2000) faced a bubble burst in 2000 due to similar reasons like low internet penetration, menial online shopper base, slower internet, inadequate infrastructure support and little acceptance of internet shopping concept. More than 1000 e-commerce business in India crumpled during this dot-com burst, making 2000-2005 a silent era of Indian e-commerce. Second wave (2006-present) has been dominated by online travel throughout its evolution, but online retail is catching up and more and more online users are showing interest in making purchase online and it claims nearly fifty percent share of non-travel B2C e-commerce.

In spite of problems discussed above, potential of India's online retail industry is huge and it can be estimated from the fact that currently it is just 7.9% of organized retail and 0.5% of overall retail. Changing lifestyles and growing internet penetration in last 5 years, are fueling India's online retail industry, which has grown nine folds from 2007-08 to 2012-13. This compounded annual growth rate (CAGR) of over 56 per cent is propelled by sales of books electronics and apparel. As per a report by CRISIL, new businesses are focusing on niche segments like grocery, jewelry, furniture and apparel, and it will further drive the market at healthy 50-55 per cent CAGR to Rs 504 billion by 2015-16. By understanding the utility of e-commerce technology, learning lessons from evolutionary past and knowing absolved present position, this additive knowledge can be extrapolated by electronic retailers to capture golden opportunity in near future.

## REFERENCES

IT Act. (2000). New Delhi: Ministry of Law, Justice And Company Affairs (Legislative Department). Retrieved from http://deity.gov.in/content/view-it-act-2000

Agarwal, H. (2014). Cash On Delivery : Should Indian Online Retailers Persist with. *Trak.in*. Retrieved from http://trak.in/ecommerce/cash-on-delivery-cod-online-payment-mode-indian-stores/

Ahmed, S., & Mahfooz, Y. (n. d.). Consolidation in the Sky- A Case Study on the Quest for Supremacy Between Jetlite And Kingfisher Airlines.

E-Commerce Is the Next Frontier in Global Expansion. (2012). *ATKearney*. Retrieved from http://www.atkearney.com/paper/-/asset_publisher/dVxv4Hz2h8bS/content/e-commerce-is-the-next-frontier-in-global-expansion/10192

Online Retail Is Front and Center in the Quest for Growth. (2013). *ATKearney*. Retrieved from https://dl.dropboxusercontent.com/u/3187612/Global Retail E-commerce Index 2013.pdf

Awad, E. M. (2012). *Electronic Commerce – From Vision to Fulfillment* (3rd ed.). New Delhi, India: PHI Learning Private Limited.

Baazee.com - India's leading online marketplace - was acquired by eBay Inc. - The World's Online Marketplace. (2005). *eBay.in*. Retrieved from http://pages.ebay.in/community/aboutebay/news/press-releases/corporate/aquisition.html

India to have 185 million mobile Internet users by June. (2014). *Bgr.in*. Retrieved from http://www.bgr.in/news/india-to-have-185-million-mobile-internet-users-by-june-iamai/

Chaffey, D. (2013). *E-Business and E-Commerce Management Strategy, Implementation and Practice* (5th ed.). New Delhi, India: Pearson Education Limited.

Chowdhury, A. (2009). IRCTC becomes the largest contributor to e-commerce. *Business Standard*. Retrieved from http://www.business-standard.com/article/technology/irctc-becomes-the-largest-contributor-to-e-commerce-109040400075_1.html

India Digital Future in Focus 2013. (2013). *ComScore*. Retrieved from http://www.comscore.com/content/download/21739/1126111/file/India-Digital-Future-in-Focus-2013.pdf

E-tail eats into Retail. Mumbai, India. (2014). *CRISIL*. Retrieved from http://www.crisil.com/pdf/research/CRISIL-Research-Article-Online-Retail-Feb14.pdf

Das, G. (2014). Cash-on-delivery : Necessary Evil. *BusinessToday*. Retrieved from http://businesstoday.intoday.in/story/cash-on-delivery-impact-on-e-commerce-companies-customers/1/202680.html

About Us. (2014). *Dqindia.com*. Retrieved from http://www.dqindia.com/

Company History - ICICI Bank Ltd. (2014a). *Economictimes.indiatimes.com*. Retrieved from http://economictimes.indiatimes.com/icici-bank-ltd/infocompanyhistory/companyid-9194.cms

Company History - Tata Communications Ltd. (2014b). *Economictimes.indiatimes.com*. Retrieved from http://economictimes.indiatimes.com/tata-communications-ltd/infocompanyhistory/companyid-11992.cms

B2C Ecommerce Climbs Worldwide, As Emerging Markets Drive Sales Higher. (2013). *Emarketer.com*. Retrieved from http://www.emarketer.com/Article/B2C-Ecommerce-Climbs-Worldwide-Emerging-Markets-Drive-Sales-Higher/1010004

Global B2C Ecommerce Sales to Hit $ 1. 5 Trillion This Year Driven by Growth in Emerging Markets. (2014). *Emarketer.com*. Retrieved from http://www.emarketer.com/Article/Global-B2C-Ecommerce-Sales-Hit-15-Trillion-This-Year-Driven-by-Growth-Emerging-Markets/1010575

How it began. (2014). *Ernet.in*. Retrieved from http://www.ernet.in/about/abouternet.html

Rebirth of e-Commerce in India. Kolkata. (2013). *Ernst & Young*. Retrieved from http://www.ey.com/Publication/vwLUAssets/Rebirth_of_e-Commerce_in_India/$FILE/EY_RE-BIRTH_OF_ECOMMERCE.pdf

Evolution of e-commerce in India. (2014). *PWC, & ASSOCHAM*. Retrieved from http://www.pwc.in/assets/pdfs/publications/2014/evolution-of-e-commerce-in-india.pdf

Facts and Information about IRCTC. (2014). *Factsninfo.com*. Retrieved from http://www.factsninfo.com/2015/06/facts-and-information-about-irctc.html

15 Landmarks in India's Digital History. (201422*feettribalworldwide.com*. Retrieved from http://22feettribalworldwide.com/15-landmarks-in-indias-digital-history/

Gopalan, R., & Ranganathan, S. S. (2014). India Retail Trends 2014. Retrieved from http://www.tatabss.com/pdf/whitepapers/india-retail-trends-2014.pdf

Digital Commerce. Mumbai. (2013). *IAMAI*. Retrieved from http://yourstory.com/wp-content/uploads/2013/05/Digital-Commerce-Report_2013.pdf

India retail: Survival of the richest? (2014). *The Economist*. Retrieved from http://www.eiu.com/industry/article/190895003/india-retail-survival-of-the-richest/2013-08-27#

Fact Sheet. (2014). *Indiamart.com*. Retrieved from http://www.indiamart.com/corporate/fact-sheet.html

Joseph, S. (2012). *E-Commerce – An Indian Perspective* (4th ed.). New Delhi: PHI Learning Private Limited.

Kalakota, R., & Whinston, A. B. (2009). *Electronic Commerce - A Managers Guide*. Delhi: Pearson Education Inc.

Kalia, P. (2013). Electronic Retailing in India: Past, Present & Future. In P. Singh (Ed.), *Retail Sector in India Opportunities and Challenges* (pp. 288–304). Amritsar, India: KG Graphics.

Kalia, P. (in press). Top e-Retailers of India: Business model and components. *International Journal of Electronic Marketing and Retailing*.

Kalia, P., Kaur, N., & Singh, T. (2015). Internet Marketing and B2C E-Commerce: The Indian Scenario. In A. Vashisht, G. Suri, & R. B. Kaur (Eds.), *Innovation Management* (pp. 127–134). Delhi, India: Excel India Publishers.

Kannan, S. (2011). IT services, future growth engine for Sify. *The Hindu*. Retrieved from http://www.thehindu.com/todays-paper/tp-business/it-services-future-growth-engine-for-sify/article2137901.ece?css=print

Kumar, K., & Mahadevan, B. (2003). Evolution of Business Models in B2C E-Commerce : The Case of Fabmall. *IIMB Management Review*, December, 23–30. Retrieved from http://www.iimb.ernet.in/~mahadev/fabmall.pdf

Kurian, B. (2000, July). Catch the shopper by the e-tail. *Business Line*, 44–47.

Laudon, K. C., & Traver, C. G. (2007). *E-commerce - Business, Technology, Society (Low Price.)*. New Delhi, India: Pearson Education Inc.

Building India: Transforming the nation's logistics infrastructure. (2010). *McKinsey & Company*. Retrieved from http://www.mckinsey.com/insights/travel_transportation/~/media/mckinsey/dotcom/insights/travel transportation/transforming indiaslogistics infrastructure/building_india-transforming_the_nations_logistics_infrastructure.ashx

Mehta, M. K. (2014). New record : 5.80 lakh e -tickets booked on IRCTC website on March 19. *The Times of India*. Retrieved from http://timesofindia.indiatimes.com/india/New-record-5-80-lakh-e-tickets-booked-on-IRCTC-website-on-March-19/articleshow/32356664.cms

E-Commerce in India: Evolution, Growth and Challenges. (2012). *MSLGroup*. Retrieved from http://mslgroup.com/insights/2012/e-commerce-in-india-evolution,-growth-and-challenges.aspx

Vision and Mission. (2014). *NASSCOM*. Retrieved from http://www.nasscom.in/vision-and-mission

E-Commerce in India. (2015). *Nishith Desai Associates*. Retrieved from http://www.nishithdesai.com/fileadmin/user_upload/pdfs/ResearchPapers/E-Commerce_in_India.pdf

Number of Internet Users 2014. (2014). Retrieved from http://www.internetlivestats.com/internet-users/#definitions

Patel, A. (2010). Concept of Mobile Agent-Based Electronic Marketplace-Safety Measures. In I. Lee (Ed.), *Encyclopedia of E-Business Development and Management in the Global Economy* (pp. 252–264). Hershey, PA: IGI Global; doi:10.4018/978-1-61520-611-7.ch025

Patnia, A. (2014). Is Indian grandfathered tax laws a roadblock for e-commerce in India? *Taxmantra.com*. Retrieved from http://taxmantra.com/is-indian-grandfathered-tax-laws-a-roadblock-for-e-commerce-in-india.html/

eCommerce in India: Accelerating growth. (2015). *PWC*. Retrieved from http://www.pwc.in/en_IN/in/assets/pdfs/publications/2015/ecommerce-in-india-accelerating-growth.pdf

Quick Facts / Milestones. Edge.in. (2014). Retrieved from http://infoedge.in/corporate-quick-facts-milestones.asp

Rajaraman, V. (2011). *Essentials of E-Commerce Technology*. New Delhi: PHI Learning Private Limited.

Schneider, G. P. (2012). *E-Commerce - Strategy, Technology and Implementation* (1st ed.). Delhi, India: Cengage Learning India Private Limited.

Recognition and Awards won by Matrimony Portal. (2014). *Shaadi.com*. Retrieved from http://www.shaadi.com/introduction/index/why-we-are-no1

Singh, J. (2011). IRCTC face of e-ticket in India. *Iamwire.com*. Retrieved from http://www.iamwire.com/2011/11/irctc-face-of-e-ticket-in-india/1862

Share of mobile phone users that use a smartphone in India from 2010 to 2017. (2014). *Statista.com*. Retrieved from http://www.statista.com/statistics/257048/smartphone-user-penetration-in-india/

India Credit Card Market Overview. (2014). *Sutherland Insights*. Retrieved from http://www.sutherlandinsights.com/india-credit-card-market-overview

Technology, Media & Telecommunications India Predictions. (2014). *Deloitte*. Retrieved from http://www2.deloitte.com/content/dam/Deloitte/in/Documents/technology-media-telecommunications/in-tmt-telecom-predictions-noexp.pdf

The Internet Economy in the G-20. Boston, USA. (2012). *The Boston Consulting Group*. Retrieved September 8, 2014, from https://www.bcg.com/documents/file100409.pdf

About Us. (2014). *Tradeindia.com*. Retrieved from http://www.tradeindia.com/AboutUs/home.html

Wollscheid, C. (2012). *Rise and Burst of the Dotcom Bubble : Causes, Characteristics, Examples*. Mittelhessen. Retrieved from http://www.grin.com/en/e-book/197166/rise-and-burst-of-the-dotcom-bubble

## KEY TERMS AND DEFINITIONS

**CRISIL:** Credit Rating Information Services of India Limited is a global analytical company providing ratings, research, and risk and policy advisory services (http://www.crisil.com/index.jsp).

**Digital Buyers:** Consumers who directly buy goods or services from a seller over the Internet using a web browser.

**Dotcom Burst:** The Dotcom bubble, also known as the 'Internet bubble' or the 'Information technology bubble was a speculative bubble of stock prices of mainly American Internet companies during the time from 1995 until 2000 (Wollscheid, 2012).

**E-Marketplace:** A virtual space which provides the infrastructure services for buyers and sellers to meet and conduct business transactions using mobile agent systems (Patel, 2010).

**ERNET:** ERNET India is the National Research and Education Network dedicated to support the needs of the research and education community within the country (http://www.ernet.in/).

**IRCTC:** Indian Railway Catering and Tourism Corporation, is a subsidiary of the Indian Railways that handles the catering, tourism and online ticketing operations of the railways (www.irctc.co.in/).

**NASSCOM:** The National Association of Software and Services Companies is a non –profit trade association of Indian Information Technology and Business Process Outsourcing industry (http://www.nasscom.in/).

**VSNL:** Videsh Sanchar Nigam Limited (VSNL), now known as Tata Communications Limited is a global telecommunications company owned by the Indian business conglomerate Tata Group. The company's infrastructure includes sub-sea, terrestrial communications networks, data centers and it provides fixed line and wireless services (http://www.tatacommunications.com/).

# Chapter 6
# An Epigrammatic View of E-Retailing in India: Prospects and Retrospects

**Parag Shukla**
*M.S. University of Baroda, India*

**Parimal Vyas**
*M.S. University of Baroda, India*

## ABSTRACT

*The Internet has changed the way many consumers shop, not just in the digital domain, but also in the physical world. E-tailing is a subset of e-commerce, which encapsulates all "commerce" conducted via the Internet. It refers to that part of e-commerce which entails the sale of product merchandise and does not include sale of services viz. Railway tickets, airlines tickets, job portals, etc. In 2012, the size of India's e-commerce market was USD 10 billion, while that of the e-tailing market was USD 0.6 billion. The current small size of e-tailing has led to it rarely being assessed on standalone basis. It is either clubbed with e-commerce or with brick & mortar retail, which, while not incorrect, does not allow for e-tailing's evaluation on its own merit. Consumer's perception regarding shopping has been changed with the introduction of internet media. Retail industry has witnessed major revolution in the changing technology oriented business scenario of the twenty-first century in India. Internet has shrunk the entire World. The rules of the game in retailing are fast changing with the introduction of Information Technology. The e-Retailing website is the front door of the online store that interacts between the e-retailer and consumers. The electronic retailing (e-Tailing, e-Retailing, internet retailing etc.) is the model of selling of retail goods using electronic media, in particular, the internet. In this research paper the authors propose to explore the factors contributing to the growth of e–Retailing in India and to investigate conceptually the issues and challenges involved in e- Retailing An attempt in this paper will also be made to study the present scenarios of e-tailing opportunities, its market, the viabilities and trends.*

DOI: 10.4018/978-1-4666-9921-2.ch006

Copyright © 2016, IGI Global. Copying or distributing in print or electronic forms without written permission of IGI Global is prohibited.

## INTRODUCTION

The Internet is just one of a range of e-commerce technologies to facilitate information exchange. The benefits of setting up an Internet presence are cost reduction, new capability, competitive advantage, communications improvement, improved control and customer service improvement. However, these benefits have yet to be fully realised as firms continue to search for the best strategies and business models on which to base their commerce activities. In India, e-tailing has the potential to grow more than hundred-fold in the next eight years to reach a value of 76 billion dollars by the year 2021. This would be possible if more number of rural people brought under the fold of internet accessing and trained to use the sophisticated way of shopping. The e-retailers should also bring confidence among the online customers by prompt delivery of goods; allowing discounts for bulk purchases, reducing delivery charges etc. Subsequently, the Indian market will attain a different outlook. E-Retailing is part of e-commerce, a term that has gained immense popularity since the advent of internet revolution, throughout the world. While e-commerce usually stands for commercial transactions or interaction among the organizations and individuals virtually, e-retailing is focused primarily on selling of goods over the internet. E-retailers intend to take advantage on it in spite of impediment and escalated competition of e-tailers. Tomorrow's high-performing businesses will use technology to strengthen their relationships with customers, leverage their data, optimize and secure their critical systems, and enable their workforces with leading tools. Technology is also enabling customers to take more control of their shopping experiences, and new approaches to shopping and fulfilment are opening the doors to competition that would not have been viable just a few years ago and it's all changing at great speed. In this chapter the authors throw a light on the current status of Indian E-tailing market and also to study positive influencing factors responsible for online shopping in India.

When a main street store builds a website, they open up opportunities to expand their market beyond geographical boundaries. The chances of losing sales from the physical shop are slight, but the potential to increase sales through their website could be enormous (Tiernan, 2000). E-Retailers have developed many innovative promotions to lure customers and there by growing the market. As one of the market trends, e-Retailing has been widely used in retail industry and growth is increasing day by day in today's scenario. E-Retailing is can be described as retailing conducted online, over the internet. The vocabulary electronic retailing that used in internet discussions as early as 1995, the term look like an almost in evitable addition to e-mail, e-business and e-Commerce, etc.

It started out way back in the year 1997 when Dell Computer got multimillion dollars of orders on the website. E-Retailing is synonymous with business- to- consumer (B2C) transaction model of e-Commerce. E-Commerce is the master field defining the e-Retailing operation. E-Commerce is a huge domain on conducting business over internet and e- Retailing is a part of it. Ecommerce means marketing, purchasing, selling, distribution and servicing with the help of electronic media like internet and other networks aided by www, email, databases etc. with the goal of commercial transactions and facilities like many alternative options, Anytime and anywhere shopping, attractive customized informative business portals, cheap and best deals, comparative analysis of attributes and prices of different available online products and services and many more. E-tailing is another name of online retailing, which mainly aims at e-shopping by online users. Singla et al. explained e-shopping where consumers perform an exchange through a computer based interface while buyer's computer interact with digital retailer to buy anything over internet. E-retailing is still at very early stage in India and still is an unorganized sector with the third party business model and without proper big brand based e-retail market.

Though computer literacy in India had increased but only 100 million (indiatechonline.com) households had Personal Computers or laptops. Widespread geographical areas and lack of proper physical infrastructure had been causing problems to Indian government to provide internet connections in all urban rural cities that caused only 66 million broadband connections, 19 million wired and 47 million through mobile could be possible to spread over India. But with the increase in computer literacy and overcoming the mental blockage regarding technical know how to operate internet, India became the 3rd largest country in the world regarding number of online users with the database of 213 million as of the year 2013 a year-on-year growth of 28%, is expected to touch 243 million by June, 2014 though the penetration rate was only 19.19%. Among them 200 million were active internet users, around 140 million represented urban India and 60 million online users' belonged to rural India as of December, 2013. More rural participations in future are expected with the aid of affordable smart phones, optic fiber infrastructure and future usage of local language content in Indian portals (IAMAI). Indian online users gradually understood many benefits of e-retailing and got attracted towards many facilities offered by e-vendors.

Online population had overcome different mental barriers as socio-cultural conservativeness, feel and touch consumer behaviour, insecurity regarding exposing personal details like credit and debit card details over the internet etc. in Indian context and became much more practical, less sentimental and with much more information has been now accepting e-retailing model in a very fast way. With enough disposable income, fast lifestyles Indian online users had been executing impulse buying behaviour which is essential for online shopping in last few years, in turn causing actual online shopping which increased revenue earned from Indian e-tail market in India which had a positive effect on country's economy, govt. revenues, urban and rural development, industrial growth and created new employment opportunities. Online buying behaviour of Indians had been quite different from traditional one and this behaviour and purchase decision process had been influenced by many socio-cultural technical positive and negative aspects in Indian context. Indian social values and cultures had impacted Indian online shopping attitude hugely which is evident from the advertising campaigns of the popular e-tailers.

## E-Tailing in India: Unlocking the Potential

In India, e-tailing has the potential to grow more than hundredfold in the next 9 years to reach a value of USD 76 billion by the year 2021. The country's growing Internet-habituated consumer base, which will comprise approximately 180 million broadband users by 2020, along with a burgeoning class of mobile Internet users, will drive the e-tailing story. E-tailing can provide employment to approximately 1.45 million people by 2021. Its growth will spur the creation of new capabilities and human skills in the areas of logistics, packaging, and technology. Additionally, such growth will promote the rise of service entrepreneurs who will have the potential to earn approximately USD 7.5 billion, annually, by 2021. It will open up international markets for the SME sector and can become an important facilitator for the growth of the telecom and domestic air cargo industries.

In India, the retail market is, at present, primarily served by traditional brick & mortar stores which make up 93% of the total market. Corporatized brick & mortar retail caters to approximately 7%, while e-tailing's share is approximately 0.1%. In the coming decade, these three retail destinations will behave differently in terms of their share of total retail sales as shown in the above figure.

As per the Figure 1: A Snapshot of Indian Retail Market Size (Technopak Analysis, 2013) the total Retail Market size was estimated to be USD 490 Billion in 2012, which is estimated to reach USD

*Figure 1. A Snapshot of Indian retail market size (Technopak Analysis, 2013)*
*Source: Technopak Analysis, 2013*
** Retail market size for 2021 is at nominal growth*

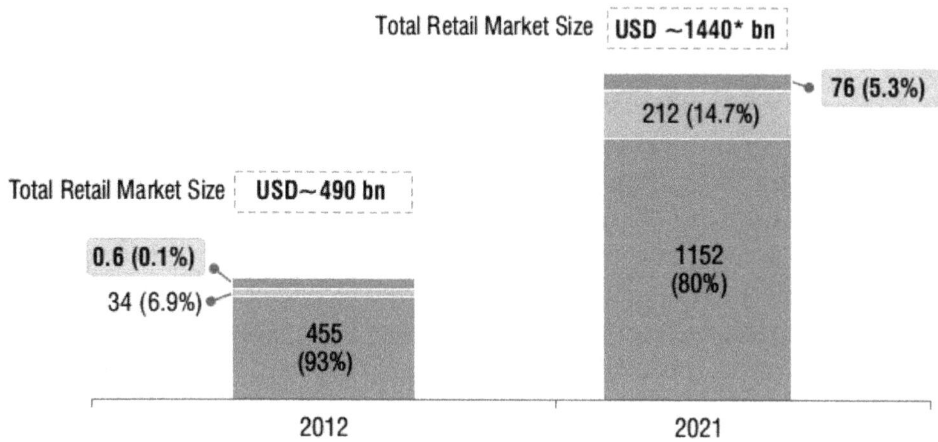


1440 Billion. Technopak estimates that, by 2021, the share of total corporatized retail, even in the best-case scenario, will increase from the current approximately 7% to 20%. This implies that, on one hand, private consumption will continue to grow annually at approximately 6%, in real terms (or 13% in nominal terms), while on the other hand traditional retail will still capture the bulk of the increase in consumption. In absolute terms, traditional retail will grow from USD 455 billion in 2012 to USD 1152 billion in 2021. The growth of traditional retail, in the current form, implies the growth of neighbourhood convenience stores in new urban centres and clusters, and the continued growth of informal retail (primarily of the Food & Grocery segment). Corporatized brick & mortar retail will increase in value from USD 34 billion to USD 212 billion by 2021, and its share of the total retail pie will just over double from the current approximately 7% to 14.7%. However, this type of brick & mortar retail will continue to face structural issues within the retailing ecosystem, which will be a challenge for retailers to address individually. The growth of e-tailing in India will be complementary to the growth of traditional retail, and in no way be at cross-purposes. On the contrary, it will improve efficiencies and reduce transaction costs in retailing and thereby boost the productivity of manufacturers (SMEs) and service providers. The potential of India's e-tailing will continue to remain untapped if the current mindset, of exclusion and seeing e-tailing as a "passing fad", prevails.

E-tailing is different from retail and therefore requires a different mindset and fresh thinking from the policy makers as well as the private sector. Thus we can summarize that the e-tailing boom can unleash tremendous potentialities in the future.

E-tailing will emerge as a viable third alternative by which corporatized retail can expand its share of the total retail pie. Technopak estimates that e-tailing in India will grow from the current USD 0.6 billion to USD 76 billion by 2021, i.e., more than hundredfold. The key reason for this disruptive growth lies in the fact that the market-enabling conditions and ecosystem creation for e-tailing will outpace the same for corporatized brick & mortar retail. This growth will offer many advantages to the Indian economy, besides bringing in immense benefits to consumers. In this light, it is imperative to have an objective debate on e-tailing. Unfortunately, the current debate on e-tailing has largely to do with e-tailing's current share of the total Indian retail pie, which is just approximately 0.1%.

In any country where e-tailing has achieved reasonable success, consumers have shown signs of evolution on two dimensions which has enabled e-tailing market's growth- access to the Internet and Internet usage beyond browsing. In India, consumers are displaying positive traction on both of these. In 2012, approximately 120 million Indian consumers accessed the Internet at least once a month (also referred to as active user base). This number is often critiqued for the quality of users. For instance, it is argued that very few (less than 15%) have access to the Internet via broadband (assuming that the number of users is equal to the number of broadband connections), and may thus be insignificant for e-tailing. This argument is not completely incorrect- the quality of Internet access does play a key role in enabling consumers to shop online. Therefore, it is important to look at access to the Internet in conjunction with the quality of access (which we will address in the subsequent point, along with how broadband access needs to be interpreted).

## The Internet-Habituated Consumer Base

The Internet browsing behaviour of Indians has dramatically changed in the past two years. This change has been almost disruptive - Indian consumers today are not only spending longer hours on the Internet, but also conducting myriad activities that were non-existent a few years ago. Internet browsing is becoming a habit for a sizeable population in urban India, i.e. cities, towns, and semi-urban clusters

## E-Tailing Enabling Infrastructure

There are two key infrastructure elements which will enable the growth of e-tailing.

### Penetration of Devices through Which to Access the Internet

The access to the Internet requires Internet-supporting devices, which can be broadly classified into PCs/laptops, mobile phones (smart phones), and tablets. The penetration of these devices is rapidly increasing .The usage of laptops and PCs is growing steadily, driven by increasing affordability and need. By the year 2020, it is projected that 150 million users will have either a laptop or a PC. However, a disruptive change is expected to be brought about by the proliferation of smart devices, i.e. smart phones and tablets. In 2012, India had over 900 million mobile subscriptions across 380 million mobile phone users. By the year 2020, mobile phone users are projected to increase to approximately 600 million. However, these mobile phone users will switch from feature phones (phones that lack data processing capability) to smart phones (phones that can process data). This will happen because of the availability of good quality smart phones at sub INR 5000 (approximately USD 100) price points. The penetration of tablets will also follow a similar trend. Currently, there are 4 million tablet users, but an equal number is getting added every year. If the trend continues, there will be 36 million tablet users by 2020. However, if tablet makers break the price barrier and make a functional tablet available at under USD 100, then the number of tablet users in India will increase manifold by 2020.

### Proliferation of Technologies Enabling Internet Access

Currently, India has nearly 24 million wired Internet subscribers comprising broadband and narrowband subscribers. Broadband connections (> 256 kbps) are 1.6 times more than narrowband connections (<

256 kbps). Often, broadband access to the Internet (approximately 15 million connections) is critiqued for having a low base relative to India's population. This is also cited as a bottleneck to e-tailing's growth. There are two key dimensions of analysis.

One is that broadband connections comprise subscriptions by households, educational institutions, public access areas, and small and medium scale enterprises. This does not include Internet access via leased lines to big corporations and government institutions.

Second, each broadband connection provides access to more than one person (referred to as user connection ratio). Households have a lower ratio compared to educational institutions or access points in public areas. At an overall level, each broadband connection provides access to four Internet users (excluding public access points). This implies that there are 60 million Indians who have access to the Internet through broadband.

The role of Mobile Internet is also very vital Internet access through mobile phones surpassed desktop-based Internet traffic in August 2012, in India. An estimated 30% of all online shopping queries were made through mobile phones in 2012. India, the second largest mobile phone market in the world, is poised to record a manifold increase in the penetration of high speed Internet, primarily driven by the rollout of 3G and 4G wireless technology. 3G services are a key driver of Internet access through mobile phones, providing high data speeds for downloads, content streaming, making video calls, etc.

## REVIEW OF LITERATURE

In today's world business houses use online business as one of the major marketing tools to increase their revenues and capture lion share of the market in a quick and effective way. Indian ecommerce and E-tailing market is growing but with a slow pace as compared to other developed global online markets. It is important to know the positive and negative influencing factors behind Indian online actual behaviour. With regard to the above a review of some relevant literature is as follows:

According to Turban (2006), e-tailing is defined as retailing conducted online, over the internet. Wang (2002) has provided a broad definition of e-tailing by defining it as the selling of goods and services to the consumer market via the internet. Zeithaml (2002) has defined that the success of e-tailing depends on the efficient web site design, effective shopping and prompt delivery. The other e-store services are delivery on real time, return and replacement process, period of filling out online orders form, speed of response time to e-customers queries. Ratchford (2001) opines that through Internet, consumers can gather information about merchandise and they compare a product across suppliers at a low cost. E-commerce offers increased market activity for retailers in the form of growing market access and information and decreased operating and procurement costs.

Myerson (1998) expressed that consumers are getting smarter in using e-tailers (and online search engines and agents) for convenience and comparison shopping. Guttmann (1998) describes several unique elements make online shopping different from the traditional in-store retail model. Besides offering convenience and expanded product variety, the online model also makes it easy for consumers to access and compare data from multiple sources. Meeker (1997), retailers might cry foul, but the new shopping paradigm they have to face is that as premium customers begin to accept the e-tail alternative in larger numbers. Hansen, J. V. (2001) in his study highlighted the fact that when a corporation begins exchanging business transactions over the internet, the internet becomes part of the corporate computer network, and then the scope of security concerns expands significantly. A variety of useful security software is available for controlling unauthorized intrusion, data corruption, and other potential vulnerabilities.

Bush et al., (2000) in his study provided initial insight as to marketer's perceptions of ethics and marketing on the Internet. The major impediment to business is the issue of security and privacy. The result showed that perceptions about security were still a major concern and that these perceptions insights be difficult to change. Over 80% of the respondents in his study indicated that organizations should develop a code of ethics for the Internet.

Sahoo, S.C. et al., (2010) in their study identified six decision–making styles in Indian environment. These are price consciousness, quality consciousness, recreational, confused by over choice, novelty consciousness and variety seeking. They do not confirm other four dimensions proposed i.e. fashion consciousness, brand consciousness, impulsiveness and brand loyalty. Young consumers between the age group of 11-20 years are most recreational in their shopping.

Rao, A.S. et al., (2010) in their study indicated that development of information technology and the growth of the communication network have radically transformed the local networks and connected them to international markets. Online buyers could gain the ability to search for products not on display, gather information without taking up are the salesperson's time and even purchase or pay for products for immediate delivery. When conducting online shopping security, reliability and trust are the factors which restrict the employees to go online.

Murugavel, D.M.V. (2010) concluded that Indian market and their reports have gone away. Many companies, who have entered both e-tailing and direct retailing based on their reports, are winding up their operations. The online retailing raises more issue them the benefits it currently offers.

The quality of products offered on line and procedures for service delivery are yet to be standardized although e-tailing has lagged in India, but hopefully in future, it would see a lot more actions as internet habit of Indian online users is on a rise and many factors are in favor of its growth.

## CRITICAL EVALUATION OF BUSINESS ENVIRONMENT FOR E-RETAILING IN INDIA

The country's Internet retailing market will reach 2 billion by 2014 with consumer electronics, toys and games growing the fastest. The travel segment sales will grow at a compound annual growth rate of nearly 38% in five year from 2009, and total $5.7 billion in 2014, according to Euro monitor. The number of active internet user rose to 52 million in Sep, 2009 from 42 million in sept, 2008 registering year- on-year growth of 19%. Claimed user (those who said they had used the internet in some from say for checking results online, during the year) is an important category for understanding further web trends, the study added. The number of people who claimed to have used the internet in 2009 stood at 71 million. Internet usage has also gone up from 9.3hrs/week to 15.7 hours/weak, a steep 70% rise, the report said. This can be attributed to innovative contact delivery, better applications and its increased use for entertainment purposes, which comprises downloading music or videos, socializing through social networking sites and expressing one's own opinions and views through micro blogging and uses generated content sites, The people in smaller town are taking Internet seriously, for deeper engagement. The survey showed that 20 million Indians use internet everyday out of this 36% of all web users are from small town. The business environment of India is best suited for e-retailing.

## OBJECTIVES OF THE RESEARCH STUDY:

The chief objective of this research is to study the Electronic retailing boom that has emerged as a new avenue to consumers for shopping. Internet penetration spread across India at a faster rate, gaining attractiveness for online buying. E-retailers intend to take advantage on it in spite of impediment and escalated competition of e-tailing. Thus, this study is undertaken to assess the factors for growth and barriers of e-tailing in India. The other objectives are:

1. To identify the factors for growth of E-tailing in India
2. To examine the Barriers of E-tailing Market in India

It is evident from the above Figure 2: Proposed Model for the Success of E-Tailers in India the most critical areas for e-retailers are security concerns, collaborations and customizations. These factors are important as they contribute a lot for the development of e-retailing.

On the basis of proposed model, following strategies are suggested to the e-retailers:

The e-retailers should analyze the characteristics of the product before offering it through online. If the product characteristic does not suit the e-retail then they should prefer the physical retail stores. The retailers should have sufficient knowledge and know-how of the hardware and software being

*Figure 2. Proposed Model for the Success of E-Tailers in India*
*Source: Model Created by Authors Based on Review of Literature*

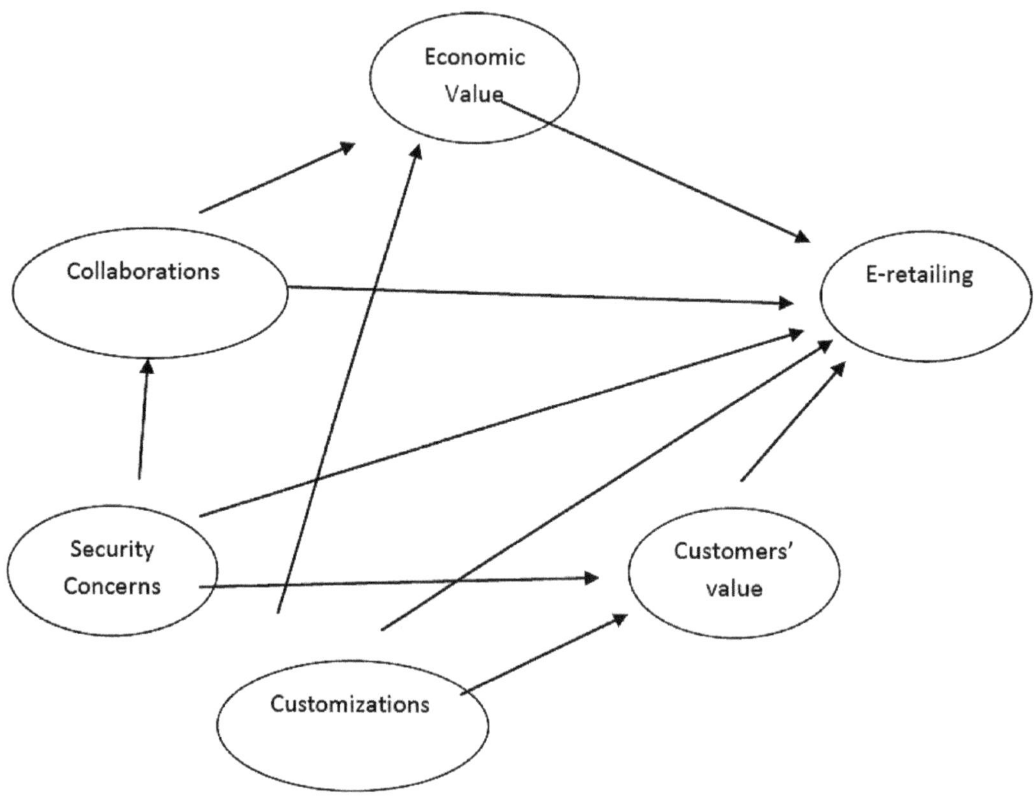

used, otherwise this can prove to be disastrous. Customer's attributes and attitudes should be taken into consideration before customization. Customization is very useful tool for providing customer value and economic value. Mostly, the firms have to collaborate with other service providers for e-retailing. The service providers should be chosen in a way that they are able to provide synergy effect. They should try to make e-shopping an enjoyable activity.

## MANAGERIAL IMPLICATIONS AND CONCLUDING REMARKS:

The current growth in e-tailing was driven by start-ups, and backed by venture capital and entrepreneurship. While the Indian e-tailing market is yet to achieve a steady state, these initial entrants have succeeded in capturing the imagination of a sizeable consuming class. These have also acted as a catalyst in the creation of an ecosystem necessary for the growth of e-tailing. E-tailing's potential cannot be tapped on the premise that investments by a few organizations will unlock this opportunity. Going forward, the projected size of e-tailing by 2021 will not be composed of pure e-tailing companies, as is largely the case today.

In this chapter the authors come up with the finding that e-tailing's opportunity will be captured by three set of corporate players:

- Some of the existing, pure e-tailing businesses will manage to build sustainable businesses and grow in size. Many new pure play e-tailing start-ups will also tap the market.
- Many of the current brick & mortar retailers (both traditional and corporatized) will succeed in viewing e-tailing not as an extension but as an important business growth driver.
- Similarly, many consumer brands will also build e-tailing businesses as a direct go-to-market approach.

E-tailing is an integrator of technology, logistics, and infrastructure, and creates a relatively efficient marketplace for vendors and consumers. At present, the Indian e-tailing market is limited by its incapability to play the role of an efficient integrator. This role has been played in other places by retailers, technology companies, venture capitalists, and private equity investors. Given the fact that the current share of corporatized retail is under 10%, and that the domestic venture capital industry is still in its infancy, policymakers will need to seek a rapprochement with investment and expertise from overseas players. E-tailing has to be viewed in the context of the profile of India that is poised to emerge over the next decade. This emerging India will comprise consumers who will have the desire, need, and conviction to use the Internet for a host of reasons, of which shopping will be one. E-tailing has been often clubbed with corporatized brick & mortar retail.

While there is no denial of the fact that it serves the same end purpose, it also cannot be denied that the entire ecosystem within which e-tailing operates is completely different from brick & mortar retail, as are its enablers. Therefore, it deserves to be considered on its own merit, instead of being clubbed with brick & mortar retail.

However, this leap of faith will not happen on its own. If e-tailing continues to be regarded by policymakers as being insignificant, and by business organizations as a "passing fad". E-tailing's current growth is like the birth of a new industry and akin to the birth of telecom and IT services in the 1990s. Both started small and recorded disruptive growth that changed our lives in many ways. In the E-tailing will have to be viewed as a vehicle that will drive efficiency, create new capabilities, and shun mediocrity. E-tailing possesses the potency to create new capabilities which India needs and offer viable employment to Indian youth over the next decade. It has the prowess to act as a catalyst and support the growth of new skills and industries. If e-tailing is ignored as a non-descript and trivial entity, it will be another case of a birth with congenital disorders, akin to brick & mortar retail.

## REFERENCES


Bush, V. D., Venable, B. T., & Bush, A. J. (2000). Ethics and Marketing on the Internet, Practitioners Perception of societal, Industry and company concerns. *Journal of Business Ethics*, *23*(3), 237–248. doi:10.1023/A:1006202107464

Digital Commerce Report (2014). Internet and Mobile Association of India [IAMAI].

Guttman, R. H., Moukas, A. G., & Maes, P. (1998). Agents as Mediators in Electronic Commerce. *International Journal of Electronic Markets*, *8*(2), 22–27. doi:10.1080/10196789800000007

Hansen, J.V. (2001). Internet commerce security: issues and models for control checking. Journal of the operational Research society, Industry and company concern, *52*(10), 1159-1164.

India Tech Online. (n. d.). Retrieved from http://www.indiatechonline.com

Meeker, M. (1997, May 28). The Internet Retailing Report. US Equity Investment Research Morgan Stanley.

Murugavel, D.M.V. (2010, August). E-tailing market scenario in India- A Bird's eye view. *Indian Journal of Marketing*.

Myerson, A. R. (1998, June 29). Comp USA: Revising Computer Retailing. *The New York Times*.

Rao, A.S., & Mehdi, M.M. (2010, July). Online user behaviour in Delhi- A factor analysis. *Indian Journal of Marketing*.

Rao, B. (1999). The Internet and the revolution in distribution: A cross-industry examination. *Technology in Society*, *21*(1), 287–306. doi:10.1016/S0160-791X(99)00018-4

Ratchford, B. T., Talukdar, D., & Lee, M. S. (2001). A model of consumer choice of the internet as an information source. *International Journal of Electronic Commerce*, *5*(3), 7–21.

Sahoo, S.C., & Dash, P.C. (2010, August). Consumer Decision Making Styles in Shopping malls- An empirical study in the Indian context. *Indian Journal of Marketing*.

Singla, B.B., Kumar, P., & Kaur, R. (2012). Online Shopping: An innovative tool of Google success.

Technopak report on E-tailing in India: Unlocking the Potential. (2013, May).

Tiernan, B. (2000). E-Tailing. Dearborn, Chicago.

Turban, E., & Gehrke, D. (2000). Determinants of e-commerce website. *Human Systems Management*, *19*, 111–120.

Turban, E., King, D., Lee, J., & Viehland, D. (2004). *Electronic Commerce A managerial perspective* (International ed.). Prentice Hall.

Wang, F., & Head, M. (2002). e-tailing: An analysis of web impacts on the retail market. *Journal of Business Strategies*, *19*(1), 73.

Wang, M. (2003). Assessment of E-Service Quality via E-Satisfaction in e-commerce globalization. *EJISDC*, *11*(10), 1–4.

Zeithaml, V. A. (2002). Service excellent in electronic channels. *Managing Service Quality*, *12*(3), 135–138. doi:10.1108/09604520210429187

## KEY TERMS AND DEFINITIONS

**E- Business:** E-business (electronic business) is the conduct of business processes on the Internet.

**E-Commerce:** E-commerce (electronic commerce or EC) is the buying and selling of goods and services, or the transmitting of funds or data, over an electronic network, primarily the Internet.

**E-Services:** An umbrella term for services on the Internet. E-services include e-commerce transaction services for handling online orders, application hosting by application service providers (ASPs) and any processing capability that is obtainable on the Web.

**E-Shopping:** It is Online shopping (sometimes known as **e**-tail from "electronic retail" or **e**-shopping) is a form of electronic commerce which allows consumers to directly buy goods or services from a seller over the Internet using a web browser.

**E-Tailing:** It is the selling of retail goods on the Internet. It is a Short form of "electronic retailing," The term seems an almost inevitable addition to e-mail, e-business, and e-commerce. E-tailing is synonymous with business-to consumer (B2C) transaction.

**Internet:** It is defined as a global computer network providing a variety of information and communication facilities, consisting of interconnected networks using standardized communication protocols.

**Multi-Channel Retailing:** Multi-channel retailing is a marketing strategy that offers your customers a choice of ways to buy products. A true multi-channel strategy covers purchases from a store, purchases from a website, telephone ordering, mail orders, interactive television, catalog ordering and comparison shopping sites. The aim of a multi-channel retailing strategy is to maximize revenue and loyalty by offering your customers choice and convenience.

Section 3

# Virtual Communities:
## The People Power in E-Retailing

# Chapter 7
# Harnessing the Potential of Virtual Communities:
## A Strategic Approach

**Dharmendra Pandey**
*Amity University, India*

## ABSTRACT

*We are living in a knowledge oriented society where empowered and well informed customers can participate, collaborate, disseminate, and channelize information and opinion among other stakeholders of an organization. Today, we have system and tools through which we can tap the expertise of a virtual group to make rational decisions. Social commerce is enabling collaborative publishing and facilitating in management of common databases for sharing knowledge. A Virtual community is a group of people with some shared interest who connect and interact with each other over a period of time using technology. A Social software regulates the activities of the participants. Prospective customers and existing consumers join these communities because they provide multifaceted opportunities and leanings to the participants. The aim of this exploratory research is to develop strategic approach to virtual communities for effective online community management and user engagement for sustainable growth.*

## 1. INTRODUCTION

Human is a social animal and we strive to look for all possible options to satisfy our social needs. We influence or get influenced at a point of time when we look for a reference point. After the advent of internet, our society has moved from individual intelligence to collective intelligence system. This fact becomes more evident when a prospective customer look for online places for a product or a service review to take a final purchase decision.

Virtual communities are social aggregations that emerge from the internet when people carry on those public discussions long enough, with sufficient human feeling, to form webs of personal relationships in cyberspace (Rheingold H., 2000).

DOI: 10.4018/978-1-4666-9921-2.ch007

Copyright © 2016, IGI Global. Copying or distributing in print or electronic forms without written permission of IGI Global is prohibited.

A Virtual community is a group of people with some shared interest who connect and interact with each other over a period of time using technology. A Social software regulates the activities of the participants.

Prospective customers and existing consumers join these communities because they provide multi-faceted opportunities and leanings to the participants.

The concept "virtual" implies that some of the traditional properties of a community is no longer a part of the "real" world. Instead that property is only virtual, which means that it looks, sounds or feels "as if" it were real but is not (Coyne, 1995; Benedict, 1991)

Virtual communities are sources of information about customer interests, trends, preferences and new product or service ideas.

Virtual communities have gained much attention from marketing professionals and researchers because they have potential to affect conversions and sales through positive word of mouth. Virtual communities are converting prospects in to customers by providing relevant product inputs through reference groups at the right time. Presence of brands in these virtual communities can greatly impact the overall profitability of a firm through effective relationship building, getting new product ideas through community based innovations.

Corporates like Micromax, a leading smartphone brand in India, crowdsourced suggestions to select a brand name for its upcoming smartphone model "Yuphoria" over virtual communities. Micromax received 1 lac entries during the campaign which resulted in positive word of mouth and ultimately good sales (see figure 1).

Consumers join these forums because it's a platform providing multifaceted opportunities to its members. Organizations can harness user generated content generating through likeminded opinion leaders to product improvement, co-creation and ultimately self-disclosure reciprocity.

## 2. OBJECTIVE

The aim of this exploratory research is to develop strategic approach to virtual communities for effective online community management and Co-creation on cross platforms for sustainable growth.

*Figure 1. Micromax Yuphoria: Crowdsourcing through virtual communities*
*Source:* gadgtes.ndtv.com

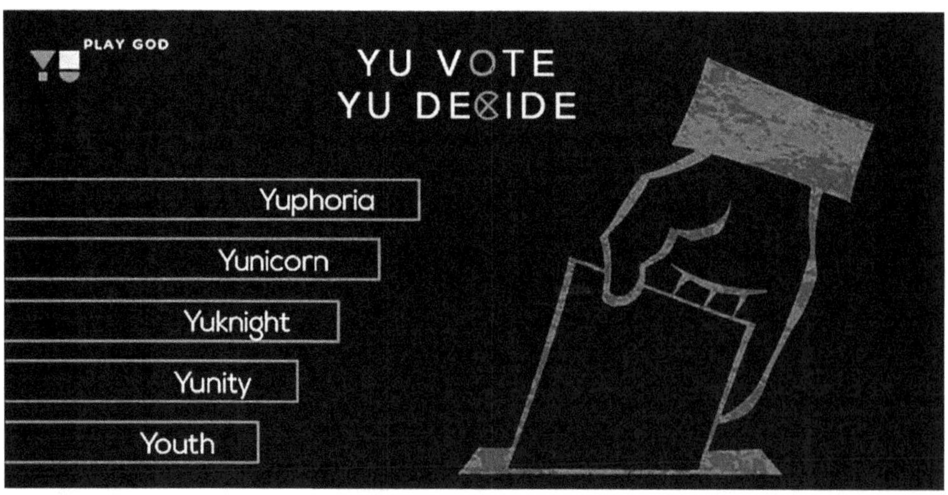

## 3. LITERATURE REVIEW

### 3.1.1. Definitions

Some key definitions by different scholars are listed below:

A. Virtual communities are social aggregations that emerge from the Internet when enough people carry on public discussions long enough, with sufficient human feeling, to form webs of personal relationships in cyberspace (Howard, 1993).
B. "Virtual Community" is a community consists of people with shared interests or goals and for whom electronic communication is a primary form of interaction (Dennis, Pootheri, & Natarajan, 1998).
C. Virtual Communities are computer mediated spaces where there is a potential for an integration of content and communication with an emphasis on member generated content (Hagel & Armstrong, 1997).
D. A Virtual community is technology mediated, persistent, environment which supports multiple interaction styles, capability for real time interaction and multi user engagement (Ho, chraefel and Chignell, 2000).
E. A virtual community can be an ideal place to ask relative strangers about information. Virtual communities tend to focus on very specific topics with relationships among members being mostly intended for information exchange about specific topics (Baym, 2000)

### 3.1.2. Classifications

Some noted classifications of Virtual Communities are listed below:

A. Virtual communities deals with human relationships and these relationships can be commercial and non-commercial (Howard Rheingold 1993, 2000)
B. Based on buying motives, a virtual community can be Consumer focused or it can be B2B focused (Hagel & Armstrong, 1997)
C. Virtual communities can be also be classified on the basis of its functioning and active memberships. We can have Non-profit and Profit as well as Company and Non-Company Virtual communities.
D. Based on the community elements like content, event and interaction classification can be: B2C, B2B, E2E (Cotheral, 2000; Warms, Cothrel & Underberg, 2000)

### 3.2. Features of Virtual Communities

Maximum cited features of virtual communities are:

A. **Participation/ Collaboration:** A new type communities is gaining momentum and acceptance on the web and which is shaping collaboration and online communication patterns and the way information is consumed and produced (Kolbitsch & Maurer, 2006).

B. **Emotional Attachment/ Loyalty:** It implies the member's attachment and relationships within virtual communities. (Blanchard, A.L., 2004). A virtual community sometimes act as a moral and emotional support. Sense of loyalty and belongingness can be possible outcomes.

C. **Reciprocity:** People discovering and sharing similar problems, requirements, experiences or opinions may feel closer and trusting without any perceived tangible gains.

D. **Period of Association within a Virtual Community:** It implies duration of association between participant and a virtual community.

## 3.3. Related Research

Earlier researches quoted the word "community" as a geographic area like a neighborhood (Well man & Gulia, 1999). Addition of "virtual" in the term means the primary mode of interaction is technology and without a physical place (Handy, 1995).

### 3.3.1. Motivation to Join a Virtual Community

Humans have a need to belong and be affiliated with others (Watson & Johnson, 1972). The implied reason is that the groups:

- Provide source of information and help in achieving goals (Watson & Johnson, 1972)
- Give rewards (Thibaut & Kelly, 1959)

According to social identity theory (Tajfel, 1978; Hogg, 1996; Turner, 1985)

People form a social identity of attitudes, values and behavioral intentions from the perceived membership in distinct self-inclusive real or imagery social groups.

### 3.3.2. Online Business Communities

Online business communities helps in effective customer relationship management and create opportunities for cross & up selling. The virtual communities creates entry barriers for competitors and exit barriers for customers (O Malley & Tynan, 2000).

Social commerce facilitated by virtual communities impacting receptivity towards other promotional cues as more and more customers are coming online for price search.

The large amount of information about pricing, competitors, and features available on the Internet also helps to create a cost transparent environment. This severely impairs a seller's ability to obtain high margins, because it turns products and services into commodities, and may damage company reputations by creating perceptions of price unfairness (Campbell C. Margaret, 1999).

### 3.3.3. Online Communities and Co-Creation

The process of community development goes hand in hand with product development (Beata, Leeming, Rowley, & Kupiec, 2007)

The business online communities facilitates engagement programs and processes among all stakeholders and help in creating unique value by providing excellent support in the entire process of co creation.

In the present scenario the locus of co-creation and innovation has shifted from products and services to "experience environments". It has become inevitable for businesses to respond to the needs and requirements of the experienced consumer.

## 4. STRATEGIC APPROACH TO VIRTUAL COMMUNITIES: (REFER FIGURE 2)

Virtual communities are the subset of Social commerce where consumers interact, collaborate, and exchange feedback, reviews, ideas within a community. Consumer participating in these communities may have these objectives:

- To get information
- To find entertainment value
- To find transactional value and
- Relationship building.

Strategically, an organization can host a virtual community on its own official websites or can create a community on the social media platforms, blogs, and forums etc. where the unique visitor's traffic is high.

### 4.1. Discussion Agenda Creation

It implies the area or topic of discussion within a community. It need to be categorically defined in sync with the organizational and community objectives.

Companies need to seed discussion agenda, moderate out negative comments and promote positive word of mouth in a virtual community.

First, an organization can provide community facilities on its own website, or it can monitor and become involved in relevant communities set up by other organizations including social media platforms. If a company sets up a community facility on its site, it has the advantage that it can improve its brand by adding value to its products. Sterne (1999) suggests that minimal intrusion should occur for better transparency, but it may be necessary for the company to seed discussion and moderate out some negative comments which may affect brand image. It may also be instrumental in increasing word of-mouth promotion of the site. (Refer Figure 2).

### 4.2. Degree of Control over Moderation Activities

Facility for free speech is inevitable in an online community but at the same time it need to be moderated for better control and to channelize discussions around the agenda to get productive outcomes in the form of ideas and suggestions. Moderation can be done at root level or at community level depending on the website where it has been hosted. In the case of an online community hosted at official website, degree of control would be high. That means admin and moderation rights can be restored and thus the

*Figure 2. Strategic approach to virtual communities*

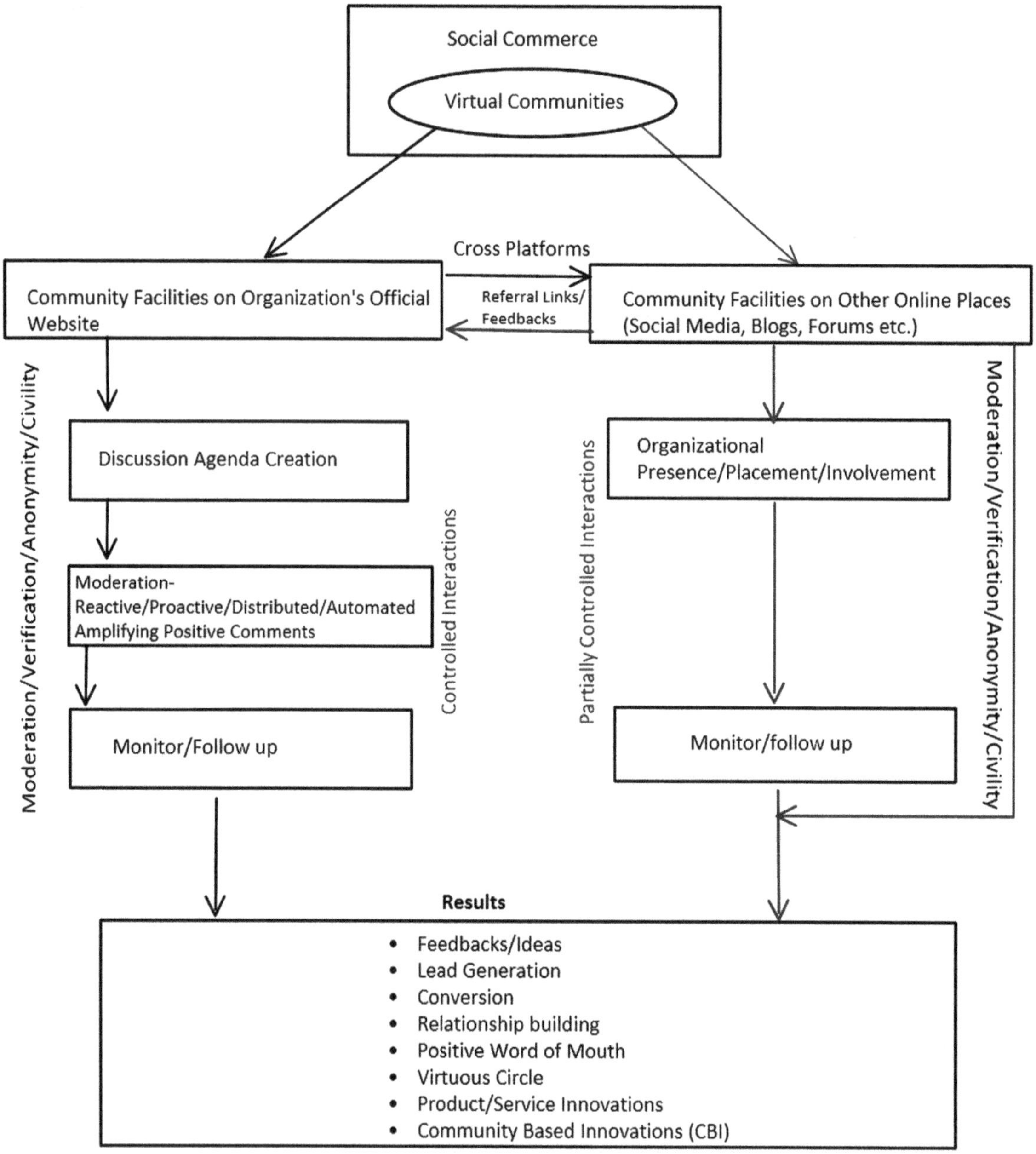


organizations have a better control over the interactions. It becomes important to handle negative comments over an issue which may go viral. Permission to the anonymous posts lies to the moderator and it depend on the level of verification required at the community level. (Refer Figure 3)

- **Moderation (Reactive/Proactive/Distributed/Automated):** Each and every comment goes for moderation to check suitability as per community guidelines laid down by the website. Possibility of degree of moderation can be high for community facilities provided at organization's own

*Figure 3. Degree of control over Moderation activities*

| | Degree of control | | | |
|---|---|---|---|---|
| | **Moderation** | **Verification** | **Anonymous Posts** | **Civility** |
| **Virtual Comunity at Organization's own website** | High | High | High | High |
| **Virtual Community at other places** | Low - Medium | Low-Medium | Low | Low |

website. For example, Dell operates virtual forums on its website as well as on other popular unofficial places. It has well-structured forum on third party sites which brings lots of traffic for the official website.

There are four important ways of doing moderation a) Reactive: using flags to differentiate good vs bad comments. b) Proactive: Following a suspicious activity and conversation to track down at the right time. c) Distributed: Provide user controlled rating system to find irrelevant and inappropriate comments. d) Automated: Use of software to moderate out obscene or irrelevant words from the conversations.

- **Verification:** Negative comments can have compounding effect on negative perception building towards a brand. Primary objective of an editor or a moderator is to verify the commenter, omit bad comments and amplify the good ones to get positive communications impact.

For better implementation, organizations need to have documented community guidelines and should have a team of moderators and editors who screen each comments on parameters like credentials, language, content, civility etc as per guidelines.

- **Anonymity:** Anonymous comments contribute a lot in search engine visibility of any website because they generate lots of keywords through user generated content. On the other hand, negative comments by an anonymous user on unofficial virtual community page can lead to intangible and tangible loss to the brand. Due to low level of moderation and verification possibility on unofficial community page, it's a challenge to control the message and its impact on its members.
- **Civility:** Voices raised need to be heard respectfully. It's all about being disagree without disrespect. For any organization, the general code of conduct pertaining to social interactions in a virtual community becomes inevitable as it may affect objectives and image of the forum. Moderators and editors play a key role here.

## 4.3. Outcomes

On both the platforms under the controlled and partially controlled interactions, an organization can achieve positive conversions, relationship building, loyalty, product / service innovations, feedbacks, ideas etc. Referral links on cross platforms play a vital role in search engine optimizations and to spread positive word of mouth.

## 5. HARNESSING COLLECTIVE AND COLLABORATIVE INTELLIGENCE: (CASE OF DELL INC.)

Collaborative intelligence is the representation of collaborative ability of an entity or a group. Organizations can become sustainable and unique by promoting better collaboration, innovation through maintaining relationships in knowledge intensive activities.

Computer giant Dell effectively manages virtual communities on cross platforms including a community based innovations (CBI) page at www.Ideastorm.com, official virtual community page hosted at community.dell.com along with community page at social media platforms like Facebook, Twitter etc. for effective collaborative exchanges (Refer Figure 4, 5 & 6).

Dell is using virtual communities focused on product development and after successful trials to implement the ideas into other areas Dell started Idea Storm, a virtual community launched in 2007 where existing and potential consumers can submit ideas to the brand.

According to Kerry Bridge, head of digital media communications EMEA and global public sector, Idea Storm has had 14,000 ideas submitted since launch, of which 4,000 were implemented and 700,000 votes on ideas.

Dell follows Co-creation process through below mentioned steps:

- Build, manage and integrate platforms for Interaction
- Aware and Inspire a target audience to participate in Co-Creation
- Involve key people of the firm in the process of Co-creation
- Gain Insight into customer activity and experience
- Foster generation of breakthrough/innovative ideas
- Initiate actions on selected ideas and follow up.

*Figure 4. Dell Community page- IdeaStorm.com to promote Community Based Innovations (CBI)*

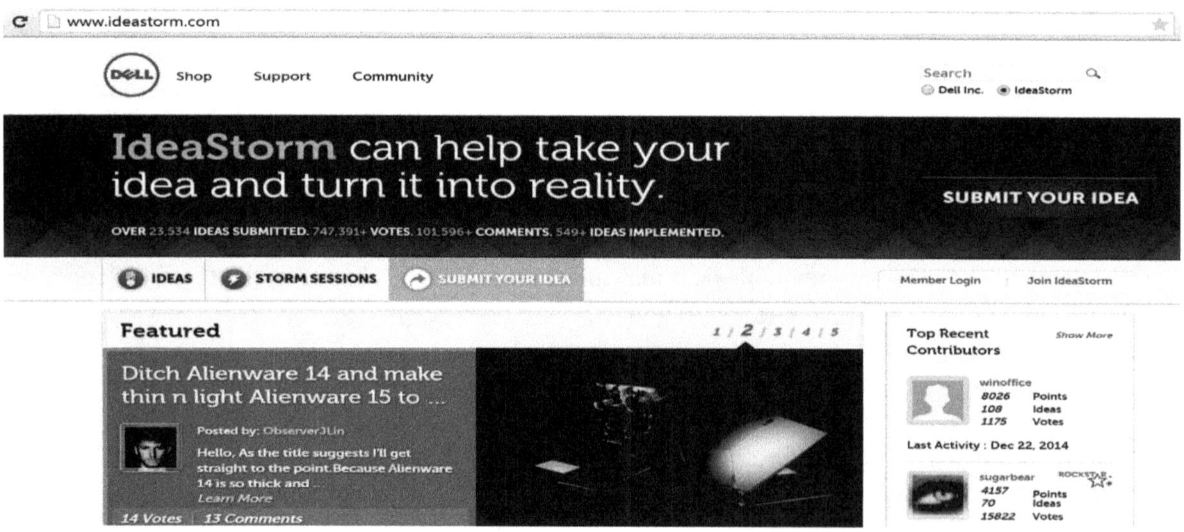

*Figure 5. Community Page hosted at Dell.com*

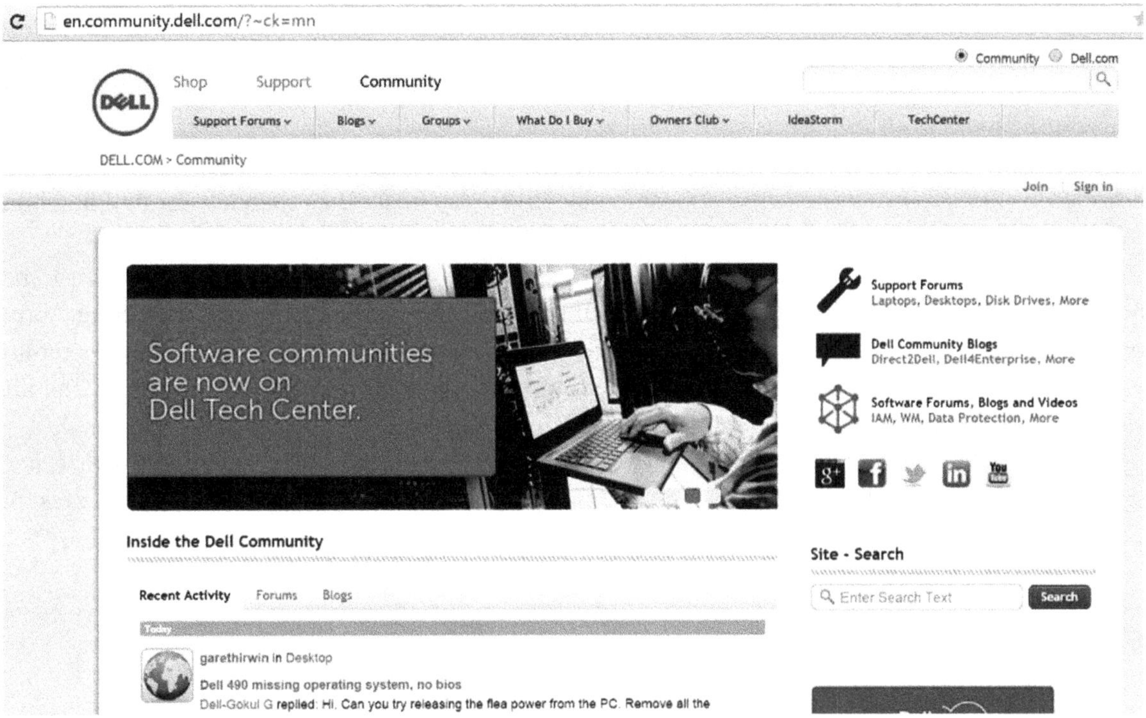


*Figure 6. Dell Online Community Page hosted at Facebook.com*

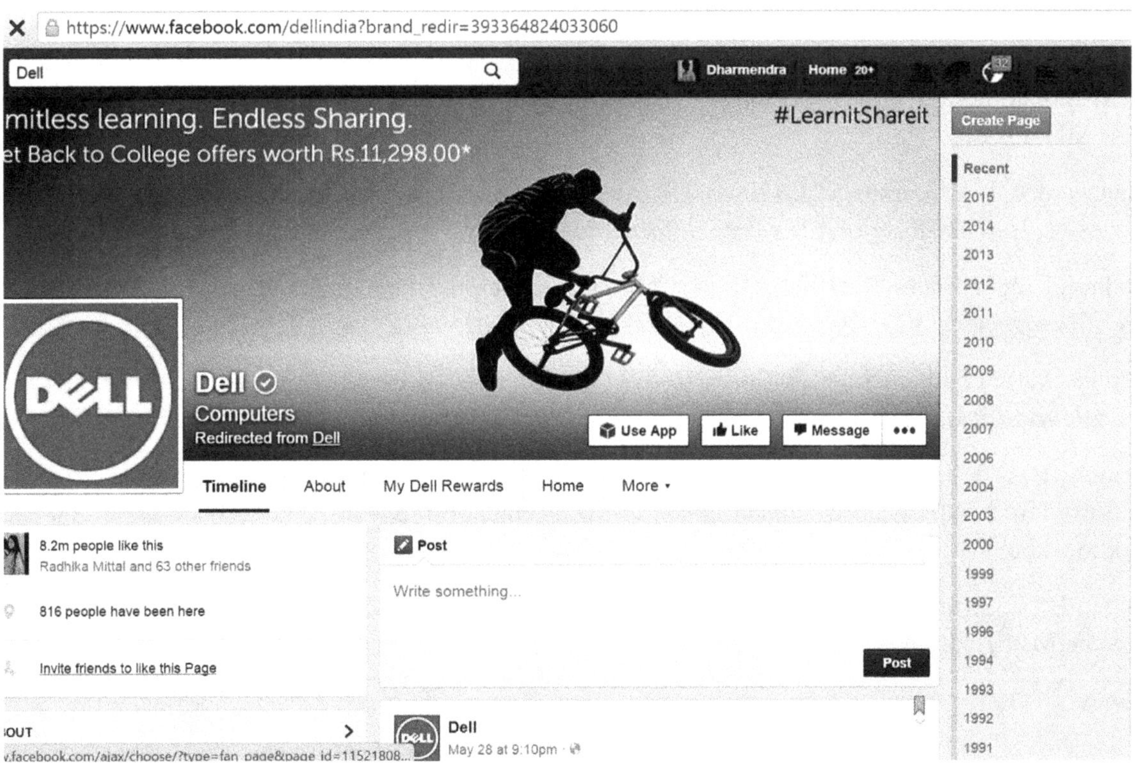

## 6. CONCLUSION

Virtual communities are web based communities with purpose of interests, transaction, fantasy or relationship. They have no physical boundaries and witnessing exponential increase in consumer participations across globe.

Virtual communities can be a worthy strategic tool through which an organization can maintain customer loyalty, achieve customer relationship objectives, can be used as channels for building brand image and can be effectively used as WOM tool.

Organizations can integrate virtual communities with their websites to differentiate their customers and personalized their relationships through e-mail response management or e-mail marketing. Virtual communities can play an important role in crowdsourcing activities and to get and new ideas through community based innovations. They can also help to improve product or service processes and after sales services to achieve better conversions and sustainable growth.

Co-creation through harnessing collaborative intelligence derived from all stakeholders with technology in place is the need of the hour. Businesses have to be present on all platforms and have to respond to experienced customers.

## REFERENCES


Armstrong, A., & Hagel, J. (1996). The real value of on-line communities. *Harvard Business Review*, *74*(3), 134–141.

Baym, N. K. (2000). *Tune in, log on: Soaps, fandom and online community*. Thousand Oaks: Sage Publications, Inc.

Blanchard, A. L. (2004). The effects of dispersed virtual communities on face-to-face social capital. In M. Huysman & V. Wulf (Eds.), *Social Capital and Information Technology* (pp. 53–74). Cambridge, MA: MIT Press.

Blanchard, A. L., & Markus, M. L. (2004). The experienced sense of a virtual community: Characteristics and processes. *The Data Base for Advances in Information Systems*, *35*(1), 65–79. doi:10.1145/968464.968470

Cothrel, J., & Williams, R. (1999). Online Communities helping them form and grow. *Journal of Knowledge Management*, *3*(1), 54–60. doi:10.1108/13673279910259394

Dennis, A. R., Pootheri, S. K., & Natarajan, V. L. (1998). Lessons from the early adopters of Web groupware. *Journal of Management Information Systems*, *14*(4), 65–86. doi:10.1080/07421222.1998.11518186

Grimes, B. (2010, December 6). 6 types of content moderation you need to know about. *BlaiseGV*. Retrieved from http://blaisegv.com/community-management/6-types-of-content-moderation-you-need-to-know-about/

Hagel, H., & Armstrong, A. G. (1997). *Net Gain: Expanding Markets through Virtual Communities*. Boston, MA: Harvard Business School Press.

Handy, C. (1995). Trust and the virtual organization. *Harvard Business Review*, *73*(3), 40–48.

Hogg, M. A. (1996). Group structure and social identity. In W. P. Robinson (Ed.), *Social groups and identities: Developing the legacy of Henri Tajfel* (pp. 65–94). UK: Butterworth-Heinemann.

Jones, S. G. (1995). Understanding community in the information age. In S. G. Jones (Ed.), *Cyber Society: Computer-mediated communication and community* (pp. 10–35). London: Sage Publications.

Kolbitsch, J., & Maurer, H. (2006). The Transformation of the Web: How Emerging Communities Shape the Information We Consume. *Journal of Universal Computer Science*, *12*(2), 187–213.

Kozinets, R. (1999). E-tribalized marketing: The strategic implications of virtual communities of consumption. *European Management Journal*, *17*(3), 252–264. doi:10.1016/S0263-2373(99)00004-3

Kozinets, R. V. (2002). The Field Behind the Screen: Using Netnography for Marketing Research in Online Communities. *Journal*, *39*(4), 61–72.

Malhotra, J.D., & Kumar, K. (Eds.), (1997, December). Evolution of a virtual community: Understanding design issues through a longitudinal study. *Proceedings of the Eighteenth International Conference on Information Systems*, Atlanta, GA, USA.

Margaret, C. C. (1999). Perceptions of Price Unfairness: Antecedents and Consequences. *JMR, Journal of Marketing Research*, *36*(2), 187–199. doi:10.2307/3152092

Meyer, H.K., & Carey, M.C. (2013). In moderation, journalism. *Practice*. doi:10.1080/17512786.2013.859838

O'Malley, L., & Tynan, C. (2000). Relationship marketing in consumer markets: Rhetoricor reality. *European Journal of Marketing*, *34*(1), 717–815.

Offitzer, A. (2014, May 29). Future of comments section: moderated and annotated. *AJR.com*. Retrieved from http://ajr.org/2014/05/29/future-comment-sections-moderated-annotated/

Othmani, L., & Bouslama, N. (2014, February 14). *The Relationship between Virtual Community and Perceived Risk in the Social-Commerce: An Exploratory Study.*

Pandey, D. (2011, August 11). Electronic commerce to social commerce. *Dharmendrapandey.com*. Retrieved from http://www.dharmendrapandey.com/2011/08/electronic-commerce-to-social-commerce_11.html

Rheingold, H. (1993). *The Virtual Community: Homesteading on the Electronic Frontier*. New York: Harper Collins.

Rowley, J., & Kupiec, T. (2007). Customer community and co creation: A case study. *Marketing Intelligence & Planning*, *25*(2), 136–146. doi:10.1108/02634500710737924

Shirin, A. (2012). Customer relationship management and customer experience management using business online communities. *JIIT.* Retrieved from http://www.jiit.ac.in/uploads/Synopsis%20-%20Shirin%20Alavi.pdf

Tajfel, H. (1978). Social categorization, social identity and social comparison. In H. Tajfel (Ed.), *Differentiation between social groups* (pp. 61–76). UK: Academic Press.

Thibaut, J. W., & Kelley, H. H. (1959). *The social psychology of groups*. New York: John Wiley & Sons.

Turner, J. C. (1978). Social comparison, similarity and ingroup favouritism. In H. Tajfel (Ed.), *Differentiation between social groups* (pp. 233–250). UK: Academic Press.

Turner, J. C. (1985). Social categorization and the self-concept: A social cognitive theory of group behavior. In E. L. Lawler (Ed.), Advances in group processes (Vol. 2, pp. 77-122). UK: JAI Press Inc.

Watson, G., & Johnson, D. (1972). *Social psychology: Issues and insights*. Philadelphia: J. B. Lippincott.

Wellman, B. (1996, April). For a social network analysis of computer networks: A sociological perspective on collaborative work and virtual community. *Paper presented at the SIGCPR/SIGMIS*, Denver, CO. doi:10.1145/238857.238860

Wellman, B., & Gulia, M. (1999). Virtual communities as communities. In M. A. Smith & P. Kollock (Eds.), *Communities in cyberspace* (pp. 167–194). New York: Routledge.

# Chapter 8
# Opinion Leaders Go Online:
## An Empirical Study on Interpersonal Influence on Purchase Intentions in E-Retailing.

**Agostino Vollero**
*University of Salerno, Italy*

**Alfonso Siano**
*University of Salerno, Italy*

**Domenico Sardanelli**
*University of Salerno, Italy*

## ABSTRACT

*"Social influence" in innovative e-retailing environments increasingly seems to have an important impact on online buying behavior. This chapter addresses this issue, focusing on the role of online opinion leaders. The opinion leadership construct has been associated with innovative behavior as well as with the early adoption of electronic shopping technologies. Despite these assumptions, little is known about online opinion leaders and their characteristics in e-retailing environments. The aim of the chapter is twofold: to identify the main features of opinion leaders in digital contexts and, by means of an exploratory empirical study, to analyse whether they have an impact on the purchase decisions of high involvement products, by explaining from where opinion leaders derive their skills.*

## INTRODUCTION

The advances of the Internet toward a "social web" configuration are beginning to have a major impact on the dynamics of purchase decisions in digital environments. Social media technologies provide a high number of platforms, such as blogs, forums, social network sites, and reputation systems where consumers can interact with each other through the dissemination of opinions regarding companies/brands and their products (Bodendorf & Kaiser, 2009; Kang & Johnson, 2013; Shi & Wojnicki, 2014).

DOI: 10.4018/978-1-4666-9921-2.ch008

Copyright © 2016, IGI Global. Copying or distributing in print or electronic forms without written permission of IGI Global is prohibited.

This is a growing area of importance particularly for e-retailing, as "social influence" seems to have a major impact on online buying behavior within Web 2.0. This chapter addresses this issue, focusing on the role of online opinion leaders.

Opinion leaders are generally considered as being crucial figures in studies on interpersonal communication, as they exert personal influence on their own informal community, above all in the domain in which their peers consider them to be experts (Katz, 1957; Childers, 1986; Flynn, Goldsmith & Eastman, 1996). The opinion leadership construct has been associated with innovative behavior (Rogers, 1983; Venkatraman, 1989; Goldsmith & Hofacker, 1991; Eastlick, 1993) as well as with the early adoption of electronic shopping technologies (O'Cass & Fenech, 2003).

Despite these assumptions, little is known about online opinion leaders and their characteristics in the e-retailing environment. The aim of the chapter is thus twofold: to identify the main features of opinion leaders and to study their current role in the online environment, analyzing whether they have an impact on the decisions of other consumers to purchase high involvement products.

The remainder of the chapter is organized as follows. We begin by describing the conceptual foundations of the main constructs considered here, namely opinion leadership and market mavenship. We then discuss the role of opinion leaders in digital contexts and define objectives of the chapter. The chapter next focuses on an empirical research study on the impact of different sources of information on the purchasing behavior of a smartphone in a simulated online setting. Several differences were found between the buying intentions of different types of consumers (opinion leaders, non-leaders, etc.). Finally the implications, research challenges and concluding remarks are presented in the last two sections.

## CONCEPTUAL BACKGROUND

The literature on opinion leadership is vast and crosses the borders of many disciplines in the social sciences. The origins of this concept can be traced back to the "two-step flow communication theory" of Katz and Lazarsfeld (1955) and the subsequent multi-step theories (e.g., Robinson, 1976; Windahl, Signitzer & Olson, 1992) that conceptualized opinion leaders as the brokers of information stemming from the mass media and as the filter of this same information to their own network of relations.

The first contributions to the debate on opinion leadership came from sociology, in which interpersonal communication became an autonomous field of study, as distinct from mass communication. In the 1940s the appreciation of interpersonal relations was one of the decisive elements in facilitating the transition from the paradigm of the "powerful mass media" (e.g., the magic bullet theory) to "limited effect" models (McQuail, 1985), such as the above-mentioned "two-step flow of communication" (see Figure 1). It was found, for example, that both the choices of voters in reference to politicians as well as those of consumers in relation to products depended more on interpersonal communication with members of their social network rather than on direct exposure to mass media (Lazarsfeld, Berelson & Gaudet, 1948; Katz and Lazarsfeld, 1955).

Primary groups (family, friends, colleagues, etc.) in which interactions are long lasting, informal and based on face-to-face relationships, constitute the networks of communication in which people are deeply involved. In these groups, people tend to change their minds collectively rather than individually, and to refer to the most influential members of their communities, which embody the "typical" group

*Figure 1. From "magic bullet theory" to two-step flow of communication*

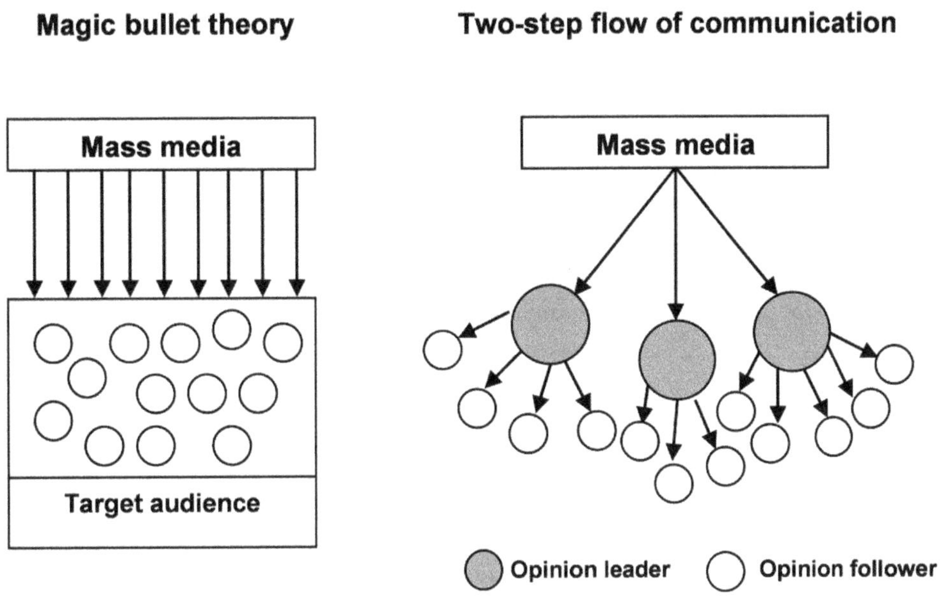


mentality. These considerations are in line with the two-step flow of communication theory (Katz and Lazarsfeld, 1955; Katz, 1957): media messages are filtered by opinion leaders, particularly receptive individuals who are then able to sort and distribute collected information to other members of their communities and groups.

Other authors have suggested variants of this initial representation, perceiving Lazarsfeld's original model as an overly mechanistic explanation of the processes of influence. For example, Windahl et al. (1992) showed that the "chain of influence" may be constituted by more than two steps, and thus it would be better to adopt a multistep model.

Also Rogers' theory of the diffusion of innovations (1983) intersects and incorporates considerations concerning the multistep flow of influence, although limited to the adoption of innovations. While the mass media are effective in promoting the adoption of the innovation to the pioneers (that is, in the initial phases of innovation), interpersonal communication is crucial in the latter stages, as less innovative individuals (usually less receptive towards the media) need to be reassured in their choices by opinion leaders.

## OPINION LEADERSHIP THEORY: MAIN ISSUES AND CONTROVERSIES

An opinion leader can thus be defined as a person who is able to influence the opinions and attitudes (and possibly behavior) of other individuals within his/her own circles of interpersonal relationships.

Opinion leadership is a distinct property that is difficult to define because it is a combination of the internal disposition of the subject – i.e. a tendency to exercise influence – and the communication role played within a given network of informal relationships. Thus, conceptualizing opinion leadership entails taking into account both individual characteristics (such as personality and expertise in a specific domain) and external factors, including the network structure and the position of the leader in this network (Summers, 1970; Baumgarten, 1975; Gnambs & Batinic, 2012).

Rogers (1983) also explained that opinion leadership is not made up of discrete states, claiming: "Influence is a matter of degree and should properly be viewed as a continuous variable, rather than a dichotomy of leaders and followers. Some individuals are looked to for advice by many of their peers; others are asked for their opinions about an innovation by only a few."

Even considering "opinion leadership" as a dichotomous construct, the resulting categories are not simply "leaders" or "followers", as the opinion seeking should be measured with a specific scale (Flynn et al., 1996)[1]. If a distinction is to be made then it should be between "leaders" and "non-leaders", and therefore between those who influence and people who do not. In fact, the two properties, opinion leadership and opinion seeking, can coexist in the same subject and in regard to the same domain, for example the same individual who provides advice on pop music may also welcome recommendations on the same topic.

Since its early conceptualization, opinion leadership has been independent of social class, as opinion leaders do not necessarily identify with the elite of the community. Generally opinion leadership is horizontal: the influence spreads between individuals on the same level; for specific areas of interest, often each social class produces its own opinion leaders.

Opinion leaders derive their influence from their interest and competence in a specific domain. However, when the influence of the leaders depends on their expertise in an area of interest, the same influence will be limited to that particular area. In this regard, a common distinction is between "generalized" and "specific" opinion leadership (Merton, 1957). Specific - or monomorphic - leaders exert influence confined to their field of interest, often because of their being experts or because deeply committed to this field. Thus, it is likely that interest and expertise in a subject plays an important role in determining the opinion leadership in the same area. Polymorphic opinion leaders are the expression of a generalized leadership, embracing various fields, which may be completely unrelated (Merton, 1957; King & Summers, 1970).

The expansion of the influence into related fields seems to largely depend on more intangible components of the personality of the leader (e.g., charisma). Several studies have revealed various characteristics of opinion leaders, which suggest a fairly consistent psychological profile. Opinion leaders are conscious about their appearance, self-centered and self-confident (Summers, 1970; Baumgarten, 1975), and show a high degree of public individuation (Chan & Misra, 1990) and a high degree of self-efficacy (Gnambs & Batinic, 2012) [2].

Finally, the propensity to opinion leadership depends on the degree of gregariousness of the subject (Katz and Lazarsfeld, 1955), defined as the number of contacts he/she has with other people. Opinion leaders need to be easily reached directly by the highest possible number of people, so that their influence may have more chance of becoming effective. Opinion leaders are in fact socially active promoters of rumors and gossip (Baumgarten, 1975; Venkatraman, 1989). The magnitude of the network of contacts does not seem to be sufficient for the recognition of the leadership. Potential followers also need to have some interest in the same area in which the leadership is expressed (Katz & Lazarsfeld, 1955; Wright & Cantor, 1967). Finally, an important factor seems to be the strategic position of the leader in his/her network.

## OPINION LEADERSHIP IN MARKETING STUDIES

### Opinion Leaders and Market Mavens

Opinion leadership is a construct that can be applied to a wide range of fields of study. Interpersonal communication and opinion leadership have gradually been recognized as fundamentally important for the transmission of information on markets, products and brands. Thus, opinion leaders also play a central role in studies on marketing, as marketplace and product information are often spread by word-of-mouth in face-to-face communications.

Marketing scholars have recognized the potential of market penetration as a result of a thorough understanding of opinion leaders. The main advantages of using opinion leaders in marketing communications are generally linked to cost reduction, increased effectiveness (due to more trust in information from peers), and positive word-of-mouth (WOM) regarding the brand (Cole, Long, Chiagouris & Gopalakrishna, 2011).

Marketing researchers have also conceptualized different types of influencers, of which the most interesting are the "product specific opinion leaders" (King & Summers, 1970) and the "market mavens" (Feick & Price, 1987), who are influential experts in the marketplace and in shopping in general.

Product-specific opinion leadership (Rogers & Cartano, 1962; King & Summers, 1970; Childers, 1986; Flynn et al., 1996) refers to opinion leadership in a specific product category, in reference to a particular consumer product, in which the opinion leader enjoys an "aura of prominence". These opinion leaders are characterized by a deep involvement in a certain type of product (King & Summers, 1970), in contrast to non-leaders, whose purchases of the same products are goal-oriented and whose involvement is only at the moment of purchase.

Product involvement also affects the type of information search performed: the opinion leaders' search for information is continuous (*ongoing search*) and not limited to a pre-purchase phase (Bloch, Sherrell & Ridgway, 1986). This information search can be done for example by regularly consulting professional magazines or specialized websites. The ongoing search also produces greater efficiency for future purchases, but at the same time increases the likelihood of impulse purchases.

Another important topic for marketers is the innovator, who adopts a product early and can exert an influence on other potential buyers. This influence can be both active, promoting conversations about the product, and passive, e.g. simply wearing his/her own latest purchase. The measure to assess how much a person can be said to be early in adopting a certain type of product is the "innovativeness" (Goldsmith & Hofacker, 1991). Some studies suggest that there is a link between innovativeness and opinion leadership (Feick & Price, 1987; Flynn *et al.*, 1996; Goldsmith, Clark & Goldsmith, 2006; Ruvio & Shoham, 2007). The nature of this link has not been fully clarified and may not be linear. This would however be in line with the claims made by Rogers (1983), that the highest concentration of opinion leaders are among the early adopters (the second category of consumers in order of innovativeness) and not among the innovators.

Another significant category of market "influence" is the market maven (Feick & Price, 1987). The area of competence of market mavens is not in terms of a single product category, but rather the market in general, in the sense that they have information on many product categories, which may or may not be related to each other, also on low-involvement products, on the shopping sites, discounts, etc. Market mavens disseminate this information among other consumers who they are in contact with, and on who they thus exert influence.

The difference from product-specific opinion leadership is qualitative, as the expertise of the market maven has more to do with the organizational aspects of the market and the distribution of the products rather than the technical aspects of the products. If the domain-specific opinion leader presents a high involvement product, the market maven presents high levels of marketplace involvement and purchasing involvement. Feick and Price (1987) clarify these features: "The definition of the market maven does not require that these individuals be early purchasers of products or necessarily even users of products about which they have information".

There are various reasons why the market maven starts a conversation about the products and the market (Feick & Price, 1987; Walsh, Gwinner & Swanson, 2004), for example a sense of duty in becoming a more "responsible" consumer (Kassarjian, 1981), and a hedonistic pleasure in conveying the information to others. The hedonistic rationale is a direct consequence of an extrovert and gregarious personality typical of market mavens (Walsh *et al.*, 2004). The collection of certain information by market mavens is determined by their exchange value in future social interactions. This assessment may both be the result of a sincere altruistic desire to help others, and the desire to gain information or other types of rewards, including the reward of being perceived positively by others (Walsh *et al.*, 2004).

The essential characteristics of this type of influential determine a set of specific attitudes and behaviors. The market mavens are self-perceived as smart buyers (Slama, Nataraajan & Williams, 1992); they pay more attention to advertising and have a positive attitude towards direct-mail advertising (Schneider & Rodgers, 1993), they plan their budget for shopping, make greater use of coupons that they pass on to friends, family and colleagues - four times more than others who have received coupons (Price, Feick & Guskey-Federouch, 1988). In addition, market mavens show an earlier awareness of new products in different product categories (Feick & Price, 1987), they frequently communicate information on retailers (Higie, Feick & Price, 1987; Abratt, Deon & Nezer, 1995), they are more aware of the value for money (Wiedmann, Walsh & Mitchell, 2001), they judge the price as a quality indicator (Lichtenstein & Burton, 1990), and show higher levels of information searches through specific media related to general consumption, such as catalogs, flyers, and consumer magazines (Feick & Price, 1987; Abratt *et al.*, 1995).

Other studies have shown that market mavenship is associated with perfectionism (Walsh & Mitchell, 2002), with innovativeness, and with the tendency to use consumption as a means of improving social status (Goldsmith *et al.*, 2006). They feel confident about their consumption choices and about their ability to see through messages aimed at misleading or deceiving consumers (Clark, Goldsmith & Goldsmith, 2008).

As for the evaluation criteria used for the selection of products (Williams & Slama, 1995), market mavens give more importance to the criteria related to the brand than criteria relating to the store.

## Opinion Leaders in Digitally-Empowering Contexts

The transformation of the media landscape has had a significant impact on redefining the concept of opinion leadership. The first question to ask is whether the Internet can be considered as a mass medium, given that the original formulation of the two-step flow considered the mass media as an influential source of opinion leaders.

In fact, the scholars who first dealt with computer-mediated communication (CMC) were from different fields than media studies (e.g. information sciences, pedagogical sciences) and they initially considered the phenomenon as being similar to interpersonal communication. Later, researchers considered CMC as more comparable to mass communication (Morris & Ogan, 1996). Also in Web 1.0 contexts, with the use of tools, such as newsgroups or forums, the communication approach may be similar to print mass media, and thus become a form of mass communication (Tsang & Zhou, 2005). Any association with the print mass media should not disregard the great differences between a one-way flow of communication and a two-way approach, typical of the digital medium. The main features of the newsgroups and blogs underpinning the mechanisms of opinion leadership are, as with the press, the asynchronicity and the prevalent use of written texts (Parks & Floyd, 1996; Vollero, 2006, 2010). Asynchronous communication enables a type of communication that is not necessarily simultaneous between issuers and recipients; thus, the contents of messages are stored in the Internet for a period that can vary from a few weeks to several years. This characteristic makes newsgroups and opinion platforms similar to a database in which it is possible to get reviews and comments on various topics over long periods. The use of written texts also tends to facilitate anonymity and, therefore, the opinions of certain individuals who would not have the courage and/or desire to interact with other individuals and to express their opinions in similar offline situations.

Some aspects of the traditional opinion leadership concept may not hold true however in the digital environment. For example, opinion leaders on Twitter usually act as agenda setters or disseminators whatever their status or particular expertise on the topic (Park, 2013). Other studies (Lyons & Henderson, 2005), instead, have described the characteristics and behavior of online opinion leaders as similar to those derived from research conducted in offline markets. These results demonstrate greater levels of involvement with the Internet than non-leaders, and support the idea that digital opinion leadership can be applied to online environments.

Similar mechanisms have been augmented with the spread of Web 2.0 features (personalization, user-generated content, etc.), thus favoring the emergence of new types of opinion leaders. As the digital media have become an increasingly important exchange platform, social interactions and influence exist in multiple forms, such as blogs, forums, social network sites, and reputation systems. In these digital environments consumers can interact with each other through the dissemination of opinions regarding companies/brands and their products (Bodendorf & Kaiser, 2009; Kang & Johnson, 2013; Shi & Wojnicki, 2014). This is a growing area of importance particularly for e-retailing, as "social influence" seems to have a major impact on online buying behavior within the Web 2.0 environment. It has also been argued that opinion leaders may act both as advocates or opponents for their peer groups, encouraging or discouraging e-shopping (O'Cass & Fenech, 2003; Kang & Johnson, 2013).

## OBJECTIVES OF THE CHAPTER

Despite many scholars recognizing the crucial role of opinion leaders and WOM mechanisms in online environments, there is a lack of empirical research concerning whether opinion leadership theories, developed in the traditional marketplace, can be applied to digital contexts (Lyons & Henderson, 2005; Cole et al., 2011).

The second part of this chapter aims to fill this gap by examining whether digital opinion leaders show similar previously researched features. The exploratory research arose from an interest in analyzing, through empirical examination, the role of opinion leaders in the choice of high involvement products (particularly, technological ones) and the effectiveness of the opinion leader in Web 2.0 environments. This research objective has been considered from two perspectives: on the one hand, an examination of opinion leadership dynamics in the online purchase of smartphones; on the other, an analysis of the impact of interpersonal and social influence on purchasing decisions. This led to the following research questions:

*Opinion leadership dynamics in the online purchase of smartphones*

**RQ 1.1:** Do opinion leaders behave differently from other people in term of online buying activities related to the smartphones?

**RQ 1.2:** Are market mavens different from the others with regard to generic purchasing dynamics?

*Impact of interpersonal and social influence on online purchasing decisions*

**RQ 2:** Compared to other factors (product attributes, price, etc.) influencing online purchasing decision, which is the strength of the impact of interpersonal and social influence?

## METHODOLOGY

Given the exploratory nature of the study, it was decided to articulate an empirical research, which could give first answers to the above-mentioned research questions. The choice of the unit of analysis - mainly university students - reflects the segment of global young people which is the most active group on the internet. In particular, Douglas and Craig (1997) argue that the sample of global youth shows a high degree of homogeneity in different countries, due to the high exposure of young people to the "global" media, and we can therefore assume that it is acceptable to our purposes.

The exploratory survey was thus administered to a sample of 327 Italian respondents via a web survey platform. The dual nature of the cognitive objective was represented by both the purchasing dynamics and the propensity to purchase smartphones online.

### Measures

In addition to the socio-demographic profile, the degree of respondents' interpersonal influence was measured, in terms both of the general marketplace, namely:

- The degree of market mavenship, by means of a scale adapted from Feick and Price (1987);
- The degree of product-specific (smartphone) opinion leadership, measured by the instrument developed by Flynn et al. (1996).

For both scales, we proceeded to test their reliability by analyzing the coefficient of Cronbach, as well as the correlation of each item with the total scale; the results support the reliability of the extrapolated dimensions (respectively $\alpha = 0.767$ and $\alpha = 0.860$), higher than the threshold conventionally fixed in the literature (i.e. 0.7 as in Nunnally and Bernstein, 1994).

As for the smartphone purchasing dynamics, various indicators were used such as the purchasing frequency, the number of smartphones owned currently, the preferred point of sale, the awareness of less known (or new) brands.

Product attributes were divided into three sub-dimensions: intrinsic attributes, that is the physical and technological product features; economic attributes (price, discount prices, sales promotions, phone company fees[3]); extrinsic attributes not concerning the product as a physical object, but rather other elements, either as auxiliary to the product (e.g., apps available in the digital store) or as symbolical benefits associated with the product.

Purchasing propensity was measured via a quasi-experiment. In the middle section of the questionnaire, a pseudo online shopping setting was represented, in which the respondents could initially see a "replica" of an Amazon page concerning the selling announcement of a smartphone and containing a product image and technical specifications. Later, the comments of previous buyers on the page, a review by Telefonino.net (an information portal on mobile phones), and, lastly, advice from family and friends were shown to respondents.

Although all the information in this section had been assembled artificially, it was structured so as to neutralize the effect of some variables, such as brand, price and smartphone design, which could have invalidated the measurement of the impact of the influence sources (friends, reviews, Amazon users, etc.) on the purchasing propensity. To prevent the smartphone offer from looking too attractive, the product was presented with good (but not too many) features, in terms of tech specifications, price and design. Hence, the smartphone brand was concealed, and the respondent was informed of this, also alerting him/her to the fact that the brand was well known. The polarity of all the influence sources was also univocally positive, as all the comments and the reviews expressed strong recommendations, in order to prevent changes in the loading of a given influence source through the influence direction.

After the presentation of all the influence sources, the purchase propensity of the smartphone was measured in terms of likelihood of purchase from 0 to 10. In addition, the respondents were asked how much importance each influence source had on their decision. The survey lasted about two months (May-June 2014), including a short pretest period (5 days – 30 respondents), during which a senior researcher had been supervising the completion of the questionnaire: in this way various questions have been reformulated and some response categories have been reordered.

## FINDINGS AND DISCUSSION

The sample was distributed relatively equally by gender (men 53% and women 47%). The average age was 33.5 years, whilst the modal age was 24. In order to create a regular distribution of classes, three age groups (up to 25 years, between 26 and 40 years, over 40 years) were identified. As a tool for data analysis, IBM SPSS 21.0 has been employed.

### General Purchasing Dynamics and Market Mavenship

The respondents were asked how frequently they used each of the sources of information on the marketplace. The most frequently performed activities were the reading of leaflets/fliers with information on the latest promotional offers (45%), and "window shopping" with a mere recreational or informative purpose (44%) even without any purchase.

The market mavenship index was trichotomized as follows: "non-mavens" (26.3% of the sample) had values between the minimum and 5.80, "moderate mavens" (36.7%) were placed between 6 and 7.80, and "market mavens" (37%) between 8 and the maximum. A bivariate analysis between the three mavenship classes and the variables concerning the general purchasing dynamics (Table 1) showed that market mavens were more committed than moderate mavens to each of the activities. Moderate mavens, in turn, dedicated more time to these activities than non-mavens.

## Specific Purchasing Dynamics and Opinion Leadership

A total of 71% of the respondents declared that they owned just one smartphone, 22% owned two, and only 7% declared that they owned three or more. More than half of respondents replaced his/her own

*Table 1. Market mavenship index and generic purchasing dynamics*

| | | Non-Mavens % | Moderate Mavens % | Market Mavens % |
|---|---|---|---|---|
| I read leaflets/fliers in order to find out about the latest offers | Never | 13.1 | 5.1 | 2.5 |
| | Rarely | 22.6 | 12.8 | 9.3 |
| | Sometimes | 33.3 | 38.5 | 27.1 |
| | Often | 20.2 | 35.0 | 29.7 |
| | Very often | 10.7 | 8.5 | 31.4 |
| I navigate specialized websites to find promotions and discounts | Never | 33.3 | 10.3 | 4.2 |
| | Rarely | 27.4 | 25.6 | 17.8 |
| | Sometimes | 26.2 | 32.5 | 19.5 |
| | Often | 10.7 | 23.9 | 33.9 |
| | Very often | 2.4 | 7.7 | 24.6 |
| I use online forums (communities) to stay informed about the latest arrivals | Never | 50.0 | 23.9 | 6.8 |
| | Rarely | 25.0 | 25.6 | 13.6 |
| | Sometimes | 11.9 | 26.5 | 17.8 |
| | Often | 9.5 | 15.4 | 29.7 |
| | Very often | 3.6 | 8.5 | 32.2 |
| I read/watch ads just out of curiosity | Never | 16.7 | 14.5 | 12.7 |
| | Rarely | 33.3 | 22.2 | 18.6 |
| | Sometimes | 29.8 | 41.9 | 34.7 |
| | Often | 17.9 | 18.8 | 23.7 |
| | Very often | 2.4 | 2.6 | 10.2 |
| I make use of coupons | Never | 59.5 | 36.8 | 33.1 |
| | Rarely | 21.4 | 32.5 | 28.0 |
| | Sometimes | 14.3 | 19.7 | 29.7 |
| | Often | 1.2 | 8.5 | 5.9 |
| | Very often | 3.6 | 2.6 | 3.4 |
| I go "window shopping" | Never | 17.9 | 5.1 | 3.4 |
| | Rarely | 22.6 | 17.1 | 23.7 |
| | Sometimes | 31.0 | 28.2 | 19.5 |
| | Often | 17.9 | 35.0 | 32.2 |
| | Very often | 10.7 | 14.5 | 21.2 |

smartphone less than once every two-three years. 24% changed it once every four years or more, 14% changed it once a year, and 10% more than once a year. More than half of the sample had bought a smartphone within the last year before the interview. A total of 25% had bought it a year earlier, 16% two to three years earlier, and 3% at least four years before the interview. A quarter of the sample used the Internet (specialized or e-commerce sites) when buying a smartphone. The remainder preferred traditional offline retailers, i.e. specialized stores and mass retail channels.

Regarding the opinion leadership index, the scores were divided into three classes: values ranging from 1 to 1.8 were included in the category of non-leaders (30.9%), from 2 to 2.8 in "moderate leaders" class (42.5%), and from 3 to 4 in opinion leaders (26.6%).

From the conjoint distribution of the market mavenship classes and the opinion leadership classes (Table 2), co-graduation was found between the two variables: there was a good correspondence between being influential with regard to the marketplace and being influential in relation to smartphones.

This was also confirmed by the fact that the Pearson correlation coefficient, calculated on the original index (not trichotomized), was equal to 0.606. Comparing the degree of opinion leadership with the generic purchasing habits, opinion leaders were found to carry out each activity more often than less influential people. In line with Feick and Price (1987), the opinion leaders in our survey had an earlier awareness of new or less known brands (Table 3).

For all the listed brands, opinion leaders claimed to know of them, in greater numbers than the less influential people. Almost half of the non-leaders (48.4%) did not recognize any of the listed brands.

*Table 2. Cross tabulation of market mavenship and opinion leadership*

| | Non-Leaders | Moderate Leaders | Opinion Leaders |
|---|---|---|---|
| Non-mavens | 60.8% | 34.2% | 5.1% |
| Moderate mavens | 33.3% | 50.5% | 16.2% |
| Market mavens | 7.2% | 40.5% | 52.3% |
| Total | 30.9% | 42.5% | 26.6% |

*Table 3. Opinion leadership and awareness of new or less known brands*

| | Non-Leaders % | Moderate Leaders % | Opinion Leaders % |
|---|---|---|---|
| Huawei | 48.4 | 63.3 | 83.8 |
| OnePlus | 2.2 | 20.3 | 46.3 |
| Xiaomi | 4.3 | 21.1 | 56.3 |
| Lenovo | 18.3 | 42.2 | 66.3 |
| Oppo | 1.1 | 20.3 | 55.0 |
| Micromax | 1.1 | .0 | 8.8 |
| Yulong | .0 | 1.6 | 3.8 |
| Zte | 1.1 | 18.8 | 52.5 |
| None of the above | 48.4 | 28.1 | 10.0 |

An opinion leader more frequently owned two or more smartphones, rather than just one, compared to non-leaders. More than half of the opinion leaders owned more than one smartphone, against 10% of non-leaders. Opinion leaders were inclined to change their smartphone more quickly. About 51% replaced the phone at least once a year, while 96% of non-leaders had not replaced their mobile phones two to three years previous to the last purchase. Opinion leaders were more likely than non-leaders to shop online, via specialized sites (such as monclick.it or stockisti.it[4]) or large e-commerce sites (such as Amazon or E-bay). Interestingly, the majority of opinion leaders preferred to shop via traditional channels, such as specialized shops and the mass retail market.

On average, respondents claimed with some confidence (average value of 7.3) to get specific information on smartphones from the Internet, consulting online forums, specialized or e-commerce sites. Discussion with friends ranked second place (5.7); and just behind was the consultation of video tutorials (5.4). The least performed activities were getting information on smartphones by talking with family members (mean score of 3.6) and from traditional media (3.9).

Comparing the mean scores of opinion leaders, moderate leaders and non-leaders, on the preferences for each source of information on smartphones, once again a rather logical picture emerges. On average, opinion leaders claimed that they (with a mean value of 9 out of 10) retrieved information on smartphones from forums and specialized sites, or by viewing videos on YouTube (8 out of 10). Compared with the least influential individuals, opinion leaders were more inclined to gather information from traditional media. Non-leaders presented a higher mean score in relation to discussions with friends (6.16), higher than the opinion leaders on the same item. Similarly non-leaders were more inclined to ask the assistant for help in stores, to discuss purchasing issues with their own partner and to accept advice from family. This corroborates the prevailing view – starting with the first formulation of the two-step-flow theory (Katz and Lazarsfeld, 1955) – that opinion leaders are more influenced by the media, than less influential subjects. In addition, the fact that the media influence on the opinion leaders consists mainly of new media, and traditional media to a lesser extent, could be explained by the fact that the highly technical information on smartphones can be presented better through web-based tools.

To measure the purchasing dynamics four pairs of Hobson's choice phrases were also presented, to which respondents were forced to take a stand between the two bounds of a certain behavior. Opinion leaders were found to be more prone to experiment with different smartphone brands and to change their smartphone even if the phone still worked. Although they tend to pay more attention to "value for money" (66.3%) than to just quality or newness apart from price (33.8%), nevertheless, they are more inclined not to care about price, spending a considerable sum just to possess a newer smartphone. In addition, opinion leaders are less prone than others to wait for some months after the product launch in order to buy the product at a more economical price. All respondents classified as opinion leaders preferred to be personally responsible for seeking out information, while only half of non-leaders (51%) took responsibility. Such findings validate the fact that the path of influence goes from opinion leaders, who collect information from disparate sources, to non-leaders, who instead tend more to rely on other people.

Our results thus show that opinion leaders appear considerably more engaged than non-leaders in terms of buying smartphones more frequently, both for themselves and as gifts, and they do this even if a previous device malfunctioned. Their passion for the product often leads them to spend more than required just to acquire the ultimate in terms of quality or newness.

## Attributes

Our survey revealed that the main attributes required for a smartphone were the price, brand reliability and battery life, while relatively less considered were the advanced functions (such as smart voice assistant, eye tracking, wireless rechargeable battery). Comparing the opinion leaders' and non-leaders' regarding these attributes, it emerges that opinion leaders gave more importance to all the attributes, with the exception of price, discount prices and brand. This indicates, on the one hand, that the opinion leaders are less interested in the price and in saving money, and, on the other, they are less biased in their judgement, considering intrinsic product attributes as a priority, and disregarding the brand.

## Purchasing Propensity

In the middle section of the questionnaire, the image of a specific purchasing situation enabled us to examine the respondents' purchasing propensity. After the respondents had been shown different images, representing an Amazon page and other information (Figure 1), respondents were asked whether or not they would buy such a product on the basis that they had the budget required.

A total of 60.8% of respondents claimed they would buy such a product. Those who answered affirmatively, were asked how likely they were to purchase the product (purchasing propensity). The mean purchasing likelihood was 7.21 out of 10 (see figure 2).

The factor that most influenced the respondents who expressed a willingness to buy, were the technical specifications (7.68 out of 10), the price (7.59) and the technical reviews on specialized websites (7.39). Advice from family (5.82) was the least decisive factor (see table 4).

### Factor Analysis

Principal component analysis of these elements revealed that, of all the latent factors, only the first two eigenvalues were consistently higher than one (2.65 and 1.77, respectively), and explained 63% of the

*Figure 2. Design of the images containing different sources of information*

*Table 4. Factors influencing purchasing decision*

| | Mean | Std. Deviation |
|---|---|---|
| Technical specifications | 7.68 | 2.252 |
| Price | 7.59 | 2.372 |
| Technical reviews on specialized websites | 7.39 | 2.062 |
| Design | 6.93 | 1.972 |
| User comments | 6.82 | 2.096 |
| Advice from friends | 6.55 | 2.326 |
| Advice from family | 5.82 | 2.829 |

total variance. Analysis of the eigenvectors of the two rotated components (with the Varimax rotation method) showed that the first component had the highest factor loadings on variables related to the intrinsic attributes of the product (technical specifications, technical reviews in specialized sites, design and price), while the second component loadings had more on sources of social influence (advice from friends and family, and user comments) (see table 5).

## Varimax Rotation Method

For each latent component extracted, factor score coefficients were calculated and used as weights for each variable in the construction of an index which represents the required factor. The index constructed from the variables that load on the first component (i.e., technical specifications, technical reviews of specialized sites, design and price) was called "sensitivity to the influence of the attributes of the product". This represents the tendency of respondents to be influenced by the functional attributes of a smartphone. This index had mean 0 and standard deviation of the scores equal to 1, since its scores correspond to the factor scores, which are expressed in units of standard deviation (i.e., they are standardized values) and tend to be distributed symmetrically around zero, which represents the average of the distribution.

The index developed from the other variables (advice from friends, advice from family and user comments) was labeled as "sensitivity to social influence", and indicates the propensity to be influenced by interpersonal relationships. Respondents were also asked to indicate, from the same sources of information presented in the previous question, which one had most influenced their choice.

*Table 5. Rotated Matrix components (sources of influence) - Varimax rotation method*

| | Component | |
|---|---|---|
| | 1 | 2 |
| Technical specifications | .834 | |
| Technical reviews in specialized sites | .777 | |
| Design | .716 | |
| Price | .646 | |
| Advice from friends | | .898 |
| Advice from family | | .893 |
| User comments | .415 | .594 |

Measuring the most influential source of information, the scores were weighted by the most important item. A linear multiple regression was thus used by placing purchasing propensity as the dependent variable, and different sources of information (weighted according to the above procedure) as independent variables (see Tables 6, 7, 8). Overall, the results demonstrate the predictive validity of the model ($F = 10.300$, $p < 0.001$).

The correlation coefficient R was quite high (0.555), thus showing a strong positive association between the information sources considered as a whole, and the purchasing propensity. The coefficient of determination $R^2$ was .308 (adj. $R^2 = 0.278$), which suggests that 30% of the variance of purchasing propensity is reproduced by its relation with all information sources.

All correlations were significant, except those with price and advice from family. The partial regression coefficients B and the standardized coefficients Beta highlight that the most decisive factors were

*Table 6. Multiple regression, model summary*

| Model | R | R Square | Adjusted R Square | Std. Error | Durbin-Watson |
|---|---|---|---|---|---|
| 1 | .555[a] | .308 | .278 | 1.792 | 1.936 |
| a. Predictors: (Constant), Advice from family, Advice from friend, Design, Price, User comments, Technical reviews in specialized sites, Technical Specifications | | | | | |
| b. Dependent Variable: purchasing propensity | | | | | |

*Table 7. Multiple regression, ANOVA*

| Model | | Sum of Squares | df | Mean Square | F | Sig. |
|---|---|---|---|---|---|---|
| 1 | Regression | 231.538 | 7 | 33.077 | 10.300 | .000[b] |
| | Residual | 520.256 | 162 | 3.211 | | |
| | Total | 751.794 | 169 | | | |
| a. Dependent Variable: purchasing propensity | | | | | | |
| b. Predictors: (Constant), Advice from family, Advice from friend, Design, Price, User comments, Technical reviews in specialized sites, Technical Specifications | | | | | | |

*Table 8. Multiple regression, parameters*

| | B | St error | Beta | t | Sig. | Tolerance | VIF |
|---|---|---|---|---|---|---|---|
| (Constant) | .912 | .841 | | 1.084 | .280 | | |
| Technical specifications | .123 | .023 | .361 | 5.286 | .000 | .918 | 1.089 |
| Design | .148 | .043 | .229 | 3.453 | .001 | .973 | 1.027 |
| Price | .044 | .030 | .096 | 1.453 | .148 | .971 | 1.030 |
| User comments | .075 | .035 | .143 | 2.112 | .036 | .936 | 1.068 |
| Technical reviews in specialized sites | .143 | .034 | .283 | 4.196 | .000 | .941 | 1.063 |
| Advice from friends | .124 | .038 | .233 | 3.228 | .002 | .819 | 1.221 |
| Advice from family | -.001 | .037 | -.002 | -.032 | .974 | .789 | 1.268 |
| a. *Dependent variable*: purchasing propensity | | | | | | | |

design, technical reviews from specialized sites, friends' advice and technical specifications, while the least important factor was the user comments. In addition, the limited importance of price can be justified by the fact that, in designing this simulated purchase environment, we tried to neutralize the impact of price on the purchase decision, ensuring that the smartphone had an average ratio quality/price with respect to its technical specifications.

The propensity of opinion leaders and market mavens to be affected by the attributes of the product or interpersonal relationships was then verified. In addition whether this propensity differed systematically from that of non-leaders or non-mavens was also examined. Thus, the means of non-leaders, moderate leaders and opinion leaders were compared in terms of their scores on the two indices, i.e. the influence of the product and social influence (Table 9). The opinion leaders were more affected, compared to those who were the least influential, by the attributes of the smartphone. Non-leaders were more affected by social influence than opinion leaders.

The same comparison was also made between the market mavens and non-mavens. The market mavens were even more affected by the attributes of the product than the opinion leaders. Non-mavens appeared to be even more influenced by personal relationships compared to non-leaders.

## IMPLICATIONS AND FUTURE RESEARCH

Further investigations are required to verify which influence sources most affect the purchasing intentions in current e-retailing settings. The high specificity of smartphones, the lack of time and information may understandably lead respondents to rely more on information sources regarding the intrinsic attributes, rather than on sources of social influence. Analyzing the most important purchasing factor, on the basis of the degree of opinion leadership of the respondents, it appears that the most influential individuals tended to report, to a greater extent than the others, the intrinsic attributes of the smartphone as decisive factors, such as the technical specifications or reviews. The least influential people instead reported, interpersonal influence sources to a greater extent than opinion leaders, such as the comments of friends and family, or of Amazon users.

The same behavioral pattern should be noted comparing market mavens and non-mavens, although it should be emphasized that non-mavens seemed to be more price sensitive than market mavens. A better understanding of the behavior of the influential individuals seems to be increasingly valuable in order to target online communication at them.

*Table 9. Mean comparison of the type of influence between opinion leaders, moderate leaders and non-leaders*

| | | **Influence of Attributes of Product** | **Social Influence** |
|---|---|---|---|
| non-leaders | Mean | -.2926500 | .1952452 |
| moderate leaders | Mean | .1184657 | -.0232023 |
| opinion leaders | Mean | .2008111 | -.2171037 |
| Total | Mean | .0000000 | .0000000 |

Moving to practical implications, we attempted to increase our knowledge of the current dynamics of consumer behavior in e-retailing, and suggest that marketers should pay attention to opinion leaders. An integrated set of communication channels could be designed targeted at opinion leaders, as well as tangible or/and intangible rewards to motivate them to make online social-network referrals.

Domain-specific opinion leaders could be employed to evaluate the concept of a product before its further development, or to pre-evaluate promotional campaigns. The various tools of interactive marketing could be very effective in persuading opinion leaders to sway other consumers towards a specific brand. In addition, given that opinion leaders are frequently innovative consumers, emphasizing product newness could help to harness their attention and to stimulate their interest.

In order to appeal to the sense of duty of market mavens, the promotional message could highlight their responsibility in explaining to others the benefits provided by the product adoption. Companies could also stimulate market mavens to participate in customer online communities that receive information about new products, thus fostering the commitment of market mavens in terms of the special status they have reached. Companies could motivate market mavens to spread information, by means of online tools, such as collaboration and opinion platforms. Companies could also appeal to the altruism of market mavens, by inviting them to let the company know which users are more in need of help, or enabling them to guide other customers through similar collaborative platforms.

One example is Vodafone Lab Italia, an online platform open to non-customers and prospects. The Vodafone Lab Forum, an online arena of discussion about technology, smartphones and computers, is an area where opinion leaders' contribution is exploited. They give advice to other users and respond quickly to their questions. The so-called Super Users have a badge alongside the nickname, often with the indication of the areas they are more expert in, and they play an active role in sustaining the company's customer relationships.

Regarding the planning of communication initiatives addressed to opinion leaders, the main difficulty seems to be the spontaneity of such subjects. On the other hand, the creation of opinion leaders for purely commercial purposes does not seem to have a positive effect and, indeed, may be counterproductive in terms of corporate image and reputation (Siano et al., 2007; Siano & Vollero, 2012).

## CONCLUSION

In many decision-making processes (for example, purchasing a product or planning a trip), personal influence often has a greater impact than the influence of the media, also in computer-mediated contexts.

In this chapter, we have highlighted that an examination of online opinion leaders is valuable, also in terms of the evolution of e-retailing channels. In an online environment the distinction between product-specific opinion leadership and market mavenship remains true: the market maven is more oriented towards a generalized and non-instrumental search for information on many kinds of products.

From a conceptual standpoint, the identification of the critical factors that characterize digital opinion leadership may help to shed light on these actors and their role in buying dynamics. This is increasingly urgent for the innovative contexts of e-retailing, which involve a variety of factors on purchase intentions.

This empirical research provides an original contribution by explaining from where opinion leaders derive their abilities. In addition, the chapter examines the appropriateness of some assumptions regarding the concept of opinion leadership within an e-retailing environment. Opinion leaders still play an important role in buying decisions, although this role needs to be interpreted in relation to the changes in market dynamics and consumer behavior introduced by Web 2.0 and the associated social media. In line with Lyengar, Van den Bulte and Valente (2011), we may argue that the customer lifetime value of opinion leaders may be higher than non-leaders because they are both heavy users and early adopters of new technology. Lastly, although various authors have stressed the high media consumption of opinion leaders (Rogers, 1983; Summers, 1970), there are fewer empirical studies in relation to new media. In our investigation, we have revealed that, of all the media, the Internet is considered to be the most influential source on smartphone purchase decisions of opinion leaders. The respondents of our survey were more likely to prefer electronic word-of-mouth (blogs, users' reviews, social media buzz and so on) to gather information on smartphones. However, they still attribute great importance to traditional word-of-mouth (e.g., opinions and suggestions from friends).

In summary, the online implementation of the two-step flow model highlights the superiority of interpersonal communication compared to mass communication during the purchasing process of non-leaders, particularly in relation to aspects of trust, which remain central elements in the marketing methods used by e-retailers.

## ACKNOWLEDGMENT

Although the views and ideas expressed in this chapter are those of Agostino Vollero, Alfonso Siano and Domenico Sardanelli, "Introduction" and "Conclusion" are attributed to Alfonso Siano, "Conceptual background", "Methodology" and "Findings and discussion" to Domenico Sardanelli, and "Opinion leadership in marketing studies", "Objectives of the chapter" and "Implications and future research" to Agostino Vollero.

## REFERENCES

Abratt, R., Deon, N., & Nezer, C. (1995). Role of the market maven in retailing: A general marketplace influencer. *Journal of Business and Psychology*, *10*(1), 31–55. doi:10.1007/BF02249268

Bandura, A. (1997). *Self-efficacy: The exercise of control*. New York: Freeman.

Baumgarten, S. A. (1975). The Innovative Communicator in the Diffusion Research. *JMR, Journal of Marketing Research*, *12*(1), 12–18. doi:10.2307/3150653

Bloch, P. H., Sherrell, D. L., & Ridgway, N. M. (1986). Consumer search: An extended framework. *The Journal of Consumer Research*, *13*(1), 119–126. doi:10.1086/209052

Bodendorf, F., & Kaiser, C. (2009). Detecting opinion leaders and trends in online social networks. *Proceedings of the 2nd ACM workshop on Social web search and mining*, ACM doi:10.1145/1651437.1651448

Chan, K. K., & Misra, S. (1990). Characteristics of the opinion leader: A new dimension. *Journal of Advertising*, *19*(3), 53–60. doi:10.1080/00913367.1990.10673192

Childers, T. L. (1986). Assessment of the Psychometric Properties of an Opinion Leadership Scale. *JMR, Journal of Marketing Research*, *23*(2), 184–188. doi:10.2307/3151666

Clark, R. A., Goldsmith, R. E., & Goldsmith, E. B. (2008). Market mavenism and consumer self-confidence. *Journal of Consumer Behaviour*, *7*(3), 238–248. doi:10.1002/cb.248

Cole, M. D., Long, M. M., Chiagouris, L. G., & Gopalakrishna, P. (2011). Transitioning from traditional to digital content: An examination of opinion leadership and word-of-mouth communication across various media platforms. *Journal of Internet Commerce*, *10*(2), 91–105. doi:10.1080/15332861.2011.571990

Douglas, S. P., & Craig, C. S. (1997). The changing dynamic of consumer behavior: Implications for cross-cultural research. *International Journal of Research in Marketing*, *14*(4), 379–395. doi:10.1016/S0167-8116(97)00026-8

Eastlick, M. A. (1993). Predictors of videotex adoption. *Journal of Direct Marketing*, *7*(3), 66–74. doi:10.1002/dir.4000070309

Feick, L. F., & Price, L. L. (1987). The Market Maven: A Diffuser of Marketplace Information. *Journal of Marketing*, *51*(1), 83–97. doi:10.2307/1251146

Flynn, L. R., Goldsmith, R. E., & Eastman, J. K. (1996). Opinion Leaders and Opinion Seekers: Two New Measurament Scales. *Journal of the Academy of Marketing Science*, *24*(2), 137–147. doi:10.1177/0092070396242004

Gnambs, T., & Batinic, B. (2012). A Personality-Competence Model of Opinion Leadership. *Psychology and Marketing*, *29*(8), 606–621. doi:10.1002/mar.20547

Goldsmith, R. E., Clark, R. A., & Goldsmith, E. B. (2006). Extending the psychological profile of market mavenism. *Journal of Consumer Behaviour*, *5*(5), 411–419. doi:10.1002/cb.189

Goldsmith, R. E., & Hofacker, C. F. (1991). Measuring Consumer Innovativeness. *Journal of the Academy of Marketing Science*, *19*(3), 209–221. doi:10.1007/BF02726497

Higie, R. A., Feick, L. F., & Price, L. L. (1987). Types and amount of word-of-mouth communications about retailers. *Journal of Retailing*, *63*(3), 260–278.

Iyengar, R., Van den Bulte, C., & Valente, T. W. (2011). Opinion leadership and social contagion in new product diffusion. *Marketing Science*, *30*(2), 195–212. doi:10.1287/mksc.1100.0566

Kang, J.-Y. M., & Johnson, K. K. P. (2013). How does social commerce work for apparel shopping? Apparel social e-shopping with social network storefronts. *Journal of Customer Behaviour*, *12*(1), 53–72. doi:10.1362/147539213X13645550618524

Kassarjan, H. H. (1981). Low Involvement: A Second Look. In K. B. Monroe & A. Arbor (Eds.), *Advances in Consumer Research* (Vol. 8, pp. 31–34). MI: Association for Consumer Research.

Katz, E. (1957). *The Two Step Flow of Communication, an Up-To-Date Report of an Hypothesis. Annenberg School for Communication, Departmental Papers (ASC)*. University of Pennsylvania.

Katz, E., & Lazarsfeld, P. F. (1955). *Personal Influence*. Glencoe, IL: The Free Press.

King, C. W., & Summers, J. O. (1970). Overlap of Opinion Leadership Across Consumer Product Categories. *JMR, Journal of Marketing Research*, *7*(1), 43–50. doi:10.2307/3149505

Lazarsfeld, P. F., Berelson, B., & Gaudet, H. (1948). *The people's choice*. New York: Columbia University Press.

Lichtenstein, D. R., & Burton, S. (1990). An assessment of the moderating effects of market mavenism and value consciousness on price-quality perception accuracy. *Advances in Consumer Research. Association for Consumer Research (U. S.)*, *17*(1), 53–59.

Lyons, B., & Henderson, K. (2005). Opinion leadership in a computer-mediated environment. *Journal of Consumer Behaviour*, *4*(5), 319–329. doi:10.1002/cb.22

McQuail, D. (1985). Sociology of mass communication. *Annual Review of Sociology*, *11*(1), 93–111. doi:10.1146/annurev.so.11.080185.000521

Merton, R. (1957). *Social Theory and Social Structure*. New York: Free Press.

Morris, M., & Ogan, C. (1996). The Internet as Mass Medium. *Journal of Communication*, *46*(1), 39–50. doi:10.1111/j.1460-2466.1996.tb01460.x

Nunnally, J., & Bernstein, I. H. (1994). *Psychometric Theory* (3rd ed.). New York: McGraw-Hill.

O'Cass, A., & Fenech, T. (2003). Web retailing adoption: Exploring the nature of internet users Web retailing behaviour. *Journal of Retailing and Consumer Services*, *10*(2), 81–94. doi:10.1016/S0969-6989(02)00004-8

Park, C. S. (2013). Does Twitter motivate involvement in politics? Tweeting, opinion leadership, and political engagement. *Computers in Human Behavior*, *29*(4), 1641–1648. doi:10.1016/j.chb.2013.01.044

Parks, M. R., & Floyd, K. (1996). Making friends in cyberspace. *Journal of Computer-Mediated Communication*, *1*(4), 80–97.

Price, L. L., Feick, L. F., & Guskey-Federouch, A. (1988). Couponing behaviors of the market maven: Profile of a super couponer. *Advances in Consumer Research. Association for Consumer Research (U. S.)*, *15*(1), 354–359.

Robinson, J. P. (1976). Interpersonal Influence in Election Campaigns Two Step-flow Hypotheses. *Public Opinion Quarterly*, *40*(3), 304–319. doi:10.1086/268307

Rogers, E. M. (1983). *Diffusion of innovations*. New York: The Free Press.

Rogers, E. M., & Cartano, D. G. (1962). Methoding of Measuring Opinion Leadership. *Public Opinion Quarterly*, *26*(3), 435–441. doi:10.1086/267118

Ruvio, A., & Shoham, A. (2007). Innovativeness, exploratory behavior, market mavenship, and opinion leadership: An empirical examination in the Asian context. *Psychology and Marketing*, *24*(8), 703–722. doi:10.1002/mar.20180

Schneider, K. C., & Rodgers, W. C. (1993). Generalized marketplace influencers' (market mavens') attitudes toward direct mail as a source of information. *Journal of Direct Marketing*, *7*(4), 20–28. doi:10.1002/dir.4000070405

Shi, M., & Wojnicki, A. C. (2014). Money talks to online opinion leaders: What motivates opinion leaders to make social-network referrals? *Journal of Advertising Research*, *54*(1), 81–91. doi:10.2501/JAR-54-1-081-091

Siano, A., & Vollero, A. (2012). Il processo di management della corporate communication: Un framework. *Sinergie Italian Journal of Management*, *88*, 73–92.

Siano, A., Vollero, A., & Siglioccolo, M. (2007). The Governance-Structure-System Model: a Framework for Corporate Communication Management. *Proceedings of 12th International Conference on Corporate and Marketing Communications* (pp. 179-210). London: Routledge.

Slama, M.E., Nataraajan, R., & Williams T.G. (1992). Market Mavens and the relationship between smart buying and information provision: An exploratory study. *Developments in marketing science, 15*, 90-93.

Summers, J. O. (1970). The Identity of Women's Clothing Fashion Opinion Leaders. *Journal of Marketing*, *7*(2), 178–185. doi:10.2307/3150106

Tsang, S. L. A., & Zhou, N. (2005). Newsgroup participants as opinion leaders and seekers in online and offline communication environments. *Journal of Business Research*, *58*(9), 1186–1193. doi:10.1016/j.jbusres.2004.05.002

Venkatraman, M. P. (1989). Opinion leaders, adopters, and communication adopters: A role analysis. *Psychology and Marketing*, *6*(1), 51–68. doi:10.1002/mar.4220060104

Vollero, A. (2006). Il two-step flow nella comunicazione in rete: gli opinion leader on-line. *Esperienze d'impresa, 2*, 49-68.

Vollero, A. (2010). *E-marketing e web communication. Verso la gestione della corporate reputation online*. Torino: Giappichelli.

Walsh, G., Gwinner, K. P., & Swanson, S. R. (2004). What makes mavens tick? Exploring the motives of market mavens' initiation of information diffusion. *Journal of Consumer Marketing*, *21*(2), 109–122. doi:10.1108/07363760410525678

Walsh, G., & Mitchell, V. W. (2002). German market mavens' decision making styles. *Journal of Euromarketing*, *10*(4), 83–108. doi:10.1300/J037v10n04_05

Wiedmann, K. P., Walsh, G., & Mitchell, V. W. (2001). The Mannmaven: An agent for diffusing market information. *Journal of Marketing Communications*, *7*(4), 195–212. doi:10.1080/13527260127413

Williams, T. G., & Slama, M. E. (1995). Market mavens' purchase decision evaluative criteria: Implications for brand and store promotion efforts. *Journal of Consumer Marketing*, *12*(3), 4–21. doi:10.1108/07363769510147218

Windahl, S., Signitzer, B., & Olson, J. T. (1992). *Using communication theory: An introduction to planned communication*. London: Sage.

Wright, C. R., & Cantor, M. (1967). The Opinion Seeker and the Avoider: Steps Beyond the Opinion Avoider: Steps Beyond the Opinion Leader Concept. *Pacific Sociological Review*, *10*(1), 33–43. doi:10.2307/1388626

## KEY TERMS AND DEFINITIONS

**(Consumer) Innovativeness:** Propensity or predisposition to buy or adopt new products.

**eWOM (Electronic Word-of-Mouth):** Any online communication made available by users (prospects or customers) that positively or negatively can affect the way a company and its brands/products are perceived.

**Interpersonal Communication:** The process of sending and receiving information between two (dyadic communication) or more people (group communication) in order to create shared meaning.

**Market Maven:** An influential expert in the marketplace and in shopping in general and not only in a specific product category.

**Opinion Avoider:** An individual who has little or no propensity to rely on the opinions of others.

**Opinion Follower:** An individual who receive information from interpersonal sources in order to evaluate current affairs, products/services, etc.

**Opinion Leader:** An individual that exerts personal influence on their own informal community, above all in the domain in which his/her peers consider him/her to be an expert.

**Self-Efficacy:** The confidence of an individual to be in possession of the necessary skills and competencies to achieve certain goals and to influence others.

## ENDNOTES

1 At the opposite pole from the opinion seeker, is the opinion avoider, who has little or no propensity to rely on the opinions of others (Wright & Cantor, 1967). Such behavior would result in an indolent and apathetic indifference to the topic or by an active boycott of the ideas of others, in order to defend the authenticity of his/her own thought.

2 The self-efficacy refers to the confidence of an individual to be in possession of the necessary skills and competencies to achieve certain goals and to influence others (Bandura, 1997).

3 Despite the fact that in many cases phone companies contracts could be activated independently of the ownership of a smartphone, fees were included within the attributes evaluated by the consumer in choosing a smartphone because frequently smartphones are sold at an economical price upon subscription of monthly/yearly plans. In these situations, fees have usually already been evaluated by the time of purchase.

4 These are two e-shops specialized in consumer electronics in Italy.

Section 4

# Hybrid Consumer Behaviour in Digital World

# Chapter 9
# The Changing Face of Shopper Behavior and E-Tailing
## The New Paradigm

**Rajesh V.**
*Retail Strategy Consulting & Knowledge Partner, India*

## ABSTRACT

*E-Tailing has captured the collective imagination of shoppers as also various entrepreneurs and of course the media. In spite of the extensive amount of material being written about E-Tailing, a comprehensive perspective is missing with regard to this sector. There is also some amount of mystery which shrouds E-Tailing because most of the operators are not profitable, notably the biggest of them all: Amazon. The chapter provides a 360 degree view about E-Tailing from a global context as also touches upon how this is influencing this sector in India. Starting from the basic premise of E-Tailing the chapter would also cover shopper behavior and the related key drivers for this business segment. It explores the various business models and their viability as also how technology impacts the shoppers and E-Tail to the extent that physical stores might no longer exist. E-Tail was based on the basic premise that this business would be more profitable than physical stores because of the savings on real estate cost as they need not open physical stores. In spite of the increasing penetration of the internet and smart phone usage, E-Tail is still in its evolution and the optimal business model is yet to be well established. The cost of fulfillment which refers to the cost required to deliver the products is turning out to be a challenge to manage and is negating the savings on real estate because of the absence of physical stores. This led to the market place model where in the E-Tailer does not hold any inventory and that is a saving for them as compared to the inventory led model where they would have to invest in the inventory. However, this has not been a major breakthrough as the investment on technology continues to be a major cost for any E-Tailer. In spite of these challenges E-Tail is considered to be the way forward largely because it is well placed to cater to some of the key shopper expectations such as - simplifying their life, value delivery, customization and speed. Although this business opportunity is aligned to some of the key customer expectations, the business model needs to be powerful as also viable and sustainable. It is in that context that any E-Tailer needs to adhere to the "Basic Retail Model" as also have a well defined revenue model. The changing dynamics of retail has led to the omni channel model where physical stores and online merge*

DOI: 10.4018/978-1-4666-9921-2.ch009

Copyright © 2016, IGI Global. Copying or distributing in print or electronic forms without written permission of IGI Global is prohibited.

*seamlessly to offer a comprehensive shopping experience. The need for this from a shopper's perspective is validated from the fact that many E-Tailers are now opening physical touch points for their customers. Clearly this is the way forward and stand alone online or offline retail might find the going tough if they do not embrace omni channel especially in the context of the changes that affect this sector such as Big Data and Analytics, Internet of things and Wearable devices, Virtual wallets and last but not the least 3D printing.*

## INTRODUCTION

E-Tailing is a sub set of the larger universe of electronic commerce or E-Commerce as it is popularly known. Any transaction or commercial activity done on the internet in a virtual manner comes under the ambit E-Commerce. The earliest instance of this is reported to be in the early 1970s. Initially online transactions were largely limited organizations and institutions and then went on to become a common activity involving the public.

Today E-Commerce spans any commercial activity across a wide spectrum and can be classified as being Business-To-Business (B2B) transaction or a Business-To-Consumer (B2C) one. This has further evolved to combinations such as Consumer to Business, Consumer to Consumer and of course online transactions with the government by the businesses as also the public. In other words such transactions are also referred to as one-to-many, many-to-one and many-to-many.

In 2014 the total global E-Commerce sales has been estimated to be more than a Trillion USD and is growing at a very fast pace. The rate of acceleration has increased in the Asia – Pacific region led by countries like China and to some extent India. This is credited to the explosion in smart phone users and has also led to the term mobile commerce. The current trends indicate that more that 40% of the internet users have engaged in some form of E-Commerce and this is bound to increase in the years to come.

E-Commerce has led to many dramatic paradigm shifts in the way business was being conducted and the best example for this is with regard to the travel industry, namely air travel. This is validated by the fact that almost a third of B2C E-Commerce in the USA or UK is pertaining to digital travel and in a developing market like India, this is as high as 75%.

Online booking and the immediate delivery of the ticket to the passenger on their computer has redefined the entire transaction process. This change led to the elimination of the requirement to print and deliver physical tickets, which is now being done by the passenger themselves. Even this is undergoing a change where there is no need for a physical, printed ticket.

This shift led to redefining the business and delivery model of airlines wherein one of the key roles of the intermediaries did not exist any longer; printing and delivery of tickets. Needless to say, technology has been a critical component which has driven such a change. However, that by itself is not the reason for such a dramatic shift.

Passenger or customer mindset is a crucial element. When one of the pioneers in low cost airlines in India introduced this concept they faced the challenge of existing customer mind sets and some practical realities. There were many potential customers who did not know how to transact online, there were many who did not have computers and internet at home and lastly very few people had printers at home. Even customers who had access to computers and printers were not comfortable transacting online because of security concerns. This led to service providers who would book and print tickets on behalf of such customers. Over a period of time with the change in the environmental factors and the customer mind sets, these intermediaries have disappeared because they do not offer any value now.

E-Tailing has also evolved in a similar manner and technology has played an important role in the success of this business segment. However, the shopper mind set and changing shopping behavior has been the catalyst for E-Tailing to become one of the fastest growing segments of business globally. Changes in shopper behavior in turn is impacted due to socio-economic factors as also several other reasons such as changes in consumption patterns, maturity levels of consumption, role of brands and branded products, etc.

This chapter will delve into the shopper mind set, their expectations and therefore their behavior with regard to pre-purchase, purchase and post-purchase. Human beings are not static and are influenced by change as also influence the change. That has been the case of E-Tailing and shopper behavior continues to influence how E-Tail changes in the years ahead. Shopper behavior such as wanting to experience the product has led to a concept called Showrooming. This refers to the shopping behavior of visiting physical stores to experience the product and get first hand information about the same after which the actual purchase is made online. This trend of shoppers wanting to have the "Touch, Feel & See" experience is now influencing E-Tailers to consider opening physical touch points or stores.

There is also a trend called as Reverse Showrooming where the shopper does the reverse. They use online resources to research about the product and narrow their choice. However, they go to a physical store to make the actual purchase. This trend has been a trigger for physical retailers to explore E-Tail and now omni channel options.

Catering to shopper expectations and being viable is the objective of the E-Tail business. However, most of the E-Tailers are reporting losses of mind blowing magnitude. In that context, the question arises as to whether this line of business will even survive in spite of shopper acceptance. On the other hand, there are examples of E-Tailers who are successful in terms of shopper base as also make profits. This leads to the question with regard to which is the right business model for a successful E-Tail venture. Apart from discussing some of the business models currently being followed, the chapter would also explore the emerging confluence of physical and virtual retail which is referred to as omni channel or multi channel retail.

The objective of this chapter is to give a comprehensive 360 degree perspective about E-Tail especially from a shopper behavior perspective. This would help understand the changing paradigms of shopping and therefore the various E-Tailing models.

## LITERATURE REVIEW

According to Turban et al. (2006) e-tailing is defined as retailing conducted online, over the internet. Zeithaml (2002) has defined that the success of e-tailing depends on the efficient web site design, effective shopping and prompt delivery. The other e-store services are delivery on real time, return and replacement process, period of filling out online orders form, speed of response time to e-customers queries. Rao (1999) e-commerce offers increased market activity for retailers in the form of growing market access and information and decreased operating and procurement costs. Myerson (1999) expressed that consumers are getting smarter in using e-tailers (and online search engines and agents) for convenience and comparison shopping. Guttman et al. (1998) describes several unique elements make online shopping different from the traditional in-store retail model. Besides offering convenience and expanded product variety, the online model also makes it easy for consumers to access and compare data from multiple sources. Moon (2004) through the different search engines, consumers save time to access to the consumption related information, and which information with mixture of images, sound, and very detailed text description to help consumer learning and choosing the most suitable product . Sheth (1983) also suggested that the consumers have two types of motives while shopping, which are functional and non-functional. The functional motives are mostly about the time, shopping place and consumer's needs, which could be like one-stop shopping to save time, the environmental of shopping place such as free parking place, lower cost of products and available to choose from widely range of products. The non-functional motives are more related with culture or social values, such as the brand name of the store.

Jarvanpaa and Todd (1997) Internet shopping and traditional shopping are sharing many similarities, at the same time, it still exists some differences between them, such as the Internet shopping could provide convenience and interactive services, and the traditional shopping could gives customers more comfortable shopping environment and good quality of products Lee and Chung (2000) Both aspect of shopping malls are trying to improving their services by learn commutatively from each other, such as traditional shopping malls provide more parking spaces, more counters, and closer to residential area in order to improve services in convenience;

## NEED OF THE STUDY

Retailers are increasingly leveraging their presence across channels of catalogue, web, stores and kiosks, to increase their share of the customer's wallet and expand across consumer segments. Recent studies on consumer shopping behaviour indicate that multichannel shoppers show a significantly higher value and frequency of purchase than single channel shoppers. Thus, the focus of modern retailing shifted to 'e-tailing', one of the most adoptive channel.

## MAIN FOCUS OF THE CHAPTER

### Issues, Controversies, Problems

Interest in E-Tailing started with a basic premise that it would be more profitable than physical or brick-and-mortar retail chains. The points which supported this view were:

- **Savings on Real Estate Cost:** This is one of the largest cost components for a physical retail chain and needs to be incurred for every store that they open. It was widely believed that E-Tail would benefit from the fact that they do not need to open many stores and that this would become a cost advantage.
- **Savings on Store Staff:** This is the next biggest cost for a retailer and is again proportional to the number of stores being operated. A similar logic to the savings on real estate cost was assumed for this as E-Tailers need not have so many frontline staff.
- **Lower Operating Costs Spread over a Larger Coverage of the Market:** The most compelling argument in favor of the E-Tail business was that the costs were not proportional to the expansion of their market coverage. That is, they can service a larger geographic area and therefore generate higher sales with the same investments made on their site, warehouse, etc.

However time has proved that while some of these costs might be lesser, there are other costs which have in some case negated the cost advantage from real estate and labor costs. One of the key elements which has redefined this perspective is the cost of fulfillment or the cost incurred to deliver the products.

In a physical store the customers tend to come, purchase and take away their purchases. In a few categories there are deliveries made to the home and some retailers even charge for the same. In certain markets like India, even physical stores do home delivery of purchases but they are only a subset of the total sales.

However, in the case of E-Tail, every purchase needs to be delivered to the customer and this has cost implications in terms of storage, packaging, delivery, cost of returns and replacements, etc. This cost of delivery remains as a constant irrespective of the purchase value and margins generated from that sale. In addition to this there is an additional cost involved when the E-Tailer offers "Cash on Delivery" (CoD) because a percentage of such orders will be cancelled when the delivery happens and there is no sale, although the cost of fulfillment has to be incurred for this transaction. In effect this is a net loss to the E-Tailer.

The other factor is with regard to the warehouse space required for an E-Tailer and the sophistication of their supply chain management systems. Although the individual store costs are saved on account of virtual presence, the cost of advanced warehouses to cater to the shoppers have led to high costs which negate the cost advantage of not having to invest in multiple physical stores.

Similarly, the savings from store staff cost is again offset because of the large number of fulfillment staff required as also the customer service centre staff who are needed to provide telephonic support and service. In addition to this an E-Tailer incurs a large cost on technology in terms of the site, content as also the hardware and software required to keep the business running.

Over the years, E-Tail has realized that there is no significant cost differential that they can leverage. This has led these operators to try out various business models and the two basic business approaches that are used in E-Tail are:

- **Inventory Led Model:** In this approach the E-Tailer holds inventory of the merchandise that they offer and leverage volume. The inventory led model is similar to the approach taken by large retail chains and the core of this approach is; Volume aggregation and Efficient Supply Chain Management. However, these involve significant investments in inventory, logistics and supply chain infrastructure.
- **Market Place Model:** The alternative approach is to back end their business with tie up with several suppliers, vendors and small traders/ retailers who hold the inventory and fulfills the orders by the customers. In this approach the E-Tailer operates more like a facilitator where he connects the buyers with the sellers. Although this approach does not require the investments in inventory, there are other business risks like lack of control over the fulfillment and variance in the level of servicing by the different suppliers, etc.

Amazon who is considered to be a benchmark with regard to E-Tail interesting uses the market place approach. More importantly, their business model now has many more components. Apart from the online retail business they are active in the internet services and offerings on the kindle eco system. Leveraging their vast network and server capabilities, they offer cloud based offerings across the globe.

Similar is the case with Alibaba, the successful Chinese B2B E-Commerce business. The visible parts of their business model are E-Tailing with TaoBao, Tmall and of course the Alibaba B2B site. However they are also present in the online payment processing space and have stakes in micro blogging sites, etc.

Therefore this space has a lot of grey areas as these E-Tailers are clearly in businesses which go far beyond online retail and most of the large global retailers today have an online presence today. Therefore clearly defining E-Tail and isolating the same from physical retail is not practically possible. In that context, the sales growth of Wal-Mart's online offering is catching up with Amazon. On the other hand Amazon is exploring opportunities in establishing physical foot prints in terms of pick up points.

The time has come when E-Tail in isolation is not a viable and sustainable option if the business aims to build scale and sustainability. The emerging trend of multi-channel and more recently omni-channel retail is the way forward in the future.

*Multi-channel retail* refers to offering multiple and alternative channels for the shoppers to make their purchases. These could be physical or virtual and are usually independent of each other.

*Omni channel* on the other hand is about creating a seamless shopper experience across the various retail channels being operated. The various shopper interfaces need to be integrated to ensure that there is no disconnect with regard to delivering what the shopper is expecting. For example; a shopper could browse on their mobile and place an order to come and physically pick up the purchases from a store.

The inevitable question is with regard to why these retailing channels have emerged and more importantly why are the physical and E-Tail models merging to offer an Omni channel solution? The answer lies in the shopper behavior and how it has changed as also the various elements and factors which continue to influence the same.

The key facets which influences shopper behavior are:

*Shopper evolution*: Shoppers evolve along the levels that have been described in the *Maslow's Hierarchy of Needs*. There are basic purchases that cater to the fundamental need of physiological needs and then to fulfill the safety needs. In under developed and developing economies most of the shoppers are preoccupied with the fulfillment of these needs. However, as economies develop and income levels increase, the shopper also evolves and moves up in the hierarchy of needs. They start aspiring to purchase products which will fulfill the higher needs. For example, a shopper in a under developed country might not be bothered about organic food whereas the same product category will find favor with shoppers in developed economies because they are purchasing such products to fulfill their belonging or esteem needs.

The other important influence on shopper evolution is the exposure to media and the extent of information they receive and process. As media access increases, the level of information to the shopper increases and this is often cross referenced between public sources as also personal sources. For example a shopper might read about a new product and then they validate the information with their circle of contacts in social media.

*So, the key element for shopper evolution is increased income levels and media exposure.*

Mature shoppers are those who have moved up the hierarchy and have a higher level of expectation from their retail experiences whether it is in terms of range, quality, price or the extent of service. Such shoppers are open to experimentation and are usually the early adopters for any changes including E-Tail.

One of the first successful categories of products which led to Amazon's success is books and music. This is a high involvement category where consumers used to prefer the browsing and reading experience while making their purchases. However, shopper evolution created a window of opportunity for Amazon to establish a beachhead.

Exposure to media and online resources led to mature shoppers to experience the book beforehand in terms of reading sample chapters, reviews, etc. Once the shopper was certain about the purchase, only the transaction remained which was fulfilled by Amazon along with a price advantage. In the years to come, their site has integrated a lot of these experiential elements in terms of reviews, samples chapters, etc., to ensure that the shopper gets all the required resources in one site. This is similar to a one stop shop in physical retail.

Shoppers across the globe are increasingly behaving in a similar manner largely because of exposure to the same or similar media. The social media explosion combined with increasing use of smart phones has made media exposure a global equalizer. This has been one of the key behavioral factors for the acceptance of E-Tail and its growth.

*Category context*: Different categories evoke varying levels of involvement, interest as also shopper response. This is closely tied in with shopper evolution and they display varying levels of interest and involvement to the same category. Apparel is a good example to illustrate this point. At a basic level if the shopper would aim to fulfill the safety need and the primary importance would be for quality and price. As the shopper evolves, these would become hygiene factors and the expectation shifts to fulfilling the belonging or esteem needs.

This would change the shopper behavior in terms of the type of products they look for, the place of purchase and their perception with regard to value.

As shoppers evolve and mature several categories tend to fall into the functional requirement space. The primary expectation while shopping for such functional categories is ease, quality and price. The shopping experience does not have a large role to play in such purchases and E-Tail has stepped into cater to this behavioral trend. Price Waterhouse Cooper's 2015 Total Retail survey has found some interesting category specific trends which illustrates this point:

- **Clothing and Footwear:** Only 30% preferred to do this online while more than 2/3rd preferred to do this in a physical store.
- **Consumer Electronics and Computers:** More than 40% did their purchases online.
- **Books, Video and Games**: More than 60% preferred to purchase this online.
- **Grocery:** Only 17% prefer to do this online.

This survey was done with more than 19,000 respondents across 19 different territories globally and clearly shows the category context of shopper behavior.

*Value definition:* Value is not only about the price. This is not an absolute factor and is driven more by perception. Value can be explained as the net of all the expenses and effort versus the benefit derived from that product. The perceived benefits as also the effort expended varies basis the shopper evolution as also the category context.

Although E-Tail sells products which are by and large the same, their service element plays a strong role in the creation of value in the shopper's mind. This is clearly one of the key drivers of various innovations by E-Tailer in the fulfillment space. Amazon, which has an offering which is similar or same to various other E-Tailers as also physical chains, is pushing the boundary with regard to delivering value in the form of ease of order and fulfillment in the shortest possible time. Apart from experimenting with drones for delivery, they are exploring the use of a one-click ordering mechanism which is based on a subscription service and is in partnership with leading brands. Called as the Amazon Dash button, this small tab can be fixed or hung and is connected through Wi-Fi. When a shopper notices that the product is running low or is finished, they need to just press the button on this tab. Their order gets processed immediately through the mobile app. This is being offered in association with brands for various categories and for example you can place a button which is in partnership with a detergent brand on the washing machine. When the detergent seems low or gets over, the shopper just presses the button and the product gets delivered.

The counter point to value is with regard to a category like apparel. In such cases the experience of the various colors, styles, etc., is more important than the speed of ordering and delivery. As such there would be no value if a solution along the lines of Amazon Dash Button was offered for this category.

*Environmental factors*: Several environmental factors have been a catalyst with regard to E-Tailing. The obvious ones are internet access and the explosion of smart phones. However, these are only the tip of the ice berg. Two other important factors which have had a profound effect on E-Tailing are:

- Payment methods and the increasing use of cashless transactions – Increasing use of credit cards led to the acceptance of online transactions in the initial stages of E-Tail and the current trend of E-Wallets and mobile wallets has only helped to increase the pace of this acceptance. The fundamental driver of this factor is the ease of payment to complete the transaction in a safe and secure manner. These payment options remove the requirement for multiple steps when processing the purchase and not only hasten the same but also makes it easy and simple.
- Global sourcing and logistics to support the same – Over the past few decades manufacturing and sourcing has no longer be restricted to domestic markets. Increasingly companies are outsourcing their manufacturing to countries like China to take advantage of lower costs. This had led to a virtuous cycle where such manufacturing bases today have built enormous scale and that helps to keep the costs low and extremely competitive. Logistics and supply chain management practices have also advanced significantly aided by technology. This translates into being able to offer a range which is not constrained by geography and that by itself has become a competitive advantage.

In the past decade or so, shoppers across the globe, especially in the younger age groups have similar buying behavior and preferences. This is largely due to the uniform media exposures that these shoppers are getting through the internet and satellite television. In a manner of speaking there is a globalization of shoppers which is underway and this is one of the key enabling factors for E-Tail as they can sell similar products and categories across countries, thereby leveraging a larger scale from centralized manufacturing and supply chain locations.

The key expectations of shoppers today revolve around the following elements and any E-Tailer who lives up to these can be confident of being successful.

*Simplify life*: The modern lifestyle involves multiple challenges and high levels of stress. Technological advancements have ironically only made the daily schedule of most shoppers more demanding and complex. In such an environment the shopper's primary expectation is to simplify their lives at least with regard to the shopping experience. This expectation is being catered to by a variety of innovations such as:

- The ease of browsing and ordering especially on the mobile.
- Seamless integration between online and offline shopping experience which has led to the evolution of omni channel solutions by physical retailers and the new trend of exploring physical touch points by E-Tailers.

- Easy check out and payment options which simplify the transaction which has been the key trigger for the development of e-wallet and online payment mechanisms.
- Faster delivery is triggering innovation in terms of use of drones, analytics to predict potential orders and have the shipment ready to move out. A recent development in the Indian E-Tail space has been to leverage the reach of local small stores as also tie up with existing operators like the postal system as also the famous *Dabbawalas* of Mumbai.

*Value delivery*: Value as detailed earlier in the chapter is about exceeding the shopper expectations and delivering a net positive experience. Although price plays a key role in value delivery, the informed shoppers today have realized that price by itself is irrelevant. Conversely very low prices tend to create an element of doubt with regard to the quality and credibility of the offering. The shoppers today expect value to be delivered on four fronts and are willing to trade off each of these to some extent if some of the other factors will offset this compromise.

- **Range:** This is one of the key components of the value perception. The shopper expects to find a wide range of products which offers them a large choice and also depth in terms of variants, sizes, etc. E-Tail is able to deliver this component of value perception far better than the physical stores because they can feature and present a larger range of products on their site than a physical store which would have size constraints. The challenge lies in being able to deliver any of the products purchased online and a market place model is better suited to do that.
- **Price:** Shopper expect online prices to be lower and therefore price has become a hygiene factor with regard to delivering value perception in E-Tail. However, this need not be a default choice especially if the E-Tailer is able to bundle other benefits as part of the value proposition. In such instances the E-Tailer need not offer deep discounts and can feature token mark downs to be in line with the shopper's expectation of online prices being lower.
- **The Shopping Experience:** This element is assuming multiple dimensions in the context of E-Tailing. Starting from the access to browsing and then the actual transaction as also the receipt of the products purchased, every stage adds to detracts to the overall experience. The increasing use of smart phones is redefining the access to an E-Tailer and has led to an explosion of apps usage.
- **Post Purchase Service and Support:** This is a very important factor in the repeat purchase and subsequent loyalty of any shopper. The challenge for an E-Tailer is to ensure that the products are delivered when promised and without any delay, while also ensuring that their fulfillment costs parameters are adhered to. Although the shopper accepts the virtual reality of the transaction, they expect some human intervention in case of any kind of service issues. The prompt redressal of any such problem, especially with some human interface adds to the experience and vice versa.

*Individuality*: Shoppers today make purchases which are not limited to functional reasons alone. This is the main reason why they expect a wide range of products to choose from. This behavior is largely influenced by the increasing spending power of shoppers. Ironically, this also creates a desire to stand apart and purchase products which reflect their individuality. This purchasing power also leads them to expect a customized experience where they are recognized and rewarded for their loyalty. This shopper expectation has led to E-Tailers customizing solutions which are driven by Big Data Analytics. E-Tail is better placed than physical stores to cater to this shopper expectation because they can identify the shopper far more easily and consistently. As compared to a physical store where the staff need to identify the shopper and offer them a customized experience, online access automatically identifies the shopper to an E-Tailer. Coupled with the enormous amount of analytical information about the shopper that is available through big data, global E-Tailers today can give very specific, targeted and relevant offerings to each shopper, individually.

*Speed*: One of the inherent characteristics of today's lifestyle is the fast pace of almost every facet in a person's life. Technology has made waiting irrelevant largely through the smart phone and internet access. Be it a search for information, communication or any kind of transaction, speed is the key expectation. E-Tailers are compelled to cater to this expectation mainly with regard to the delivery of products. Apart from various other fulfillment initiatives, E-Tailers are today experimenting with innovations such as predictive picking. Amazon has been working on using shopper data and past buying behavior to predict what they would shop as soon as they log into the site and start browsing. This enables their fulfillment centre to pick the product from their vast warehouses and keep it ready for shipping as soon as the shopper hits the confirmation button. This shopper expectation is also intertwined with the expectation of simplifying life. As the pace of life picks up because of lifestyle changes, the time taken for functional chores is seen to be boring and irritating by the customers. A speedy solution to being able to complete such functional chores would always be welcome and have a high value perception.

Very clearly E-Tail as a business proposition has several elements which are aligned to the key expectations of shoppers today. Their value proposition can be tailored to fulfill a few or even all the above mentioned expectations. However, catering to any shopper expectation invariably leads to cost and the question for E-Tailers is whether these costs are worth the returns. It is therefore imperative that that the business should have a powerful value proposition which is also viable and sustainable. This is where a robust business model comes into play and any E-Tailer who does not have a well defined business model will not succeed in the long run.

## SOLUTIONS AND RECOMMENDATIONS

Factoring in the shopper evolution and their key expectations, it is easy to understand why businesses are leaning more and more towards the Omni channel model. However, a business can still be only an E-Tailer and still succeed. Regardless of whether the business wants to adopt a pure play E-Tail model or an Omni channel one, they need to keep in mind that retail lies at the heart of both these approaches. The "Basic Retail Model" is a simple guiding principle to build the basic blocks of a retail business whether it is physical, virtual or a combination of these (see Figure 1).

- **Truly Different Store:** The first step in creating this self sustaining cycle of success is to create a truly different E-Retail site. This could be in terms of the range, user interface, pricing, services, etc. The underlying principle being that the shopper should perceive the difference when they browse the site, make their purchases and it should add to the overall experience. This is easier said than done as the pace of technological changes picks up and everyone would find it easy to duplicate something being done.
- **Better Value:** As discussed earlier in the chapter, value is not about low prices only. Many E-Tailers tend to operate on the premise that discounts and low prices is a de facto requirement.

*Figure 1. Basic retail model*

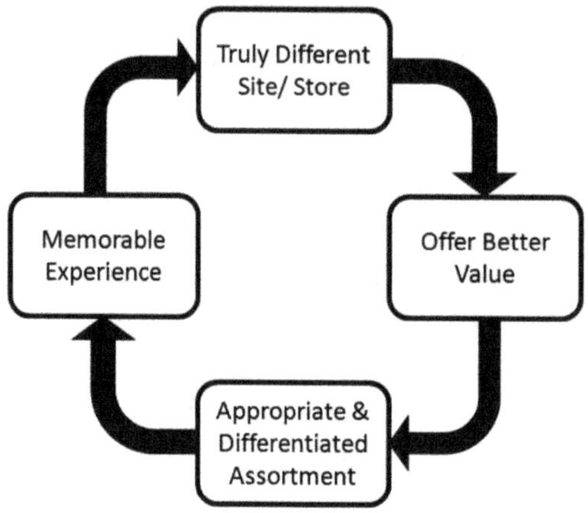


This is misguided and they should examine the various components of value in the context of shopper evolution as also the category context. Value can also be in the form of a different site and a fantastic user interface.

- **Appropriate and Differentiated Assortment:** This is a very powerful part of the model. The core to any retail business is products being offered and the customer's desire to purchase the same. Unless the customer gets a relevant range, there is no reason for them to patronize a site. This is both an opportunity and a challenge with regard to E-Tail because it is possible to offer the whole universe on any site. However, the challenge would be to fulfill the purchases of any shopper. As such, E-Tail needs to strike a fine balance between the range of products being offered and the actual inventory being managed to ensure fulfillment. Although the assortment being offered should be appropriate and relevant to the shopper, a part of this range should be unique and different. This not only helps in building loyalty through repeat visits but also helps to create a truly different store as also establish the value perception. Needless to say, the actual fulfillment of purchases is crucial to this element.
- **Memorable Experience:** The primary tipping point for consumers to start experiencing the self service formats was the 'Touch, Feel & See' factor. In a similar manner the catalyst for E-Tail has been the novelty and ease of purchasing. In the case of E-Tail this element has multiple dimensions. The first one is the user interface when browsing the site, searching for the products, making the selection and finally processing the payment even if it is cash on delivery. Ironically this experience is not under the control of the E-Tailer alone. Poor internet connectivity, problems with the shopper's computer or smart phone, issues regarding their credit or debit cards, etc., can spoil this experience. Successful E-Tailers need to factor in all these variables and endeavor to avoid any unpleasant experience while the shopper is browsing. Next and most important is the experience with regard to receiving the product on time and in a proper condition. Here the role of the delivery person assumes paramount importance and E-Tailers who invest in this space would definitely create a powerful competitive advantage. The last experiential element is with regard to the handling of returns, complaints, etc., this is again an enormous opportunity to create a difference and leave behind a memorable experience. In today's context of social media and instant sharing

of information, the experience factor can be a double edged sword. A truly memorable experience leads to positive word of mouth and generates lots of goodwill. Alternatively any shortcomings are quickly pointed out and publicized.

The "Basic Retail Model" helps to define a powerful value proposition which could become a long term competitive advantage. However, that is not enough for the sustenance and viability of an E-Tailer. The business needs to generate profits and do so consistently. In order to do that an E-Tailer needs to build their offering by becoming the best in at least one of the four components of the model. An E-Tailer has the choice of being known for:

- Their range of products
- The price
- Their service and shopper experience

All three involve investments and trying to be the best on all these fronts is not a long term viable strategy. Although low prices are the easiest approach to take, it is rarely sustainable unless the business builds such enormous scale that the low prices can be supported by exceptionally low sourcing costs. In the absence of deep pockets and also massive scale, it would be better for an E-Tailer to explore one of the other two options; range and/ or service.

This does not mean that the E-Tailer can focus on one element while completely ignoring the other two. They need to focus on excelling in one while ensuring basic hygiene levels in the others.

The other side of the coin with regard to a sustainable business is with regard to revenues. Depending on the model being followed the E-Tailer has the option to choose revenue streams. Inventory led models leverage the power of volume aggregation and lower cost of sourcing. Market place models generate revenues from various fees including advertising on the site. One common indicator for any E-Tailer's business is Gross Merchandise Value (GMV). This is the total value of all the products they have sold and indicates the potential revenue of the E-Tailer, regardless of the model they follow.

## FUTURE DIRECTIONS

There are several technological advancements which might redefine the way retail and E-Tail function. The important developments that will impact online shopping are –

*Integrated customer view through Big Data and analytics*: Identifying the shopper to know about their buying behavior as also the likes and dislikes is becoming easier by the day. In the past the shopper had the freedom to identify themselves or remain anonymous. This is no longer an option especially with regard to E-Tail. The shopper needs to log in to make purchases and that by default identifies them and tracks their buying behavior. This could be in terms of pages browsed, products viewed, purchased, cancelled, etc. With the increasing use of smart phones and mobile apps, this understanding now goes beyond only the shopping behavior. A shopper's mobile number is emerging as their unique identity and is used across a variety of online usage. This is also linked to their social media use and the emerging e-wallets. Big data refers to the analysis of a wide range of disparate data sets from social media use, online shopping, online payments, made, credit usage, etc. This is leading to far higher levels of shopper understanding and customizing the offerings to cater to their requirements as also influencing their shopping in certain instances. This is obviously leading to concerns about privacy and in some instances exerting undue influence on the shopper. This trend is only going to increase although it is expected that there will be strict legal guidelines put into place to protect the individual.

*Internet of Things and Wearable devices*: Chips have started invading most devises being used today and the trend is to be able to link these to the internet. This will enable a connected environment which offers several benefits starting from connectivity and access. This trend will soon get linked to the E-Tail businesses to offer speed and convenience in transactions. The Amazon Dash and Tab discussed earlier in the chapter is a classic example of such a development. Apple and Samsung have introduces smart watches and Google is bringing the Google Glass. These are called as wearable devices and connect the user to the internet without having to pick up and use something like a phone. Gesture commands, voice commands, etc., will start to integrate the use and working of such devices to the daily routine of a person. This technological development will make access to an E-Tail site easier and can also be spontaneous. For example, if a shopper wearing a Google glass notices someone wearing a dress they like, they can use the same device to search for a similar dress and even order it online immediately.

*Virtual wallets*: These are the next stage of evolution in cashless commerce. A shopper transfers money to their virtual wallet and then spends it online or even transfers it from mobile to mobile as the need may be. This can even be based on credit and replace credit cards. This development will go hand in hand with that of wearable devices to increase the pace of acceptance of E-Tail globally as shoppers can complete their transactions spontaneously, easily and in a fast manner.

*Social Media and Customer Engagement*: Traditional loyalty programs using cards is now no longer relevant. The primary purpose of such a card was to have a single identifying factor in the form of a unique number which can then be linked to any transaction made by the customer for easy analysis. The smart phone revolution has led to a shopper's mobile number to become that unique identifying number. This is also easier to use as the number is automatically linked to any activity done using the smart phone. Since shoppers are using the same device for all their browsing, social media and online transaction activities, their mobile number becomes a common bridge to link these disparate databases. Sophisticated tools and software are available today and are being developed which is able to do this detailed analysis and generate the insights about customers. Ironically such analysis might lead to a situation where the E-Tailer might know their shoppers better than the shopper themselves. A study with regard to the applicability of such customer analysis showed that based on the data available a social media site would know their user as much or even slightly better than their own spouse. Needless to say, such insights about the shopper is going to lead to highly targeted and customized offerings which will yield very high response rates.

*3D Printing*: This technology is slowly moving away from a niche space into the mainstream. The application of 3D printing is not confined to any particular space or sector. It spans from doctors having printed out tissues used for surgeries, edible pizza being made, car parts being printed and even a house being made using a large scale 3D printer. One international lifestyle retailer had offered a range of accessories which was made using 3D printing. The primary constraint in this trend has been the cost of the printer which is coming down steadily and might soon enable such printers to become a common household device. In such a context the shoppers might want to purchase the design details and prefer to print out the products at home after customizing the same as per their preferences. In such a scenario physical stores might actually have no role to play and all the shopping for designs would happen only from an E-Tailer.

## CONCLUSION

In conclusion, the demarcation between E-Tail and physical retail is already fuzzy and they would merge and integrate into each other in the future. The rapid developments in technology and shopper evolution might even change the fundamental construct of a purchase transaction wherein the shopper is not purchasing the end product at all and creates the product at their end.

Even if that does not happen, the integration between physical and virtual shopping is definitely not far away. Retailers would leverage physical stores to deliver the experience while using the online space for transaction processing and fulfillment. Thus, the end of stand along physical retail as also pure E-Tail is not far away, the sustainable alternative that will endure will ultimately be Omni Channel Retail.

## REFERENCES

Guttman, R. H., Moukas, A. G., & Maes, P. (1998). Agents as Mediators in Electronic Commerce. *International Journal of Electronic Markets*, *8*(1), 22–27. doi:10.1080/10196789800000007

Information Economy Report. (2015). *Unlocking the Potential of E-commerce for Developing Countries.* Retrieved from http://unctad.org/en/PublicationsLibrary/ier2015_en.pdf

Jarvenpaa, S. L., & Todd, P. A. (1996). Consumer Reactions to Electronic Shopping on the World Wide Web. *Journal of Electronic Commerce*, *1*(2), 59–88. doi:10.1080/10864415.1996.11518283

Lee, K., & Chung, N. (2000). Effect of virtual reality-driven shopping mall and consumer's purchase intention. *Korean Management Review*, *29*(3), 377–405.

Maxwell, J., & Brewster, M. (2015). Price Waterhouse Cooper's Total Retail survey. *PriceWaterhouseCooper.* Retrieved from http://www.pwc.com/gx/en/retail-consumer/retail-consumer-publications/global-multi-channel-consumer-survey/index.jhtml

Metters, R., & Walton, S. (2007). Strategic supply chain choices for multi-channel Internet retailers. *Service Business*, *1*(4), 317–331. doi:10.1007/s11628-006-0016-5

Moon, B.-J. (2004). Consumer adoption of the internet as an information search and product purchase channel: some research hypotheses. *Int. Journal of Internet Marketing and Advertising, 1*(1).

PricewaterhouseCooper. (2015). *2015 Total Retail survey.* http://www.pwc.com/gx/en/retail-consumer/retail-consumer-publications/global-multi-channel-consumer-survey/index.jhtml#

Rajesh, V. (2010). *The Indian reTALEs*. India: Unicorn Publishers.

Rao, B. (1999). The Internet and the revolution in distribution: A cross-industry examination. *Technology in Society*, *21*(3), 287–306. doi:10.1016/S0160-791X(99)00018-4

Sheth, J. N. (1983). An integrative theory of patronage preference and behaviour. In W. R. Darden & R. F. Lusch (Eds.), *Patronage behavior and retail management* (pp. 9–28). Orlando, FL: Elsevier.

Turban, E., King, D., Viehland, D., & Lee, J. (2006). *Electronic Commerce: A Managerial Perspective, International*. Upper Saddle River, NJ: Prentice Hall.

Information Economy Report, Unlocking the Potential of E-commerce for Developing Countries. (2015). *UNCTAD*. Retrieved from http://unctad.org/en/PublicationsLibrary/ier2015_en.pdf

Zeithaml, V. A. (2002). Service excellent in electronic channels. *Managing Service Quality*, *12*(3), 135–139. doi:10.1108/09604520210429187

# Chapter 10
# Discernment of Youth towards E-Retailing in Asian and Gulf Marketing Territories

**Soney Mathews**
*INTI-IU, Malaysia*

**Seema Varshney**
*Waljat College of Applied Sciences, Oman*

**Jagdeep Singh Jassel**
*INTI-IU, Malaysia*

## ABSTRACT

*Internet has created an opportunities for businesses especially retailers to stay connected with customers in the era of globalization. The customers can make purchases in a faster and convenient manner with the use of internet. E- Retailing is becoming very prominent and is being accepted by every age group across the world over the last few decades. Customers are embracing the shift from physical store to virtual store for purchase of products. E- Commerce has been grown very fast because of many advantages associated with buying on internet because of lower transaction and search cost as compared to other types of shopping. Through online shopping consumers can buy faster, more alternatives and can order product and services with comparative lowest price. (Cuneyt and Gautam 2004). This research paper will focus on youth of different social, national cultural backgrounds and their perception and attitude towards e-retailing .This also attempts to find out the important factors that make them loyal towards a particular marketer, without personal interaction.*

## INTRODUCTION

Internet has created an opportunities for businesses especially retailers to stay connected with customers in the era of globalization. The customers can make purchases in a faster and convenient manner with the use of internet. The Internet is becoming an increasingly important channel for conducting business and attracting clients. The Internet enables businesses to reach new markets and new consumers.

DOI: 10.4018/978-1-4666-9921-2.ch010

Copyright © 2016, IGI Global. Copying or distributing in print or electronic forms without written permission of IGI Global is prohibited.

However, merely 'reaching' new consumers is not enough; it is also necessary to retain them and earn their loyalty (Eduard & Frederic, 2007).

E-Retailing is becoming very prominent and is being accepted by every age group across the world over the last few decades. Customers are embracing the shift from physical store to virtual store for purchase of products. The exponential increases in online shopping and the unprecedented rate of growth in the number of retailers selling online have created an extremely competitive marketplace where most e-retailers have yet to turn a profit (David M. & Richard T 2000).

The trend of e-commerce has been increased rapidly in the recent years with the development of internet and due to the easy accessibility of internet usage. Easy access to internet has driven consumers to shop online in fact according to the University of California, Los Angeles (UCLA) communication policy (2001), online shopping is third most popular activity on the internet after email using and web browsing.

E- Commerce has been grown very fast because of many advantages associated with buying on internet because of lower transaction and search cost as compared to other types of shopping. Through online shopping consumers can buy faster, more alternatives and can order product and services with comparative lowest price. (Cuneyt & Gautam 2004).

As e-commerce is growing rapidly, marketers and retailers are prudently analyzing the consumers' attitude and behavior towards the online shopping and are spending millions of dollars to assist all the demographics of online shoppers. Internet shopping accounts for less than 1% of all purchases in South-East Asia—a region twice as populous as America, where the proportion is nearly 10%. But surging smartphone use and a broadening middle class mean the market is set to multiply; perhaps fivefold by 2018, reckons Frost & Sullivan, a consulting firm.

The growth of internet has brought a rapid changes in the buying behavior of consumers. E-retailing has become an emerging preference of all consumers. Retailing with youth is also becoming exciting and challenging for marketers in the 21st Century. The younger generation of today have become more associated with technology. Their inclination towards technology have engaged them in online shopping. There are major changes in their buying behavior too. They are moving towards easy mode of buying through e retailing rather than physical retailing.

This research paper will focus on youth of different social, national cultural backgrounds and their perception and attitude towards e-retailing .This also attempts to find out the important factors that make them loyal towards a particular marketer, without personal interaction. This research study is focused on three countries i.e. India, Malaysia and Oman. The study adds value to the literature review of youth perception and attitude towards e-retailing and also e-satisfaction and e-trust.

The objectives of conducting this research are:

- To study the e-factors influencing perception and attitude of youth towards e-retailing;
- To understand the relationship between the e-factors and e-satisfaction of youth towards e-retailing;
- To understand the relationship between the e-factors and e-trust of youth towards e-retailing;
- To study the relationship between e-satisfaction, e-trust and e-loyalty of youth towards e-retailing.

## REVIEW OF LITERATURE

### E-Retailing in the 21st Century

Purchasing habits fluctuate over time with every generation, but because of increased access to new technology and uncertainty due to world events and insecure futures, the consumer trends of generations have changed. In order for businesses to appeal to these consumers, it is important to understand what these buying habits are, how they have changed, and what techniques can be utilized to expand sales among consumer segments.

Online shopping is a growing phenomenon worldwide and with increase in internet penetration India too is witnessing a surge in online shopping. Consumer buying behavior is a widely researched area but online buying behavior is a relatively new field of study. Marketers are trying to understand the online buying behavior of Indian consumers so that they can look out for new ways of identifying distinct profitable customer segments and targeting them better. Marketers need to know who are the online customers, what are they buying online and why, what prevents them from buying online, what other factors affect their online buying behavior, does social media have any influence on their buying behavior (Indrila & Rupa 2014).

There are various benefits to consumers while purchasing through online. The benefits include ability of a better price when compared to price range offered by merchants, access to a wider choice of merchandise, being open for 24*7 and the convenience of not having to drive to a physical store. But despite that the online shopping cannot replace the experience of shopping in a retail store or the entertainment value of going to a mall or market.

A customer who knows exactly what he or she wants can look it up online, read and compare the information, and purchase from the site that offers the best price or service. But a shopper, who is uncertain what to look for, or who just enjoys browsing through items on display, will prefer a retail store where the merchandise can be seen, handled and sampled. Many people who are currently familiar with computers and do feel comfortable using the Internet to shop and are likely to change their purchasing habits.

E-retailing is when a marketer selling goods and services through the use of internet. E-retailing is also called as e-tailing. E-retailing is promoted widely as a convenient avenue for shopping. Shopping online can economize on time and effort hy making it easy to locate merchants, find items, and procure offerings (Sridar Balasubramanian. 1997). Consumers do not have to leave their home nor travel to find and obtain merchandise online. They can also browse for items by category or online store.

Success for retailers in the next few years is going to be defined by "Retail Agility", the ability to take advantage of the emergence of a plethora of new markets, channels, products and customer segments which shows no signs of abating. The rapid expansion of sales and marketing channels—more social commerce, gaming commerce, and mobile to name just a few—will continue. At the same time, customers will prefer to patronize retailers who provide an integrated but distinct experience across channels. (Akshay Borawake, Siddharth Asokan, & Sat Vijayaraghavan, n. d.).

The Internet-based retail channels generally offer the consumer a convenient way to explore a broader range of products and product attributes and to compare features and prices. Shopping online helps customers and ensures the health of a growing economy by ensuring that businesses can offer a wider variety of certain items, allow less likelihood of impulse buying, offer convenience for those who do not have time to drive to the mall or outlet stores, and offer product reviews (Smith and Rupp, 2003).

Understanding how the Internet is different has been widely researched in order to help establish how retailers can unlock its potential, either as an alternative or as a complementary retail channel (Rowley, 1996; Morganosky, 1997; Hart, Doherty & Ellis, 2000). Unfortunately, the Internet in its current technological form is a poor service delivery medium because it lacks the capacity for direct personal interaction enjoyed by the most non-internet- based services. Regardless of the Internet's growth and enormous use for marketing purposes, various researchers have reported poor perception of e-service (Kolesar & Galbraith, 2000; Darian & Wiman, 2001; Burke, 2002), and many blunders seem to occur because e-companies fail to deliver real added value services to the customers, and to meet their expectations (Zott, Amit & Donlevy 2000).

Today, we witness the fact that online shopping sites render us the opportunity of easy shopping without taking a lot of hassles. Evolved and effective, eCommerce solutions now drive success of an enterprise. (Kapil Gupta, 2014) The benefits of e-commerce/ e-retailing is:

- There is no time barrier for shopping online. As it is available 24x7, people can log in at any time to buy or sell their products.
- Provides instant information about the products or services.
- Online shopping solutions have facilitated the reduction of costs (both online and offline) for promotions and marketing.
- It is feasible in every manner and it reduces the labor cost and the delivery time.
- Customers are informed about new products through on time alerts.
- Ecommerce development saves the time of consumers as well as the sellers.
- Customer frustration can be avoided.

## Techno-Savvy Consumer towards E-Retailing

Today's consumers are more techno savvy and they always use internet to purchase products and services. They expect their online journey of buying behavior to be smooth. The retailers should also give the consumers unlimited experience. This becomes a challenging factor for the retailers. They are spending a lot on research to understand the mindset of the consumers towards e-retailing across the world. E-retailing is becoming an essential element in retailing and is slowly replacing physical retailing.

The articles by Katharine King (2006) shares research into 18-24-year-old 'urbanites', described by media magnate Rupert Murdoch as 'digital natives' because they have grown up in the era and know nothing else. Forty eight per cent of this group agree with the statement 'When I need information the first place I look in on the internet' and 99% of them own a mobile phone. They consider themselves to be under time pressure and 40% agree there are too many brands, making choice more complicated. The research also identified 10 expectations embedded in young people's lives. Among these are an interesting life full of meaningful experiences; success in multiple areas, not just career; and to be at the hub of a large friendship network.

## Youth Sophistication

Youth at present are getting more inclined to technology and due to this their attitude towards buying behavior is also changing. They are 24/7 attached with internet and are more sophisticated to technology.

They find this tool to be more effective and faster. Youth affiliation towards technology is considered as a lifestyle change and almost all marketers are considering this to be an opportunity towards business prosperity.

Youth in many countries are using the Internet for shopping because they are triggered by diverse attitudes and motivations. Young consumers are seeking value, temporal or short benefits, flexibility, and possibility of exploring products in online environments. Youth always search for convenience in online transactions as it gives them flexibility to browse websites at leisure time. According to a research done in Taiwan it was found that website design, website reliability, website security, and website customer service are the four dominant characteristic factors that influence consumer perceptions of online purchasing. Besides, the four types of online buyers (trial, occasional, frequent and regular online buyers) have different perceptions of these website characteristics. (Indrila & Rupa 2014).

## Overview of E-Retail Market in India, Malaysia, and Oman

India's retail market value was estimated at $520 billion in 2013, and is expected to grow to $950 billion by 2018. With a CAGR currently pegged at 13%, the Indian e-commerce market is expected to grow the fastest within the Asia-Pacific Region – with its market size doubling every 2-2.5 years. This certainly gives us reason for deep introspection. While the global growth rate of online shoppers is estimated at 8-10%, India currently has more than 10 million online shoppers. Though 70% of India's e-commerce market is related to travel (flights, hotel bookings, etc.), electronics and apparels are by far the most important categories in terms of sales. The key driver Indian e-commerce is the rapid increase of broadband internet penetration, which is growing at a whopping 20% every year. The rising standards of the mushrooming middle-class with high disposable incomes, coupled with the urban influence on rural aspirations, have led to an exponential growth of the internet culture in India (Ajay 2015). The way the business is moving and the increasing thrust on e-commerce is re-proving the country's consumption story. E-commerce or e-tailing is the recent paradigm that retailers have had to also confront and already 75 per cent of retailers have adopted e-commerce in some form and globally, retailing has already graduated to a multi-channel, omni-channel retail industry. "E-commerce has emerged out of nowhere and forced retailers to adapt (Ramnath Subbu 2015).

Cloud security company Trend Micro says Malaysians are embracing the web for shopping in increasing numbers. It released a survey revealing that eight of 10 Malaysian Internet users are shopping online. Researcher Nielsen has predicted that Malaysia's online shopping market will hit 5 billion ringgit ($1.5 billion) by 2015. "The rapid growth of online shopping worldwide together with the immense increase of money changing hands in the cyberspace, especially after the reduction of the Online Interbank GIRO (IBG) to 10 sen, will attract more cyber criminals to target online shoppers," said Trend Micro SEA region MD Goh Chee Hoh (Inside Retail Asia 2015). Internet retailing recorded strong current value growth in 2014 due to its convenience. Other than its 24/7 availability, it also offers a huge product portfolio with regular price promotions, fueled by competition among the top players. Thus, consumers are able to shop at anytime and anywhere whenever the mood takes them (Euromonitor, 2015).

Consumers in the Sultanate of Oman are now gradually exploring online shopping options, according to the 2014 Online Shopping Behaviour Study conducted by MasterCard. Nearly 20 per cent of those surveyed indicated they access the internet for online shopping, of which 80 per cent said they were highly satisfied with their online shopping experience (Mastercard survey, 2014). A new Arab Advisors Group survey of Oman's Internet users revealed that around 19.4% of the adult Internet users in the country buy products, pay for services or pay bills online through e-commerce. A new major survey of the Internet users in Oman was conducted by the Arab Advisors Group between January 2014 and April 2014. The survey revealed that around 19.4% of adult Internet users in Oman buy products and pay for services and bills online. The Arab Advisors Group conservatively estimates the number of these e-commerce users to be around 180 thousand users.

## E-FACTORS AND CONCEPTUAL RESEARCH FRAMEWORK

### E-Relationship

Customer e-relationship is always a matter of concern for the retailer. Maintaining an online relationship is called as e-relationship. A marketer while providing e-retailing need to have a favorable e-relationship with the customer. If the consumers are not happy with the service provided they need to improve the e-relationship to retain the customer. The marketer should also attempt to retain a long term relationship. There are few factors which is considered while understanding customer e-relationship. The main factors are like creating a favorable customer relationship, attempts to improve customer relationship, maintain long-term relationship and treating customers as partners (see figure 1).

*Figure 1. E-Relationship factors*

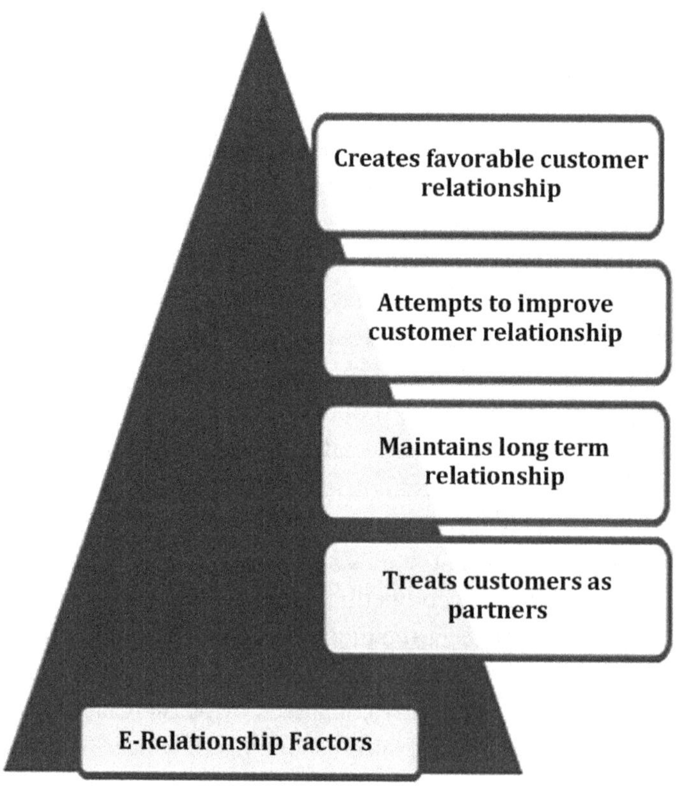

The retailer should always connect with the customer to develop a continuous loyalty. Therefore relationship marketing plays an important role. Relationship marketing theory suggests that it is more valuable for a retailer to invest effort in developing and maintaining close and long-lasting relationships with customers rather than attracting short-term, discrete transactions. Customers in such relationships are found to purchase more, to be willing to pay more for goods and/or services, to exhibit a high tendency to trust, to become emotionally attached to that firm, and to refer customers to the firm (Kumar V., Bohling, & Ladda, 2003; Reichheld & Schefter, 2000).

Kolesar and Galbraith (2000) suggest that establishing a relationship with customers is harder to achieve in an e-retail transaction because alienation makes it harder to create the kind of bond that is often enjoyed between other service providers and their customers. They argue that because the Internet as a medium is less personal than other retail channels, surrogates for direct personal interaction must be provided in an e-retail transaction. Kolesar and Galbraith (2000) further argue that establishing e-retail relationships desired by customers may become easier as consumer values regarding Internet relationships evolve. Interestingly, they conjecture that these values might first emerge among the technologically progressive youth, which helps justify our choice of student samples.

## E-Perceived Value

E-Perceived value means the worth that a product or service has in the mind of the consumer. Customer e-perceived value is an important concept in Marketing. The consumer's e-perceived value of a good or service affects the price that he or she is willing to pay for it. It is the inner feeling of the individual. It's a sense of how customers think and feel. Under e-perceived value we always consider value of money and value of time. Both becomes an important element while evaluating the e-perceived value. By understanding the e-perceived value, the attributes of consumers can be decided and this will benefit the marketers on a larger scale.

## E-Efficiency

E-efficiency is the ability of the e-retailers to do something with quality. It's the relationship between the retailer's and customers' expectations towards product delivery. Under e-efficiency factors like product delivery, customer handling and customer retention is considered. Every consumers consider these factors to be the most important ones and avoid ineffective behaviors.

## E-Fulfillment

E-fulfillment is a level of customer satisfaction. Every customer is highly satisfied when the marketer provided him product or service of his expectations. E-fulfillment is achieved when the e-retailers provide a speedy customer delivery along with a complete flexibility. This will lead to best customer experience.

## E-Privacy

E-privacy is of high priority to every online customers. Honesty followed by the retailers is an important element under e-privacy. Every retailer should also have a centric privacy policy to protect the customers. The retailers should also have a proper technology to implement the e-privacy.

Privacy is one of the key determinants of trust and of success. Internet user privacy is an growing concern. Every consumer desire a greater control over the transmission and use of their personal data. Consumers who do business with companies online are vulnerable in three general ways: (1) the data on their computer may be compromised, (2) the data transfer to an online business may be compromised, and (3) the data stored by the business may be compromised. When consumers are connected to the Internet, information on their personal computers is increasingly vulnerable to intrusions and theft. If a firewall is not installed, it is possible for thieves to hack into consumers' hard drives. The installation of spyware distributed as viruses attached to e-mail makes it possible for third parties to view the content of a consumer's hard drive and track movement through the Internet. Consumers' information is also at risk when they visit Web sites and/or complete transactions online. When consumers provide credit card and personal information to Web sites, this information can be intercepted if the transfer is not encrypted using SSL (secure socket layer) protocols. Privacy can also be compromised with cookies that allow others to track clickstream history. Another threat to consumer privacy occurs after a company obtains consumer data. In some cases, companies have not kept their promises not to share the data with third parties. However, more serious threats for identity theft include employees stealing data that is electronically stored, or thieves directly hacking into company databases and stealing personal or financial data, such as consumer credit card or Social Security information (George, Andrew & Shalini, 2004).

## E-Information

E-information is internet based information. Every retailer should provide in depth information about the product or the services to the customers. E-information includes complete information about product availability, the confidentiality level of buying the product and product recommendations.

Consumers shopping on-line are overwhelmed by the amount of the digital information provided to them. They tend to prioritize the delivered content for processing. In this regard, on-line customer reviews have become an indispensable part of product research during on-line shopping (Grau, 2008). Since on-line consumer reviews are perceived as sincere sources of information, they are favoured among other sources. The credibility of attributed to on-line consumer reviews is extremely high. These reviews ease identification by providing a peer review especially for utilitarian consumers. When consumers are provided with a trustworthy peer recommender's review, they do not only use the information provided to evaluate alternatives but also for decreasing their degree of search effort for the entire decision making process (Smith, Menon & Sivakumar, 2005). In this regard, peer or editorial recommendations are reported as more trustworthy than sponsored ads. In more detail, provision of user-oriented product information is coupled by recommendations of previous consumers. As an informant, on-line consumer reviews give user-oriented product information, while as a recommender, they provide positive, negative or neutral signal of product popularity (Park, Lee & Han 2007) as well as the performance evaluation of the e-tailer in keeping his/her promises. Sellers also provide product related information and also provide on-line consumer reviews information to the buyers.

## E-Trust

Trust is defined as one's willingness to rely on a trading partner with confidence (Moorman, Deshpande, & Zaltman, 1993), Liu, F., Dixon, M. & Murphy, J. (2002) Trust improves commitment and customer satisfaction (Bauer et al.,2002), therefore trust building is not only crucial for traditional businesses but for on-line businesses as well (Handy, 1995). High levels of trust have been reported to increase both purchase intention and customer loyalty (Chen and Barnes, 2007). E-tailers aim to build brand loyalty and trust by the provision of a proxy for reviews of previous customers through the use of e-commerce-based word-of-mouth (eWOM) systems (James, 2008, McWilliams, 2000). Consumers shopping on-line have been reported to lack trust in the legitimacy of on-line stores (Novak et al., 1999).

Lee and Turban (2001) define consumer trust in Internet shopping as "the willingness of a consumer to be vulnerable to the actions of an Internet merchant in an Internet transaction, based on the expectation that the Internet merchant will behave in certain agreeable ways, irrespective of the ability of the consumers to monitor or control that Internet merchant" (p. 79).

There are two common themes emerge from the literature about trust: first of all it represents a willingness to accept vulnerability, a belief about the behavioral intentions of others and positive expectations about the outcomes of another party's behavior; and secondly, trust is generally agreed to be a dynamic process, which can be slow to build yet can quickly be destroyed (Yoon, 2002). While trust is effective in developing a better understanding of exchange behavior, the dual nature of this construct makes it problematic, for trust comprises both a global (attitudinal/affective) component and a situational one (Butler, 1991 cited in O'Malley, 2003). For the purposes of the present study, a definition of trust which specifically relates to e-retailing is sought.

Within the retailing literature, it is commonly agreed that there are two key conditions necessary for trust to develop: risk and interdependence of the consumer and the retailer (Chen and Dhillon, 2003; Rousseau et al., 1998). This notion of vulnerability, uncertainty and dependence is elaborated on by Jarvenpaa, Tractinsky and Vitale (2000) who link it to a consumer's lack of control over the purchasing situation, and suggest trust to be a governance mechanism in the retailer-consumer exchange relationship. As far as e-retailing is concerned, several researchers have posited that trust is an important element of intentions to adopt business- to-consumer e-commerce (Grabner-Kraeuter, 2002; Pavlou, 2002; Vinton, 2001).

During on-line shopping, although decision maker may find more information and a wider variety of alternatives, credibility of information source and trustworthiness of retailer often present important bottlenecks (Kim & Benbasat, 2003).

## E-Satisfaction

Customers level of satisfaction while purchasing products online is termed as e-satisfaction. E-satisfaction has an impact towards e-loyalty. E-satisfaction can be build up on high level of satisfaction or low level of satisfaction. Understanding the level of e-satisfaction of customers has become an essential element under consumer behavior.

E-Satisfaction is received by a retailer, when e-relationship, e-perceived value and e-efficiency is fulfilled effectively. Once e-satisfaction is achieved, the retailer can fulfill e-loyalty or in other words e-satisfaction leads to e-loyalty. A number of studies have proposed the link between e-satisfaction and e-loyalty (e.g. R. Anderson & Srinivasan, 2003; Shankar, Smith, & Ragaswamy, 2003).

## E-Loyalty

A major challenge facing Internet retailers is in the area of customer loyalty or e-loyalty which, following R. Anderson and Srinivasan (2003), is defined as 'the customer's favorable attitude toward an electronic business, resulting in repeat purchasing behavior' (p. 125). A number of research authors have argued that understanding how to develop loyalty is fundamentally important to all online retailers Goode & Harris (2007), Reichheld (2001), Reichheld & Schefter (2000), Zeithaml, Parasuraman, & Malhotra (2002). Likewise, Harris and Goode (2004) argue that loyalty development for online retailers is 'both more difficult and more important than in offline retailing' (p. 139). The high importance placed on online loyalty is because of the competitive nature of the online market and the ever-increasing number of online retailers. The Internet also makes it relatively easy and less costly for consumers to search for alternative suppliers and to comparison-shop, as well as giving them the ability to switch suppliers at the click of a button. This makes it even more important to build and maintain customer loyalty online (Rafiq, Fulford, & Xiaoming Lu 2013).

Harris and Goode (2004) argue that loyalty development for online retailers is 'both more difficult and more important than in offline retailing' (p. 139). The high importance placed on online loyalty is because of the competitive nature of the online market and the ever-increasing number of online retailers.

Loyalty is widely regarded in the literature as an important contributory factor to a firm's profitability. For instance, Reichheld and Schefter (2000) suggest that an increase of only 5% in customer retention rates can increase profits by 25% to 95%. Customer loyalty positively influences profitability both by helping to reduce marketing costs (particularly the cost of acquiring new customers) and by increasing sales per customer.

## CONCEPTUAL RESEARCH FRAMEWORK

Based on the e-factors a conceptual research framework is developed. This study tests the conceptual model depicting the e- factors of perception and attitude of youth towards e-satisfaction and e-trust. The model also analyses the relationship between e-satisfaction and e-loyalty and also the relationship between e-trust and e-loyalty. The overall research framework is shown in Figure 2.

### Hypotheses

Based on the research framework two (2) hypothesis is developed. The following is a list of the hypotheses that are presented in the theoretical model that was empirically tested in this study.

**Hypothesis 1:** e-loyalty of youth in general is a positive function of e-satisfaction.
**Hypothesis 2:** e-loyalty of youth in general is a positive function of e-trust.

## RESEARCH DESIGN

### Survey Instrument

The survey instrument includes a question asking respondents to assess the perception of e-retailing. The survey instrument consisted utilize a 5-point Likert type scale. Included: strongly disagree to strongly agree.

*Figure 2. Research framework: E-Loyalty*

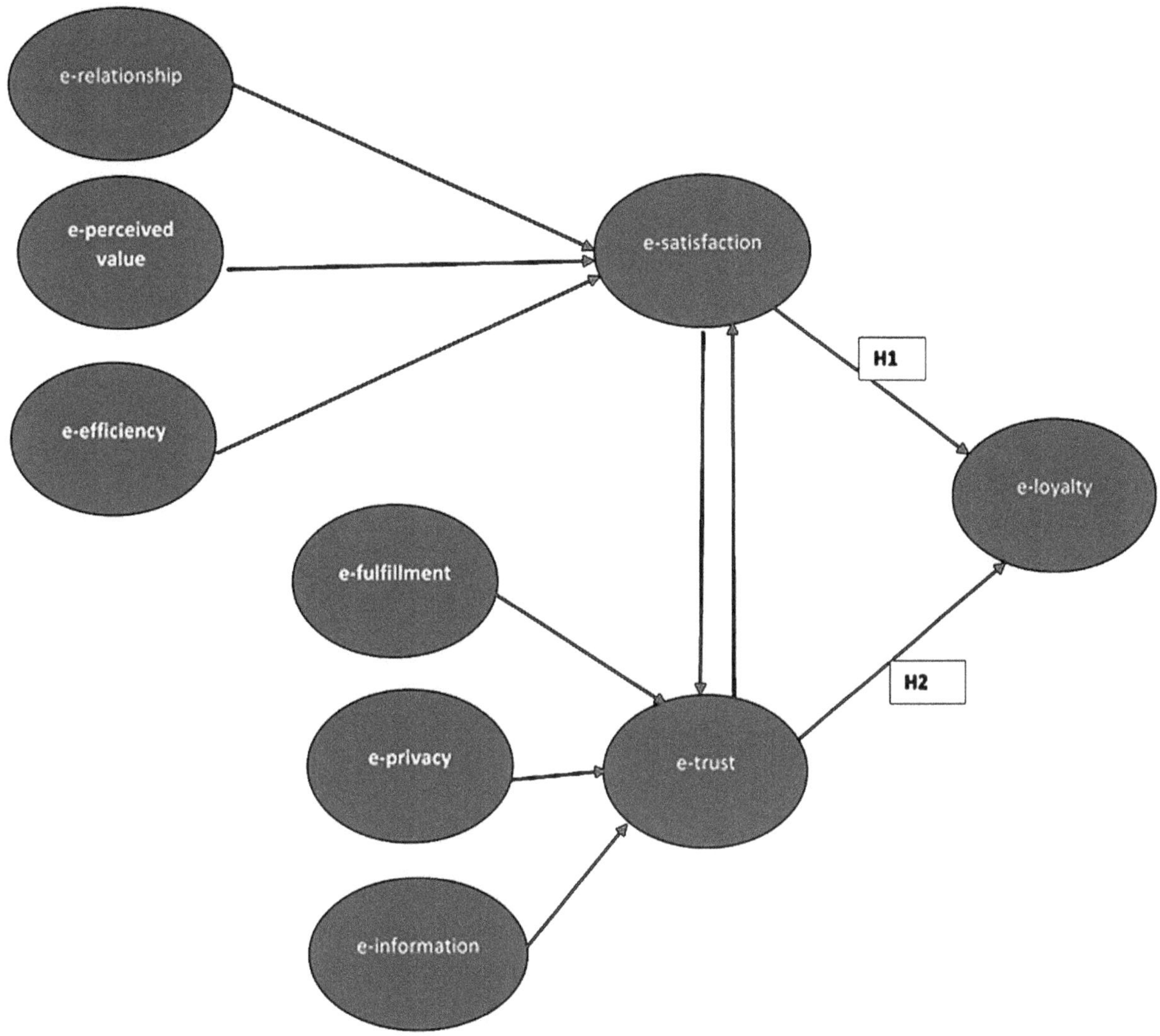


## Data Collection

A self-administered survey questionnaire were used to collect data. The questionnaire were stamped with sequential numbers and were randomly distributed to youth in Malaysia, India and Oman.

## Sample

One way to determine sample size is to use already published tables that set out the sample size of a particular set of criteria. The first table considered for this study is the Krejice and Morgan (1970) table for determining sample size for a Finite Population. According to Krejice and Morgan (1970) a sample of 384 is an appropriate size to be considered as representative statistical sample in empirical research for a population of above 75,000 or 1,000,000.

Likewise, Yamane (1967) cited in Israel (2013) proposed a simplified formula which calculated sample size using a set criteria of ?5% precision level with 95% confidence level and P=0.5. Based on this criteria also for a population of above 100,000 a sample size of 400 is appropriate.

The sample for study will include youth in selected regions of Malaysia, India and Oman who are at least 19 years of age. The age group of youth is taken under two age brackets i.e. 19-24 years and 25-30 years. The targeted usable sample size for this study was set around 408 respondents.

## Research Approach

Inductive and deductive are two approaches which are often associated with research methods. Inductive approach is described as theory-building process which starts with the observation of specific phenomena and generalizing of the phenomenon of the study (Wilson, 2010). In other words, by undertaking inductive approach researchers seek to make observations of the study and then may be to contribute it to development of a new theory. Conversely, deductive approach applies a well-known theory to develop hypotheses and then design strategy to measures those hypothesis (Collins, 2010; Wilson, 2010).

The present study is based on deductive approach which is often associated with quantitative research. Deductive approach allows the researcher to use theoretical application analyse the research findings or to make observations (Collins, 2010; Wilson, 2010). Furthermore, with deductive approach it will enable to test the propositions made by the hypotheses and relationship between the key concepts.

# SOLUTION AND RECOMMENDATIONS

## Discussion Solution

Multivariate analysis is conducted for data analysis and to identify the relationship amongst different variables and how it influences Satisfaction and trust of the youth customers. E-Loyalty is the end result of e-satisfaction and e-trusts when customers are buying products through e-retailing (see table 2).

## Demographic Profile of Respondents

This study covered the demographic profile of the 408 respondents. Gender and age of the responses were collected from the sample comprised of 408 respondents. The respondents were aged between 19 and 30 years. 59% of the respondents were male and 41% female.

*Table 1. Statistics*

| | | Gender | Age Group | Race | Occupation: | Monthly Income |
|---|---|---|---|---|---|---|
| N | Valid | 408 | 408 | 408 | 408 | 408 |
| | Missing | 0 | 0 | 0 | 0 | 0 |

*Table 2. Demographic profile of respondents*

| Category | Frequencies | Percentages |
|---|---|---|
| **Gender (N=408)** | | |
| Male | 240 | 59.0 |
| Female | 168 | 41.0 |
| **Age (N=408)** | | |
| 19-24 | 188 | 46.0 |
| 25-30 | 220 | 54.0 |

## Analysis of E-Satisfaction Constructs

Before testing the overall confirmatory measurement model, the measurement of each sub-dimension of the e-satisfaction and other constructs should be assessed individually. The confirmatory measurement model to be tested that the e-satisfaction is a three-factor structure composed of (1) e-relationship, (2) e-perceived value, and (3) e-efficiency. Further dissection of the model indicates that these three factors are correlated and that there are 9 observed variables. Four observed variables loaded onto e-relationship, two observed variables loaded onto e-perceived value and three observed variables loaded onto e-efficiency. In addition, errors of measurement associated with each observed variable were uncorrelated. The overall measurement fit of the e-satisfaction construct was tested by a confirmatory factor analysis. The items and the result of the confirmatory factor analysis of sub-dimension of the e-satisfaction are presented in Table 1. Table 3 presents the completely standardized coefficients (i.e., both the latent and observed variables are standardize), the indicator reliabilities and the error variances for each indicator. The composite indicator reliabilities and variance extracted estimates were calculated using the formula recommended by Fornell and Larcker (2010). As presented in table 3, all of the composite reliabilities were above .7 and all variance extracted estimates were above .5.

## Analysis of E-Trust Constructs

The confirmatory factor analysis was performed by specifying the posited relationships of the observed variables to the underlying three dimensions of e-trust, with the dimensions allowed to inter-correlate freely. The covariance matrix was used as the input data for the confirmatory factor analysis; the confirmatory measurement model to be tested that e-trust is a three-factor structure composed of (1) e-fulfillment (3 indicators) (2) e-privacy (3 indicators) (3) e-information (4 indicators). Further dissection of the model indicates that these three factors are correlated and there were 10 observed variables. After assessing the unidimensionality of each sub-dimension individually, the overall measurement fit of the e-trust construct was tested by a confirmatory factor analysis. The items and the result of the confirmatory factor analysis of sub-dimension of the e-trust are presented in Table 4. As presented in Table 4, all of the composite reliabilities were above .7 and all variance-extracted estimates were above .5.

After measuring the adequacy of the individual items, the composite reliability score and variance extracted estimate for each latent factor was assessed. The composite reliability score and variance extracted estimate for each latent variable (construct) were generated from completely standardized

*Table 3. Composite Reliability and validity of the e-satisfaction variables (n=408)*

| Constructs and Indicators | Standardized Loading | Reliability | Error Variance |
|---|---|---|---|
| ***E-Relationship*** | | **.89*** | **.73**** |
| Creates favorable customer relationship. | .84 | .69 | .33 |
| Attempts to improve customer relationship. | .79 | .65 | .28 |
| Maintains long term relationship. | .88 | .78 | .24 |
| Treats customers as partners. | .85 | .71 | .28 |
| ***E-Perceived Value*** | | **.83*** | **.61**** |
| Perceived value of money. | .79 | .61 | .42 |
| Perceived Value of time. | .74 | .58 | .44 |
| ***E-Efficiency*** | | **.85*** | **.65**** |
| Product Delivery. | .75 | .56 | .47 |
| Complaint Handling. | .91 | .83 | .17 |
| Customer Retention. | .76 | .58 | .41 |
| * Composite reliability | | | |
| ** Variance extracted estimate | | | |

*Table 4. Composite reliability and validity of the e-trust variables (n=408)*

| Constructs and Indicators | Standardized Loading | Reliability | Error Variance |
|---|---|---|---|
| ***E-Fulfillment*** | | **.89*** | **.63**** |
| Speedy customer delivery. | .67 | .45 | .55 |
| Flexibility. | .91 | .82 | .18 |
| Best Customer Experience. | .82 | .68 | .32 |
| ***E-Privacy*** | | **.79*** | **.56**** |
| Maintain honesty with buyers. | .67 | .45 | .55 |
| Follows customer centric privacy policy. | .78 | .61 | .39 |
| Privacy enhance technology. | .79 | .62 | .38 |
| ***E-Information*** | | **.88*** | **.64**** |
| Complete information about product availability. | .78 | .61 | .39 |
| Based on the information, I feel confident to buy. | .91 | .83 | .17 |
| Based on the information, I can recommend the products. | .8 | .65 | .35 |
| I feel the websites are overloaded with information. | .7 | .48 | .52 |
| * Composite reliability | | | |
| ** Variance extracted estimate | | | |

LISREL estimates and calculated by the formula provided by Fornell and Larcker (2010). As shown in Table 5, most of the composite reliabilities were above .7. Most of the variance extracted estimates were also above .50. However, the composite reliability scores that are between .60 and .70represent the lower limit of acceptability (Hair, Anderson, Tatham & Black, 2008). Therefore, these values were accepted as marginally reliable measurement scales.

## Test of Hypothesis 1

**Hypothesis 1:** E-loyalty of youth in general is a positive function of e-satisfaction.

Hypothesis 1 formulated from the theoretical framework stated that the more e-satisfaction leads to higher positive influence on e-satisfaction. In table 6, It can be noted that the Pearson correlation generate a value of 0.336 at $p<0.001$. Therefore, it can be deduced that there is a positive correlation between e-satisfaction and e-loyalty, hence confirming hypothesis 1 that e-loyalty of youth in general is a positive function of e-satisfaction.

*Table 5. Composite reliability and validity of overall measurement model*

| Constructs and Indicators | Standardized Loading | Reliability | Variance Extracted Estimate |
|---|---|---|---|
| ***e-satisfaction*** | | **.85*** | **.66**** |
| X1 | 0.81 | 0.66 | 0.34 |
| X2 | 0.8 | 0.65 | 0.35 |
| X3 | 0.83 | 0.68 | 0.32 |
| ***e-trust*** | | **.79*** | **.56**** |
| X4 | 0.71 | 0.5 | 0.5 |
| X5 | 0.77 | 0.6 | 0.4 |
| X6 | 0.76 | 0.58 | 0.42 |
| Note: * Composite reliability, ** Variance extracted estimate, X1-e-relationship, X2-e-perceived value, X3-e-efficiency, X4-fulfillment, X5-e-privacy, X6-e-information. | | | |

*Table 6. E-satisfaction and e-loyalty correlations*

| | | E-Loyalty | E-Satisfaction |
|---|---|---|---|
| E-Loyalty | Pearson Correlation | 1 | .336** |
| | Sig. (2-tailed) | | .000 |
| | N | 408 | 408 |
| E-Satisfaction | Pearson Correlation | .336** | 1 |
| | Sig. (2-tailed) | .001 | |
| | N | 408 | 408 |
| **. Correlation is significant at the 0.01 level (2-tailed). | | | |

**Hypothesis 2:** E-loyalty of youth in general is a positive function of e-trust.

Hypothesis 2 formulated from the theoretical framework stated that the more-trust leads to higher positive influence quality of e-loyalty. In table 7, It can be noted that the Pearson correlation generate a value of 0.768 at $p<0.001$. Therefore, it can be deduced that there is a positive correlation between e-trust and e-loyalty, hence confirming hypothesis 1 that e-loyalty of youth in general is a positive function of e-trust (see tables 8-11).

*Table 7. E-trust and e-loyalty correlations*

| | | E-Loyalty | E-Trust |
|---|---|---|---|
| E-Loyalty | Pearson Correlation | 1 | .768** |
| | Sig. (2-tailed) | | .000 |
| | N | 408 | 408 |
| E-Trust | Pearson Correlation | .768** | 1 |
| | Sig. (2-tailed) | .000 | |
| | N | 408 | 408 |
| **. Correlation is significant at the 0.01 level (2-tailed). | | | |

*Table 8. Variables entered/removed[a]*

| Model | Variables Entered | Variables Removed | Method |
|---|---|---|---|
| 1 | e-satisfaction, e-trust[b] | | Enter |

a. Dependent Variable: e-loyalty
b. All. requested variables entered.

*Table 9. Model summary*

| Model | R | R Square | Adjusted R Square | Std. Error of the Estimate |
|---|---|---|---|---|
| 1 | .799[a] | .770 | .585 | 0.409 |

a. Predictors: (Constant), e-satisfaction, e-trust

*Table 10. ANOVA[a]*

| Model | | Sum of Squares | df | Mean Square | F | Sig. |
|---|---|---|---|---|---|---|
| 1 | Regression | 15.120 | 3 | 5.040 | 7.870 | .000[a] |
| | Residual | 29.460 | 46 | .064 | | |
| | Total | 44.580 | 49 | | | |

a. Dependent Variable: e-loyalty
b. Predictors: (Constant), e-satisfaction, e-trust

*Table 11. Coefficients*[a]

| Model | | Unstandardized Coefficients | | Standardized Coefficients | t | Sig. |
|---|---|---|---|---|---|---|
| | | B | Std. Error | Beta | | |
| 1 | (Constant) | 1.264 | 0.320 | | 3.643 | .000 |
| | e-satisfaction | .592 | .135 | .265 | 4.385 | .020 |
| | e-trust | .672 | .185 | .153 | 3.632 | .010 |

a. Dependent Variable: e-loyalty

## Hierarchical Multiple Regression (HMR) Analysis

This multiple regression analysis has been carried out to measure whether there is any association between dependent variable e-loyalty and independent variable namely e-satisfaction and e-trust. The overall predictability of the model is shown above. F test of 7.870 (sig. = 0.000) shows that the overall regression is significant. The R square of 0.799 shows that 79.9% of the variation e-loyalty is explained by the regression. The regression has a strong fit.

Table 11 shows the relationship between dependent variable and each independent variable. The two variables e-satisfaction and e-trust are significantly correlated with e-loyalty. Here, t value of "e-satisfaction" = 4.385 (Sig. = 0.020), e-satisfaction has a positive significant influence on e-loyalty at 5% level. T value of "e-trust" = 3.632 (Sig. = 0.010), e-trust has a positive significant influence on e-loyalty at 5% level.

The past few decades, tourism has come to be viewed as the key to economic development. Malacca Government take the challenge to develop the community become the tourism innovation (Othman, A., 2013). After doing survey and analysis with SPSS, the results has summarizes are as above. The level of awareness of the residency of the community along Malacca find with the frequency, HMR and SEM. From the analysis we found the positive results with the different groups. This chapter presents the summary, discussion of the findings of the study. In the first section of the chapter, a summary and discussion of the hypotheses testing are presented. Finally, the chapter concludes with suggestions and recommendations.

## DISCUSSION OF THE RESULTS AND IMPLICATION

In the 21st Century, every retailers biggest problem is to make young online buyers to get always connect with the retailers. During online shopping satisfaction and trust becomes an important factor to increase loyalty. This study developed "e-loyalty model" that investigated how e-satisfaction and e-trust has an impact on e-loyalty. The satisfaction level of youth towards e-retailing is analyzed in detail. The study specially focused on e-retailing behavior of youth across India, Malaysia and Oman.

The sample for this study was proportionally stratified on the basis of the number of populations in the pre-selected regions in relation to acceptance of technology while buying products that covered counties and cities in the state. The study addressed the effects of e-retailing on the youth. Respondents were asked to complete a survey based on their perception towards e-retailing and their satisfaction was observed.

The result was a final usable sample size of 408 youth from three different countries. Under this research study, two main components e-satisfaction and e-trust is focused to understand e-loyalty.

The result from this research study clearly demonstrate that e-satisfaction and e-trust has a substantial impact on e-loyalty. The retailers in particular should strongly consider all the factors to maintain a positive relationship with youth. This suggest that e-retailers need to focus of all the e-factors as all the factors have a high impact factor in order to have effective commitment towards brand loyalty.

E-trust is also important and cannot be neglected by the retailers. Youth mainly builds trust towards e-retailers based on e-fulfillment, e-privacy and e-information. Considering these e-factors a new dimension of e-trust can be formed.

This research study indicates the youth attitude and shows that they mainly consider satisfaction and trust while purchasing goods online. Therefore, the retailers should essentially build in strong long-lasting with young customers. Amazingly there is a link between the two e-factors to reach e-loyalty. Analyzing the link between these two main factors (e-satisfaction and e-trust) every retailer should logically increase the customer satisfaction and trust whereby the youth will start believing the company and will continue to connect with them for a longer time. In other words greater the e-satisfaction and e-trust greater will be e-loyalty.

Moreover, the results of the study also found that e-retailing has created a greater impact on the youth and their buying behavior. The overall findings of this study indicate that there is a positive impact of e-trust and e-loyalty.

This research study has managerial implications for designing e-retailing strategies and thereby e-retailers can potentially increase their customer loyalty. Every online retailers can evaluate their own web site based on the consumer expectations.

## CONCLUSION

Today, the demographics in favor of youth are enormous. While we can quibble about the size or the purchasing power of the youth, the size is still extremely interesting to a host of marketers both global and local. Yet, many marketers have bitten the dust in their quest to crack the youth market. Perhaps some of them are ahead of their time. As mentioned in the research, the shopaholic youth has a preference towards e-retailing. They slowly are shifting towards e-retailing due to time constrain and their preferences are getting closer towards e-retailing. This is because of the comfort provided to them by the e-retailers. Across the world, the youth started to use internet purchases. There is a close relationship with e-satisfaction and e-trust. These two variables lead to e-loyalty. E-satisfaction and e-trust can lead to e-loyalty. If e-retailing companies can understand the needs of their customers specially the youth, they can present products and services to strengthen their competitive advantage.

## FUTURE RESEARCH

Retailers are showing a great interest towards younger generation as there is a wide scope of trade in this demographic group. Both academicians and industrialists are conducting different researches to understand their e-behavior and pattern of e-purchasing behavior of youth. This study though, claims to be in-depth analysis of youth behavior, offers a fertile area for further research. Some of them are as follows:

- A research can be made to understand the pattern of e-retiling buying behavior of youth across the world.
- An in-depth study can be conducted to understand the youth purchasing behavior towards physical retailing and e-retailing.

## REFERENCES

Anderson, J. R., & Gerbing, D. W. (2010). Structural equation modeling in practice: A review and recommended two-step approach. *Psychological Bulletin*.

Anderson, R., & Srinivasan, S. S. (2003). E-satisfaction and e-loyalty: A contingency framework. *Psychology and Marketing*, *20*(2), 123–138. doi:10.1002/mar.10063

Anderson, R., & Srinivasan, S. S. (2003). E-satisfaction and e-loyalty: A contingency framework. *Psychology and Marketing*, *20*(2), 123–138. doi:10.1002/mar.10063

Arab advisors Group. (2014). Retrieved from http://www.arabadvisors.com/Pressers/presser-150614.htm

Balasubramanian, S. (1997). Two Essays in Direct Marketing [PhD Dissertation]. Yale University, New Haven, CT.

Bearden, W. D., Sharma, S., & Teel, J. E. (2012). Sample size effects on chi-square and other statistical used in evaluating causal models. *JMR, Journal of Marketing Research*.

Bollen, K. A. (2011). *Structural equations with latent variables*. New York: Wiley.

Bramall, C., Schoefer, K., & McKechnie, S. (2004). The determinants and consequences of consumer trust in e-retailing: A conceptual framework. *Irish Marketing Review*, *17*(1&2), 13–22.

Burke, R. R. (2002). Technology and the Customer Interface What Consumers Want in the Physical and Virtual Store. *Academy of Marketing Science Journal*, *30*(4), 411–432. doi:10.1177/009207002236914

Byrne, B. M. (2011). *Structural Equation Modeling with LISREL, PRELIS, and SIMPLIS: basic concepts, allocations, and programming*. Mahwah, New Jersey: Lawrence Erlbaum Associates Inc.

Chen, S. C., & Dhillon, C. S. (2003). Interpreting dimensions of consumer trust in e-commerce. *Information Technology Management*, *4*(2/3), 303–318. doi:10.1023/A:1022962631249

Collins, H. (2010). *Creative research*. Lausanne: AVA Academia.

Darian, J. C., Tucci, L. A., & Wiman, A. R. (2001). Perceived Salesperson Service Attributes and Retail Patronage Intentions. *International Journal of Retail & Distribution Management*, *29*(5), 205–213. doi:10.1108/09590550110390986

David, M. S., & Richard, T. H. (2000). E-satisfaction: An initial examination. *Journal of Retailing*, *76*(3), 309–322. doi:10.1016/S0022-4359(00)00035-X

Doxey, G. V. (2011). In the Impact of Tourism*: The Travel Research Association, Sixth Annual Conference Proceedings*.

Fornell, C., & Larcker, D. F. (2010). Evaluating structural equation models with unobservable variables and measurement error. *JMR, Journal of Marketing Research.*

Fransi, E. C., & Viadiu, F. M. (2007). A study of e-retailing management: Analysing the expectations and perceptions of Spanish consumers. *International Journal of Consumer Studies, 31*(6), 613–622. doi:10.1111/j.1470-6431.2007.00623.x

Grabner-Kraeuter, S. (2002). The role of consumers' trust in *online shopping. Journal of Business Ethics, 39*(1-2), 43–50. doi:10.1023/A:1016323815802

Grau, J. (2008). Consumer Interactions: Social Shopping, Blogs and Reviews. New York, NY: eMarketer Inc.

Gupta, K. (2014). Why eCommerce is a must for a 21st Century Business? Retrieved from https://www.linkedin.com/pulse/20140819070607-3179967-why-ecommerce-is-a-must-for-a-21st-century-business

Hair, J. F., Jr., & Anderson, R. L. Tatham, & Black, W. C. (2008). Multivariate Data Analysis. New York: Macmillan

Handy, C. (1995). Trust and The Virtual Organization. *Harvard Business Review, 73*, 40–50.

Harris, L. C., & Goode, M. M. H. (2004). The four levels of loyalty and the pivotal role of trust: A study of online service dynamics. *Journal of Retailing, 80*(2), 139–158. doi:10.1016/j.jretai.2004.04.002

Hart, C. A., Doherty, N. F., & Ellis-Chadwick, F. E. (2000). Retailer Adoption of the Internet: Implications for Retail Marketing. *European Journal of Marketing, 34*(8), 954–974. doi:10.1108/03090560010331441

Internet Retailing in Malaysia. (2015). *Euromonitor.* Retrieved from http://www.euromonitor.com/internet-retailing-in-malaysia/report

Israel, G. D. (2013). Determining Sample Size. *Program Evaluation and Organizational Development.* IFAS, University of Florida. Retrieved from http://edis.ifas.ufl.edu/pd006

James, A. (2008). More online shoppers take the word of anonymous product reviewers.

Jarvenpaa, S. L., Tractinsky, N., & Vitale, M. (2000). Consumer trust in an internet store. *Information Technology Management, 1*(1—2), 45–71. doi:10.1023/A:1019104520776

Kim, D., & Benbasat, I. (2003). Trust-related arguments in Internet stores: A framework for evaluation. *Journal of Electronic Commerce Research, 4*, 49–64.

King, K. (2006). Youth: Lifestyle, Expectation and Media. *Young Consumers, 7*(2), 22–29. doi:10.1108/17473610610701466

Kolesar, M. B., & Galbrait, R. W. (2000). A Service Marketing Perspective on E-Retailing: Implications for E-Retailers and Directions for Further Research. *The Internet Research: Electronic Networking Applications and Policy, 10*(5), 424–438. doi:10.1108/10662240010349444

Krejcie, R., & Morgan, D. (1970). Determining Sample Size for Research Activities. *Educational and Psychological Measurement*, 30, 607-610. Retrieved from http://home.kku.ac.th/sompong/guest_speaker/KrejcieandMorgan_article.pdf

Kumar, V., Bohling, T. R., & Ladda, R. N. (2003). Antecedents and consequences of relationship intention: Implications for transaction and relationship marketing. *Industrial Marketing Management*, *32*(8), 667–676. doi:10.1016/j.indmarman.2003.06.007

Lee, M. K. O., & Turban, E. (2001). A Trust Model for Consumer Internet Shopping. *International Journal of Electronic Commerce*, *6*, 75–91.

Liu, F., Dixon, M., & Murphy, J. (2002). Ramizwick & T. Ping, (Ed.), Exploring Online Buying and Online Trust in China (pp. 336-342). Association for Consumer Research, Valdosta, GA.

Malaysians increasingly shop online. (2015). *Inside Retail Asia.* Retrieved from http://insideretail.asia/2013/08/23/malaysians-increasingly-shop-online/

McWilliams, G. (2000). Building strong brands through online communities. *MIT Sloan Management Review*, *41*, 43–54.

Milne, G. R., Rohm, A. J., & Bahl, S. (2004). Consumers' Protection of Online Privacy and Identity. *The Journal of Consumer Affairs*, *38*(2), 217–232. doi:10.1111/j.1745-6606.2004.tb00865.x

Mishra, S. (n. d.). A Conceptual Framework for creating customer value in e-retailing in India. South Asian. *Journal of Management*, *16*(4), 127–147.

Moorman, C., Deshpande, R., & Zaltman, G. (1993a). Factors Affecting Trust in Market Research Relationships. *Journal of Marketing*, *57*(1), 81–101. doi:10.2307/1252059

Novak, T. P., Hoffman, D. L., & Peralta, M. (1999). Building Consumer Trust in Online Environment: The Case for Information Privacy. *Communications of the ACM*, 1999, 42.

O'Malley, L. (1003). Relationship marketing. In S. Hart (Ed.), *Marketing Changes.* London: Thomson Learning.

Oman shows promise for online shopping growth: MasterCard Survey. (n. d.). *Mastercard.com.* Retrieved from http://newsroom.mastercard.com/mea/press-releases/oman-shows-promise-for-online-shopping-growth-mastercard-survey/

Ozturkcan, S., & Gul Gursoy (2014). On-Line Reviews' Impact on Trust Building. *Proceedings of the Global Conference on Business and Finance, 9*(1), 350-360.

Park, D.-H., Lee, J., & Han, I. (2007). The Effect of On-Line Consumer Reviews on Consumer Purchasing Intention: The Moderating Role of Involvement. *International Journal of Electronic Commerce*, *11*(4), 125–148. doi:10.2753/JEC1086-4415110405

Pavlou, P. A. (2002). What drives electronic commerce? A theory of planned behaviour perspective. *Best Paper Proceedings of the Academy of Management,* Denver. CO.

Pizzutti, C., & Von, D. (2011). Perception of justice after recovery efforts in internet purchasing: The impact of consumer trust and loyalty towards retailing sites and online shopping in general. *Brazilian Administration Review*, *8*(3), 225–246. doi:10.1590/S1807-76922011000300002

Puri, A. (2015). Is E-commerce Replacing Physical Retail In India? 27. Jan, 2015, Retrieved May 6, 2015, from http://www.joneslanglasalleblog.com/realestatecompass/real-estate/2015/01/ecommerce-replacing-physical-retail-india/

Rafiq, M., Fulford, H., & Lu, X. (2013). Building customer loyalty in online retailing: The role of relationship quality. *Journal of Marketing Management*, *29*(3-4), 494–517. doi:10.1080/0267257X.2012.737356

Reichheld, F. F., & Schefter, P. (2000). E-loyalty. Your secret weapon on the web. *Harvard Business Review*, *78*(4), 105–113.

Retail Agility: Catalyst to Successful Retailing in the 21st Century. (n. d.). *Throughtworks*. Retrieved from http://assets.thoughtworks.com/articles/retail_agility_21st_century.pdf)

Rousseau, D., Sitkin, S. B., Burt, R. S., & Camerer, C. (1998). Not so different after all: A cross-discipline view of trust. *Academy of Management Review*, *23*(3), 393–404. doi:10.5465/AMR.1998.926617

Shankar, V., Smith, A., & Rangaswamy, A. (2003). Customer satisfaction and loyalty in online and offline environments. *International Journal of Research in Marketing*, *20*(2), 153–175. doi:10.1016/S0167-8116(03)00016-8

Smith, A. D., & Rupp, W. T. (2003). Strategic Online Customer Decision Making: Leveraging the Transformational Power of the Internet. *Online Information Review*, *27*(6), 418–432. doi:10.1108/14684520310510055

Smith, D., Menon, S., & Sivakumar, K. (2005). On-line Peer and Editorial Recommendations, Trust, and Choice in Virtual Markets. *Journal of Interactive Marketing*, *19*(3), 15–37. doi:10.1002/dir.20041

Subbu, R. (2015, May 10). Organised retail reorganising in India. *The Hindu*. Retrieved from http://www.thehindu.com/business/Industry/retail-sector-in-india/article7188691.ece

Sun, P.-C., & Lin, C.-M. (2010). Building customer trust and loyalty: An empirical study in a retailing context. *Service Industries Journal*, *30*(9), 1439–1455. doi:10.1080/02642060802621478

Vinton, M. (2001). Trust and quality are key to thriving on the web today. *Marketing*, *14*(June), 12.

Wang, F., Head, M. M., & Archer, N. A. (2000). Relationship building model for the web retail marketplace. *Journal of Internet Research*, *10*(5), 374–384. doi:10.1108/10662240010349381

Yoon, S.-J. (2002). The antecedents and consequences of trust in online-purchase decisions. *Journal of Interactive Marketing*, *16*(2), 47–63. doi:10.1002/dir.10008

Zigmund, W. G. (2012). *Business Research Methods* (5th ed.). Fort Worth, TX: The Dryden Press.

Zott, C., Amit, R., & Donlevy, J. (2000). Strategies for Value Creation in E-Commerce: Best Practices in Europe. *European Management Journal*, *18*(5), 463–475. doi:10.1016/S0263-2373(00)00036-0

# Section 5

# Communicating and Delivering Value Online

# Chapter 11
# Engaging your Global Social Media Audience:
## A Framework for E-Retailers

**Leila Samii**
*Aurora University, USA*

## ABSTRACT

*The global reach of social media provides opportunities for e-Retailers. Implementing a global social media strategy maximizes the efficiency of the exchange of information between the target audience and the brand. Information acquisition provides e-Retailers with knowledge about their target audience, while information dissemination spreads awareness about the brand to the target audience. As a result, e-Retailers leveraging user content on social media enable the development of strategic global engagement to reduce cultural complexities. The REALLY framework develops a foundation to leverage user-generated content using standardization for multilayered social media campaigns for e-Retailers. Roxy's global social media campaign is used as a case example to analyze global social media strategy and internationalization.*

## INTRODUCTION

There is no question of the vast size and global reach of social media. The potential for e-Retailers to spread content on social media is limitless across applications and country borders. In fact, in the US 52% of adults are using at least two social media platforms (Duggan, Ellison, Lampe Lenhart & Madden, 2015). There is a need for a foundational understanding of social media concepts to leverage global strategy independent of social media channels.

The extensive reach of social media has changed the way people communicate across countries and cultures. The range and speed of social media supports e-Retailers in the efficient exchange of information with consumers across markets through a global strategy. Marketing has evolved from traditional one-way and two-way broadcasting strategies to a more dynamic social strategy creating multi-way communication between the brand and consumer (Piskori, 2010).

DOI: 10.4018/978-1-4666-9921-2.ch011

Copyright © 2016, IGI Global. Copying or distributing in print or electronic forms without written permission of IGI Global is prohibited.

The multi-way communication is not limited to channels or borders. Opportunities are created for e-Retailers to listen to the content being posted from the social media community. The exchange of information between the consumer and e-Retailer creates a dialogue for both sides to learn about one another. Many brands have been utilizing social media; however they do so from a country to country perspective, limiting the full potential of social media. Social media should be standardized to reach a global audience. Using a global strategy on social media enables e-Retailers to maximize their efficiency and social media community.

Social media applications are global platforms with limitless barriers to enter into the space. The optimal approach to global social media strategy has created complexity amongst brands. There are mixed results as to the optimal approach for implementing either a global or multi-domestic social media strategy. There is gap in the literature discussing social media strategy from a global lens however extending theory from multiple disciplines creates a holistic understanding of global social media strategy. For example, global strategy versus multi-domestic strategy has been discussed in the international business literature with support for both. A global strategy emphasizes standardization across countries to increase economies of scale (Levitt, 1983) while a multi-domestic strategy emphasizes adaptation from country to country to customize for the specific market (Ohmae, 1989). Both multi-domestic and global strategies have their benefits and drawbacks; however adapting and standardizing parts of the business units seems most reasonable (Quelch & Hoff, 1993). Looking specifically at social media, it is beneficial for e-Retailers to leverage the global reach of their social media message through a comprehensive strategy.

Through a global social media strategy, complexities of culture will become a challenge. Therefore, there is a need for strategies to be developed to leverage user generated content and reduce cultural complexities. Many brands have leveraged user generated content to efficiently spread brand awareness around their company. In fact, listening to the content being spread on social media provides learning opportunities for e-Retailers to understand more about their community in their specific industry. Through the careful listening and analysis of user posts e-Retailers can develop engagement strategies for their community. An e-Retailer's brand image can be reflected through a strategic social media campaign leveraging user global engagement.

This chapter develops a model for social media strategy after surveying internationalization research. A global social media model is presented to capitalize on user generated content for a global strategy. The proposed REALLY framework developed by the author is a holistic approach for managing cultural challenges while maximizing the true global reaches on social media. This chapter is organized in the following: first an introduction into the theoretical concepts that guide global social media are presented, then a framework for successful global e-Retailing on social media is proposed. Next, Roxy Quicksilvers' Dare Yourself campaign is analyzed as a case example and finally the new social internationalization process is revealed to guide the process.

## BACKGROUND

### Global Social Media

In a report conducted by Nielsen, it was discovered that personal computer and mobile phone users spend more time on social media sites than on any other site (Nielsen, 2012). Alongside search engine optimization, social media leads the promotional marketing strategy mix in lead generation for companies

(Hubspot, 2013). Social media sites are formed by user generated content (UGC) added to a specific Web 2.0 application (Kaplan & Haenlein, 2010). Social media leverages the online community to create UGC on the dynamic global platform. In an effort to increase traffic on the Web 2.0 about a specific brand, users share content about their own perceptions of the brand. The information that is shared varies between positive or negative, short or long, with or without visual content. There are multiple types of content that users create that are all dependent on their experience with the brand. In some cases, consumers are creating or adding to conversations about a brand without ever having an interaction with the brand. UGC is inevitable on social media.

Social media content is shared on various platforms to people with similar interests. Due to social media, the first touch point a consumer experiences with a brand may or may not originate from the brand. In many instances, a consumer will have pre-conceived notions that guide their brand experience from another customer's experience with the brand (Bruhn, Schoenmueller & Schafer, 2012). The landscape of social media is a global borderless platform and if UGC is not managed it will be detrimental to e-Retailers. Successful brands leveraging the multi-way communication use strategies which enlist users to create content around the e-Retailer with a clear message to help with the brand image.

The generation of a brand with full control of their image fully is long gone (Barwise & Meehan, 2010). Social media users from across the globe have a larger say in an e-Retailers brand image. Customer demand and business imperatives are truly global with the increase in Web 2.0 (Iacobucci, Arabie, & Bodapati, 2000) and even more so with the rise of social media applications and usage. Social media users adopt and colonize on each one of the platforms to develop communities including members from all over the world. According to the Internet World Stats (2015) Facebook has over 1 billion subscribers with over 93% daily active users from 210 different countries and territories. Social media applications have been commonly compared to population sizes of countries from around the world. The one difference between physical countries and social media applications are the limitless size and minimal barriers to enter onto the social media sites for people from various cultures. Comparatively, China and India are the only countries that surpass the population of Facebook, the leading social media site, in terms of "citizens" (United States Census, 2015).

The vast range and speed of information spreading through the Web 2.0 is as fast as any consumers connection speed. Thus, the virality or sharing of content quickly spreads from country to country through social media. The global reach of social media sites has blurred the geographic lines that differentiate countries due to the openness of communication and spread of information on the Web 2.0. Social media applications encourage a large marketplace for exchange of goods, services and ideas across the borderless world. The Web 2.0 has created "an invisible continent" (Ohmae, 2000) enabling firms to reveal information about their brand prior to entering the market, while obtaining market knowledge and acquiring information about consumers in a given country (Prashantham, 2005).

The openness of social media on the Invisible Continent not only has limited barriers for users to enter, but also for firms to create a strong presence to communicate brand messages. Therefore, once on social media sites, a brand is now open to most countries on the online marketplace which is facilitated by the Web 2.0 (Ohmae, 2000). For e-Retailers, the openness of social media creates many opportunities as an e-Retailer brand becomes global with no barriers for a brand or consumer to become a part of the social media continent. E-Retailers posting on social media should focus their social media marketing on a global strategy to maximize the spread of a message.

In an effort to minimize cultural blunders, many e-Retailing firms have focused their attention on dividing their social media accounts on a country to country basis or through a fragmented organizational structure. Research has shown language is an important cultural factor for consumer acceptance of social media content (Singh, Lenhert, & Bostick, 2012) and supports the fragmented social media organization structure. However, the efficiency of social media is lost if the firm does not implement a centralized social media organizational strategy. E-Retailing firms should focus on implementing a global social media strategy to leverage all of the benefits of social media for a competitive advantage in the global marketplace (Etgar & Rachman-Moore, 2010).

## Internationalization

Johanson and Vahlne (1977) first introduced the Uppsala model of internationalization as an incremental approach to selling abroad. Traditionally, internationalization is explained as gradual transition into foreign markets based upon the market knowledge, market commitment, commitment decisions and current activities of the firm. The gradual international process was thought to be vital factor in decreasing the liability of foreignness and the costs associated with uncertainty of doing business in foreign markets (Zaheer, 1995). However, since the Uppsula model was introduced the business environment has changed and the borderless world has decreased the importance of foreign market entry and expansion strategies (Johanson & Vahlne, 2009). The growth of the internet and social media infrastructure has generated highly connected global businesses. Highly connected brands in the marketplace are interconnected with a brand presence on social media building consumer brand awareness. On the other hand, brands have more knowledge about the consumer and the industry. The information a brand learns through social media decreases a brand's liability of foreignness with the details of the marketing environment.

The Invisible Continent has changed the process in which brands move abroad and learn about the markets' they are entering. Internationalization is important for position-building in a foreign network, not only for market entry (Axelsson & Johanson, 1992). The exchange of content on the internet has strengthened information acquisition about the market so e-Retailing businesses develop stronger positioning strategies. Firms leverage the Internet to acquire knowledge and for resource building for a better understanding of the market (Loane, 2006), while social media provides a deeper layer of consumer knowledge. The e-Retailer acquires a more individualized perspective of the target audience to have a better understanding of their consumers. By expanding an e-Retailers' social media presence for researching the marketing environment, consumers are more likely to passively notice the brand on social media through their personal community more than on the Web 2.0.

Social media facilitates a large exchange of personal and brand related information in developing connections. On social media, observable exchanges of information and conversations are the norm which leads to relationship building between the brand and its social media community. The information processed by the brand aids in understanding the environment of a country. As a result, the internet has increased network relationships (Mathew, Healy & Ali, 2006) and has become a prominent factor for internationalization (Coviello & Munro, 1997). The parallel between network relationships and communities reveal the constant formation of social media sites and social networks. Social media communities have created network relationships with the various levels of the brand's social media community, which will be discussed in more detail later in the chapter. A social media community includes the users that are a prominent driving factor of the information that populates a brand's social media page.

The exchange of information and the relationship building is vital to the success of a global brand and should be utilized to market brand products. International marketing knowledge, cross border customer knowledge and customer acquisition are facilitated by the internet (Mathew et al., 2006). E-Retailing brands using search engine portals leverage the access of international customers towards a pathway for internationalization. The process of internationalization through the internet is beneficial for selling products. On the other hand, brands learn specifically about the marketplace while consumers can learn about certain products and services through a brand's owned social media site.

## Information Exchange

Social media enables brands to access cultural and market knowledge despite the cultural and geographical proximity or psychic distance (Arenius, 2005; Child, Ng & Wong, 2003). Facilitation of brand knowledge is made possible with social media applications on the internet for information dissemination, information about their brand, and information acquisition, market knowledge for the brand (Prashantham, 2005). Information acquisition and information dissemination create efficiency for marketing teams in e-Retailing.

Information dissemination enables consumers to be familiar with a brand prior to them entering the country's market. The knowledge about the brand is not necessarily communicated through brand related content, yet a person may learn about the company by coincidence on social media through the users' community. Since social media is borderless, users constantly are stumbling on content without intending to do so. Although important for the consumer to learn about the brand, if the message is not clear or if the message is misinterpreted by the consumer the brand could lose a customer. In the worst case scenario, the consumer would spread negative content due to mixed messages. Therefore, brands need to prepare for unintentional views of their social media content, on top of intentional views.

The information transfer on social media has many benefits, however problems can arise from the large exchange of user generated content on social media. In a local context, a social media campaign can be executed with minimal brand complexity due to similarities in culture. The cultural values and meaning are more simplistic for brand congruence within the mind of the consumer in a local context. However in a global setting, the message has a large potential to create brand complexity with the varying cultural factors despite language barriers.

Social media thought has focused on the need for a decentralized social media organization structure. Language has been suggested to be an important component for social media success (Singh et al., 2012). There leaving the organizational structure of social media within companies fragmented on a country to country basis based on language. However, with the advancements in technology, web browsers automatically translate websites, therefore although language is an important factor for consideration it is adjusted for by the web browser. Moreover, social media sites adjust for the language barrier to the users preferred language, such as Twitter (Twitter, 2015). Therefore, the more important factor to address on social media is the cultural context and the message that is communicated through the global platform to leverage a centralized organizational structure. The message and meaning on social media is interpreted by users based on factors including communal norm, marketing promotion element, character narrative and communication forum (Kozinets, Valck, Wojnicki, & Wilner, 2010). Thus, the interpretation of the message by the consumer, when communicated through social media, has the possibility of misinterpretation if the cultural message is not in sync with the cultural norms. Social media communication through the spread user-produced content creates a complex cultural process with many voices. A global strategy with a centralized social media organization structure is the best method of leveraging the efficiency of social media, if and only if the brand capitalizes on consumer posts.

Adding another layer to the cultural marketing mix is the proliferation of user generated content (UGC) posted on social media. The free flow of information now has given consumers more control

(Ohmae, 2000). Companies that listen to their community are leading the social media revolution for three reasons: first, brands understand their consumers' wants and needs through information acquisition, second, brands are using the user generated content to create a brand image, and third, via information dissemination brands are communicating with their consumers. E-Retailing brands that capitalize on information acquisition and dissemination are successful.

UGC can create complexity for brand management. Negative brand comments on social media left unaddressed have the potential to go viral on the internet (Burmann, 2010). For example, on a United flight a passenger watched one of the employees accidentally break his guitar. The passenger went through many channels within United for reimbursement. The passenger never was compensated and as a result he created a YouTube video with over 14 million views to date titled "United Breaks Guitars"[1] . On the other side, positive comments are vital to the success of e-Retailing brands on social media with generating information around the brand.

E-Retailers capitalizing on information acquisition through consumer posts on social media have the potential to learn about their target audience. The information acquisition about the consumer provides vital knowledge for the best approach for communicating a message to the target audience. For example, UGC that is posted by consumers helps e-Retailers determine their positioning strategy both on- and offline.

The message and positioning strategy for a brand becomes dynamic once content is posted on social media channels, even with a global marketing strategy. The global presence on social media channels presents a challenge to manage all of the various cultural factors for a cohesive brand image. The global brand image must be strategically positioned to spread the brand message and capture the cultural idiosyncrasies. Therefore, brands that encourage user generated branding disentangle the potential cultural problems that arise with a global marketing strategy. The e-Retailing brand using UGB is now communicating messages to the target audience in the accurate cultural context. The meaning associated with the messages developed through UGB capitalizes on relatable content to a specific country.

## GLOBAL SOCIAL MEDIA STRATEGY

### REALLY Framework

As a result of the evolution of information transfer through the openness of social media, e-Retailers are still learning how to leverage content and their resources. As a result of the advances in social media channels and data, the author has developed a framework to be used at various stages of the social media strategy. The proposed framework was developed to maximize the efficiency of posting social media content through the REALLY social media framework. The framework should constantly be referred to during all parts of the social media strategy, whether introducing a social media strategy or campaign or during the maturity phase of a social media strategy. The REALLY framework is a holistic framework which leverages each of its factors for social media success utilizing a global strategy. Social media is global with information exchange from all over the world. The REALLY framework develops a foundation for strategic global social media campaigns.

The REALLY framework is an acronym that stands for Research, Engagement, Analysis, Listening, Learning and You and each part of the framework has interchangeable factors that complement one another. For example, information is acquired about the target audience and the industry which shape the social media campaign. The information about the target audience can pin point users to help leverage and spread the campaign message. Furthermore, social media opportunities are determined from industry voids in the marketplace that e-Retailing brands can capitalize on. The REALLY framework can be adapted to all social media channels which is important with the changes in popularity of social media for a global strategy.

Research, is one of the most important aspects of social media. Figure 1 reveals the various parts of the REALLY framework. Research is acquiring information about the industry and the target audience to develop an understanding of the marketplace. The Research portion incorporates the rest of the framework and should consistently be evolved to change with the advancements in technology channels. During the Research phase, e-Retailers should listen, learn and analyze information about the target audience, influencers, competitors, set goals and objectives, define a message and finally analyze their own brand. Through Listening on social media e-Retailers are acquiring information from user generated content about their brand. As a result, e-Retailers are learning information about their target audience, industry and their own brand through the eyes of the consumers. The Listening and Learning piece is invaluable to e-Retailers because it provides unsolicited feedback from the consumers. The Research, Listening and Learning should be analyzed to have a deeper understanding about the UGC so e-Retailers can leverage the content for engagement. E-Retailers now have the appropriate information to engage the customers on the right channels and with the right message. Finally, e-Retailers should create a message for the social media campaign that encompasses the brand image or the You of the REALLY Framework.

Moreover, the REALLY framework has many varied parts of the framework that are included throughout the 5 factors of the framework. Each factor of the REALLY framework should be referred to throughout the entirety of the process. To truly understand the e-Retailers global audience, it is important to constantly update the REALLY framework and extend the best process for your specific brand. Since social media success is specific to the online target audience, what works for one brand, may not always work for another brand and vice versa. Therefore, the REALLY framework was created for brands to recognize the peculiarities of their specific social media community and tactics, despite cross- cultural differences. The holistic approach to social media needs to be utilized for success on social media.

*Figure 1. REALLY framework*

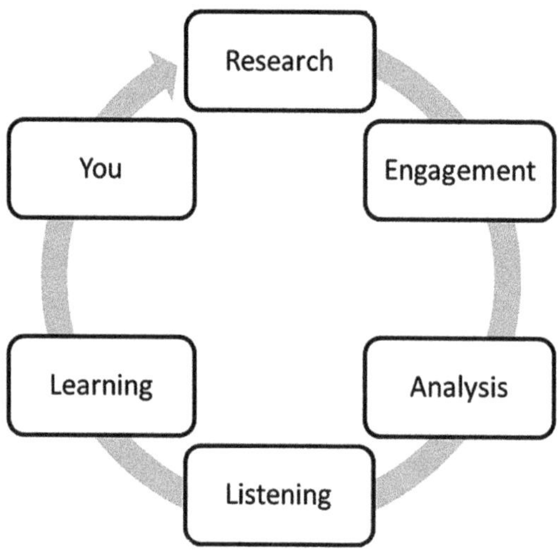

The REALLY framework has dynamic factors that reveal the peculiarities of the target audience to create segments based on the behaviors of the social media community. Table 1 reflects the specific factors within the REALLY framework that should be leveraged to develop a comprehensive strategy or campaign. For instance, the Target Audience should be researched and analyzed to reveal opportunities for content and social media channels to develop a global message. The research of the target audience should reflect the commonality of what is deemed as important for the target audience. The communication and etiquette of the specific community should be researched to determine the message that should be communicated. In some instances, it may seem that the cultural factors are important, however the audience will discount the cultural differences in the message if it positioned correctly based on the community standards. Therefore, understanding the community through research is much more vital and telling than defining cross cultural factors.

e-Retailers can observe the best positioning for a global message through their research analysis and listening to the interactions that occur in the community. Influencers in the community should be researched, analyzed and listened to learn trends in the e-Retailing industry from content to new channels being used for communication. Moreover, brands should engage with Influencers to develop relationships to create a larger network and to spread a larger message. Table 1 reveals the different factors that should be incorporated throughout the REALLY framework.

The information in the table reveals action items that should be analyzed when implementing the REALLY framework. Though the factors will be specific to the organization, all of the factors should be a focus to stay relevant.

## Target Audience

Research is fundamental to any social media strategy and should be incorporated throughout all levels of a social media strategy. Through Research, the community will reveal the communication mediums that the e-Retailer should utilize, content that is valued and the overall etiquette amongst the community members. As discussed, social media messages should be positioned with a global audience and have a dynamic voice to resonate with all of the community.

Starting with the target audience, e-Retailing brands should research the information to successfully communicate and engage on social media. Engaging with the target audience is one of the most involved tasks since one misstep could cause detrimental problems to the brand. The customer is king (Okanawo,

*Table 1. REALLY framework with factors to address*

| Research | Engagement | Analysis | Listening | Learning | You |
|---|---|---|---|---|---|
| e-Retailing Industry | Influencers | Target Audience | e-Retailing Industry | Positive WOM | Brand Image |
| Target Audience | Brand Advocates | Influencers | Influencers | Negative WOM | UGB |
| Influencers | Consumers | Brand | Consumers | Influencers | Social Responsibility |
| | Empowering | | | Competitor TA Posts | Objectives/Goals |
| | UGB | | | | |

2009) reflects the need for brands to fully understand their target audience to deliver them the current information. The analysis of the target audience is vital for positioning the brand message to connect with the global consumer.

One approach to understand the many various global voices of the target audience is to analyze the consumers from a dynamic approach that moves beyond primarily traditional demographic analysis. Defining the target audience has shifted to segmenting the market through holistic classifications of the target audience including psychographics and behavioral factors (Kaplan & Haenlein, 2010; Li &Bernoff, 2008; Mangold & Faulds, 2009; Muntinga, Moormán & Smit, 2011). The increase in data capturing through social media allows for sophisticated segmentation allowing for messages that resonate with the consumers with similarity in their lifestyles. Employing information such as user behaviors and characteristics deepens the focus of user information more than primarily population statistics and cultural factors.

Demographics are defining factors about a person however they are static or slow to change features. Some examples of demographics include age, gender and income level. Next, psychographics are descriptive factors about an individual person that is usually generalized to a group. Some examples of psychographics include personality, lifestyle and attitude. Finally, behaviors relates to the consumer's usage pattern of a product. The behaviors include, but are not limited to loyalty, purchase behavior and rate of use. Typically, geography is included in the list however geographic distances have been decreased by modern technology (Child, Ng and Wong, 2003) especially with social media. The consumers' motivation to interact with the e-Retailer rewards the brand with appropriate messaging and content. The brand now knows more about the customer and their lifestyle that is deeper than a generalization of cultural norms of a group of individuals. Social media has provided a more definitive knowledge base of the dynamic consumer across cultures.

Social media usage is a popular determinant of the target audience on social media. Typologies of users social media interaction was developed and created a deeper understanding of the consumers (Li & Bernoff, 2008). The Social Technographic Profile, commonly referred to as the Groundswell Tools reveals 6 typologies of social media users. From the most active and influential to the ones non-active on social media are: creators, critics, joiners, collectors, spectators and inactives. The Groundswell tool reveals social media usage by general demographics determined by Age, Country and Gender. The Groundswell tool creates a snapshot of the user base determined by their usage of social media, despite the cultural differences. Analyzing the usage of social media is vital to a social media strategy. An e-Retailer overlooking the type of social media user could fail to engage with the users by requesting the users to interact with the e-Retailer's social media channel in a method that is unfamiliar to them. One step further than interactions of social media use is determining the motivations driving social media use by the community. Expanding on the Groundswell typologies, the Consumers' Brand Related Activity, COBRA, develop motivations of social media use. Table 2 shows the three drivers of engagement from the COBRA Motivations are consumers (low engagement), contributors (middle engagement) and creators (high engagement) of users based upon motivations of use (Muntinga, et al., 2011). Motivations provide e-Retailers a deeper understanding of how to leverage the different types of social media users from across the globe.

In instances that e-Retailing companies do not have access to the actual Groundswell data for their company, the tool has general data per age, gender and country. Therefore, it is possible to deduce a general understanding of the motivations of their target audience. Table 2 is a template for generalizing the Groundswell tools information into the COBRA typologies.

*Table 2. Groundswell social technographic profiles to COBRA typologies*

| | Groundswell Social Technographic Profiles |
|---|---|
| Creator | Creator |
| | Critic |
| Contributor | Collector |
| | Joiner |
| Consumer | Spectator |
| | Inactive |

Determining motivations of your social media users becomes easier when generalized in terms of the Groundswell tool in comparison to the COBRA typologies. The Groundswell tool and COBRA typologies should be used as a starting guide for your research and engagement, however it is a general resource.

Finally, the behaviors of the target audience should be taken into consideration. Target audience behaviors on social media should focus on loyalty to the e-Retailing brand as referenced in Table 1. Brand loyalty facilitates engagement and recommendation of the e-Retailing company by the consumer (Capozzi & Zipfel, 2012). The increased engagement through social media enables the e-Retailing brand to nurture relationships and build deeper relationships with its consumers. In fact, a deeper relationship with the e-Retailer is expected by the customer (Falkow, 2010). Brand loyalty fosters trust between the brand and the consumer with the deeper relationship (Capozzi & Zipfel, 2012). Since social media develops community networks, e-Retailing brands should capitalize on the information dissemination of the consumer to their community about the e-Retailer, creating brand advocates (Booth & Matic, 2011). As a result, brands should determine the loyalty of their customers to their e-Retailing brand to leverage the brand advocates.

Moreover, it is recommended that e-Retailing brands use listening tools to learn and analyze the target audience. There are many listening tools on the market today including Hootsuite, Google Alerts, TweetDeck and Talk Walker (Safko, 2010). Each tool provides information to learn more about keyword searches and context of the conversation related to e-Retailing brands on social media sites. By listening to the target audience e-Retailers have the ability to develop a global message that resonates with many social media users. The information provided from the listening tools develops a holistic understanding of the target audience to determine voids the company can fill.

Once listening tools are set in place, research should be conducted and analyzed based on some of the following factors being discussed by the target audience: keywords, frequency of posts, sentiment and popular channels. More detailed information on factors to analyze can be found on ReallyLeila.com under "e-Retailing Challenges and Opportunities in the Global Marketplace" with the Password: REALLY. The target audience information of behaviors on social media will present opportunities for e-Retailers on social media.

To stay relevant on social media, it is important to constantly track the target audience demographics, psychographics and behavioral factors.

Research has consistently explained success factors of social media marketing strategy (i.e. Kaplan & Haenlein, 2010; Mangolds & Faulds, 2009; Piskorski, 2011; Safko, 2012) and specifically on the social network site, Facebook (Vries, Gensler & Leeflang, 2012). Certain characteristics have been examined to attract more interactivity with the brand on social media sites. The number of likes, vivid-

*Table 3. Target audience factors to measure*

| | Factors to Measure |
|---|---|
| Demographic Factors | Age |
| | Gender |
| | Income |
| | Marital Status |
| | Geographic Location |
| Psychographic Factors | Social Media Usage |
| | Social Media Motivations |
| Behavioral Factors | Loyalty |
| | Keywords |
| | Frequency of Posts |
| | Sentiment |
| | Popular Channels |

ness, interactivity, content and position all have relationships with the number of likes and comments on a page. Through the analysis of engagement of the community and the brand, it efficiently determines the positioning of social media for a global audience.

## INFLUENCER MARKETING

Influencers are typically thought leaders creating content on social media and therefore are commonly also known as Creators and/or Mavens (i.e. Foster, West & Francescucci, 2011; Yang, 2013). For the scope of this chapter we will use the term Influencers to address the group of people creating content and have social media clout. Influencers typically are up with the new trends in the industry and have large communities on social media. The Influencers are vital for e-Retailing social media for a few reasons: trust, clout, knowledge of community and trends.

Influencers should be observed to discover advancements in the industry both on- and offline. E-Retailers should listen to Influencers to understand trends in the industry and monitor the norms of the culture on social media channels (Kumar & Mirchandani, 2012). Similar to the Consumer target audience, some important factors to analyze the Influencer on include their target audience, content, themes and community. After the information is analyzed for the Influencers in the industry, voids and opportunities should be noted for the e-Retailer to implement.

Once the e-Retailers analyze the Influencers, they should leverage Influencers to spread a brand's message to the Influencer's community (Booth & Matic, 2011; Kaplan & Haenlein, 2011; Kumar & Mirchandani, 2012). Typically, Influencers will have a larger community and know how to communicate with their audience, therefore the global message will resonate more so with the Influencers gloal audience. Consumers trust information spread from peers through word of mouth more than from advertisements in general (Senecal & Nantel, 2004). Moreover, Influencers spread targeted messages through knowledge of their community culture. For e-Retailing brands, targeting Influencers are vital to help spread the message to the Influencers network. Since the Influencer already has a strong community, the call to action for the e-Retailer fosters a dialogue between the Influencers community and the Influencer. As a result, the community is hearing from a familiar voice in a relatable cultural context (Kumar and Mirchandanu, 2012). The Influencers clout and knowledge of their community will increase brand congruence through trust and recognition of appropriate message context.

## Objectives and Goals

Objectives and goals define the brand goal and the various tactics to use. The opportunities presented by the target audience and the Influencers will provide a clear pathway to moving forward with social media. The strategic objectives and goals should reflect the research of the social media landscape in the industry (Keller, 1993), as well as the typologies of users and motivations. Defining the objectives and a clear message should parallel the brand image to support the vision of the company. Enlisting Influencers to communicate the message will preserve the e-Retailers brand image.

As discussed, social media is dynamic and attracts various types of users with different motivations to participate online. Successful social media strategies and campaigns leverage the various types of social media users. Having a one-size-user-fits-all approach to a social media campaign will not be as successful at imprinting the brands message onto the consumer. E-Retailers would be most successful with a multilayered social media campaign to create a greater affinity to the brand. As the campaign strategy is determined the e-Retailer should take into consideration the lack of control around the conversation. Therefore, the e-Retailer should leverage UGB to shift the social media community's conversation around a specific topic.

## User Generated Branding

Although brands cannot control messages on social media entirely, they can influence the message with stimulation of consumer-related content about the brand. E-Retailers leveraging consumer generated content around the brand efficiently develop the brand image and message with the help of the community (Gensler, Völckner, Thompkins & Wiertz, 2013). Strategic campaigns efforts and sponsoring content aimed at influencing user generated content creates a central point for conversation on social media to create User Generated Branding (UGB) (Burmann, 2010). User generated branding has been successful for many brands. For example, the ALS Challenge was a successful example of a brand leveraging UGC to create a UGB. The ALS challenge was an effort to spread awareness about ALS by stimulating consumer related content around the non-profit. The ALS challenge dared consumers to dump buckets of ice over their head to raise awareness around the ALS disease. Participants then would tag their network of friends on social media and challenge them to dump buckets of ice water over their head and then tag their friends. The challengers whom did not follow through with the ALS challenge were required to make a donation. According to the ALS Association (2015), the ALS challenge raised $21.7mllion, became a household name throughout the campaign and created more awareness around ALS. Moreover, the campaign focused the users around a central point for conversation to leverage their UGC and develop a UGB.

Social media campaigns enlist many different types of social media users to participate. Many e-Retailer leverage the various types of social media users and motivations to spread targeted contextual messages. For instance, the Influencers are the ones constantly creating content online and are the users that participate with the most engagement. Therefore, Influencers should be targeted to help spread the word around a social media campaign (Kaplan & Haenlein, 2011; Kumar & Mirchandani, 2012). The clout of the Influencers will motivate other Creators and Consumers to participate with a social media campaign.

### Social Responsibility

Observations of social media campaign reflect the execution and perceived objectives aiming to better the community or a cause typically are successful. Emotional arousal is triggered by e-Retailing brands improving the community. It is important for the message of the social media campaign to be clear and meaningful to the user for participation. Multilayered social media campaigns with a socially responsible component have been successful. As an example, discussed earlier, the ALS challenge #IceBucketChallenge went viral with 17 million videos created by users for the challenge with 10 billion views and on Facebook along 28 million Facebook users were talking about the challenge in less than 3 months (ALS, 2015). The emotional arousal coupled with the social responsibility objective created a clear message to support ALS.

Social media has changed selling strategies (Mangold & Faulds, 2009). In e-Retailing, the importance of using social media for selling should not be isolated from the social responsibility. In fact, the social media objectives should align with the social responsibility of the e-Retailer, as will be discussed later in a case. Therefore, marketing objectives are somewhat different on social media than on traditional marketing channels, as with social media the purchase decision is heavily weighted on the brand image versus the actual product. The approach to marketing has become more implicit with social media. Brand's that have a positive image and are known to do "good" for society are typically successful brands.

The social media campaign must have a clear contextual message resonating with many cultures and the varying types of social media users. Very limited brands have created a successful truly global social media campaign. Quicksilver's brand Roxy has created a global campaign that has targeted 80 countries.

## ROXY #DareYourself GLOBAL SOCIAL MEDIA STRATEGY

### Introduction

Social media produces the exchange of information and many companies have leveraged the use of content spread around a brand. Roxy Quiksilver capitalized on the global social media user generated content to spread a positive brand image. Similar to many other e-Retailing brands, Roxy has disrupted the internationalization process with a strong global brand image prior to entering the specific country market with physical locations or products. Brands can refer to Roxy's global social media implementation as a framework to determine the country market potential prior to fully investing in the market.

Roxy is a subsidiary of Quiksilver and sells primarily girls and women clothing for extreme sports such as surfing, swimming and skiing. Quiksilver, the parent company of Roxy, has trend setting brands including DC Shoes, Silver Edition, Fidra, Raisons, Radio Fiji labels, Roxy and Quiksilver. As one of the top players in action sportswear, Quiksilver brands focus on clothing for outdoor sports. Since 1969, Quiksilver has been changing the action sports lifestyle from the type of fabric used in their clothes to their social media marketing success.

Quiksilver introduced Roxy to fill a void in the niche market of active wear for women, specifically action sports clothing. The name Roxy is known as a trendy brand among active women for the outdoors. Roxy brand is limited to primarily sports clothing, while selling some shoes, boots and hand bags. When Roxy was first introduced in 1990, Quiksilver noticed the need for a women's line with the proliferation of women surfers. Action sportswear was never the same for women after Roxy entered the retail landscape.

## REALLY Framework Strategy

Social media is one of Roxy's strengths. Roxy conveys the brand image of an active lifestyle coupled with emotional messages daring women to push themselves to the limits. As a result, Roxy determined an opportunity in the marketplace to leverage social media. The *Dare Yourself* campaign was launched as a multilayered social media campaign to promote the Roxy brand image. The campaign attracted various types of social media users.

## Research

The information acquired through research of the target audiences' behaviors and psychographics facilitated a high arousal and empowering campaign. The Dare Yourself campaign was targeted to women aged 18-28. Interestingly, a Pew report by Brennar and Smith (2013) compared social media usage by age group in a sample of countries. In every country that was analyzed, the 18-29 year olds participated in social media considerably more that 30-49 and 50+. The differentiation of social media usage by age changes the message being communicated. Age segmentation towards marketing is a more rational and better approach to marketing than traditional ideas of country to country. Therefore, empowering women in the 18-28 age group was important and on target, especially when referring to the COBRA typologies as noted in Table 5 (Munting et al., 2010). Roxy's research of the target audience presented opportunities for solid social media objectives and a targeted message.

The global social media campaign was inspirational to women from all over the world and all walks of life. The Dare Yourself campaign aimed to challenge and fill the void of women athletes. Roxy capitalized on the opportunity to encourage women to reach their goals beyond their limits and to think about the future. Further, it inspired women to change the world and dismiss gender roles, culture, language and geography. Roxy did not put limits on the campaign, so women would not put limits on their entry.

The Roxy Dare Yourself campaign examined from the Research perspective of the REALLY framework reveals the type of e-Retailing Industry and the defined Target Audience in terms of age, gender, location and keywords.

*Table 4. Roxy's research for the Dare Yourself campaign from the REALLY framework*

| Research | Roxy |
|---|---|
| e-Retailing Industry | Women's Active Wear |
| Target Audience | 18-29 year olds, the Americas, Europe, Latin America, South Asia and North Asia, active women, athletic, competitive, high achievers. |

*Table 5. Roxy's engagement for the Dare Yourself campaign from the REALLY framework*

| Engagement | Roxy |
|---|---|
| Creators | Video submission; Personal identity, integration and social interaction, empowerment and entertainment |
| Consumers | Voting; Information, entertainment and remuneration |
| Empowering | Creators increasing their voice through their submissions |

## Engagement

The Engagement of the REALLY framework that was created through the Roxy *Dare Yourself* campaign was dependent on the research and analysis of the community. Roxy created the *Dare Yourself* multilayered UGB campaign and attracted various types of social media users while empowering women. As referenced in Table 5, the Roxy Dare Yourself campaign was a 2-Phased campaign. In the first phase of the campaign, women were encouraged to enter the contest two ways by submitting 1) a one-minute video or 2) writing a 150-word essay with pictures showing how they "Dare" themselves every day. The premise of the contest was to make women aware of their lives and their potential. In the second phase of the campaign, the rest of the community was encouraged to vote on their favorite video and/or pictures and essays. The 2 phases or multilayered campaign attracted many participants to create content from all over the world with different social media behaviors and motivations.

The *Dare Yourself* campaign was launched in key countries in the Americas, Europe, Latin America, South Asia and North Asia. Moreover, the contestants of the campaign were only permitted to be submitted in 11 languages: English, French, German, Russian, Japanese, Traditional Chinese, Korean, Indonesian, Thai, Portuguese and Spanish.

The explanation of the Roxy Dare Yourself campaign in terms of the Engagement of the REALLY framework reveals the level of engagement of the social media user and the action item based on the motivation.

## Analysis, Listening and Learning

The Dare Yourself campaign had a clear message and was successfully targeted to the defined audience. Alexa a credible site for website analysis defines website and online demographics and psychographics. Based on Alexa's ranking system, Roxy website visitors are primarily females with a large portion having a college degree and some having some type of college for Roxy. The Alexa ranking is in line with the target audience that was selected for the *Dare Yourself* campaign. The *Dare Yourself* campaign had 4,000 submissions as noted in Table 6. The number of entries was substantial for girls aged 18-28 to be curating original content. These women created content about themselves and sent in videos on how they challenge themselves every day. The creation of information is difficult to do and it reflects that there are a large number of women aged 18-28 years that are creating content on social media.

Roxy's Dare Yourself campaign could be concluded as successful. For one, Roxy's communities all consist of tens of thousands and hundreds of thousands of users. Further, the large Roxy community reveals a robust social media strategy creating a solid foundation for a social media campaign. Klout a widely used social media tool that determines the influence a brand has on social media through social

*Table 6. Roxy's analysis, listening and learning for the Dare Yourself campaign from the REALLY framework*

| Analysis | Roxy |
|---|---|
| Target Audience | 75 countries, 11 languages<br>Creators- 4,000 entries<br>Contributors- 100,000 votes<br>Creators, Consumers and Contributors- 750,000 views |
| Influencers | Klout score is 66 (top 5%) |
| Brand | Active, fun, women oriented, pushing women to the limit. |
| Positive WOM | Spread of the campaign revealed positive WOM |

network analysis (Klout, 2015). Roxy has a Klout score of 66. According to Klout, any user that has a score of 65 or higher is in the top 5% of social media users. Therefore Roxy is considered an Influencer on social media revealing their strength of engaging users.

The *Dare Yourself* campaign was launched to create a community for women aged 18-28. With 75 countries being represented in the campaign, while it was only launched in a group of countries in 11 languages, it stimulated a large number of users to generate content. During the second phase of the campaign, there were 100,000 votes in the first week of the voting phase and 750,000 views of the contest. Interestingly, the numbers and the strategy of the launch of the campaign attracted each type of social media user and their motivations for using social media. The Roxy brand looked into the voids that were present in the active wear clothing space and determined there was a need to empower women to challenge their daily routine.

The analysis of the Roxy case in terms of the Analysis, Listening and Learning of the REALLY framework details the results of the campaign as a result of the Dare Yourself Campaign.

Interestingly, when looking at the motivations of social media users the *Dare Yourself* campaign parallels the motivations of social media users. Creators are motivated in social media for personal identity, integration and social interaction, empowerment and entertainment. The *Dare Yourself* campaign drove personal identity, integration and empowerment in their creators that submitted their videos. Women were empowered through their personal identity by showing the world how they dare themselves on a daily basis.

The number of people that voted in the first week of the consumer voting contest was 100,000. There were 100,000 community members that were interested in the *Dare Yourself* campaign and wanted to contribute, yet did not want to create original content. Users that are contributors want to join social media and share information. There is a large number of contributors on social media and it is vital to any social media campaign to include them in your social media strategy. Through listening, Roxy learned the different types of social media users.

Roxy targeted the contributors in social media by asking the users to vote on the creators that submitted to the *Dare Yourself* campaign. The contributors have social media motivations that include personal identity, integration and social interaction and entertainment. Through the *Dare Yourself* campaign, Roxy targets the contributors by asking the Contributors to involve themselves through voting for the best *Dare Yourself* videos and pictures. Although Contributors did not create original content, they were still motivated by the entertainment factor and identifying with the Creators.

The *Dare Yourself* contest was extremely large. For a company of its size, the success of having 4,000 contest contestants and 100,000 contributors that voted is quite substantial. However, there were a number of consumers that did not want to contribute or create, yet they were still interested in the campaign. Although most of these Consumers are not possible to identify, the sheer number of views of the *Dare Yourself* campaign, 750,000 views, reflect the strong need to also appeal to the motivations of the Consumer. Based on the success of the Dare Yourself campaign, Figure 2 reflects the different type of users and their motivations: Creators, Contributors and Consumers and Action items for an e-Retailer to implement for a social media campaign.

## You

Roxy set out to accomplish four objectives in their Dare Yourself campaign (C.Beeson, personal communication, January 28, 2013):

1. To connect with their audience globally.
2. To build and broaden their online, and global community primarily through their nearly 3 million followers on Facebook.
3. To complement the surf and snow categories and lifestyles.
4. To inspire girls.

*Figure 2. Social media users, roles and action items for a social media campaign*

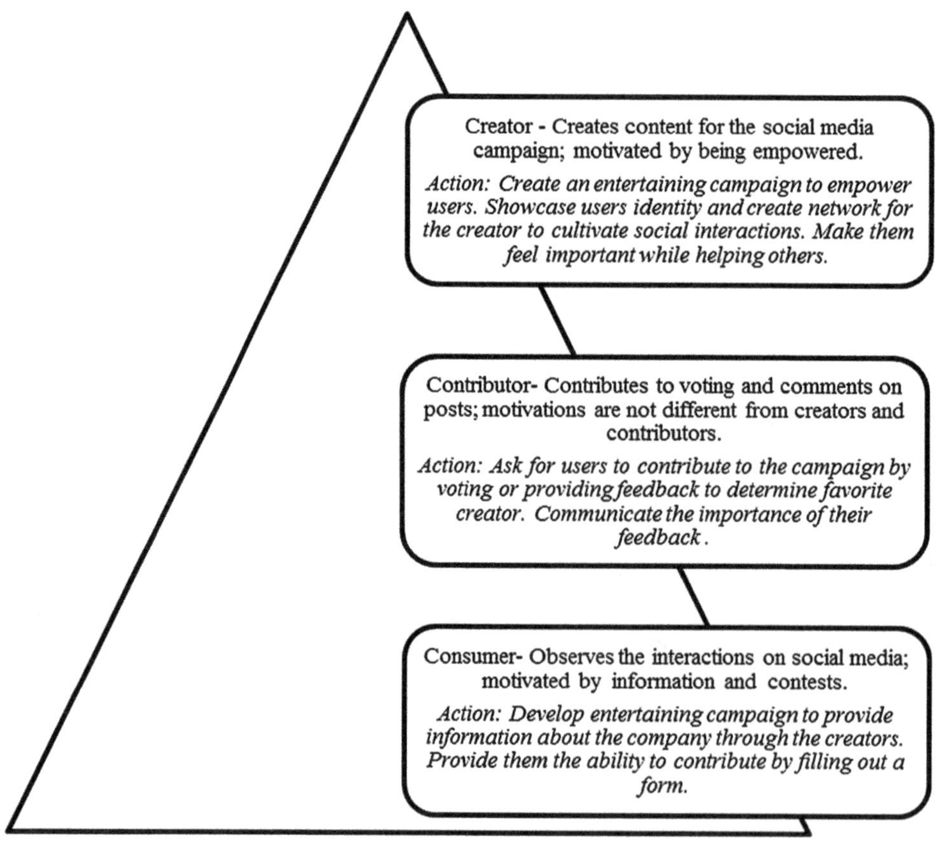

The objectives were important to empower girls creating an emotional connection to the brand. Moreover, the objectives were in line with the brand image and included a sense of social responsibility. The Roxy Dare Yourself campaign message was: "what it means to live every day as an adventure to show the mark you want to leave on the world" (Roxy, 2013).

As spoken about earlier, Roxy took a multilayered approach to target the various motivations of the target audience to satisfy their objectives. The multilayered approach to the campaign was shown to be imperative to the success of the campaign and to the UGB strategy. In the first phase of the campaign there were 4,000 entries submitted from all over the world. The content created on social media around the Roxy was quite substantial as detailed in Table 7.

The explanation of the Roxy Dare Yourself campaign from the "You" perspective is shown in Table 7. The information reflects Roxy's brand image, leveraging UGB, social responsibility and their objectives and goals.

Roxy standardized their promotional strategy of the *Dare Yourself Campaign.* Roxy limited their campaign to 11 languages and launched the same campaign throughout their key markets. Roxy communicated the same message to their global market of 18-28 year old women. Moreover, Roxy promoted their campaign through print advertising, social/online advertising, retail marketing and PR with the same message and brand image across the globe. Interestingly, there was no need to change their campaign from country to country based on cultural differences.

Consequently, the organizational structure on social media was centralized to one social media account per channel. During the time of the campaign, Roxy had only one social media channel per application (i.e. one Facebook account in English, one YouTube account in English). They did not have various social media accounts per language or country. Interestingly, they have a large social media community on each of the channels supporting the centralized social media structure. Contrary to previous research, the success of the campaign was not dependent on the social media channel language, the UGB controlled for the cultural and community differences.

Finally, at the time of the campaign, Roxy was only selling in 19 countries (United States, Argentina, Australia, Canada, Chile, Colombia, Costa Rica, Ecuador, French Polynesia, Guam, Guatemala, Honduras, Mexico, New Zealand, Nicaragua, Panama, Peru, Puerto Rico and Venezuela), however they had an overwhelmingly large response from 75 countries. The sheer number of responses from countries outside of their authorized retailers signals another phenomenon that is occurring in social media, a change in the internationalization process. In many countries that were represented in the campaign, the brand Roxy was not present. However, with the virality of content and UGB, users are learning about brands through social media. Roxy has created a market through their positive brand image and successful global social media campaign prior to physically entering the market by stimulating conversation through UGB.

*Table 7. Roxy's You for the Dare Yourself campaign from the REALLY framework*

| You | Roxy |
|---|---|
| Brand Image | Consistent across all marketing channels, print and digital. |
| UGB | Leveraging the target audience to create content with video submissions and asking consumers' to vote. |
| Social Responsibility | Challenging women to better and dare themselves. |
| Objectives/Goals | Connecting with global audience, build and broaden social media community, complement brand and inspire girls. |

## SOCIAL INTERNATIONALIZATION

We define social internationalization as a process of the exchange of information and ideas through social media. Social media has changed e-Retailing through social internationalization. Traditional international business theory suggests internationalization and location selection as incremental with specific stages for determining the best market for expansion (Vahlne and Johanson, 1977). However with the rise of social media usage has evolved the internationalization process. The information exchanged on social media between users and the e-Retailer is more dynamic and descriptive. Firms should be flexible and evolve based on the customers' needs (Tallman and Shenkar, 1992). Consumers can be analyzed in more depth on social media since there is a platform for users to reveal information about themselves. The Web 2.0 as a platform connects e-Retailers and consumers, but social media provides more insight to the e-Retailer about the consumers. Social internationalization facilitates discussion and information dissemination around the e-Retailer to develop a market with a social media campaign. Moreover, information acquisition is leveraged for location selection by e-Retailers based on customer needs.

Prior to social media and the internet, brand awareness was limited to the retailer having a physical presence in a country. However, the *Dare Yourself* campaign supports the revelation of the change in internationalization. Social Internationalization is only in it's the beginning phases as more e-Retailers learn the methods to leverage information dissemination and acquisition. Future research should look into social internationalization in more detail.

## CONCLUSION

Social Internationalization has changed the e-Retailing process. The traditional internationalization process has evolved from bricks-and-mortar sequential expansion to e-Retailing and developing market potential through social media. The potential of social media should be leveraged for the success of the e-Retailer. Through following the REALLY framework, e-Retailers can capitalize on the target audience to develop multilayered UGB social media campaign.

This chapter focused on global strategic approaches to social media campaigns to leverage UGC across all social media channels across various countries. To capitalize on the efficiency of social media and its global reach, e-Retailers should use a global strategy instead of looking at social media contrasts in an individual country approach. It must be noted, social media channels are constantly changing and foundational knowledge of global social media is important to understand the emerging patterns. Therefore the information presented is applicable to all channels and countries. Technology is ever changing, thus e-Retailers that are nimble will be successful by having knowledge in the underlying frameworks that guide global social media.

## REFERENCES

Arenius, P., Sasi, V., & Gabrielsson, M. (2006). Rapid Internationalization enabled by the Internet: The case of a knowledge intensive company. *Journal of Entrepreneurship*, 279-290.

Axelsson, B., & Johanson, J. (1992). *Foreign market entry: The textbook vs the network view*. London: Routledge.

Barwise, P., & Meehan, S. (2010). The one thing you must get right when building a brand. *Harvard Business Review*, December, 80–84.

Berger, J. (2012). *Contagious: Why things catch on*. New York: Simon and Schuster.

Bodapati, Arabie, & Palmer, R. A. (2004). How managers perceive the impacts of information technologies on contemporary practices: Reinforcing, enhancing or transforming? *Journal of Relationship Marketing*, 3(4), 7–26.

Booth, N., & Matic, J. (2011). Mapping and leveraging influencers in social media to shape corporate brand perceptions. *Corporate Communications*: An *International Journal (Toronto, Ont.)*, 16(3), 184–191.

Brennar, J., & Smith, A. (2013). *Social Networking*. Washington, D.C.: Pew Internet.

Bruhn, M., Schoenmueller, V., & Schäfer, D. B. (2012). Are social media replacing traditional media; is brand equity creation? *Management Research Review*, 770-790.

Burmann, C. (2010). *A call for user-generated branding*. Brand Management.

Capozzi, L., & Zipfel, L.B. (2012). The conversation age: the opportunity for public relations. *Corporate Communications: An International Journal*, 17(3), 336 – 349.

Carroll, D. (2015, January 9). United Breaks Guitars. *Dave Carrol Music*. Retrieved from http://www.davecarrollmusic.com/music/ubg/

Child, J., Ng, S. H., & Wong, C. (2002). Psychic Distance and Internationalization: Evidence from Hong Kong Firms. *International Studies of Management & Organization*, 32(10), 36–56.

Duggan, M., Ellison, N., Lampe, C., Lenhart, A., & Madden, M. (2015, January 9). Social Media Site Usage 2014. *Pew Research Center*. Retrieved from http://www.pewinternet.org/2015/01/09/social-media-update-2014/?utm_content=buffer68e1e&utm_medium=social&utm_source=twitter.com&utm_campaign=buffer

Erikson, E. (1968). *The Psychosocial stages of development*. London: Norton & Company.

Etgar, M., & Rachman-Moore, D. (2010). Geographical Expansion by International Retailers: A Study of Proximate Markets and Global Expansion Strategies. *Journal of Global Marketing*, *23*(1), 5–15. doi:10.1080/08911760903439560

Evans, L. (2010). *Social media marketing: Strategies for engaging in Facebook, Twitter & other social media*. Indianapolis: Que Publishing.

Facebook users of the world. (2015, May 4). *Internet World Stats*. Retrieved from http://www.internetworldstats.com/facebook.htm

Falkow, S. (2010). PR Trends 2010: Branded Content. *The Proactive Report*.

Foster, M., West, B., & Francescucci, A. (2011). Exploring social media users segmentation and online brand profiles. *Journal of Brand Management*, 19(1), 4-17.

Gensler, V., Völckner, F., Liu-Thompkins, Y., & Wiertz, C. (2013). Managing brands in the social media environment. *Journal of Interactive Marketing, 27*(4), 242–256. doi:10.1016/j.intmar.2013.09.004

Hubspot. (2013). Revealing charts from the 2013 state of inbound marketing. *Hubspot.*

Iacobucci, D., Arabie, P., & Bodapati, A. V. (2000). Recommendation Agents on the Internet. *Journal of Interactive Marketing, 14*(3), 2–11. doi:10.1002/1520-6653(200022)14:3<2::AID-DIR1>3.0.CO;2-J

Impact of the Ice Bucket Challenge. (2015, April 15). *ALS Association.* Retrieved from http://www.alsa.org/news/archive/impact-of-ice-bucket-challenge.html

Johanson, J. & Vahlne, J. (1977). The internationalization of the firm- A model of knowledge development and increasing foreign market commitments. *Journal of International Business*, 8, 22-32.

Johanson, J. & Vahlne, J. (2009). The Uppsala internationalization process revisited: From liability of foreignness to liability to outsidership. *Journal of International Business Studies*, 40(9), 1411-1431.

Kaplan, A., & Haenlein, M. (2010). Users of the world, unite! The challenges and opportunities of social media. *Business Horizons, 53*(1), 59–68. doi:10.1016/j.bushor.2009.09.003

Keller. (1993). Conceptualizing, measuring, and managing customer-based brand equity. *Journal of Marketing*, 1993, 1-22.

Klout. (2013). *Klout.* Retrieved from Klout: www.klout.com

Kozinets, V., de Valck, K., Wojnicki, A. C., & Wilner, S. J. S. (2010). Networked narratives: Understanding word-of-mouth marketing in online communities. *Journal of Marketing, 74*(2), 71–89. doi:10.1509/jmkg.74.2.71

Kumar, V., & Mirchandi, R. (2012). Increasing he ROI of Social Media Marketing. *Sloan Management Review*, 54(1), 55.

Levitt, T. (1983). The globalization of markets. *Harvard Business Review,* 1983.

Li, C., & Bernoff, J. (2011). *Groundswell.* Cambridge: Forrester.

Loane, S. (2006). The Role of the Internet in the Internationalisation of small and medium sized companies. *Journal of International Entrepreneurship*, 33(4), 263–277.

Mangold, W. G., & Faulds, D. J. (2009). Social Media: The new hybrid element of the promotion mix. *Business Horizons, 52*(4), 357–365. doi:10.1016/j.bushor.2009.03.002

Mathews, S., Healy, M., & Ali, Y. (2006). A comparative evaluation of the Internet's influence on international market penetration and development growth strategies of Australian SME's. *Proceedings of the Australia & New Zealand Marketing Academy Annual Conference.* Brisbane.

Muntinga, D. G., Moorman, M., & Smit, E. G. (2011). Introducing COBRAs Exploring motivations for brand-related social media use. *International Journal of Advertising, 30*(1), 13–46. doi:10.2501/IJA-30-1-013-046

Coviello, N., & Munro, H. (1997). Network relationships and the internationalisation process of small software firms. *International Business Review.*

Ohmae, K. (1989, June). Managing in a Borderless World. *Harvard Business Review.*

Ohmae, K. (2000). *The Invisible Continent.* New York, NY: Harper Business.

Okonkwo, U. (2009). Sustaining the luxury brand on the Internet. *Journal of Marketing*, 16, 303–310.

Piskorski, M. J. (2011). Social Strategies That Work. *Harvard Business Review.* PMID:22111430

Prashantham, S. (2005). Toward a Knowledge-Based Conceptualization of Internationalization. *Journal of International Entrepreneurship, 3*(1), 37–52. doi:10.1007/s10843-005-0304-5

Quelch, J.A., & Hoff, E.J. (1993). Customizing Global Marketing. In R.Z. Aliber, & R.W. Click (Eds.), *Reading in international business: A decision approach.* Cambridge: Massachusetts Institution of Technology.

Roxy. (2015). Retrieved from www.roxy.com

Safko, L. (2012). *The Social Media Bible.* Hoboken: John, Wiley & Sons.

Samii, L. (2015). e-Retailing Challenges and Opportunities in the Global Marketplace. *ReallyLeila.* Retrieved from http://reallyleila.com/2015/05/31/e-retailing-challenges-and-opportunities-in-the-global-marketplace/

Senecal, S., & Nantel, J. (2004). The influence of online product recommendations on consumers' online choices. *Journal of Retailing*, 80(2), 159-169.

Singh, N., Lenhert, K., & Bostick, K. (2012). Usage: Insights into reaching consumers worldwide. *Thunderbird International Business Review*, 54(5), 683-700. doi:10.1002/tie.21493

The State of the media: The social media report 2012. (2012). *Nielsen.*

Twitter, Inc. (2012). Retrieved from www.twitter.com

U.S. and World Population Clock. (2015, May 30). *US Census Bureau.* Retrieved from http://www.census.gov/popclock/

Vries, L., Gensler, S., & Leeflang, P. (2012). Popularity of brand posts on brand fan pages: An investigation of the effect of social media marketing. *Journal of Interactive Marketing*, 26(2), 83-91.

Yang, H. (2013). Market mavens in social media: Examining young Chinese consumers' viral marketing attitude, eWOM and behavior. *Journal of Asia-Pacific Business, 14*(2), 154–178. doi:10.1080/10599231.2013.756337

Zaheer, S. (1995). Overcoming the Liability of Foreignness. *Academy of Management Journal, 38*(2), 341–363. doi:10.2307/256683

## KEY TERMS AND DEFINITIONS

**Centralized Social Media Organizational Strategy:** Creating a social media strategy with only one account per social media application (i.e. Twitter, Facebook, Pinterest) in one language.

**Culture:** A group of people with similar ideas and beliefs to the exchange of information, behaviors and norms that guides their understanding of messages.

**Global Social Media Strategy:** A social media strategy maximizing the potential of social media with standardization of messages.

**Information Acquisition:** Knowledge transfer from an industry, market, country and/or consumer to a company to decrease liability of foreignness and complexities.

**Information Dissemination:** Knowledge transfer about a company to a market, country and/or consumer to create awareness.

**Internationalization:** The process of cross border movements of a company.

**Multilayered Strategy:** Attracting various types of social media audiences based on their patterns of social media usage and motivations.

**Social Internationalization:** Creating awareness around a brand through information dissemination on social media prior to selling products overseas.

**User Generated Branding:** Leveraging social media users to spread user generated content around a brand by the brand strategically stimulating discussion through a social media campaign.

**User Generated Content:** Social media participants creating unsolicited content on social media applications.

# Chapter 12
# Role of Media in Success of E-Tailing

**Surabhi Singh**
*IMS Ghaziabad, India*

## ABSTRACT

*This chapter proposes to bring forth insights as how media contributes in e-tailing. The success of online retailers owe to the role which media plays in changing the consumer mind. India's retail market value was estimated at $520 billion in 2013, and is expected to grow to $950 billion by 2018. With a CAGR currently pegged at 13%, the Indian e-commerce market is expected to grow the fastest within the Asia-Pacific Region – with its market size doubling every 2-2.5 years. This certainly gives us reason for deep introspection. While the global growth rate of online shoppers is estimated at 8-10%, India currently has more than 10 million online shoppers. With the evolution of the online marketplace, sites like Flipkart, Snapdeal, Jabong and Myntra are thriving which has risen the practice of buying goods online. The media has definitely played vital role in shaping the online retail business.*

## INTRODUCTION

In 2012, India's Gross Domestic Product (GDP) was USD 1.7 trillion, at current prices, of which private consumption constituted nearly 60%. USD 490 billion was the size of the merchandise retail market in India, which accounted for nearly half of private consumption. The high share of private consumption in India's economy, which is not expected to change much in the coming decade, also implies that India's retail growth rate will mirror the country's GDP growth rate. E-commerce in India took off with an entry of portals, including many focused on travel, media and jobs. The governments' drive to open the sector for FDI in B2B business and bring e-commerce to the front has caused a number of major players to venture into India. Today, E bay, Amazon, Jabong and some serious Indian players are giving these physical retailers a run for their money.

Flipkart and Snapdeal's recent fund-raising exercise has also embarked the significance of investors in e-commerce. The change in government and the stride of positive sentiment across the nation has led to growing faith in India and Indian business models. The governments' initiative to simplify regulations and make India a business-friendly nation is definitely benefiting e-commerce.

DOI: 10.4018/978-1-4666-9921-2.ch012

Copyright © 2016, IGI Global. Copying or distributing in print or electronic forms without written permission of IGI Global is prohibited.

Though 70% of India's e-commerce market is related to travel (flights, hotel bookings, etc.), electronics and apparels are by far the most important categories in terms of sales. The key driver in Indian e-commerce is the rapid increase of *broadband internet penetration,* which is growing at a whopping 20% every year. The rising standards of the growing middle-class with high disposable incomes have led to an exponential growth of the internet culture in India.

This is very significant to the Indian retail sector. The internet has given Indian consumers access to a wide range of products and services, even in places where the reach of brick-and-mortar shopping complexes are not possible. Also, the availability of a much wider range of products when compared to physical retail stores, coupled with relatively lower price leads to increase demand for online retail. Many big companies are rising to the challenge and adopting smarter strategies to guard their space. The likes of Tata, Future Group and Reliance are expanding their reach by foraying into e-commerce via alliances with leading online players. Indian retailers have clearly read the writing on the wall. As the competition grows, multi channel approach in delivering a unified and consistent customer experience will increase.

When it was recognized that the mail order catalogue was an effective means of presenting products to customers, televised shopping channels emerged which exploited the medium of television to enhance and convey details of the products to customers. The advent of credit cards also made this process of payment even easier. It also made it possible for the customer to pay for an item, even though the customer did not, at the specific time of the sale, actually have the money in hand to pay for it. Another practice also set the stage for online retailing: cross-border shopping. In the United States, where every state and region may have a different rate of sales tax, it is common for customers to drive across a state line in order to purchase items at a lower sales tax rate. In Europe, the same may apply by crossing national borders to purchase items such as liquor, cigarettes or perfume where tax or duty is lower: customers enjoy tax-free shopping. As soon as online shopping became available, customers immediately recognized the great advantages of being able to ignore state or national boundaries.(Chandra et. al., 2002)

The online commerce enables social interactions across many channels. The platform has several components- Channel Interface, core commerce platform, social commerce platform, integration layer, functional modules, and master data management. The channels are like click and collect, Kiosks, in store displays. The channel interface services provide the mechanism to use the commerce platform as channel for shopping. This platform offers functions which enable shopping such as product catalog and listing, check out, order processing and fraud check, payment and promotions. The layer called integration layer provides services and adapters that integrate with line of business applications and enterprise services built of diverse technology platforms. Functional modules include LOB services and components for order management, inventory management and promotion. The other component, Master Data Management offers a total view of data across channels. It enables ease of management and analytics.

Improving the total experience is the way to success. The media plays a major role in shaping the online retailing. Social commerce platform help in other social functions like reviews and ratings (integration with bazaarvoice and viewpoints), social connect (Facebook and Twitter), rewards (Groupon and LivingSocial), social analytics (Google analytics), social sharing and social benchmarking (Facebook and Twitter). Interface implementations are enabled using adapters for service providers. Many of retailers have social media presence via facebook, Twitter, pinterest.

Twitter's Buy buttons has significantly shifted the social network's role in the relationship between consumers and businesses, and disrupt the way in which we have thought about path-to-purchase. The close knit relationship gets strengthened with the help of such social networks. Further customer interests are developed with the help of blogs and wikis also by online retailers. The online interface enables the marketers to develop targeted promotion for customers.

The ability to interact with consumers directly on platforms they were already using to connect with one another was the new leading edge in customer service. As more and more companies began to establish Facebook and Twitter accounts, dialogue on these platforms shifted from interpersonal communications to share the opinions and experiences about brands.

The influence of the internet, especially via social networking, on people's purchasing behavior has grown over the years. Retailers, who depended on traditional stores to drive sales, have found that the *reach of social media* extends beyond generating visibility; it is also a channel to generate revenue. Social media being the next logical marketing arena has prompted retailers to shift a percentage of their marketing dollars to this space. The recent launches of shopping functions in the social network (i.e. Facebook's and Twitter's "buy" buttons) indicate that the acceptability of media for retail has emerged as mandatory.

Retailers that have already started participating in the trend include Nordstrom and Target, which are using Home Depot, (RED), and Burberry, which are using Twitter's buy button.

In recent years, social media has become both a source of retail inspiration and a medium for increasing sales and website traffic. Many ecommerce sites are reporting "higher conversion rates" from customers referred by social networks. The retailers can develop the vibrant micro community in social media which results in increased sales. Social media enables to build the awareness, create the hype of the product and fill the gaps in sales cycle. The scope of promotion gets expanded through this media. Social Media management tools save the time of online retailers. Crowdsourcing enables to speed up the innovation in the product in line with the needs of community. TESCO had used crowdsourcing to introduce new flavor of ice cream by seeking suggestions from customers. The success of online retailing lies in allowing customers to build the brand through participation and promotion. Interactivity with customer give the necessary exposure to brand and promotion is strengthened. Smart business practices are employed to give offers and rewarding the existing customers. Social media creates the environment where customer is valued and loyalty is enhanced. This makes the online retailers aware about their deficiencies in the form of customer feedback given through social network. The social media enable them to provide information about in-store events and e commerce deals. Retailers can create the urgency for discounted items by sharing such news across the network. The promotions of products are possible by advertising but purchases are driven by social networking. This network enables customers to evaluate the peers and sharing of experts. The brands are defined by creating the awareness of their experiences. The likes on Facebook also give the recommendations to customers. The check in services of mobile phone can also be used for multiple reasons. This may be to earn points, to inform their friends, to maintain a timeline etc.

There are sections of consumers who still prefers brick and mortar store. For this, online retailer can convince the customer that the products not available in stores are available online.

One of the reason the customer interact through social media is to learn about products and promotions. The extensive search of products can be possible with internet media. Online retailers require three main things- Shopping cart, secure server and payment processing. Shopping cart is software which keeps track of what the users selects to buy from website. The secure server helps provide protection against the loss of information. Payment processing options are also used in the online transaction by customer. In online retailing designing the promotion campaign means right use of social media platform. The benefits of media use for such online business allow course corrections and increases website traffic.

The media has the vital role in growth of online retailing in India. E-tailing has achieved reasonable success in countries and consumers have shown growth on two factors which has enabled e-tailing market's growth. The Internet access and usage of internet. In India, consumers are displaying positive impact on both of these. Consumption based pricing can be further studied by Marketer through social network. Social graphs are used to show the network of relationships and connections between people on a social networking platform.

Meaningful information can be obtained from social graph analysis. This is useful from the perspective of user's interest. The strategy adopted by retailers is to create the urgency for discounted items with limited offer and increase sales across the network. The website like Pinterest is of importance to retailers owing to their ability to target audience with specific interest. The mobile proliferation with social networking component is also being exploited by retailers. Applications such as Wiket make customers to advise products, share and get rewarded in form of virtual points. Many companies are using different operating models including partnering with online marketplaces or set up their online stores in retail business. The operating models include *Marketplace and pick-up & drop* where the seller partner with leading marketplaces to set up dedicated online stores on latter's website. The seller has to manage the inventory and drive the sales. Although sellers have little control on pricing and customer experience. Another model is *Self owned inventory* where the ecommerce players own the inventory. This model provides better post purchase customer experience and fulfillment. It provides smooth operations due to ready information on inventory, supply chain and shipments. The third model is *Private Label* which reflects a business where online retailers set up its own brands. This model gives offer of wide ranges of products and prices. Margins are higher in this format. The fourth model is *White Label* which includes setting up branded online store managed by the online commerce player. In this case the brand has the responsibility to generate website traffic and provide better services. It helps in building the trust and provides the control of brand and product experience. In recent scenario now the smartphones are increasingly replacing PCs for online shopping. According to some industry experts over 50% of orders are getting placed through mobile apps which leads to customer loyalty of brands. Most of mobile transactions include the entertainment like booking movie tickets and music downloads. The online retailers use television, social media for attracting customers with the concept of sales on weekends, holidays and festivals. There is a recent trend of newer products such as grocery, healthcare, hygiene, healthcare products being purchased online. Similarly Indian jewelry has also been in demand. The few factors need to be evaluated before entering new online retail business. They are market size, e commerce readiness, scope of growth, barriers to entry, competition.

## BACKGROUND

In the age of web 2.0 and almost omnipresent broadband internet connections, a large majority of the online public are communicating with each other through a new medium. Apart from e mail and instant messengers they communicate through the medium of blogs, micro blogging websites and social networking websites like Facebook, Twitter, LinkedIn and many others (Ahuja, 2010)

In 2015 e commerce players see mobile commerce as the most preferred route with mobile wallet as preferred way of payment. With 4G services expected to be launched in 2015, internet penetration is likely to take significant leap which will give boost to mobile commerce. Changes in lifestyle and shopping choices will see buyers preferring online and mobile channel over physical channel to save time ad seek range and comparative pricing. For mobile wallets improvements on payments front with multiple payment instruments with multiple authentication layers will help the consumer with seamless mobile experience. (www.pwc.in)

As per reports Customers are 71% more likely to purchase a product when referred by a social media channel.

With the entry of e commerce behemoths such as Amazon and Alibaba the competition is expected to further intensify. Both these international players come with deep pockets and patience to drive the Indian e commerce market. Also their strong domain knowledge and best practices from their international experience give them the additional edge. Additionally these companies have been parts of markets where they have seen the e commerce market evolve and are aware of challenges and strategies to address issues thereof. (www.pwc.in)

Web 2.0 enables users to interact, collaborate and share content, ideas and companies to improve sales and marketing (Boesler, 2012)

Interest graphs provide marketers with a better opportunity to generate revenue than social graphs. (Hossain, 2012)

Facebook leads with retail companies, with 97 per cent of the top 250 Internet retailers in the United States on the site. They also have a huge presence on Twitter, YouTube and Pinterest, and are growing in both followers and engagement. The bottom line: The world's largest retail brands are spending a lot of time and money on building their social networks as a key component of their overall e-commerce strategy. For small businesses, the opportunity may be even more significant. With growing technological advancements in the e-commerce industry, it has never been easier or more accessible for small- and medium-sized businesses to create a site and leverage social media to build a customer base.(www.theglobeandmail.com)

The Internet usage of Indians has dramatically changed in the last few years. This change has been almost disruptive as Indian consumers today are not only spending longer hours on the Internet, but also conducting many activities that were non-existent a few years ago. Internet browsing is becoming a habit for a population in urban India, i.e. cities, towns, and semi-urban clusters. In India, the retail market is, at present, primarily dominated by traditional brick & mortar stores which is around 93% of the total market. Corporatized brick & mortar retail is 7%, while e-tailing's share is 0.1%. In the coming decade, these three retail models may behave differently in terms of their share of total retail sales (Source: Technopak Analysis) (see figure 1).

As per Technopak's estimates, India's GDP growth, in real terms, will average nearly 6% over the next decade. This growth will therefore translate to an increase in merchandise retail market, from the current ~USD 490 billion, to USD 810 billion, by 2021, in real terms, and USD 1.4 trillion in nominal terms (assuming a 7% inflation rate) (see figure 2).

In 2012, 120 million Indian consumers accessed the Internet at least once a month (also referred to as active user base). This number is often critiqued for the quality of users. For instance, it is argued that very few (<15%) have access to the Internet via broadband (assuming that the number of users is equal to the number of broadband connections), and may thus be insignificant for e-tailing. This argument is not

*Figure 1. Indian retail market size*

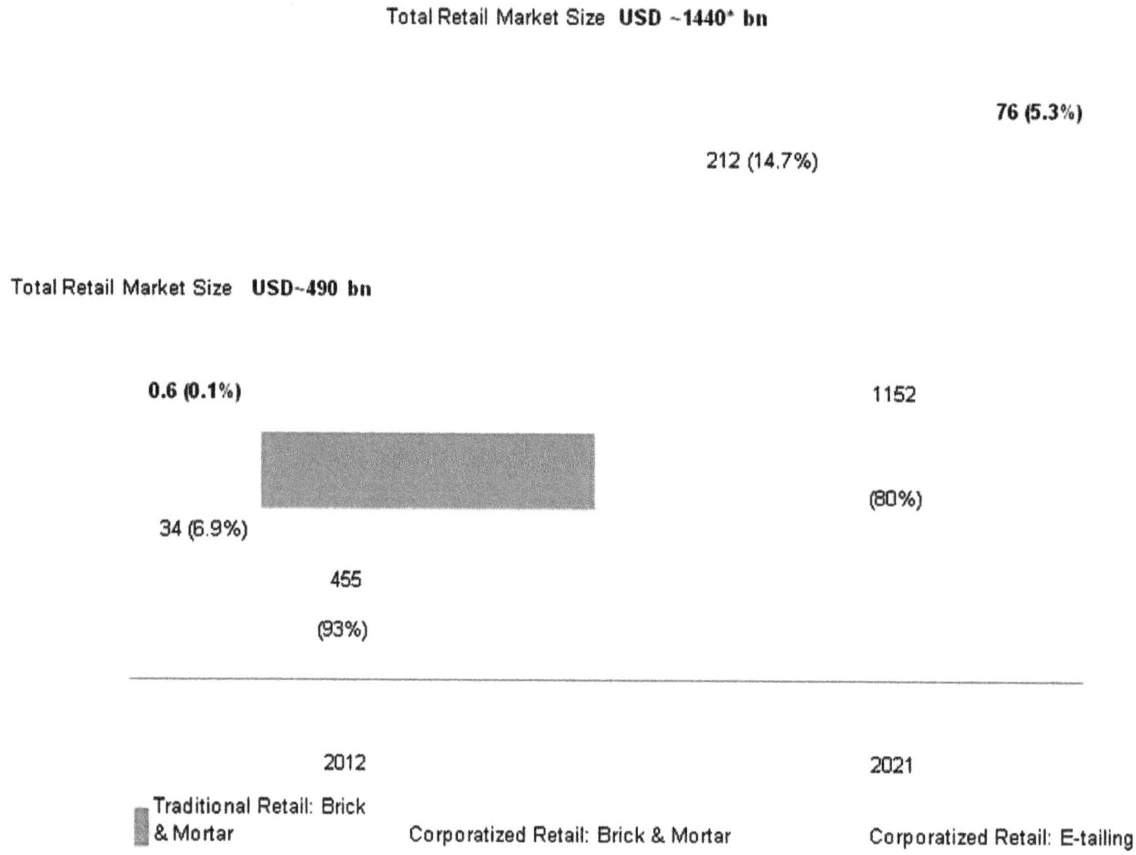


*Figure 2. Usage of social networking sites in retail*

completely incorrect- the quality of Internet access does play a key role in enabling consumers to shop online. Therefore, it is important to look at access to the Internet in conjunction with the quality of access.

Corporatized brick & mortar retail will increase in value from USD 34 billion to USD 212 billion by 2021, and its share of the total retail pie will just over double from the current 7% to 14.7%. However, this type of brick & mortar retail will continue to face structural issues within the retailing ecosystem, which will be a challenge for retailers to address individually. These issues viz. real estate, labor, sourcing and supply chain, were extensively debated in Technopak's previous whitepaper on Foreign Direct Investment (FDI) in retail, and its impact on the Indian retail sector, and the Indian economy at large. (Source: Technopak Analysis) (see figure 3).

There are two key reasons why such trends emerge. The first is India's demography- India is predominantly young with a median age of 26 years. This will continue to be the case for the next ten years, with the projected median age of 29 years in 2020. By 2020, 40% of India would have been born after the launch of the Internet and mobile phones in the country. Thus, for a sizeable mass of Indians, access to the Internet and the use of mobile phones will be a norm to which they won't have to make transition to, unlike previous generations. For these young consumers, spending time on the Internet will be as normal as watching television is for today's consumers. This key pillar is thus quickly falling into place to facilitate the growth of India's e-tailing sector. (Technopak Analysis)

Online retailers use social network platform to target relevant ads based on a customer's demographics, age groups and interest. The online platforms enable social interactions across multiple online channels. This has several channels for order capturing such as websites, mobile applications, catalogs, click & collect, PoS, kiosks, interactive TV, in store displays and call center (www.infosys.com) (see figure 4).

It has been said that 'social media is seen by many marketers as the next gold rush' (Kaplan, 2010)

Improving the total experience is the way to success. The media plays a major role in shaping the online retailing. Online retailers will have to evolve their offering to meet the needs, wants and desires

*Figure 3. E-tailing market in other countries*

| | E-tailing Market (USD bn) | | E-tailing (% of Retail) | |
|---|---|---|---|---|
| Country | 2008 | 2012 | 2008 | 2012 |
| US | 140 | 225 | 3.6% | 5% |
| UK | 65 | 85 | 8.6% | 13% |
| China | 16 | 180 | ~1% | 6% |

*Figure 4. Transition to online channels*

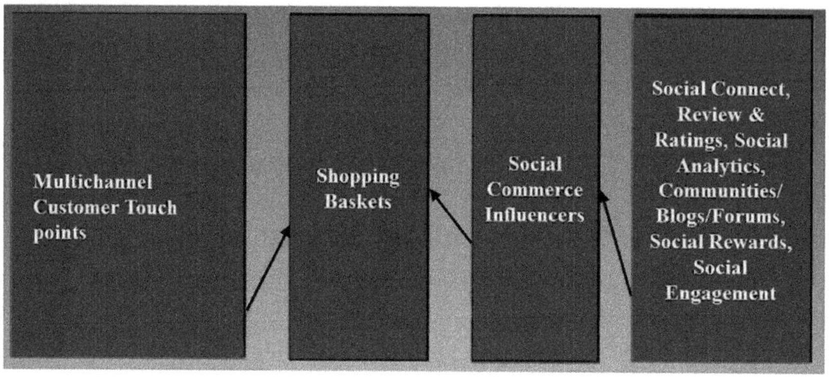


of consumers and media will promote the e tailing experience. Several online grocery stores such as BigBasket, Local Banya, ZopNow, Ekstop, Veggi Bazaar are experimenting with different business and delivery models. (Economic Times)

Online consumers in India are deal seeking value hunters, UBS said in an April 2015 research report on India's consumer sector.

Social networks have started to play a significant role in the growth of the e-commerce business. The maturity of social media and its reach across masses and classes makes it a suitable platform for online sales. Social media pages provide information regarding new products in the market, user reviews and ratings of the product, recommendations, share products, etc. Every 30 seconds, e-commerce industry generates $1.2 million revenue with Facebook, Pinterest and Twitter contributing $5,483, $4,504 and $4,308 respectively. 32 In 2013, 39% of Facebook users liked brand pages to research products while 74% of consumers rely on social media for product-related guidance.

In 2013, social media giants Facebook, Twitter and Pinterest together accounted for 75 percent of social generated e-commerce sales, according to a BI Intelligence study. The study also found that 39% of Facebook users follow brands to research products while 74 percent of consumers rely on social media to guide their purchases. Several online fashion retailers are now using social media to create unique campaigns that drive better user engagement, by directing followers to their websites and hence increasing sales. Such is the potential of this discovery-led shopping that, few of these brands have even brought social media into their offline stores. Meanwhile there are few of our international fashion brands making the right use of social media: Burberry, Kate spade etc (www.blogmobstac.com) With the entry of e commerce such as amazon and alibaba, the competition is expected to grow. Indian retailers are aiming to continue their focus on expanding sellers and selection of their platforms innovating on many touchpoints and provide delivery services. (www.pwc.in)

The internet penetration in India as a percentage of population as on Dec 2014 is 19% as compared with 87% in USA. As the potential of internet use in India increases, the potential for growth of e tailing will increase. In China this is 47%. (www.pwc.in)

The social media provides a platform for e-tailers to engage with customers for:

- Advertisement
- Building brand awareness

*Figure 5. Top 10 countries in terms of population and corresponding e-households (Source: E Commerce Foundation 2014)*

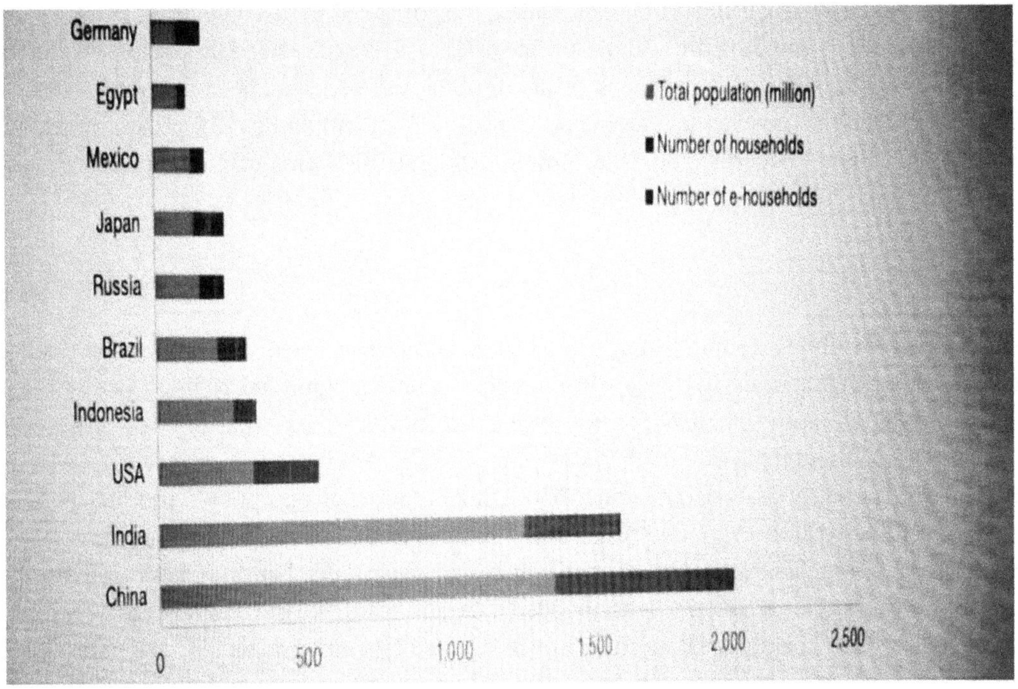


- Developing a community of trusted users
- Spreading Word-of-Mouth
- Customer feedback (see figure 5).

India's internet penetration with total e households at 46 million against China's 207 million is one of the reasons behind India's poor sales growth (see figure 6).

*Figure 6. Internet penetration as percentage of population (2014) (Source: Internet Livestats website accessed on Dec, 2014)*

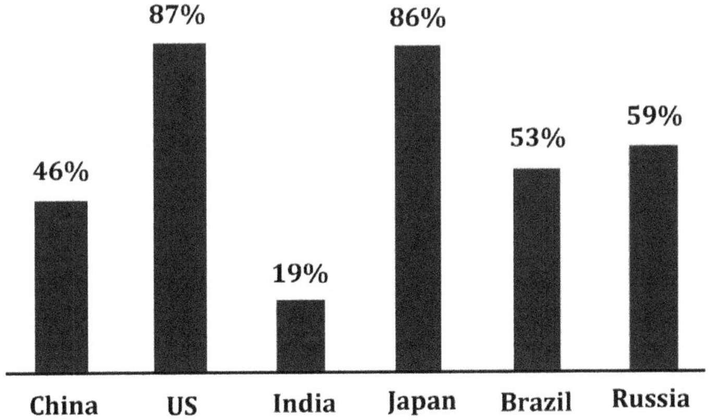

In relation with its population only 19% Indians use the internet. This indicates the potential of internet use in India and as internet penetration increases the potential of growth for online retail will increase.

Global biggies like Amazon and Alibaba has taken the competition to a new level. E-tailers are differentiating themselves by providing innovative service offerings like one-day delivery, 30-day replacement warranty, cash on delivery (CoD), cashback offers, mobile wallets, etc. The supply chain has improved significantly and e-tailers are even leveraging on the services of Indian Post for greater reach across the country. In 2014, Indian Post collected ` 2.8 billion through CoD option of payment.

## ISSUES

The issues related to online retailing is managing omnichannel* experience. Omni-channel retailing is a relatively new concept that refers to the development of a seamless approach to the consumer experience through all available shopping channels, such as brick-and-mortar stores, smartphones, tablet computers, personal computers, direct mail, television, radio, catalog, and the likes. The channels used by customer must be treated efficiently as constant updation on information of company's product is to be taken care of. The customer if not responded on time owing to absence of proper media, the retail business via internet goes in vain. The strategies to make customer experience better and better in totality is the buzzword for today's online market. Experience led transactions make the business grow higher profits. The global leaders like Amazon are continually refining their customer service offering to suit the nature of product. Amazon's Mayday feature enables the customer getting the personal assistance with their kindle products. The delivery experience has also to be improved as lack of integrated logistics lead to increase in dissatisfaction of online buyers (see figure 7).

Online retailing has many issues as Indian consumers have faith on in store shopping. The customers find it more reliable than online shopping. The e tailing requires best practices like user experience, offers and rewards, exclusive content, customer engagement, customer service, High search engine ranking,

*Figure 7. Revolution in retail*

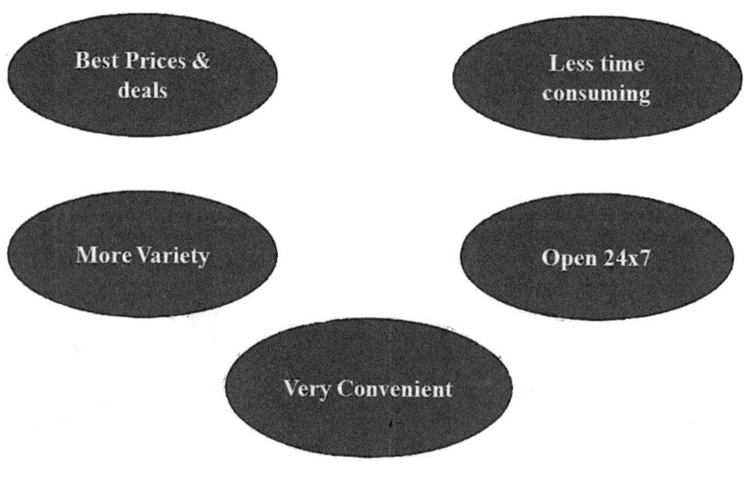

business opportunity in data etc. According to Forrester research, an independent research firm, only 14% online buyers were there in 2013. Although in other countries the percentage of online buyer is higher. The following are the issues with online retailers-

1. **High Competition:** There are several players doing the same business in almost the same way. With high competition the profitability is decreasing due to aggressive pricing strategies, heavy discounts and offers, free delivery, high commissions to affiliates and vendors during sale period.
2. **Poor Logistic and Supply Chains:** E-commerce companies live on the reach and the ability to stock more items than physical stores as these are their biggest differentiators.
3. **Payments:** E-commerce companies have to offer a wide variety of payment options including CoD, credit and debit card, internet banking, among others. 60-70% of the payments are made using the CoD option in India as customers fear to share information online and do not trust the website for secure payments.

Online retailing has become the fastest growing segment having grown at around 56% over 2009-2014. By 2020 the online retail in India is expected to account for 3% of total retail (see figure 8).

## CONTROVERSIES

There have been incidents of controversies where online retailers have been lashed out by public. Flipkart had recently pulled out of controversial deal with Airtel as it was violating net neutrality. Net neutrality means service providers should treat all traffic equally. Users should be able to access all websites at the same speed and cost.

*Figure 8. Do you recall reading a positive/negative review customer service in any of following?*

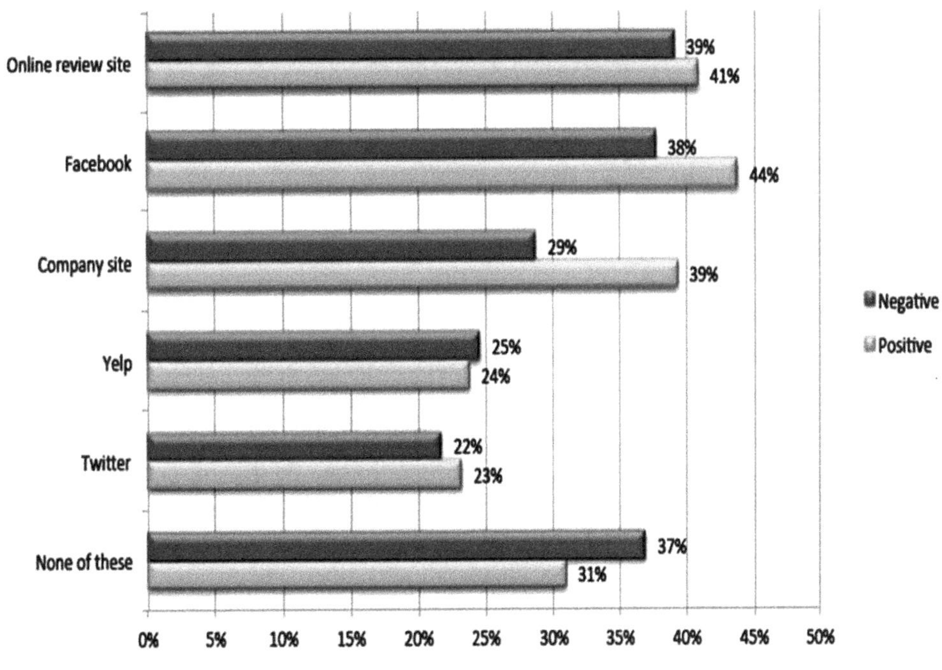

Today, manufacturers and retailers running brick-and-mortar stores are anxiously asking the government to intervene with the creation of a regulatory body to stop e-retailers from undercutting prices. Physical retailers are definitely feeling the challenge by the marketing blitz of their online counterparts, and the question of whether e-commerce is kicking out brick-and-mortar retailers looms large.

## PROBLEMS

The media usage for consumers is mostly for socializing so it disturbs people if marketing offers are made to them through online companies. The company's social media page should be different than website else customer does not favor them. The media requires constant innovation in online retailing so that customer feel connected. The proactiveness of media in online retail is one of the biggest challenge in today's scenario. The innovativeness in the online company promotion is the winning factor of e marketing. Several online stores have shut down as customers did not favour them. It's quite challenging to fulfill the expectation of online customers and adapting the products with their varied needs. The competition amongst online retailers has brought the significant changes in demand of products. The customer wants to remain undisturbed as he uses social media for socializing. The media has often extensively been used for promotion purposes. The online retailing has the problem of identifying the ways to satisfy the customer. The need of constant innovation and differentiation has created the demand of dynamism in online business. The review, ratings and opinion of product becomes instant which decreases the product return rate. The customer gets discouraged by number of pages before 'add to cart'. The excessive problems faced by customers in usage of media leads to decline in business of online retail.

## SOLUTIONS AND RECOMMENDATIONS

Online retailing best practices are realized and this serves as best selling channel. To get the maximum benefit from online channel the companies must adopt different innovative ideas and operating models including joining other retailers for mutual gain. This mode enables the e marketing on social networks whose potential is higher than word of mouth marketing. The overall promotion and merchandising leads to increased average order value. Online customers trust feedback from consumer base than marketer. The utilization of media must be made to increase customer engagement and interactivity. Consumers have faith on like minded consumers more than marketers. Recommendations from consumers (via likes on Facebook) are more effective in building positive image of online brand. Online retailers will have to evolve their offering to meet the needs, wants and desires of consumers and media will promote the e tailing experience. The online consumer would like to have the fruitful experience in retailing. Social interactions and referrals lead to increase in website traffic. There is a need to build the trust quotient and demographics as older generation people rarely would like to pay to someone whom they do not know.

There is a need of integrated media system where e tailing should be promoted and internet accessibility is also to be taken care of. Online retailers must capitalize the business opportunities presented by social media. The content management is significant in e tailing business. The analytic tools can further be used to acquire information of customer choice of trends. It becomes easy to see how data drives the relevance of any product and thereby leads to more sales. Data analysis can lead to cracking customer mind in promoting its products. It is necessary to ensure that proper stock is available to meet the demand of online market. Online retailers must offer online experience that is constant, entertaining and up-to-date. The media used by online marketers must be extended customer service. The content has to be innovative. Analytical tools enable to decipher the sentiments contained within data. The data analytic tools must facilitate the company to listen and understand its customers on website. The automated monitoring system need to be set up as sometimes the comments of blogs or twitter if not responded results in dilution of brand. Retailers need to capitalize the potential opportunities of Facebook which has more than 1 billion active users. Multiple touch points can be used to satisfy the customers. Companies need to work on technology advancement in tier 2 and 3 cities (see figure 9).

## FUTURE RESEARCH DIRECTIONS

The further study can be made to strengthen the usage of media in online retailing. The factors inhibiting the customer adoption can be studied. The interface in digital retailing is significant in getting web traffic and customer satisfaction. Website optimization is also necessary element in Retailer's promotion strategy. They must offer proven method to address them in a cost-effective and usable manner, unifying the contact channels into a measurable, data-driven single communication interface. This chapter will suggest efforts which will enable online retailers in their growth acceleration. Compared with China, India has more online retailers with their own business models. The further research may be carried out to sort out the gaps in online retail business.

## CONCLUSION

The internet users have increased from 20 million in 2004 to nearly 250 million in 2014. This shows that online users have increased. This shift emphasizes the relevance of India's digital economy. The connectivity has been the outcome of technology revolution in India which has given access to enormous

*Figure 9. Brand building differentiation and digital customer experience*

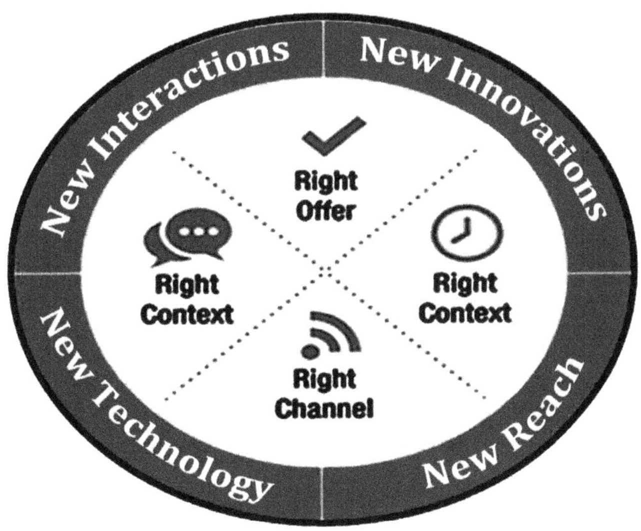

information. This connectivity will bring the change in the format of retailing. The media use has to be intensified and rigorous attempts have to be made by companies. The online retailers must work on customer experience, technological advancements, delivery experience and convergence of offline and online channels. The company must plan an effective media strategy to increase the social interaction in online retailing. The increase of Smartphone ownership has led to social media revolution in market. The newer technologies like virtual walls and virtual mirrors will help the improvement of retail experience and therefore the consumption are enhanced. The role played by media is to enhance the participation of customers in online commerce. Virtual mirrors will make the customers try on clothes/ accessories before buying them. Further virtual walls will help them to check the bar codes of items on electronic wall using their mobile phones. One retailer TESCO has already adopted this technology. In India another retailer Home Shop 18 has introduced first virtual shopping wall and even in International airport this technology has been used. 'Experiential Retail' is the holy mantra of the Indian shopper, and in the coming years, every retailer will do everything it can to turn the whole shopping experience into an entertainment experience. India's overall online retail opportunity is extensive coupled with demographic trend, rising internet saturation and strong growth is expected. The significant role of Media cannot be denied in the overall marketing of online retailing. Most of the social medias are maximizing the utility of online retailers in current Market. Small businesses are realizing the potential to expand sales across the country by enhancing online strategies while curtailing stores and a focus on bricks and mortar. Social media is no longer a channel within the marketing mix. If it is used to its full potential, it will be an essential part of a company's business plan and, for retailers in particular, a fully incorporated part of an overall online sales strategy. Many companies, especially startups, no more consider social media and e-commerce as disconnected strategies, but instead are looking to social networks such as Facebook that offer a combination of data, analytics and payment technology to aid open doors to a new era of online retailing. As customers progress from research to purchase to fulfillment stages, their expectations change fast. Online retailers need to understand the drivers of changes and adapt their offer accordingly. They have to work constantly on brand positioning. There is huge potential for online companies to exploit the growing internet user base and advanced technologies. However this will not take place without overcoming the operational, regulatory and digital challenges.

## REFERENCES


Ahuja, V., & Medury, Y. (2010). Corporate blogs as e CRM tools- Building customer engagement through content management. *Journal of Database Marketing & Customer Strategy and Management*, *17*(2), 91–105. doi:10.1057/dbm.2010.8

Background paper future of e commerce web. (n. d.) Retrieved from http://www.assocham.org/upload/event/recent/event_1113/Background_Paper_Future_of_e-Commerce_web.pdf

Bennett, S. (2014).How Much Online Business Is Done Every 30 Seconds? Incredible E-Commerce Statistics! Retrieved from http://www.adweek.com/socialtimes/ real-time-ecommerce/499958

Boesler, M. (2012). The state or world economy. *Business Insider.* Retrieved from http://www.businessinsider.com/world-bank-world-economy-2012

Chandra, P., Satish, Sunitha, G. (2012). E-Tailing – The Mantra of Modern Retailer's Success. *Journal of Arts, Science & Commerce*, *3*(2).

Digital impact on in store shopping research studies. (2014, October). Google. Retrieved from https://think.storage.googleapis.com/docs/digital-impact-on-in-store-shopping_research-studies.pdf

E tailing in India. (n. d.). Technopak Whitepaper. Retrieved from http://www.technopak.com/files/E-tailing_in_India.pdf

Ecommerce in India- Accelerating growth. (n. d.). *PWC.* Retrieved from https://www.pwc.in/en_IN/in/assets/pdfs/publications/2015/ecommerce-in-india-accelerating-growth.pdf

Hariharan, G. (2008). Profile and perception of retail consumers. *Indian Journal of Marketing*, *38*(2).

Hossain, N. (2012). Why the Interest graph is a Marketer's best friend. *Mashable.com.* Retrieved from http://mashable.com/2012/06/19/Interest-graph-marketer

Infographic: The importance of social media in e-commerce. (n d.). Retrieved from http://www.thedrum.com/news/2014/02/16/

Kamboj, D., & Nair, S. (2014). Social Media in Retail Industry. *Infosys Lab Briefings*, *12*(1).

Kaplan, M., & Haenlein, M. (2010). Users of the world, unite! The challenges and opportunities of SocialMedia. *Business Horizons*, *53*(1), 59–68. doi:10.1016/j.bushor.2009.09.003

Key Challenges facing retailers in the online world. (n. d.). Retrieved from http://www.artificial-solutions.com/wp-content/uploads/protected/wp_retail-challenges.pdf

Laxmi, Prabha, G. (2007). The prospects and problems of Indian Retailing. *Indian Journal of Marketing*, *37*(10).

Pearson, M. (2012). Social Media plays growing role in online retailing. Retrieved from http://www.theglobeandmail.com/report-on-business/small-business/sb-marketing/sales/social-media-plays-growing-role-in-online-retailing/article4179338

Shih, C. (2009). *Facebook is the future of CRM* (p. 12). Customer Relationship Management.

Sikri, S., & Wadhwa, D. (2012). Growth and Challenges of retail industry in India. *Asia Pacific Journal Of Marketing And Management Review*, 1(1).

Swamy, V. (2010). Creating a buzz in social CRM. *Silicon India*, 22-23.

# Chapter 13
# Omnichannel Retailing

**Gulnaz Banu P.**
*NIFT-Bengaluru, India*

**Gokulakannan P.**
*NIFT-Bengaluru, India*

## ABSTRACT

*Tremendous growth of information technology led to the rise of a new form of retailing, the digital retailing, (includes e-commerce and m-commerce), which offers value, convenience and tons of information. Mostly, customers experience digital and conventional retailing distinctly. For a customer to appreciate 'The brand', it is necessary for him to experience it, no matter through which channel he interacts with 'The brand'. Here, Omnichannel strategy, which uses digital media as its backbone, is an integrated sales experience that melds the advantages of physical stores with the information rich-experience of online shopping. An Omnichannel strategy enables the customer to get what he wants anyhow, anytime and anywhere through options like Click and Collect Store, order from a public space, browse in store-order online, browse online-get at store and in-store GPS, information centre etc. From a retailer's perspective, it offers him a single customer view (SCV) that helps in understanding what the customers want. An effective integration of field intelligence and digital media data facilitates excellent control over the stocking of products. Integration of channels enables a retail store to fulfil an online order, thus the volume of products going into decline stage is reduced. Also it becomes easy to either risk pool the inventory and deliver from one point or reduce warehousing and deliver from the store. As a result, capital investment is optimised. To adopt omnichannel, it is necessary to understand the psychology of digital shoppers, customer touch points and actionable channels preferred by the customers. The SCV offered by omnichannel ensures that the brand makes its customers appreciate, enjoy and remain connected to the brand.*

## INTRODUCTION

In the modern era governed by consumers, the retailers constantly innovate themselves to meet the consumers' demands. Due to digitalisation, it can be seen a lot of retailers operating through brick and mortar stores, making their products available online through third party e-commerce retailers or themselves going online. Despite the booming e-tailing sector, retailers are able to get only less than

DOI: 10.4018/978-1-4666-9921-2.ch013

Copyright © 2016, IGI Global. Copying or distributing in print or electronic forms without written permission of IGI Global is prohibited.

5% of their overall sales through e-commerce ("Why is omnichannel," 2015). Thus it's a necessity to develop an edge over the competitors in providing service to the consumers and achieving operational efficiency. Also it is inevitable that the consumer should embrace the brand rather than the channels currently he is experiencing. Omnichannel retailing, which is at the nascent stage, integrates the online and the brick and mortar channel to give the customer a jaw-dropping shopping experience. On the other hand, the company gets a single customer view to facilitate achieving operational excellence. In order to establish omnichannel, it is quintessential to understand the consumers. This chapter aims to provide a background on omnichannel retailing, modes of omnichannel, its benefits and challenges to implement. Understanding the customers being the primary step towards omnichannel, the chapter also incorporates a brief account of Indian online shoppers as a result of the study undertaken.

## BACKGROUND

According to A.T. Kearney Ltd, 2014 a multi-channel shopper is more loyal and spends more than a single-channel shopper. More the channels a retailer offers, more the customer uses the channels and more loyal the customer is to the retailer. For traditional retailers, presence in multiple channels has become a necessity in order to maximise the 'affective memory potential' of the brand's show rooming, visual display, advertisement, marketing campaigns, Web rooming and Screen stacking (Taylor Nelson Sofres (TNS), 2014). As it stands, Presence in multiple channels was the answer of traditional retailers to fast growing online pure plays. In the competition against online pure plays, the ability to get orders to customer quickly is a vital tool. Thus integration across channels facilitates the retailers to fulfil the order swiftly from the stores located geographically proximate to the customer. According to Baker. H. Jay, 2012 by integrating, a retailer can also leverage stores as distribution centres and pick up points for online orders, point of purchase returns and also as experience centres for e-commerce platform. A study by L2.Inc, 2015 has shown that a return of product purchased online to stores lead to increase in value capture as customers tend to purchase on impulse in-store.

## OMNICHANNEL RETAILING

Is Omnichannel an e-commerce ecosystem supported by the stores or a store environment that is assisted by the online channel? It is neither of the above as, Omnichannel retailing is a retail environment built by integrating both online and offline channels to improve customer serviceability and enable the customer experience the brand. Omnichannel strategy, which uses digital media as its backbone, can be defined as *an integrated sales experience that melds the advantages of physical stores with the information rich-experience of online shopping* (Rigby. D, 2011). An Omnichannel strategy enables the customer to get what he wants *anyhow, anytime and anywhere* through options like Click and Collect Store, order from a public space, browse in store-order online, browse online-get at store etc.

## CRITICAL FACTORS IN OMNICHANNEL RETAILING

According to John Polcari, 2014, for omnichannel to be successfully established there are four critical factors:

- Understand the customer
- Determine the necessary channels
- Support cross – company communication
- Act on knowledge

This chapter explains about the online shoppers and their needs, their motivation towards online shopping and their channel preferences with the help of the findings of exploratory research conducted with a structure questionnaire. Also, it deals with the different modes (channels) of omnichannel retailing with the information gathered through interviewing supply chain professionals of two leading lifestyle companies in India.

## UNDERSTANDING ONLINE SHOPPERS

Based on the study conducted, to understand the online shoppers of lifestyle products (with 100 valid and usable samples out of 163 obtained), the following points were assimilated.

Out of the usable samples, 10% of the respondents have never shopped online and don't foresee themselves to shop lifestyle products online. The remaining respondents can be classified into four categories (Capgemini, 2014):

1. True Online shoppers-8% of the respondents
2. Value shoppers – 34% of the respondents
3. Socially influenced shoppers - 20% of the respondents
4. Variety seeking shoppers- 28% of the respondents

## TRUE ONLINE SHOPPERS

The true online shoppers enjoy the rich information that the digital media provides. Their inclination towards online shopping is driven by the detailed product description available, which they find difficult to get at stores. Also their tendency to look for latest trends, comparing the offerings of different brands aids their frequent online shopping. On an average, the conversion ratio (no. of purchases in a time period/ the frequency of visiting the digital portal in a time period) of the true shoppers is above 0.35 with the sample mean being 0.2. It is noted that age and gender are not compelling factors in influencing the higher degree of online shopping.

## VALUE SHOPPERS

In growing e-commerce markets like India where e-tailers are in the pursuit of capturing the market through attractive deals, it is no wonder to find high percentage of value conscious shoppers. When the primary motive of this category of shoppers is to grab the offers, they are also influenced by extensive promotional marketing campaigns. Value conscious shoppers extensively compare other available product offerings and they regard that the restrictions at stores for comparison is a matter of concern.

While Students and young professionals form the major part of value shoppers, there is no significant difference between the genders. In addition, 60% of this group expect themselves to spend more in online shopping in the future.

## SOCIALLY INFLUENCED SHOPPERS

20% of the respondents who can be referred to as socially influenced shoppers make use of the reviews and social media to get opinion on the products in the consideration set. They fall completely in the age group of less than 35 years. The exposure to social media, extensive use of internet makes them socially engaged on their shopping too. Besides the respondents also feel prefer shopping online because it is the trend of the present. It is to be noted that men are more socially influenced than women when it comes to shopping online.

## VARIETY SEEKING SHOPPERS

The other class of online shoppers are the variety seekers who predominantly shop online because of its luxury in variety. They dwell in detail about the product description, compare product offerings at disposal and choose digital portals to satisfy their needs because of the ease of comparison. Women extensively seek variety while men are more direct in their shopping.

## ISSUES FACED BY SHOPPERS IN ONLINE AND STORE SHOPPING

Online shoppers, in general, face problems at the time of the delivery of the product. 45% of the respondents are either in a situation (like meetings) they cannot collect the product or not at the destination of delivery when the product is up for delivery. Meanwhile, 31% of online shoppers have frequently faced delays in delivery.

At stores, 24% of respondents do not get the required level of details on the product. Also 31% of respondents feel they don't get an instant recognition in forms of cash back and discounts on the next purchase at stores.

## CHANNEL PREFERENCES OF ONLINE SHOPPERS

It is found that 47% of online shoppers are willing to browse and order the product through digital media and collect it at their home or office. Omnichannel by integration eases the operation of this mode as the product can be picked up at stores proximate to the delivery point.

Of those who faced problems during the delivery of products, around 50% respondents are open to collect the product at the nearest brand's outlet (click and collect).

Around 50% of the respondents, who frequently faced above issues at store, are willing to visit the store and order the product online through their gadgets or store tablets to get it delivered to required destination (Visit the store – get the product anywhere mode) .

A look at the issues in both the formats, shows the need for improving serviceability and more importantly consumers are open to trying new approaches like click and collect, visit the store-order online (which can happen through omnichannel strategy) (see figure 1).

## DIFFERENT MODES OF OMNICHANNEL RETAILING

### Satisfying Online Orders through Physical Stores

In this mode of supply chain, an online order is catered from the stores nearer to the location of the customer. When the customer orders online, the integration of the online and offline channels enable the stores to know about the customer demand. Thus the demand can be met from the store nearby rather from a warehouse. The required product could be picked up from the warehouse only if the stores

*Figure 1. Simple supply chain of omnichannel*

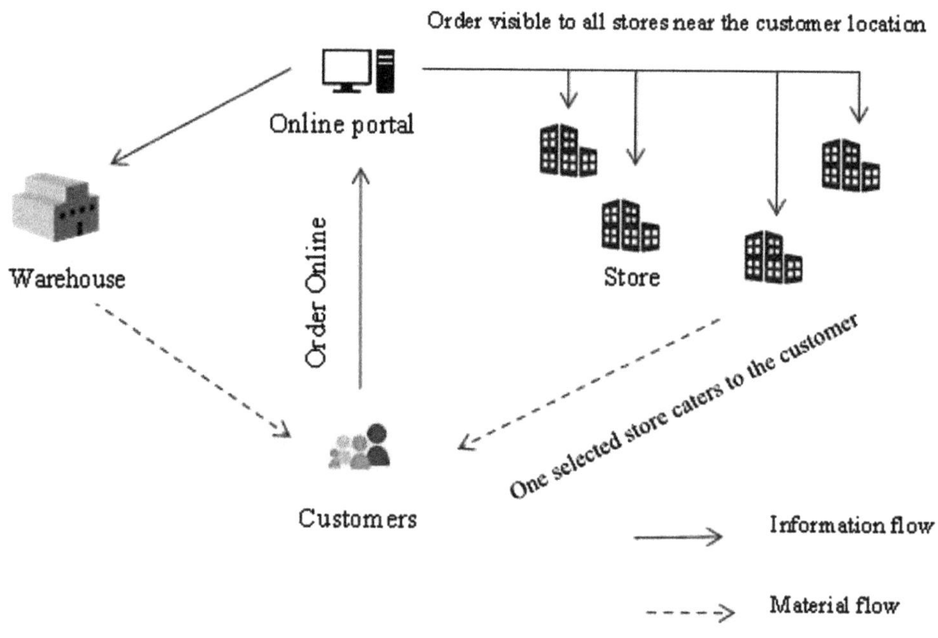

nearby do not have the inventory of that product. Which store should satisfy the customer's need? The answer is obvious – the store nearer to the customer. But proximity is not the only influencing variable (see figure 2).

When the store to cater to the customer is selected, the no. of days the stock lying at the store should be considered. It is noted that the store where the stock age is high should be prioritised in order to bolster the store sales in that product line. With many retailers operating in different formats like owned and operated stores, franchise stores, multi brand outlets with varying profit margins, the consideration of profit margin from the stores at proximity becomes critical. The store with higher profit margin will be given importance.

The next important factor to be looked into is the rate of sales at the stores and the lead time to replenish the stock. If the lead time of replenishment or the rate of sales (ROS) is higher, it may lead to a loss of sales at the stores. Thus stores with moderate or low ROS should be selected if the lead time is high. Finally the cost involved in delivering the product from these stores should be considered and an optimum trade-off between the cost and other factors should be achieved.

The costs involved in delivering the product should be evaluated based on the following variables:

1. No. of walk-ins at the store in specific time periods;
2. Man-power required in servicing the in-store customers;
3. Opportunity cost of potential sales lose if the store person is to deliver the product;
4. Cost in logistics; or
5. Cost that will be incurred if a supply chain partner delivers the online order and added commission on Cash on Delivery orders.

After all the above considerations, the store, whose sales can be improved and that offers better profit margin at lower cost and no loss of sales (ideally) should be selected.

*Figure 2. Selecting the store to cater: Flow chart*

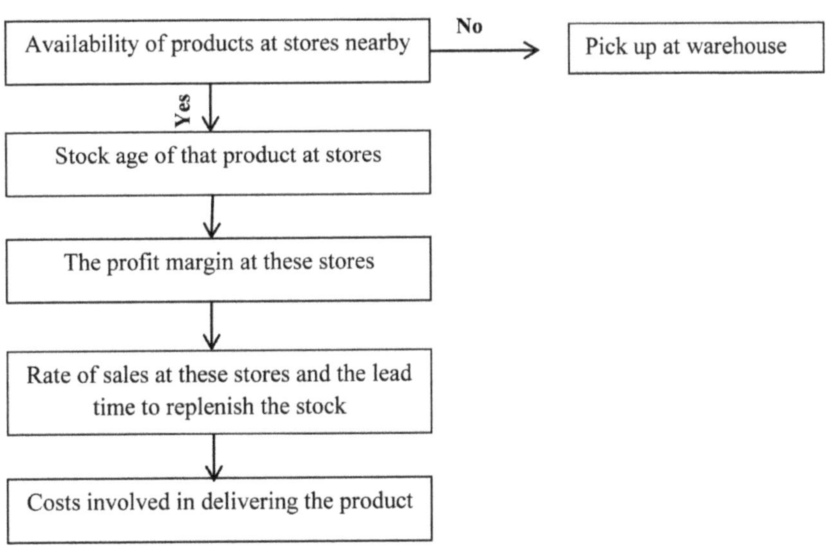

Because of the improved sell through at a particular store, the working capital in form of inventory will go down by at least 10%. This mode of omnichannel is highly profitable and easily executable.

## CLICK AND COLLECT

As discussed already, more shoppers are willing to collect their online orders at the nearest brand's outlet. It paves way for 'click and collect mode' through front end integration. When the product is ordered online, the product can be delivered to the store of customer's choice from where the customer will collect. This is also a profitable mode as it offers following advantages:

1. Increases the footfalls to the store which can be capitalised by cross selling through efficient customer engagement.
2. Improves serviceability to customers and connects the customer to the brand.
3. Gives the customer an opportunity to experience the product and even return it back easily if it doesn't meet his requirements.
4. Reduces the cost incurred in delivery of the product.

## VISIT THE STORE: GET THE PRODUCT ANYWHERE

This mode facilitates stores to reduce the loss of a potential customer. The customer who visits the store may not find the appropriate fit or may perceive he can get better offers on next purchase if he shops online. To avoid a situation of losing a customer, the omni-stores provides the customer an opportunity to order the product at store or online through store's smart hand gadgets and receive the product at the required destination.

Since omnichannel brings all the product lines of an organisation under one roof, a product specific customer need not visit a particular store that offers the specific range of products as he can visit the omni-store nearby, browse through the catalogue of products to order his requirement and the product can be shipped directly to customer. This mode gives higher penetration for organisations that have multiple brands.

## SEE AT A PUBLIC SPACE: GET THE PRODUCT ANYWHERE

Reports suggest that frequent flyers enjoy the advertisements at airports. Why waste the customer's attraction gained? Provide him a QR code and an easier way to order the product he got attracted to. Omnichannel retail of this mode ensures that no customer attracted to or interested in an offering goes without the product. The product ordered with a QR code can be delivered anywhere, anytime by integrating the channels and live updating of the order to point of pick up (store/ warehouse/ distribution centre).

Meanwhile, this mode requires huge backend operations like generating QR Codes for thousands of products, communicating the service to the customers in an effective way.

## PRE-REQUISITES TO SET UP OMNICHANNEL

1. A strong and an efficient IT enabled backend and support system.
2. A customer database that offers single customer view to understand a customer's needs, preferences and motivation.
3. Logistics support (either owned by the company or outsourced).
4. Co-operation from third party retailers who are willing to give live updates of inventory (or at least on daily basis).
5. Manpower with skill sets to set up, execute and efficiently manage the system.
6. Experts believe that Economies of scale can be achieved with larger brands, product categories and product lines under one roof.

## BENEFITS OF IMPLEMENTING OMNICHANNEL STRATEGY

- Single customer view (SCV) provided by omnichannel enables the organisation to treat a customer as one across all channels and thus gives a better understanding of the customer.
- SCV helps in forecasting the demand close to 100% accuracy and thus manage inventory better.
- Omnichannel retailing improves the rate of sales at stores. Thus stagnated working capital in the form of inventory can be reduced.
- Because of the integration across all stores and all channels, an online shopper can return a product to any omni-store (not constrained by location or place of purchase) or through e-commerce logistics at his convenience. This improved serviceability makes the customer experience and enjoy the brand.
- Increased understanding of the customers, which at present is of great use in e-commerce, can be shared with the brick and mortar stores to facilitate up selling and cross selling. A future, in which once the customer enters a store (wherever), the sales person will instantaneously know the shopper's details, preferences and weak points, is not distant.
- Besides serviceability and capital reduction, omnichannel makes accounting and book keeping easier in a multi brand company. Since all the brands and product categories are under one roof, numerous accounts currently maintained for all brands goes down to one.
- With third party e-tailers targeting market penetration with huge markdowns, offers and deals, their value based pricing strategy are expected to down in few years. Thus companies resorting to omnichannel retailing will look lucrative at that point of time because of their compelling service and similar pricing when the markdowns of e-tailers reduce. The absence of e-tailers in the physical environment also gives a niche edge for omnichannel retailers due to their superior serviceability (see figure 3).

*Figure 3. Flow chart: Steps to set up an Omnichannel*

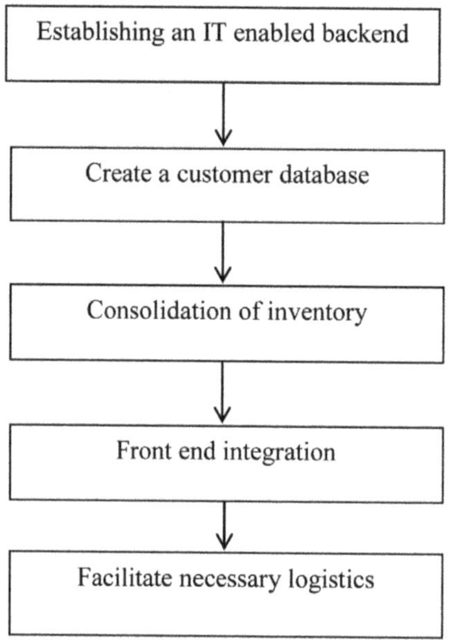


## SETTING UP OMNICHANNEL

### Establishing an IT Enabled Backend

As said earlier, the IT enabled backend should be strong and efficient enough to set up execute and manage the entire omnichannel ecosystem. It should be well equipped with capital, technology and manpower for efficient functioning. The IT enabled backend should be capable enough to feed front end and the planning team with relevant and accurate information. The success of the omnichannel lies on the efficiency of the IT system.

### Create a Customer Database

The customer database is the second major determinant of the success of omnichannel. For example, in the present scenario, when the same customer visits all channels and all retail formats, he is perceived as 3 customers (one customer each across online channel, owned store and third party retailers). Subsequently his demand for one is treated as 3. But the omnichannel database should be good enough to offer a single customer view.

The database should be sufficient enough to provide information on the category of customers one falls under, his preferences, shopping pattern, previous purchases and his touch points. The database should give IT, the information on how to customise the product page of the online portal. The products shown up to the customer should follow the algorithm below:

- Track the IP address of the customer.
- Find the category of customers he falls under.

- Display the products according to customer's nature.
- Display the products that are available at stores nearer to the location of the IP address.
- Do not display a product only if it is not available at any store nearer to the locality and at the warehouse.

When the same customer accesses the online portal from a different location to that of pervious purchases, in order to avoid a situation of non-conversion, it is safer to display products available at stores near to the location of access and at stores near to previous point of delivery of goods.

### Consolidation of Inventory

In order to execute omnichannel effectively inventory allocated for all channels and stores should be treated as one. At any point of time, the quantity of stock available at all the locations and across all retail formats should be known. Only with the knowledge of available inventory at all places, costs involved in meeting the customer demand can be found and an appropriate store can be selected to deliver the goods.

The major challenge in this stage is to convince the third party retailers like franchisees, multi brand outlets and e-tailers to facilitate live updating of their stock quantity.

## FRONTEND INTEGRATION

Like backend, the frontend especially all stores offering the brand's product, should be integrated. This will provide a seamless experience to the customers. Customers should be able to collect or return the product at any of the brand's outlet. A store should be able to look at the inventory of another proximate store of the same brand.

Government taxation are a stumbling block to this currently in countries like India where inter store transfer owned by the brand is possible via Stock Transfer Note. But transfer of goods from franchise stores to brand owned store will lead to double taxation as two bills are generated from the same product. Also varying General Sales Tax (GST) among states do not support this system even though customer and the store lie at proximity but within the boundaries of two adjacent states.

## FACILITATE NECESSARY LOGISTICS

The last mile distribution can be taken care of by own logistics of the company with sufficient manpower or be outsourced. The problem with outsourcing the logistics lies in the bargaining power of the logistics partner. The logistics companies, in general, charge for every service offered (pick up of product, delivery at required destination and collecting the money on cash on delivery orders). To deploy own logistics, the company should receive sufficient online orders from a particular region with significant frequency to achieve the economies of scale.

## COST CENTRES

There are three major drivers of cost in omnichannel system. They are as follows:

- IT enabled manpower (requires Hardware, technology and skilled manpower).
- A project management team.
- Frontend (requires manpower, logistics and warehousing).

Setting up an omnichannel requires high amount of capital investment. The major part of this capital investment will go into building the necessary backend.

Since the omnichannel provides an opportunity to capture more online shoppers and retain the existing offline shoppers, reduce the working capital, inventory carrying cost and subsequent reduction in financing costs, experts believe that the time taken to recover the investment will be relatively lesser.

## CHALLENGES

1. **Organisational Challenge (Forrester Consulting, 2014):** To counter the threat posed by Online pure players, retailers developed e-commerce capabilities rapidly which are often inelastic to adapt to new process of omnichannel. As a result, the status quo of siloed online and offline platforms hinder the establishment omnichannel. The retailers should bring many stakeholders including CMO, VP ecommerce, CIO, head of sales, head of supply chain and head of Business development on same page to ensure the smooth implementation and functioning of the omnichannel strategy.
2. **Attribution of Sales (Ownership) Challenge:** When an offline platform fulfils online order or vice versa, who shall be attributed for the sale? How should the compensation plan for the sales force be devised, is another challenge to the retailers.
3. **Technology and Integration Challenges:** Integration of back- office technology to enable sharing of consumer data, analytics is very complex that it requires a revamped retail order management system to connect POS, ecommerce, ERP and retail mainframe systems. Huge investment in technology is required to overcome the challenges of integration. Also lengthy timelines of implementation might paralyse the retailer.
4. **Operational Challenge:** Real time inventory accuracy across stores and distribution centres is very important to put omnichannel strategy into operation. Retailers are limited by their business model (multiple store formats- Owned and operated stores, franchise owned- brand controlled, franchise owned and operated stores, large format stores) to have access to real time inventory data.
5. **Executional Challenge:** Sales force is another important part of an organisation. The sales force should be properly trained and well informed about the strategy as they are one of the key drivers for customer satisfaction.

## CONCLUSION

69% of respondents foresee themselves spending more in online channel in the future. So an efficient execution of omnichannel retailing will put the company at the top of the chart because it paves way to achieve accuracy in demand & inventory management and achieve operation excellence. Once a database to understand the customers and the channel preferences is established, companies should educate their people about the system and encourage inter department interactions of retail planners, supply chain managers, retail's regional managers and e-commerce wing managers to effectively work for the omnichannel setup. Experts believe that the future lies in the omnichannel retailing in order to satisfy and retain the customers overfed with opportunities to fulfil their demands.

## REFERENCES

Consulting, C. (2014). *Digital shopper relevancy: A Research report.* Paris: Levine, Ted.

Customer Desires vs Retailer Capabilities: Minding the omni-channel commerce gap. (2014, January). *Accenture and Forrester Consulting.*

Five omnichannel fundamentals for driving foot traffic. (2015). *The Daily Tuesday, L2.inc.*

Kearney, A. T. (2014). *Crafting an Omnichannel Strategy.* Chicago: Michael Brown & Mike Moriarty.

Omnichannel Importance. (2014). *TNS New Zealand and StopPress.*

Polcari, J. (2014, September). Four critical success factors for omnichannel retailing. *ChiefMarketer.com.* Retrieved from http://www.chiefmarketer.com/four-critical-success-factors-omnichannel-marketing/

Rigby, D. (2011, December). The future of shopping. *Harvard Business Review.* Retrieved from https://hbr.org/2011/12/the-future-of-shopping

Trunick, P. A. (2015). Omni-channel Strategies: Customer-controlled Supply Chains. *Material Handling & Logistics, 70*(1), 21–23.

Understanding the Multi-channel shopper. (2012, April). *Verde Group and Baker Retailing Center.*

Why is omnichannel retailing so important for Bed Bath & Beyond? (2015). *Trefis Team, Forbes.*

# Chapter 14
# Competing Through Logistics Management:
## Studies on E-Retailing in China

**Yaqiong Lu**
*Xi'an Jiaotong-Liverpool University, China*

**Zheng Liu**
*Xi'an Jiaotong-Liverpool University, China*

**Lei Ma**
*Nanjing University of Science & Technology, China*

## ABSTRACT

*In the past 10 years, e-commerce and e-retailing have developed rapidly in China, the largest emerging country. Due to the increasingly more competition in this industry, a fast and reliably delivery is important to win customer satisfaction. Despite of the fact that many e-retailing companies are running virtual network by outsourcing logistics to third parties, there is also a trend for companies to establish their own logistics channels. In fact, self-owned logistics can be an effective approach of marketing and customer relationship development, and thus provide competitive advantage. This chapter focuses on how Chinese e-retailing companies compete through logistics management. It starts with an introduction of e-retailing and logistics management from practice and literature perspectives. Then, there are cases studies into successful Chinese re-retailing companies with a highlight on their logistics management models and customer satisfaction based on initial survey. Further discussion will address the critical issues of logistics management in e-retailing.*

## INTRODUCTION

In the last decade, China has revealed great development of e-commerce, especially in the B2C market. According to China E-Commerce Research Centre, the e-commerce market reached the total scale of 1.8851 trillion in 2013 with an increase rate of 42.8%, compared to 1.3205 trillion in 2012. E-commerce has now occupied 8.04% of the total domestic consumption%. Statistics imply that e-commerce is

DOI: 10.4018/978-1-4666-9921-2.ch014

Copyright © 2016, IGI Global. Copying or distributing in print or electronic forms without written permission of IGI Global is prohibited.

gradually changing the lifestyles of individuals, and e-retailing, especially B2C, may play an increasingly significant role in the future. Along with the expansion of B2C, some challenges and problems emerge, such as network security, online payment, and logistics service. At present, most researches focus on network security and online payment, while there is no significant improvement in the aspect of logistics service. Admittedly, logistics service is a vital part of the whole industry chain of e-commerce. Some leading Chinese B2C company such as JD has built their own logistics to enhance the capability of logistics service. At the same time, traditional logistics enterprises are attempting to take advantages of B2C market. Although the scale of logistics has experienced significant development, yet researches on the evaluation of the quality of B2C logistics services have not formed. Under these circumstances, it is quite important to establish such systems and methods to help improve the logistics services of e-retailing companies. Based on this background, this chapter will focus on how Chinese e-retailing companies compete through logistics. Specifically, it will address the following issues: 1) What are the current business models of logistics management in Chinese e-retailing companies? 2) How to evaluate the performance of e-retailing logistics from customer perspective, consisting of speed, feasibility, service attitude and quality? 3) How can e-retailing companies improve their logistics management to meet customer need?

## LITERATURE REVIEW

Current literature can be reviewed from the areas of e-retailing, logistics management and service quality. In particular, it will find out how theories are built along with the retailing sectors from traditional model towards e-commerce. In addition, the role of logistics management is critical in supply chain management, as companies sometimes complete by providing fast logistics with high quality. Since e-retailing nowadays is more customer focus, the service quality and how it is linked with customer satisfaction has also attracted academic research. Key theories along with assessment models can help to generate further studies on the emerging issues.

### E-Business and E-Retailing

The theory of e-retailing can be explored as a combination of retailing and e-business to achieve company competitive advantage, with studies based on Porter's frameworks (1980, 1985) – cost leadership and uniqueness, and supply chain management and operations, in particular risk management. Retailer business as a service sector is highly influenced by customer acceptance. The central competitive advantages of traditional food retailing business are regarded as price, quality (including customer service) and convenience (Morschett et al., 2006). The key success factors of retailer in e-commerce are highlighted as the quality of customer reception, as explored in the French grocery "drive-in" sales outlet (Colla and Lapoule, 2012). The topics of supply chain and relationship management are also covered in e-retailing. For example, Zairi and Al-Mashari (2002) has systematically evaluated partnerships between retailers and suppliers with a focus on quick response, vendor managed inventory and efficient consumer response. In addition to supply partnerships studies, there are some theories on evaluating e-retailing effectives and efficiency from operations management perspectives. These works include Barsauska et al.'s (2008) assessment on the impact of cost position on supply management, Min and Wolfinbarger's (2005) examination on three strategic issues – early mover advantages, bricks, and clicks combination in market efficiency, Wen et al.'s (2003) model of evaluating e-commerce efficiency with data envelopment analysis method, and Lu and Hung's data envelopment analysis approach of combining outputs and inputs into e-retailing companies (Lu and Hung, 2011). E-commerce is also associated with risk due to virtual management. While investigating into the consumer attitudes towards virtual environment of local retail market, researchers find that customer may be in favor of e-retailing if influence by particular social groups (Liao and Shi, 2009). This finding has linked internet-based e-retailing with the theory of reasoned action (Fishbein & Ajzen, 1975). In terms of the strategic management of e-retailing, franchising is suggested as an appropriate way of expansion (Watson et al., 2002).

## Logistics Management

Logistics management is considered important to both intra- and inter-firm process. The concept of logistics has combined information flow, product flow, service and finance in a chain, as extension from a firm to its partners (Christopher, 1998). The functional activates of logistics include transportation, facility structure, inventory management, material handling and communication and information (Williamson et al, 1990), which are integrated together (Kotler, 2003). Manufacturing companies are seeking for effective ways of logistics management in order to remain profitable (Zudor et al, 2014). Meanwhile, the changing and globalization industry dynamics has driven service sectors such as retailing companies to implement new technologies of logistics management (Rendo & Ficko, 2010). Some have suggested that retailing companies' competitive advantage can be achieved by managing materials follow and physical distribution with IT (Kotler, 2003), while examples have showed that real-time data gathering can develop sophisticated warehouse data to exchange with suppliers (Colla & Dupuis, 2002). Studies have been conducted to exam the performance effect of IT in logistics functions, including warehouse management system (Hill & Scudder, 2002). Recent research also explores the association between digitized logistics activities bundles and logistics performances in terms of cost and service improvement (Lai et al., 2010), and solution for information management (Zudor et al., 2014). While some companies keep logistics as core business, there is also a trend of logistics outsourcing in order to reduce cost and improve customer service (Knemeyer & Murphy, 2004). However third-party logistics management is associated with risk of relationship failure (Kremic et al, 2006), and there are studies to examine how relationship risk influences the evaluation on logistics service provider (Tsai et al., 2012). Researchers have also pointed out that physical distribution services remain determinants of product return in e-retailing business (Rao et al., 2014), and efficiency is a significant moderator of the impact of logistics performance on customer loyalty (Ramanathan, 2010).

## E-Retailing and Logistics

The relationship of e-retailing and logistics has also been explored recently, since e-retailing is a combination of e-commerce and retailing, which heavily relies on logistics. According to Colla and Lapoule (2012), the success of retailer in e-commerce largely comes from customer acceptance, of which logistics is a key component. As defined by Zairi and Al-Mashari (2002), the critical linkage between e-retailers and suppliers are vendor managed inventory, swift response and efficient consumer response. E-retailers are seeking ways to manage logistics in order to earn more money and increase the degree of customer satisfaction (Zudor et al, 2014).

## Service Quality

Quality here refers to the nature that products can meet customers' requirement. As service is intangible and its operation process and consumption process happen at the same time, service cannot be stored. The measurement of service quality does not fix standards of tangible products. Thus, service quality should be evaluated in both the outcome and the process. Numerous studies into e-retailing have suggested that customer satisfaction is one of the key success factors, and therefore it is important to review the theories and models of service quality in particular. Determinants such as accessibility, communication, credibility, understanding, appearance and availability are highlighted in e-commerce service quality (Cox & Dale, 2001), while marketing services, logistics services, operations services and collaboration services are identified as integral parts of e-commerce business service quality (Yang et al., 2006). By survey into Chinese e-retailers, it is found that reliability in service quality and purchasing experience as dominant customer satisfaction factors (Subramanian et al., 2014).

To trace back to the studies of service quality, one of the early model PZB was proposed by Parasuraman et al (1985) with the aim of analyzing service quality problems. The core concept is that customers are deciders of service quality so that enterprises should meet demand of customers by closing five gaps, which influence service quality evaluation. As Figure 1 illustrates, gap 5 is the core of the whole model, which indicates the gap between customers' expectation and perceived quality. It is the outcome

*Figure 1. PZB service quality model*
*Adapted from Parasuraman et al., 1985*

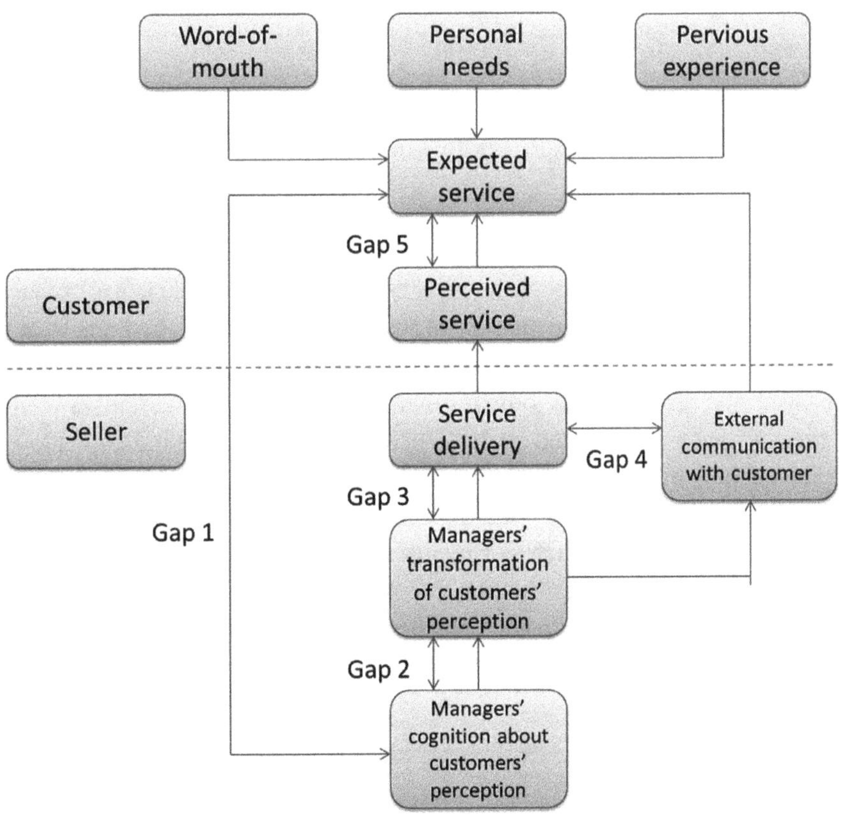

of the cumulative effect of other four gaps. Therefore, to bridge this gap, exposing of other four gaps' essential reason is required. PZB service quality model is a direct and effective tool to find out the gap of service concept between service provider and costumer. By identifying these gaps, enterprises could generate strategies or methods, and ensure the consistence of the expected quality and real quality. As a result, consumers would provide useful comments on the service quality and the customer satisfaction would thereby be improved. This model provides a theoretical framework to measure service quality. Additionally, it can be utilized to further study the root of the problems and help to find the solution.

Based on previous research, Parasuraman et al. (1988) later developed an instrument named "SERVQUAL" to help measure service quality. There are five service quality dimensions identified by "SERVQUAL". These dimensions are tangibles, reliability, responsiveness, assurance, and empathy. By considering these five dimensions, customers could effectively evaluate the quality of products or services. In practical operations, these five dimensions each consists of several concrete questions in terms of questionnaire, by which researchers could acquire the information from consumers. More specifically, 22 related factors could be generated from customers' responses, including consumers' expected value, experienced value, and the lowest acceptable value. Service quality is marked by combining another questionnaire, scores given by consumer, and integrated computation. SERVQUAL is the basic framework on service quality study, researchers in different area could modify with specific standards in accordance to practical requirements. The formula of SERVQUAL Model is:

$$SQ = \sum_{j=1}^{5} W_j \sum_{i=1}^{22} \left(P_i - E_i\right), \quad i = 1,2,3,\ldots,\ n, \quad n = 22, \quad j = 1,2,3,4,5$$

$P_i$ : Score of consumer's perception for factor i

$E_i$ : Score of consumer's expectation for factor i

$W_j$ : Weight of dimension j

A third model - the Logistics Service Quality Model - is a commonly used one to measure the logistics service quality which based on the perception of consumer. It was first published by Mentzer et al (1989). On the basis of the researches of logistics marketing and delivery, Mentzer et al. (1989) chose 3 dimensions – timeliness, accessibility, and quality, out of total 26 factors as indicators to evaluate physical distribution service quality. In 1997, Bienstock et al. furtherly studied on PDSQ (Physical Distribution Service Quality), and thereby divided service quality into process and outcome parts. They measured the quality from several prospective, such as timeliness, delivery status of products, and effectiveness, developed a quantitative method to construct the measurement model, and also conducted some experiments to test and verify this model. According to researches of Mentzer et al. (2001), a more complete LSQ model can be given on the basis of product market dominant by consumers.

## Service Evaluation in China

In the past twenty years, Chinese researchers have also developed logistics service evaluation theories based on western studies. For example, Wang (2000) developed four evaluation indicators for logistics service, namely time, cost, quantity and quality. Tian (2001) raised the view that logistics service quality can be measured from two angles - external customers and internal customers respectively. Although Chinese researchers start late in the field of logistics service quality evaluation, they focus more on the implementation of theory to the actual situation in China, and therefore provide more theoretical support for this study - the logistics performance of e-retailers in China.

# E-RETAILING LOGISTICS MANAGEMENT IN CHINA: CASE STUDIES

E-retailing is developing fast in China with the emerging of large companies and SMEs. To investigate on the e-retailing logistics management in China, four representative companies are selected for in-depth studies. They are Taobao, Dangdang, JD and Suning. Some general features of these companies are listed in Table 1. Case studies will focus on its logistics management process and performances, with an analysis of supplier management, inventory management, delivery, and customer service management. Cross-case analysis will be conducted to address and key successful factors and challenges of e-retailing logistics management.

## Case One: Taobao

Wholly owned by Alibaba Group (established in 1999 Hangzhou), Taobao was launched in 2003 to provide C2C (mainly) shopping platforms. While China's credit card system was immature at that stage, Alibaba Group introduced the online paying system named Alipay. In 2005, Taobao became the leading C2C company in China. In 2008, Taobao furtherly introduced B2C platform Tmall, to expand its current C2C business model. In 2009, its transaction exceeded RMB 200 billion (USD 29 billion). Taobao currently has more than 500 million product listings, serving more than 210 million registered users. The Alimama, an online advertising exchange network, and Koubei, China's leading classified listing

*Table 1. Case companies' profile*

| Companies | Main Products | Logistics Types | Data Source |
|---|---|---|---|
| Case One (Taobao) | Merchandise products | Third party (domestic) | www.taobao.com; Williamson and Wang, 2014; Liu, 2013; Ma, 2010; Zhang, 2011 |
| Case Two (Dangdang) | Books, Merchandise products | Third party (domestic, overseas) Self-built (domestic) | www.dangdang.com; Dong, 2005; |
| Case Three (JD) | Electric devices, Merchandise products | Self-built (domestic) Third party (domestic, overseas) | www.jd.com; Ren & Dong, 2013; Huang, 2010; Wang, 2011 |
| Case Four (Suning) | Electric devices, Home appliance | Self-built (domestic) | www.suning.com; Yu et al., 2008; |

website, are parts of Taobao platform. According to Taobao, its mission is to facilitate an e-commerce ecosystem for partners and consumers. It has reduced the role of controlling activities in the platform, while encouraging shop owners to take initiatives.

While focusing on its core competence of building up C2C trading platform, Taobao outsourced its logistics management since establishment. When an order is placed, both sellers and buyers can choose the logistics company who are partnered with Taobao. The information will be passed directly to the logistics company, who will then in charge of the complete delivery. It is true that with third-party logistics partners, Taobao can concentrate on its core business, and developing more value added activities; however there is also criticism of this model. Firstly, although sellers and buyers can both select the logistics company, in reality it is mainly the sellers who make the decisions. Sometimes buyers have no choice but to pay high delivery fee, due to the unequal buyer-seller relationship. Secondly, the delivery process is completely operated by third parties without control from Taobao. Sellers sometimes pack the products wrongly, and logistics companies sometimes cannot follow the standards of storing and transporting. Once a product is delivered in bad condition (such as damaged, different from description, or delayed), it is not clear who should take responsibility, and thus the refund process is complicated. Thirdly, although Taobao treats the third-party logistics companies (such as Shunfeng, Yunda, Yuantong) as strategic partners by signing agreements, the standard of selecting these partners is not clear. Some logistics companies behave unprofessionally, according to customers' complain. Packages are damaged, or staff being unfriendly, which eventually brings Taobao bad reputation. Fourthly, the current logistics industry in China is still developing, and there are remote areas where logistics service cannot reach customers. Due to lacking of information sharing between logistics companies and Taobao, the delivery status sometimes cannot be predicted. As customers cannot trace back the delivery, when deliveryman arrives, it is normal that no one is present to receive the parcel. This causes further problems of re-delivery and refund. According to a survey on female customer's satisfaction in March 2010, conducted by Sina.com, Taobao's delay in delivery, wrong delivery and unfriendliness of deliveryman are the biggest problems. Some customers have decided to buy products from B2C companies who are Taobao's competitors.

## Case Two: Dangdang

Established in 1999 Beijing, Dangdang is a B2C e-commerce company in China. In the early years, Dangdang mainly sold books online, and it soon became China's largest book e-retailers. With brand recognized by customers, it then expanded to a board product range of fashion cloths, cosmetic products and home products. Apart from selling products with Dangdang brand, it also operates the Dangdang marketplace program, allowing third-party merchants to sell products with this online platform. With 15 years of experience in e-retailing, Dangdang has developed an integrated supply chain, by building close relationship with major suppliers in China. Therefore, it can complete in terms of providing cheap products with high diversity.

With the aim of providing customers "more choices, low prices," Dangdang has developed close relationship with suppliers. It has 3000 main suppliers, who can deliver 300,000 types of products with the lowest price. Since 2005, Dangdang has expanded its business from selling books to other merchandized products. Due to the long lasting supplier relationship, it remains cost competitive. In terms of book sector, it can offer 30% lower price than physical book stores. As for the home devices, it also becomes successful through collaboration with larger suppliers and acquiring electronic device selling e-retailers such as 010buy.com.

The inventory system of Dangdang is its prioritized operations concern. Tt has built distribution center in Beijing, Shanghai, Guangzhou, Chengdu, Wuhan, Zhengzhou and Wuxi. To quickly meet the customers' requirement, it has expanded warehouses to cover major areas of China. In 2014, it built a new stock with the capacity of over 6.5 million units of books and general merchandise products. With the launches of new logistic centers in Beijing, Dangdang can improve its delivery speed to customer in Beijing area. Dangdang further upgrades hardware and software, including using ERP system over all storages. According to Dangdang, a better inventory management can reduce delivery failure, and fasten delivery time, thus eventually achieve customer satisfaction. However, it is commented that Dangdang need to integrate its inventory management system in different areas. Meanwhile, though advanced software and self-developed ordering system can help to improve logistics performance, the expanding of storage can increase cost. Thus Dangdang should balance its inventory capacity and cost by implementing innovative technology and management system.

In terms of delivery, Dangdang mainly uses third-party companies, and keep a small amount of self-built delivery in 192 major cities in China. The main concern is to save cost, for the reason that most orders are small and fragmented. Dangdang's delivery is often criticized by customers as slow and unreliable. Sometimes, due to Dangdang's lack of control over third-party collaborators, customers cannot track the delivery status. Dangdang's suppliers also mention its delay of inventory information management. Realizing the problems, Dangdang has made improvement through closely working with delivery companies, evaluating their performance, and training. In terms of international delivery, Dangdang chooses reliable third-parties such as EMS.

Dangdang has developed mobile payment system, refund system, order tracking system, customized book ordering and online reading service. Customers can choose whether paying directly online, or payment on arrival.

## Case Three: JD

JD is the largest online retailing company in China with a market share 54.3% in 2014. Established in 2004 Beijing, it provides customers B2C online shopping experience. While mainly selling electric devices, it also offers a wide selection of products at competitive prices. In order to control over the logistics and to meet customer satisfaction, JD has built its own nationwide fulfillment infrastructure and last-mile delivery network. JD offers payment options and comprehensive customer services. It has established strong relationships with suppliers. JD has expanded rapidly recently. The number of products it offers has grown from 1.5 million stock keeping units in 2011 to 25.7 million in 2013. Currently it has 47.4 million active customer accounts to fulfill 323.3 million orders.

JD has close relationship with its major suppliers. JD makes sure that brand certification and quality inspection are guaranteed before choosing suppliers. Examples of its brand suppliers are main electric OEMs, Standard Klasse Gut (a supplier of fashion & high quality kitchen appliances), Mixmind Art & Design Co, Ltd (a clothing supplier), and Mary Ching (a British-Chinese brand of footwear). In addition to selling JD products, it also provide platform for third-party shop owners.

Highly valuing the logistics management, JD has built the largest storages in China e-commerce industry. In 2014, it has operated 97 warehouses with an aggregate gross floor area of 1.8 million square meters, 1,808 delivery stations and 715 pick-up stations over 40 Chinese cities. The whole inventory management is highly depended on IT system. As customers' orders grow rapidly, JD has to continuously invest on warehouses as fast as possible.

Domestic delivery is mainly self-operated by JD. Currently it has 62,000 full-time employees in charge of delivery, refund process, and other services. JD offers its customer 4 delivery service choices: 1) 211 arrival within limited time: If an order is placed before 11am (in some cities 10am), the delivery can be completed on the same day. If an order is made before 11pm, the delivery will be done before 3pm the next day. By the end of 2014, this service has covered 134 district/towns in China. 2) Next day arrival: For orders placed before a certain time, delivery will be completed the next day. This service has covered 866 district/towns in China. 3) Fast arrival: This is a highly customized service. Customers can choose to get their order within 3 hours by paying additional fee. So far, this service is available in 6 cities including Beijing, Shanghai, Guangzhou, Chengdu, Wuhan and Shenyang. 4) Night arrival: This is another customized service. Customers can choose to receive their products between 7pm and 10pm by paying extra fee. This service is available in 6 cities, same as fast arrival service. In addition to self-operated logistics, JD also collaborates with third logistics companies for areas outside Beijing, Shanghai and Guangzhou. JD collaborates with large electric home appliance manufacturer (such as Haier) in logistics management, for the reason that these OEMs already own well-structured delivery and service system. Also with international logistics companies such as UPS, DHL and EMS, JD currently can ship its products to 78 countries and regions.

For customers, tracking can be made on JD parcels with emails and online system. JD has built pick-up stations, where customers can directly get their parcels after receiving a message from JD. JD offers returns and refunds for most items within 30 days of receiving. There is a general procedure for refund. Other services such as after-sales maintenance are also available.

## Case Four: Suning

Suning Appliance Co. Ltd. was established in 1990 Nanjing. After 10 years of selling home electric appliance mainly, it entered e-commerce in 2005 by launching Suning.com, a B2C platform. The company combines physical stores and virtual online system together. Based on Suning Appliance Co. Ltd.'s well-recognized brand and integrated logistics system with 1000 distribution centers and 3000 aftersales service centers in 30 provinces, it soon becomes a top 3 e-retailer in China. Suning also provides platform for third party shop owners.

Suning has strong control over the whole logistics system, from supplier selection, warehouse management, delivery to customer service. Based on the success of Suning physical retailing store, it main products are still electric devices. While keep long relationship with thousands of global electric OEMs, it further expands product range to home appliances by collaborating with suppliers or third-party sellers. During collaboration, Suning provides supports on operations strategy, project management and brand management. According to one of its suppliers, Three Squirrel, there are 6 reasons (advantages) why suppliers choose Suning as B2C platform. 1) Favorable policy: There is no entry fee for suppliers. Suning has a standard to choose suppliers of high quality, to avoid direct competition. Suppliers can operate first, and pay Suning later. 2) Professional service: Suppliers who collaborated with Suning will receive professional guidance, such as pricing strategy and online promotion. 3) Integration of online and offline operations: Due to the fact that Suning online platform is extended from its physical stores, Sunning has the advantage of combining online and offline sales. As its suppliers, this "physical store + e-commence + service" model is a good way to share resources and to promote brand. 4) Resource advantage: there is information sharing system between Suning and its suppliers. 5) Brand advantage:

Due to the success of Suning store with a brand value of 956.86 billion RMB, its online platform can also be trusted by suppliers and customers potentially. 6) Convenience: Suning provides quick financing model, warehouse and logistics systems around China.

Suning has a strong capability of warehouse management and delivery. The logistics system is name "Suning Cloud". It has more than 80 warehouses for large electric appliance for both online orders and Suning physical stores. Moreover, it has built 10 warehouses for small items, each using advanced technology. However, due to the transit from Suning physical store to e-commerce, still there are some problems of integrating the inventory system.

Suning's delivery is completed self-operated. In 2013, its delivery capacity was 50000 staff and 10000 vehicles. For large electric appliance, the delivery system is shared online and offline (Suning store) with 60 delivery centers. For small items, Suning has a separate team of 2000 people and 208 delivery centers. It believes that a strong delivery team can meet customer requirement, as most electric appliance will be checked by the staff and customer on arrival. Due to the rapid increasing of orders (both online and offline in stores), it needs to continuously upgrade the delivery capability, while coordinating the delivery system for online and offline orders.

Suning has developed its own paying system. Customers can pay online, or on arrival with POS in 27 cities. Suning distinguishes itself form other e-retailers by owning 1600 physical facilities, such as EXPO superstores (a combination of electric appliance stores, department stores, restaurants and cinemas), franchised stores and customer experience centers. Customers can walk in to see the products, whereas suppliers can promote their brands. With 4000 service centers and 24 hour call center, Suning has strong capability in aftersales service. This highly interactive model among suppliers, Suning and customers is a unique model in B2C business in China.

## Cross-Case Analysis

From the above case studies, it is seen that logistics management should meet companies' overall strategy, and sometimes provide competitive advantage. Table 3 is a summary of companies' activities along the logistics system of supplier relationship, inventory management, delivery and customer relationship, with a highlight on the core operations concerns or in-house operations.

Taobao, as a platform for C2C trading, focuses mainly on information management (such as interface improvement) and ecosystem maintaining, and therefore it completely outsources the logistics management to third-party collaborators. However, there are some challenges due to Taobao's lacking of control, incomplete information sharing system and bad performance of logistics companies. Therefore it should improve information system, and set up standards while selecting the logistics partners. Dangdang's logistics management highlights supplier relationship and building large warehouses, with delivery mainly outsourced. In this way, it can achieve low cost, and meeting the variety of customer requirement (to avoid out-of-stock by adopting capacity leading demand approach). To balance the inventory cost and delivery cost, it chooses to outsource major parts of delivery. However, its lack of control over delivery and sometimes quality failure is criticized by customers. JD highly values logistics management, and mainly adopts a self-operated system in China. It has built large warehouses across the country; employing staff specialized in packaging, delivering, refund and after-sales service. It provides a variety of delivery chooses for customer, including fast arrival, night arrival and pick-up stations. Though JD's self-built logistics system can ensure of quality and control over the whole process, still the company are facing the financing challenges for the cost of large warehouse, distribution network and labor.

They also face competitions from both e-retailers and third-party logistics companies. Suning adopts a highly vertical integrated logistics system, due to Suning Appliance Co. Ltd.'s well-established logistics competence. It strictly selects suppliers and maintains long-term relationship. Suning also has physical stores, experience superstores and service centers to meet the customer need. This integrated system can ensure of customer satisfaction and quality, but also face some problems. Suppliers (especially third party sellers) sometimes lack of control for its operations. Also as customer mainly recognize Suning for its electric home appliances (due to the success of Suning Appliance Co. Ltd.), it still need to promote other product range. In addition, in the transit stage, Suning needs to set priorities of core competence, while improving the online system (see table 2).

*Table 2. Summary of case company logistics management with key activities*

| Company | Supplier | Inventory | Delivery | Customer |
|---|---|---|---|---|
| Case One | No major suppliers due to C2C model. | Operated by third-party logistics companies. | - Completely outsourced to third-party logistics companies as partners.<br>- Taobao lacks control over the delivery process.<br>- Information share is incomplete. | - Taobao' own paying system.<br>- Failure in delivery status tracking.<br>- Buyers have to negotiate with sellers and sometimes logistics companies for refund. |
| Case Two | - Long term close relationship with major suppliers to cut down cost.<br>- Collaboration with a diversity of suppliers to achieve broader product range.<br>- Acquiring e-retailers to expand product range quickly. | - Establishing large storage in major cities.<br>- Capacity leading demand approach.<br>- Advanced ERP and information system, however lack of coordination. | - Mainly outsourced to third-party distributors, while keep small capacity of self-delivery to cut down cost.<br>- Improving delivery quality by training and assessing collaborator's performance. | - Dangdang's own ordering and refund system.<br>- Choices of paying directly or on arrival.<br>- Sometimes failure in delivery status tracking. |
| Case Three | - Close relationship with OEM manufacturers and brand suppliers.<br>- JD and third-part sellers | - Establishing large storages.<br>- Facing the challenges of cost and customer order increasing. | - Self-operated delivery for domestic orders of JD products.<br>- Integrated process of packaging, delivery, refund, and after-sales service with tracking system<br>- A variety of delivery choice, e.g. fast arrival, night arrival.<br>- Third-party logistics partners in some areas, and for large electric home appliance. | - JD's own ordering and refund system.<br>- Different delivery choices.<br>- JD's pick-up stations.<br>- Standard procedure for refund.<br>- Other after-sales services. |
| Case Four | - Suning and third-party sellers.<br>- Suning has strong supply network on electric devices, before entering B2C business.<br>- Close relationship with suppliers/sellers, including training and collaboration. | - Self-built warehouse for large electric appliance, combined online and offline (store) orders.<br>- Separate warehouse for small parcels (online)<br>- Advanced information system | - Self-built delivery team, combining online and offline orders for large electric appliance<br>- Separate self-built delivery team for small items.<br>- However the team needs expanding quickly due to order increasing. | - Suning's own paying system.<br>- Choices of paying online, or on arrival with POS, and pick up at Suning stores.<br>- Suning physical stores, franchisees, and customer experience centers.<br>- 4000 after-sales service centers. |

*Table 3. Value result for factors*

| Factors | 1 or 2 Tier Cities | Factors | 3 or 4 Tier Cities | Factors | During "11.11" |
|---|---|---|---|---|---|
| V13 | 9.2 | V02 | 9.02 | V02 | 8.6 |
| V12 | 9.1 | V14 | 8.96 | V04 | 8.57 |
| V02 | 8.96 | V13 | 8.93 | V01 | 8.56 |
| V14 | 8.93 | V25 | 8.89 | V13 | 8.56 |
| V25 | 8.93 | V12 | 8.8 | V12 | 8.46 |
| V01 | 8.83 | V24 | 8.65 | V14 | 8.43 |
| V09 | 8.8 | V01 | 8.46 | V20 | 8.21 |
| V20 | 8.73 | V04 | 8.43 | V25 | 8.08 |
| V04 | 8.65 | V09 | 8.43 | V11 | 8.02 |
| V24 | 8.63 | V11 | 8.2 | V24 | 7.86 |
| V18 | 8.56 | V05 | 7.84 | V09 | 7.82 |
| V11 | 8.16 | V08 | 7.72 | V10 | 7.68 |
| V05 | 8.08 | V03 | 7.67 | V23 | 6.68 |
| V03 | 7.9 | V20 | 7.67 | V08 | 6.8 |
| V17 | 7.86 | V17 | 7.65 | V05 | 6.62 |
| V10 | 7.73 | V10 | 7.62 | V03 | 6.58 |
| V08 | 7.71 | V23 | 7.11 | V22 | 6.52 |
| V23 | 7.47 | V22 | 7 | V26 | 6.38 |
| V06 | 7.34 | V18 | 6.96 | V06 | 6.02 |
| V27 | 7.31 | V27 | 6.85 | V27 | 6.02 |
| V26 | 7.3 | V26 | 6.79 | V07 | 5.98 |
| V22 | 7.29 | V15 | 6.64 | V28 | 5.89 |
| V16 | 6.98 | V07 | 6.58 | V19 | 5.42 |
| V07 | 6.82 | V28 | 6.54 | V21 | 5.42 |
| V15 | 6.7 | V16 | 6.39 | V18 | 5.34 |
| V21 | 6.66 | V19 | 6.27 | V16 | 5.12 |
| V19 | 6.41 | V21 | 6.25 | V15 | 5.08 |
| V28 | 6.31 | V06 | 6.12 | V17 | 4.89 |
| Average | 7.91 | Average | 7.57 | Average | 6.94 |

## IMPROVING SELF-BUILT LOGISTICS MANAGEMENT: STUDIES ON CUSTOMER SATISFACTION

Since the aim of e-retailing logistics management is to meet customer requirement, it is important to study into consumer behavior. Here we select JD (Case Three) as example to build linkage between logistics performance and customer satisfaction. JD is under rapid development and has self-built logistics service, and therefore studies into JD can potentially be extended to a general understanding of self-built logistics management in Chinese e-retailing industry. This study (conducted between September 2014 and May 2015) adopts quantitative method (survey into customers based on questionnaire from the service quality model). From data analysis, further improvement suggestions are made to JD's logistics management.

## Data Analysis from Survey

Combining SERVQUAL model with specific example of JD, we generated 6 dimensions and 28 factors (v01 – v 28) as important issues that influence consumers' experience.

1. Transparency. Customers can receive quick, accurate and seasonable logistics information during experiencing B2C e-commerce logistics service. The company makes efforts to eliminate information asymmetric between suppliers and customers by informing customers the important logistic status. This dimension is evaluated by complete instruction (v01), detailed information about products (v02), and logistics process reference (v03)
2. Completeness. The company provides a fully functional ordering system that customers can carry out simple and fast operations. The company also offers flexible and various logistics service to cater for different demands. It has reasonable measurements towards emergencies. Completeness can be further indicated through user-friendly operations process (v04), various methods of payment (v05), various methods of receiving products (v06), various methods of changing and returning (v07), and complete treatment measures (v08).
3. Reliability. The ability of logistics service offered by the B2C e-commerce company is reliable. Staffs who provide such service honor promises that offer accurate logistics service and protect personal privacy. Reliability can be assessed by accurate order processing (v09), good protection for trade information (v10), good protection for personal information (v11), accurate product processing (v12), good protection for products (v13), and good product packaging (v14).
4. Timeliness. It refers to the time and speed of logistics service provided by the B2C e-commerce company. Whether the company can solve problems and meet customers' demand in time is vital here. This dimension is assessed by swift order processing (v15), swift switch from order processing to consignment (v16), swift reply for logistics service (v17), delivery in promised time (v18), and swift error processing (v19).
5. Economy. The cost of logistics service contains not only the cost itself but also the cost-effective degree. In addition, when customers change and return goods, whether logistics cost afforded by firms is also a point customers concern. Economy can be judged by charge reasonable price for logistics service (v20), high cost-effective logistics service (v21) and charge reasonable price for change and return (v22).
6. Empathization. B2C e-commerce Company can provide logistics service for the sake of customers. Moreover, the company tries it best to build the brand image and gain loyalty by keeping good relationship with customers and positive attitudes to meet customers' needs. This dimension can be evaluated by enough value-added service (v23), good Q&A mechanism (v24), good attitude to customers (v25), professional logistics service (v26), complete measures dealing with errors (v27), and good outcome in dealing with errors (v28).

With a questionnaire developed based on these 28 factors, survey is conducted into 3 parts: delivery address is in 1 or 2 tier cities, 3 or 4 tier cities and customers do online shopping during the time period of "11.11" (the November 11 event, when massive promotion sales take place in China e-commerce). Logistics quality is marked as 5 degrees, 1-2 points for strongly disagree, 3-4 points for disagree, 5-6 points for neutral, 7-8 points for agree and 9-10 for strongly agree.

Survey result (Table 3) shows that customers are basically satisfied with JD logistics service, since the average scores in all 3 conditions fell in "agree", yet there are still some differences according to the values of final results against each factor.

Firstly, in 2014, the official weibo of JD announced that the sales revenue during "11.11" was 2.5 billion RMB and the total amount for sales orders were more than 6.8 million. According to the data, the average score of values during "11.11" (6.94) is much smaller than customers in 1 or 2 tier cities (7.91) and customers in 3 or 4 tier cities (7.57). It illustrates that customers' satisfaction degree to JD logistics service during "11.11" is lower than ordinary days. The data suggests that JD logistics service quality is impacted by huge orders. Except for the shortage of logistics system existing, the lowest scores of factors appear in the outcome of dealing with errors (5.89), swift error processing (5.42), delivery in promised time (5.34), swift switch from order processing to consignment (5.12), swift order processing (5.08) and swift reply for logistics service (4.89). The factors with lowest values can be generalized into 2 aspects: speed and error. From random interview to customers about the status of speed and error of JD logistics service during "11.11", we found that almost everyone complained about the delivery delay and inaccuracy. It shows that JD is not capable for abnormal conditions and the emergency response plan is not effective enough. The total amount for sales orders in 2014 during "11.11" was as 3 times as many as the number in 2012 and it reached the highest level of 2013 by 12am in 11th. In other words, it can be seen that the trading volume of "11.11" increases annually so that the pressure for JD increases as well. It is urgent for JD to optimize the operation mode during abnormal time period. Otherwise, the "logistics jam" will get worse. Moreover, "11.11" is a good opportunity to develop new customers because there may be potential customers attracted by huge discount. If they are not satisfied with the logistics service, they may not shop on JD anymore. Likewise, "11.11" is only a representative for special time periods, JD will also encounter problems during some festivals like the Spring Festival, during which customers are likely to stock up on necessities.

Secondly, by comparing the evaluation condition of customers in 1 or 2 tier cities with customers in 3 or 4 tier cities, it can be seen that there are 11 factors belongs to the domain of "strongly agree" for customers in 1 or 2 tier cities while only 6 factors for customers in 3 or 4 tier cities. Primarily, customers in 3 or 4 tier cities are not quite content with the order process compared to customers in 1 or 2 tier cities. This is because the part related to 3 or 4 tier cities in the information system is not thorough enough. Some information may be missed during logistics tracking so that customers cannot get the feedback in time and follow the delivery process. Thus, JD should improve its information system. Then, customers are not quite satisfied with the logistics fee. They think JD does not charge reasonable price for logistic service. As is known that the average income of customers in 3 or 4 tier cities are generally lower than 1 or 2 tier cities, customers in 3 or 4 tier cities are more price-sensitive. JD may give them discount for logistics price, for example, shipping free if they spend over 2000 RMB on an order. Compared to the profit, loss in logistics fee is insignificant. In addition, such discount is also attractive to price-sensitive customers, which will help to marketing in 3 or 4 tier cities. When it comes to the factor "delivery in promised time", because JD does not own logistics centers in 3 or 4 tier cities, it has to cooperate with third party storage companies. Since the third party storage is not directly managed by JD, it is hard to guarantee the quality. Therefore, JD needs to strengthen cooperation with third party storage companies and set standard. If they cannot meet the requirement, JD has the right to terminate the agreement. Finally, dissatisfaction with "complete instruction" and "use-friendly operation process" can be classified into the same category-inferior user experience of webpage. Since customers in 3 or 4 tier cities start later than 1 or 2 tier cities in the field of online shopping, their degree of familiarity with online shopping is lower. As a result, such customers prefer more specific instruction and straightaway interface. It will be convenient for them if JD improves the operation process.

Thirdly, there are factors that customers are not satisfied in all 3 conditions (in the domain of "neutral"). Obviously, "swift error processing" and "outcome in dealing with errors" are in the intersection. It seems that JD is weak in dealing with errors, both for speed and the final outcome. Although it is difficult to avoid errors thoroughly due to huge orders, errors have a bad effect on users' experience and JD's reputation. Therefore it is crucial for JD to lift the speed of error processing and improve the quality of error treatment. It should carefully collect customers' feedback to find out the reasons of failure.

## Self-Built vs. Third-Party Logistics

JD chooses the self-built logistics mode and combines it with third party storage companies. Logistics can cooperate closely with other business link in order to assure long term stable profits. For industries under intense competition (such as e-commerce), self-built logistics is beneficial to the control of supply and retail channel. More narrowly, it helps to plan management process, increase logistics effectiveness and decrease circulation expense. For large-scale e-commerce companies, self-built logistics integrate the logistics with fund flow and information flow more closely so that improves the work efficiency. Also it realizes the strategy integration of material and component purchase, delivery and production support, by which means to reduce the occupation of funds, lower the cost.

On the other hand, self-built logistics increases the investment burden and weaken the ability to resist market risk. To run self-built logistics, companies need to inject heavily in establishing logistics centers, transportation facilities and related human capital. In consequence, the e-commerce company must reduce the input in other links which is likely to result in management incompetence. For some small-scale e-commerce companies, they even cannot keep normal operation because of the large investment proportion in self-built logistics. In addition, for most e-commerce companies, logistics department is only a back office and they are not professional in this area. In this case, self-built logistics force e-commerce companies to do what they are not expert in. It often requires managers spending too much time, energy and resource to support. As the result, the logistics effectiveness is low and management control is difficult.

Third party storage also has a couple of strengths. Generally, the core business of an e-commerce company will not be logistics. Also, logistics are its specialty. Since the emerging third party storage engages verities types of logistics projects, it can integrate the logistics resource to lower cost and improve logistics effectiveness. Third party storage can be business advantage. Since e-commerce companies engage in different industries, the demand of logistics service is also multifarious. For example, fresh products require cold storage and dangerous chemicals require safe storage. Meeting such different demand is the fundamental of third party storage logistics, while e-commerce companies cannot achieve it by self-built logistics. Third party storage can also decrease the influence of logistics facilities hysteresis. Logistics department in small-scale companies is lack of coordination with external resources. When the core business of e-commerce companies develops rapidly, logistics system need to follow up. At the moment, self-built logistics is often hysteretic because of the restriction of facilities. As a result, it is the time to ask help from third party storage. Third party storage also has the advantage in information network, which contribute to improving the customers' satisfaction degree. It can make use of enhance the ability of processing orders and shorten the response time to customer demand by powerful and convenient information network.

On the other hand, the control ability over logistics of e-commerce companies decreases. Because of the intervention of third party storage weakens the control ability over logistics, the risk of losing control over logistics may occur. In addition, managers may try to shift the responsibilities onto each other internal the e-commerce companies due to the existence of the third party. Since third party storage faces more than one e-commerce companies, the trade secrets are likely to be released during providing service to other competitors. The cooperation between the third party storage and e-commerce companies is a long term relationship. If the third party storage operates improperly, it will influence the operation of e-commerce companies as well.

## Suggestions on Improving E-Commerce Logistics Service in China

There are several other suggestions as extension from JD's studies to e-commerce logistics in general: 1) Make inductive strategies. The government should provide promotion of logistics development by establishing regulations to coordinate e-commerce companies and logistics companies. Policies can be made on specifying logistics industry and setting a general goal of logistics development. 2) Enhance the construction of hardware and software. Modern logistics system can effectively reduce intermediate links, time of circulation and time of circulation. E-commerce companies or logistics companies should pay attention to methods automation, management institutionalization and delivery information. 3) Establishing standard logistics system. Along with the spread of e-commerce around the world, logistics internationalization is the inexorable trend. E-commerce companies or logistics companies should be geared to international standards, including logistics terms, barcodes and equipment. 4) Train logistics talents. The introducing of advanced e-commerce logistics in to China involves trade economy, management, packaging and computer technology, which brings forward higher requirements logistics employees. E-commerce companies or logistics companies should train logistics talents because of the significant influence of staff quality and management level. 5) Construct the e-commerce logistics network. The high efficient e-commerce logistics relies on the effective logistics network. The efficiency of logistics network restricts the efficiency of logistics system. E-commerce companies or logistics companies should focus on 3 networks: physical logistics network, virtual network and customer marketing network.

# CONCLUSION

Along with the development of B2C, E-commerce and e-retailing becomes a hot issue as a new type of business model. Since most e-retailing companies do not have physical stores and its delivery all relies on logistics, logistics service evaluation becomes a vital part of customer experience. This chapter has analyzed e-retailing logistics management following a "from theory to practice" order. Literature review has been conducted in the area of e-retailing, logistics and customer satisfaction (service quality), which provide conceptual framework for the topics of e-retailing logistics management. We then have selected 4 representative cases from the Chinese e-retailing business, namely Taobao, Dangdang, JD and Suning. Though they are all successful and expanding quickly, the approaches of logistics management are different. Taobao completely outsources logistics management, to keep its core business of information platform development as a C2C company. Dangdang mainly outsource the delivery process, whiling keeping its own warehouse, to cut down cost and to remain quick responsive to market (capacity leading demand strategy). JD mainly use self-built logistics system in warehouse and delivery management, to promote its brand and build customer relationship. Suning adopts a highly vertical integrated logistics system, due to the fact that B2C service is expanded from its traditional physical store operations. In order to assessment e-retailing logistics performance, we have conducted survey studies into JD's customers. Results show that JD's self-built logistics has several advantages, such as strong ability of control over each link of supply chain and keep strong competitiveness. On the contrary, it requires high prior-period investment and the degree of specialization is not high enough to support system management before logistics system has been perfected. Third party storage enhances the ability of processing orders and shortens the response time to customer demand by powerful and convenient information network. However, it makes the control ability over logistics of e-commerce companies decrease and be likely to release e-commerce companies' information. Possible solutions are making inductive strategies by government, enhancing the construction of hardware and software, establishing standard logistics system, training logistics talents and constructing the e-commerce logistics network by e-commerce companies or logistics companies. Our suggestions based on case companies can potentially be extended to other e-retailing companies. The analysis and findings can also be useful in terms of theory contribution and managerial implementation.

## ACKNOWLEDGMENT

This research is supported by the National Natural Science Foundation of China (Grant No. 71272164). We also would like to express our sincere thanks to all participants for this survey study.

## REFERENCES

Barsauskas, P., Sarapovas, T., & Cvilikas, A. (2008). The evaluation of e-commerce impact on business efficiency. *Baltic Journal of Management*, *3*(1), 71–91. doi:10.1108/17465260810844275

Bienstock, C. C., Mentzer, J. T., & Bird, M. M. (1996). Measuring physical distribution service quality. *Journal of the Academy of Marketing Science*, *25*(1), 31–44. doi:10.1177/0092070397251004

Christopher, M. (1998). *Logistics and supply chain management: Strategies for reducing cost and improving services* (2nd ed.). London: Pitman Publisher.

Colla, E., & Dupuis, M. (2002). Research and managerial issues on global retail competition: Carrefour/Wal-Mart. *International Journal of Retail & Distribution Management*, *30*(2), 103–111. doi:10.1108/09590550210418128

Colla, E., & Lapoule, P. (2012). E-commerce: Exploring the critical success factors. *International Journal of Retail & Distribution Management*, *40*(11), 842–864. doi:10.1108/09590551211267601

Cox, J., & Dale, B. G. (2001). Service quality and e-commerce: An exploratory analysis. *Managing Service Quality*, *11*(2), 121–131. doi:10.1108/09604520110387257

Dong, Y. (2005). Dangdang: Enhanced delivery speed. *International Business*, B04.

Hill, C.A., & Scudder, G.D. (2002). The use of electronic data interchange for supply chain coordination in the food Industry. *Journal of Operations Management*, *20*(4), 375–387.

Huang, K. (2010). JD's logistics competition. Retrieved from http://tech.sina.com.cn/i/2010-05-15/01544189077.shtml

Knemeyer, A. M., & Murphy, P. (2004). Evaluation the performance of third-party logistics arrangements: A relationship marketing perspective. *Journal of Supply Chain Management*, *40*(1), 722–740. doi:10.1111/j.1745-493X.2004.tb00254.x

Kotler, P. (2003). *Marketing Management* (11th ed.). New Jersey: Pearson Education.

Kremic, T., Tukel, O. I., & Rom, W. O. (2006). Outsourcing decision support: A survey of benefits, risks, and decision factors. *Supply Chain Management. International Journal (Toronto, Ont.)*, *11*, 467–482.

Lai, K., Wong, C. W. Y., & Cheng, T. C. E. (2010). Bundling digitized logistics activities and its performance implications. *Industrial Marketing Management*, *39*(2), 273–286. doi:10.1016/j.indmarman.2008.08.002

Liao, Z., & Shi, X. (2009). Consumer prospections of internet-based e-retailing: An empirical research in Hong Kong. *Journal of Services Marketing*, *23*(1), 24–30. doi:10.1108/08876040910933066

Liu, C. (2013). The problems and solutions of Taobao's logistics model. *Shangqing*, 47.

Lu, W.-M., & Hung, S.-W. (2011). Exploring the efficiency and effectiveness in global e-retailing companies. *Computers & Operations Research*, *38*(9), 1351–1360. doi:10.1016/j.cor.2010.12.009

Ma, N. (2010). The optimized design of C2C third-party logistics network: Case of Taobao. *China Business & Trade*, 22.

Mentzer, J. T., Flint, D. J., & Hult, G. T. M. (2001). Logistics service quality as a segment-customized process. *Journal of Marketing*, *65*(4), 82–104. doi:10.1509/jmkg.65.4.82.18390

Mentzer, J. T., Gomes, R., & Krapfel, R. E. (1989). Physical distribution service: A fundamental marketing concept. *Journal of the Academy of Marketing Science*, *17*(4).

Min, S., & Wolfinbarger, M. (2005). Do early movers, clicks, and mortars, and generalists prevail in E-commerce? *Journal of Business Research*, *58*, 1030–1039. doi:10.1016/j.jbusres.2004.02.005

Morschett, D., Swoboda, B., & Schramm-Klein, H. (2006). Competitive strategies in retailing – an investigation of the applicability of Porter's framework for food retailers. *Journal of Retailing and Consumer Services*, *13*(4), 275–287. doi:10.1016/j.jretconser.2005.08.016

Parasuraman, A., Zeithaml, V. A., & Berry, L. L. (1985). A conceptual model of service quality and its implications for future research. *Journal of Retailing*, *49*(1), 41–50.

Parasuraman, A., Zeithaml, V. A., & Berry, L. L. (1988). SERVQUAL: A multiple-item scale for measuring consumer perceptions of service quality. *Journal of Retailing*, *64*(1), 12–40.

Porter, M. (1980). *Competitive strategy: Techniques for analyzing industries and competitors*. New York: Free Press.

Porter, M. (1985). *Competitive advantage—Creating and sustaining superior performance*. New York: Free Press.

Ramanathan, R. (2010). The moderating roles of risk and efficiency on the relationship between logistics performance and customer loyalty in e-commerce. *Transportation Research Part E, Logistics and Transportation Review*, *46*(6), 950–962. doi:10.1016/j.tre.2010.02.002

Rao, S., Rabinovich, E., & Raju, D. (2014). The role of physical distribution services as determinants of product returns in internet retailing. *Journal of Operations Management*, *32*(6), 295–312. doi:10.1016/j.jom.2014.06.005

Ren, B., & Dong, X. (2013). The study on self-built logistics system of electronic commerce enterprise: 360buy as a case. *Logistics Sci-Tech*, *1*, 104–108.

Rendo, S., & Ficko, D. (2010). New logistics technologies in improving customer value in retailing service. *Journal of Retailing and Consumer Services*, *17*(3), 216–223. doi:10.1016/j.jretconser.2010.03.012

Subramanian, N., Gunasekaran, A., Yu, J., Cheng, J., & Ning, K. (2014). Customer satisfaction and competitiveness in the Chinese e-retailing: Structural equation modeling approach to identify the role of quality factors. *Expert Systems with Applications*, *41*(1), 69–80. doi:10.1016/j.eswa.2013.07.012

Tian, Y. (2001). Logistics quality management. *Logistics technology, 24*(2), 3-8.

Tsai, M., Lai, K., Lloyd, A. E., & Lin, H. (2012). The dark side of logistics outsourcing – Unraveling the potential risks leading to failed relationships. *Transportation Research Part E, Logistics and Transportation Review*, *48*(1), 178–189. doi:10.1016/j.tre.2011.07.003

Wang, S. (2011). Selling large home electrics appliance becomes JD's headache. Retrieved from http://www.56products.com/News/2011-9-14/34519KC711E7B615712.html

Wang, Z. T. (2000). *Modern logistics*. China: China Goods and materials publisher.

Watson, A., Kirby, D. A., & Egan, J. (2002). Franchising, retailing and the development of e-commerce. *International Journal of Retail & Distribution Management*, *30*(5), 228–237. doi:10.1108/09590550210426390

Wen, H. J., Lim, B., & Huang, H. L. (2003). Measuring e-commerce efficiency: A data envelopment analysis (DEA) approach. *Industrial Management & Data Systems*, *103*(9), 703–710. doi:10.1108/02635570310506124

Williamson, K. C., Spiter, D. M., & Bloomberg, D. J. (1990). Modern logistics systems: Theory and practice. *Journal of Business Logistics*, *11*(2), 65–86.

Williamson, P. & Wang, J. (2014). Alibaba group's Taobao: From intermediary to ecosystem enabler. *Judge Business School Case Centre* (Ref. 314-139-1), University of Cambridge.

Yang, Y., Humphreys, P., & McIvor, R. (2006). Business service quality in an e-commerce environment. *Supply Chain Management. International Journal (Toronto, Ont.)*, *11*(3), 195–201.

Yu, M., Zhang, L., & Yu, X. (2008). Some thoughts of Suning's logistics model. *Modernization of Management*, *6*, 30–32.

Zairi, M., & Al-Mashari, M. (2002). E-commerce based supply chain management: A proposed model based on retailing experience. *Computer & Information Science*, 61 – 84.

Zhang, W. (2011). A study on Taobao's logistics delivery problems. *Work and Study Abroad,* May.

Zudor, E. I., Kemeny, Z., Ekart, A., Buckingham, C. D., & Monostori, L. (2014). *A solution for information management in logistics operations of modern manufacturing chains*. Paper presented at the 8th International Conference on Digital Enterprise Technology – Disruptive Innovation in Manufacturing Engineering towards the 4th Industrial Revolution (pp. 337 – 344).

# Chapter 15
# Taxation Policy Measures for E- Retailers

**Sana Moid**
*Amity University, India*

## ABSTRACT

*The internet has already revolutionized many aspects of modern business and living and promises to bring even more radical future changes. In contrast, tax laws are normally slow to changing realities. It is anticipated that trade in tangible (physical) goods with e- commerce will not introduce problems. However, trade in intangible (electronic or digital) goods can be problematic because they will be difficult if not impossible to track. The chapter discusses the important concepts woven around the idea of taxing e tailing transactions and aims at coming up with a conclusion which will help further to determine the appropriate tax policies for e retailers keeping in mind the global framework. The chapter aims at discussing the concept of Internet Taxation, E- Retailing laws and regulations in Global Context. The chapter also discusses broad outlines relating to taxability of E Retailing transactions from VAT and CST angle under different scenarios and arguments in favor and against of taxing the e tailing transactions. The chapter also discusses important acts passed in different economies for taxing online retailers including Marketplace Fairness Act 2013 and Internet Tax Freedom Act. It is concluded by discussing the possible effects of the online retail tax. It could be argued that e- commerce for most part will not require new tax principles. Existing principles still apply only the old ways of doing things need to be digitized. The internet and e- commerce certainly does introduce some new business models and products that would not have been possible with old technology. And in some case, new laws may be required or old laws amended. Trade in intangibles or goods that are in digital format promises to be the main problem area.*

## 1. INTRODUCTION

As more purchases are made over the Internet, states are looking for new ways to collect taxes on online sales. There is a common misperception that the U.S. Constitution prohibits states from taxing internet sales. This is not true. States may impose sales and use taxes on such, even when the retailer in outside the state. However, if the seller does not have a constitutionally sufficient connection ("nexus") to the state, then the seller is under no enforceable obligation to collect the tax and remit it to the state. The purchaser is still generally responsible for paying the tax, but few comply and the tax revenue goes uncollected.

DOI: 10.4018/978-1-4666-9921-2.ch015

Copyright © 2016, IGI Global. Copying or distributing in print or electronic forms without written permission of IGI Global is prohibited.

From the inception of the internet until the late 1990s, it was free of regulations by government in the United States at all levels and also free on any specifically targeted tax levies, duties, imposts or license fees. By 1996, however, that began to change, as several US states and municipalities began to see internet services as a potential source of tax revenue. The 1998 Internet Tax freedom Act halted the expansion of direct taxation of the internet, grandfathering existing taxes in ten states. In United States alone, some 30,000 taxing jurisdictions could otherwise have claim to taxes on a piece of the Internet. The law, however, did not affect sales axes applied to online purchases. These continue to be taxed at varying rates depending on the jurisdiction, in the same way that phone and mail orders are taxed. The absence of direct taxation of the internet does not mean that all transactions taking place online are free of tax, or even that internet is free of all tax. In United States, nearly all online transactions are subject to one form of tax or the other. The Internet Tax Freedom Act merely precludes states in the United States from imposing their sales tax or any other kind of gross receipts tax, on certain online services. E- Retailing transactions are growing by leaps and bounds, day by day, because of convenience, choice, cost competitiveness and transparency being offered. The growth of E- Commerce is reducing the ability of federal, state and local governments to raise revenue from traditional sources in traditional ways. Consequently, legislatures are reassessing specific tax policies with respect to e-commerce and asking how such policies may impede or facilitate economic objectives. With increase in volume and value of these transactions, naturally it is important to explore the possibility of levy of VAT or CST as the case may be and to investigate about possible evasion of tax.

The chapter discusses these important concepts woven around the idea of e tailing and taxation policy measures and aims at coming up with a conclusion which will help further to determine the appropriate tax policies for e retailers keeping in mind the global framework.

The chapter aims at discussing about the following points:

1. The concept of Internet Taxation.
2. Broad outlines relating to taxability of E Retailing transactions from VAT and CST angle under different scenarios including:
    a. Taxation policy when E- Retailers act only as a facilitator and does not own any material on his own.
    b. Taxation policy where the E- Retailers purchases the material on his own and then re sells to the buyers.
    c. Taxation policy when the E- Retailers holds the material of the seller as an agent in his custody.
3. Global taxation policy for e retailers
4. Discussion of important acts passed in different economies for taxing online retailers including Marketplace Fairness Act 2013 (Passed in USA to make it easier for states to collect web sales taxes).
5. Arguments in favor and against of taxing the e tailing transactions.
6. Possible effects of the online retail tax

## 2. BACKGROUND

Though there exists no standard definition for the term e-commerce, it is generally used in the sense of denoting a method of conducting business through electronic means rather than through conventional physical means. Such electronic means include 'click &buy' methods using computers as well as 'm-commerce' which make use of various mobile devices or smart phones. This term takes into account not just the act of purchasing goods and /or availing services through an online platform but also all other activities which are associated with any transaction such as:

- Delivery
- Payment facilitation
- Supply chain and service management

E-commerce has defied the traditional structure of businesses trading with consumers bringing to the fore various business models which has empowered consumers.

Some of the common business models which are facilitated by e- commerce are as follows:

1. **B2B:** E–Commerce has enabled various businesses to build new relationships with other businesses for efficiently managing several of their business functions. B2B e- commerce could comprise of various models, which may include distribution services, procurement services, digital /online market place like services etc. India Mart.com is one such B2B online market place which provides a platform for businesses to find other competitive suppliers.
2. **C2C:** Traditionally consumers have had dealings with other consumers, but only few of those activities were in a commercial sense. E-commerce has made it possible to bring together strangers and providing a platform for them to trade on. For example, portals such as eBay and Quikr enables consumers to transact with other consumers.
3. **C2B:** This relatively new model of commerce and is a reverse of the traditional commerce models; here consumers (i.e. individuals) provide services/goods to businesses and create value for the businesses. This type of transaction can be seen in internet forums where consumers provide product development ideas or in online platforms where consumers provide product reviews which are then used for advertisement purposes.
4. **B2B2C:** A variant of the B2C model wherein there is an additional intermediary business to assist the first business transact with the end consumer. This model is poised to do much better. Provided upon request only in a web based commerce with the reduced costs of having an intermediary. For instance, Flipkart, one of the most successful e- commerce portals provides a platform for consumers to purchase a wide variety of goods such as electronic goods, apparels, books and music CDs. Further, apart from businesses providing intermediary services such as that of Flipkart a lot online platforms tie up with payment gateway facilitators who provide a platform for the processing of payments.
5. **B2C:** Direct dealings between businesses and consumers have always existed; however with the emergence of e-commerce such transaction have gained further momentum. In a traditional B2C model, the distribution channel typically starts with manufacturer and goes through a distributor/ wholesaler to retailer, who interacts with the end customer. However, in an online model one finds the manufacturer or the intermediary directly trading with the consumer.

## 3. LITERATURE REVIEW

Alison Shelton, an economic researcher from the American Association of Retired Persons Public Policy Institute, argues that sales tax provides about 25 percent, on average, of state and local tax revenues. These taxes go uncollected on many Internet sales. This is because the Supreme Court has placed limits on the states' abilities to require certain out-of-state merchants to collect the tax. Moreover, consumers have failed to carry out their legal responsibilities to submit the sales tax to their home states. Thus under the existing laws related to sales tax, identical products may be taxed differently depending on whether they are purchased over the Internet, through a catalogue, or in a traditional "mortar-and-bricks" store. Traditional retailers accuse that this situation confers a price advantage on catalogue and Internet retailers (Shelton, 2001).

The sales tax base for state and local governments is shrinking because of the expanded use of services not subject to sales tax and legislatively granted exemptions. These services include purchases made through the Internet, telephone, and catalogs (Bruce & Fox, 2001). E-commerce is merely one of the casual factors in the reduction.

Many states rely on sales tax revenue and are afraid that with the growth of Internet Commerce, they stand to lose billions of dollars in revenue on the state and local level. In a recent Congressional Research Service (CRS) Report for Congress, the U.S. Supreme Court sees the enforcing and collection of taxes by state and local governments as too much of a burden, not worth the bother. "Based on CRS calculations of state and local sales tax revenue as a portion of total tax revenue, Washington, Tennessee and Arizona are the states and local jurisdictions most reliant on the sales tax. In those states over 40% of total tax revenue is derived from the sales tax" (Maguire, 2005).

Former congressman Jack Kemp in an article, Cal-Tax Digest states that he believes the "Internet is a driving force in the American and World economies. The current federal tax code is a confusing and corrupting burden on our economy. Certain factions are seeking to impose a new national framework of Internet taxation that may contain the same flaws as the current federal code and that may be unconstitutional" (Kemp, 2000).

Li (2000) provides a technical and policy analysis of the Canadian Goods and Services Tax (GST) in the context of e-commerce and suggests some options for reform. Even though the GST has had a bad reputation in Canada and its integrity is now threatened by growing online cross-border shopping, based on the revenue potential of the GST, a re- placement is highly unlikely, and a cleaned-up or reformed GST is more practical. Thus the government should take advantage of the opportunity presented by e-commerce to reform the GST.

In an application of the substance over form doctrine to the international e-commerce taxation issue, Ngoy (2003) proposes an approach consisting of applying what is called here the permanent establishment (PE) function test to e- commerce infrastructures in order to see whether they qualify for being fiscally treated as PE, if they pass the concerned test. The study concludes that some of them substantially have the same function as the category of office PE, and they should be fiscally treated as this category of PE no matter the form they have.

## 4. INTERNET TAXATION

Since from the penetration of use of Internet in the late 90s, it was free from all regulations(especially tax levies, duties, imposts or license fees etc.) by respective governments but in 1996, countries start thinking the use of Internet services as a potential source of tax revenue and to look into the same, United States in the year 1998 came with "Internet Tax Freedom Act" to intervene the policy of taxation on use of internet services, however did not affect sales taxes applied to online purchases. The Internet Tax Freedom Act merely precludes the states in United States from imposing their sales tax, or any other kind of gross receipts tax, on certain online services. There have been various types of taxes earlier to "Internet Tax Freedom Act" which were levied on purchase and sale of goods but now after implementation of act all these taxes become a part of internet taxation on all transactions of products online which are as follows:

1. **Internet Access Tax:** Internet access tax is the tax levied on access of Internet Service Provider charges taken from users. ISPs taxation was earlier an informal form of tax which was either under sales tax or service tax in different states but after Internet Tax Freedom Act it became a part of internet taxation.
2. **Telecom Service Tax:** Telecom service tax is the tax levied on the use of different modes of internet access (like regular phone line, ISDN, DSL, cable, wireless, satellites etc.) for sale and purchase of goods online.
3. **Franchise Tax:** Franchise tax was traditionally levied on all services and utilities but it has been found that generally the organisations transfer this tax burden to internet service provider (ISPs), their customer or both. To remove this barrier Internet Tax Freedom Act put a restriction on this multiple taxation by including this tax under Internet taxation category.
4. **Bit Tax and E-Mail Tax:** Bit tax is another constituent of Internet taxation which is levied on the usage of data. More specifically this tax is calculated as per number of bits used in volume for online transactions. Bit tax also includes E-mail tax which is based on email sent or received specifying number of messages and their particular data sizes as well. However e-mail tax has been posed to various hurdles and hence it was later banned under Internet Tax Freedom Act by United States.
5. **Bandwidth Tax:** Bandwidth tax was started with a concept based on different speed of one's Internet connection and was conceptualized to be levied on ratio scale as per the bandwidth and speed of connection but it was also banned by the Internet Tax Freedom Act later.

### 4.1. Basic Principles of Internet Taxation

Taxation policy for E- Retailing transactions should be based on the following seven criteria:

1. The system should be equitable: taxpayers in similar situations who carry out similar transactions should be taxed in the same way.
2. The system should be simple: administrative costs for the tax authorities and compliances costs for tax payers should be minimized as far as possible.
3. The rules should provide certainty for the taxpayer so that the tax consequences of a transaction are known in advance: taxpayers should know what is to be taxed and when- and where the tax is to be accounted for.

4. Any system adopted should be effective: it should produce the right amount of tax at the right time and minimize the potential for tax evasion and avoidance.
5. Economic distortions should be avoided: corporate decision makers should be motivated by commercial rather than tax considerations.
6. The system should be sufficiently flexible and dynamic to ensure that tax rules keep pace with technological and commercial developments.
7. Any tax arrangements adopted domestically and any changes to existing international taxation principles should be structured to ensure a fair sharing of the Internet tax base among countries, particularly important as regards division of the tax base between developed and developing countries.

## 5. FUNDAMENTALS ON TAXATION OF E-COMMERCE

Apparently a number of taxation issues are not fresh or unique to electronic commerce but have already evolved in conventional commerce, which increasingly banks on new modes of communications and progressively crosses national borders.

- **Neutrality:** Taxation should seek to be neutral and equitable between forms of e-commerce and between conventional and e-commerce, so as to avert double taxation or unintentional non-taxation.
- **Efficiency:** Compliance costs to business and administration costs for governments should be derogated as far as possible.
- **Certainty and Simplicity:** Tax rules should be clear and simple to interpret, so that taxpayers know where they stand.
- **Effectiveness and Fairness:** Taxation should produce the right amount of tax at the right time and the potential of evasion and avoidance should be belittled.
- **Flexibility:** Taxation systems should be flexible and dynamic to ascertain they keep pace with technological and commercial developments.

## 6. TAXING OF E RETAILING TRANSACTIONS

### 6.1. Broad Outlines Relating to Taxability of E Retailing Transactions from VAT and CST Angle under Different Scenarios in India

E Retailing transactions are growing by leaps and bounds, day by day, because of convenience, choice, cost competitiveness and transparency being offered. VAT departments in the States of Karnataka and Telangana (India) have raised the issue of taxability of E- Retailing transactions and doubts about evasion of tax. It is apprehended that E- Retailing firms may be forced to leave the Country unless and until clear and transparent guidelines are issued in this direction, without any arbitrariness and possibility for different interpretations which will lead to painful, costly and time consuming litigation. Leading E- Commerce giant Amazon has already indicated that they may leave the State of Karnataka or even Country, if the tax related arbitrariness hits their operations. This would result in loss of jobs, affect growth of the economy and add to impression in the minds of international community that the tax practices in India are not stable and do not allow them to carry out the business in a predictable manner. Therefore, it is the need of the hour for the State Governments to come out with clear cut and transparent guidelines on E- Retailing transactions.

Basically, E- Retailers can carry out three types of transactions:

1. *Where the E- Retailers acts only as a facilitator,* in which he does not own any materials on his own, but allows the buyers to purchase the materials through his web site, in terms of the agreement between E- Retailers and the Seller who owns the materials. In this case, E- Retailer is purely a commission agent and out of the purview of the VAT or CST Acts. The liability towards VAT or CST in such a case would be as under:
    a. The taxability to either VAT or CST, depends upon the materials movement by seller, as he is required to deliver the materials to the buyer. In case the seller is required to make delivery of the goods to the buyer situated in the other State, consequent to the order placed by the buyer on the website of E- Retailers, then the seller is required to remit CST on the sale price of goods to the VAT department of the State from where the materials are moved. For eg, the seller is in the state of Maharashtra and buyer is in the state of Kerala. Then the materials are required to be transferred from Maharashtra to Kerala consequent to sale transaction carried out by the buyers on the E- Retailer's website. The seller in the state of Maharashtra is required to remit CST to the VAT department of Maharashtra State.
    b. Alternatively, if the seller and buyers are both in the state of Maharashtra, then the material movement will be within the State of Maharashtra and the seller is required to remit VAT to the State of Maharashtra. No liability arises on the E- Retailers, as he does not own the materials and therefore not transferring any property in goods to the buyer.
    c. Material movement decides the mature of levy- If it is interstate movement, the seller is required to remit CST. In case of intra- state movement, the seller is required to remit VAT. The right to levy VAT or CST accrues to the State wherein the materials are moved.
2. *Where the E- Retailer purchases the materials on his own and then re-sells to the buyers,* then the liability would be on the E- Retailers for discharge of VAT or CST as the case may be, which is explained hereunder:
    a. In case the material movement is within the same state, then the E- Retailer is required to remit VAT on the sale transaction to the VAT department of the State where the materials are located. For e.g. If the buyer is in the State of Kerala and places order on the website of the E- Retailer and if the E- Retailer holds the materials in his godown in the State of Kerala and makes delivery to the buyer, then the E- Retailer is required to remit VAT to Kerala
    b. In case the material movement is from one state to another state, then the E- Retailer is required to remit CST to the state from where the material movement is initiated on account of sale transaction. For e.g. A buyer in Kerala places order on website of E- Retailer. Consequently, the E Retailer who holds stock of the materials in the State of Karnataka is required to make delivery of the goods to the buyer in the State of Kerala. Since interstate movement is involved, the seller is required to remit CST to the state of Karnataka.
    c. The crux of the issue is- liability for VAT or CST arises in the State from where the materials are delivered. If the E- Retailer holds his materials in the state of Karnataka, then whether the buyer is in the State of Karnataka or Kerala, the liability to discharge VAT or CST on the part of E- Retailer accrues to the State of Karnataka.

d. However, if the E- Retailer holds materials in the State of Kerala also, and delivers the materials to the buyer in the State of Kerala, then the liability arises in the State of Kerala and E- Retailer is required to remit VAT to the State of Kerala. Even though the web site related infrastructure of the E- Retailer is located in the State of Karnataka, no liability arises in the state of Karnataka, as there is no material movement from the State of Kerala.

3. *Third alternative is- Where the E- Retailer holds the materials of the Seller as an agent in his custody.* In such a case, the E- Retailer is an agent of the seller and discharges the liability on behalf of the seller. Here again, the material movement determines the taxability of the transaction to VAT or CST.
   a. The E- Retailer holds the materials of the seller in his godown in Karnataka. Then he would be required to move the materials either to other States or within the State of Karnataka, based on the location of the buyer.
   b. If the buyer is located in the State of Karnataka, then the material movement will be within the State of Karnataka and E- Retailer is required to remit VAT to the state of Karnataka, on behalf of the seller.
   c. If the buyer is located in the state of Kerala, then the material movement is to be done from the State of Karnataka to Kerala, which becomes a CST sale and E-Retailer is required to remit CST to the State of Karnataka, on behalf of the Seller.
4. The basic issue that is to be understood in the subject is- State where the materials are lying and from where the movement is initiated for delivery to the buyer, whether inter state or intra-state is competent to levy VAT or CST, depending upon the movement. Location of E- Retailer in a state does not automatically casts obligation on him or empower the State to levy VAT or CAT, if the material is lying in other State and movement on account of sale is from that of other state.
5. If the State VAT authorities are under the impression that location of E- Retailer in their casts liability on him, irrespective of the location of the materials and their movement, guidelines or instruction under such impression would result in disputes which would consume lot of time, energy and money of the E- Retailers.

## 6.2. European Union

The member countries of the European Union use Value Added Tax rather than sales tax. The basis of the value added to a good or service at each stage of the production and distribution chain determines the tax. The tax is collected through a system of partial payments which allows firms to deduct for their VAT accounts the amount of tax that they paid on their commercial purchases. This system makes the tax neutral no matter how many transactions were made.The important thing to note, what makes it comparable to the US sales tax, is that the VAT is paid by the final consumer based upon a percentage in addition to the final price of the good or service. The supplier of the good or service then submits the VAT paid to the national tax administration.

The European Union addressed the issue of taxation on online purchases through legislation in May 2002 in the form of an amendment to the sixth VAT Directive. The objective of the amendment was to create a level playing field for EU businesses with respect to the indirect taxation of electronic commerce. While promoting fairness, it was also the EU's goal to make compliance for businesses, including non EU businesses, as easy and straightforward as possible. These objective fall in line with the EU's overriding purpose to promote a single market and fair competition.

## 6.3. Taxing Internet Sales under the Current US System

Sales tax is implemented at the state and local levels of governments in the United States. Currently, forty five states charge sales taxes on various types of retail sales. Of these states, thirty three of them authorize local governments to collect various forms of sales tax. The combination of state and local sales tax regulations results in more than 7500 taxing jurisdictions imposing some form of sales tax in the US. Citizens are technically supposed to pay tax on all internet purchases under current US law. However, unless the retailer is required to collect this tax due to nexus, individuals are supposed to self report and pay the tax themselves. Most consumers do not self report tax on their internet purchases. Consumers can easily avoid reporting this because the states do not pursue collecting the tax due to how cost effective it would be. For most purchasers, this is considered one of the benefits of purchasing items online. The tax that US citizens are supposed to pay and report on their internet purchases from retailers that do not collect sales tax is called an equivalent use tax. By definition, a use tax is a tax imposed on the use of certain goods that are bought outside the taxing authority's jurisdiction.

The use tax is essentially the same as the sales tax except that it requires the consumer, rather than the retailer, to report the tax and essentially the same because tax rates are the same for both. States have relied on use taxes to collect tax on internet sales, because they are often prohibited from requiring out of state retailers to collect sales tax. Unfortunately, these efforts have been largely ineffective. This is mainly because most consumers do not know about the tax, consumers think the amount due is too small to justify the paperwork, and the consumers know that the states have been lax in enforcing payment on the use tax. Internet retailers are, however, required to collect sales tax on items sold to consumers in states where the retailer has a substantial nexus. The Supreme Court determined that substantial nexus essentially means that the retailer must have a substantial physical presence n the taxing stage. There has been extensive litigation between retailers and state governments over whether those retailers have substantial nexus with the state. Additionally, it has led retailers to remove distribution centers and offices from certain states to avoid meeting the substantial nexus requirement.

The substantial nexus requirement can lead to several inequalities. It puts brick and mortar and click and order retailers at 5-10% worth of sales tax that brick companies must charge may not seem like a lot, but when inherently narrow profit margins in the retail industry are taken into account, it is plain to see why local "brick" businesses struggle to compete against internet retailers. Another argument raised in opposition to the "click only advantage" is that the internet retailers use state funded resources to assist them in commerce while at the same time do not collect sales tax that would be used to fund those resources. Some examples of the resources used by internet retailers are the construction and maintenance of roads, state consumer protection agencies, and police and fire protection. The loophole also disproportionately affects lower income households as research shows that low income consumers are less likely to shop online than more affluent consumers.

### 6.3.1. Legislative Efforts to Fix the Tax Loophole

In recent years there have been a number of bills introduced at both the state and federal level attempting to close the loophole that allows internet retailers to avoid collecting sales tax when they do not nexus with the consumer's state. These proposed laws are often called "Amazon Law's" or "Amazon Taxes"; named after the large internet retailer like Wal- Mart, Best Buy, and Target continue to push legislators to close the loophole that allows retailers like Amazon to avoid collecting sales tax. Retailers such as these are at a competitive disadvantage when competing against companies like Amazon because their brick and mortar stores give them nexus with states, which requires them to collect sales tax on all of their internet and in store sales. States have continued to introduce bills attempting to close sales tax on all of their internet and in store sales. States have continued to introduce bills attempting to close the loophole with varying results. New York, Rhode Island, North Carolina, Illinois, Arkansas, Connecticut, California, South Dakota and Colorado are among the states that have passed legislation addressing the loophole. The corporations negatively affected by this type of legislation, such as Amazon, have filed suit in federal court challenging the constitutionality of many of these "Amazon Taxes". The big issue in these suits is whether the retailers affected by this type of legislation meet the "substantial nexus" requirement set forth in Quill. Some states, like New York, have attempted to establish "substantial nexus" through the independent in state websites that the out of state retailers use to promote their sales. Several state courts have ruled that this method of establishing "substantial nexus" through the independent in state websites that the out of state retailers use to promote their sales. Several state courts have ruled that this method of establishing "substantial nexus" is constitutional. In 2002, a state-led initiative established the Streamlined Sales and Use Tax Agreement in an effort to simplify and align sales tax policies among the states. This in turn would reduce the burden of tax compliance and make the implementation of a system to tax internet sales more feasible.

## 7. MARKETPLACE FAIRNESS ACT 2013

The purpose of the legislation is to provide States with the ability to enforce their existing state and local sales and use tax laws in a way that does not unduly burden e-commerce. The legislation does not require States to collect sales and use taxes. Instead, the legislation gives States the ability to collect – or decide not to collect – sales and use taxes from the online retailers rather than rely on individuals to accurately report their online purchases.

Under the Marketplace Fairness Act, States can begin collecting these sums by adopting one of the following options:

- Become a Member State of the Streamlined Sales and Use Tax Agreement.
- Adopt Minimum Simplification Requirements.
- The legislation recognizes that States should not be required to conform to a one- size-fits-all model.
- Any State may collect sales and use taxes if they adopt minimum simplification requirements.
- Authority to collect begins on the first day of the calendar quarter that is at least 6 months after the State enacts legislation to implement the minimum simplification requirements to provide sellers with additional notice of the collection requirement. Supporters argue that small sellers will not be unduly burdened by the act since the legislation exempts sellers with less than $1,000,000 in gross remote sales. Opponents argue that the Act would allow states to impose massive regulation and taxation requirements on online businesses outside their jurisdictions, would place difficult compliance hurdles on online businesses, and would lead to higher costs for consumers.

The Marketplace Fairness Act of 2013 authorizes each member state under the Streamlined Sales and Use Tax Agreement (the multi-state agreement for the administration and collection of sales and use taxes adopted on November 12, 2002) to require all sellers not qualifying for a small-seller exception (applicable to sellers with annual gross receipts in total U.S. remote sales not exceeding $1 million) to collect and remit sales and use taxes with respect to remote sales under provisions of the agreement, but only if the agreement includes minimum simplification requirements relating to the administration of the tax, audits, and streamlined filing. The bill defines "remote sale" as a sale of goods or services into a state in which the seller would not legally be required to pay, collect, or remit state or local sales and use taxes unless provided by the act.

## 7.1. What Does This Mean for the Retail Industry?

Traditional retailers are only required to collect taxes in states where their stores are located. The process is simple as there are only a few tax rates to deal with. If the MFA is made into a law, it will require online stores to collect taxes based on the customer's location. This could result in online retailers dealing with over 9600 different tax collecting jurisdictions, including state and local governments. Logistically, this will turn out to be a major hurdle for businesses, especially due to the various unique tax rates and rules for each government.

From a consumer's point of view, shopping online just gets more expensive if the consumer resides in a state that collects sales tax. Another effect of this bill could be the rise in sales of e- commerce companies based outside USA. For example, if a consumer orders a product from a store based out of Canada, the store won't be liable to collect and deposit sales tax to the state in which the consumer is located.

Given the impact on the retail industry is significant, retailers will need to b able to actively measure changes to revenue based on this Act. While having a test control is a good strategy for retailers that might have physical presence in some states, many pure online retailers will have to measure the impact of the passing of the Act with more complex methods to account for other variations. The price advantage that these retailers have will be negated, provided they have more data on their customer's shopping behavior. In this case, they can improve their pricing strategies using price optimization models. Managing costs will be even more important. Companies like Amazon are using this opportunity to improve their logistics to have better shipping facilities by increasing their presence locally.

At a macroeconomic level this would imply an overall increase in costs for consumers and will have the potential to impact other related industries such as logistics. Due to changes in customer behavior, people opting to shop in store could drive revenue down for logistics companies due to reduced needs in shipping. The act might spur online retailers to invest more in physical presence. This could replace some of the lost revenue as the retailers would need to service these offline locations.

## 8. CHALLENGES OF TAXING E- RETAILING TRANSACTIONS

In the recent past, E-commerce transactions continue to challenge tax administrations given the often multi jurisdictional nature of the transactions and the potential anonymity of the parties. Often transactions are concluded over the internet which pose challenges as regards place of residence of the contracting parties, place of conclusion of contracts, acceptance of the offer, characterization of the income generated etc. Absence of specific guidelines in this regard result in Revenue taking a very myopic view of the matter lest there should be ostensible loss to the exchequer and taxpayers using the AAR as a favorable destination to buy insurance against any potential tax risk.

Ordinarily, the taxability of traditional modes in the hands of the non-residents is based on the source rule. Business profits are ordinary taxed in the source country only if the overseas entity creates a Permanent Establishment ('PE'). Generically speaking, PE is defined to mean a fixed place of business through which the business of an enterprise is wholly or partly carried on. Such concepts become irrelevant in the context of E-commerce transactions in absence of physical location.

Settled principles of law and fact get questioned basis the form of the transaction being an e-commerce arrangement. A pertinent example to deliberate upon would be that of provision of digitized goods such as software or music to be downloaded for use by the recipient or access to web based documents. Characterization of income generated from the same to be in the nature of royalty taxable in most jurisdictions or business profits not taxable in absence of creation of a PE would be the typical bone of contention. It is an accepted phenomenon that should the same good be sold in non-digitized form (physical form e.g. a book or a CD or mere subscription of journals) it would be regarded as sale of goods not resulting in royalty. The mere alteration in the form of the transaction leads to differing interpretations with the Revenue using its unilateral discretion to tax - causing hardship to businesses. Ideally speaking, the rules for taxability should be neutral to the form of the transaction being in the nature of an E-commerce transactions or transactions through conventional modes. Unfortunately, tax laws do not move in tandem with technological advancements, which results in ambiguity and in turns causes unwarranted litigation.

Challenges of taxing E- Retailing transactions could be summarized as follows (see table 1).

## 9. PROS AND CONS OF TAXING E- RETAILING TRANSACTION

E-Commerce is defined as all the commercial transactions that take place over the Internet, including retail sales of products and services, advertising, and business to business commerce. One thing is clear: electronic commerce will grow to account for hundreds of billions of dollars a year in sales. E- Retailing is poised to takeoff as consumers take advantage of comparison shopping, niche markets, and, importantly, the tax free status of goods bought and sold over the internet. The debate over Internet taxation started several years ago, when Internet was at its earliest stages. In 1998, US Congress passed the Internet Freedom Act, which imposed a 3 year moratorium on new Internet taxes. Presently, states can still tax income earned through Internet service providers. States can also apply local business license taxes to a service provider when it is located in the same jurisdiction, and collect sales taxes on products brought over the internet, if the taxes are imposed in the same manner as taxes on mail order products. The Internet Freedom Act also set up the National Advisory Commission on Electronic Commerce to recommend a course of action for Internet taxation.

### 9.1. On One Side of the Fence

E- commerce growth will produce sales tax numbers that are simply too large to ignore. Due to Internet's income generating potential, state and local policy makers are hard at work opposing any limits on their efforts to reap revenue from the Internet for their treasuries. These groups want to stop the loss of tax revenue through remote sales of items over the internet and are pushing for a variety of changes to

*Table 1. Challenges taxing electronic commerce activities*

| | Types of Challenges | Enforcement of tax legislation to assure authority for: | Application of tax legislation to identify: | Principles challenged in taxing online income |
|---|---|---|---|---|
| 1. | *Establishing Identification* | Has a transaction occurred – where has it taken place and by whom?<br>(Pinto, 2005, p.1) | • the 'virtual' geographical boundaries<br>• location of Taxpayers<br>• vendors engaged in EC<br>• location of business<br>• Taxable entity<br>• Whether electronic transaction is for supply of goods/services<br>• Of the permanent establishment<br>(Pinto, 2005, p.2; Chen & Wang, 2010). | • Of the taxing points as disintermediation takes place<br>• Residence of individual or company<br>• Place of the Source of income<br>• Permanent Establishments<br>• Characterising the nature of income<br>(Li, 2000, p.8; Pinto, 2005; Chen & Wang, 2010). |
| 2. | *Establishing Assurance* | • Appropriate records kept for EC business<br>• Collection of taxes in EC<br>• GST being imposed on the state where final consumption occurs<br>(Pinto, 2005, p.3) | That transaction took place<br>(Chen & Wang, 2010) | That principles of tax are upheld e.g. neutrality, fairness, equity<br>(Li, 2000, Pinto, 2005; Chen & Wang, 2010) |
| 3. | *Establishing Accessibility* | • To electronic records<br>• To tax havens<br>• To state of final consumption | • Electronic records for audit of sales revenue<br>• Customs Procedures<br>(Chen & Wang, 2010, p.24-26) | International tax treaties<br>(Li, 2000, p.10) |
| 4. | *Establishing authority of tax legislation* | • Collection of taxes<br>• Enforcement of penalties<br>• Enforcing existing laws in an online business<br>• Can the existing tax legislations stand in Court for EC cases? | • Applying income tax concepts to EC environment<br>(Chen & Wang, 2010; Pinto, 2005, p.3). | Income Tax Concepts<br>(Li, 2000, p.5) |

the current tax codes. The main reason put forward is that the increased acceptances of online retailing could potentially decrease the tax offers of cities and states. The potentially taxable e- commerce events include access to the Internet; digitized services sold on the Internet; and tangible goods and services sold on the Internet.

Advocates claim that America's tax free e commerce really amounts to tax evasion. Citing a similar struggle with the mail order industry, they argue that states lose $ 4 billion in sales taxes annually from catalog sales since states, cities and countries lack authority to capture sales taxes on catalog sales if the mail order business is headquartered out of state.

Should the call for Internet taxation fail, some state and local officials have argued that they may be forced to raise other taxes to make up for lost revenue. Or request the federal government to cover for the budgetary shortfall. Sales taxes account for up to 40 percent of state revenues.

Another important argument put forward by pro tax supporters is the alleged unfair advantages Internet has over traditional retailers. Exempting "e- tailers" from sales tax is said to give them a competitive advantage over regular retailers. They point that there is no fundamental reason to provide favored treatment to online transactions over similar types of transactions offline. Since other services that are important to the growth of the economy are taxed, there is no reason to favor Internet access and e- commerce. Thus, calling for the composition of tax on all Internet sales would ensure the protection of two things: the revenue base, as well as "main Street" businesses.

## 9.2. On the Other Side

Opponents fear that the imposition of taxes would slow the growth and opportunity of e- commerce, just before it fully gains a foothold among consumers. They fear that introducing taxes now might seriously impede the Internet's growth at a critical stage of early development. Extending the moratorium will enable e-commerce which is relatively new and emerging industry, a chance to develop without market distortions caused by haphazard tax structure. The anti tax camp argues that the Internet, by its very nature cannot be regulated or controlled. Policy makers and business opposing Internet taxes argue that the Internet should remain a global free trade zone, unencumbered by overlapping and discriminatory taxes imposed by the country's taxing jurisdictions. However, if taxes are imposed on Internet commerce, this zone of freedom and opportunity will become enmeshed in government bureaucracies. Another important contention is that the Internet is inherently non geographic. The decentralized nature of the Internet makes it impossible to establish the precise geographic route or endpoints taken by any single transmission. This makes every internet transmission vulnerable to multiple taxation that could stop this rapidly growing medium in its tracks. Although state and local governments enjoy a significant amount of freedom in determining their tax policies, their tax discretion does not extend beyond their geographic boundaries. Taxing the internet may also drive away the dot coms to locations that do not tax them, if we impose taxes that reduce their business. Many of the companies engage in commerce over the Internet do not have to be physically located in the United States. An exodus of e commerce companies could impact the growth of Internet related jobs, a loss that could hurt the economy. Other opponents argue that compliance with thousands of differing local tax rates, would be unduly burdensome on out of state companies, especially for small businesses or for sellers of information goods that are delivered online and often do not have even customer's mailing address. Some argue that the Internet stimulates purchases at retail stores and through catalogs.

## 10. CONCLUSION

These are just some of the issues involving taxation and electronic commerce. It could be argued that e-commerce for the most part will not require new tax principles. And in some cases, new laws may be required or old laws amended. Trade in intangibles or goods that are in digital format promises to be the main problem area. These goods are easily moved electronically across the internet. This is likely to be an area where a multilateral approach is required. By its nature, the parties to such transactions are likely to come from disparate jurisdiction. Establishing tax suites in these cases may be problematic.

The principles of taxation are challenged in online trading. The difficulty in applying the tax definitions to the online environment has shaped legal dilemmas. However this can be overcome. The important issues require legal resolution. The 'emergence of international and global tax dimensions have been subject to continuous negotiations throughout their history in response to changing forms and functions of society'.

Extant tax laws in India do not specifically provide for rules for determining taxability of E-commerce transactions. Certain countries like Singapore, UK and the USA have enacted specific tax legislations to deal with various aspects like levy of VAT, taxability in cases of location of websites in or outside the local jurisdiction, withholding taxes, permanent establishment issues, etc. At India level, the Government of India had set up the High Powered Committee ('HPC') to analyze and recommend the issues relating to E-commerce and the Committee had submitted its report in February 2001. The HPC has also emphasised the need for neutrality between taxation of E-commerce and the commerce carried on in traditional manner. One of the important recommendations is that the concept of PE be abandoned and a serious attempt should be made within OECD and UN to find an alternative to the concept of PE. The alternative recommended by the Committee is based on "base erosion" approach which requires taxation of any payment to a foreign enterprise, if it is tax deductible in the hands of a taxpayer in the source country.

Such initiative on the part of the Government is a step in the right direction; however, there has not been any significant traction on the same and it merely continues to have guidance value. The need to the hour is to give shape to the guidelines with appropriate inputs from all the stakeholders to avoid unwarranted litigation and at the same time protect interests of the Revenue.

## REFERENCES

Bruce, D., & Fox, W. (2001). *State and Local Sales Tax Revenue Losses from E-Commerce: Updated Estimates.* Retrieved from http://cber.bus.utk.edu/ecomm/Ecom0901.pdf

Chen, S., & Wang, J. S. (2010). Tax Evasion and Fraud Detection: A Theoretical Evaluation of Taiwan's Business Tax Policy for Internet Auctions. *Asian Social Science, 6*(12), 23-35. Retrieved from http://www.ccsenet.org/journal/index.php/ass/article/view/7067/6242

Kemp, J. (2000). *Governors' Scheme to Tax Internet is Questionable and Unsound.* Retrieved from http://www.caltax.org/MEMBER/digest /mar2000/mar00-2.htm

Li, J. (2000). E-Commerce Tax Policy in Australia, Canada and the United States. *Wales Law Journal, 23*(2), 313–329.

Maguire, S. (2005). *Congressional Research Service: Report for Congress: State and Local Sales and Use Taxes and Internet Commerce.* Retrieved from http://www.ipmall.info/hosted_resources/crs/RL31252_050128.pdf

Ngoy, J. M. (2003). Is international e-commerce an HIV tax issue? *International Journal of Services Technology and Management, 4*(1), 53. doi:10.1504/IJSTM.2003.002571

Pinto, D. (2005). Ten Tax Issues Relating to conducting business in cyberspace. *Journal of Internet Banking and Commerce, 10*(1), 1-9. Retrieved from http://www.arraydev.com/commerce/jibc/

Shelton, A. (2001). *Should State and Local Government Tax E-commerce.* Retrieved from http://www.aarp.org/research/economy/taxation/aresearch-import-393-INB41.htm

Section 6

# Case Study

# Chapter 16
# Case Study E-Tailing Health Services in India

**Bobby Kurian**
*Jain University, India*

## ABSTRACT

*This case study has been developed to promote understanding the e-tailing of health services. E-health web portal provides a new medium for information dissemination, interaction and collaboration among institutions, health professionals, health providers and the public. This case study provides a founders perspective in setting up and running a medical website that offers online health care services to customers across the world. The case study discusses the challenges and issues faced by the founders and also the promoter's perspective on the lucrativeness of offering e-tailing services. Using this case study an attempt is made to stress the importance of a flexible e-tailing business model specific to the services offered and need of periodic assessments to ensure that the business runs profitable.*

## INTRODUCTION

Three IT professionals with 15 years of e-commerce experience decided to come together and launch an e-commerce company in 2010. The idea was to launch an online health portal aiming to educate, guide, and help patients make informed health decisions. They pooled in their savings and funded the company. The strategy behind the formation of this company was to take advantage of the booming medical tourism in India. Several features have positioned India as an ideal healthcare destination including cost effective healthcare solutions, availability of skilled healthcare professionals, and advanced healthcare treatments.

The idea of an e-commerce company providing health services online was relatively new. The company's initial approach was to reach out to those users who were interested in availing quality medical treatment information online. The e-health portal which was launched on June, 2010 acted as an online guide to let users know the details of hospitals in their locality. Initially, company's focus was on the revenues from advertisement. The revenue was mainly expected from the advertisements (Google Ads and hospital Ads). The internet portal platform and the underlying business model changed multiple times as the founders tried various ways to boost up company's online business.

DOI: 10.4018/978-1-4666-9921-2.ch016

Copyright © 2016, IGI Global. Copying or distributing in print or electronic forms without written permission of IGI Global is prohibited.

## BACKGROUND

Shopping has assumed a brand-new look, thanks to the vast number of ecommerce sites today. Accessibility, ease of purchase, value shopping, and enhanced security contribute to the wave of shopping sprees at today's online shopping malls. Mind boggling discounts and promotional attractions lure new Internet consumers and convince shoppers to return and spend even more of their budgets online.

Initially only few items sold well on the Web. Books, CDs and personal computers were among the first to find their niche in electronic commerce, and subsequently the first to achieve major sales. But later, everything that you can and cannot get in a store find its place in online sites. There are now many businesses that sells 'only available on internet' products which one can't get elsewhere. Many brick-and-mortar stores now turning into multichannel merchants (who own brick-and-mortar stores, and Internet sites) and Internet-only businesses. Sites are now becoming mobile friendly and m-commerce or app based online shopping are now a trend.

E-tailing also known as E-retailing had its start in 1996, when Amazon.com launched its virtual market place where goods from producers are directly sold to intended buyers. This move totally commercialized the internet. The next year, in 1997, Dell Systems hit headlines when it made a record profit by selling its computer goods via online. Many other ventures like Barnes & Noble, 3M, Target, Compustore, Costco, etc., joined in.

In simple terms E-tailing refers to the selling of retail goods on the Internet. It's a business-to-consumer (B2C) transaction. There are many reasons consumers get logged into E-Tailing websites. Many find attractive pricing options on these sites. Some value the time saved for the purchase while others get attracted due to the ease in which one can compare and choose the right products. Also the deals and the quick delivery to home make the virtual e-tailing marketplace more attractive. In today's highly dynamic market environment it's not only the price but the also the customer experience that has huge potential to influence the purchases. These days, the e-tailing stores are giving many brick and mortar stores a run for their money. In order to keep its market share many well know brick and mortar shops are either becoming active partners in the e-tailing business or starting their own e-tailing business that's based on a hybrid model.

In the year 2000, India focused E-tailing business started gaining ground. The economic surge and young high earning individuals were the early targets. Slowly as the Indian economy started showing steady growth more players started entering the field. Thriving job markets in Indian Metros and a unbelievable pace of outsourcing to India with changing life styles created an apt atmosphere for the e-tailing business to flourish. Also was the government infrastructure build-up especially lower internet charge and availability of cheap and quality internet band width and had major impact on the e-tailing process. The smart phone users as well as laptop ownership among the youth started growing in a mind boggling rate.

PWC, in its 2014 report shows that more than 16% of the total population in India is online and the percentage is expect to double in the coming years. The same report also shows the fast racing pace in which the E-Commerce and E-Tailing are growing in India. PwC research suggests that the E-Tailing share in India with respect to Re-tailing currently at a mere .5% is expected to grow to 3% by 2020.

A whitepaper published by Technopak titled "E-tailing in India, 2013" raises two key infrastructure elements which are must (and often outside the scope of businesses) to enable the growth of e-tailing. The first element is the penetration of devices through which to access the Internet. Usage of PCs, laptops, tablets, and smartphones had become more affordable and penetration of these devices is rapidly increasing. The second key item is the explosion of technologies enabling Internet access. Now mobile internet and broadband access are becoming cheaper for a large section of the households and with the roll out of 3G and 4G wireless technology, accessing internet using mobile devices become common.

Over these years e-tailing business in India grown into different sub-types like those offering general e-stores, specialized e-stores, e-malls, manufacture direct selling models, e-broker models, e-auctions and the latest those providing e-services direct to the consumers.

E-Tailing services means providing services to the customers directly. Providing online exam coaching, Visa services, Health Services, etc. are examples of E-Tailing services business. Providing health services online started early in the United States when an online company called 'WebMed.com' started reaching out to consumers with an striking tagline 'Better Information, Better Health'. Sooner many companies like Mayoclinic.com, askmydoctor.com etc started. Most of these online healthcare offering services concentrated on providing credible information about health subjects that matter to the consumers.

The advantage of internet to find out quality and cost efficient treatment facilities spurred the growth of Medical tourism business. Some like to call Medical Tourism as 'Medical value travel' since it refers to patients seeking healthcare beyond the borders. Earlier it was the APAC region that attracted much the medical value travel especially Singapore and Thailand. Slowly as the Indian economy started making smart moves, much interest was generated on the low cost quality care available in India.

Over the last 5 year period, stunning figures were reported about foreign patients availing heath care in India. India became one of the most sought after destination for medical tourists across the globe due to the affordable cost, talented specialists and globally accredited hospitals. Another reason was the Ayurveda Hospitals & Yoga centres, something India owns exclusively.

A brief report on healthcare, telemedicine and medical tourism in India (2015) published by ASA & Associates, a Delhi based chartered accountants firm, suggest healthcare revenue in India is set to reach US$280 billion by 2020.The report suggest that the current size of the healthcare industry represent a US$40 billion industry and 71% of it comes from the hospitals. Those in high demand are orthopedic joint replacement surgery and open heart surgery available in India at an affordable rate. Another blooming area is related cosmetic surgery and infertility treatments, since these procedures do not have proper medical insurance schemes available at patient's home country making it a costly affair to handle.

KPMG, one of the largest consulting firm in the world, published its 2014 India Analysis report that clearly underlined the reasons why foreign travellers choose India as their treatment destination. 40% of the stakeholders surveyed agreed on the advanced medical technology available in India. Ministry of India - tourism department's statistics on patients availing treatment facilities in the period 2009-2012 shows about 6.5 million medical foreign tourist travel in the year 2012 alone and numbers are showing considerable growth. The KPMG report does a comparison and points out the affordability of the treatment packages in India compared to other countries. KPMG India analysis put the savings into the range of 30% to 70% when compared to countries like USA and UK.

India's prestige as a credible treatment destination is on a rise. The health care sector in India has becomes one of the largest business segment. The industry comprises not only hospitals and clinics but also medical tourism, telemedicine and clinical trials. The company in this case study tried to tap into the medical tourism opportunity using an attractive online portal. However having a website was not enough; it should be able to win consumer confidence.

## KEY SUCCESS FACTORS FOR E-TAILING BUSINESS

E-tailing as a new form of retailing that bring businesses of all sizes to levels of national and international growth. Tiernan, Bernadette (2000) conclude that a well-received e-tail efforts incorporate up-to-the-moment trend analyses, broad project management, promising technical design, insightful customer responsiveness, smart marketing and sales, solid security, and more.

Many large as well as small businesses are making big moves onto the Internet. German market research organization yStats.com published a report titled “The World’s Leading E-Commerce Companies 2014” which contained a list of top ten e-Commerce companies in terms of revenue. Amazon.com was credited with No.1 ecommerce seller in the world followed by JD.com and Walmart.com. Indian story was not different. Funded by large global investors, the e-tailing market in India is skyrocketing. As per Redseer consulting company research report titled “E-Tailing Market in India, 2011”, horizontal players that sell products across all verticals, dominate the Indian e-tailing market . The key players are Amazon, Snapdeal and Flipkart which contribute majority of the e-tailing sales. There are niche players operating in the vertical segment like home products, fashion and health care products, but these constitute a small portion of the market presently, but are growing swiftly.

The mantra for e-tailing success depends on taking a long-range view. Businesses entering the e-tailing market must recognize the potential in niche segments and provide services that are understandable. Their websites must be brilliant, informative, and functional to give consumers a great shopping experience. The site should allow forming a meaningful connection with your customers if you ever want them to return, and if you want them to spread the good news about you. The e-tailing business model must have an intense customer focus. Meeting what the customers need, ensuring happy customer experience and making appropriate changes to the process to win customer loyalty are all important in e-tailing.

Plenty of literature was available on the key considerations that E-tailing websites should look into, to be successful. As the areas of study related to the E-tailing websites were very extensive, author decided to confine the scope of the paper to briefly touch on six categories.

### User Appeal of the E-Tailing Website

When designing an e-commerce site, it is tempting to ignore users of the site and follow up standard templates that are available or copy designs from other competing sites. But customers often depend on websites that are simple and to the point. The website should be attractive and user-friendly to satisfy the user. The design that matters is the inclusion of appealing high quality images and content the customer is interested in.

Many online visitors consider online shopping - be it for services or products, as a real stress buster. If the site is designed in an engaging way, they are sure to make the purchase. By making site intuitive, the obstacles that deter purchase decisions are largely reduced.

To build a customer-centred web site the creators also need to understand the environment in which people will access the site. The environment includes the physical environment (e.g. light levels), the socio-cultural environment (e.g. sharing of information) and the technical environment (e.g. browser version). David Travis (2003) explains an appealing e-commerce site as probably with one or more of the following:

1. **Useful:** It does something that is hard to do in any other way.
2. **Flexible:** It allows you to solve a problem in more than one way.
3. **Memorable:** It is easy to remember how to do most things.
4. **Quick to Learn:** Most people can get going with the system fairly quickly.
5. **Fun to Use:** Using the product is fun in its own right,
6. **Attractive:** It is engaging to look at.
7. **Efficient:** It helps you get things done more quickly or more cheaply.
8. **Simple:** The most important things can be done in one or two steps.

## Security Aspects of E-Tailing Website

E-commerce Security is implemented to protect e-commerce assets from unauthorized access, use, alteration, or destruction. It has got different dimensions that include integrity protection that generally includes prevention against unauthorized data modification, authenticity, confidentiality, and protection of privacy. The most important ones were related to the payment gateways. Transmitting credit card data over secure channels was the utmost importance of every customer in the site. They look for the 'https' secure channel links as well as the certificate banners displayed to make sure that they are not dealing with a fake website. The consumer wants to ensure that the payment made reach its intended recipient and the site provides his a receipt for the same. The customer also wants to ensure that service will be delivered to him as promised. Normally website provides customer service and helpline numbers for the customers to follow up in case of delay in delivering the services. Most of the e-commerce sites does store the data in encrypted form to avoid data being compromised by hackers.

E-commerce provider takes multiple security strategies to reduce the risk of external site attacks that can compromise the security significantly. Awareness of the risks and the implementation of multi-layered security protocols, detailed and open privacy policies and strong authentication and encryption measures will help to assure the consumer and insure the risk of compromise of security breech at a minimal level (Eamonn, 2015).

Organizations like CERT and SANS published a guideline documents to help develop secure websites. Standards like ISO 17799, COBIT, etc., provide detailed instruction to implement enterprise security. As cyber criminals get more and more sophisticated in deceptions and hacking, its important for e-tailing site to be aware of the dangers of security risk and the impact it will have on their business.

## Design Architecture of the E-Tailing Website

Many times the e-commerce site designers focus on functionality than thinking about the customers who will be actually deciding the business success. The web designers make beautiful workflows and incorporate superb functionalities and freeze the design and hand it over for launch. Such frozen platforms or architecture create big mishaps later as they are not easy to be changed on the run, and may need to shut down, thereby making the site unavailable to the users. Hence it's critical for any web site managers to spent adequate time on capturing requirements, and then freeze the underlying architecture.

Adaptability, flexibility and responsiveness to the changing requirements and conditions is the most essential characteristic required for any e-tailing company (Barnes et al, 2001).Flexibility in the design structure of the site highly significant too. It needs to be clearly distinguished from screen layouts – the individual pages that the customer sees on screen. (Travis, 2003).The architecture issues need to be resolved before the detailed screen design – or you may find yourself with an information architecture that cannot evolve to include your next range of products, your new ways of working, or the new delivery channels you decide to introduce in a few years' of time. Retrofitting these features will be expensive and will almost certainly confuse returning customers who have got used to your earlier site.

## Marketing through the E-Tailing Website and Search Engine Optimization

For any business, marketing is the key mantra to reach target audience. And in E-commerce space, learning who your target viewers are and how to 'get your customer spot you' is exceptionally critical. Today, more than 300 billion of searches are made online to gather information. Vanessa Fox (2010) in her book 'Marketing in the Age of Google' describe search as the 'Entry Point of the Web'.

Herbert Simon (1971) was right in his prediction about information abundance. He highlighted the issue with this statement: "…in an information-rich world, the wealth of information means a dearth of something else: a scarcity of whatever it is that information consumes. What information consumes is rather obvious: it consumes the attention of its recipients. Hence a wealth of information creates a poverty of attention and a need to allocate that attention efficiently among the overabundance of information sources that might consume it."

More than 90 percent of the online population uses a search engine to find products, services, and information. Search Engine Optimization (SEO) plays a huge part in increasing brand visibility, bringing in new customers as well as existing ones, and generating interest from targeted audiences. (Leena, 2015). For online retailers, it creates a powerful viewer traffic, which naturally results in increased sales. Kirthi Kalyanam (2002) posits that e-marketing is about enabling relational exchanges in digital networked and interactive environments and discuss about the development of the e-marketing mix by enabling the holistic consideration of various e-marketing functions. Janal (2000), in Dan Janal's Guide to Marketing on the Internet, give out a set of checklist on best practices of online advertising. Lorrie Thomas (2011),explains different types of online advertisings possibilities including Vertical Search (specific search engines like yellow pages),Display Advertising (banner ads),E-Mail Marketing, Viral Marketing (also referred to as word-of-mouth marketing), News Sites (AdWords),Blog Marketing, Behavioral Advertising, Social Media Advertising and Affiliate Marketing.

Search-engine optimization, or SEO, is the process getting the site listed in top ranking when one does searches in major search engines, including Google, Yahoo, and MSN. Such organic searches are generally free and it takes good programmic skills and patience to get them listed on the search engine pages. The processes of getting into SEO give rise to the emergence of a skillset among experts known as Social media optimization technique. Many along with SEO uses the paid service of PRC which meant pay per click. Quality score optimization, or QSO, talks about quality score improvement that being considered by many search engine algorithms to be listed in its search results. Optimization of meta tags are also crucial. It's the meta tag magic that gives all the description and details when a search result was displayed directly underneath the title tag. Thus Meta tags must have compelling statements about the service or product offered at the site. However as the search algorithms became smarter, there influence in getting better visibility reduced (Kristopher B. Jones, 2008).

## Cost Saving Model

Many Internet startups failed because their business models and strategies were flawed. In their purest form, the initial (pioneering) phase in the application of business models and strategies for an internet startup is the perceived opportunity to transform an industry. New Internet-based firms would challenge the established firms in an industry or sector and drive change based on the innovative use of technology to deliver low pricing and radical improvements in service levels. Most startups obtained equity-based funding or venture capital support and ran at an operating loss as they spent massive amounts of money on advertising to attract customers. (Steve Elliot, 2002),

Joseph. H. Wen et al, (2001) identify two major Web site design strategies: `informational/ communicational design strategy' and `on-line/transactional design strategy.' The models for informational/ communicational design strategy include brand awareness and image building, cost saving, promotion, and infomediary. The models for on-line transactional design strategy include brokerage, retail, mall, advertising, subscription, community, manufacturer, and customization.

By directly meeting information needs of the customer an e-tailing site can offer its consumers productivity saving and if the strategy in place, a better cost effective deals can be displayed to the user. Rather than reaching out to certain vendors by offline or personal contacts and discussing the users need, a well-designed site provide option for the user to aim to the right spot the customer is interested in. If the displayed information is appropriate and attractive deals are clubbed with the information, then the customer will be very much attracted to the site and perform business transactions.

## Trust Factor

Trust is not merely the exchange of objects. Rather, it emerges as a result of sustained interaction in which the parties continually take note of the coherence between their held paradigm (of trust or mistrust) and the actual behavior of the partner in the interaction (Stuart Barnes,et al,2001). But the issue with web world is that interactions are short lived. This may that web based organizations would need to set up elaborate structures of help desk, guarantees and guarantors – compliance through contracts and agreements to evolve into a trusted business partner

David Travis (2003) defines E-commerce trust indicators to measure the success of an e-commerce venture. He broadly classifies it into three categories as conversion rate, fulfillment, and customer retention. Conversion rate is simply the percentage of customers who do what you want them to do as a result of using your site: this might be purchasing a product, Fulfillment is about more than just making sure the product arrives punctually. What customers are looking for is some feedback that their order has been placed and is being dealt with. It makes no sense to have an easy-to-use web site if week-long delays are introduced at the delivery stage. Customer retention can be tracked by the number of clients coming back into the site. Khalid Adiri et al (2008) propose in their paper titled 'The Human Face of E-Business' that in B2C e-commerce applications it is very important to take cultural aspects into consideration when designing an e-commerce Web site. Appropriate and culturally sensitive website allows users to stay long and hooked to the site and thereby incrementing the trust factor. Selecting photos of customer service representatives and displaying their contact details in the targeted markets represent an easy way to enhance the vendors' trustworthiness.

Jaclyn Easton (1999) of strikeitrich.com provides an interesting narration. Jaclyn describe the rules that were applied at Amazon.com that have contributed enormously are,

1. Obsess over your customers.
2. Remember that the Web is an infant.
3. If you make one customer unhappy, he won't tell five friends— he'll tell 5,000 on social media, newsgroups and so on.

Researchers have highlighted the lack of a common model for trust in e-commerce, mainly due to the multi-dimensional nature. Petrovic.O et al, (2003) mentions trust levels during transaction phases as information phase (where Trust in built), agreement phase (where trust is confirmed), and settlement phase (where trust is maintained). In this research work, trust is divided into 6 key elements namely 'state of the art security', 'merchant legitimacy', 'fulfillment', 'tone and ambience', 'control', and collaboration. These elements combine to create site loyalty.

In any e-commerce business the transaction may be divided into three phases (Schmid, 1993; Zbornik, 1996): information, agreement and settlement. In the Information phase, customers collect information about products and services. Finding an attractive and compelling information package satisfies the customer to go into the next phase which is the agreement phase. In the agreement phase value propositions with competitors and other choices are debated and negotiated. The phase is crucial and cultivates a 'customer binding' by establishing a healthy business relationship between supplier and buyer that will eventually lead to a contract, payment, delivery and so on. Once this phase over, settlement phase begins which is the last step. The physical delivery of services/products happens here and it's were customer satisfaction matters.

## RESEARCH METHODOLOGY

The following figure (Figure 1) explain the conceptual framework followed for this research study

Two main sources of data were used for this chapter:

1. Interviews with the people responsible for bring up an e-tailing website (e-health services) to determine the reasons behind the initiative, their experiences in setting up and managing the e-commerce platform, and their future plans;
2. Literature Reviews on e-tailing business.

## CASE STUDY CONTEXT

The case study analysis is organized in different headings. This is to provide an overview of the e-health business, to present the challenges faced by the business (e.g., expand markets, competition, technology, product planning, strategic planning, marketing, manage the supply chain etc.), and to show how to plan for the future in the e-tailing world. The case covers an e-tailing company's transition in different stages. This study offers an owner's perspective from the relevant business angles and ways to sustain

*Figure 1. Conceptual framework*

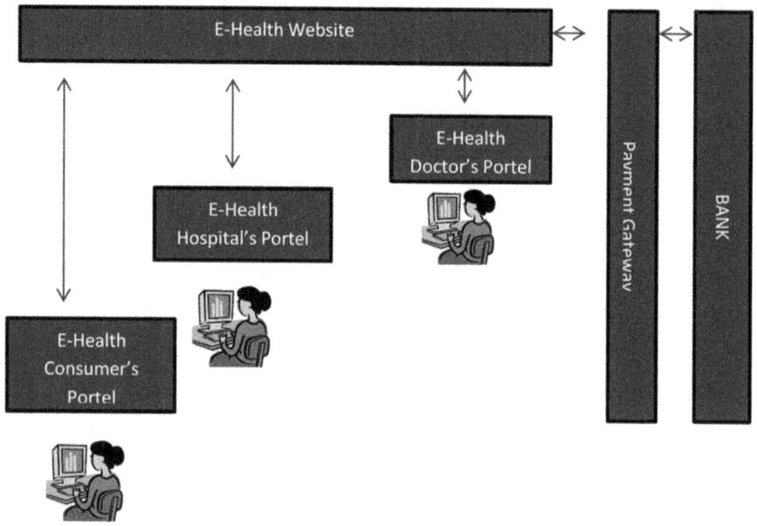


its business. This case demonstrates that a rich website with nice animation or high end graphics won't give profit. By examining this case, an attempt is made to educate on the significance of developing right business model in the highly imitable e-tailing environment

The e-health portal had two critical components: a B2C element (Business to Consumer) and a B2B element (Business to Business). B2C portal as displayed in the Figure 2 above has direct dealing with customers who want to receive medical services from the site. The consumers pay when they book a treatment assistance service through the site as per their requirement. The B2B portal allows hospitals and consultants/clinics to associate with the company for a yearly fee and offer their services through the portal. The company also tied up with players including leading medical pharmacies, hotel chains and foreign exchange institutions to offer discounts to users.

The company started with a vision to be remembered as most trustworthy and compassionate health care facilitator around the globe. Company's mission statement read 'best affordable medical treatment for customers around the world'

The core services offered includes:

1. Comprehensive Information (Hospital, Doctor and Treatment Details);
2. VISA Assistance;
3. Treatment Scheduling -Doctor's Appointments and Procedure planning;
4. Airport Pick up and Drop;
5. Accommodation assistance near the hospital;
6. Interpreter services;
7. Forex facilities;
8. Post Treatment Follow ups;
9. Recreational Trips.

Amenities and facilities offered by our associated hospitals:

*Figure 2. Business to customer health services*

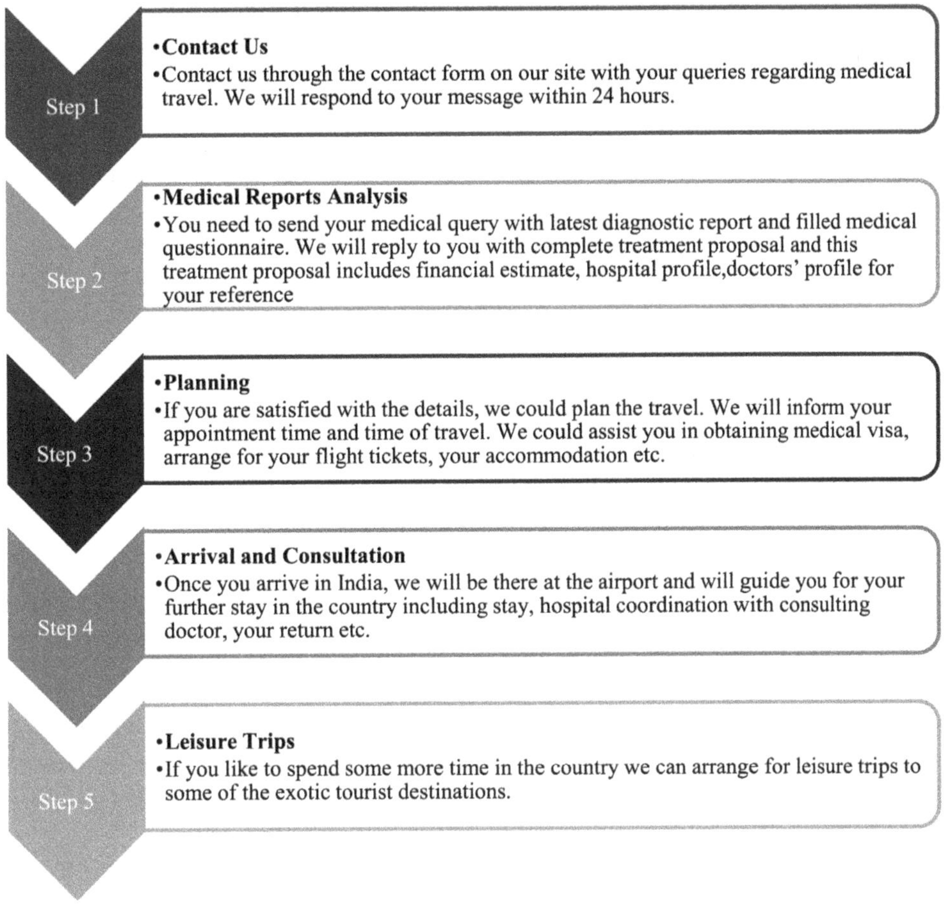


1. Quick and complimentary review of medical reports;
2. Dedicated patient coordinator to take care of all your requirements;
3. Language interpreters;
4. Assistance with visa formalities and other regulatory approvals;
5. Choice of deluxe suites, single and twin-sharing rooms;
6. Complimentary stay for one attendant during hospital admission;
7. Choice of international cuisines to suit your taste;
8. TVs with international entertainment channels;
9. 24-Hour Pharmacy and Healthcare store ensuring that all medicines are authentic and stored as per the required standards. The store also has a convenience store section catering to your other daily needs like toiletries;
10. 24x7 room service;
11. Gift and souvenir shop so that you take good memories along with good health;
12. In-house salon and spa to spruce you up.

The standard process flow of the e-health offer is shown in the flow chart shown in Figure 3.

*Figure 3. Standard process flow chart of the online health services company*

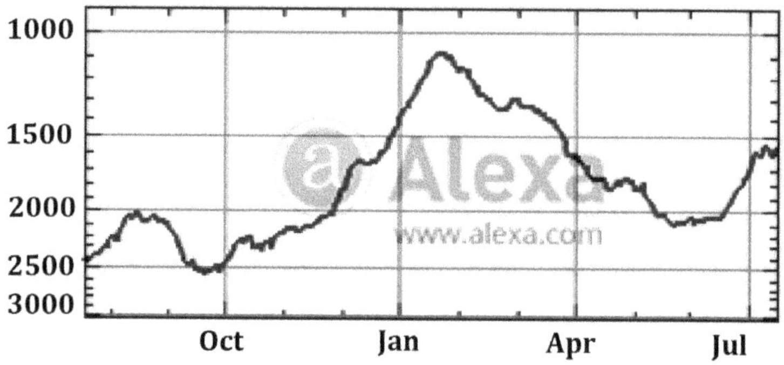


The company started with a solid, interactive and smooth user interface with easily navigable menus and professional with high quality images. The site boasted of a polished design that can be viewed even from a smart phone with 5 inch screen size .The site provided a simple, streamlined shopping cart, with an integrated secure payment gateway system from a leading vendor.

## EVOLUTION OF A PROFITABLE E-HEALTH SERVICE STRATEGY

From a case study perspective, the following passages are divided into three stages. This is to showcase the importance of key factors. In each stage, there were certain road blocks faced by the company. The below passage will explain the steps implemented by its founders at each stage to keep the business grow and achieve healthy revenue flow.

**Stage 1:** Informative site for Medical Treatment in India.

When the company started this e-service business, there were hardly any players in the market. In the beginning the site was offering hospital advertisements and providing doctor/hospital information free of charge. The idea was to be an online health portal aiming to help patients to make informed health decisions. The founders worked hard to build a data bank of the hospitals and physicians in each locality. Any customers who want to get treated for a symptom are asked to browse through the site and find out the best possible match of the category of specialties. Once the specialty is identified the location preferred is shown. Once the location is selected, then the hospital or doctor in that location for the chosen specialty is listed with contact information. There is also search directly by the hospital name or doctor name or the specialty.

Without any mentionable unique value proposition to the customers, this e-tailing of health services did not worked well. The website recorded a low traffic during its 9 month period after inception. Below Figure (Figure 4) shows the Alexa Traffic Ranks recorded in 2011-12 period. [Alexa.com is a wholly owned subsidiary of Amazon.com and specializes in the commercial web traffic data and analytics]. Alexa web traffic graph for 2011-12 period shows there were around 1500 visitors on average thorough the year which is a low traffic rate for an e-tailing service offering.

*Figure 4. Alexa traffic ranks recorded in 2011-12 period*

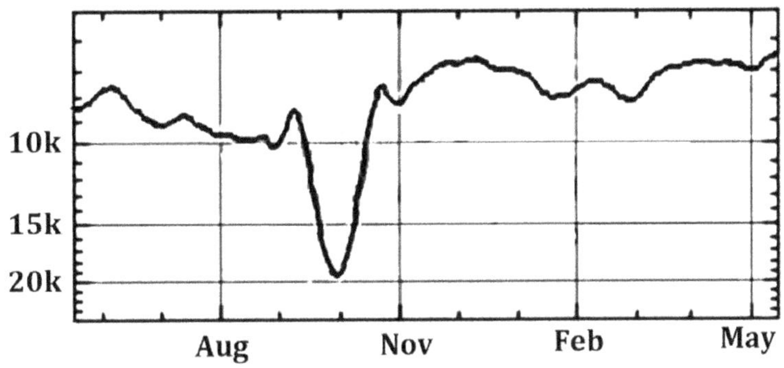


**Stage 2:** Setting a Unique Selling Point.

The idea of getting into e-tailing of health services was new in India. But the search and getting the hospital information was not difficult. The entrepreneurs considered such offerings as less attractive since these are easy to find using a Google search with descriptions. The returns on investment (ROI) from the portal were unimpressive. The revenue generated by such sites were based on the site traffic and traditionally such web site gave minimal returns.

The founders decided to add value to the website customers. They introduced a concept of 'Happy Hospital Care' for needy patients. The idea was to make the hospital admissions to final discharge, hassle-free. To make this concept a success, the founders invested in forming tie-up with leading private practitioners and specialty hospitals. Funding for web portal enhancements and marketing were quickly available, since the medical tourism boom in India attracted more venture capital fund flows into the company.

The founders redesigned the entire site. They transformed the portal to a more 'dynamic' site than a 'stand-alone' one. By 'dynamic', it meant not only information of health providers, but more of supporting services for a fee. The motto was to make hospital admission to hospital discharge processes (inpatient procedures) easy and economical. To make these services cost effective for the consumers, the company set up 'partnerships' with leading hospitals and private medical consultants. The partnership was based on a commission basis. To take care of those with insurance claims, the idea of tying up with insurance firms also mooted. Considering the huge medical tourism demand in India a visa support facility and foreign traveler assistance team was set up. The team consisted members with knowledge of different spoken languages. As part of other premium services offered, pick up from airports to the nearest treatment location, were arranged. Also a special officer was assigned to the patient to take care of the foreign traveler's arrival formalities at the airport. Another premium facility offer provided best in class accommodation to people accompanying the patient.

There was also well-ness products that are mainly focused for tourists who want to avail the traditional healing techniques available in India. There were exclusive Ayurveda treatment offers to interested parties including Body Detoxification Package, Rejuvenation Package, Weight loss/Slimming Program and Pancha karma Therapy, etc. Such programs are conducted in exotic resorts in south India and sold at a premium price package. In order to make effective customer connect, company setup an online chat assistance service to guide the users. The site also added latest medical news and upcoming health & medical events using its blogs and social media pages.

The company's Alexa traffic ranking improved after implementing many value add features to the website. The Figure (Figure 5) shows the Alexa traffic pattern for the year 2012-13.

Even with a good traffic rate of 10000 visits, the site did not generate much revenue and the founders were facing an uphill task of informing the investors why the system not working.

**Stage 3:** With SEO and Aggressive Marketing.

The entrepreneurs wondered why such a great idea of affordable online health solution service was not clicking. They had the right strategic vision. The company used enough marketing tools to get more hospital and doctors added to its portfolio services. The site was well personalized. Price packages are affordable and competitive. The website has nice user interface and easily accessible menu design. The payment gateway was offered by a leading service provider. The payment processes were completely secure and safety was guaranteed. Still some gaps remain that blocked the site success.

Founders wondered what need to be done next to make company profitable. They decided to do a deep market analysis again and tasked a research firm to do this part. Research firm after meticulous studies of the market and the site offerings, finally arrived at one major reason why the business not taking off. The firm described the issue as – "Not getting the right customers landed on the portal". Even though the site traffic was good, the site was not getting into the eyes of serious customers.

Armed with the survey firm's suggestion, the team decided to use aggressive online marketing and advertising. Activities like Search Engine Optimization (SEO) and Marketing are employed and started giving them results. The company also spread its brand by targeting communications, including both online and offline channels, with an aggressive promotional campaign. Rather than the casual online visitors, the focus was on to the 'serious visitor' who want treatment advice.

All these activities made a dramatic rise in the website traffic and in 2013 the site saw a decent daily traffic of around 40000 user hits (Figure 6). The services availed by the customer shot up and around 152 treatment services were offered in that period.

**Stage 4:** Incorporating the TRUST Factor.

The site traffic saw great improvement. However the conversion of site traffic into sales (of health services) was not up to mark. Much of the profit generated was spend on advertisement. The company

*Figure 5. Alexa traffic pattern for the year 2012-13*

*Figure 6. Alexa traffic pattern in the year 2013-2014*

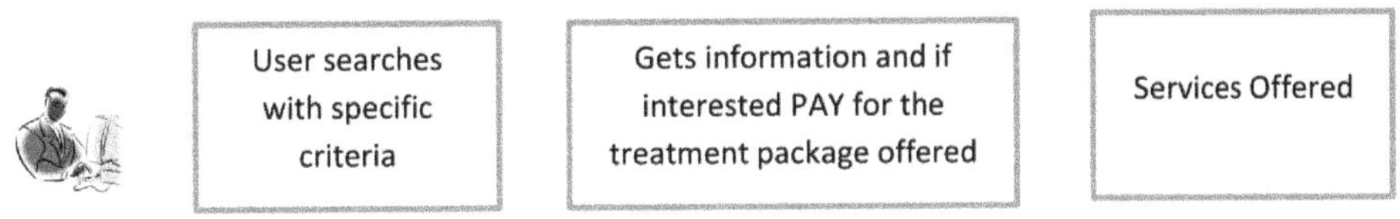


founders started debating why a website with such high traffic is not giving good financial returns. After discussing with experts and other veterans in the e-tailing field they understood that building up strong trust, the TRUST factor, is missing in their business model.

They decided to alter the below process (Figure 7).

To gain trust and invite more clients, an idea of free consultation was mooted. The strategy was to offer a free medical advice and screening through the website. The website provided an option for the user to scan and upload medical reports, and this later get analyzed by an expert medical team which will send a free online consultation voucher to the user. The user using this voucher will log on to an audio conference provided in the site. The user discusses his medical problems with the appropriate medical staff and an initial analysis is provided free of cost. Based on the reports, different options available to the patient were described. If the user decides to proceed further, then the payment and other formalities were initiated. The user has the liberty to spend much time discussing online with the practitioner and clear the doubts before availing paid services.

The new process flow is shown in Figure 8.

As the volume of such requests increased the company setup a dedicated 24/7 call center to answer the queries and appointed specialist doctors. These doctors constituted a team to assess and evaluate the reports uploaded and draft initial health advice for each user. This service did not prescribe any medicines or treatment procedures.

As more and more customers got connected to the portal and consultation with doctor, the call volume increased. Around 30% of such callers later availed paid services. The site traffic further boosted by mouth to mouth publicity and many patients from abroad started availing the premium services. The site is now running at good profit with around 45 paid patient services per month from India and abroad. Many Health magazines run the company advertisements. The dedicated software team takes care of the mobile application and regular upgrading of the website. The mobile app is popular among all the mobile platforms, and mobile apps are turning out to be the most used technology for availing the health services.

The company has now plans to enter in the field of Infertility management and treatment by comprehensive range of infertility services. Fertility treatments are expensive abroad. In India, there were

*Figure 7. Updated business process flow*

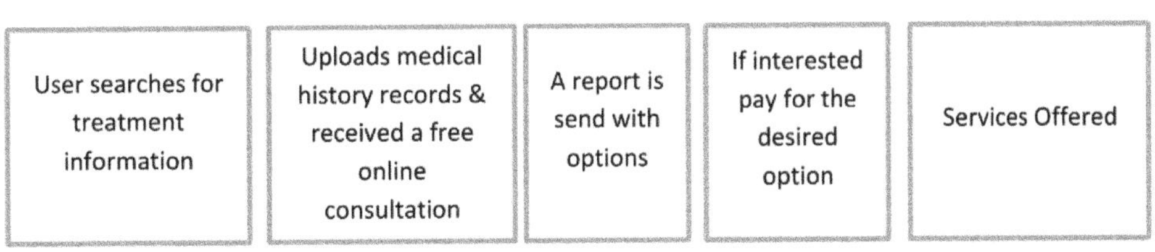

*Figure 8. Business process flow further fine-tuned*

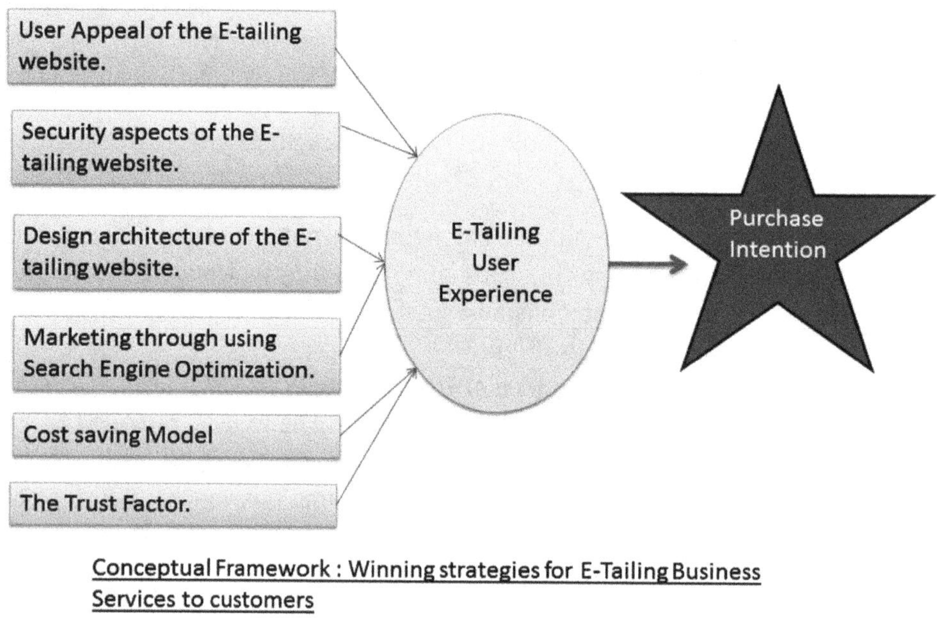


a number of good hospitals offering economical assisted reproductive therapy. As per the expansion plans, the company plans to come up with an exclusive and dedicated web portal to help people with fertility issues. The company is in talks with leading fertility experts to offer customized fertility care packages and treatment financing plans for its customers. The idea was to utilize low cost fertility care and offer packages to needy customers by cutting down expensive IVF/fertility treatment costs without compromising the quality of treatment.

## CONCLUSION

The purpose of this paper is to present and explain the fine-tuning of e-tailing practices by an online health service provider in each of the above three phases. As detailed in the case study, the idea of having a business model is absolutely important to the success of any e-tailing business. But to add is the extreme importance of building the trust with online customers, since the company is living in the virtual web and making a personal 'connection' can do wonders. Investing significantly in customer service and winning their 'trust' is the key to the success of any e-tailing firm. To make the e-tailing business a success one need to continuously observe at your back end and make changes as necessary. Search engine optimization and online/offline marketing campaigns targeting the 'right' customer base are unconditionally required for the online business to grow. With all of these in places, it will be easier to attain the vision of being a successful and useful e-tailing business serving a large pool of satisfied and happy customers.

## REFERENCES

Aldiri, K., Hobbs, D., & Qahwaji, R. (2008). The Human Face of E-Business: Engendering Consumer Initial Trust Through the Use of Images of Sales Personnel on E-Commerce Web Sites. *International Journal of E-Business Research*, *4*(4).

Barnes, S., & Hunt, B. (2001). *E-Commerce and V-Business*. Oxford, Great Britain: Reed Educational and Professional Publishing.

Bijlani, J. (2015). eCommerce in India: Accelerating growth. *PWC*. Retrieved from http://www.pwc.in/assets/pdfs/publications/2015/ecommerce-in-india-accelerating-growth.pdf

Bisen, A., Singh, P., & Anand, A. (2013, May). E-tailing in India: Unlocking the Potential (White Paper). *Technopak*. Retrieved from http://www.technopak.com/files/E-tailing_in_India.pdf

Dan, J. (2000). *Dan Janal's Guide to Marketing on the Internet*. New Jersey: John Wiley & Sons Publishing, Inc.

David, T. (2003). *E-Commerce Usability: Tools and Techniques to Perfect the On-Line Experience*. UK: Taylor & Francis Publishing.

Eamonn, R. (2015). Major Security Issues in Ecommerce. *WebScience*. Retrieved from http://webscience.ie/docs/Webscience White Paper-Security Issues in E-Commerce.pdf

Elliot, S. (2002). *Electronic Commerce: B2C Strategies and Models*. UK: Wiley & Sons Ltd.

Fox, V. (2010). *Marketing in the Age of Google*. New Jersey: John Wiley & Sons, Inc.

Gordon, S. (2004). E-Commerce: A Control and Security Guide. Hoboken, New Jersey: John Wiley & Sons.

Jaclyn, E. (1999). *Profiles of 23 Incredibly Successful Websites You've Probably Never Heard Of*. Manhattan, New York: McGraw-Hill Publishing.

Jing, Y. (2009). On-line Payment and Security of E-commerce. *Proceedings of the China International Symposium on Web Information Systems and Applications*.

Kalyanam, K., & McIntyre, S. (2002). The E-Marketing Mix: A Contribution of the E-tailing Wars. *Journal of the Academy of Marketing Science*, *30*(4), 487–499. doi:10.1177/009207002236924

Kristopher, J. (2008). *SEO: Your visual blueprint for effective Internet marketing*. Indianapolis, IN: Wiley Publishing Inc.

Kulkarni, S. (2015), A brief report of Healthcare, Telemedicine and Medical Tourism in India. Retrieved from http://www.asa.in/pdfs/surveys-reports/Healthcare-Telemedicine-and-Medical-Tourism-in-India.pdf

Leena, O. (2015). *Retail Websites Are in Need of E-Commerce SEO*. Retrieved from http://www.webfly.com/retail-websites-are-in-need-of-e-commerce-seo/

Medical Value Travel in India. (2014). *KPMG Research Report*. Retrieved from www.kpmg.com/IN/en/IssuesAndInsights/ArticlesPublications/Documents/KPMG-FICCI-Heal-Sep2014.pdf

Niranjanamurthy, M., & Dharmendra, C. (2013). The study of E-Commerce Security Issues and Solutions. *International Journal of Advanced Research in Computer and Communication Engineering*, *2*(7).

Petrovic, O., Ksela, M., Fallenböck, M., & Kittl, C. (2003). *Trust in the Network Economy*. New York: Springer Publishing. doi:10.1007/978-3-7091-6088-6

Schmid, B. (1993). Elektronische märkte. *Journal of Economic computer science,* 35(1).

Simon, H. (Ed.), (1971). Computers, Communications, and the Public Interest. Designing Organizations for an Information-Rich World. Baltimore, Maryland: The Johns Hopkins Press.

Thomas, L. (2011). *Online Marketing*. USA: The McGraw-Hill Companies, Inc.

Tiernan, B. (2000). *E-Tailing*. Chicago, IL: Dearborn Financial Publishing.

Wen, H.J., Chen, H.-G., & Hwang, H.-G. (2001). E-commerce Web site design: strategies and models. *Information Management and Computer Security*, 9(1). Retrieved from http://www.csus.edu/indiv/c/chingr/mis182/ecomwebsitedesign.pdf

Zbornik, S. (1996). *Electronic markets and electronic hierarchies*. Konstanz, Germany: UVK Verlagsgesellschaft mbH.

## KEY TERMS AND DEFINITIONS

**Alexa Traffic Ranking:** Alexa is an Amazon company that provides commercial data traffic analysis. Alexa traffic rankings provide traffic data and global rankings for the websites.

**Forex:** Foreign exchange market for trading currencies.

**Infomediary:** A combined form of Information and intermediary. This mean getting specialized knowledge about the customers that help their producers to fine tune their marketing.

**Medical Tourism:** People touring to other countries in search of affordable treatment.

**ROI (Return on Investment):** A performance measurement for assessing the benefit to the investor from his investment.

**SEO (Search Engine Optimization):** SEO is a form of digital marketing where efforts are made by companies to show up its website in the first listings while doing searches using a search engine.

**Telemedicine:** Remote delivery of health care services by using telecommunication technology.

**Unique Selling Point:** The unique propositions that a brand offers to its customers.

# Compilation of References


15 Landmarks in India's Digital History. (201422*feettribalworldwide.com*. Retrieved from http://22feettribalworldwide.com/15-landmarks-in-indias-digital-history/

2014 China mobile shopping report (brief edition). (2014). *iResearch*. Retrieved from http://www.iresearchchina.com/samplereports/6112.html

82% Sina Weibo users shop online. (2014). *China Internet Watch*. Retrieved from http://www.chinainternetwatch.com/11199/sina-weibo-users-shop-online/

A new era in buying Retail in China's digital age. (2013). *PwC (PricewaterhouseCoopers)*. Retrieved from http://www.pwccn.com/webmedia/doc/635334251818697593_consulting-retail-china.pdf

About Us. (2014). *Dqindia.com*. Retrieved from http://www.dqindia.com/

About Us. (2014). *Tradeindia.com*. Retrieved from http://www.tradeindia.com/AboutUs/home.html

Abratt, R., Deon, N., & Nezer, C. (1995). Role of the market maven in retailing: A general marketplace influencer. *Journal of Business and Psychology*, *10*(1), 31–55. doi:10.1007/BF02249268

Adams, R. B., & Ferreira, D. (2007). A theory of friendly boards. *The Journal of Finance*, *62*(1), 217–250. doi:10.1111/j.1540-6261.2007.01206.x

Addressing the Tax Challenges of the Digital Economy. (2014). OECD Library. Retrieved from http://www.oecd-ilibrary.org/taxation/addressing-the-tax-challenges-of-the-digital-economy_9789264218789-en

Agarwal, H. (2014). Cash On Delivery : Should Indian Online Retailers Persist with. *Trak.in*. Retrieved from http://trak.in/ecommerce/cash-on-delivery-cod-online-payment-mode-indian-stores/

Agarwal, J., & Wu, T. (2015). Factors influencing growth potential of e-commerce in emerging economies: An institution-based N-OLI framework and research propositions. *Thunderbird International Business Review*, *57*(3), 197–215. doi:10.1002/tie.21694

Ahmad, N., Haleem, A., & Syed, A. A. (2012). Compilation of critical success factors in implementation of enterprise systems: A study on Indian organisations. *Global Journal of Flexible Systems Management*, *13*(4), 217–232. doi:10.1007/s40171-013-0019-8

Ahmed, S., & Mahfooz, Y. (n. d.). Consolidation in the Sky- A Case Study on the Quest for Supremacy Between Jetlite And Kingfisher Airlines.

Ahuja, V., & Medury, Y. (2010). Corporate blogs as e CRM tools- Building customer engagement through content management. *Journal of Database Marketing & Customer Strategy and Management*, *17*(2), 91–105. doi:10.1057/dbm.2010.8

AIMC - Association for the research In Communication Media. (n. d.). 15 encuesta AIMC a usuarios de Internet. Retrieved from http://www.aimc.es/-Navegantes-en-la-Red-.html

Aldiri, K., Hobbs, D., & Qahwaji, R. (2008). The Human Face of E-Business: Engendering Consumer Initial Trust Through the Use of Images of Sales Personnel on E-Commerce Web Sites. *International Journal of E-Business Research*, *4*(4).

Amit, R., & Zott, C. (2001). Value creation in e-business. *Strategic Management Journal*, *22*(6/7), 493–520. doi:10.1002/smj.187

Anderson, J. R., & Gerbing, D. W. (2010). Structural equation modeling in practice: A review and recommended two-step approach. *Psychological Bulletin*.

Anderson, R. E., & Srinivasan, S. S. (2003). E-satisfaction and e-loyalty: A contingency framework. *Psychology and Marketing*, *20*(2), 123–138. doi:10.1002/mar.10063

Anderson, W. P., Chatterjee, L., & Lakshmanan, T. R. (2003). E-commerce, transportation, and economic geography. *Growth and Change*, *34*(4), 415–432. doi:10.1046/j.0017-4815.2003.00228.x

Antoniou, G., & Batten, L. (2011). E-commerce: Protecting purchaser privacy to enforce trust. *Electronic Commerce Research*, *11*(4), 421–456. doi:10.1007/s10660-011-9083-3

Arab advisors Group. (2014). Retrieved from http://www.arabadvisors.com/Pressers/presser-150614.htm

Arenius, P., Sasi, V., & Gabrielsson, M. (2006). Rapid Internationalization enabled by the Internet: The case of a knowledge intensive company. *Journal of Entrepreneurship*, 279-290.

Armstrong, A., & Hagel, J. (1996). The real value of on-line communities. *Harvard Business Review*, *74*(3), 134–141.

Ash, C., & Burn, J. (2003). Assessing the benefits from e-business transformation through effective enterprise management. *European Journal of Information Systems*, *12*(4), 297–308. doi:10.1057/palgrave.ejis.3000476

ASSOCHAM. (2012). *State of e-commerce in India*. Retrieved from http://www.assocham.org/arb/general/Comscore%20ASSOCHAM-report-state-of-e-commerce-in-india.pdf

Awad, E. M. (2012). *Electronic Commerce – From Vision to Fulfillment* (3rd ed.). New Delhi, India: PHI Learning Private Limited.

Axelsson, B., & Johanson, J. (1992). *Foreign market entry: The textbook vs the network view*. London: Routledge.

Ayres, I., & Braithwaite, J. (2001). *Responsive Regulation: Transcending the Deregulation Debate*. Oxford University Press.

B2C e-commerce as percentage of global GDP from 2009 to 2018. (2014). *Statista*. Retrieved from http://www.statista.com/statistics/324612/b2c-e-commerce-as-percentage-of-gdp-worldwide/

B2C Ecommerce Climbs Worldwide, As Emerging Markets Drive Sales Higher. (2013). *Emarketer.com*. Retrieved from http://www.emarketer.com/Article/B2C-Ecommerce-Climbs-Worldwide-Emerging-Markets-Drive-Sales-Higher/1010004

B2C e-commerce sales worldwide from 2012 to 2018. (2014). *Statista*. Retrieved from http://www.statista.com/statistics/261245/b2c-e-commerce-sales-worldwide/

Baazee.com - India's leading online marketplace - was acquired by eBay Inc. - The World's Online Marketplace. (2005). *eBay.in*. Retrieved from http://pages.ebay.in/community/aboutebay/news/pressreleases/corporate/aquisition.html

Background paper future of e commerce web. (n. d.) Retrieved from http://www.assocham.org/upload/event/recent/event_1113/Background_Paper_Future_of_e-Commerce_web.pdf

Bai, B., Law, R., & Wen, I. (2008). The impact of website quality on customer satisfaction and purchase intentions: Evidence from Chinese online visitors. *International Journal of Hospitality Management*, *27*(3), 391–402. doi:10.1016/j.ijhm.2007.10.008

Balasubramanian, S. (1997). Two Essays in Direct Marketing [PhD Dissertation]. Yale University, New Haven, CT.

Bandura, A. (1997). *Self-efficacy: The exercise of control.* New York: Freeman.

Banker, R., Bardhan, I. R., Chang, H., & Lin, S. (2006). Plant information systems, manufacturing capabilities, and plant performance. *Management Information Systems Quarterly*, *30*(2), 315–337. doi: 10.2307/25148733

Barnes, S., & Hunt, B. (2001). *E-Commerce and V-Business.* Oxford, Great Britain: Reed Educational and Professional Publishing.

Barsauskas, P., Sarapovas, T., & Cvilikas, A. (2008). The evaluation of e-commerce impact on business efficiency. *Baltic Journal of Management*, *3*(1), 71–91. doi:10.1108/17465260810844275

Barwise, P., & Meehan, S. (2010). The one thing you must get right when building a brand. *Harvard Business Review*, December, 80–84.

Basu, T., Barik, D., & Arokiasamy, P. (2013, August 26-31). Demographic Determinants of Economic Growth in BRICS and selected Developed Countries, *Paper presented at the XXVII IUSSP International Population Conference (IUSSP 2013)*, BEXCO, Busan, Republic of Korea.

Baumgarten, S. A. (1975). The Innovative Communicator in the Diffusion Research. *JMR, Journal of Marketing Research*, *12*(1), 12–18. doi:10.2307/3150653

Baym, N. K. (2000). *Tune in, log on: Soaps, fandom and online community.* Thousand Oaks: Sage Publications, Inc.

Bearden, W. D., Sharma, S., & Teel, J. E. (2012). Sample size effects on chi-square and other statistical used in evaluating causal models. *JMR, Journal of Marketing Research.*

Beckett, R. C. (2005). Collaboration now a strategic necessity. Handbook of Business Strategy, 6(1), 327–332. doi: 10.1108/08944310510558124

Bendoly, E., Soni, A., & Venkataramanan, M. A. (2004). Value chain resource planning: Adding value with systems beyond the enterprise. *Business Horizons*, *47*(2), 79–86. doi:10.1016/j.bushor.2003.08.004

Bennett, S. (2014).How Much Online Business Is Done Every 30 Seconds? Incredible E-Commerce Statistics! Retrieved from http://www.adweek.com/socialtimes/ real-time-ecommerce/499958

Berger, J. (2012). *Contagious: Why things catch on.* New York: Simon and Schuster.

Berman, J. (2014). Alibaba's Opportunities May Spell Trouble for eBay and Amazon. *TheStreet.com.* Retrieved from http://www.thestreet.com/story/12968357/1/alibabas-challenges-and-opportunities-may-spell-trouble-for-ebay-and-amazon.html

Beynon-Davies, P. (2004). *E-business.* New York, NY: Palgrave Macmillan.

Bhagat, S., & Bolton, B. (2009). *Corporate Governance and Firm Performance: Recent Evidence.* Retrieved from http://www.econ.upf.edu/docs/seminars/bhagat.pdf

Bhatt, G., & Emdad, A. (2001). An analysis of the virtual value chain in electronic commerce. *Logistics Information Systems*, *14*(1/2), 78–84. doi:10.1108/09576050110362465

Bienstock, C. C., Mentzer, J. T., & Bird, M. M. (1996). Measuring physical distribution service quality. *Journal of the Academy of Marketing Science*, *25*(1), 31–44. doi:10.1177/0092070397251004

Bigné-Alcañiz, E., Ruiz-Mafé, C., Aldás-Manzano, J., & Sanz-Blas, S. (2008). Influence of online shopping information dependency and innovativeness on internet shopping adoption. *Online Information Review*, *32*(5), 648–667. doi:10.1108/14684520810914025

Bigne, E., Carla, R., & Sanz, S. (2005). The Impact of Internet User Shopping Patterns and Demographics. *Journal of Electronic Commerce Research*, *6*(3), 193–209.

Bijlani, J. (2015). eCommerce in India: Accelerating growth. *PWC.* Retrieved from http://www.pwc.in/assets/pdfs/publications/2015/ecommerce-in-india-accelerating-growth.pdf

Bilgihan, A., Okumus, F., Nusair, K., & Bujisic, M. (2014). Online experiences: Flow theory, measuring online customer experience in e-commerce and managerial implications for the lodging industry. *Information Technology & Tourism*, *14*(1), 49–71. doi:10.1007/s40558-013-0003-3

Bisen, A., Singh, P., & Anand, A. (2013, May). E-tailing in India: Unlocking the Potential (White Paper). *Technopak.* Retrieved from http://www.technopak.com/files/E-tailing_in_India.pdf

Blanchard, A. L. (2004). The effects of dispersed virtual communities on face-to-face social capital. In M. Huysman & V. Wulf (Eds.), *Social Capital and Information Technology* (pp. 53–74). Cambridge, MA: MIT Press.

Blanchard, A. L., & Markus, M. L. (2004). The experienced sense of a virtual community: Characteristics and processes. *The Data Base for Advances in Information Systems*, *35*(1), 65–79. doi:10.1145/968464.968470

Bloch, P. H., Sherrell, D. L., & Ridgway, N. M. (1986). Consumer search: An extended framework. *The Journal of Consumer Research*, *13*(1), 119–126. doi:10.1086/209052

Bodapati, Arabie, & Palmer, R. A. (2004). How managers perceive the impacts of information technologies on contemporary practices: Reinforcing, enhancing or transforming? *Journal of Relationship Marketing*, 3(4), 7–26.

Bodendorf, F., & Kaiser, C. (2009). Detecting opinion leaders and trends in online social networks.*Proceedings of the 2nd ACM workshop on Social web search and mining*, ACM doi:10.1145/1651437.1651448

Boesler, M. (2012). The state or world economy. *Business Insider.* Retrieved from http://www.businessinsider.com/world-bank-world-economy-2012

Bollen, K. A. (2011). *Structural equations with latent variables.* New York: Wiley.

Booth, N., & Matic, J. (2011). Mapping and leveraging influencers in social media to shape corporate brand perceptions. *Corporate Communications*: An*International Journal (Toronto, Ont.)*, 16(3), 184–191.

Bramall, C., Schoefer, K., & McKechnie, S. (2004). The determinants and consequences of consumer trust in e-retailing: A conceptual framework. *Irish Marketing Review*, *17*(1&2), 13–22.

Brashear, T. G., Kashyap, V., Musante, M. D., & Donthu, N. (2009). A profile of the Internet shopper: Evidence from six countries. *Journal of Marketing Theory and Practice*, *17*(3), 267–282. doi:10.2753/MTP1069-6679170305

Brennar, J., & Smith, A. (2013). *Social Networking.* Washington, D.C.: Pew Internet.

Broekhuizen, T., & Huizingh, E. (2009). Online purchase determinants: Is their effect moderated by direct experience? *Management Research News*, *32*(5), 440–457. doi:10.1108/01409170910952949

Bruce, D., & Fox, W. (2001). *State and Local Sales Tax Revenue Losses from E-Commerce: Updated Estimates.* Retrieved from http://cber.bus.utk.edu/ecomm/Ecom0901.pdf

Bruhn, M., Schoenmueller, V., & Schäfer, D. B. (2012). Are social media replacing traditional media; is brand equity creation? *Management Research Review*, 770-790.

Building India: Transforming the nation's logistics infrastructure. (2010). *McKinsey & Company*. Retrieved from http://www.mckinsey.com/insights/travel_transportation/~/media/mckinsey/dotcom/insights/travel transportation/transforming indiaslogistics infrastructure/building_india-transforming_the_nations_logistics_infrastructure.ashx

Burke, R. R. (2002). Technology and the Customer Interface What Consumers Want in the Physical and Virtual Store. *Academy of Marketing Science Journal*, *30*(4), 411–432. doi:10.1177/009207002236914

Burke, R. R.Burke & Raymond R. (1997). Do You See What I See? The Future of Virtual Shopping. *Journal of the Academy of Marketing Science*, *25*(4), 352–360. doi:10.1177/0092070397254007

Burmann, C. (2010). *A call for user-generated branding*. Brand Management.

Bush, V. D., Venable, B. T., & Bush, A. J. (2000). Ethics and Marketing on the Internet, Practitioners Perception of societal, Industry and company concerns. *Journal of Business Ethics*, *23*(3), 237–248. doi:10.1023/A:1006202107464

Byrne, B. M. (2011). *Structural Equation Modeling with LISREL, PRELIS, and SIMPLIS: basic concepts, allocations, and programming*. Mahwah, New Jersey: Lawrence Erlbaum Associates Inc.

Cao, J., Yu, X., & Zhang, Z. (2015). Integrating OWA and data mining for analyzing customers churn in e-commerce. *Journal of Systems Science and Complexity*, *28*(2), 381–392. doi:10.1007/s11424-015-3268-0

Capozzi, L., & Zipfel, L.B. (2012). The conversation age: the opportunity for public relations. *Corporate Communications: An International Journal*, 17(3), 336 – 349.

Carlton, D. W., & Fischel, D. R. (1983, May). The Regulation of Insider Trading. *Stanford Law Review*, *35*(5), 857–895. doi:10.2307/1228706

Carroll, D. (2015, January 9). United Breaks Guitars. *Dave Carrol Music.* Retrieved from http://www.davecarrollmusic.com/music/ubg/

Castro-Schez, J. J., Miguel, R., Vallejo, D., & Lopez-Lopez, L. M. (2011). A highly adaptive recommender system based on fuzzy logic for B2C e-commerce portals. *Expert Systems with Applications*, *38*(3), 2441–2454. doi:10.1016/j.eswa.2010.08.033

Chaffey, D. (2013). *E-Business and E-Commerce Management Strategy, Implementation and Practice* (5th ed.). New Delhi, India: Pearson Education Limited.

Chandra, P., Satish, Sunitha, G. (2012). E-Tailing – The Mantra of Modern Retailer's Success. *Journal of Arts, Science & Commerce*, *3*(2).

Chang, H. H., & Chen, S. W. (2008). The impact of online store environment cues on purchase intention: Trust and perceived risk as a mediator. *Online Information Review*, *32*(6), 818–841. doi:10.1108/14684520810923953

Chang, J., & Samuel, N. (2004). Internet shopper demographics and buying behavior in Australia. *Journal of American Academy of Business*, *5*(1/2), 171–176.

Chang, M. K., Cheung, W., & Lai, V. S. (2005). Literature derived reference models for the adoption of online shopping. *Information & Management*, *42*(4), 543–559. doi:10.1016/S0378-7206(04)00051-5

Chan, K. K., & Misra, S. (1990). Characteristics of the opinion leader: A new dimension. *Journal of Advertising*, *19*(3), 53–60. doi:10.1080/00913367.1990.10673192

Chellappa, R. K., & Pavlou, P. A. (2002). Perceived information security, financial liability and consumer trust in electronic commerce transactions. *Logistics Information Management*, *15*(5/6), 358–368. doi:10.1108/09576050210447046

Chen, S., & Wang, J. S. (2010). Tax Evasion and Fraud Detection: A Theoretical Evaluation of Taiwan's Business Tax Policy for Internet Auctions. *Asian Social Science, 6*(12), 23-35. Retrieved from http://www.ccsenet.org/journal/index.php/ass/article/view/7067/6242

Chen, G. (2012). The use of electronic brokerage systems in China: A modified e-Commerce model. *Canadian Journal of Administrative Sciences*, *29*(1), 99–109. doi:10.1002/cjas.213

Chen, J. E., Pan, S. L., & Ouyang, T. H. (2014). Routine reconfiguration in traditional companies' e-commerce strategy implementation: A trajectory perspective. *Information & Management*, *51*(2), 270–282. doi:10.1016/j.im.2013.11.008

Chen, S. C., & Dhillon, C. S. (2003). Interpreting dimensions of consumer trust in e-commerce. *Information Technology Management*, *4*(2/3), 303–318. doi:10.1023/A:1022962631249

Childers, T. L. (1986). Assessment of the Psychometric Properties of an Opinion Leadership Scale. *JMR, Journal of Marketing Research*, *23*(2), 184–188. doi:10.2307/3151666

Childers, T. L., Carr, C. L., Peck, J., & Carson, S. (2001). Hedonic and utilitarian motivations for online retail shopping behaviour. *Journal of Retailing*, *77*(4), 511–535. doi:10.1016/S0022-4359(01)00056-2

Child, J., Ng, S. H., & Wong, C. (2002). Psychic Distance and Internationalization: Evidence from Hong Kong Firms. *International Studies of Management & Organization*, 32(10), 36–56.

China mobile shopping market GMV hit RMB167.64 Bn in 2013 with fast growing penetration. (2014). *iResearch.* Retrieved from http://www.iresearchchina.com/views/5405.html

China online shopping GMV soars 47.1%. (2014). *iResearch.* Retrieved from http://www.iresearchchina.com/views/5826.html

China online shopping market slows down while mobile buying outbursts. (2014). *iResearch.* Retrieved from http://www.iresearchchina.com/views/5548.html

China sees more sophisticated online shoppers. (2014). *Nielsen.* Retrieved from http://www.nielsen.com/content/dam/nielsenglobal/cn/docs/Nielsen%202014%20China%20online%20shopper%20trends_EN_Client%20Version.PDF

China's e-tail revolution: Online shopping as a catalyst for growth. (2013). Mckinsey & Co. Retrieved from https://www.mckinsey.com/~/media/McKinsey/dotcom/Insights%20and%20pubs/MGI/Research/Productivity%20Competitiveness%20and%20Growth/China%20e-tailing/MGI_China_e-tailing_Full_report_March_2013.ashx

China's pied piper. (2006). *The Economist.* Retrieved from http://www.economist.com/node/7942225

Chinese spend big on cross-border Internet shopping. (2015). *Xinhua.* Retrieved from http://www.china.org.cn/business/2015-03/31/content_35211611.htm

Chiu, P. H., Kao, G. Y. M., & Lo, C. C. (2010). Personalized blog content recommender system for mobile phone users. *International Journal of Human-Computer Studies*, *68*(8), 496–507. doi:10.1016/j.ijhcs.2010.03.005

Cho, J. (2004). Likelihood to abort an online transaction: Influences from cognitive evaluations, attitudes, and behavioral variables. *Information & Management*, *41*(7), 827–838. doi:10.1016/j.im.2003.08.013

Chowdhury, A. (2009). IRCTC becomes the largest contributor to e-commerce. *Business Standard*. Retrieved from http://www.business-standard.com/article/technology/irctc-becomes-the-largest-contributor-to-e-commerce-109040400075_1.html

Christopher, M. (1998). *Logistics and supply chain management: Strategies for reducing cost and improving services* (2nd ed.). London: Pitman Publisher.

Chun, S. H., Rhee, B. D., Park, S. Y., & Kim, J. C. (2011). Emerging dual channel system and manufacturer's direct retail channel strategy. *International Review of Economics & Finance*, *20*(4), 812–825. doi:10.1016/j.iref.2011.02.006

Clark, R. A., Goldsmith, R. E., & Goldsmith, E. B. (2008). Market mavenism and consumer self-confidence. *Journal of Consumer Behaviour*, *7*(3), 238–248. doi:10.1002/cb.248

Clemes, M. D., Gan, C., & Zhang, J. (2014). An empirical analysis of online shopping adoption in Beijing, China. *Journal of Retailing and Consumer Services*, *21*(3), 364–375. doi:10.1016/j.jretconser.2013.08.003

Coglianese, C., Healey, T. J., Keating, E. K., & Michael, M. L. (2004). *The Role of Government in Corporate Governance*. Regulatory Policy Program Center for Business and Government.

Cole, M. D., Long, M. M., Chiagouris, L. G., & Gopalakrishna, P. (2011). Transitioning from traditional to digital content: An examination of opinion leadership and word-of-mouth communication across various media platforms. *Journal of Internet Commerce*, *10*(2), 91–105. doi:10.1080/15332861.2011.571990

Colla, E., & Dupuis, M. (2002). Research and managerial issues on global retail competition: Carrefour/Wal-Mart. *International Journal of Retail & Distribution Management*, *30*(2), 103–111. doi:10.1108/09590550210418128

Colla, E., & Lapoule, P. (2012). E-commerce: Exploring the critical success factors. *International Journal of Retail & Distribution Management*, *40*(11), 842–864. doi:10.1108/09590551211267601

Collins, H. (2010). *Creative research*. Lausanne: AVA Academia.

Comor, E. (2000). Household Consumption on the Internet: Income, Time, and Institutional Contradictions. *Journal of Economics*, *34*(1), 105.

Company History - ICICI Bank Ltd. (2014a). *Economictimes.indiatimes.com*. Retrieved from http://economictimes.indiatimes.com/icici-bank-ltd/infocompanyhistory/companyid-9194.cms

Company History - Tata Communications Ltd. (2014b). *Economictimes.indiatimes.com*. Retrieved from http://economictimes.indiatimes.com/tata-communications-ltd/infocompanyhistory/companyid-11992.cms

Constantinides, E. (2004). Influencing the online consumer's behaviour: The web experiences. *Internet Research*, *2*(2), 111–126. doi:10.1108/10662240410530835

Constantinides, E., & Fountain, S. J. (2008). Web 2.0: Conceptual foundations and marketing issues. *Journal of Direct, Data and Digital Marketing Practice*, *9*(3), 231–244. doi:10.1057/palgrave.dddmp.4350098

Constantinides, E., Romero, C. L., & Gomez, M. A. (2010). Effects of web experience on consumer choice: A multicultural approach. *Internet Research*, *20*(2), 188–209. doi:10.1108/10662241011032245

Constantinides, E., Romero, L. R., & Boria, M. A. G. (2008). Social media: A new frontier for retailers? *European Retail Research*, *22*(1), 1–28. doi:10.1007/978-3-8349-8099-1_1

Consulting, C. (2014). *Digital shopper relevancy: A Research report*. Paris: Levine, Ted.

Corbitt, B. J., Thanasankit, T., & Yi, H. (2003). Trust and e-commerce: A study of consumer perceptions. *Electronic Commerce Research and Applications*, *2*(3), 203–215. doi:10.1016/S1567-4223(03)00024-3

Cothrel, J., & Williams, R. (1999). Online Communities helping them form and grow. *Journal of Knowledge Management*, *3*(1), 54–60. doi:10.1108/13673279910259394

Coviello, N., & Munro, H. (1997). Network relationships and the internationalisation process of small software firms. *International Business Review*.

Cox, J., & Dale, B. G. (2001). Service quality and e-commerce: An exploratory analysis. *Managing Service Quality*, *11*(2), 121–131. doi:10.1108/09604520110387257

Crain, N., & Crain, W. M. (2010, September). *The Impact of Regulatory Costs on Small Firms*. Retrieved from https://www.sba.gov/sites/default/files/The%20Impact%20of%20Regulatory%20Costs%20on%20Small%20Firms%20%28Full%29.pdf

Cui, M., & Pan, S. L. (2015). Developing focal capabilities for e-commerce adoption: A resource orchestration perspective. *Information & Management*, *52*(2), 200–209. doi:10.1016/j.im.2014.08.006

Cunningham, I., & Cunningham, W. (1973). The urban in-home shopper: Socio-economic and attitudinal characteristics. *Journal of Retailing*, *49*(1), 42–57.

Customer Desires vs Retailer Capabilities: Minding the omni-channel commerce gap. (2014, January). *Accenture and-ForresterConsulting*.

Dam, H. K., & Ghose, A. (2015). Mining version histories for change impact analysis in business process model repositories. *Computers in Industry*, *67*, 72–85. doi:10.1016/j.compind.2014.10.005

Dan, J. (2000). *Dan Janal's Guide to Marketing on the Internet*. New Jersey: John Wiley & Sons Publishing, Inc.

Darian, J. C., Tucci, L. A., & Wiman, A. R. (2001). Perceived Salesperson Service Attributes and Retail Patronage Intentions. *International Journal of Retail & Distribution Management*, *29*(5), 205–213. doi:10.1108/09590550110390986

Das, G. (2014). Cash-on-delivery : Necessary Evil. *BusinessToday*. Retrieved from http://businesstoday.intoday.in/story/cash-on-delivery-impact-on-e-commerce-companies-customers/1/202680.html

David, M. S., & Richard, T. H. (2000). E-satisfaction: An initial examination. *Journal of Retailing*, *76*(3), 309–322. doi:10.1016/S0022-4359(00)00035-X

David, T. (2003). *E-Commerce Usability: Tools and Techniques to Perfect the On-Line Experience*. UK: Taylor & Francis Publishing.

Dehning, B., Richardson, V. J., & Zmud, R. W. (2007). The financial performance effects of IT-based supply chain management systems in manufacturing firms. *Journal of Operations Management*, *25*(4), 806–824. doi:10.1016/j.jom.2006.09.001

Delfmann, W., Albers, S., & Gehring, M. (2002). The impact of electronic commerce on logistics service providers. *International Journal of Physical Distribution & Logistics Management*, *32*(3), 203–222. doi:10.1108/09600030210426539

Dellarocas, C. (2003). The digitization of word of mouth: Promise and challenges of online feedback mechanisms. *Management Science*, *49*(10), 1407–1424. doi:10.1287/mnsc.49.10.1407.17308

DeLone, W. H., & McLean, E. R. (2004). Measuring e-commerce success: Applying the DeLone & McLean information systems success model. *International Journal of Electronic Commerce*, *9*(1), 31–47. doi: 10.1080/10864415.2004.11044317

Dennis, A. R., Pootheri, S. K., & Natarajan, V. L. (1998). Lessons from the early adopters of Web groupware. *Journal of Management Information Systems, 14*(4), 65–86. doi:10.1080/07421222.1998.11518186

Department for Business Innovation & Skills. (2013, October). *A Strategy For Future Retail: Industry and Government Delivering in Partnership.* Retrieved from https://www.gov.uk/government/uploads/system/uploads/attachment_data/file/252383/bis-13-1204-a-strategy-for-fut ure-retail-industry-and-government-delivering-in-partnership.pdf

Dholakia, R., & Uusitalo, O. (2002). Switching to Electronic Stores: Consumer characteristics and the perception of shopping benefits. *International Journal of Retail & Distribution Management, 30*(10), 459–469. doi:10.1108/09590550210445335

Digital Commerce. Mumbai. (2013). *IAMAI.* Retrieved from http://yourstory.com/wp-content/uploads/2013/05/Digital-Commerce-Report_2013.pdf

Digital Commerce Report (2014). Internet and Mobile Association of India [IAMAI].

Digital impact on in store shopping research studies. (2014, October). Google. Retrieved from https://think.storage.googleapis.com/docs/digital-impact-on-in-store-shopping_research-studies.pdf

Dong, Y. (2005). Dangdang: Enhanced delivery speed. *International Business,* B04.

Douglas, S. P., & Craig, C. S. (1997). The changing dynamic of consumer behavior: Implications for cross-cultural research. *International Journal of Research in Marketing, 14*(4), 379–395. doi:10.1016/S0167-8116(97)00026-8

Dowling, G. R., & Staelin, R. (1994). A model of perceived risk and intended risk-handling activity. *The Journal of Consumer Research, 21*(1), 119–134. doi:10.1086/209386

Doxey, G. V. (2011). In the Impact of Tourism*: The Travel Research Association,Sixth Annual Conference Proceedings.*

Duggan, M., Ellison, N., Lampe, C., Lenhart, A., & Madden, M. (2015, January 9). Social Media Site Usage 2014. *Pew Research Center.* Retrieved from http://www.pewinternet.org/2015/01/09/social-media-update-2014/?utm_content=buffer68e1e&utm_medium=social&utm_source=twitter.com&utm_campaign=buffer

E tailing in India. (n. d.). Technopak Whitepaper. Retrieved from http://www.technopak.com/files/E-tailing_in_India.pdf

Eamonn, R. (2015). Major Security Issues in Ecommerce. *WebScience.* Retrieved from http://webscience.ie/docs/Web-science White Paper-Security Issues in E-Commerce.pdf

Eastlick, M. A. (1993). Predictors of videotex adoption. *Journal of Direct Marketing, 7*(3), 66–74. doi:10.1002/dir.4000070309

E-commerce Europe. (2013, October 24). *Round Table Amsterdam: E-commerce in Europe - Challenges and Opportunities.* Retrieved from http://www.ecommerce-europe.eu/news/2013/10/round-table-amsterdam-e-commerce-in-europe-challenges-and-opportunities

Ecommerce in India- Accelerating growth. (n. d.). *PWC.* Retrieved from https://www.pwc.in/en_IN/in/assets/pdfs/publications/2015/ecommerce-in-india-accelerating-growth.pdf

E-Commerce in India. (2015). *Nishith Desai Associates.* Retrieved from http://www.nishithdesai.com/fileadmin/user_upload/pdfs/ResearchPapers/E-Commerce_in_India.pdf

eCommerce in India: Accelerating growth. (2015). *PWC.* Retrieved from http://www.pwc.in/en_IN/in/assets/pdfs/publications/2015/ecommerce-in-india-accelerating-growth.pdf

E-Commerce in India: Evolution, Growth and Challenges. (2012). *MSLGroup.* Retrieved from http://mslgroup.com/insights/2012/e-commerce-in-india-evolution,-growth-and-challenges.aspx

E-Commerce Is the Next Frontier in Global Expansion. (2012). *ATKearney*. Retrieved from http://www.atkearney.com/paper/-/asset_publisher/dVxv4Hz2h8bS/content/e-commerce-is-the-next-frontier-in-global-expansion/10192

eCommerce: China's consumption growth engine. (2014). *Morgan Stanley*. Retrieved from http://online.barrons.com/articles/ecommerce-chinas-consumption-growth-engine-1415323378

Economic Action Plan (2015). Retrieved from http://www.budget.gc.ca/2015/docs/plan/budget2015-eng.pdf

Elliot, S. (2002). *Electronic Commerce: B2C Strategies and Models*. UK: Wiley & Sons Ltd.

Erikson, E. (1968). *The Psychosocial stages of development*. London: Norton & Company.

E-tail eats into Retail. Mumbai, India. (2014). *CRISIL*. Retrieved from http://www.crisil.com/pdf/research/CRISIL-Research-Article-Online-Retail-Feb14.pdf

Etgar, M., & Rachman-Moore, D. (2010). Geographical Expansion by International Retailers: A Study of Proximate Markets and Global Expansion Strategies. *Journal of Global Marketing*, *23*(1), 5–15. doi:10.1080/08911760903439560

Evangelista, P., & Sweeney, E. (2006). Technology usage in the supply chain: The case of small 3PLs. *International Journal of Logistics Management*, *17*(1), 55–74. doi:10.1108/09574090610663437

Evans, L. (2010). *Social media marketing: Strategies for engaging in Facebook, Twitter & other social media*. Indianapolis: Que Publishing.

Evans, P. B., & Wurster, B. S. (1997). Strategy and the new economics of information. *Harvard Business Review*, *75*(5), 70–83. PMID:10170332

Evolution of e-commerce in India. (2014). *PWC, & ASSOCHAM*. Retrieved from http://www.pwc.in/assets/pdfs/publications/2014/evolution-of-e-commerce-in-india.pdf

Facebook users of the world. (2015, May 4). *Internet World Stats*. Retrieved from http://www.internetworldstats.com/facebook.htm

Fact Sheet. (2014). *Indiamart.com*. Retrieved from http://www.indiamart.com/corporate/fact-sheet.html

Facts and Information about IRCTC. (2014). *Factsninfo.com*. Retrieved from http://www.factsninfo.com/2015/06/facts-and-information-about-irctc.html

Falkow, S. (2010). PR Trends 2010: Branded Content. *The Proactive Report*.

Fama, E. F. (1980). Agency problems and the theory of the firm. *Journal of Political Economy*, *88*(2), 288–307. doi:10.1086/260866

Fam, K. S., Foscht, T., & Collins, R. D. (2004). Trust and the online relationship: An exploratory study from New Zealand. *Tourism Management*, *25*(2), 195–207. doi:10.1016/S0261-5177(03)00084-0

Fang, H., Zhang, J., Bao, Y., & Zhu, Q. (2013). Towards effective online review systems in the Chinese context: A cross-cultural empirical study. *Electronic Commerce Research and Applications*, *12*(3), 208–220. doi:10.1016/j.elerap.2013.03.001

Fang, H., Zhang, J., Sensoy, M., & Magnenat-Thalmann, N. (2014). Reputation mechanism for e-commerce in virtual reality environments. *Electronic Commerce Research and Applications*, *13*(6), 409–422. doi:10.1016/j.elerap.2014.08.002

Fan, Q., Yul Lee, J., & In Kim, J. (2013). The impact of web site quality on flow-related online shopping behaviors in C2C e-marketplaces: A cross-national study. *Managing Service Quality: An International Journal*, *23*(5), 364–387. doi:10.1108/MSQ-11-2012-0150

Feick, L. F., & Price, L. L. (1987). The Market Maven: A Diffuser of Marketplace Information. *Journal of Marketing*, *51*(1), 83–97. doi:10.2307/1251146

Fichman, R. (2004). Going beyond the dominant paradigm for information technology innovation research: Emerging concepts and methods. *Journal of the Association for Information Systems*, *5*(8), 314–355.

Five omnichannel fundamentals for driving foot traffic. (2015). *The Daily Tuesday, L2.inc.*

Flavián, C., & Guinalíu, M. (2006). Consumer trust, perceived security and privacy policy: Three basic elements of loyalty to a web site. *Industrial Management & Data Systems*, *106*(5), 601–620. doi:10.1108/02635570610666403

Fleder, D., & Hosanagar, K. (2009). Blockbuster culture's next rise or fall: The impact of recommender systems on sales diversity. *Management Science*, *55*(5), 697–712. doi:10.1287/mnsc.1080.0974

Flynn, L. R., Goldsmith, R. E., & Eastman, J. K. (1996). Opinion Leaders and Opinion Seekers: Two New Measurament Scales. *Journal of the Academy of Marketing Science*, *24*(2), 137–147. doi:10.1177/0092070396242004

Fornell, C., & Larcker, D. F. (2010). Evaluating structural equation models with unobservable variables and measurement error. *JMR, Journal of Marketing Research.*

Foster, M., West, B., & Francescucci, A. (2011). Exploring social media users segmentation and online brand profiles. *Journal of Brand Management*, 19(1), 4-17.

Foucault, B. E., & Scheufele, D. A. (2002). Web vs campus store? Why students buy textbooks online. *Journal of Consumer Marketing*, *19*(5), 409–423. doi:10.1108/07363760210437632

Fox, V. (2010). *Marketing in the Age of Google*. New Jersey: John Wiley & Sons, Inc.

Fransi, E. C., & Viadiu, F. M. (2007). A study of e-retailing management: Analysing the expectations and perceptions of Spanish consumers. *International Journal of Consumer Studies*, *31*(6), 613–622. doi:10.1111/j.1470-6431.2007.00623.x

Furnell, S. (2004). E-commerce security: A question of trust. *Computer Fraud & Security*, *2004*(10),10–14.

Garner, S.J. & Thompson H.A. (1986). Patient perceived risk in the purchase of physician services. *Journal of Professional Services Marketing*, 1, 149-159.

GDP Data. (2015). *The World Bank*. Retrieved from http://data.worldbank.org/indicator/NY.GDP.MKTP.CD

Geffen, C. A., & Rothenberg, S. (2000). Suppliers and environmental innovation: The automotive paint process. *International Journal of Operations & Production Management*, *20*(2), 166–186. doi:10.1108/01443570010304242

GEMI (Global Environmental Management Initiative). (2004). *Forging new links: enhancing supply chain value through environmental excellence*. Retrieved from http://www.gemi.org/supplychain/resources/ForgingNewLinks.pdf

Gensler, V., Völckner, F., Liu-Thompkins, Y., & Wiertz, C. (2013). Managing brands in the social media environment. *Journal of Interactive Marketing*, *27*(4), 242–256. doi:10.1016/j.intmar.2013.09.004

Gibbs, J., Kraemer, K. L., & Dedrick, J. (2003). Environment and Policy Factors Shaping Global Ecommerce Diffusion: A Cross-Country Comparison. *The Information Society*, *19*(1), 5–18. doi:10.1080/01972240309472

Global B2C Ecommerce Sales to Hit $ 1. 5 Trillion This Year Driven by Growth in Emerging Markets. (2014). *Emarketer.com*. Retrieved from http://www.emarketer.com/Article/Global-B2C-Ecommerce-Sales-Hit-15-Trillion-This-Year-Driven-by-Growth-Emerging-Markets/1010575

GMV of China online shopping hit unexpected 268.37 billion Yuan in Q2 2012. (2012). *iResearch*. Retrieved from http://www.iresearchchina.com/views/4394.html

Gnambs, T., & Batinic, B. (2012). A Personality-Competence Model of Opinion Leadership. *Psychology and Marketing*, *29*(8), 606–621. doi:10.1002/mar.20547

Gökmen, A. (2012). Virtual business operations, e-commerce & its significance and the case of Turkey: Current situation and its potential. *Electronic Commerce Research*, *12*(1), 31–51. doi:10.1007/s10660-011-9084-2

Goldsmith, R. E., Clark, R. A., & Goldsmith, E. B. (2006). Extending the psychological profile of market mavenism. *Journal of Consumer Behaviour*, *5*(5), 411–419. doi:10.1002/cb.189

Goldsmith, R. E., & Hofacker, C. F. (1991). Measuring Consumer Innovativeness. *Journal of the Academy of Marketing Science*, *19*(3), 209–221. doi:10.1007/BF02726497

Gonzalez, J. S. (1998). *The 21st century Intranet*. Upper Saddle River, NJ: Prentice Hall.

Gopalan, R., & Ranganathan, S. S. (2014). India Retail Trends 2014. Retrieved from http://www.tata-bss.com/pdf/whitepapers/india-retail-trends-2014.pdf

Gordon, S. (2004). E-Commerce: A Control and Security Guide. Hoboken, New Jersey: John Wiley & Sons.

Grabner-Kraeuter, S. (2002). The role of consumers' trust in online-shopping. *Journal of Business Ethics*, *39*(1-2), 43–50. doi:10.1023/A:1016323815802

Grant, K., Edgar, D., Sukumar, A., & Meyer, M. (2014). "Risky business": Perceptions of e-business risk by UK small and medium sized enterprises (SMEs). *International Journal of Information Management*, *34*(2), 99–122. doi:10.1016/j.ijinfomgt.2013.11.001

Grau, J. (2008). Consumer Interactions: Social Shopping, Blogs and Reviews. New York, NY: eMarketer Inc.

Greene, W. (2014, January 16). E Commerce in South east Asia: Opportunities for Continued Growth in 2014. *Tigermine.com*. Retrieved from http://www.tigermine.com/2014/01/16/e-commerce-southeast-asia-opportunities-challenges-growth-2014/

Griffis, S. E., Rao, S., Goldsby, T. J., & Niranjan, T. T. (2012). The customer consequences of returns in online retailing: An empirical analysis. *Journal of Operations Management*, *30*(4), 282–294. doi:10.1016/j.jom.2012.02.002

Grimes, B. (2010, December 6). 6 types of content moderation you need to know about. *BlaiseGV*. Retrieved from http://blaisegv.com/community-management/6-types-of-content-moderation-you-need-to-know-about/

Guan, S. U., Tan, S. L., & Hua, F. (2004). A modularized electronic payment system for agent-based e-commerce. *Journal of Research and Practice in Information Technology*, *36*(2), 67–87.

Gunasekaran, A., & Ngai, E. W. T. (2008). Adoption of e-procurement in Hong Kong: An empirical research. *International Journal of Production Economics*, *113*(1), 159–175. doi:10.1016/j.ijpe.2007.04.012

Guo, S., Wang, M., & Leskovec, J. (2011, June). The role of social networks in online shopping: information passing, price of trust, and consumer choice.*Proceedings of the 12th ACM conference on Electronic commerce,*San Jose, CA (pp. 157-166). ACM. doi:10.1145/1993574.1993598

Gupta, K. (2014). Why eCommerce is a must for a 21st Century Business? Retrieved from https://www.linkedin.com/pulse/20140819070607-3179967-why-ecommerce-is-a-must-for-a-21st-century-business

Guttman, R. H., Moukas, A. G., & Maes, P. (1998). Agents as Mediators in Electronic Commerce. *International Journal of Electronic Markets*, *8*(2), 22–27. doi:10.1080/10196789800000007

Hagel, H., & Armstrong, A. G. (1997). *Net Gain: Expanding Markets through Virtual Communities*. Boston, MA: Harvard Business School Press.

Hair, J. F., Jr., & Anderson, R. L. Tatham, & Black, W. C. (2008). Multivariate Data Analysis. New York: Macmillan

Hamad, H., Elbeltagi, I., Jones, P., & El-Gohary, H. (2015). Antecedents of B2B e-commerce adoption and its effect on competitive advantage in manufacturing SMEs. *Strategic Change*, *24*(5), 405–428. doi:10.1002/jsc.2019

Handy, C. (1995). Trust and the virtual organization. *Harvard Business Review*, *73*(3), 40–48.

Handy, C. (1995). Trust and The Virtual Organization. *Harvard Business Review*, *73*, 40–50.

Hansen, J.V. (2001). Internet commerce security: issues and models for control checking. Journal of the operational Research society, Industry and company concern, *52*(10), 1159-1164.

Hariharan, G. (2008). Profile and perception of retail consumers. *Indian Journal of Marketing*, *38*(2).

Harris, L. C., & Goode, M. M. H. (2004). The four levels of loyalty and the pivotal role of trust: A study of online service dynamics. *Journal of Retailing*, *80*(2), 139–158. doi:10.1016/j.jretai.2004.04.002

Hart, C. A., Doherty, N. F., & Ellis-Chadwick, F. E. (2000). Retailer Adoption of the Internet: Implications for Retail Marketing. *European Journal of Marketing*, *34*(8), 954–974. doi:10.1108/03090560010331441

Hartono, E., Holsapple, C. W., Kim, K. Y., Na, K. S., & Simpson, J. T. (2014). Measuring perceived security in B2C electronic commerce website usage: A respecification and validation. *Decision Support Systems*, *62*, 11–21. doi:10.1016/j.dss.2014.02.006

Herbig, P. (1998). *Handbook of Cross-cultural Marketing*. New York, NY and London: International Business Press.

Hermes, N. (2000). Fiscal decentralisation in developing countries. *De Economist*, *148*(5), 690–692.

Higie, R. A., Feick, L. F., & Price, L. L. (1987). Types and amount of word-of-mouth communications about retailers. *Journal of Retailing*, *63*(3), 260–278.

Hill, C.A., & Scudder, G.D. (2002). The use of electronic data interchange for supply chain coordination in the food Industry. *Journal of Operations Management*, *20*(4), 375–387.

Hirschheim, R., Welke, R., & Schwarz, A. (2010). Service-oriented architecture: Myths, realities, and a maturity model. *MIS Quarterly Executive*, *9*(1), 37–48.

Hofacker, C. R. (2001). *Internet Marketing* (3rd ed.). New York: Wiley.

Hofstede, G. (1991). *Cultures and Organizations: Software of the Mind*. London: McGraw-Hill.

Hogg, M. A. (1996). Group structure and social identity. In W. P. Robinson (Ed.), *Social groups and identities: Developing the legacy of Henri Tajfel* (pp. 65–94). UK: Butterworth-Heinemann.

Holiday benchmark data alert. (2015, January 5). IBM. Retrieved from http://www-01.ibm.com/software/marketing-solutions/benchmark-hub/alert.html

Holsapple, C. W., & Singh, M. (2000). Toward a unified view of electronic commerce, electronic business, and collaborative commerce: A knowledge management approach. *Knowledge and Process Management*, *7*(3), 151–164. doi:10.1002/1099-1441(200007/09)7:3<151::AID-KPM83>3.0.CO;2-U

Hong, W., & Zhu, K. (2006). Migrating to Internet-based e-commerce: Factors affecting e-commerce adoption and migration at the firm level. *Information & Management*, *43*(2), 204–221. doi:10.1016/j.im.2005.06.003

Ho, S. C., Kauffman, R. J., & Liang, T. P. (2011). Internet-based selling technology and e-commerce growth: A hybrid growth theory approach with cross-model inference. *Information Technology & Management*, *12*(4), 409–429. doi:10.1007/s10799-010-0078-x

Hossain, N. (2012). Why the Interest graph is a Marketer's best friend. *Mashable.com*. Retrieved from http://mashable.com/2012/06/19/Interest-graph-marketer

How it began. (2014). *Ernet.in*. Retrieved from http://www.ernet.in/about/abouternet.html

How Tmall.com fills China's dinner tables with global. (2014). *Alizila*. Retrieved from http://www.alizila.com/how-tmallcom-fills-chinas-dinner-tables-global-food

Hsu, P. F. (2013). Integrating ERP and e-business: Resource complementarity in business value creation. *Decision Support Systems*, *56*, 334–347. doi:10.1016/j.dss.2013.06.013

Hua, N., Morosan, C., & DeFranco, A. (2015). The other side of technology adoption: Examining the relationships between e-commerce expenses and hotel performance. *International Journal of Hospitality Management*, *45*, 109–120. doi:10.1016/j.ijhm.2014.12.001

Huang, K. (2010). JD's logistics competition. Retrieved from http://tech.sina.com.cn/i/2010-05-15/01544189077.shtml

Huang, C. Y., Tzeng, G. H., & Ho, W. R. J. (2011). System on chip design service e-business value maximization through a novel MCDM framework. *Expert Systems with Applications*, *38*(7), 7947–7962. doi:10.1016/j.eswa.2010.12.022

Huang, J., Jiang, X., & Tang, Q. (2009). An e-commerce performance assessment model: Its development and an initial test on e-commerce applications in the retail sector of China. *Information & Management*, *46*(2), 100–108. doi:10.1016/j.im.2008.12.003

Huang, T. C., Lee, T. J., & Lee, K. H. (2009). Innovative e-commerce model for food tourism products. *International Journal of Tourism Research*, *11*(6), 595–600. doi:10.1002/jtr.731

Huang, Z., & Benyoucef, M. (2013). From e-commerce to social commerce: A close look at design features. *Electronic Commerce Research and Applications*, *12*(4), 246–259. doi:10.1016/j.elerap.2012.12.003

Hubspot. (2013). Revealing charts from the 2013 state of inbound marketing. *Hubspot*.

Hwang, Y., & Kim, D. J. (2007). Customer self-service systems: The effects of perceived web quality with service contents on enjoyment, anxiety, and e-trust. *Decision Support Systems*, *43*(3), 746–760. doi:10.1016/j.dss.2006.12.008

Iacobucci, D., Arabie, P., & Bodapati, A. V. (2000). Recommendation Agents on the Internet. *Journal of Interactive Marketing*, *14*(3), 2–11. doi:10.1002/1520-6653(200022)14:3<2::AID-DIR1>3.0.CO;2-J

Ibarra, L., Partida, A., & Aguilar, D. (2015). Electronic commerce as a business strategy: Impact in consumption habits in Hermosillo, Sonora's inhabitants. *Procedia: Social and Behavioral Sciences*, *175*, 275–282. doi:10.1016/j.sbspro.2015.01.1201

Iizuka, K., Iizuka, Y., & Suematsu, C. (2013). E-business process modeling issues: From the viewpoint of inter-organizational process efficiency and information sharing. *Procedia Computer Science*, *22*, 820–827. doi:10.1016/j.procs.2013.09.164

Impact of the Ice Bucket Challenge. (2015, April 15). *ALS Association*. Retrieved from http://www.alsa.org/news/archive/impact-of-ice-bucket-challenge.html

India @ Digital Bharat. (2015). *BCG and IAMAI*. Retrieved from http://www.bcgindia.com/documents/file180687.pdf

India Credit Card Market Overview. (2014). *Sutherland Insights*. Retrieved from http://www.sutherlandinsights.com/india-credit-card-market-overview

India Digital Future in Focus 2013. (2013). *ComScore*. Retrieved from http://www.comscore.com/content/download/21739/1126111/file/India-Digital-Future-in-Focus-2013.pdf

India retail: Survival of the richest? (2014). *The Economist*. Retrieved from http://www.eiu.com/industry/article/190895003/india-retail-survival-of-the-richest/2013-08-27#

India Tech Online. (n. d.). Retrieved from http://www.indiatechonline.com

India to have 185 million mobile Internet users by June. (2014). *Bgr.in*. Retrieved from http://www.bgr.in/news/india-to-have-185-million-mobile-internet-users-by-june-iamai/

Infographic: The importance of social media in e-commerce. (n d.). Retrieved from http://www.thedrum.com/news/2014/02/16/

Information Economy Report, Unlocking the Potential of E-commerce for Developing Countries. (2015). *UNCTAD*. Retrieved from http://unctad.org/en/PublicationsLibrary/ier2015_en.pdf

Information Economy Report. (2015). *Unlocking the Potential of E-commerce for Developing Countries*. Retrieved from http://unctad.org/en/PublicationsLibrary/ier2015_en.pdf

Internet Retailing in Malaysia. (2015). *Euromonitor*. Retrieved from http://www.euromonitor.com/internet-retailing-in-malaysia/report

Israel, G. D. (2013). Determining Sample Size. *Program Evaluation and Organizational Development*. IFAS, University of Florida. Retrieved from http://edis.ifas.ufl.edu/pd006

IT Act. (2000). New Delhi: Ministry of Law, Justice And Company Affairs (Legislative Department). Retrieved from http://deity.gov.in/content/view-it-act-2000

Iyengar, R., Van den Bulte, C., & Valente, T. W. (2011). Opinion leadership and social contagion in new product diffusion. *Marketing Science*, *30*(2), 195–212. doi:10.1287/mksc.1100.0566

Iyer, K. N. S., Germain, R., & Frankwick, G. L. (2004). Supply chain B2B e-commerce and time-based delivery performance. *International Journal of Physical Distribution & Logistics Management*, *34*(8), 645–661. doi:10.1108/09600030410557776

Jaclyn, E. (1999). *Profiles of 23 Incredibly Successful Websites You've Probably Never Heard Of.* Manhattan, New York: McGraw-Hill Publishing.

James, A. (2008). More online shoppers take the word of anonymous product reviewers.

Janita, I., & Chong, W. K. (2013). Barriers of B2B e-business adoption in Indonesian SMEs: A literature analysis. *Procedia Computer Science*, *17*, 571–578. doi:10.1016/j.procs.2013.05.073

Jarvenpaa, S. L., & Todd, P. A. (1996). Consumer Reactions to Electronic Shopping on the World Wide Web. *Journal of Electronic Commerce*, *1*(2), 59–88. doi:10.1080/10864415.1996.11518283

Jarvenpaa, S. L., Tractinsky, N., & Vitale, M. (2000). Consumer trust in an internet store. *Information Technology Management*, *1*(1—2), 45–71. doi:10.1023/A:1019104520776

Jensen, M. C., & Meckling, W. H. (1976). Theory of the firm: Managerial Behavior, Agency costs and ownership structure. *ScienceDirect*. Retrieved from http://www.sciencedirect.com/science/article/pii/0304405X7690026X

Jensen, M.C. (2002). Value Maximization, Stakeholder Theory, and the Corporate Objective Function. *Business Ethics Quarterly*, 12(1).

Jing, Y. (2009). On-line Payment and Security of E-commerce. *Proceedings of theChina International Symposium on Web Information Systems and Applications.*

Jobber, D. (2007). *Principles and practice of marketing* (5th ed.). London: McGraw Hill.

Johanson, J. & Vahlne, J. (1977). The internationalization of the firm- A model of knowledge development and increasing foreign market commitments. *Journal of International Business*, 8, 22-32.

Johanson, J. & Vahlne, J. (2009). The Uppsala internationalization process revisited: From liability of foreignness to liability to outsidership. *Journal of International Business Studies*, 40(9), 1411-1431.

Johnson, M. W., Christensen, C. M., & Kagermann, H. (2008). Reinventing your business model. *Harvard Business Review*, *86*(12), 51–59. PMID:18543808

Joines, J., Scherer, C., & Scheufele, D. (2003). Exploring Motivations for Consumer Web use and their implications for Ecommerce. *Journal of Consumer Marketing*, *20*(2), 90–108. doi:10.1108/07363760310464578

Jones, S. G. (1995). Understanding community in the information age. In S. G. Jones (Ed.), *Cyber Society: Computer-mediated communication and community* (pp. 10–35). London: Sage Publications.

Joseph, S. (2012). *E-Commerce – An Indian Perspective* (4th ed.). New Delhi: PHI Learning Private Limited.

Kalakota, R., & Robinson, M. (2001). *E-business 2.0: Roadmap for success.* Boston, MA: Addison–Wesley.

Kalakota, R., & Whinston, A. B. (2009). *Electronic Commerce - A Managers Guide.* Delhi: Pearson Education Inc.

Kalia, P. (2013). Electronic Retailing in India: Past, Present & Future. In P. Singh (Ed.), *Retail Sector in India Opportunities and Challenges* (pp. 288–304). Amritsar, India: KG Graphics.

Kalia, P. (in press). Top e-Retailers of India: Business model and components. *International Journal of Electronic Marketing and Retailing.*

Kalia, P., Kaur, N., & Singh, T. (2015). Internet Marketing and B2C E-Commerce: The Indian Scenario. In A. Vashisht, G. Suri, & R. B. Kaur (Eds.), *Innovation Management* (pp. 127–134). Delhi, India: Excel India Publishers.

Kalyanam, K., & McIntyre, S. (2002). The E-Marketing Mix: A Contribution of the E-tailing Wars. *Journal of the Academy of Marketing Science*, *30*(4), 487–499. doi:10.1177/009207002236924

Kamboj, D., & Nair, S. (2014). Social Media in Retail Industry. *Infosys Lab Briefings*, *12*(1).

Kang, J.-Y. M., & Johnson, K. K. P. (2013). How does social commerce work for apparel shopping? Apparel social e-shopping with social network storefronts. *Journal of Customer Behaviour*, *12*(1), 53–72. doi:10.1362/147539213X13645550618524

Kannan, S. (2011). IT services, future growth engine for Sify. *The Hindu.* Retrieved from http://www.thehindu.com/todays-paper/tp-business/it-services-future-growth-engine-for-sify/article2137901.ece?css=print

Kaplan, A. M., & Haenlein, M. (2010). Users of the world, unite! The challenges and opportunities of Social Media. *Business Horizons*, *53*(1), 59–68. doi:10.1016/j.bushor.2009.09.003

Kasemsap, K. (2015d). Implementing business intelligence in contemporary organizations. In A. Haider (Ed.), Business technologies in contemporary organizations: Adoption, assimilation, and institutionalization (pp. 177–192). Hershey, PA, USA: IGI Global. doi:10.4018/978-1-4666-6623-8.ch008

Kasemsap, K. (2015a). The role of e-business adoption in the business world. In N. Ray, D. Das, S. Chaudhuri, & A. Ghosh (Eds.), *Strategic infrastructure development for economic growth and social change* (pp. 51–63). Hershey, PA, USA: IGI Global. doi:10.4018/978-1-4666-7470-7.ch005

Kasemsap, K. (2015b). The role of electronic commerce in the global business environments. In F. Cipolla-Ficarra (Ed.), *Handbook of research on interactive information quality in expanding social network communications* (pp. 304–324). Hershey, PA, USA: IGI Global. doi:10.4018/978-1-4666-7377-9.ch019

Kasemsap, K. (2015c). The role of information system within enterprise architecture and their impact on business performance. In M. Wadhwa & A. Harper (Eds.), *Technology, innovation, and enterprise transformation* (pp. 262–284). Hershey, PA, USA: IGI Global. doi:10.4018/978-1-4666-6473-9.ch012

Kasemsap, K. (2015e). The role of business analytics in performance management. In M. Tavana & K. Puranam (Eds.), *Handbook of research on organizational transformations through big data analytics* (pp. 126–145). Hershey, PA, USA: IGI Global. doi:10.4018/978-1-4666-7272-7.ch010

Kasemsap, K. (2015f). The role of data mining for business intelligence in knowledge management. In A. Azevedo & M. Santos (Eds.), *Integration of data mining in business intelligence systems* (pp. 12–33). Hershey, PA, USA: IGI Global. doi:10.4018/978-1-4666-6477-7.ch002

Kasemsap, K. (2015g). Implementing enterprise resource planning. In M. Khosrow-Pour (Ed.), *Encyclopedia of information science and technology* (3rd ed., pp. 798–807). Hershey, PA, USA: IGI Global. doi:10.4018/978-1-4666-5888-2.ch076

Kassarjan, H. H. (1981). Low Involvement: A Second Look. In K. B. Monroe & A. Arbor (Eds.), *Advances in Consumer Research* (Vol. 8, pp. 31–34). MI: Association for Consumer Research.

Katsanakis, I., & Kossyva, D. (2012). C-business: A theoretical framework for the implementation of co-opetition strategy in e-business. *Procedia: Social and Behavioral Sciences*, *58*, 259–268. doi:10.1016/j.sbspro.2012.09.1000

Katz, E. (1957). *The Two Step Flow of Communication, an Up-To-Date Report of an Hypothesis. Annenberg School for Communication, Departmental Papers (ASC)*. University of Pennsylvania.

Katz, E., & Lazarsfeld, P. F. (1955). *Personal Influence*. Glencoe, IL: The Free Press.

Kearney, A. T. (2012). *E-commerce is the next frontier in global expansion*. Retrieved from http://www.atkearney.com/documents/10192/348450/2012-E-Commerce-Index.pdf/83c81d46-fa4f-4421-850a-ef501d92afbd

Kearney, A. T. (2013). *Online retail is front and central in the quest for growth*. Retrieved from http://www.atkearney.com/documents/10192/3609951/Online+Retail+Is+Front+and+Center+in+the+Quest+for+Growth.pdf/f6693929-b2d6-459e-afaa-3a892adbf33e

Kearney, A. T. (2014). *Crafting an Omnichannel Strategy*. Chicago: Michael Brown & Mike Moriarty.

Keeney, R. L. (1999). The value of internet commerce to the customer. *Management Science*, *45*(4), 533–542. doi:10.1287/mnsc.45.4.533

Keller. (1993). Conceptualizing, measuring, and managing customer-based brand equity. *Journal of Marketing*, 1993, 1-22.

Kemp, J. (2000). *Governors' Scheme to Tax Internet is Questionable and Unsound*. Retrieved from http://www.caltax.org/MEMBER/digest /mar2000/mar00-2.htm

Ke, X., & Sun, Q. (2014). Study of CSF in China's B2C E-commerce based on expert evaluation. *Journal of Electronic Commerce in Organizations*, *12*(2), 31–45. doi:10.4018/jeco.2014040103

Key Challenges facing retailers in the online world. (n. d.). Retrieved from http://www.artificial-solutions.com/wp-content/uploads/protected/wp_retail-challenges.pdf

Kim, D. J., Ferrin, D. L., & Rao, H. R. (2008). A trust-based consumer decision-making model in electronic commerce: The role of trust, perceived risk, and their antecedents. *Decision Support Systems*, *44*(2), 544–564. doi:10.1016/j.dss.2007.07.001

Kim, D., & Benbasat, I. (2003). Trust-related arguments in Internet stores: A framework for evaluation. *Journal of Electronic Commerce Research*, *4*, 49–64.

Kim, M. J., Chung, N., & Lee, C. K. (2011). The effect of perceived trust on electronic commerce: Shopping online for tourism products and services in South Korea. *Tourism Management*, *32*(2), 256–265. doi:10.1016/j.tourman.2010.01.011

King, C. W., & Summers, J. O. (1970). Overlap of Opinion Leadership Across Consumer Product Categories. *JMR, Journal of Marketing Research*, *7*(1), 43–50. doi:10.2307/3149505

King, K. (2006). Youth: Lifestyle, Expectation and Media. *Young Consumers*, *7*(2), 22–29. doi:10.1108/17473610610701466

Klang, D., Wallnöfer, M., & Hacklin, F. (2014). The business model paradox: A systematic review and exploration of antecedents. *International Journal of Management Reviews*, *16*(4), 454–478. doi:10.1111/ijmr.12030

Klein, R., Rai, A., & Straub, D. W. (2007). Competitive and cooperative positioning in supply chain logistics relationships. *Decision Sciences*, *38*(4), 611–646. doi:10.1111/j.1540-5915.2007.00172.x

Klout. (2013). *Klout*. Retrieved from Klout: www.klout.com

Knemeyer, A. M., & Murphy, P. (2004). Evaluation the performance of third-party logistics arrangements: A relationship marketing perspective. *Journal of Supply Chain Management*, *40*(1), 722–740. doi:10.1111/j.1745-493X.2004.tb00254.x

Kolbitsch, J., & Maurer, H. (2006). The Transformation of the Web: How Emerging Communities Shape the Information We Consume. *Journal of Universal Computer Science*, *12*(2), 187–213.

Kolesar, M. B., & Galbrait, R. W. (2000). A Service Marketing Perspective on E-Retailing: Implications for E-Retailers and Directions for Further Research. *The Internet Research: Electronic Networking Applications and Policy*, *10*(5), 424–438. doi:10.1108/10662240010349444

Koo, D. M., Kim, J. J., & Lee, S. H. (2008). Personal values as underlying motives of shopping online. *Asia Pacific Journal of Marketing and Logistics*, *20*(2), 156–173. doi:10.1108/13555850810864533

Korgaonkar, P. A., & Karson, E. J. (2007). The influence of perceived product risk on consumers' e-tailer shopping preference. *Journal of Business and Psychology*, *22*(1), 55–64. doi:10.1007/s10869-007-9044-y

Kotb, A., Roberts, C., & Stoner, G. (2013). E-business in accounting education in the UK and Ireland: Influences on inclusion in the curriculum. *The International Journal of Management Education*, *11*(3), 150–162. doi:10.1016/j.ijme.2013.05.002

Kotler, P. (2003). *Marketing Management* (11th ed.). New Jersey: Pearson Education.

Koyuncu, C., & Bhattacharya, G. (2004). The impacts of quickness, price, payment risk, and delivery issues on on-line shopping. *Journal of Socio-Economics*, *33*(2), 241–251. doi:10.1016/j.socec.2003.12.011

Kozinets, R. (1999). E-tribalized marketing: The strategic implications of virtual communities of consumption. *European Management Journal*, *17*(3), 252–264. doi:10.1016/S0263-2373(99)00004-3

Kozinets, R. V. (2002). The Field Behind the Screen: Using Netnography for Marketing Research in Online Communities. *Journal*, *39*(4), 61–72.

Kozinets, V., de Valck, K., Wojnicki, A. C., & Wilner, S. J. S. (2010). Networked narratives: Understanding word-of-mouth marketing in online communities. *Journal of Marketing*, *74*(2), 71–89. doi:10.1509/jmkg.74.2.71

Krejcie, R., & Morgan, D. (1970). Determining Sample Size for Research Activities. *Educational and Psychological Measurement*, 30, 607-610. Retrieved from http://home.kku.ac.th/sompong/guest_speaker/KrejcieandMorgan_article.pdf

Kremic, T., Tukel, O. I., & Rom, W. O. (2006). Outsourcing decision support: A survey of benefits, risks, and decision factors. *Supply Chain Management. International Journal (Toronto, Ont.)*, *11*, 467–482.

Kristopher, J. (2008). *SEO: Your visual blueprint for effective Internet marketing*. Indianapolis, IN: Wiley Publishing Inc.

Kulkarni, S. (2015), A brief report of Healthcare, Telemedicine and Medical Tourism in India. Retrieved from http://www.asa.in/pdfs/surveys-reports/Healthcare-Telemedicine-and-Medical-Tourism-in-India.pdf

Kumar, V., & Mirchandi, R. (2012). Increasing he ROI of Social Media Marketing. *Sloan Management Review*, 54(1), 55.

Kumar, K., & Mahadevan, B. (2003). Evolution of Business Models in B2C E-Commerce : The Case of Fabmall. *IIMB Management Review*, December, 23–30. Retrieved from http://www.iimb.ernet.in/~mahadev/fabmall.pdf

Kumar, K., & van Dissel, H. G. (1996). Sustainable collaboration: Managing conflict and cooperation in interorganizational systems. *Management Information Systems Quarterly*, *20*(3), 279–300. doi:10.2307/249657

Kumar, V., Bohling, T. R., & Ladda, R. N. (2003). Antecedents and consequences of relationship intention: Implications for transaction and relationship marketing. *Industrial Marketing Management*, *32*(8), 667–676. doi:10.1016/j.indmarman.2003.06.007

Kurian, B. (2000, July). Catch the shopper by the e-tail. *Business Line*, 44–47.

Lai, J. Y., Kan, C. W., & Ulhas, K. R. (2013). Impacts of employee participation and trust on e-business readiness, benefits, and satisfaction. *Information Systems and e-Business Management*, *11*(2), 265–285.

Lai, K., Wong, C. W. Y., & Cheng, T. C. E. (2010). Bundling digitized logistics activities and its performance implications. *Industrial Marketing Management*, *39*(2), 273–286. doi:10.1016/j.indmarman.2008.08.002

Laudon, K. C., & Laudon, J. P. (2005). *Management information systems: Managing the digital firm*. Upper Saddle River, NJ: Prentice Hall.

Laudon, K. C., & Traver, C. G. (2007). *E-commerce - Business, Technology, Society (Low Price.)*. New Delhi, India: Pearson Education Inc.

Laudon, K. C., & Traver, C. G. (2009). *E-Commerce Business. Technology. Society* (5th ed.). New Jersey: Prentice Hall.

Laudon, K. C., & Traver, C. G. (2009). *E-commerce: Business, technology and society*. Upper Saddle River, NJ: Prentice Hall.

Laux, V. (2008). Board independence and CEO turnover. *Journal of Accounting Research*, *46*(1), 137–171. doi:10.1111/j.1475-679X.2008.00269.x

Laxmi, Prabha, G. (2007). The prospects and problems of Indian Retailing. *Indian Journal of Marketing*, *37*(10).

Lazarsfeld, P. F., Berelson, B., & Gaudet, H. (1948). *The people's choice*. New York: Columbia University Press.

Lee, G. G., & Lin, H. F. (2005). Customer perceptions of e-service quality in online shopping. *International Journal of Retail & Distribution Management*, *33*(2), 161–176. doi:10.1108/09590550510581485

Lee, K., & Chung, N. (2000). Effect of virtual reality-driven shopping mall and consumer's purchase intention. *Korean Management Review*, *29*(3), 377–405.

Lee, M. K. O., & Turban, E. (2001). A Trust Model for Consumer Internet Shopping. *International Journal of Electronic Commerce*, *6*, 75–91.

Leena, O. (2015). *Retail Websites Are in Need of E-Commerce SEO.* Retrieved from http://www.webfly.com/retail-websites-are-in-need-of-e-commerce-seo/

Lee, S., & Lim, G. G. (2005). The impact of partnership attributes on EDI implementation success. *Information & Management*, *42*(4), 503–516. doi:10.1016/S0378-7206(03)00153-8

Levitt, T. (1983). The globalization of markets. *Harvard Business Review,* 1983.

Leyton, D., Pino, J. A., & Ochoa, S. F. (2015). EBTAM: Technology acceptance in e-business environments. *Information Systems and e-Business Management, 13*(2), 211–234. doi: 10.1007/s10257-014-0255-2

Li, K., Idemudia, E. C., Lin, Z., & Yu, Y. (2012). A framework for intermediated online targeted advertising with banner ranking mechanism. *Information Systems and e-Business Management, 10*(2), 183–200. doi:10.1007/s10257-010-0134-4

Liang, T., Ho, Y., Li, Y., & Turban, E. (2011). What drives social commerce: The role of social support and relationship quality. *International Journal of Electronic Commerce*, *16*(2), 69–90. doi:10.2753/JEC1086-4415160204

Liang, T., & Huang, J. (1998). An empirical study on consumer acceptance of products in electronic markets: A transaction cost model. *Decision Support Systems*, *24*(1), 29–43. doi:10.1016/S0167-9236(98)00061-X

Liao, Z., & Shi, X. (2009). Consumer prospections of internet-based e-retailing: An empirical research in Hong Kong. *Journal of Services Marketing*, *23*(1), 24–30. doi:10.1108/08876040910933066

Li, C., & Bernoff, J. (2011). *Groundswell*. Cambridge: Forrester.

Lichtenstein, D. R., & Burton, S. (1990). An assessment of the moderating effects of market mavenism and value consciousness on price-quality perception accuracy. *Advances in Consumer Research. Association for Consumer Research (U. S.)*, *17*(1), 53–59.

Li, F., Pieńkowski, D., van Moorsel, A., & Smith, C. (2012). A holistic framework for trust in online transactions. *International Journal of Management Reviews*, *14*(1), 85–103. doi:10.1111/j.1468-2370.2011.00311.x

Li, J. (2000). E-Commerce Tax Policy in Australia, Canada and the United States. *Wales Law Journal*, *23*(2), 313–329.

Lim, H., & Dubinsky, A. J. (2004). Consumers' perceptions of e-shopping characteristics: An expectancy-value approach. *Journal of Services Marketing*, *18*(6), 500–513. doi:10.1108/08876040410561839

Li, N., & Zhang, P. (2002), Consumer online shopping attitudes and behavior: an assessment of research. *Proceedings of 8th Americas Conference on Information System* (pp. 508-517).

Ling, K. C., Chai, L. T., & Piew, T. H. (2010). The effects of shopping orientations, online trust and prior online purchase experience toward customers' online purchase intention. *International Business Research*, *3*(3), 63–75. doi:10.5539/ibr.v3n3p63

Lin, I. C., & Chang, C. C. (2009). A countable and time-bound password-based user authentication scheme for the applications of electronic commerce. *Information Science*, *179*(9), 1269–1277. doi:10.1016/j.ins.2008.12.026

Lin, L. M., & Hsia, T. L. (2011). Core capabilities for practitioners in achieving e-business innovation. *Computers in Human Behavior*, *27*(5), 1884–1891. doi:10.1016/j.chb.2011.04.012

Lin, Z. (2014). An empirical investigation of user and system recommendations in e-commerce. *Decision Support Systems*, *68*, 111–124. doi:10.1016/j.dss.2014.10.003

Liu, C. (2013). The problems and solutions of Taobao's logistics model. *Shangqing*, 47.

Liu, F., Dixon, M., & Murphy, J. (2002). Ramizwick & T. Ping, (Ed.), Exploring Online Buying and Online Trust in China (pp. 336-342). Association for Consumer Research, Valdosta, GA.

Liu, B., Cao, S. G., & He, W. (2011). Distributed data mining for e-business. *Information Technology Management*, *12*(2), 67–79. doi:10.1007/s10799-011-0091-8

Liu, C., & Arnett, K. P. (2000). Exploring the factors associated with website success in the context of electronic commerce. *Information & Management*, *38*(1), 23–33. doi:10.1016/S0378-7206(00)00049-5

Liu, C., & Guo, Y. (2008). Validating the end-user computing satisfaction instrument for online shopping systems. *Journal of Organizational and End User Computing*, *20*(4), 74–96. doi:10.4018/joeuc.2008100104

Liu, X., He, M., Gao, F., & Xie, P. (2008). An empirical study of online shopping customer satisfaction in China: A holistic perspective. *International Journal of Retail & Distribution Management*, *36*(11), 919–940. doi:10.1108/09590550810911683

Loane, S. (2006). The Role of the Internet in the Internationalisation of small and medium sized companies. *Journal of International Entrepreneurship*, 33(4), 263–277.

Loed, W. (2014). 10 reasons why Alibaba blows away Amazon and EBay. *Forbes.com.* Retrieved from http://www.forbes.com/sites/walterloeb/2014/04/11/10-reasons-why-alibaba-is-a-worldwide-leader-in-e-commerce/

Lohse, G., Bellman, S., & Johnson, E. (2000). Consumer buying behaviour on the Internet: Findings from panel data. *Journal of Interactive Marketing*, *14*(1), 15–29. doi:10.1002/(SICI)1520-6653(200024)14:1<15::AID-DIR2>3.0.CO;2-C

Lu, W.-M., & Hung, S.-W. (2011). Exploring the efficiency and effectiveness in global e-retailing companies. *Computers & Operations Research*, *38*(9), 1351–1360. doi:10.1016/j.cor.2010.12.009

Lu, X. H., Huang, L. H., & Heng, M. S. H. (2006). Critical success factors of inter-organizational information systems: A case study of Cisco and Xiao Tong in China. *Information & Management*, *43*(3), 395–408. doi:10.1016/j.im.2005.06.007

Lyons, B., & Henderson, K. (2005). Opinion leadership in a computer-mediated environment. *Journal of Consumer Behaviour*, *4*(5), 319–329. doi:10.1002/cb.22

Ma, N. (2010). The optimized design of C2C third-party logistics network: Case of Taobao. *China Business & Trade*, 22.

Maguire, S. (2005). *Congressional Research Service: Report for Congress: State and Local Sales and Use Taxes and Internet Commerce.* Retrieved from http://www.ipmall.info/hosted_resources/crs/RL31252_050128.pdf

Maher, M., & Andersson, T. (1999). Corporate Governance: Effect on Firm Performance and Economic Growth. *ECGI.* Retrieved from http://www.ecgi.org/research/accession/cgeu.pdf

Maity, M., & Dass, M. (2014). Consumer decision-making across modern and traditional channels: E-commerce, m-commerce, in-store. *Decision Support Systems*, *61*, 34–46. doi:10.1016/j.dss.2014.01.008

Malaysians increasingly shop online. (2015). *Inside Retail Asia.* Retrieved from http://insideretail.asia/2013/08/23/malaysians-increasingly-shop-online/

Malhotra, J.D., & Kumar, K. (Eds.), (1997, December). Evolution of a virtual community: Understanding design issues through a longitudinal study. *Proceedings of the Eighteenth International Conference on Information Systems*, Atlanta, GA, USA.

Mangold, W. G., & Faulds, D. J. (2009). Social Media: The new hybrid element of the promotion mix. *Business Horizons*, *52*(4), 357–365. doi:10.1016/j.bushor.2009.03.002

Marchet, G., Perego, A., & Perotti, S. (2009). An exploratory study of ICT adoption in the Italian freight transportation industry. *International Journal of Physical Distribution & Logistics Management*, *39*(9), 785–812. doi:10.1108/09600030911008201

Margaret, C. C. (1999). Perceptions of Price Unfairness: Antecedents and Consequences. *JMR, Journal of Marketing Research*, *36*(2), 187–199. doi:10.2307/3152092

Markus, M. L. (2004). Technology management: Using IT to drive organizational change. *Journal of Information Technology*, *19*(1), 4–20. doi:10.1057/palgrave.jit.2000002

Mathews, S., Healy, M., & Ali, Y. (2006). A comparative evaluation of the Internet's influence on international market penetration and development growth strategies of Australian SME's. *Proceedings of the Australia & New Zealand Marketing Academy Annual Conference*. Brisbane.

Matopoulos, A., Vlachopoulou, M., & Manthou, V. (2007). Exploring the impact of e-business adoption on logistics processes: Empirical evidence from the food industry. *International Journal of Logistics Research and Applications*, *10*(2), 109–122. doi:10.1080/13675560701427270

Maxwell, J., & Brewster, M. (2015). Price Waterhouse Cooper's Total Retail survey. *PriceWaterhouseCooper*. Retrieved from http://www.pwc.com/gx/en/retail-consumer/retail-consumer-publications/global-multi-channel-consumer-survey/index.jhtml

McKnight, D. H., Choudhury, V., & Kacmar, C. (2002). The impact of initial consumer trust on intentions to transaction with a website: A trust building model. *The Journal of Strategic Information Systems*, *11*(3/4), 297–323. doi:10.1016/S0963-8687(02)00020-3

McQuail, D. (1985). Sociology of mass communication. *Annual Review of Sociology*, *11*(1), 93–111. doi:10.1146/annurev.so.11.080185.000521

McWilliams, G. (2000). Building strong brands through online communities. *MIT Sloan Management Review*, *41*, 43–54.

Medical Value Travel in India. (2014). *KPMG Research Report*. Retrieved from www.kpmg.com/IN/en/IssuesAndInsights/ArticlesPublications/Documents/KPMG-FICCI-Heal-Sep2014.pdf

Meeker, M. (1997, May 28). The Internet Retailing Report. US Equity Investment Research Morgan Stanley.

Mega trends 2015. (2015) *Making sense of a world in motion* Retrieved from http://www.ey.com/Publication/vwLUAssets/ey-megatrends-report-2015/$FILE/ey-megatrends-report-2015.pdf

Mehrabian, A., & Russell, J. (1974). *An Approach to Environmental Psychology*. Cambridge, MA: MIT Press.

Mehta, M. K. (2014). New record : 5.80 lakh e -tickets booked on IRCTC website on March 19. *The Times of India*. Retrieved from http://timesofindia.indiatimes.com/india/New-record-5-80-lakh-e-tickets-booked-on-IRCTC-website-on-March-19/articleshow/32356664.cms

Mentzer, J. T., Flint, D. J., & Hult, G. T. M. (2001). Logistics service quality as a segment-customized process. *Journal of Marketing*, *65*(4), 82–104. doi:10.1509/jmkg.65.4.82.18390

Mentzer, J. T., Gomes, R., & Krapfel, R. E. (1989). Physical distribution service: A fundamental marketing concept. *Journal of the Academy of Marketing Science*, *17*(4).

Merton, R. (1957). *Social Theory and Social Structure*. New York: Free Press.

Metters, R., & Walton, S. (2007). Strategic supply chain choices for multi-channel Internet retailers. *Service Business*, *1*(4), 317–331. doi:10.1007/s11628-006-0016-5

Meyer, H.K., & Carey, M.C. (2013). In moderation, journalism. *Practice*. doi:10.1080/17512786.2013.859838

Michaelidou, N., Siamagka, N. T., & Christodoulides, G. (2011). Usage, barriers and measurement of social media marketing: An exploratory investigation of small and medium B2B brands. *Industrial Marketing Management*, *40*(7), 1153–1159. doi:10.1016/j.indmarman.2011.09.009

Miller, R. R. (1998). *Selling to Newly Emerging Markets*. New York: Quorum Books.

Milne, G. R., Rohm, A. J., & Bahl, S. (2004). Consumers' Protection of Online Privacy and Identity. *The Journal of Consumer Affairs*, *38*(2), 217–232. doi:10.1111/j.1745-6606.2004.tb00865.x

Min, S., & Wolfinbarger, M. (2005). Do early movers, clicks, and mortars, and generalists prevail in E-commerce? *Journal of Business Research*, *58*, 1030–1039. doi:10.1016/j.jbusres.2004.02.005

Mishra, S. (n. d.). A Conceptual Framework for creating customer value in e-retailing in India. South Asian. *Journal of Management*, *16*(4), 127–147.

Mishra, V. (2011). The influence of e-business alliance network on e-business firm's performance: An exploratory study. *Journal of Service Science Research*, *3*(2), 153–184. doi: 10.1007/s12927-011-0007-5

Miyazaki, A. D., & Fernandez, A. (2001). Consumer perceptions of privacy and security risks for online shopping. *The Journal of Consumer Affairs*, *35*(1), 27–44. doi:10.1111/j.1745-6606.2001.tb00101.x

Modahl, M. (2000). *Now or never*. New York: Harper Collins.

Moon, B.-J. (2004). Consumer adoption of the internet as an information search and product purchase channel: some research hypotheses. *Int. Journal of Internet Marketing and Advertising, 1*(1).

Moorman, C., Deshpande, R., & Zaltman, G. (1993a). Factors Affecting Trust in Market Research Relationships. *Journal of Marketing*, *57*(1), 81–101. doi:10.2307/1252059

Morosan, C. (2014). Toward an integrated model of adoption of mobile phones for purchasing ancillary services in air travel. *International Journal of Contemporary Hospitality Management*, *26*(2), 246–271. doi:10.1108/IJCHM-11-2012-0221

Morris, M., & Ogan, C. (1996). The Internet as Mass Medium. *Journal of Communication*, *46*(1), 39–50. doi:10.1111/j.1460-2466.1996.tb01460.x

Morschett, D., Swoboda, B., & Schramm-Klein, H. (2006). Competitive strategies in retailing – an investigation of the applicability of Porter's framework for food retailers. *Journal of Retailing and Consumer Services*, *13*(4), 275–287. doi:10.1016/j.jretconser.2005.08.016

Mukhopadhyay, S. K., & Setoputro, R. (2004). Reverse logistics in e-business: Optimal price and return policy. *International Journal of Physical Distribution & Logistics Management*, *34*(1), 70–89. doi:10.1108/09600030410515691

Mulhern, F. (1997). Retail Marketing: From distribution to integration. *International Journal of Research in Marketing*, *14*(2), 103–124. doi:10.1016/S0167-8116(96)00031-6

Mummalaneni, V., & Meng, J. (2009). An exploratory study of young Chinese customers' online shopping behaviors and service quality perceptions. *Young Consumers*, *10*(2), 157–169. doi:10.1108/17473610910964732

Muntinga, D. G., Moorman, M., & Smit, E. G. (2011). Introducing COBRAs Exploring motivations for brand-related social media use. *International Journal of Advertising*, *30*(1), 13–46. doi:10.2501/IJA-30-1-013-046

Murugavel, D.M.V. (2010, August). E-tailing market scenario in India- A Bird's eye view. *Indian Journal of Marketing*.

Myerson, A. R. (1998, June 29). Comp USA: Revising Computer Retailing. *The New York Times*.

Narang, R., & Singh, S. (2014). Quality of Work Life and Service Quality. In A. Goyal (Ed.), Innovation in Services Marketing and Management: Strategies for Emerging Economies (pp. 265-290). Hershey, PA, USA: IGI Global. doi:10.4018/978-1-4666-4671-1.ch015

Narang, R. (2010). Psychographic segmentation of youth in the evolving Indian retail market. *International Review of Retail, Distribution and Consumer Research*, *20*(5), 535–557. doi:10.1080/09593969.2010.520508

Narang, R. (2011). Examining the role of various psychographic characteristics in apparel store selection: A study of Indian youth. *Young Consumers: Insights and Ideas for Responsible Marketers*, *12*(2), 133–144. doi:10.1108/17473611111141597

Narang, R., Polsa, P., Soneye, A., & Fuxiang, W. (2015). Impact of hospital atmosphere on perceived health care outcome. *International Journal of Health Care Quality Assurance*, *28*(2), 129–140. doi:10.1108/IJHCQA-12-2013-0142 PMID:26335166

Ngoy, J. M. (2003). Is international e-commerce an HIV tax issue? *International Journal of Services Technology and Management*, *4*(1), 53. doi:10.1504/IJSTM.2003.002571

Nguyen, H. O. (2013). Critical factors in e-business adoption: Evidence from Australian transport and logistics companies. *International Journal of Production Economics*, *146*(1), 300–312. doi:10.1016/j.ijpe.2013.07.014

Nicholls, A., & Watson, A. (2005). Implementing e-value strategies in UK retailing. *International Journal of Retail & Distribution Management*, *33*(6), 426–443. doi:10.1108/09590550510600852

Niranjanamurthy, M., & Dharmendra, C. (2013). The study of E-Commerce Security Issues and Solutions. *International Journal of Advanced Research in Computer and Communication Engineering*, *2*(7).

Norris, G., Hurley, J., Hartley, K., Dunleavy, J., & Balls, J. (2000). *E-business and ERP: Transforming the enterprise*. New York, NY: John Wiley & Sons.

Novak, T. P., Hoffman, D. L., & Peralta, M. (1999). Building Consumer Trust in Online Environment: The Case for Information Privacy. *Communications of the ACM*, 1999, 42.

Number of Internet Users 2014. (2014). Retrieved from http://www.internetlivestats.com/internet-users/#definitions

Nunnally, J., & Bernstein, I. H. (1994). *Psychometric Theory* (3rd ed.). New York: McGraw-Hill.

Nurmilaakso, J. M. (2008). Adoption of e-business functions and migration from EDI-based to XML-based e-business frameworks in supply chain integration. *International Journal of Production Economics*, *113*(2), 721–733. doi:10.1016/j.ijpe.2007.11.001

O'Cass, A., & Fenech, T. (2003). Web retailing adoption: Exploring the nature of internet users Web retailing behaviour. *Journal of Retailing and Consumer Services*, *10*(2), 81–94. doi:10.1016/S0969-6989(02)00004-8

Offitzer, A. (2014, May 29). Future of comments section: moderated and annotated. *AJR.com*. Retrieved from http://ajr.org/2014/05/29/future-comment-sections-moderated-annotated/

Ogata, K., & Futatsugi, K. (2010). Proof score approach to analysis of electronic commerce protocols. *International Journal of Software Engineering and Knowledge Engineering*, *20*(2), 253–287. doi:10.1142/S0218194010004712

Ohmae, K. (1989, June). Managing in a Borderless World. *Harvard Business Review*.

Ohmae, K. (2000). *The Invisible Continent*. New York, NY: Harper Business.

Oh, S. (2010). New role-based access control in ubiquitous e-business environment. *Journal of Intelligent Manufacturing*, *21*(5), 607–612. doi:10.1007/s10845-008-0208-z

Ojo, M. (2010). Building on the Trust of Management: Overcoming the Paradoxes of Principles Based Regulation. Law and Prosociality, 30(7).

Ojo, M. (2013, December 28). *Audits, Audit Quality and Signaling Mechanisms: Concentrated Ownership Structures*. Paper presented at the 2014 IBFR Conference, May 27 - 30 2014 San Jose Costa Rica. Retrieved from http://www.theibfr.com/ARCHIVE/ISSN-1941-9589-V9-N2-2014.pdf

Ojo, M., (2011). Co-operative and Competitive Enforced Self Regulation: The Role of Governments, Private Actors and Banks in Corporate Responsibility. *Journal of Financial Regulation and Compliance, 19*(2).

Okonkwo, U. (2009). Sustaining the luxury brand on the Internet. *Journal of Marketing*, 16, 303–310.

O'Malley, L. (1003). Relationship marketing. In S. Hart (Ed.), *Marketing Changes*. London: Thomson Learning.

O'Malley, L., & Tynan, C. (2000). Relationship marketing in consumer markets: Rhetoricor reality. *European Journal of Marketing*, *34*(1), 717–815.

Oman shows promise for online shopping growth: MasterCard Survey. (n. d.). *Mastercard.com*. Retrieved from http://newsroom.mastercard.com/mea/press-releases/oman-shows-promise-for-online-shopping-growth-mastercard-survey/

Omar, M., Bathgate, I., & Nwankwo, S. (2011). Internet marketing and customer satisfaction in emerging markets: The case of Chinese online shoppers. *Competitiveness Review: An International Business Journal*, *21*(2), 224–237. doi:10.1108/10595421111117489

Omnichannel Importance. (2014). *TNS New Zealand and StopPress*.

Onetti, A., Zucchella, A., Jones, M. V., & McDougall-Covin, P. P. (2012). Internationalization, innovation and entrepreneurship: Business models for new technology-based firms. *Journal of Management and Governance*, *16*(3), 337–368. doi:10.1007/s10997-010-9154-1

Online Retail Is Front and Center in the Quest for Growth. (2013). *ATKearney*. Retrieved from https://dl.dropboxusercontent.com/u/3187612/Global Retail E-commerce Index 2013.pdf

Organisation for Economic Co-operation and Development. (2010). Summary of Key Points and Conclusions. *Proceedings of the conference on Empowering E-Consumers: Strengthening Consumer Protection in the Internet Economy*.

Organization for Economic Co-operation and Development. (2010). Summary of Key Points and Conclusions. Proceedings of the conference on Empowering E-Consumers: Strengthening Consumer Protection in the Internet Economy.

Osawa, J. (2013). Alibaba isn't the Amazon of China. *Wall Street Journal*. Retrieved from http://blogs.wsj.com/digits/2013/10/16/alibaba-isnt-the-amazon-of-china/

Osawa, J. (2014). Alibaba: A mix of Amazon, eBay and PayPal with a dash of Google- how the Chinese company came to dominate Chinese e-commerce. *Wall Street Journal*. Retrieved from http://www.wsj.com/articles/SB100014240527 02303546204579440472954450720

Osawa, J. (2014). How to understand Alibaba's business model. *Marketwatch.com.* Retrieved from http://www.marketwatch.com/story/how-to-understand-alibabas-business-model-2014-03-15-94855847

Osmonbekov, T., & Gruen, T. (2013). Manufacturer–reseller e-business arrangements: The impact of inequity on relationship performance and the moderating role of dependence. *Industrial Marketing Management*, *42*(6), 872–879. doi:10.1016/j.indmarman.2013.05.013

Osterwalder, A., Pigneur, Y., & Tucci, C. L. (2005). Clarifying business models: Origins, present, and future of the concept. *Communications of the Association for Information Systems*, *16*(1), 1–25.

Othmani, L., & Bouslama, N. (2014, February 14). *The Relationship between Virtual Community and Perceived Risk in the Social-Commerce: An Exploratory Study.*

Ozturkcan, S., & Gul Gursoy (2014). On-Line Reviews' Impact on Trust Building. *Proceedings of the Global Conference on Business and Finance,9*(1), 350-360.

Palacios, J. J. (2003). Globalization and e-commerce: Diffusion and impacts in Mexico. I-Ways. *Digest of Electronic Commerce Policy and Regulation*, *26*, 195–205.

Palopoli, L., Rosaci, D., & Ursino, D. (2006). Agents' roles in B2C e-commerce. *AI Communications*, *19*(2), 95–126.

Palumbo, F., & Herbig, P. (1998). International Marketing Tool: The Internet. *Industrial Management & Data Systems*, *98*(6), 253–261. doi:10.1108/02635579810228381

Pan, E.J. (2003). Harmonization of U.S – E.U Securities Regulation: The Case for a Single European Securities Regulator Law and Policy in International Business

Pandey, D. (2011, August 11). Electronic commerce to social commerce. *Dharmendrapandey.com.* Retrieved from http://www.dharmendrapandey.com/2011/08/electronic-commerce-to-social-commerce_11.html

Pang, C., Yen, D. C., & Tarn, J. M. (2007). Exploring online shoppers'e-trust in China. *Human Systems Management*, *26*(3), 193–198.

Pan, Y., & Zinkhan, G. M. (2006). Determinants of retail patronage: A meta-analytical perspective. *Journal of Retailing*, *82*(3), 229–244. doi:10.1016/j.jretai.2005.11.008

Papaioannou, E., Assimakopoulos, C., Sarmaniotis, C., & Georgiadis, C. K. (2013). Investigating customer satisfaction dimensions with service quality of online auctions: An empirical investigation of e-Bay. *Information Systems and e-Business Management, 11*(2), 313–330. doi:10.1007/s10257-012-0202-z

Papazoglou, M. P., & Ribbers, P. M. A. (2006). *E-business: Organizational and technical foundations.* Chichester, UK: John Wiley & Sons.

Parasuraman, A., Zeithaml, V. A., & Berry, L. L. (1985). A conceptual model of service quality and its implications for future research. *Journal of Retailing*, *49*(1), 41–50.

Parasuraman, A., Zeithaml, V. A., & Berry, L. L. (1988). SERVQUAL: A multiple-item scale for measuring consumer perceptions of service quality. *Journal of Retailing*, *64*(1), 12–40.

Parise, S., & Guinan, P. J. (2008). Marketing using Web 2.0. In *Proceedings of the 41st Hawaii International Conference on System Sciences.* Washington, DC: IEEE Computer Society Press.

Park, C. S. (2013). Does Twitter motivate involvement in politics? Tweeting, opinion leadership, and political engagement. *Computers in Human Behavior*, *29*(4), 1641–1648. doi:10.1016/j.chb.2013.01.044

Park, C. W., & Lessig, V. P. (1977). Students and housewives: Differences in susceptibility to reference group influence. *The Journal of Consumer Research*, *4*(2), 102–110. doi:10.1086/208685

Park, D.-H., Lee, J., & Han, I. (2007). The Effect of On-Line Consumer Reviews on Consumer Purchasing Intention: The Moderating Role of Involvement. *International Journal of Electronic Commerce*, *11*(4), 125–148. doi:10.2753/JEC1086-4415110405

Parker, C. (2007). M eta Regulation: Legal Accountability for Corporate Social Responsibility. In D McBarnet, A Voiculescu, & T Campbell (Eds.), The New Corporate Accountability: Corporate Social Responsibility and the Law. Cambridge University Press.

Parks, M. R., & Floyd, K. (1996). Making friends in cyberspace. *Journal of Computer-Mediated Communication*, *1*(4), 80–97.

Patel, A. (2010). Concept of Mobile Agent-Based Electronic Marketplace-Safety Measures. In I. Lee (Ed.), *Encyclopedia of E-Business Development and Management in the Global Economy* (pp. 252–264). Hershey, PA: IGI Global; doi:10.4018/978-1-61520-611-7.ch025

Pathak, B., Garfinkel, R., Gopal, R. D., Venkatesan, R., & Yin, F. (2010). Empirical analysis of the impact of recommender systems on sales. *Journal of Management Information Systems*, *27*(2), 159–188. doi:10.2753/MIS0742-1222270205

Patnia, A. (2014). Is Indian grandfathered tax laws a roadblock for e-commerce in India? *Taxmantra.com*. Retrieved from http://taxmantra.com/is-indian-grandfathered-tax-laws-a-roadblock-for-e-commerce-in-india.html/

Pavlou, P. A. (2002). What drives electronic commerce? A theory of planned behaviour perspective. *Best Paper Proceedings of the Academy of Management,* Denver. CO.

Pearson, M. (2012). Social Media plays growing role in online retailing. Retrieved from http://www.theglobeandmail.com/report-on-business/small-business/sb-marketing/sales/social-media-plays-growing-role-in-online-retailing/article4179338

Petrovic, O., Ksela, M., Fallenböck, M., & Kittl, C. (2003). *Trust in the Network Economy*. New York: Springer Publishing. doi:10.1007/978-3-7091-6088-6

Pinto, D. (2005). Ten Tax Issues Relating to conducting business in cyberspace. *Journal of Internet Banking and Commerce, 10*(1), 1-9. Retrieved from http://www.arraydev.com/commerce/jibc/

Pisano, G. P., & Verganti, R. (2008). Which kind of collaboration is right for you? *Harvard Business Review*, *86*(12), 78–86.

Piskorski, M. J. (2011). Social Strategies That Work. *Harvard Business Review*. PMID:22111430

Pizzutti, C., & Von, D. (2011). Perception of justice after recovery efforts in internet purchasing: The impact of consumer trust and loyalty towards retailing sites and online shopping in general. *Brazilian Administration Review*, *8*(3), 225–246. doi:10.1590/S1807-76922011000300002

Polcari, J. (2014, September). Four critical success factors for omnichannel retailing. *ChiefMarketer.com*. Retrieved from http://www.chiefmarketer.com/four-critical-success-factors-omnichannel-marketing/

Poon, S., & Swatman, P. M. C. (1998). A combined-method study of small business Internet commerce. *International Journal of Electronic Commerce*, *2*(3), 31–46. doi:10.1080/10864415.1998.11518314

Popper, B. (2014). Alibaba has more sales than Amazon and eBay combined, but will Americans trust it? China's biggest internet company has filed for its US IPO. *The Verge.com*. Retrieved from http://www.theverge.com/2014/5/7/5690596/meet-alibaba-the-ecommerce-giant-with-more-sales-than-amazon-and-ebay

Porter, M. (1980). *Competitive strategy: Techniques for analyzing industries and competitors*. New York: Free Press.

Porter, M. (1985). *Competitive advantage—Creating and sustaining superior performance*. New York: Free Press.

Posts tagged 'Tmall'. (2014). *Yipitdata*. Retrieved from http://yipitdata.com/tag/tmall/

Prasad, C., & Aryasri, A. (2009). Determinants of shopper behaviour in e-tailing: An empirical analysis. *Paradigm*, *13*(1), 73–83. doi:10.1177/0971890720090110

Prashantham, S. (2005). Toward a Knowledge-Based Conceptualization of Internationalization. *Journal of International Entrepreneurship*, *3*(1), 37–52. doi:10.1007/s10843-005-0304-5

Pressman, A. (2014). Alibaba a threat to eBay, Amazon outside the U.S., not within. *Yahoo Finance*. Retrieved from http://finance.yahoo.com/news/alibaba-aims-at-ebay-and-amazon-outside-of-the-united-states-173757037.html

Price, L. L., Feick, L. F., & Guskey-Federouch, A. (1988). Couponing behaviors of the market maven: Profile of a super couponer. *Advances in Consumer Research. Association for Consumer Research (U. S.)*, *15*(1), 354–359.

PricewaterhouseCooper. (2015). *2015 Total Retail survey.*http://www.pwc.com/gx/en/retail-consumer/retail-consumer-publications/global-multi-channel-consumer-survey/index.jhtml#

Puri, A. (2015). Is E-commerce Replacing Physical Retail In India? 27. Jan, 2015, Retrieved May 6, 2015, from http://www.joneslanglasalleblog.com/realestatecompass/real-estate/2015/01/ecommerce-replacing-physical-retail-india/

Quarterly Retail E-commerce Sales. (2015). *U.S. Department of Commerce*. Retrieved from https://www.census.gov/retail/mrts/www/data/pdf/ec_current.pdf

Quelch, J.A., & Hoff, E.J. (1993). Customizing Global Marketing. In R.Z. Aliber, & R.W. Click (Eds.), *Reading in international business: A decision approach.* Cambridge: Massachusetts Institution of Technology.

Quick Facts / Milestones. Edge.in. (2014). Retrieved from http://infoedge.in/corporate-quick-facts-milestones.asp

Qu, W. G., Pinsonneault, A., Tomiuk, D., Wang, S., & Liu, Y. (2015). The impacts of social trust on open and closed B2B e-commerce: A Europe-based study. *Information & Management*, *52*(2), 151–159. doi:10.1016/j.im.2014.07.002

Qu, Z., Wang, Y., Wang, S., & Zhang, Y. (2013). Implications of online social activities for e-tailers' business performance. *European Journal of Marketing*, *47*(8), 1190–1212. doi:10.1108/03090561311324282

Rabinovich, E., & Bailey, J. P. (2004). Physical distribution service quality in internet retailing: Service pricing, transaction attributes, and firm attributes. *Journal of Operations Management*, *21*(6), 651–672. doi:10.1016/j.jom.2003.11.004

Rabinovich, E., Knemeyer, A. M., & Mayer, C. M. (2007). Why do Internet commerce firms incorporate logistics service providers in their distribution channels? The role of transaction costs and network strength. *Journal of Operations Management*, *25*(3), 661–681. doi:10.1016/j.jom.2006.05.012

Rafiq, M., Fulford, H., & Lu, X. (2013). Building customer loyalty in online retailing: The role of relationship quality. *Journal of Marketing Management*, *29*(3-4), 494–517. doi:10.1080/0267257X.2012.737356

Rai, A., Patnayakuni, R., & Seth, N. (2006). Firm performance impacts of digitally enabled supply chain integration capabilities. *Management Information Systems Quarterly*, *30*(2), 225–246.

Rai, A., Sambamurthy, V., & Agarwal, R. (2008). How CIOs can enable governance of value nets. *MIS Quarterly Executive*, *7*(4), 193–204.

Raisinghani, M. S., Meade, L., & Schkade, L. L. (2007). Strategic e-business decision analysis using the Analytic Network Process. *IEEE Transactions on Engineering Management*, *54*(4), 673–686. doi:10.1109/TEM.2007.906857

Rajaraman, V. (2011). *Essentials of E-Commerce Technology*. New Delhi: PHI Learning Private Limited.

Rajesh, V. (2010). *The Indian reTALEs*. India: Unicorn Publishers.

Ramanathan, R. (2010). The moderating roles of risk and efficiency on the relationship between logistics performance and customer loyalty in e-commerce. *Transportation Research Part E, Logistics and Transportation Review*, *46*(6), 950–962. doi:10.1016/j.tre.2010.02.002

Rao, A.S., & Mehdi, M.M. (2010, July). Online user behaviour in Delhi- A factor analysis. *Indian Journal of Marketing*.

Rao, B. (1999). The Internet and the revolution in distribution: A cross-industry examination. *Technology in Society*, *21*(1), 287–306. doi:10.1016/S0160-791X(99)00018-4

Rao, P. (2002). Greening the supply chain: A new initiative in South East Asia. *International Journal of Operations & Production Management*, *22*(6), 632–655. doi:10.1108/01443570210427668

Rao, S., Rabinovich, E., & Raju, D. (2014). The role of physical distribution services as determinants of product returns in internet retailing. *Journal of Operations Management*, *32*(6), 295–312. doi:10.1016/j.jom.2014.06.005

Rashidirad, M., Soltani, E., & Salimian, H. (2014). Do contextual factors matter? A missing link between competitive strategies–dynamic capabilities alignment and e-business value. *Strategic Change*, *23*(1/2), 81–92. doi:10.1002/jsc.1961

Ratchford, B. T., Talukdar, D., & Lee, M. S. (2001). A model of consumer choice of the internet as an information source. *International Journal of Electronic Commerce*, *5*(3), 7–21.

Raymond, L., Bergeron, F., Croteau, A. M., & St-Pierre, J. (2015). Developing absorptive capacity through e-business: The case of international SMEs. *Journal of Small Business Management*, *53*, 75–94. doi:10.1111/jsbm.12192

Rebirth of e-Commerce in India. Kolkata. (2013). *Ernst & Young*. Retrieved from http://www.ey.com/Publication/vwLUAssets/Rebirth_of_e-Commerce_in_India/$FILE/EY_RE-BIRTH_OF_ECOMMERCE.pdf

Recognition and Awards won by Matrimony Portal. (2014). *Shaadi.com*. Retrieved from http://www.shaadi.com/introduction/index/why-we-are-no1

Reibstein, D. J. (2002). What attracts customers to online stores, and what keeps them coming back? *Journal of the Academy of Marketing Science*, *30*(4), 465–473. doi:10.1177/009207002236918

Reichheld, F. F., & Schefter, P. (2000). E-loyalty. Your secret weapon on the web. *Harvard Business Review*, *78*(4), 105–113.

Remarque, R. (2013). *Africa E commerce: Beyond the Hype*. Retrieved from http://www.siliconafrica.com/african-e-commerce/

Ren, B., & Dong, X. (2013). The study on self-built logistics system of electronic commerce enterprise: 360buy as a case. *Logistics Sci-Tech*, *1*, 104–108.

Rendo, S., & Ficko, D. (2010). New logistics technologies in improving customer value in retailing service. *Journal of Retailing and Consumer Services*, *17*(3), 216–223. doi:10.1016/j.jretconser.2010.03.012

Retail Agility: Catalyst to Successful Retailing in the 21st Century. (n. d.). *Throughtworks*. Retrieved from http://assets.thoughtworks.com/articles/retail_agility_21st_century.pdf)

Retail sales worldwide will top $22 trillion this year. (2014). *eMarketer*. Retrieved from http://www.emarketer.com/Article/Retail-Sales-Worldwide-Will-Top-22-Trillion-This-Year/1011765

Rezaei, R., Chiew, T. K., & Lee, S. P. (2014). A review on e-business interoperability frameworks. *Journal of Systems and Software*, *93*, 199–216. doi:10.1016/j.jss.2014.02.004

Rheingold, H. (1993). *The Virtual Community: Homesteading on the Electronic Frontier*. New York: Harper Collins.

Rigby, D. (2011, December). The future of shopping. *Harvard Business Review*. Retrieved from https://hbr.org/2011/12/the-future-of-shopping

Riley, C. (2014). Alibaba is not the Amazon of China. *CNN Money*. Retrieved from http://money.cnn.com/2014/09/15/investing/alibaba-amazon-china/

Risk Based Security. (2013). *Data Breach Quick-view: An Executive's Guide to 2013 Data Breach Trends*. Retrieved from https://www.riskbasedsecurity.com/reports/2013-DataBreachQuickView.pdf

Robinson, J. P. (1976). Interpersonal Influence in Election Campaigns Two Step-flow Hypotheses. *Public Opinion Quarterly*, *40*(3), 304–319. doi:10.1086/268307

Rogers, E. M. (1983). *Diffusion of innovations*. New York: The Free Press.

Rogers, E. M., & Cartano, D. G. (1962). Methoding of Measuring Opinion Leadership. *Public Opinion Quarterly*, *26*(3), 435–441. doi:10.1086/267118

Rosaci, D., & Sarne, G. M. L. (2014). Multi-agent technology and ontologies to support personalization in B2C e-commerce. *Electronic Commerce Research and Applications*, *13*(1), 13–23. doi:10.1016/j.elerap.2013.07.003

Rousseau, D., Sitkin, S. B., Burt, R. S., & Camerer, C. (1998). Not so different after all: A cross-discipline view of trust. *Academy of Management Review*, *23*(3), 393–404. doi:10.5465/AMR.1998.926617

Rowley, J., & Kupiec, T. (2007). Customer community and co creation: A case study. *Marketing Intelligence & Planning*, *25*(2), 136–146. doi:10.1108/02634500710737924

Rox, H. (2007). Top reasons people shop online may surprise you. *Associatecontent.com*. Retrieved from http://www.associatedcontent.com/article/459412/top_reasons_people_shop_online_may.html?cat=3

Roxy. (2015). Retrieved from www.roxy.com

Ruvio, A., & Shoham, A. (2007). Innovativeness, exploratory behavior, market mavenship, and opinion leadership: An empirical examination in the Asian context. *Psychology and Marketing*, *24*(8), 703–722. doi:10.1002/mar.20180

Sacconi, L. (2004). *Corporate Social Responsibility (CSR) as a Model of 'Extended' Corporate Governance: An Explanation Based on the Economic Theories of Social Contract*. Reputation and Reciprocal Conformism.

Safa, N. S., & Ismail, M. A. (2013). A customer loyalty formation model in electronic commerce. *Economic Modelling*, *35*, 559–564. doi:10.1016/j.econmod.2013.08.011

Safko, L. (2012). *The Social Media Bible*. Hoboken: John, Wiley & Sons.

Sahoo, S.C., & Dash, P.C. (2010, August). Consumer Decision Making Styles in Shopping malls- An empirical study in the Indian context. *Indian Journal of Marketing*.

Samii, L. (2015). e-Retailing Challenges and Opportunities in the Global Marketplace. *ReallyLeila*. Retrieved from http://reallyleila.com/2015/05/31/e-retailing-challenges-and-opportunities-in-the-global-marketplace/

Saraf, N., Langdon, C. S., & Gosain, S. (2007). IS application capabilities and relational value in interfirm partnerships. *Information Systems Research*, *18*(3), 320–339. doi:10.1287/isre.1070.0133

Savrul, M., Incekara, A., & Sener, S. (2014). The potential of e-commerce for SMEs in a globalizing business environment. *Procedia: Social and Behavioral Sciences*, *150*, 35–45. doi:10.1016/j.sbspro.2014.09.005

Sawhney, M., & Khosla, S. (2014). Alibaba vs. Amazon: Who will win the global e-commerce war? *Forbes.com.* Retrieved from http://www.forbes.com/sites/forbesleadershipforum/2014/09/22/alibaba-vs-amazon-who-will-win-the-global-e-commerce-war/

Schiffman, L. G., & Kanuk, L. L. (1997). Consumer Behaviour (6th ed). Englewood Cliffs, NJ: Prentice-Hall International.

Schiffman, L., & Kanuk, L. (2003). *Consumer Behaviour* (8th ed.). New Jersey: Prentice Hall.

Schmid, B. (1993). Elektronische märkte. *Journal of Economic computer science,* 35(1).

Schneider, G. P. (2012). *E-Commerce - Strategy, Technology and Implementation* (1st ed.). Delhi, India: Cengage Learning India Private Limited.

Schneider, K. C., & Rodgers, W. C. (1993). Generalized marketplace influencers' (market mavens') attitudes toward direct mail as a source of information. *Journal of Direct Marketing*, *7*(4), 20–28. doi:10.1002/dir.4000070405

Schoder, D., & Yin, P. L. (2000). Building firm trust online. *Communications of the ACM*, *43*(12), 73–79. doi:10.1145/355112.355127

Senecal, S., & Nantel, J. (2004). The influence of online product recommendations on consumers' online choices. *Journal of Retailing*, 80(2), 159-169.

Seo, H. J., Lee, Y. S., Hur, J. J., & Kim, J. K. (2012). The impact of information and communication technology on skilled labor and organization types. *Information Systems Frontiers*, *14*(2), 445–455. doi:10.1007/s10796-010-9276-7

Shankar, V., Smith, A., & Rangaswamy, A. (2003). Customer satisfaction and loyalty in online and offline environments. *International Journal of Research in Marketing*, *20*(2), 153–175. doi:10.1016/S0167-8116(03)00016-8

Share of mobile phone users that use a smartphone in India from 2010 to 2017. (2014). *Statista.com.* Retrieved from http://www.statista.com/statistics/257048/smartphone-user-penetration-in-india/

Sharma, A., & Sheth, J. (2004). Web-based marketing. The coming revolution in marketing thought and strategy. *Journal of Business Research*, *57*(7), 696–702. doi:10.1016/S0148-2963(02)00350-8

Shelton, A. (2001). *Should State and Local Government Tax E-commerce.* Retrieved from http://www.aarp.org/research/economy/taxation/aresearch-import-393-INB41.htm

Sheng-jun, Y. (2011). Educational Policies and Economic Growth in BRICs: Comparative Perspectives. *Journal of US-China Public Administration*, *8*(2), 188–197.

Shergill, G. S., & Chen, Z. (2005). Web-based shopping: Consumers' attitudes towards online shopping in New Zealand. *Journal of Electronic Commerce Research*, *6*(2), 79–94.

Sheth, J. N. (1983). An integrative theory of patronage preference and behaviour. In W. R. Darden & R. F. Lusch (Eds.), *Patronage behavior and retail management* (pp. 9–28). Orlando, FL: Elsevier.

Shih, C. (2009). *Facebook is the future of CRM* (p. 12). Customer Relationship Management.

Shih, H. Y. (2012). The dynamics of local and interactive effects on innovation adoption: The case of electronic commerce. *Journal of Engineering and Technology Management*, *29*(3), 434–452. doi:10.1016/j.jengtecman.2012.06.001

Shi, M., & Wojnicki, A. C. (2014). Money talks to online opinion leaders: What motivates opinion leaders to make social-network referrals? *Journal of Advertising Research*, *54*(1), 81–91. doi:10.2501/JAR-54-1-081-091

Shimp, T. A., & Sharma, S. (1987). Consumer ethnocentrism: Construction and validation of the CETSCALE. *JMR, Journal of Marketing Research*, *24*(August), 280–289. doi:10.2307/3151638

Shim, S., Eastlick, M. A., Lotz, S. L., & Warrington, P. (2001). An online prepurchase intentions model: The role of intention to search. *Journal of Retailing*, *77*(3), 397–416. doi:10.1016/S0022-4359(01)00051-3

Shirin, A. (2012). Customer relationship management and customer experience management using business online communities. *JIIT.* Retrieved from http://www.jiit.ac.in/uploads/Synopsis%20-%20Shirin%20Alavi.pdf

Shleifer, A., & Vishny, R. W. (1986). Large shareholders and corporate control. *Journal of Political Economy*, *94*(3), 461–488. http://scholar.harvard.edu/files/shleifer/files/lg_shareholders.pdf doi:10.1086/261385

Siano, A., & Vollero, A. (2012). Il processo di management della corporate communication: Un framework. *Sinergie Italian Journal of Management*, *88*, 73–92.

Siano, A., Vollero, A., & Siglioccolo, M. (2007). The Governance-Structure-System Model: a Framework for Corporate Communication Management.*Proceedings of 12th International Conference on Corporate and Marketing Communications* (pp. 179-210). London: Routledge.

Sikri, S., & Wadhwa, D. (2012). Growth and Challenges of retail industry in India. *Asia Pacific Journal Of Marketing And Management Review*, 1(1).

Sillence, E., Briggs, P., Harris, P., & Fishwick, L. (2006). A framework for understanding trust factors in web-based health advice. *International Journal of Human-Computer Studies*, *64*(8), 697–713. doi:10.1016/j.ijhcs.2006.02.007

Simon, H. (Ed.), (1971). Computers, Communications, and the Public Interest. Designing Organizations for an Information-Rich World. Baltimore, Maryland: The Johns Hopkins Press.

Singh, J. (2011). IRCTC face of e-ticket in India. *Iamwire.com*. Retrieved from http://www.iamwire.com/2011/11/irctc-face-of-e-ticket-in-india/1862

Singh, M., & Byrne, J. (2006). Performance evaluation of e-business in Australia. *The Electronic Journal of Information Systems Evaluation*, *8*(1), 71–80.

Singh, N., Lenhert, K., & Bostick, K. (2012). Usage: Insights into reaching consumers worldwide. *Thunderbird International Business Review*, 54(5), 683-700. doi:10.1002/tie.21493

Singla, B.B., Kumar, P., & Kaur, R. (2012). Online Shopping: An innovative tool of Google success.

Sin, L., & Tse, A. (2002). Profiling internet shoppers in Hong Kong: Demographic, psychographic, attitudinal and experiential factors. *Journal of International Consumer Marketing*, *15*(1), 7–29. doi:10.1300/J046v15n01_02

Sivanad, C., Geeta, M., & Sulep, M. (2004). Barriers to mobile Internet banking services adoption: An empirical study in Klang Valley of Malaysia. *Internet Business Review*, *1*, 1–17.

Slama, M.E., Nataraajan, R., & Williams T.G. (1992). Market Mavens and the relationship between smart buying and information provision: An exploratory study. *Developments in marketing science, 15*, 90-93.

Smith, C. (2014). Here's why Alibaba is becoming a huge threat to Amazon and eBay. *BusinessInsider.com.* Retrieved from http://www.businessinsider.com/why-alibaba-is-becoming-a-huge-threat-to-amazon-and-ebay-2014-8

Smith, A. D., & Rupp, W. T. (2003). Strategic Online Customer Decision Making: Leveraging the Transformational Power of the Internet. *Online Information Review*, *27*(6), 418–432. doi:10.1108/14684520310510055

Smith, D., Menon, S., & Sivakumar, K. (2005). On-line Peer and Editorial Recommendations, Trust, and Choice in Virtual Markets. *Journal of Interactive Marketing*, *19*(3), 15–37. doi:10.1002/dir.20041

Snir, E. M. (2001). Liability as a catalyst for product stewardship. *Production and Operations Management*, *10*(2), 190–206. doi:10.1111/j.1937-5956.2001.tb00078.x

Sohrabi, B., Mahmoudian, P., & Raeesi, I. (2012). A framework for improving e-commerce websites usability using a hybrid genetic algorithm and neural network system. *Neural Computing & Applications*, *21*(5), 1017–1029. doi:10.1007/s00521-011-0674-7

Spelich, J. W. (2014). Alibaba's head has a plan to save post offices around the world. Retrieved from http://qz.com/203912/ali-babas-e-commerce-head-has-a-plan-to-save-post-offices-around-the-world/

Spulber, D. (2014). *The Innovative Entrepreneur*. New York, Cambridge: Cambridge University Press. doi:10.1017/CBO9781107239012

Srivastava, A. (2009). Electronic signatures and security issues: An empirical study. *Computer Law & Security Report*, *25*(5), 432–446. doi:10.1016/j.clsr.2009.05.007

Stableford, S., & Mettger, W. (2007). Plain language: A strategic response to the health literacy challenge. *Journal of Public Health Policy*, *28*(1), 71–93. doi:10.1057/palgrave.jphp.3200102 PMID:17363939

Statistical report on Internet development in China internet report. (2014). *China Internet Network Information Center (CNNIC)*. Retrieved from http://www1.cnnic.cn/IDR/ReportDownloads/201404/U020140417607531610855.pdf

Strader, T. J., & Shaw, M. J. (1999). Consumer cost differences for traditional and Internet markets. *Internet Research*, *9*(2), 82–92. doi:10.1108/10662249910264819

Straub, D., & Watson, R. (2001). Research commentary: Transformational issues in researching IS and net-enabled organizations. *Information Systems Research*, *12*(4), 337–345. doi:10.1287/isre.12.4.337.9706

Subbu, R. (2015, May 10). Organised retail reorganising in India. *The Hindu*. Retrieved from http://www.thehindu.com/business/Industry/retail-sector-in-india/article7188691.ece

Subramanian, N., Gunasekaran, A., Yu, J., Cheng, J., & Ning, K. (2014). Customer satisfaction and competitiveness in the Chinese e-retailing: Structural equation modeling approach to identify the role of quality factors. *Expert Systems with Applications*, *41*(1), 69–80. doi:10.1016/j.eswa.2013.07.012

Subramani, M. R. (2004). How do suppliers benefit from IT use in supply chain relationships? *Management Information Systems Quarterly*, *28*(1), 45–74.

Summers, J. O. (1970). The Identity of Women's Clothing Fashion Opinion Leaders. *Journal of Marketing*, *7*(2), 178–185. doi:10.2307/3150106

Sun, P.-C., & Lin, C.-M. (2010). Building customer trust and loyalty: An empirical study in a retailing context. *Service Industries Journal*, *30*(9), 1439–1455. doi:10.1080/02642060802621478

Su, Q., & Chen, L. (2015). A method for discovering clusters of e-commerce interest patterns using click-stream data. *Electronic Commerce Research and Applications*, *14*(1), 1–13. doi:10.1016/j.elerap.2014.10.002

Swamy, V. (2010). Creating a buzz in social CRM. *Silicon India*, 22-23.

Swamynathan, G., Wilson, C., Boe, B., Almeroth, K., & Zhao, B. (2008). Do social networks improve e-commerce? A study on social marketplaces. In *Proceedings of the First Workshop on Online Social Networks*. New York, NY: ACM Press. doi:10.1145/1397735.1397737

Swinyard, W. R., & Smith, S. M. (2003). Why people (don't) shop online: A lifestyle study of the Internet consumer. *Psychology and Marketing*, *20*(7), 567–597. doi:10.1002/mar.10087

Tajfel, H. (1978). Social categorization, social identity and social comparison. In H. Tajfel (Ed.), *Differentiation between social groups* (pp. 61–76). UK: Academic Press.

Tan, F. B., Yan, L., & Urquhart, C. (2007). The effect of cultural differences on attitude, peer influence, external influence and self-efficacy in actual online shopping behavior. *Journal of Information Science and Technology*, *4*(1).

Tan, F. T. C., Pan, S. L., & Zuo, M. (2014). The role of organisational interdependencies and asset orchestration in business integration: A case study of M.com. *International Journal of Information Management*, *34*(6), 780–784. doi:10.1016/j.ijinfomgt.2014.07.004

Technology, Media & Telecommunications India Predictions. (2014). *Deloitte*. Retrieved from http://www2.deloitte.com/content/dam/Deloitte/in/Documents/technology-media-telecommunications/in-tmt-telecom-predictions-noexp.pdf

Technopak report on E-tailing in India: Unlocking the Potential. (2013, May).

Technopak. (2012). *E-tailing In India–pushing the retail frontier*, Retrieved from http://www.rasci.in/downloads/2012/e-tailing_%20india_pushing_retail_frontier.pdf

Teo, T. S. H., & Yu, Y. (2005). Online buying behavior: A transaction cost economics perspective. *Omega: The International Journal of Management Science*, *33*(5), 451–465. doi:10.1016/j.omega.2004.06.002

The Internet Economy in the G-20. Boston, USA. (2012). *The Boston Consulting Group*. Retrieved September 8, 2014, from https://www.bcg.com/documents/file100409.pdf

The State of the media: The social media report 2012. (2012). *Nielsen*.

The Tech Faq. (2008). *Top reasons why people shop online*. Retrieved from http://www.thetechfaq. com/2008/09/29/top-reasons-why-people-shop-online/,Thetechfaq.com

The world's next e-commerce superpower. (2011). BCG (The Boston Consulting Group). Retrieved from https://www.bcg.com/documents/file91905.pdf

Theodosiou, M., & Katsikea, E. (2012). Antecedents and performance of electronic business adoption in the hotel industry. *European Journal of Marketing*, *46*(1/2), 258–283. doi:10.1108/03090561211189329

Thibaut, J. W., & Kelley, H. H. (1959). *The social psychology of groups*. New York: John Wiley & Sons.

Thomas, B., Miller, C., & Simmons, G. (2015). An examination of regional policy implications pertaining to SME e-business adoption in South-East Wales. *Strategic Change*, *24*(5), 429–446. doi:10.1002/jsc.2020

Thomas, L. (2011). *Online Marketing*. USA: The McGraw-Hill Companies, Inc.

Tian, Y. (2001). Logistics quality management. *Logistics technology, 24*(2), 3-8.

Tian, Y., Ye, Z., Yan, Y., & Sun, M. (2015). A practical model to predict the repeat purchasing pattern of consumers in the C2C e-commerce. *Electronic Commerce Research*, *15*(4), 571–583. doi:10.1007/s10660-015-9201-8

Tian, Z., Zhang, Z., & Guan, X. (2013). A new evolution model for B2C e-commerce market. *Information Technology Management*, *14*(3), 205–215. doi:10.1007/s10799-013-0159-8

Tiernan, B. (2000). E-Tailing. Dearborn, Chicago.

Tiernan, B. (2000). *E-Tailing*. Chicago, IL: Dearborn Financial Publishing.

Tigre, P. B. (2003). E-commerce readiness and diffusion: The case of Brazil. I-Ways. *Digest of Electronic Commerce Policy and Regulation*, *26*, 173–183.

Tirole, J. (2006). *The Theory of Corporate Finance*. Princeton, Oxford: Princeton University Press.

Tomlinson, M. (2000). Tackling e-commerce security issues head on. *Computer Fraud & Security*, *2000*(11), 10–13. doi:10.1016/S1361-3723(00)11017-6

Tong, X. (2010). A cross-national investigation of an extended technology acceptance model in the online shopping context. *International Journal of Retail & Distribution Management*, *38*(10), 742–759. doi:10.1108/09590551011076524

Trunick, P. A. (2015). Omni-channel Strategies: Customer-controlled Supply Chains. *Material Handling & Logistics*, *70*(1), 21–23.

Tsai, M., Lai, K., Lloyd, A. E., & Lin, H. (2012). The dark side of logistics outsourcing – Unraveling the potential risks leading to failed relationships. *Transportation Research Part E, Logistics and Transportation Review*, *48*(1), 178–189. doi:10.1016/j.tre.2011.07.003

Tsang, S. L. A., & Zhou, N. (2005). Newsgroup participants as opinion leaders and seekers in online and offline communication environments. *Journal of Business Research*, *58*(9), 1186–1193. doi:10.1016/j.jbusres.2004.05.002

Turban, E., & Gehrke, D. (2000). Determinants of e-commerce website. *Human Systems Management*, *19*, 111–120.

Turban, E., King, D., Lee, J., & Viehland, D. (2004). *Electronic Commerce A managerial perspective* (International ed.). Prentice Hall.

Turban, E., King, D., Viehland, D., & Lee, J. (2006). *Electronic Commerce: A Managerial Perspective, International.* Upper Saddle River, NJ: Prentice Hall.

Turban, E., Lee, J., King, D., & Chung, H. M. (2000). *Electronic commerce: A managerial perspective*. Upper Saddle River, NJ: Prentice Hall.

Turner, J. C. (1985). Social categorization and the self-concept: A social cognitive theory of group behavior. In E. L. Lawler (Ed.), Advances in group processes (Vol. 2, pp. 77-122). UK: JAI Press Inc.

Turner, J. C. (1978). Social comparison, similarity and ingroup favouritism. In H. Tajfel (Ed.), *Differentiation between social groups* (pp. 233–250). UK: Academic Press.

Twitter, Inc. (2012). Retrieved from www.twitter.com

U.S. and World Population Clock. (2015, May 30). *US Census Bureau.* Retrieved from http://www.census.gov/popclock/

UNCTAD, (2015). *Unlocking the Potential of E commerce for Developing Countries* Information Economy Report.

Understanding the Multi-channel shopper. (2012, April). *Verde Group and Baker Retailing Center.*

Vachon, S., Klassen, R. D., & Johnson, P. F. (2001). Customers as green suppliers: managing the complexity of the reverse supply chain. In J. Sarkis (Ed.), *Greening Manufacturing: From Design to Delivery and Back* (pp. 136–149). Sheffield, UK: Greenleaf Publisher. doi:10.9774/GLEAF.978-1-909493-22-3_11

Vaithianathan, S. (2010). A review of e-commerce literature on India and research agenda for the future. *Electronic Commerce Research*, *10*(1), 83–97. doi:10.1007/s10660-010-9046-0

Van Vliet, P., & Pota, D. (2001). Understanding online retail: A classification of online retailers. *Journal of Computer Information Systems*, *41*(2), 23–29.

Venkatraman, M. P. (1989). Opinion leaders, adopters, and communication adopters: A role analysis. *Psychology and Marketing*, *6*(1), 51–68. doi:10.1002/mar.4220060104

Vijayasarathy, L. R., & Jones, J. M. (2000). Print and Internet catalog shopping: Assessing attitudes and intentions. *Internet Research, 10*(3), 191–202. doi:10.1108/10662240010331948

Vinton, M. (2001). Trust and quality are key to thriving on the web today. *Marketing, 14*(June), 12.

Vision and Mission. (2014). *NASSCOM*. Retrieved from http://www.nasscom.in/vision-and-mission

Vollero, A. (2006). Il two-step flow nella comunicazione in rete: gli opinion leader on-line. *Esperienze d'impresa, 2*, 49-68.

Vollero, A. (2010). *E-marketing e web communication. Verso la gestione della corporate reputation online*. Torino: Giappichelli.

Volusion. (2006). *Ebusiness and its significance in today's marketplace*. Retrieved from http://www.volusion.com/ecommerce-blog/articles/e-business-solution-e-commerce

Vries, L., Gensler, S., & Leeflang, P. (2012). Popularity of brand posts on brand fan pages: An investigation of the effect of social media marketing. *Journal of Interactive Marketing*, 26(2), 83-91.

Walsh, G., Gwinner, K. P., & Swanson, S. R. (2004). What makes mavens tick? Exploring the motives of market mavens' initiation of information diffusion. *Journal of Consumer Marketing, 21*(2), 109–122. doi:10.1108/07363760410525678

Walsh, G., & Mitchell, V. W. (2002). German market mavens' decision making styles. *Journal of Euromarketing, 10*(4), 83–108. doi:10.1300/J037v10n04_05

Wang, F., & Head, M. (2002). e-tailing: An analysis of web impacts on the retail market. *Journal of Business Strategies, 19*(1), 73.

Wang, S. (2011). Selling large home electrics appliance becomes JD's headache. Retrieved from http://www.56products.com/News/2011-9-14/34519KC711E7B615712.html

Wang, S. (2012). A dynamic model of trust in online shopping. *Proceedings of the2012 AICI International Conferenceon Artificial Intelligence and Computational Intelligence* (pp. 296-303). Berlin Heidelberg: Springer. doi:10.1007/978-3-642-34240-0_39

Wang, X., & Ren, Z. J. (2012). How to compete in China's E-commerce market. *Sloan Review*. Retrieved from http://sloanreview.mit.edu/article/how-to-compete-in-chinas-e-commerce-market/

Wang, Z. T. (2000). *Modern logistics*. China: China Goods and materials publisher.

Wang, C. L., Ye, L. R., Zhang, Y., & Nguyen, D. D. (2005). Subscription to fee-based online services: What makes consumer pay for online content? *Journal of Electronic Commerce Research, 6*(4), 301–311.

Wang, F., Head, M. M., & Archer, N. A. (2000). Relationship building model for the web retail marketplace. *Journal of Internet Research, 10*(5), 374–384. doi:10.1108/10662240010349381

Wang, H. J., & Wu, H. (2011). Supporting process design for e-business via an integrated process repository. *Information Technology & Management, 12*(2), 97–109. doi:10.1007/s10799-010-0076-z

Wang, M. (2003). Assessment of E-Service Quality via E-Satisfaction in e-commerce globalization. *EJISDC, 11*(10), 1–4.

Wang, S. (2001). Designing information systems for electronic commerce. *Industrial Management & Data Systems, 101*(6), 304–314. doi:10.1108/EUM0000000005580

Wang, X. (2012). Foreign direct investment and innovation in China's e-commerce sector. *Journal of Asian Economics, 23*(3), 288–301. doi:10.1016/j.asieco.2010.11.007

Watson, A., Kirby, D. A., & Egan, J. (2002). Franchising, retailing and the development of e-commerce. *International Journal of Retail & Distribution Management, 30*(5), 228–237. doi:10.1108/09590550210426390

Watson, G., & Johnson, D. (1972). *Social psychology: Issues and insights*. Philadelphia: J. B. Lippincott.

Wellman, B. (1996, April). For a social network analysis of computer networks: A sociological perspective on collaborative work and virtual community. *Paper presented at the SIGCPR/SIGMIS*, Denver, CO. doi:10.1145/238857.238860

Wellman, B., & Gulia, M. (1999). Virtual communities as communities. In M. A. Smith & P. Kollock (Eds.), *Communities in cyberspace* (pp. 167–194). New York: Routledge.

Wen, H.J., Chen, H.-G., & Hwang, H.-G. (2001). E-commerce Web site design: strategies and models. *Information Management and Computer Security*, 9(1). Retrieved from http://www.csus.edu/indiv/c/chingr/mis182/ecomwebsitedesign.pdf

Wen, H. J., Lim, B., & Huang, H. L. (2003). Measuring e-commerce efficiency: A data envelopment analysis (DEA) approach. *Industrial Management & Data Systems, 103*(9), 703–710. doi:10.1108/02635570310506124

Wheeler, B. C. (2002). NEBIC: A dynamic capabilities theory for assessing net-enablement. *Information Systems Research, 13*(2), 125–146. doi:10.1287/isre.13.2.125.89

Why is omnichannel retailing so important for Bed Bath & Beyond? (2015). *Trefis Team, Forbes*.

Whysall, P. (2000). Retailing and the internet: A review of ethical issues. *International Journal of Retail & Distribution Management, 28*(11), 481–489. doi:10.1108/09590550010356840

Wiedmann, K. P., Walsh, G., & Mitchell, V. W. (2001). The Mannmaven: An agent for diffusing market information. *Journal of Marketing Communications, 7*(4), 195–212. doi:10.1080/13527260127413

Wigand, R. T., Benjamin, R. I., & Birkland, J. (2008). Web 2.0 and beyond: Implications for electronic commerce. In *Proceedings of the 10th International Conference on Electronic Commerce*. New York, NY: ACM Press. doi:10.1145/1409540.1409550

Williamson, P. & Wang, J. (2014). Alibaba group's Taobao: From intermediary to ecosystem enabler. *Judge Business School Case Centre* (Ref. 314-139-1), University of Cambridge.

Williamson, K. C., Spiter, D. M., & Bloomberg, D. J. (1990). Modern logistics systems: Theory and practice. *Journal of Business Logistics, 11*(2), 65–86.

Williams, T. G., & Slama, M. E. (1995). Market mavens' purchase decision evaluative criteria: Implications for brand and store promotion efforts. *Journal of Consumer Marketing, 12*(3), 4–21. doi:10.1108/07363769510147218

Windahl, S., Signitzer, B., & Olson, J. T. (1992). *Using communication theory: An introduction to planned communication*. London: Sage.

Witt, R. E. (1970). *Group Influence on Consumer Brand Choice*. The University of Texas: Bureau of Business Research.

Wollscheid, C. (2012). *Rise and Burst of the Dotcom Bubble : Causes, Characteristics, Examples*. Mittelhessen. Retrieved from http://www.grin.com/en/e-book/197166/rise-and-burst-of-the-dotcom-bubble

Wright, C. R., & Cantor, M. (1967). The Opinion Seeker and the Avoider: Steps Beyond the Opinion Avoider: Steps Beyond the Opinion Leader Concept. *Pacific Sociological Review, 10*(1), 33–43. doi:10.2307/1388626

Wu, J. H., & Hisa, T. L. (2008). Developing e-business dynamic capabilities: An analysis of e-commerce innovation from I-, M-, to U-commerce. *Journal of Organizational Computing and Electronic Commerce, 18*(2), 1–17. doi:10.1080/10919390701807525

Wu, J. N., Zhong, W. J., & Mei, S. E. (2011). Application capability of e-business, e-business success, and organizational performance: Empirical evidence from China. *Technological Forecasting and Social Change*, *78*(8), 1412–1425. doi:10.1016/j.techfore.2011.03.023

Wu, J., Li, L., & Xu, L. D. (2014). A randomized pricing decision support system in electronic commerce. *Decision Support Systems*, *58*, 43–52. doi:10.1016/j.dss.2013.01.015

Xia, Y., & Zhang, G. P. (2010). The impact of the online channel on retailers' performances: An empirical evaluation. *Decision Sciences*, *41*(3), 517–546. doi:10.1111/j.1540-5915.2010.00279.x

Xu, Y., & Paulins, V. A. (2005). College students' attitudes toward shopping online for apparel products: Exploring a rural versus urban campus. *Journal of Fashion Marketing and Management*, *9*(4), 420–433. doi:10.1108/13612020510620795

Yan, B. N., Lee, T. S., & Lee, T. P. (2015). Analysis of research papers on e-commerce (2000–2013): Based on a text mining approach. *Scientometrics*, *105*(1), 403–417. doi:10.1007/s11192-015-1675-6

Yang, H. (2013). Market mavens in social media: Examining young Chinese consumers' viral marketing attitude, eWOM and behavior. *Journal of Asia-Pacific Business*, *14*(2), 154–178. doi:10.1080/10599231.2013.756337

Yang, Y., Humphreys, P., & McIvor, R. (2006). Business service quality in an e-commerce environment. *Supply Chain Management. International Journal (Toronto, Ont.)*, *11*(3), 195–201.

Yang, Z., & Jun, M. (2002). Consumer perception of e-service quality: From internet purchaser and non-purchaser perspectives. *The Journal of Business Strategy*, *19*(1), 19–41.

Yau, O. H. M. (1988). Chinese cultural values: Their dimensions and marketing implications. *European Journal of Marketing*, *22*(5), 44–57. doi:10.1108/EUM0000000005285

Yoon, C. (2009). The effects of national culture values on consumer acceptance of e-commerce: Online shoppers in China. *Information & Management*, *46*(5), 294–301. doi:10.1016/j.im.2009.06.001

Yoon, S.-J. (2002). The antecedents and consequences of trust in online-purchase decisions. *Journal of Interactive Marketing*, *16*(2), 47–63. doi:10.1002/dir.10008

Youderian, A. (2014). Alibaba vs. Amazon: An in-depth comparison of two eCommerce giants. *Ecommercefuel.com.* Retrieved from http://www.ecommercefuel.com/alibaba-vs-amazon/

Young Kim, E., & Kim, Y. K. (2004). Predicting online purchase intentions for clothing products. *European Journal of Marketing*, *38*(7), 883–897. doi:10.1108/03090560410539302

Yousafzai, S. Y., Pallister, J. G., & Foxall, G. R. (2003). A proposed model of e-trust for electronic banking. *Technovation*, *23*(11), 847–860. doi:10.1016/S0166-4972(03)00130-5

Yu, X. H., Guo, X. T., & Yao, Q. Y. (2011). The effect of online word-of-mouth in electronic markets: An investigation of the culture differences in the Chinese and US contexts. *Proceedings of the2011 International Conferenceon Management Science and Engineering (ICMSE),* Piscataway, New Jersey (pp. 34-40). IEEE.

Yu, M., Zhang, L., & Yu, X. (2008). Some thoughts of Suning's logistics model. *Modernization ofManagement*, *6*, 30–32.

Yu, T., & Wu, G. (2007). Determinants of internet shopping behaviour: An application of reasoned behaviour theory. *International Journal of Management*, *24*(4), 744–762.

Zaheer, S. (1995). Overcoming the Liability of Foreignness. *Academy of Management Journal*, *38*(2), 341–363. doi:10.2307/256683

Zairi, M., & Al-Mashari, M. (2002). E-commerce based supply chain management: A proposed model based on retailing experience. *Computer & Information Science*, 61 – 84.

Zbornik, S. (1996). *Electronic markets and electronic hierarchies*. Konstanz, Germany: UVK Verlagsgesellschaft mbH.

Zeithaml, V. A. (2002). Service excellent in electronic channels. *Managing Service Quality*, *12*(3), 135–138. doi:10.1108/09604520210429187

Zhang, W. (2011). A study on Taobao's logistics delivery problems. *Work and Study Abroad*, May.

Zhang, T., Agarwal, R., & Lucas, H. C. (2011). The value of IT-enabled retailer learning: Personalized product recommendations and customer store loyalty in electronic markets. *Management Information Systems Quarterly*, *35*(4), 859–881.

Zhang, Y., Bian, J., & Zhu, W. (2013). Trust fraud: A crucial challenge for China's e-commerce market. *Electronic Commerce Research and Applications*, *12*(5), 299–308. doi:10.1016/j.elerap.2012.11.005

Zhang, Y., Deng, X., Wei, D., & Deng, Y. (2012). Assessment of e-commerce security using AHP and evidential reasoning. *Expert Systems with Applications*, *39*(3), 3611–3623. doi:10.1016/j.eswa.2011.09.051

Zhao, Z. J., & Gutierrez, J. A. (2002). Customer Service Factors Influencing the Internet Shopping in New Zealand. Retrieved from http://proceedings.informingscience.org/InSITE2004/017zhao.pdf

Zhao, D., Savage, S. J., & Chen, Y. (2008). Ownership, location and prices in Chinese electronic commerce markets. *Information Economics and Policy*, *20*(2), 192–207. doi:10.1016/j.infoecopol.2008.02.001

Zhu, F., & Zhang, X. (2010). Impact of online consumer reviews on sales: The moderating role of product and consumer characteristics. *Journal of Marketing*, *74*(2), 133–148. doi:10.1509/jmkg.74.2.133

Zhu, K. (2004). The complementarity of information technology infrastructure and ecommerce capability: A resource-based assessment of their business value. *Journal of Management Information Systems*, *21*(1), 167–202.

Zhu, K., & Kraemer, K. L. (2005). Post-adoption variations in usage and value of e-business by organizations: Cross-country evidence from the retail industry. *Information Systems Research*, *16*(1), 61–84. doi:10.1287/isre.1050.0045

Zigmund, W. G. (2012). *Business Research Methods* (5th ed.). Fort Worth, TX: The Dryden Press.

Zott, C., Amit, R., & Donlevy, J. (2000). Strategies for Value Creation in E-Commerce: Best Practices in Europe. *European Management Journal*, *18*(5), 463–475. doi:10.1016/S0263-2373(00)00036-0

Zudor, E. I., Kemeny, Z., Ekart, A., Buckingham, C. D., & Monostori, L. (2014). *A solution for information management in logistics operations of modern manufacturing chains*. Paper presented at the 8th International Conference on Digital Enterprise Technology – Disruptive Innovation in Manufacturing Engineering towards the 4th Industrial Revolution (pp. 337 – 344).

Zuo, W., Huang, Q., Fan, C., & Zhang, Z. (2013). Quality management of B2C e-commerce service based on human factors engineering. *Electronic Commerce Research and Applications*, *12*(5), 309–320. doi:10.1016/j.elerap.2013.03.005

# About the Contributors

**Shailja Dixit** has a PhD in Management and is a Gold Medalist in her Management Program. She is working as Associate Professor in the Department of Management at Amity University, Lucknow, India. Her research interests include social media, women entrepreneurship, consumer research, consumer decision making, and branding. She has more than 25 research papers published in reputed international peer reviewed journals. She is currently associated with many reputed journals as Reviewer and Editor.

**Amit Kumar Sinha** has a PhD in Business Economics. He is working with the Business School, at Amity University, Lucknow, India. His research interests include Corporate Governance, Corporate Disclosure, Micro Finance, E-commerce, Digitalization of Banking and Financial Services. He is associated with several peer reviewed reputed journals as reviewer and member of editorial board. He has more than 12 research papers published with reputed peer reviewed journals.

* * *

**Thomas W. Cline** is a professor of marketing and statistics in the Alex G. McKenna School at the Saint Vincent College and a doctoral consultant for statistical methods at Robert Morris University's School of Health Sciences. He teaches courses in consumer behavior, marketing research, statistical methods, advertising and promotion, and strategic marketing. Dr. Cline has published numerous articles in academic journals, including the Journal of Advertising, the Journal of Consumer Psychology, the Journal of Economic Psychology, Psychology & Marketing, and the Journal of Marketing Communications. Dr. Cline and his colleagues won the 2003 Young Contributors Award for best paper in the Journal of Consumer Psychology. Dr. Cline is widely cited in the popular press, including by USA Today, Psychology Today, CBS News, The LA Times, MSNBC, and The Washington Times. Dr. Cline is a coauthor of *Consumer Behavior*, a 2015 South-Western/Cengage Learning textbook. He has also coauthored *Consumer Behavior: Science & Practice*, the International Edition in 2011.

**Jagdeep Singh Jassel** is working as the Dean of the Faculty of Business, Communication and Law (FOBCAL), at the INTI-International University in Malaysia. He has more than 15 years of work experience in various industries, ranging from manufacturing, to hospitality, to education. His experience includes managerial roles in a human resource function, spearheading training and development initiatives, managing labour relations, HR consulting, and also academics. Worked with a number of multinational companies, including ICI Paints Malaysia, Avillion Hotels International and Samsung Corning Malaysia.

Within academia, he has served as a Senior Officer in the Human Resource Office, Senior Lecturer, Head of Programme, Associate Dean, and Acting Dean. Dr. Jagdeep is a qualified trainer, certified by Deloitte Consulting Group, UK.

**Prateek Kalia** is a PhD Scholar in the Department of Research, Innovation & Consultancy at I.K Gujral Punjab Technical University, India. His area of research is in electronic retail and consumer behaviour. He has earned a B.Sc. and MBA. In the past, he has worked as a Deputy General Manager at PICTCL, Government of Punjab, India.

**Kijpokin Kasemsap** received his BEng degree in Mechanical Engineering from King Mongkut's University of Technology Thonburi, his MBA degree from Ramkhamhaeng University, and his DBA degree in Human Resource Management from Suan Sunandha Rajabhat University. He is a Special Lecturer in the Faculty of Management Sciences, Suan Sunandha Rajabhat University, based in Bangkok, Thailand. He is a member of the International Association of Engineers (IAENG), the International Association of Engineers and Scientists (IAEST), the International Economics Development and Research Center (IEDRC), the International Association of Computer Science and Information Technology (IACSIT), the International Foundation for Research and Development (IFRD), and the International Innovative Scientific and Research Organization (IISRO). He also serves on the International Advisory Committee (IAC) for the International Association of Academicians and Researchers (INAAR). He has numerous original research articles in top international journals, conference proceedings, and book chapters on business management, human resource management, and knowledge management, published internationally.

**Navdeep Kaur** works as an Assistant Professor in the Department of Business Management, Guru Nanak Dev Engineering College.

**Bobby Kurian** holds a post graduate diploma in Software Enterprise Management from IIM, Bangalore, a Bachelor of Technology in Computer Science from Kannur University and is currently a Doctoral Student (Management) at Jain University, Bangalore India. He is an entrepreneur and is engaged in setting up a startup firm in Bangalore, India, focusing exclusively on open-source based software solutions.

**Bo Liang** is an Assistant Professor of Marketing at the Alex G. McKenna School of Business, Economics and Government at Saint Vincent College. Her research interests are in the areas of consumer information search, learning, and decision making in online environments. Specifically, she employs web analytics, content analysis, social network analysis, data visualization, and statistical modeling tools to analyze online consumer-generated data sets to better understand consumer learning and decision-making and their sociological underpinnings, generating insights to inform theory as well as practice in the area of marketing.

**Zheng Liu** is a lecturer in the International Business School Suzhou, Xi'an Jiaotong-Liverpool University. She gained her Ph.D at the Institute for Manufacturing, University of Cambridge with the research topic "The Development of Inter-firm Trust in Different National Culture Contexts: cases from the animation game industry." Her current research interests include cross-culture management, supply chain, and the creative industry.

**Yaqiong Lu** is currently studying BSc Economics in the Suzhou International Business School, Xi'an Jiaotong-Liverpool University. She has a great interest in e-commerce business models, such as, service quality evaluation models and logistics models, including the Logistics Service Quality Model, the SERVQUAL Model and Lean Six Sigma. In a recent research project, she conducted a survey of customers' satisfaction with China's e-retailers. The result can provide an approach to measure the logistics performance of e-commerce companies in China, so that the companies can improve their logistics service aiming at specific problems.

**Lei Ma** joined the Department of Public Affairs of Nanjing University of Science & Technology in March 2009. She is a professor and the head of Centre for Innovation & Development at Nanjing University of Science & Technology. Following an early career in industry, she was the senior economist in the Hanzhou Branch of China mobile group from 2005 to 2008, a sales manager from 1998 to 1999, and a senior consultant from 2000 to 2005 in the Shanghai branch of the France BULL Group. She gained her Master degree in 1996 and a PhD. degree in 2003 from the School of Economics & Management, Nanjing University of Science & Technology. She was a post-doctor from 2003 to 2005 at School of Economics & Management of Zhejiang University. She was an academic scholar from 2008 to 2009 at the Center for International Manufacturing (CIM) at the University of Cambridge. Dr. Ma's research interests are in technological innovation, enterprise's habitual domains, and science and technology policy.

**Zhongyu Ma** is the deputy-director of the State Information Centre (SIC). His job is mainly focused on policy-making and advising on decision-making for State Council, the Central Government and the State Development of Reform Commission in industrial and social development, development planning and investment policies, etc. All his decisions are directed to setting China on the way towards sustainable development. At the same time, he works as a professor at the School of Natural Resources and Environment at Renmin University of China, engaged in research on recycling economy, ecology, climate change, and sustainable urban and rural development. He also worked at the Institute of Ecology and Resource Management at the University of Edinburgh (UK) from 1993 to 1995. He has published over 80 papers and 20 books, both in English and Chinese. He has attended and organized numerous national and international conferences, including the International Workshop of Poverty and Environment in Beijing in 2004; the 3rd World Water Forum in Kyoto in 2003; the World Water Symposium in Stockholm in 2003; the 7th Session of UNCSD on Sustainable Tourism in New York in 1999; the International Symposium of Sustainable Agricultural Technology in Beijing in 1997; System-Oriented Research in Agriculture and Rural Development in France in 1994; and the Integrated Resource Management for Sustainable Agriculture in Beijing in 1993, among others. Dr. Ma has organized and directed several research teams and completed more than 50 research projects in the areas of resource management, carrying capacity assessment, climate change, poverty alleviation and recycling economy, and ecotourism and natural heritage conservation. Dr. Ma obtained his Ph.D. in agricultural science in 1992 from Northwestern Agricultural University in China. Between 1996 and 2000, he worked at the Chinese Academy of Agricultural Sciences as the leading scientist in the area of rural sustainable development. In 2000, he was transferred to Renmin University of China to establish the School of Natural Resources and Environment and works in the school. In 2004, he was selected to be the deputy director of Commission of Development and Reform in Ningxia and promoted to a deputy-general of the Ningxia Provincial Government, and director of the Ningxia Policy Research Center in 2012.

**Soney Mathews** is working as an Associate Professor in the Faculty of Business, Communication and Law (FOBCAL) at the INTI-International University, Malaysia. She has 19 years of teaching and research experience. Her areas of interest are in research, especially marketing, youth marketing and consumer behavior. She has published many research papers in both international and national journals.

**Sana Moid** is presently designated as a AP II at the Amity Business School, Lucknow Campus, Amity University. Her area of research includes investment, SME exchange working, creative accounting and tax planning.

**Ritu Narang** is an Assistant Professor in the Department of Business Administration, University of Lucknow. She has done her Ph. D. and D.Lit. in Business Administration and was at the top of the merit list of MBA students in 1989. She was awarded 'The Best Research' Award among the Teachers by the University of Lucknow in 2010. Two of her research papers have been awarded 'The Best Research Paper' in International Conferences, including one organized by Oxford Business School. Twice she has been a Senior Distinguished Fellow at Hanken School of Economics, Helsinki. Dr. Narang has successfully completed two Major Research Projects sponsored by the University Grants Commission, New Delhi. Her papers have been presented at various national and international conferences including the Academy of Marketing Science World Marketing Conference, the POMS Annual Conference, the Centre for Marketing in Emerging Economies (Annual Conference of the Emerging Markets Conference Board), the Indian Academy of Management, the Conference on Retailing in Asia Pacific (The Oxford Institute of Retail Management), the American Marketing Association's Services Special Interest Group International Conference, among others. Dr. Narang has several publications in various international journals such as the International Review of Retail, the journal of Distribution and Consumer Research, the International Journal of Case Studies in Management, the International Journal of Health Care Quality Assurance, Clinical Governance: An International Journal, the Young Consumer, the International Journal of Management in Education, the journal of Quality Assurance in Education, and Vikalpa. She has done an Indian adaptation of a book on Organization Behaviour published by Pearson Publishers. Two of her books are currently under publication. She has published several chapters in national and international books. She has reviewed several research papers for international journals and has done an Indian adaptation of a book on Organizational Behaviour. Dr. Narang has also been involved in delivering invited talks to managers of public and private sector organizations including Tata Consultancy, RDSO, State Bank of India, etc. She has been involved in various administrative assignments at the University of Lucknow. She is the former Director MBA Retail Management, Co-OSD, Institute of Management Sciences, to name a few.

**Marianne Ojo** has published numerous international-based publications which include peer-reviewed books, ISI accredited, as well as other accredited journal articles, book chapters and conference proceedings papers. During her career, her work has not only found international acceptance, but also received most cited commendations. The author currently works as a visiting professor and post-doctoral researcher as well as a university lecturer and visiting scholar at several institutions which include North West University, South Africa and she also supervises graduate and non-graduate students. She is also affiliated with several institutions in the United States, as well as the Legal Scholarship network. Furthermore, she serves as a reviewer for various scientific and academic journals which have been accredited with the highest credentials at an international level. Her previous academic commitments include Visiting Scholarship at the University of Heidelberg, Insolvency and Research work at Lessing Trebing Bert, Frankfurt, Research Fellow at the Center for European Law and Politics University of Bremen (2007 – 2010), Teaching Associate and Graduate Teaching Assistant at Oxford Brookes University (2004 – 2007). She has also collaborated with several other authors, as well as contributed in several consultation and academic exercises with the Bank of International Settlements. These include Strengthening the Resilience of the Banking Sector: Proposals to Strengthen Global Capital and Liquidity Regulations (March 2010), International Framework for Liquidity Risk Measurement, Standards and Monitoring: Corporate Governance and Internal Controls, Measures Aimed at Mitigating Pro cyclical Effects of Capital Requirements (Aug 2010) and Measures Aimed at Enhancing the Loss Absorbency of Regulatory Capital (Aug 2010).

**Dharmendra Pandey** is a marketing learner, educationist, researcher, blogger, technology enthusiast, ex-salesman and has more than 10 years of rich experience in industry and academics. He is currently associated with Amity University, Lucknow, India, as an Assistant Professor of Marketing.

**Leila Samii** is an Assistant Professor at Aurora University in the Masters of Digital Marketing and Analytics Program and adjuncts in the Harvard Extension School. She holds a Ph. D. in International Business and Marketing with a focus on Social Media Marketing. Her research focuses on global social media marketing, investigating the link between brand image and social media from a global context. With an expertise in social media and international business, Leila has extensive knowledge on earned media and has developed various global frameworks focusing on cost effective strategies for social media. Leila has explored and published in this emerging field of study. Leila is owner and managing director of a social media marketing consulting firm, ReallyLeila LLC, which focuses on educating small and medium-sized enterprises on aligning their social media goals with their current business objectives. Leila is passionate about social media and teaching others the ins and outs of social media in easy to understand manner. She has managed a number of projects on creating social media marketing strategies and campaigns.

**Domenico Sardanelli** is a PhD student in Marketing Management and a Graduate Research Assistant in Research Methods in Social Science and Digital Marketing at the University of Salerno (Italy). He graduated with full marks in 2014. Domenico's current research interests include online consumer behaviour and word-of-mouth marketing.

**Parag Shukla** (M.Com, PGDMM, UGC- NET, SET) is a PhD Scholar and working as an Assistant Professor in the Faculty of Commerce at the M.S.University of Baroda, Department of Commerce and Business Management, Gujarat, India. He received his Bachelors and Masters Degree with specialization in Marketing Management from the M.S.University of Baroda, India. His area of research is in the field of Retailing. His experience includes content analysis with the television and media research industry. He currently teaches courses of management in various under graduate and post graduate levels in the University. He has presented and published several research papers in different areas of Retailing and Marketing in various National and International refereed Journals and conference proceedings. He is currently working on a recent research project entitled "An Empirical Investigation of Experiential Value vis-a-vis Usage Attitude of Selected Mobile Shoppers in the State of Gujarat". He has also received other accolades in his research papers from various academias. Mr. Shukla is the recipient of the Best Business Academic of the Year Award (BBAY) where he won the Silver Medal for his research paper in 69th International All India Commerce Conference, which is widely recognized in Indian Education and Retail Industry.

**Alfonso Siano** is a Professor and Chair of Corporate Communications and Marketing Communications at the University of Salerno (Italy) where he is Founder and Chair of the Doctoral Programme in Marketing and Communications. He has previously been Researcher and Lecturer in Management at the University of Rome 'La Sapienza.' He teaches and carries out research in corporate communication and reputation, marketing communications, arts and heritage marketing, and digital marketing. He has published 8 books and several book chapters. He has published in a wide range of international academic journals, including the Journal of Marketing Communications, Corporate Communications: an International Journal, the Journal of Brand Management, the Journal of Communication Management, the International Studies of Management and Organization, and the Museum Management and Curatorship.

**Surabhi Singh** (M COM, MCA, PGDBA, and PhD Scholar from AMU) is specialized in marketing with an overall experience of 14 years in corporate, as well as teaching. She has additional qualifications of an Advanced Diploma in Management which is equivalent to M Phil, and a certificate in guidance. She has been actively involved in research, teaching, training and consultancy. She is the recipient of IMS Noida's Award of 'A Grade Faculty' and recently received an award from UK Journal for case writing. She won the best paper award in a National Conference at one of the premier business schools. She has also received other accolades in her research papers from various academias. She has edited three books and 29 papers in various National and International refereed Journals and conference proceedings. She is also a reviewer in few International Journals. Currently she is associated with IMS Ghaziabad as Asstt Professor-Marketing.

**Tejinderpal Singh** works as an Assistant Professor at the University Business School of Panjab University, Chandigarh.

**Prashant Trivedi** is pursuing doctoral research in area of green marketing, and has also worked as an Asst. Professor in area of management for four years and has corporate experience of three plus year after completing an MBA in 2006. He has conducted over three hundred educational seminars and personality development workshops.

**Yanbin Tu** is a Professor of Marketing at Robert Morris University. He is also a Chutian Scholar and Visiting Professor at Jianghan University. He earned his doctoral degree at the University of Connecticut. He has worked for the Bank of Shanghai for three year. Dr. Tu has taught at Simon Fraser University in Canada and at UConn as an instructor. His research interests cover e-commerce, database marketing, CRM, and financial services marketing. He has publications in leading business journals such as the International Journal of Electronic Commerce, Decision Support Systems, and Applied Economics.

**V. Rajesh** has been an integral part of the transformation of Indian retail. He has been a part of successfully introducing several modern retail formats in India starting with supermarkets in the mid 90's and various other mass merchandise, lifestyle and specialty stores. Rajesh has handled varied functional roles, especially the marketing and customer service function at a CXO level which involved strategy formulation, also the roll out and execution of multiple startups. He has written several articles and case studies for leading publications and has authored of one of India's first hands-on books on Indian retail titled "The INDIAN reTALEs." Rajesh is now active in the knowledge space and engaged in sharing his extensive expertise through Strategic Consulting assignments and Training programs. As part of this knowledge sharing initiatives, he has authored a second book on career success titled "Out Of Syllabus".

**Seema Varshney** has worked as an Assistant Professor for the Waljat Colleges of Applied Sciences, Muscat, Sultanate of Oman, for the past 8 years. She has 15 years of teaching experience for both Post-Graduate and Undergraduate students. Other than teaching she has an interest towards research and published research papers in national and international journals. She has an interest towards Community Service Committee Programs and is actively involved in community service in Muscat.

**Agostino Vollero**, PhD, is an Assistant Professor for the Department of Political, Social and Communication Studies, at the University of Salerno (Italy), where he teaches E-marketing. His primary research interests are in the areas of digital marketing, corporate communication and corporate reputation. He has published two books and various articles in leading Italian and international journals, including Journal of Brand Management and Journal of Marketing Communications.

**Parimal Hariom Vyas** is working as an acting Vice-Chancellor and Pro-Vice Chancellor and as a Joint Professor of Management Studies, & Professor in the Department of Commerce and Business Management, Faculty of Commerce, The Maharaja Sayajirao University of Baroda, Vadodara. He has completed the FDP at the Indian Institute of Management, Ahmedabad, and has a Ph. D. (Commerce) and M. Com. (Management). He has more than 30 years of teaching experience. He has held many positions at the M. S. University of Baroda, including Professor of Commerce and Business Management, Faculty of Commerce; Former Dean, Faculty of Commerce; Former Head of the Department, Department of Commerce and Business Management, Faculty of Commerce; Former Principal, M. K. Amin Arts, Science and Commerce College; and Joint Professor, Faculty of Management Studies.

# Index

## O



## P



## R



## S



## T

## U



## V



## Y

# Information Resources Management Association

IRMA INTERNATIONAL

# Become an IRMA Member

Members of the **Information Resources Management Association (IRMA)** understand the importance of community within their field of study. The Information Resources Management Association is an ideal venue through which professionals, students, and academicians can convene and share the latest industry innovations and scholarly research that is changing the field of information science and technology. Become a member today and enjoy the benefits of membership as well as the opportunity to collaborate and network with fellow experts in the field.

## IRMA Membership Benefits:

- **One FREE Journal Subscription**
- **30% Off Additional Journal Subscriptions**
- **20% Off Book Purchases**
- Updates on the latest events and research on Information Resources Management through the IRMA-L listserv.
- Updates on new open access and downloadable content added to Research IRM.
- A copy of the Information Technology Management Newsletter twice a year.
- A certificate of membership.

## IRMA Membership $195

Scan code to visit irma-international.org and begin by selecting your free journal subscription.

Membership is good for one full year.

www.irma-international.org

www.ingramcontent.com/pod-product-compliance
Lightning Source LLC
LaVergne TN
LVHW060411300926
849162LV00006B/1398
* 9 7 8 1 4 6 6 6 9 9 2 1 2 *